FOR REFERENCE

Do Not Take From This Room

Archaeology in America

Archaeology in America
An Encyclopedia

Volume 4
West Coast and Arctic/Subarctic

Francis P. McManamon, General Editor
Linda S. Cordell, Kent G. Lightfoot,
and George R. Milner, Editorial Board

GREENWOOD PRESS
Westport, Connecticut • London

Library of Congress Cataloging-in-Publication Data

Archaeology in America : an encyclopedia / Francis P. McManamon, general editor ; Linda S. Cordell, Kent
G. Lightfoot, and George R. Milner, editorial board.
    v. cm.
  Includes bibliographical references and index.
  Contents: v. 1. Northeast and Southeast — v. 2. Midwest and Great Plains/Rocky Mountains — v. 3.
Southwest and Great Basin/Plateau — v. 4. West Coast and Arctic/Subarctic.
  ISBN 978–0–313–33184–8 (set : alk. paper) — ISBN 978–0–313–33185–5 (v. 1 : alk. paper) — ISBN
978–0–313–33186–2 (v. 2 : alk. paper) — ISBN 978–0–313–33187–9 (v. 3 : alk. paper) — ISBN
978–0–313–35021–4 (v. 4 : alk. paper)
  1. United States—Antiquities—Encyclopedias. 2. Excavations (Archaeology)—United States—
Encyclopedias. 3. Historic sites—United States—Encyclopedias. 4. Archaeology—United States—
Encyclopedias. 5. Canada—Antiquities—Encyclopedias. 6. Excavations
(Archaeology)—Canada—Encyclopedias. 7. Historic sites—Canada—Encyclopedias. 8. Archaeology—
Canada—Encyclopedias. I. McManamon, Francis P. II. Cordell, Linda S. III. Lightfoot, Kent G., 1953– IV.
Milner, George R., 1953–
  E159.5.A68   2009
  973.03—dc22   2008020844

British Library Cataloguing in Publication Data is available.

Library of Congress Catalog Card Number: 2008020844
ISBN: 978–0–313–33184–8 (set)
        978–0–313–33185–5 (vol. 1)
        978–0–313–33186–2 (vol. 2)
        978–0–313–33187–9 (vol. 3)
        978–0–313–35021–4 (vol. 4)

First published in 2009

Greenwood Press, 88 Post Road West, Westport, CT 06881
An imprint of Greenwood Publishing Group, Inc.
www.greenwood.com

Printed in the United States of America

The paper used in this book complies with the
Permanent Paper Standard issued by the National
Information Standards Organization (Z39.48–1984).

10 9 8 7 6 5 4 3 2 1

Cover: These Haida mortuary poles were created in the mid 19th century and express the attributes of their
high ranking dead at the top. A Haida watchman is standing beneath the poles, Gwaii Haanas National
Marine Conservation Area, Ninstints, British Columbia, Canada. For a related essay about nearby
archaeological sites, see Aubrey Cannon, "The Namu Site and Prince Rupert Harbour Sites: 11,000 Years of
Human Adaptation and Settlement."

CONTENTS

VOLUME 4: WEST COAST AND ARCTIC/SUBARCTIC

ENTRIES FOR THE WEST COAST

California

Hawai'i

Pacific Northwest and Southeastern Alaska

ENTRIES FOR THE ARCTIC/SUBARCTIC

West Coast Region

INTRODUCTION

This section of *Archaeology in America* includes essays about archaeological sites along and a bit inland of the West Coast from California to southeastern Alaska, and also includes Hawai'i. The section is subdivided into three parts distinguished by their natural environments and human histories: California, Hawai'i, and the Pacific Northwest coast and coastal mountains from Oregon to southeastern Alaska. California's varied environments range from ocean coast and offshore islands to desert to broad, fertile river valleys to rugged foothills and sharp, young mountains. Hawai'i is a distinctive, complex island ecosystem with a wide range of environments delimited by variation in elevation and rainfall. The northern portion of the West Coast region encompasses the coast and coastal mountain ranges of Oregon, Washington, British Columbia, and southeastern Alaska. The coast of this portion of the region contains many inlets and embayments, and in the northern half, many islands.

We have focused these essays on the most important and interesting archaeological sites within the West Coast region. Many of the sites described in the essays can be visited or artifacts from them and exhibits about them can be seen in museums throughout the region. In the list of further information that ends each essay, interested readers can learn where to find additional resources about the sites described in essays and other, similar sites and topics.

The articles in the West Coast section of *Archaeology in America* include twenty-one general essays on topics that cover ancient or historic time periods. The section also includes thirty-nine essays focusing on particular sites or areas associated with certain kinds of archaeological sites.

The West Coast region as defined for this volume encompasses a very long north-south axis from southern California to southern Alaska; it also extends far into the Pacific to include Hawai'i. Therefore, we have arranged the essays in groups according to sub-regions of California, Hawai'i, and the Pacific Northwest. This will allow readers who are interested mainly in the archaeology of one of these areas to find all the essays for different regions in the same section of the volume. Each of the subsections includes a short introductory essay.

KEY FOR WEST COAST—CALIFORNIA REGIONAL MAP

1. Tsuari, Patrick's Point State Park
2. Lava Bed National Monument and Tule Lake Area
3. Point St. George
4. Point Reyes National Seashore and Tomales Bay State Park
5. Emeryville and West Berkeley shell mounds
6. Brazil Mound
7. Ahwahnee village site, Yosemite National Park
8. Hospital Rock, Sequoia and Kings Canyon National Parks
9. The Cross Creek site
10. Santa Cruz quarries, Prisoners Harbor, and Christy Ranch sites
11. Eel Point, Nursery, and Lemon Tank, San Clemente Island
12. El Presidio de Santa Barbara State Historic Park and Goleta Slough sites
13. Topanga Canyon, Malaga Cove, and Serra Springs
14. Windsong Shores
15. Joshua Tree National Park
16. Petaluma Adobe State Historic Park
17. Presidio de San Francisco Park, Golden Gate National Recreation Area
18. La Purisima Mission State Historic Park
19. Sutter's Fort State Historic Park and Old Sacramento
20. Bodie State Historic Park
21. Mission San Diego de Alcala
22. Avila Adobe, El Pueblo de Los Angeles Historical Monument
23. Mission San Antonio
24. Mission San Buenaventura
25. Fort Ross State Historic Park
26. Farallon Islands, Farallon National Wildlife Refuge and Gulf of the Farallones National Marine Sanctuary
27. Marshall Gold Discovery State Historic Park
28. Malakoff Diggins State Historic Park
29. Walnut Grove and Locke
30. S.S. *Frolic* shipwreck, Point Cabrillo Lighthouse and Preserve
31. Manzanar National Historic Site
32. Wildrose Charcoal Kilns
33. Gunther (Indian) Island, Humbolt Bay
34. Olompali State Historic Park
35. Borax Lake site and Clear Lake Basin
36. Patterson Mound
37. Hotchkiss
38. Blossom Mound
39. Chaw'se, Indian Grinding Rock State Historic Park
40. Daisy Cave, San Miguel Island
41. Arlington Springs, Santa Rosa Island
42. Little Harbor and Soapstone Quarries, Santa Catalina Island
43. Chumash Painted Cave State Historic Park
44. Pitas Point
45. Calico Hills Archaeological District
46. Little Blair Valley Pictographs, Anza Borrego State Park, San Diego Desert
47. Big and Little Petroglyph Canyons, Coso Rock Art National Historic Landmark
48. Blythe Geoglyphs
49. Carrizo Painted Rock Pictographs, Carrizo Plain National Monument
50. Hemet Maze Stone, Riverside
51. Vasco Cave, Vasco Regional Preserve
52. Chitactac-Adams Heritage County Park
53. Bodega Bay

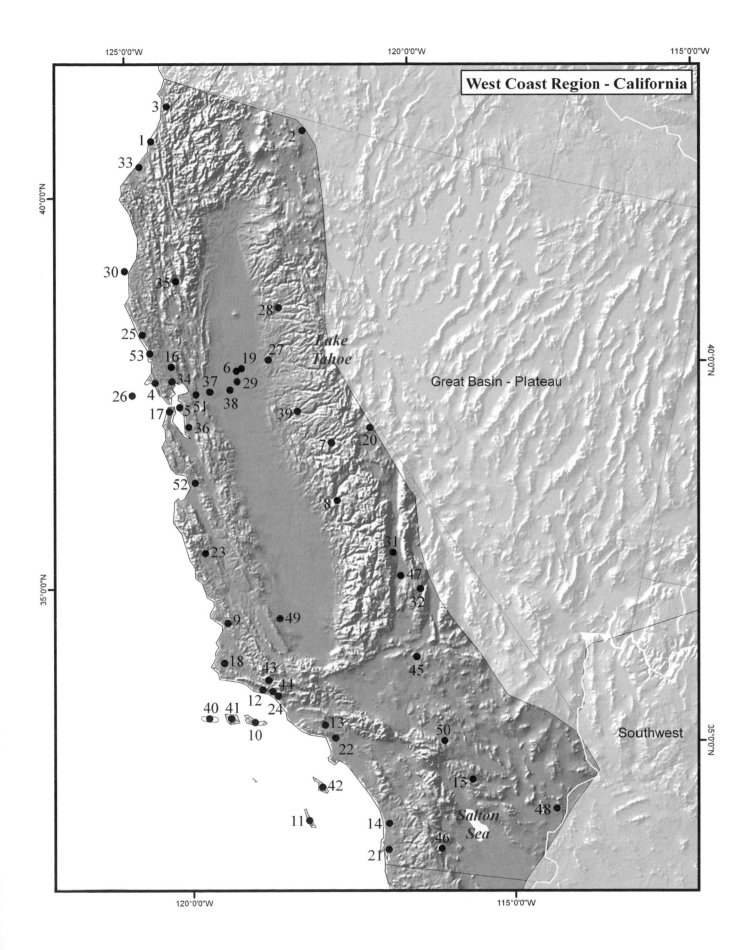

West Coast Region - California

Lake Tahoe

Great Basin - Plateau

Salton Sea

Southwest

CALIFORNIA

The area encompassed by the modern state of California has a rich archaeological record from ancient, as well as historic times. There are reliably dated coastal sites in southern California from before 13,000 years ago (see the essays on the early sites along the Pacific coast and sites on the northern and southern Channel Islands). Following the initial colonization of the area, human populations adapted to the varied environments in many different ways that are recorded in the archaeological sites throughout the area.

California's historic period archaeological sites reflect exploration, colonization, and resource exploitation efforts in both the southern and northern areas of the state. The initial extended contact, following a few recorded early coastal encounters with European explorers, was with Spanish missionaries from the south and southwest (see the essay on early European exploration and encounters). The Franciscan mission system, established during the 1760s and lasting until the 1830s, has left archaeological and architectural traces from San Diego to Sonoma. From the north, Russian traders and colonists, initially based in Alaska, established an outpost at Fort Ross on the northern Californian coast and remained there until the mid-nineteenth century. Those interested in the Russian colonial efforts and sites will also want to read the essay on Sitka in the Pacific Northwest section, as well as the general essay on Russian colonial activities in the Arctic-Subarctic section of this volume.

More recent historic period sites associated with Euro-American exploitation of California's natural resources and with events as recent as World War II (see the essay that includes a section on the Manzanar National Historic Site internment camp) also can be found in this section.

ENTRIES FOR THE CALIFORNIA REGION

The Archaeology of California

Early Peopling of the Pacific Coast of North America

Hunter-Gatherer Peoples of California

Rock Art Sites in California

Native American Perspectives of California Archaeology

European Exploration and Early Encounters with California Indians

Spanish and Mexican Colonization of Alta California

The Russian Colonization of California

Historical Archaeology after American Annexation

Shipwrecks and Submerged Sites of California and the Northwest Coast

Point St. George, Tsurai (Patrick's Point State Park), and Other Sites

Lava Bed National Monument, Tule Lake Area, and Other Sites

Clear Lake Basin and the Borax Lake Site

Point Reyes National Seashore Sites, Olompali and McClure Sites

Patterson, Emeryville, West Berkeley, and Other Shell Mound Sites

The Blossom Mound, Brazil Mound, and Hotchkiss Sites

Yosemite National Park, Indian Grinding Rock State Historic Park, and Sequoia and Kings Canyon National Parks

Ancient and Historic Sites from Santa Cruz to San Luis Obispo

The Cross Creek Site

Arlington Springs, Daisy Cave, Santa Cruz Quarries, and Other Sites

Eel Point, Little Harbor, Soapstone Quarries, and Other Sites

Goleta Slough Area Sites, Pitas Point Site, and Chumash Painted Cave State Historic Park

Topanga Canyon, Malaga Cove, Serra Springs, and Other Sites

Windsong Shores and Other Sites

Coso Rock Art, China Lake, and Sites in Joshua Tree National Park

Sonoma, Petaluma Adobe, and Olompali State Historic Parks

Presidio de San Francisco Park, Golden Gate National Recreation Area

Mission San Diego de Alcala, La Purisima State Historic Park, and Other Historic Sites

Old Sacramento, Sutter's Fort, and Walnut Grove/Locke Sites

Bodie State Historic Park, Wildrose Kilns, and Manzanar National Historic Site

THE ARCHAEOLOGY OF CALIFORNIA

The first people to arrive in California may have come from the interior—the traditional explanation—or by boat from the northern Pacific coast. Either way, they reached the coast at least as early as 13,200 years ago, making California one of the first places in the Americas for which we have reliably dated human occupation. At the end of the last Ice Age, California was cooler and wetter than it is today, but its great physiographic variability contributed to its many distinct ecological zones, just as it currently does. The high Sierra Nevada and northern ranges were forbidding and covered in snow, and great pine forests extended far into southern California. But initial settlers found natural resources to support them in the estuaries, littoral zones, river systems, forests, grasslands, and even extensive lakes in what are now deserts scattered about the region.

Once in the region, people never left, although countless migrations and population shifts occurred; numerous documented archaeological sites tell their story. Many of these sites were formally recorded during the twentieth century, but a good many have been destroyed by the state's cities and highways. Nonetheless, an extremely rich archaeological record remains, consisting of spectacular obsidian quarries, major rock art sites, huge geoglyphs on the desert floors, thick coastal shell middens, and great numbers of small sites where food processing and tool making occurred. Most sites are not obvious to the public, because the tribes of California did not use stone or other permanent materials to construct their homes, nor did they build huge monuments. Yet archaeologists have learned a great deal from simple residential sites about diverse ancient lifeways in the region.

Indeed, California is renowned for having been home to some of the most mobile and small-scale hunter-gatherer societies, along with some of the most politically and economically complex systems ever developed by hunter-gatherers. It was home to folks who practiced limited agriculture in the eastern deserts, groups who were fully maritime in orientation (plying the seas in oceangoing plank canoes and participating in intensive trade networks), and tribes that were part of the famed Northwest Coast culture area centered in present-day Washington and British Columbia.

California also has a rich archaeological record from the historic period. The Franciscan mission system was established during the 1760s and endured into the 1830s, bringing many indigenous peoples into direct and often oppressive contact with European practices, goods, and diseases. Twenty-one missions from San Diego to San Francisco Bay placed an indelible stamp on Native cultures. Russians gained a temporary foothold in northern California, competing for a few decades with the Spanish in an effort to secure territory and economic gains. At Fort Ross, north of San Francisco, Russians set up a small community and fort (1812–41) and brought along Aleutian hunters from Alaska. These hunters labored for the Russians, harvesting a wealth of sea otter pelts from the cold California Pacific waters. Then came the Gold Rush of the late 1840s, which led to the first major European interactions with interior Native Californians. Ishi, the so-called last wild Indian of California, was a member of one of the interior tribes, which were virtually wiped out by land-hungry gold rushers (and their successors) who gravely mistreated them. The public can visit dozens of sites throughout the region that are associated with the colonial and gold rush eras (for example, Fort Ross State Historic Park, La Purisima Mission State Historic Park, and Marshall Gold Discovery State Historic Park).

HISTORY OF RESEARCH AND MAJOR THEMES

Late in the 1800s through about 1920, amateur archaeologists and pioneering professionals discovered major coastal sites around San Francisco Bay, the Santa Barbara coast, the Channel Islands, and other locales. Thus began excavations that would place burials—as well as tools, ornaments of shell and bone, basketry, and many other goods—in museums in the United States and Europe (for example, at the Musée de l'Homme in Paris).

For decades, archaeology in the region focused on the simple reconstruction of culture histories; the naming and relative dating of distinct phases and major migrations (or cultural replacements) in the past; and the nature of human adaptations to local ecological conditions. Scholars such as David Banks Rogers, Nels Nelson, Max Uhle, and Richard Olsen investigated many large coastal middens and cemeteries, using the cruder field methods dominant in that era. Despite the damage done to some sites by rapid fieldwork often unfettered by the screening of archaeological site fill to recover small artifacts and other important recovery techniques, these early archaeologists retrieved invaluable data that otherwise would never have been recovered before the construction of modern roads and buildings damaged or destroyed many archaeological sites in sections of the coast.

More rigorous research, guided by theoretical and systematic behavioral questions about the past, marked the "new" archaeology of the 1960s. Findings associated with recent investigations in major sub-regions of California are highlighted below. Research-oriented archaeology focuses on dynamic topics, such as the early peopling of the Pacific coast. It is now considered reasonable to posit that the peopling of the continent could have followed a coastal pathway.

The coastal-migration approach reverses conventional thinking and places some of the first Americans on the California coast, rather than on the Great Plains. The Arlington Canyon skeleton from Santa Rosa Island (northern Channel Islands) is more than 13,000 years old, and occupants of Daisy Cave (on nearby San Miguel Island) were making a living in the coastal environment at least 11,600 years ago. They had to have reached the islands in boats and been familiar with marine resources, so the hypothesis has been advanced that they traveled south from the Bering Sea—skirting Alaska, British Columbia, and the northwestern United States—to arrive in California before 13,500 years ago. The largely undisturbed Channel Islands (part of Channel Islands National Park) are among the best places to continue to look for such evidence.

Another major research theme for the region is the emergent political complexity among a few of the more populous groups, such as the Chumash. Politically complex hunter-gatherers have been identified in relatively few areas around the world—among them south Florida, the northwest coast, and California. Archaeological evidence for massive craft specializations, such as stone drill making and shell bead making, among the Channel Islands Chumash have revealed a complex form of labor organization unusual among hunter-gatherers. Also evident for the channel region are major exchange systems governed by shell bead money and complex boating technology that contributed to notable wealth differences and the stabilization of Chumash leadership (chiefs). Status was inherited, and people lived in permanent villages sites along the densely populated coasts. Numerous studies of the region's archaeological record have focused on the emergence and perpetuation of these complex economic and political features. Similar research about political complexity is emerging in a few other areas of the state.

Exacting paleoclimatic research studies in California that focus on the delicate balance between human populations and fragile resources offer valuable lessons for examining today's deteriorating ecosystems. Important archaeological studies of the dynamics of multi-ethnic communities—such as Fort Ross, where Russians, Aleutians, and the local California Kashaya Pomo lived together—are also underway. The contemporary relevance of enhancing our understanding of multi-ethnic communities is clear. And historic archaeologists are productively investigating the rich material record of buildings and artifacts from the missions, presidios, forts, gold-mining sites, and urban Chinatowns extending from the 1760s to the late 1800s, reclaiming the lost details of many individual and community histories.

REGIONAL SYNTHESES

Except for a few tribes that practiced the planting of maize and beans near the Colorado River in extreme eastern and southeastern California, all of the indigenous peoples of the region were hunters and gatherers. Within this broad category, however, many different lifeways were practiced.

Deserts

In the east and south central areas of California, encompassing some of the driest and harshest deserts in the United States, people were relatively mobile hunter-gatherers, shifting location to take advantage of seasonal patterns of abundance in water, plants, and small animals. Cohabiting social groups stayed comparatively small, so as not to overtax sparse resource patches.

These regions are generally referred to as the southern desert and the Mojave Desert, extending into the western margin of the Great Basin (toward Nevada). Despite the challenges presented by harsh heat and modest water supplies, small populations lived there for thousands of years, and some of the most striking images and densest concentrations of rock art in North America were created by these populations. The China Lake (Coso) area of the northern Mojave encompasses the Big and Little Petroglyph canyons, which contain hundreds of rock art panels and many thousands of individual images made by multiple generations of Shoshone and Paiute and their ancestors.

Petroglyphs are images pecked into the rock; elsewhere in California, pictographs (paint or pigments applied to the rock face) are generally more common. Many of the images at Coso are stylized or naturalistic representations of desert animals—principally horned sheep. The rock art has been variously interpreted as resulting from the activities of shamans engaged in ceremonial rites or vision quests, or possibly the work of hunters imagining their targets. However, since so much of the art consists of other kinds of images, including abstract (geometric) and anthropomorphic images (costumed figures, figures with headdresses or staffs, stick figures), a singular focus on hunting magic seems unlikely. The meaning of rock art always poses challenges to its interpreters; most likely, multiple classes of rock artists produced images for multiple purposes—some mundane and some sacred.

Also in the locality are the Coso Volcanic Fields, some of the more intensively used obsidian quarry sources in a state rich with volcanic glass. There are hundreds of distinct source areas, and this material was widely sought for making razor-sharp stone tools. Coso obsidian has been found at sites in far-flung parts of central and southern California, constituting one of the region's most important traditional trade goods—particularly prior to AD 1000. Since tools made of this obsidian, such as projectile points, were so heavily traded between about 2000 BC and AD 1000, some scholars suggest that a peak of large-game hunting occurred in this period—maybe linked to the florescence of rock art in the same vicinity.

The California deserts also feature hundreds of geoglyphs, also known as intaglios—large figures created by the careful configuration of sand, pebbles, and rocks on the ground surface, exposing the lighter-colored desert soils below. The various images of human and animal figures scattered throughout these arid lands include some of the largest in the world, including one human figure more than 50 meters long, north of Blythe. Others are found near Needles and Parker, and south into Baja California. Along with large rock alignments, some of which are almost 200 meters long, these striking features are reminiscent of the great geoglyphs of Nazca in Peru and those of the Atacama Desert in Chile. The California desert regions are also remarkable for their early (more than 9,000 years ago) fluted-point assemblages from the shores of extinct lakes, and for the local manufacture and use of ceramics by highly mobile hunter-gatherer populations after about AD 1300.

Central Valley

The southern portion of the Central Valley of California (the San Joaquin Valley) was apparently an important route for coastal-interior trade throughout prehistory, and large villages of Yokuts lived there at the time of European contact, the beginning of the historic period. Settlement was densest in the vicinity of river systems and large, marshy areas, such as ancient Tulare Lake. It is clear that unbroken occupation in the Tulare Lake locus extended back to 10,000 or more years ago, based on significant archaeological discoveries (including at least 270 fluted projectile points—more than have been found in the rest of California combined). Extinct late Pleistocene species, such as *Bison antiquus*, Columbian mammoth, and sloth, have also been recovered there.

San Diego Coast

The coast near San Diego is marked by a series of large estuary systems, the greatest such concentration in the state. Estuaries were a magnet for plant and animal species, including shellfish and birds, and the rich amalgamations of desirable resources attracted early human populations—the so-called San Dieguito people. Scholars have not fully resolved whether the first people to arrive came from the desert interior, where the drying and eventual disappearance of late Pleistocene lakes forced migrations to the better-watered and resource-rich coastal zones, or whether coastal populations may have expanded into the region from other parts of California, such as the Santa Barbara Channel.

Unlike nearby coastal populations, however, these groups' ecological adaptations remained oriented largely toward terrestrial and estuary species through some 9,000 years of prehistory. Less open-ocean fishing or sea mammal hunting occurred than in many areas, such as the Channel Islands, the Santa Barbara coast, and parts of northern California. Evidence (such as cremation burials and manufacture of local ceramics) points to continuing desert influence, especially in the northern San Diego area. Scholars are currently debating whether many coastal estuaries were abandoned during the Holocene due to major erosion or siltation events, driving some populations back inland.

Southern Channel Islands

The southern Channel Islands had a strong orientation toward the sea from an early date. The Eel Point site (on San Clemente Island) was occupied as early as 8,200 years ago. The Little Harbor site (on Santa Catalina Island) was an important residential site later in the Holocene and was one of the earliest sites on the south coast to be subjected to intensive ecological and paleoenvironmental analyses.

Early island populations consumed high proportions of shellfish, fish, and marine mammals; these proportions varied according to local marine conditions. Studies of ecological contexts and resource acquisition patterns have now been conducted for hundreds of island sites. People lived in modest-size villages or moved seasonally across less bountiful landscapes in small food-gathering groups as climate and resources (including fresh water) allowed.

By tracing the distribution of a unique type of olivella shell bead, scholars have proposed a long-distance southern islands interaction sphere that may have connected the southern Channel Islands with Shoshonean speakers on the adjacent mainland and as far away as the Great Basin 5,000 years ago. Large soapstone quarries on Santa Catalina Island were exploited to make large vessels (ollas), bowls, and comals for trade with neighbors during the late and historic periods.

On the nearby Los Angeles and Orange county coasts, Shoshonean speakers lived in many near-coast communities and maintained strong ties to the desert interior, as evidenced through their burial practices (cremations) and trade relations. The Mojave Trail connects the coast to the Hohokam area of southern Arizona. Shell bracelets, baked clay figurines, and projectile points that originated in the Arizona desert are found at Late Holocene coastal sites in this mainland region. Scholars debate whether these folks arrived and displaced preceding populations some 1,500 years ago, when use of the bow and arrow was spreading—or perhaps much earlier, around 5,000 years ago, when the southern interaction sphere emerged.

Northern Channel Islands and Santa Barbara Coast

The northern Channel Islands and Santa Barbara Channel area were the territory of the Chumash and their predecessors. Evidence suggests they occupied the area without displacement for at least 13,000 years.

California's earliest reliably dated burial and the earliest shell midden are both found on the northern Channel Islands, at the sites of Arlington Springs (Santa Rosa Island) and Daisy Cave (San Miguel Island), respectively. The skeletal remains are incomplete and have been known as both "Arlington Man" and "Arlington Woman," reflecting inconclusiveness about the individual's sex. The skeleton was found in an isolated inhumation (human burial) excavated in 1960 by Phil Orr from deep Arlington Canyon strata. The bones and associated materials have been confidently dated to about 13,200–13,500 years ago, making the individual essentially contemporary with the Clovis people of the interior American West. Locally, he or she may have been part of a larger population occupying ancient Santarosae Island (the name for the four northern islands conjoined at the end of the Pleistocene, when sea levels were much lower). A millennium or more later, perhaps some of her or his descendants lived at the more westerly Daisy Cave.

These cave/rockshelter dwellers clearly had access to boats and gathered many resources from nearshore and kelp bed areas, including shellfish and fish. It had long been argued that the first occupants of the Americas had a strong terrestrial orientation, but the careful analysis of the Daisy Cave deposits on San Miguel Island demonstrates that people adapted quite early to littoral and marine ecosystems.

From Malibu to Morro Bay, hundreds of other sites along the Chumash mainland coastline exhibit this same strong marine orientation. At the time of contact with Europeans the Chumash of the islands and mainland coastal zones had one of the highest population densities ever recorded for hunter-gatherers—more than six people per square kilometer. By contrast, in interior or arid lands, hunter-gatherers typically lived at densities of 0.01 to 0.1 person per square kilometer.

The late period Chumash are known for a number of other cultural features that are well documented by data from hundreds of sites. For example, the Chumash were among the most politically complex hunter-gatherer groups in world prehistory, operating as a simple chiefdom with inherited leadership roles and wealth differences. This kind of complexity without agriculture is rare anywhere in the world. They were also among the most economically specialized of all North American societies, making drilled shell beads by the millions at a series of village sites on the islands after AD 1150. The beads came to serve as a legitimate money, or standard of value, that governed countless transactions in an active island-mainland-inland trade system throughout the centuries before the Spanish missions altered traditional culture.

Moreover, people filling in the landscape gave up their mobility along the most bountiful coasts, occupying village sites of 100–500 people year-round in the later periods. Thus many of the sites are large and consist of deep accumulations of refuse. The mainland Chumash, including subgroups in the Santa Barbara coast region and the interior Kern County region, produced spectacular polychrome pictographic rock art. Lastly, the Chumash are renowned for their sophisticated plank canoe, which was crucial in the development of their political and trade systems. Several lines of archaeological data indicate the canoe was invented at roughly AD 500 and became important in the local political economy by AD 1000.

San Francisco Bay

The San Francisco Bay region, with its productive and massive bay and estuary ecological zones, was first occupied at least 4,000 years ago. Various processes, including rising sea levels and extensive development, may have destroyed earlier sites.

The preserved sites are dominated by large, deep shell mounds along bay shores. It has been suggested that these were not only residential locales—representing hundreds or thousands of years of kitchen refuse from good-sized populations anchored to these spots—but also politically and ceremonially important markers on the landscape. According to this idea, these were places where leaders sought to attract followers, where ancestors were buried, and where important rituals were conducted. Among the most conspicuous of these large mounds were the Emeryville and Ellis Landing shell mounds (now largely destroyed). Late in prehistory (about AD 1000), many of these bayside sites were abandoned, and most people evidently moved inland. Large local populations may have overtaxed the animal resources so severely that a long-term move was necessary.

Northern California

Northern California consists of a few major zones, including the territory of the Pomo north of San Francisco, the far north coast, and the interior north. This vast area is a bit less studied than other regions.

The Borax Lake site (near Clear Lake) is among the earliest sites in the American West and is sometimes referred to as a type site for the Paleoindian period (ca. 11,000 years ago) because of its distinctive stone tool assemblage. It also has Early (8,000 years ago) and Middle Holocene (3,000–5,000 years ago) components. Acorn economies may have been important in the oak-rich areas of this zone as early as 7,000 years ago—much earlier than once thought, and perhaps earlier than anywhere else in the state. Acorns were undeniably the most important plant food in pre-contact California, so early tangible evidence for this resource (the grinding tools) is of great interest. During the last few thousand years, the area was occupied by the Clear Lake Pomo and several other Pomo subgroups. Like the Chumash, the Pomo were specialized bead makers for their region, lived in good-sized permanent villages, and had inherited ranks and occupations. Fort Ross, a Russian outpost, was established in Kashaya Pomo territory on the coast during the early 1800s.

The far north coast is part of the famed northwest coast culture area. The Yurok, Karuk, Hupa, and other groups exhibited clear affinities with the art, architecture, and political organization of the Northwest. Salmon dominated the diet, and large permanent villages were located along major river systems in thick redwood forests. Rank and wealth varied across households, feasts were important in status competitions, and many important artifacts were part of ritual and economic exchange systems.

Many other areas of the state also supported thriving Native populations; there is not space to do them justice here. For example, high alpine villages have been found in the White Mountains of eastern California; probable house structures are marked by rock rings. The western flanks of the Sierra Nevada Mountains were rich in seeds and acorns and a wide array of other resources, and thousands of plant-processing sites marked by bedrock mortars are scattered throughout the region. Visitors can view one of the most impressive plant-processing sites in the American West at Indian Grinding Rock State Historic Park, near Jackson.

Further Reading: Arnold, Jeanne E., and Julienne Bernard, "Negotiating the Coasts: Status and the Evolution of Boat Technology in California," *World Archaeology* 37 (2005): 109–131; Erlandson, Jon M., and Terry L. Jones, eds., *Catalysts to Complexity: Late Holocene Societies of the California Coast* (Los Angeles: UCLA Cotsen Institute of Archaeology, 2002); Hildebrandt, William R., and K. McGuire, "The Ascendance of Hunting during the California Middle Archaic: An Evolutionary Perspective," *American Antiquity* 67 (2002): 231–256; Lightfoot, Kent G., *Indians, Missionaries, and Merchants: The Legacy of Colonial Encounters on the California Frontiers* (Berkeley: University of California Press, 2004); Moratto, Michael J., *California Archaeology*, 2nd printing (Salinas, CA: Coyote Press, 2004); Whitley, David S., *The Art of the Shaman: Rock Art of California* (Salt Lake City: University of Utah Press, 2000).

Jeanne E. Arnold

EARLY PEOPLING OF THE PACIFIC COAST OF NORTH AMERICA

For decades most archaeologists saw the colonization of the Americas as a strictly terrestrial enterprise, with small hunting bands trekking across the frozen plains of Beringia near the end of the Pleistocene, through a fabled ice-free corridor and into the heartland of North America.

In this traditional view, the first Americans (Paleoindians) were big-game hunters who only settled the Pacific coast after large game were hunted out of interior regions; people migrated down river valleys to the western edge of the continent, then gradually adapted to life by the sea. In this model, the fully maritime, or seafaring, peoples who occupied much of the Pacific coast when Europeans first explored the area were thought to have developed in just the last few thousand years.

Recently, however, archaeologists have shown that maritime peoples occupied much of the Pacific coast—including numerous offshore islands—by the end of the Pleistocene, between 13,000 and 9,000 years ago. This has led many scholars to suspect that a coastal migration around the north Pacific Rim may have contributed to the earliest human settlement of the Americas.

The notion that the Pacific coast was settled relatively late in the long history of the Americas resulted, in part, from a global sea level rise of roughly 125 meters (approximately 410 feet) since the end of the last glacial period, about 20,000 years ago. Rising seas have obscured a series of vast submerged landscapes, including the shorelines and coastal lowlands that would have been home to most early maritime peoples 8,000 or more years ago. Dramatic changes in Pacific coast landscapes have almost certainly submerged or destroyed many early coastal sites, contributing to anthropological perceptions that coastal economies and maritime adaptations developed relatively late in human history.

In the last 10–20 years, these ideas have been challenged by an accumulation of archaeological, geological, and paleoecological evidence that shows that (1) anatomically modern humans (*Homo sapiens sapiens*) used boats to settle island Southeast Asia and Australia at least 50,000 years ago, and more distant archipelagos in Melanesia and the Ryukyu Islands by 35,000 to 40,000 years ago; (2) a coastal migration route around the North Pacific was open by approximately 16,000 years ago; (3) people who were adapted to the coastal environment (paleocoastal) had settled several Pacific coast areas by at least 13,000 to 11,000 years ago; and (4) the antiquity of coastal settlement—including colonization of some offshore islands that could only be reached by boat— occurred as early as Paleoindian settlement in interior areas. These and other findings have forced a re-evaluation of traditional terrestrial models for the Pleistocene colonization of the Americas. Consequently, they have transformed the Pacific coast from a peripheral area for Paleoindian studies to a major focus of current research on the peopling of the New World.

Despite the difficulties involved in finding early archaeological sites along the Pacific coast, recent research has identified important coastal localities in the Pacific Northwest, southern California, and Baja California that shed considerable light on the nature of early human settlement along the Pacific coast of North America. The earliest of these, found on California's Channel Islands, may also support the idea that a coastal migration around the North Pacific contributed to the peopling of the Americas.

THE PACIFIC NORTHWEST

In the thickly forested landscapes of the Northwest Coast region, the search for early coastal sites is especially complicated due to regional and local variation in glacial history, isostatic and tectonic movements, sea-level changes, and marine erosion. From northern California to southern British Columbia, where the effects of glaciation and isostatic adjustments are less pronounced, a history of massive subsidence earthquakes appears to have destroyed most early coastal sites. Further north, especially along the convoluted and protected coastlines of southeast Alaska and northern British Columbia, a number of recent discoveries hint at the presence of an ancient maritime tradition that spans at least 11,000 years.

In southeast Alaska, these sites include well-known occupations at the Ground Hog Bay, Hidden Falls, and On Your Knees Cave sites, where evidence for early coastal foraging and maritime activities is attested to by the settlement of islands, the lack of terrestrial alternatives, and the long-distance transport of obsidian from the Suemez Island source on the outer coast. At On Your Knees Cave, the importance of marine resources is also demonstrated by a diverse array of marine fauna and the isotopic content detected in human skeletal remains found at the site, which show a strong marine signature.

On Haidi Gwaii (Queen Charlotte Islands) in British Columbia, detailed interdisciplinary reconstruction of ancient coastal landscapes has combined with archaeological investigations to document an impressive array of early coastal sites dating between about 11,000 and 9,000 years ago. Many of these sites have been found in the modern intertidal zone or along raised beaches, where they have been impacted by marine erosion. Intact remnants of some sites suggest a widespread maritime tradition that included the use of boats and harpoons and an economy based on seal and sea otter hunting, fishing, shellfishing, and other activities.

Underwater work has also documented the presence of a vast submerged coastal landscape flooded by rapidly rising seas about 10,000 years ago. Off Haida Gwaii, for instance, a Canadian team identified evidence of ancient river channels, a delta, and submerged forests over 50 meters below sea level. Auger sampling of the sea floor along this submerged river channel even produced a chipped-stone artifact from a depth of 55 meters that may be a remnant of a site occupied more than 10,500 years ago.

THE CALIFORNIA COAST AND THE CHANNEL ISLANDS

The southern California coast is renowned for the antiquity and abundance of early shell middens and other evidence for coastal occupations. On or near the mainland coast, a handful of fluted points have been found, testifying to the presence of Paleoindians in the area. Unfortunately, none of these are from stratified and well-dated contexts or associated with larger assemblages that could tell us more about the origins and lives of these enigmatic people.

Scores of sites dating between about 10,000 and 8,000 years ago have also been found along the California coast, however, documenting a widespread presence of people who lived adjacent to estuaries and productive rocky shorelines up and down the coast. On the mainland, many of these Early Holocene sites—including the Cross Creek site in San Luis Obispo County—contain an abundance of estuarine shells and grinding stones (manos and metates), suggesting a dual economy dominated by the use of shellfish and small seeds. Bones of fish, sea mammals, sea birds, and land mammals hint at a broader economy, including maritime capabilities more clearly expressed in early sites on the Channel Islands.

Located between about 20 and 80 kilometers from the mainland, California's Channel Islands provide some of the most intriguing evidence for early maritime adaptations in the New World. The earliest of these sites are the terminal Pleistocene occupations of Arlington Springs (on Santa Rosa Island) and Daisy Cave (on San Miguel), both on islands that could not have been settled without seaworthy boats. The Paleoindian occupation of these sites represents the earliest evidence for seafaring and maritime peoples in the Americas.

In 1959 Phil Orr of the Santa Barbara Museum of Natural History discovered several human bones eroding from the walls of an ancient arroyo about 11 meters (37 ft) below the rim of Arlington Canyon. The bones, which are not a complete skeleton, have been known as both "Arlington Man" and "Arlington Woman," reflecting the incompleteness of the skeleton and inconclusiveness about the individual's sex. The skeletal remains were associated with charcoal initially dated to about 10,000 radiocarbon years (approximately 11,500 years ago), but recent re-dating of organic remains from the Arlington Springs site suggest that the Arlington Canyon individual may have died closer to 13,000 years ago. This is roughly the same age as Clovis sites in the continental interior, demonstrating that maritime Paleoindian (or paleocoastal) peoples had also settled the Channel Islands by this time.

Evidence for an early coastal settlement of California's Channel Islands also comes from Daisy Cave, which overlooks a remote and rugged stretch of rocky coast. Daisy Cave (CA-SMI-261) is a narrow fissure about 11 meters long and 1–2 meters wide, associated with a small rockshelter about 4 meters by 5 meters wide and a dense shell midden on the slope in front of the cave and rockshelter. The cave provides shelter from strong winds that buffet San Miguel much of the year. Because offshore waters drop off relatively steeply, Daisy Cave remained relatively close to the coast throughout the Holocene. Since the terminal Pleistocene, in fact, this unique combination of shelter and proximity to rich coastal resources repeatedly attracted maritime peoples.

The oldest shell midden in North America, Daisy Cave contains evidence for human occupation by paleocoastal people beginning about 11,600 years ago. Aside from a few nondescript stone tools and tool-making debris, the archaeological remains recovered from the earliest occupation consist almost entirely of marine shells. These show that paleocoastal peoples foraged for abalones, mussels, turban snails, and other shellfish in nearby rocky, intertidal habitats. Despite the limited nature of the occupation, these materials tell us that Paleoindians lived along the coast, relied on seafoods, and explored offshore islands much earlier than most archaeologists would have believed possible 20 years ago.

Between 10,000 and 8,500 years ago, people visited Daisy Cave repeatedly and left behind a much broader range of materials with which to reconstruct their lives. These extensive Early Holocene strata have produced a variety of well-preserved artifacts and faunal remains associated with early maritime peoples, including numerous expedient stone tools; a few projectile points and bifaces; bone gorges (bipoints) that are the oldest fishhooks known from the Americas; more than 1,600 woven sea grass artifacts; beads made from olivella shells; tens of thousands of marine shells and fish bones; and occasional bones of sea otter, seals, and sea birds. The artifacts and faunal remains suggest that paleocoastal peoples were capable of taking a full range of marine resources and that their economy was fully maritime as much as 10,000 years ago.

Important evidence for a well-established maritime occupation also comes from numerous other early Channel Island shell middens dated between about 10,000 and 8,000 years ago, including an important site at Eel Point on San Clemente Island (dated to about 9,000 years ago). Because most of these sites are located some distance from their contemporary coastlines—with the intervening coastal lowlands submerged by rising post-glacial seas—they probably represent a small fraction of the early sites that once existed on the Channel Islands.

CEDROS ISLAND AND BAJA CALIFORNIA

That the early Channel Island sites may represent a broader paleocoastal tradition along the arid coasts of North America is supported by recent work on Cedros Island off the Pacific coast of Baja California. Here, Matthew Des Lauriers identified two shell middens (the Cerro Pedregoso and Richard's Ridge sites) roughly contemporary with the terminal Pleistocene and Early Holocene occupations at Daisy Cave.

Until about 10,000 years ago, Cedros Island was connected to the mainland, so its settlement may not have required seaworthy boats. Like the early Channel Island sites, however, these early Cedros shell middens contain the remains of marine shellfish, fish, and seals, indicating the presence of a very early and relatively eclectic maritime economy. Several other coastal shell middens in Baja California were also occupied between about 10,000 and 8,000 years ago, suggesting that coastal fishing peoples may have lived along much of the Pacific coast at a very early date.

CONCLUSIONS

There is still much to be learned about the earliest human settlement of the Pacific coast, where post-glacial sea level rise, landscape changes, and marine erosion pose major challenges for archaeologists interested in early maritime peoples. Despite these problems, recent archaeological work along the Pacific coast has continued to push back the antiquity of the earliest coastal settlements, expanded the geographical distribution of such coastal sites, and documented that paleocoastal peoples used boats to colonize a number of offshore islands. In recent years, an increasing amount of geological and archaeological evidence has emerged. This evidence suggests that a coastal migration may have contributed to the initial colonization of the Pacific coast during the late Pleistocene. However, further research is needed to determine whether such a coastal migration (or migrations) actually took place, including careful interdisciplinary research under the sea, on the largely unexplored terrestrial landscapes that lie submerged off the Pacific coast of North America.

Further Reading: Des Lauriers, Matthew R., "Terminal Pleistocene and Early Holocene Occupations of Isla de Cedros, Baja California, Mexico," *Journal of Island and Coastal Archaeology* 1(2) (2006): 255–270; Dixon, E. James, *Bones, Boats, and Bison* (Albuquerque: University of New Mexico, 1999); Erlandson, Jon M., *Early Hunter-Gatherers of the California Coast* (New York: Plenum, 1994); Erlandson, Jon M., "Anatomically Modern Humans, Maritime Adaptations, and the Peopling of the New World," in *The First Americans: The Pleistocene Colonization of the New World*, edited by Nina Jablonski (San Francisco: Memoirs of the California Academy of Sciences, 2002); Fedje, D. W., and Mathewes, R. W., eds., *Haida Gwaii: Human History and Environment from the Time of Loon to the Time of the Iron People* (Vancouver: University of British Columbia Press, 2005); Fladmark, Knut R., "Routes: Alternate migration corridors for Early Man in North America," *American Antiquity* 44 (1979): 55–69; Johnson, John R., Thomas Stafford, Jr., Henry Ajie, and Don P. Morris, "Arlington Springs Revisited," *Proceedings of the 5th California Islands Conference*, edited by D. Browne, K. Mitchell, and H. Chaney (Santa Barbara, CA: Santa Barbara Museum of Natural History, 2002), 541–545.; Rick, Torben C., Jon M. Erlandson, René L. Vellanoweth, and Todd J. Braje, "From Pleistocene Mariners to Complex Hunter-gatherers: The Archaeology of the California Channel Islands," *Journal of World Prehistory* 19 (2005): 169–228.

Jon M. Erlandson

HUNTER-GATHERER PEOPLES OF CALIFORNIA

When Spanish explorers first entered California in the early 1500s, there were an estimated 350,000 people living in California, making it one of the most densely populated regions in Native North America. Though such high population ratios are typically associated with agricultural communities, the majority of the state's inhabitants practiced an unusual, yet highly successful form of hunting and gathering unique to the Americas. California was divided into a bewildering number of small, politically distinct groups that were highly local in their outlook and divided linguistically, and the ways in which these people lived was as varied as the California landscape itself. Groups ranged from highly mobile peoples of the southwestern deserts to semi-sedentary villagers of the north coastal temperate rainforests.

Despite the fractured nature of the sociopolitical landscape and the great diversity in ethnographic and prehistoric traditions, people were connected through wide-ranging trade and exchange. They shared a similar subsistence base and way of life that was deeply rooted in the past. These commonalities in the face of such variable circumstances make California hunter-gatherers unique, distinctive, and endlessly fascinating.

SOCIOPOLITICAL ORGANIZATION
One of the most characteristic elements of California aboriginal groups was their sociopolitical organization. Unlike in much of the rest of North America, large, politically unified tribes were rare. The majority of Native California groups were organized in smaller political units, sometimes referred to as "tribelets," particularly in the northern part of the state. Slightly less prevalent were residential kin groups (defined by some form of family organization)—common among Takic-speaking peoples, such as the Cahuilla, Luiseno, and Diegueno in southern California. District organization, which included multiple local units unified in a larger organization, takes a distant third among the types of sociopolitical organizations observed among California's aboriginal peoples when they first encountered Europeans.

Tribelets, or village communities, were small, politically independent, landholding units consisting of 100–500 people living within a few villages—or more than a few, perhaps up to twenty. It has been estimated that there were somewhere between 500–1000 tribelets in California at contact, and tribelets tended to be larger and more densely populated in areas with abundant and diverse resources.

While connected with other tribelets by marriage ties, regional ceremonies, and trade relationships, each tribelet exhibited a highly local way of life from day to day. People traveled to hunt, gather, and trade, but overall, their outlook was squarely centered on their village of birth. Villages included one or more households of kinsmen who were related through male descent. These households often owned particular subsistence areas, including productive acorn groves and fishing locations. Individual households fiercely defended their rights to these places—and they, not chiefs, held control over them.

Chiefs typically resided in the tribelet's largest, principal village. Traditionally, chiefly position was hereditary, but chiefly position did not equate to chiefly power. Chiefs—usually senior males—were respected, but their role was that of an advisor. They organized major gatherings, helped settle disagreements, and coordinated defensive action, but they could not act without a consensus of respected elders within the community.

Though it is impossible to say when tribelet organization first developed in California, it is likely that this form of social organization has very ancient roots. We know from the archaeology that the earliest Californians were broad-spectrum hunter-gatherers—extremely mobile groups who relied on a wide variety of foods for their existence, moving over the landscape seasonally as resources became available.

Over time, people began to focus on particular resources and settle down, particularly along the food-rich coast and rivers. As populations increased, territories became increasingly circumscribed. The origins of tribelets may be associated with these events—manifested archaeologically in an increase in the number and size of sites and regionalization that occurred at different times in different parts of the state. Tribelets may have developed as populations grew and household groups came together to defend their territory and resources.

SUBSISTENCE ECONOMY
In the past, agriculture was not necessary to live well in California, provided one had the knowledge and skills necessary to extract the bounty of the region's natural resources. California hunter-gatherers were experts at living off the land. They knew when and where food could be gathered, hunted, or caught, and organized their lives along an annual subsistence round that took advantage of this cycle.

In the spring, people focused on gathering roots, budding plants, and berries. This continued in the summer, which was also a time when people engaged in seasonal smelt fishing and marine-mammal hunting along the coast. The fall was a critical time for harvesting mass quantities of acorns (or pinyon nuts in the deserts) and migrating salmon in the north. Migrating waterfowl were plentiful during this time as well. In the lean winter months, people came together for ceremonies and other community events, relying on stored foods to survive.

An inspiring list of foods was taken by California hunter-gatherers, though each group had a particular

Tribal territories of California groups, by Kathleen Montgomery. [Courtesy of Far Western Anthropological Research Group, Inc., 2007]

focus, depending on the ecology of the local region. Elk and deer were important wherever they were available, as were various species of fish, and the diet was supplemented with all manner of smaller mammals, birds, seeds, nuts, bulbs, fruits, berries, and insects. Salmon was a key resource in the northern part of the state, particularly in the fall.

Along the coast and estuaries, a wide variety of shellfish species were harvested; the substantial shell mounds along San Francisco Bay and other estuaries attest to centuries, even millennia of shellfish consumption by Native groups. Other coastal resources include seals, sea lions, offshore and inshore fishes, and the occasional beached whale. In marshy zones, waterfowl, crayfish, mollusks, and turtles were key foods. In deserts, people also relied on antelopes, jackrabbits, lizards, mesquite, cactus, and yucca in the lowlands, and bighorn sheep and pinyon nuts in the uplands.

Acorns were a staple throughout California, even in the salmon-rich north and along the coast, where marine foods were abundant. (Pinyon nuts took a similar role in the desert.) Though there are fifteen oak species in the state, certain species were preferred by Native people for their taste, particularly the Tan Oak. Acorns are rich in carbohydrates and fat, and are comparable to maize and wheat in nutritional content. While acorn crop size varies from year to year, usually enough of one species was available during harvest time to last an entire year. Acorns were gathered in the fall and stored in baskets inside of houses or in large, raised outdoor granaries. They were removed from storage and processed on an as-needed basis. Such storage provided insurance against starvation, which could be a problem in the lean winter months, when obtaining other foods could be extremely difficult.

In order to be digested in large quantities, acorns require extensive processing to remove their bitter tannic acids. In most of California, this involved an elaborate procedure involving shelling, pounding, and grinding acorns into a meal (usually with mortars and pestles), followed by leaching with water in a shallow, sandy depression or basket. The processed food was then cooked by placing heated stones in the meal, which was finally eaten as a mush or bread.

Acorns were probably part of the Native Californian diet very early in time. They were incorporated into the diet as early as 10,000 years ago at some sites, then became a staple over most of the state by approximately 3,000 years ago. In general, labor-intensive processing of acorns and other foods became more important over time. This is what archaeologists refer to as intensification—where a wider range of foods— many of which took a long time to prepare—are eaten. As populations increased and territories became more circumscribed, access to resources became more limited—while at the same time, more mouths had to be fed. Though acorn processing was long and tedious, their predictability and storability made them an excellent and reliable food source, and this would have been very important to hunter-gatherers under such conditions.

LANGUAGE

At the time of contact with Europeans, between sixty-five and eighty mutually unintelligible languages were spoken in California, making it one of the most linguistically diverse locations on the planet. There are few places where as many languages were spoken in such a small area, with only coastal Papua New Guinea rivaling this cacophony of tongues. Like other aspects of Native California society, language was intensely local. An indefinite but surely staggering number of dialects were spoken, and this is likely related to the territoriality characteristic of community groups.

So how can this remarkable mosaic of languages be explained? This question has fascinated anthropologists since the turn of the twentieth century, when many of these rapidly disappearing languages were being salvage recorded. Historical linguistics (or the study of language change through time) addresses how and when these languages first came to California and what this tells us about human populations in the past. Though oversimplified and temporally inexact, such analyses have been very influential in California archaeology, and archaeological models typically take into account linguistic events and processes.

Most Native Californian languages are related to other languages spoken throughout the Americas—some very far away. Thus it is believed that some of the languages represent shifting territories or population migrations of peoples to California. The languages of California are divided into six major stocks, or superfamilies, including Hokan, Penutian, Yukian, Algic, Na-Dene, and Uto Aztecan.

Hokan languages are believed to be the most ancient in California, likely spoken over the majority of the state before Penutian-speaking people spread in central California and forced Hokan speakers to its edges. Yukian languages were spoken north of San Francisco Bay. As they do not appear to have any relationship to languages spoken outside of this area, they may have developed in California. Algic (Algonquian) and Na-Dene (Athabascan) languages are spoken in northwestern California and are believed to be associated with migrations of northern groups of peoples into California as late as 1,500–700 years ago. Another late arrival is the Uto-Aztecan group of languages, which was widely distributed in southern California and is associated with an expansion of desert-adapted peoples in the last thousand years.

TRADE AND EXCHANGE

There are abundant historic period ethnographic accounts of trade and exchange between tribal groups in California. Many of these transactions involved the movement of resources within a group's territory to a neighboring group that lacked them—often occurring within formal gatherings, such as feasts or dances. These ceremonies helped to cement ties between the groups, lessening the potential for territorial conflict.

One survey of the ethnographic literature found that the most commonly reported items traded in California, in decreasing order, were marine shell beads, baskets, salt, hides and pelts, bows, acorns, fish, and obsidian, although nearly every item conceivably procured or manufactured by Native California people was also reported as a trade commodity. Unfortunately, many of these goods do not preserve well in the archaeological record, leaving archaeologists the task of unraveling prehistoric relationships by focusing on better-preserved materials.

The two most-studied durable items are beads manufactured from marine shell and obsidian tools and their waste debris. Archaeologists traditionally focus on shell and obsidian because they provide chronological information (by the use of radiocarbon dating for shell and hydration rim measurement for obsidian). Additionally, obsidian can be readily traced to its point of origin through aspects of its chemical composition, and recent isotope studies have indicated that marine shells can be similarly sourced.

Marine shell beads are found in archaeological sites within every region of California, the Great Basin, and the Southwest. Their small size and durability meant they were easily carried, either directly or through intervening middlemen, across great distances. They have been found in 10,000-year-old desert archaeological sites, hundreds of miles from the coast, indicating that coastal California people had established trade relationships with interior populations at a very early date. Shell beads were highly valued, and strings of them were used as money in some areas in later years. The most ubiquitous type of bead was that fashioned from the olive snail (*Olivella* spp.), and the archaeological record shows pronounced preferences for different olivella bead forms across space and time. These changing fashions not only provide an indirect dating method (known as seriation, a method used to establish a relative chronology by comparing stylistic changes), but they also allow archaeologists to infer trading affinities between groups.

Obsidian has been well studied for its chronological resolution as well for its ability to be chemically sourced to specific volcanic glass flows, several of which are located within California. Similar to the shell beads, obsidian tools were also shaped to suit changing tastes and their stylistic variation can be investigated. The archaeological record demonstrates that obsidian was widely traded, in distinct directional patterns. There is also abundant evidence demonstrating that the demand for obsidian fluctuated through time, peaking between about 3,000 and 1,000 years ago, after which trade sharply declined.

Although prehistoric Californians traded a wide variety of resources, there is little evidence for any group engaging in trade-related activities as their economic focus. Certain groups may have controlled a resource, such as an obsidian quarry, but did not focus their activities exclusively on acquiring or trading the resource. Still, trading reached quite sophisticated levels in some places.

The trails used by these traders linked village to village, forming a network that spread beyond the state. Many of the trails were subsequently used by early Euro-American explorers, fur traders, and settlers, eventually forming some of today's modern highways. In some areas, particularly in the California desert, portions of these prehistoric trails are still visible.

MATERIAL CULTURE

The material culture of California hunter-gatherers was diverse and often quite specialized. In general, technology became more specialized over time as people focused on particular resources and became less mobile; there are more less-portable artifact types late in time.

Houses ranged from the permanent to the ephemeral. In the Northwest, rectangular semi-subterranean plank structures were constructed with split, hewn redwood planks. These houses were often named and were known to have been lived in for hundreds of years. In the Central Valley, people lived in round, semi-subterranean lodges held up with a large center post. Conical brush houses were used in other parts of the state. When mobile, groups constructed wickiups, small frame shelters with circular footprints covered in basketry mats or bark. Sweat houses are a distinct feature of the region. They were typically substantial earth- or plank-covered structures that were heated by fire (never steam). They were used by men for daily purification, and women were only admitted for special ceremonies. The oldest houses in California consist of packed floors radiocarbon dated to approximately 8,000 years ago. Most, if not all, early houses were circular. Multi-family or communal houses were rare in Native California. In most of the state, houses were typically small and inhabited by single household families. This was undoubtedly the predominant pattern in the ancient past as well.

Boats were a major form of transportation along California's coast and waterways. Wooden dugout canoes were used in the Northwest, including both river forms and larger, oceangoing varieties. Tule balsas were canoe-shaped rafts constructed of rushes that had been lashed together and were widely used in California. The *tomol*, or sewn-plank canoe, was unique to the southern California coast, in particular the Santa Barbara Channel area, and used by the Chumash in ancient and historic times.

Tomols could be up to 9 meters (30 ft) long and were constructed of redwood driftwood. The wood was hewn into small planks, sewn together in a canoe shape using plant fiber string, and sealed with asphaltum (a naturally occurring, gluey tar). They were owned by hereditary chiefs and wealthy individuals who controlled a long-distance exchange network between the mainland and the Channel Islands, where shell beads were manufactured. Archaeologists have discovered asphaltum plugs and other artifacts related to the *tomol* in regional sites that are approximately 1,300 years old.

A wide range of food-procurement technology was used throughout California. Hunting tools and techniques included snares, deadfalls, throw stones, spears, darts, *atl atl*s (dart-throwing sticks or boards), and bows and arrows. The bow and arrow was a late technological innovation that spread unevenly across California. It is thought that it appeared around 1,500 years ago in the northern portion of the state, probably from the Columbia Plateau, and spread to the deserts. This technology apparently reached the central and southern coasts later, by about 800 years ago. The bow and arrow was a more powerful weapon than the *atl atl* and dart it replaced, allowing for greater accuracy at longer distances—and probably altering hunting strategies. With the powerful but less accurate spears and *atl atl*/darts, Native people likely hunted in large groups and relied on ambushing game. The bow and arrow allowed for a new, solitary style of hunting.

Fishing gear included a suite of ingenious devices and methods. Buckeye and soap-root poisons were used to stun fish in many locations, as was the spear, a simple yet effective device. Deep-sea fish were captured with the hook and line, but this form of fishing was relatively rare. A wide variety of nets were used. Basketry traps, used in conjunction with weirs, were effective methods of capturing large numbers of spawning salmon. In the Northwest, some weirs, such as the famous Kepel fish dam, were very large, annual, multi-community efforts overseen by Yurok ritual leaders. Sea mammals were hunted with antler toggling harpoons, which were sometimes tipped with stone arrows to improve their effectiveness.

Ethnographically, acorns and small seeds were ground primarily using mortars and pestles. Bedrock mortars, ubiquitous in California, are communal plant-processing locations where women ground acorns. Mortars and pestles had replaced flat milling stones and manos across the state by around 4,500 years ago. Traditionally this change is thought to represent a dietary shift from small seeds (milling stones and manos) to intensive acorn processing (mortars and pestles). However, there is growing evidence that milling stones may have been used for acorn processing as well—and that, rather than a wholesale shift in the diet, this change may simply reflect a less mobile way of life among hunter-gatherers.

California Native peoples are rightly famous for their basketry. Baskets ranged from the utilitarian to true works of art. Baskets, made with both twining and coiling techniques, are lighter and more portable than pottery, which is rare in California. Women wove special designs into some of the fancier pieces, and many of these designs are distinctive of particular locations. Food and other items were stored and transported in baskets, some of which were very large. Many specialized types of baskets exist with specific food serving, cooking, collecting and processing uses, including very finely woven baskets, which were used as water carriers. Other basket types included those used as bird and fish traps, caps (worn by women throughout California), baby carriers, and sandals (in desert locations).

Not all aspects of the material culture, of course, were purely functional. Many rites and ceremonies were associated with food pursuits, such as the annual World Renewal Ceremony. Glimpses of the incredibly rich ritual and religious life of California Native peoples can be seen in the archaeology. Pipes, rattles, rock art, and artifacts with no known function are tantalizing clues to the supernatural life of California hunter-gatherers, which undoubtedly has roots very deep in the past. Though hunting and gathering is no longer practiced in California, many of these ancient traditions have been passed along to later generations and continue to be an important part of California Native American culture today.

Further Reading: Fagan, Brian, *Before California: An Archaeologist Looks at Our Earliest Inhabitants* (Lanham, MD: Rowman and Littlefield, 2003); Heizer, Robert F., and Albert B. Elsasser, *The Natural World of the California Indians* (Berkeley: University of California Press, 1980); Heizer, Robert F., and M. A. Whipple, eds., *The California Indians: A Source Book*, 2nd ed. (Berkeley: University of California Press, 1971); Kroeber, A.L., *Handbook of the Indians of California* (New York: Dover Publications, 1976) (reprint of Bulletin 78 of the Bureau of American Ethnology of the Smithsonian Institution, 1925); Heizer, Robert F., ed., *Handbook of North American Indians Volume 8: California* (Washington, DC: Smithsonian Institution, 1978); Moratto, Michael J., *California Archaeology* (Orlando, FL: Academic Press, 1984).

Shannon Tushingham and Allika Ruby

ROCK ART SITES IN CALIFORNIA

The landscape of California contains many visual images created by the people who lived on the land in ancient times and for thousands of years prior to their encounter with Western society. Many of these images, or fragments of the original images, remain to this day. They provide a window to the past, prompting questions like "Who made them?" "How old are they?" and the ever-present "What do they mean?"

WHAT IS ROCK ART?
For many, the term "rock art" conjures an image of the beautiful wall murals in Lascaux Cave in France, or Altamira in Spain, or possibly some of the large human-like figures found on desert ground surfaces in Baja California or the American Southwest. While many of these images do represent art in our cultural view, rock art had a much deeper meaning to the Native peoples who made it: it connected them with the natural world. Thus, the term "art" is a misnomer but is so ingrained into vocabulary worldwide that it is difficult to use a different label. Rock art comprises designs, motifs, and patterns that humans have placed in the natural landscape. California rock art is usually found on boulders in the open air, but can also be in rock shelters and small caves. It is found in three distinct varieties characterized by the method that produced the images.

A hunting petroglyph found in the Coso Ranges.   [Garry C. Gillette]

The most common type of rock art in California is the petroglyph, an engraving that is pecked, scratched, incised, or abraded into the rock surface, typically removing the darker, natural patina, leaving an image that stands out from the surrounding area. Petroglyphs are found on sandstone, schist, basalt, granite, and even lava tuff. The pecked marks were made by either direct or indirect hitting of the rock surface with a harder rock or hammerstone. These tools have often been identified by archaeologists and rock art researchers as quartz or chert. Sharpened chert or obsidian was probably used to make the scratches.

Pictographs are paintings made by combining natural minerals or other material for color (which is first ground to a powder in a stone mortar) with a liquid (referred to as a binder). Colors included black (charcoal), red and orange (hematite [iron oxide] or cinnabar), white (kaolin clay), yellow (limonite), and sometimes blue and green (copper). To make the paint, Natives combined the minerals or other materials with a binder, such as blood, egg white, spring water, plant gum, or vegetable oils. The paint was often applied with fingers or a simple brush made from a small mammal tail. All the images on a pictograph panel may be the same color (usually red or black), or may use a combination of colors. At some sites, the images may have been pecked into the rock surface and then painted.

The most uncommon form of rock art are geoglyphs—earth forms also known as intaglios and rock alignments. Geoglyphs are found in the dry desert where the sand has blown away, exposing the hard dirt (or desert floor), which comprises small pebbles. The pebbles, darkened from their exposure to the sun, are scraped away in patterns to outline large images in the lighter soil: figures such as mountain lions, human figures, and serpents. Geoglyphs are large; one human figure measures 52 meters in length. Rock alignments are also found in the desert and consist of arrangements of small stones in patterns on the ground surface.

The type of rock art that is found in California is usually representative of a specific geographical location (for example, petroglyphs are often found in the desert).

HOW OLD IS IT?

Frequently asked questions include "How old is it?" and "How do you know?" While the field of rock art dating is still in its infancy, some images can be dated, and others can be associated with a specific time period.

A petroglyph found in the Coso Ranges.   [Garry C. Gillette]

Certain pictographs can be dated with a radiocarbon method if they have carbon-containing matter (charcoal, or an organic binder such as blood, plant gum, or fat, for example). The process has been perfected so that only a very minute sample of the paint (0.5 mg) is required for testing. This type of dating is only useful on a small percentage of pictographs.

Other methods can predict a maximum possible date or a minimum possible age. The subject matter of a panel may determine the oldest possible date. As an example, the image of a man on horseback indicates that the rock art was made after the historic period reintroduction of the horse in California by the Spaniards in 1769. The appearance of a bow and arrow is archaeologically dated AD 500, and a sailing ship image can only be as young as the first explorers sailing off the coast of California (1542). The environment can also give clues to the relative age of rock art. Pictographs, often occurring in rock shelters and small caves, are exposed to coastal climates; they can only be preserved a few hundred years. Petroglyphs in the open desert environment darken with time; the lighter pecked images are younger than those with a darker patina. The sequential layering of rock art images, one over the other, also indicates that the lowest element is the oldest.

Perhaps the oldest rock art in California are petroglyphs that are referred to by some researchers as the Pit and Groove tradition. These are similar to other areas of the far West and are believed to be thousands of years old. They comprise cupules (small dimples on boulders), concentric circles, and PCNs (Pecked Curvilinear Nucleated forms, which are circles or ovals that have raised centers).

WHO MADE IT, AND WHAT DOES IT MEAN?

Perhaps the most challenging question is "What do the images mean?" Much of the rock art in California was the result of ritual experiences. Cupules are found at numerous sites. Oral traditions, collected by researchers (ethnographers) shortly after contact with Euro-Americans, indicate that cupules held different meaning to different tribal groups. To the Pomo, they were the vestiges of fertility rituals, and to several northeastern California groups, they were known as rain rocks and considered helpful in controlling the weather. Cupules were incorporated by the Hupa into their calendar stones, which helped them determine seasons and kept their world in balance.

To a large extent, California rock art is believed to have been made by shamans or medicine doctors to preserve a

Warrior (?) petroglyphs found in the Coso Ranges.   [Garry C. Gillette]

record of their vision quests, or trance experiences, in which they entered the supernatural world to obtain supernatural power. Animal figures represented spiritual helpers, and human-like figures (anthropomorphs) represented the shamans who were in a trance.

Early ethnographers have recorded several accounts of rights of passage rituals that included the making of rock art images on nearby boulders. The ritual for Luiseno (Riverside County) girls is reported to have concluded with the young women running to a nearby boulder and painting the image of their spirit helper (rattlesnake) as diamond chains in red paint. These ethnographic accounts, when studied by rock art researchers, present many clues, often in the form of metaphors to the meaning of rock art. Other rock art sites in California are believed to represent weather control rituals and possible boundary markers. Some rock art researchers interpret various petroglyphs as hunting magic, placed on boulders by Natives to increase their success in the hunt.

WHERE ARE THE SITES?

The first historical record of a rock art site in California are drawings by Joseph Goldsborough Bruff made in 1850, in Lassen County. By 1929 Julian Steward had increased the known sites in California to 129. Rock art has now been identified in all California counties, and new sites continue to be recorded. Many of these sites are on private and protected property.

Out of respect to the cultures that created them and preservation concerns, only a few of publicly accessible rock art sites in California are presented here. Many of these sites are considered sacred sites, and Native groups still approach them with great respect and reverence as a connection to the natural world and their ancestors. It is everyone's responsibility to help preserve these sites from the past for the future. Please, when visiting a site, do not touch, walk on, or apply any substance to rock art.

SITES OPEN TO PUBLIC VISITATION

Little Blair Valley Pictographs

These red pictographs in Anza Borrego State Park in the San Diego desert are the visible remnants of the girls' puberty initiation rituals of the Kumeyaay, which marked their transition into womanhood and their being eligible for marriage. The site consists mainly of two panels of diamond chains and zigzag lines. A few other images are also present. The last recorded known girls' puberty ritual in southwestern California took place in the 1890s.

For a brochure with directions for the hike to view the pictographs, contact the Anza Borrego State Park Visitor Center, 200 Palm Canyon Drive, Borrego Springs, CA 92004, (760) 767-5311.

Blythe Geoglyphs

These geoglyphs are located on a terrace above the California side of the Colorado River. They were made by Yuman-speaking peoples who made ritual pilgrimages from the south to visit their place of creation. The figures were made at the locations of mythic events and were meant to represent beings that were involved in the rituals. The figures represented at the Blythe geoglyphs commemorate Mastamho, the creator-deity; his helper spirit, the mountain lion; and perhaps even his evil twin brother, Kaatar. It has been determined by archaeological dating that these geoglyphs are

about 1,100 years old. For visiting information, consult the BLM Web site: http://www.blm.gov/az/yfo/intaglios.htm.

Painted Cave Pictographs

Located in the foothills just east of Santa Barbara is one of the most outstanding and well-known pictograph sites in California. The geometric images are painted in red, black, and white, and represent the supernatural world of the Chumash Indians. These Indians occupied the area from Topanga Canyon in Los Angeles County, north to San Luis Obispo and east to the San Joaquin Valley. Researchers have determined that the images were painted (and repainted) at different times. While some researchers believe that the images in the cave represent the visions of shamans during a trance state—such as the zigzag lines attributed to represent the rattlesnake, the spirit helper of the shaman—others see them as depictions of the sun, a solar eclipse, and other solar events. The painted cave is believed to be no more that 1,000 years old—and probably more recent, based on wind erosion studies. The paintings are gradually being reclaimed by nature. Additional information and directions for a visit to Painted Cave can be found on the Web site of the Santa Barbara Museum of Natural History: http://www.sbnature.org.

Carrizo Painted Rock Pictographs

Located in San Luis Obispo County, the Painted Rocks represent the largest known Chumash pictograph site. During the early part of the twentieth century, much of the site was destroyed by vandalism; yet, early photographs indicate a brilliant display of images that include human figures in a ceremonial dance in red, black, and white; four men in a *tomal* (planked Chumash canoe); rattlesnakes; turtles; seals; and many other images that were painted by shamans. Many of the paintings are believed to be 2,000 to 3,000 years old, but some may have been placed there less than 500 years ago.

Painted Cave is open for daily visits July 15–March 1, with tours only from March 1 to the end of May. The site is closed to all visits from June to July 15 to protect nesting birds. For further information, contact the Goodwin Educational Center at (805) 475-2131.

Hemet Maze Stone

This petroglyph site, near Hemet in Riverside County, along with similar maze depictions (some as pictographs in red paint) in northern San Diego County, is an anomaly in California rock art. It is not known which culture is responsible for such images. Several are not complete mazes, but all the panels comprise complex grid-like patterns, often appearing as the only image. The Hemet Maze is deeply engraved or pecked into the vertical side of a granite boulder.

For additional information, contact the Riverside County Regional Park and Open Space District at (951) 955-4319.

Coso Petroglyphs

The Coso ranges in the California Great Basin are the home to what is probably the most impressive and largest concentration of petroglyphs in the state. The images depict hundreds of bighorn sheep, shamans, human figures, medicine bags, geometric figures, and other petroglyphs. Most of the petroglyphs are thought to be 1,000–1,500 years old, but some may date back thousands of years. They were made by Numic-speaking Shoshone, Northern and Southern Paiute, and Kwaiisu peoples. Current interpretations identify the images as being made by shamans during weather control rituals, with a competing hypothesis that they represent hunting magic. These petroglyphs have enjoyed great preservation, as they are located within the boundaries of the China Lake Naval Weapons Center at Ridgecrest.

They may only be visited through guided tours arranged by the Maturango Museum, 100 E. Las Flores Avenue, Ridgecrest, CA 93555, (619) 375-6900, http://www.maturango.org.

Chaw'se

Located in the Sierra Foothills near Jackson, Chaw'se Grinding Rock State Park is the site of the largest (1,185) collection of Bed Rock Mortars (BRMs) in California, and is one of a very few sites known to combine petroglyphs with mortars. The site is the traditional area of the Northern Sierra Miwok. The carvings, which include animal and human tracks, circles, and wavy lines, are believed to be 2,000–3,000 years old. The petroglyphs are protected by a fence; a deck still offers a good view of the overall rock outcropping. The park includes a reconstructed Miwok village and roundhouse; several Native American events take place yearly. School tours are also available.

For information on visiting Chaw'se, contact Indian Grinding Rock State Park, 14881 Pine Grove-Volcano Road, Pine Grove, CA 95665, (209) 296-7488.

Vasco Caves

Located in the Vasco Regional Preserve, and administrated by the East Bay Regional Park District, is a grouping of sandstone boulders that contain pictographs of eagles, hawks, and other more abstract markings. The area is known to have been inhabited for nearly 10,000 years, and the red and black pictographs may have been placed there by a mixture of cultures, including Bay Miwok, Valley Yokut, and possibly Ohlone (whose trade routes were nearby).

Access to the site is through limited guided tours arranged through East Bay Parks at (510) 636-1684. Additional information is found on their Web site, http://www.ebparks.org.

Chitactac-Adams Heritage County Park

This small Santa Clara County Park is located in the southern part of the county, on the site of an Ohlone village along Uvas Creek. The interpretive park includes a visitor's shelter that displays information about the lifeways of the people who lived there for at least the last 2,500 years. In addition to interpretive signs throughout the park, some direct the visitor to view rock art consisting of concentric circles and cupules. There are numerous bedrock mortars (BRMs). Park docents give several tours for schoolchildren each week, and public programs are scheduled throughout the year.

For additional information and school tours, please contact Santa Clara County Park Interpretive Office, (408) 323-0107.

Lava Beds National Monument

The rock art of this northern California area consists of both petroglyphs and pictographs. The Modoc peoples who inhabited the area are more culturally connected to those of the Columbia Plateau than with California and the Great Basin, and this is evident in the content of the images, which are primarily geometric designs—human, animal, and other figures. One of the public sites is Petroglyph Point, which was an island before Tule Lake was drained in the twentieth century. Petroglyph Point is one of the most extensive petroglyph sites in California, with over 5,000 images, and is believed to have been created by shamans. Some of the images may also have been made during puberty and fertility rituals. Climate studies show that, except for only brief periods between 6,400 and 5,700 years ago, between 5,400 and 2,600 years ago, and within the last 500 years, the island was submerged. The lack of any Modoc cultural images from the last 500 years (such as horses) leads researchers to believe that the pictographs at Lava Beds were probably made between 1,500 and 400 years ago.

Visitors are also directed to view rock art at Big Painted Cave and Symbol Bridge. Limited tours of the pictographs at Fern Cave are available between May and October, with advance reservations from the Monument Visitors Center, where a brochure, "Images in Stone," is also available. Call (530) 667-8100 to make a reservation. Additional information is also found on their Web site, http://www.nps.gov/labe.

Further Reading: Clottes, Jean, *World Rock Art* (Los Angeles: The Getty Institute, 2002); Gillette, Donna, "The Rock Art of Chitactac-Adams Heritage Park and Environs," *A Gathering of Voices*, Santa Cruz County History Journal 5 (2002): 117–129; Grant, Campbell, *The Rock Paintings of the Chumash* (Berkeley: University of California Press, 1965); Heizer, Robert F., and Martin A. Baumhoff, *Prehistoric Rock Art of Nevada and Eastern California* (Berkeley: University of California Press, 1962); Loendorf, Lawrence L., Christopher Chippindale, and David Whitley, *Discovering North American Rock Art* (Tucson: University of Arizona Press, 2005); Smith, Gerald A., and Steven M. Freers, *Fading Images; Indian Petroglyphs of Western Riverside County* (Riverside, CA: Riverside Museum Press, 1994); Whitley, David S., *The Art of the Shaman: California Rock Art* (Salt Lake City: University of Utah Press, 2000).

Donna L. Gillette

NATIVE AMERICAN PERSPECTIVES
OF CALIFORNIA ARCHAEOLOGY

Since the entrance of non-Natives into the Americas, indigenous people have struggled to protect their past, survive in the present, and ensure their future. With the growth of non-Native communities across what is now the United States, numerous cultural sites have been destroyed in order to make room for these expanding populations without local Native American tribal input. In recognition of this destruction, the United States government adopted various laws to protect those sites and provide mechanisms to limit the impact of ground-disturbing activities. The discipline of anthropology, and the subdiscipline of archaeology, grew out of the discovery of these cultural sites as investigators attempted to create explanations for the objects they encountered.

Because of California's large population growth and the spreading of urban centers into previously undeveloped areas, cultural resource management (CRM) and archaeology have become a booming business in the state. Because California is such a large and environmentally diverse state, different types of landowners exist. For example, tribes in northern California most often work with federal land agencies (National Park Service, Bureau of Land Management, U.S. Forestry Service, and so on) over logging and water projects and their impact on sacred sites. Tribes in central California work with a number of federal land agencies, but also with a mixture of large private land tracts (for example, ranches, farms, vineyards) and a growing number of community development projects where sacred sites exist. Tribes in southern California are most heavily impacted by a large number of development projects on both small and large parcels of private land. As they are planned for construction across the state, even cell phone towers and cable lines can trigger the need for archaeological work.

A number of Native California tribal members who work in cultural resource protection related to us a number of key issues about the current state of California archaeology. The most common concerns California Native people raised were the exclusion of Native people from the recovery of archaeological materials; the lack of consultation about the cultural sites and the interpretations created about these indigenous places—preconceived notions that California tribal cultures are extinct, leaving only archaeologists qualified to discuss them; the fact that the quality of California archaeology has significantly diminished because of the for-profit CRM firms and their relationship with developers; the ineffectiveness of the current laws to protect the cultural sites; and the need to acknowledge past wrongs and work together toward better education. Tribes and archaeologists really share a common

goal in protecting traditional cultural sites and preserving stories about the past to teach future generations.

ARCHAEOLOGISTS AS GATEKEEPERS: IDENTITY AND ACCESS

Native Californian participants related to us how California archaeologists use their authority and knowledge to deny tribal members access to their ancestors' cultural material—even going so far as to reject a tribal member's statement of cultural heritage.

For example, when discussing the possible visit of a Gabrielino/Tongva community member to view her ancestors' remains under the care of a particular archaeologist in his laboratory, the archaeologist was hesitant to arrange the visit because, as he put it, "She hasn't proven her Gabrielino heritage to me yet." As a faculty member at a public institution, it is not his job to ask people to prove their heritage in order to have access to the collection.

Some archaeologists view California tribal members as claiming an identity to which they have no right. Native people have been called "delusional Mexicans" who practice traditions that they invented. This is especially hurtful when most California Native people are of mixed heritage due to the mission system and Spanish conquest. Less than 100 years ago, laws allowed an average person to take children from their Native parents, purportedly for their own protection.

Sam Dunlap, tribal-council member of the Gabrielino/Tongva Nation, provided another example of how archaeologists act as gatekeepers of Native Californian identity. At a 2007 cultural-sensitivity training class sponsored by the county of Riverside, an archaeologist complained that he shouldn't have to consult with Cahuilla tribes. He proclaimed that the Cahuilla were non-existent after 1940, and those who identify as Cahuilla today practice reinvented cultural traditions and are not really Cahuilla. Although those present quietly dismissed this comment, no one rose to challenge his comment, even if they did not agree.

This kind of comment stems from the unfounded perception that Native cultures are static and cemented in time. Some people seem to believe that Natives or any other group can lose their culture if they incorporate foreign (European) ideas and objects into traditional (primitive) lifeways. In reality, culture is always changing and at any given moment represents the accumulation of hundreds of changes, sometimes spurred by outside influences, over thousands of years.

Lalo Franco, the cultural and historic resources director for the Tachi Yokut tribe, described how an archaeologist attempted to exclude Native people from an archaeological

Lake Cachuma, California, and the surrounding landscape.　[Wendy Giddens Teeter]

site in Kern County. The site was over 1,000 years old and—since it was in a remote area—considered pristine. The archaeologist urged Kern County officials to forbid Native Americans from going to the site, because they might ruin it. The archaeologist stated that the Native community hadn't known about the site previously, and now that he had found it, there was a sudden interest. Franco objected to the archaeologist's inaccurate characterization of the Native community's relationship to the site. Franco states that they always knew about the site but were unable to utilize it in a traditional way, because a gate blocked their access. Furthermore, the Native community understands the fragile condition of the site and is not going to destroy it, especially since they view the site as sacred.

These examples show how archaeologists consider themselves experts of an extinct Indian past and presume that modern Native Americans have no interest in the past and are unable to preserve it. This paternalistic viewpoint is furthered when archaeologists imply Native Americans are unable to

understand the implications their decisions will have regarding their cultural materials and history. In reality Native people have always been interested in their past and preserve it by passing traditional knowledge and history down to their children.

DIFFERENCES IN SITE SIGNIFICANCE DEFINITIONS AND LACK OF CONSULTATION

State and federal laws dictate that impacts to the environment, including archaeological, historical, and cultural sites, caused by public construction projects must be documented and in many cases also mitigated. It is hoped that with this documentation, sites will be protected or the impact to sites minimized. However, many California Native Americans report having witnessed shoddy archaeological work completed, resulting in final reports that do not truly describe the significance and number of sites that may be affected by the work proposed.

For example, a Karuk tribal member described how, a few years ago in northern California, a road was to be constructed through an acorn-gathering area. Ground stone and other related artifacts were visible and prominent on the surface. The archaeologist in charge of accessing the APE (area of potential effects) defined the area as extending only 4.2 meters (14 ft) on either side of the proposed road. To the contrary, tribal members determined the APE to be 305 meters (1000 ft) above and below the proposed road cut. This area was not recognized as significant, because it only had ground stone (milling equipment) present. When the road was constructed, whole sites where destroyed. Had the archaeologist consulted and incorporated tribal members' comments into the APE, nonrenewable cultural sites would have been avoided and protected.

Another Karuk tribal member described another way in which tribal consultation is being avoided. She has noticed that many federal agencies have increased their use of programmatic agreements (PAs). PAs are agreements between federal, state, and local agencies with the California State Historic Preservation Office (SHPO) that clarify how cultural resources will be managed. The creation and signing of these PAs are often done without the consultation of Native California tribes. Since only signatories to the PA can change it, tribes are unable to have their concerns regarding site management addressed early and with authority.

LACK OF CULTURAL SENSITIVITY
Native Californian people hold traditional sites in high esteem. In acknowledgment of this sacredness, many Native Californians leave offerings of prayers and gifts while on archaeological sites. Consequently, they request that all those present on a site act in a respectful manner, even if they do not hold the same view of sacredness. This request is not always honored, however.

Joyce Perry, an Acjacheman tribal member, reported how the offerings she had placed on an archaeological site she was monitoring were mistreated. She found her gifts scattered one day when she arrived at the site. When she asked what happened, she was told that one of the archaeologists working at the site had stomped all over the offerings. When others at the site asked the person disturbing the offerings to stop, explaining that the offerings were medicine placed by a tribal member, the archaeologist cursed about the offerings.

The county of Riverside has established a set of minimum requirements of education and experience for archaeologists and anyone performing cultural-resource analysis in the county. These requirements are based on those used by the National Park Service (36 CFR Part 61). Anyone working as an archaeologist, field surveyor, or researcher must also complete a cultural sensitivity training program.

With completion of the minimum requirements, archaeologists are then placed on the county's list of approved archaeologists. The irony is that as long as you take the sensitivity class and meet the minimum requirements, you are approved; you don't have to practice what you've learned. The archaeologist who claimed that the real Cahuilla were extinct will continue to work status quo. Leslie Mouriquand, Riverside's county archaeologist, noted that there is no legal way the county can keep him off the approved list; it can't screen for personal views. Additionally, since cultural resource management firms are not licensed, there are few avenues to lodge formal complaints against archaeologists, despite the damage they can cause.

THE PROBLEM WITH CURRENT LOCAL, STATE, AND FEDERAL LAWS
The Riverside County requirement is just one in a long line of well-intentioned laws and regulations that have been created in order to improve the protection of Native sites in California but have no teeth. In other words, California tribal members have little recourse against CRM practitioners who fall short of legal compliance. Of course, another problem is that the laws are often written to make legal compliance fairly easy, but the results still fall far below the intention (or spirit) of consultation and cooperation.

TRIBAL MONITORING
The identification and mitigation of cultural resources can add significant expense to a development project. In order to limit the time and money needed for this phase of construction, some Native Californians believe, a development company and a CRM firm will come to an agreement that specific kinds of cultural materials found in a project area represent little significance. Under the California Environmental Quality Act (CEQA), the Native American monitoring program was created to prevent this type of deception and to ensure the protection of cultural resources. During any ground-disturbing activity where Native American remains or artifacts might be encountered, a Native American monitor, preferably from the local Native community, is present to ensure the ethical treatment of items found. If human remains or cultural items are encountered, tribal monitors have the ability to stop work.

Even with this preventative system in place, there is little oversight of the monitoring process. Tribal monitors, similar to archaeologists working on CRM projects, are often selected and paid for by the developer, which can lead to ethical dilemmas. As Julie Tumamait, a Chumash tribal member, said to us, "Some people are monitoring for monitoring's sake; just for the money and are not even consulting with Native people about the work they are doing."

Additionally, monitors are not required by California law to be archaeologically trained or culturally certified. A monitor may be culturally knowledgeable, but if the site was not previously identified by the local Native American community, the monitor may defer to the archaeologist's interpretation of the site's archaeological significance. Conversely, if a tribal monitor is archaeologically trained but not culturally knowledgeable, the monitor may disregard a culturally constructed feature because it is not considered significant archaeologically. Both types of monitors can hinder site protection.

REAL CHANGE?

Many Native Californians are well aware of the loopholes in current laws and have supported legislation to fill in the gaps. Fred Collins, spokesman for the Northern Chumash Tribal Council, stated that with the passage of Senate Bill 18 (SB18) in 2005 was an important step for California tribes. The new law gives California tribes the opportunity to comment on changes to city and county land-use plans. This enables tribes to communicate with all the city and county governments and work very closely with them to form better protocols. By bringing tribes in at the planning stage of a development and before any ground is disturbed, it is hoped that cultural sites can be identified and avoided. However, as with many other cultural resource laws, there is no punishment or fines for counties and cities that do not consult with tribes. When there is inadequate compliance, or the law fails to protect, the next step is often expensive litigation.

WHERE DO WE GO FROM HERE?

Even with problems, a few tribal cultural-resource directors stated that they can see a changing of the tide in the archaeologists' relationship to Native Californian communities. Gregg Castro, T'rowt'raahl Salinan/Rumsien Ohlone, and member of Society for California Archaeology's (SCA) Native American Programs Committee—told us that SCA "has come a long way from where they were," but still has a long way to go.

Although this SCA Programs Committee compiles a resource book titled *Sourcebook on Cultural Resources Management, Archaeology, and Cultural Heritage Values* to be used by archaeologists and Native American communities, Lalo Franco considers the book solely as a way for SCA members to be seen as good people. The SCA has also developed one of the strongest codes of ethics, by which it expects its members to abide. Franco believes that the policies and suggestions discussed in the book will not be sustained until SCA members and other archaeologists recognize the impact that their work and their predecessors' activities have had on the Native American communities whose past they study.

APOLOGY

Although Franco gets asked to be on Native American advisory boards for a number of organizations and agencies, he told us that he turns these invitations down, because he sees them "as trying to put a bandage on the damage and hurt" that the archaeologists have caused Native communities. Franco wants to see an apology from archaeologists. Only then will Native communities regain trust in the archaeologists' sincerity.

Franco's belief that an apology will improve the situation in California is not off base. Similar apologies have been instrumental in improving relationships between Native Americans and archaeologists in other parts of the country. In Desireé R. Martinez's research of interactions between federal agency archaeologists and Pacific Northwest tribal representatives, real dialogue didn't start until all federal employees involved in government-to-government discussions, including the head commanding officer, acknowledged the history of poor communication and appalling treatment endured by Pacific Northwest nations under the federal agency. Although the federal employees making the acknowledgment were not the people who began the ill treatment, they were the inheritors of the situation and thus guilty by association. The Pacific Northwest tribes were distrustful of federal agencies and their employees until they received an apology for the tribes' past treatment. Only then could tribal members be sure that the federal agency was sincere about wanting to include them in creation of federal land management plans.

ACKNOWLEDGEMENT OF DIFFERING WORLDVIEWS

Even with an apology, archaeologists must acknowledge that their view of the archaeological record is very different from that of Native Californians. This view affects their communication with tribal community members. Franco and Castro think that by viewing a cultural site as strictly archaeological, archaeologists create a real disconnect between the artifacts and the Native Californian communities who still hold them in high regard.

Castro explains that this divide is exacerbated by the difference in the view of time. Archaeologists don't understand why Native Californians can be so attached to old artifacts; Californian tribal communities consider their cultural sites—and the materials found in them—sacred and vital to their history and present-day survival. To see the two as separate not only objectifies the artifacts and human remains, but also dehumanizes the represented people, both past and present.

INCREASED TRIBAL PARTICIPATION

Gregg Castro believes that this disconnect can be rectified with the increased presence of Native Californians at archaeological conferences and meetings. Although some Native people who have attended SCA conferences have been disgusted by how their history was presented, Castro argues that increased participation will create change and combat the perception of Native people as abstractions. It is not necessary for Native Californians to agree with archaeologists' interpretations.

EDUCATION

Almost all Native California participants cited the need to educate the students—the future archaeologists—on how to work with tribal communities. Castro explains that after a session at the 2007 SCAs that he had helped put together, students provided positive feedback. They stated that they hadn't known the impact archaeology had had on Native Californian communities and were grateful for the education.

Leo Carpenter Jr. agrees with Castro but emphasizes the importance of educating Native Californians in the -ologies (biology, archaeology, geology) as well. Carpenter said to us that some archaeological and scientific techniques are useful, and Native Californians need to "encourage and invest in our peoples in order to protect our resources and sacred sites." He is working with the Bureau of Land Management in Northern California to create a stewardship program that will train California tribal members to use archaeological methods to protect sites. The documentation of sites through these methods can help Native Californian communities in court cases. Ultimately, Carpenter believes, Native Californians have to be patient and open to educating themselves and those with whom they come in contact.

Further Reading: California Native American Heritage Commission Web site, http://www.nahc.ca.gov (online 2005); Deloria, Vine Jr., "Indians, Archaeologists, and the Future," *American Antiquity* 57(4) (1992): 31–33; King, Thomas F., *Thinking About Cultural*

Resource Management: Essays From the Edge (Walnut Creek, CA: AltaMira Press, 2002); Martinez, Desiree R., "Overcoming Hindrances to Our Enduring Responsibility to the Ancestors: Protecting Traditional Cultural Places," *American Indian Quarterly* 30(3) (2006); McGuire, Randall, "Why Have Archaeologists Thought Real Indians Were Dead and What Can We Do About it?" in Thomas Biolsi and Larry Zimmerman, eds., *Indians and Anthropologists: Vine Deloria, Jr. and the Critique of Anthropology* (Tucson: University of Arizona Press, 1997); Perry, Joyce, and Lynn Gamble, "Hate Crimes on Sacred Sites in Southern California: An American Indian Experience," *Society for California Archaeology Newsletter* 36(2) (2002): 10–13; Zimmerman, Larry, "Remythologizing the Relationship between Indians and Archaeologists," in *Native Americans and Archaeologists: Stepping Stones to Common Ground*, edited by Nina Swidler, Kurt Dongoske, Roger Anyon, and Alan Downer (London: AltaMira Press, 1997), 44–56.

Desireé Reneé Martinez and Wendy Giddens Teeter

EUROPEAN EXPLORATION AND EARLY ENCOUNTERS WITH CALIFORNIA INDIANS

Early European exploration of the California coast and subsequent cross-cultural encounters between seafarers and California Indians is documented in a rich historical record. Chronicles of European voyages of exploration to Alta California before permanent Spanish settlement in 1769, which includes four Spanish expeditions between 1542 and 1603 and the Englishman Sir Francis Drake's visit in 1579, offer the first outsiders' ethnographic glimpses of California's indigenous populations. The voyages are also the earliest examples of culture contact on North America's West Coast.

Archaeological remains from the interactions between European voyagers and California Indian hunter-gatherers present a unique opportunity to study sixteenth-century intercultural engagement in California. Twentieth-century excavations of indigenous sites in northern California have unearthed evidence of the encounters in the form of European and Asian artifacts found within wholly Native contexts of coastal village sites. These archaeological sites, some of which can be visited today, illuminate a fascinating chapter in the history of Native American and European culture contact.

Five documented European voyages of exploration to Alta California occurred before the Spanish permanently colonized the region in 1769. These consist of four voyages on behalf of the Spanish crown, including expeditions by Cabrillo-Ferrelo (1542–43), Unamuno (1587), Cermeño (1595), and Vizcaíno (1602–03); and one five-week sojourn by the Englishman Sir Francis Drake and his vessel, the *Golden Hind*, in 1579.

It is important to keep in mind, however, that from 1565 to the early nineteenth century, the long-standing route of the

Manila trade between the Philippines and Acapulco usually made landfall in northern California after a north Pacific crossing, then followed the California coast south to Mexico. These annual voyages may have resulted in undocumented encounters between Europeans engaged in the Manila trade and California Indians over several hundred years.

The first Spanish voyage explored Alta California from September 1542 to March 1543, initially under the leadership of Juan Rodríguez Cabrillo, and later under the leadership of Bartolomé Ferrelo, after Cabrillo's death in January 1543. The Spaniards may have explored as far north as the Oregon border, and they had extensive interactions with various California Indian groups, mostly in southern California. There is no firsthand account of the voyage, but two abbreviated accounts were compiled after the voyage. The existing accounts record one violent episode between the Spaniards and the Northern Diegueño near San Diego, but encounters were otherwise peaceful ones that included regular bartering of cloth and other unspecified trade goods for provisions. There was also at least one instance where a female ruler of several villages in the Santa Barbara Channel area (likely Barbareño Chumash), spent two nights aboard the Spanish flagship. There are no known material remains of the expedition or any of the interactions.

Sir Francis Drake and his ship, the *Golden Hind*, landed somewhere on the California coast during summer 1579. He and his crew spent five weeks preparing the vessel for a long Pacific crossing. Scholars debate the precise location of the landfall, but most agree it was within Coast Miwok territory,

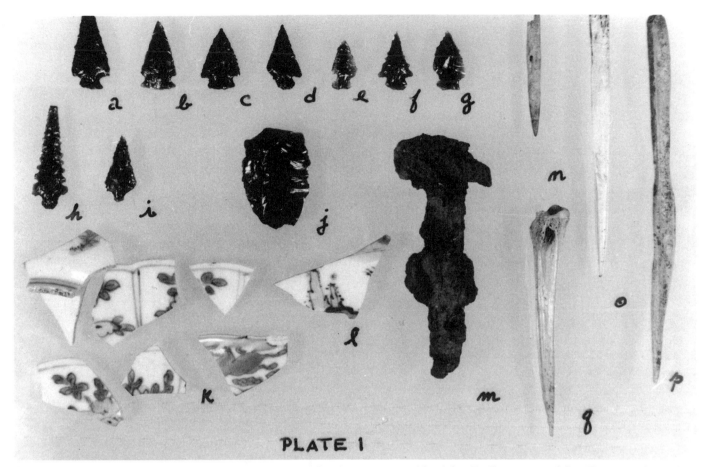

Artifacts from CA-MRN-308, now in Point Reyes National Seashore, excavated by Adan E. Treganza and San Francisco State College in 1958. [Courtesy of the Phoebe Apperson Hearst Museum of Anthropology and the Regents of the University of California (Ms283)]

and was likely in Drakes Bay. Accounts of Drake's interactions with the Coast Miwok are documented in several accounts—notably, *The World Encompassed by Sir Francis Drake* and Hakluyt's *Famous Voyage* account. The episode is fascinating, because the Drake documents consistently record a series of unusual and highly ritualized scenes after *Golden Hind's* arrival in California.

After anchoring, a lone individual in a canoe addressed the crew with an oratory greeting. Afterward, the crew observed the Native inhabitants weeping and scratching their faces. Later came a well-known incident in which the California Indians "crowned" Drake as their "king," followed by more crying, shrieking, weeping, and scratching.

Most scholars agree that the Native inhabitants' actions are consistent with some variation of the Kuksu or Ghost Dance rites, traditional forms of mourning ceremony that were a regular part of the ritual calendar and took place during the summer months. This interpretation suggests the Coast Miwok perceived the English as returned spirits or ghosts of dead ancestors, or as individuals who had arrived to participate in the ceremonial context of the Kuksu and Ghost Dance performances. This pro-

vides the cultural context for making sense of how the voyagers were received by the Coast Miwok, as well as how they may have perceived material remains from later visitors.

After Drake, the next European visit to California was by Pedro de Unamuno in October 1587. On a return voyage from the Philippines to Acapulco, a small *frigata* commanded by Unamuno made a two-day landfall near Morro Bay, north of San Luis Obispo. After anchoring their ship, the Spaniards briefly explored the surrounding inland area. Although they observed several Obispeño Chumash villages, the only direct encounter occurred in a violent confrontation between the Native inhabitants and the Spaniards and their Filipino crew that resulted in casualties to both sides. Unamuno and his crew subsequently retreated to their ship and resumed their voyage, which they continued without further incident.

Eight years after Unamuno's voyage, the Spanish Manila galleon *San Agustín*—under the command of Sebastian Rodriguez Cermeño and carrying a diverse cargo of Chinese export trade goods, including porcelain, silk, and other luxury items—wrecked in Drakes Bay (known to the Coast Miwok as Tamál-Húye), California, in November 1595, while

Archaeologists from the University of California, Berkeley, excavating CA-MRN-232 on the bluff above Estero de Limantour in 1949, now part of Point Reyes National Seashore.   [Courtesy of the Phoebe Apperson Hearst Museum of Anthropology and the Regents of the University of California (Ms079)]

en route from the Philippines to Mexico. From an archaeological standpoint, this event resulted in one of the most intriguing cases of intercultural engagement in early California history.

The *San Agustín* anchored in the bay to re-provision and assemble a small launch for coastal exploration, but was driven ashore during a storm after its arrival. The Spaniards were forced to modify the launch to accommodate the whole eighty-member crew for the return to Mexico. For more than a month, both before and after *San Agustín*'s wreck and while completing modifications to the launch, Cermeño's crew interacted with the indigenous Coast Miwok population.

The encounters were documented in an account written by Cermeño upon his return to Mexico, as well as several other contemporary declarations. The documents record daily observations and events from the voyage, and Cermeño made brief ethnographic observations about the indigenous populations.

The surviving Spaniards successfully continued their voyage, but abandoned *San Agustín* and its cargo. From the Coast Miwok perspective, this was likely just the beginning of their interaction with the shipwreck itself; small-scale collecting, opportunistic salvage, or possibly systematic exploitation likely continued for some time. The month-long interaction between Spanish sailors and Coast Miwok hunter-gatherers left the richest archaeological record of early culture contact in California, including a considerable quantity of introduced European and Asian material culture reused by Coast Miwok villagers.

Following their departure from Tamál-Húye, Cermeño and his crew briefly encountered two California Indian groups as they traveled south to Mexico—first the Obispeño, or Purismeño Chumash, near San Luis Obispo; and later, the Island Chumash off Santa Rosa Island, in the Santa Barbara Channel. During both encounters, the Chumash groups approached the launch in their own boats, and the Spaniards traded cloth for desperately needed provisions. Cermeño recorded these interactions as simple and uneventful trading encounters.

Large iron fasteners, possibly from the *San Agustín*, located during University of California, Berkeley, excavations at Point Reyes. [Courtesy of the Phoebe Apperson Hearst Museum of Anthropology and the Regents of the University of California (Ms079)]

Sebastían Vizcaíno's expedition, which explored Alta California from November 1602 to January 1603, was the last European expedition to visit California before permanent Spanish colonization in the late eighteenth century. In San Diego, a Northern Diegueño group approached the Spaniards as a large force, displaying aggressive posturing, while several women wept in a greeting similar to that recorded by Drake in northern California more than 20 years earlier. Further north, Gabrielinos at Catalina Island greeted Vizcaíno's crew, invited them ashore, and provided provisions; later, Island Chumash in the Channel Islands approached the Spaniards in canoes. At Monterey, the northernmost encounter with California Indians that Vizcaíno recorded, Ohlone peoples visited the voyagers several times, but Vizcaíno did not record specific details of the encounters.

One Native oral tradition that recorded a pre-colonization European encounter in California comes from the Kashaya Pomo—closely related neighbors of the Coast Miwok, to the north. Their story, told by elder Essie Parrish to Berkeley linguist Robert L. Oswalt in 1958, records their first perceptions of a European sailing ship as a large bird traveling across the water, signaling the end of the world. Although we cannot know if this tradition refers to a specific encounter, its real value is that it gives us a glimpse of the California Indian perspective of early encounters, albeit filtered through many generations of oral tradition. In that regard, the story gives us insight into how at least one indigenous group made sense of their initial contact with European outsiders.

At present most of the known archaeological evidence of early European explorers in California comes from California Indian sites in northern California and consists of introduced European and Asian material remains incorporated by Coast Miwok hunter-gatherers into their daily practice. With the possible exception of a few miscellaneous objects (notably, a 1567 English silver sixpence excavated from the Coast Miwok village site of Olompali in 1974 and attributed by some to Drake, and a sixteenth-century Japanese spear tip of unknown origin from a site near San Quentin Cove), the majority of the archaeological evidence for early European voyages is from Cermeño's shipwreck, *San Agustín*.

The wreck site itself has yet to be located, although efforts to locate *San Agustín*'s remains are underway by researchers from the University of California at Berkeley, the National Park Service, and the National Oceanic and Atmospheric Administration. Current archaeological evidence for the shipwreck, and for the cross-cultural encounter between the European explorers and the Coast Miwok, is indirect and consists of objects from the ship excavated from Coast Miwok sites on land.

University of California archaeologists excavated seven Coast Miwok village and midden sites surrounding modern-day Drakes Bay from 1940 to 1951. Their primary interest was to locate artifacts from the firmly dated *San Agustín* shipwreck to provide a chronometric marker for refining the area's culture history. Later researchers from San Francisco State College (now University) and other institutions excavated at Point Reyes from the mid-1950s to the early 1970s, uncovering several additional sites with material from *San Agustín*. Unlike the Berkeley archaeologists, these researchers were primarily interested in finding evidence of Sir Francis Drake's possible 1579 landfall.

Archaeological remains from *San Agustín* mostly consist of blue and white underglaze Chinese-export porcelain, including dishes, bowls, plates, and other ceramic vessels. The porcelain shards excavated from Coast Miwok sites around Tamál-Húye fall into at least three distinct categories.

The most numerous is a fine ware type that came to be known as *kraaksporcelein* (a Dutch term referring to the type of vessel engaged in the Asian trade), or Kraak porcelain. This type of ware was produced in China's porcelain center at Jingdezhen for export to the West and is characterized by pale blue designs on a white body.

In addition to Kraak porcelain, another late-sixteenth-century porcelain type found at Point Reyes sites was produced at provincial kilns in Fujian province. It is often referred to as Swatow ware (an erroneous term referring to the port of Swatow, or Shantou, in Guangdong, which did not actually export porcelain during the sixteenth and seventeenth centuries). In contrast to Kraak porcelain, Swatow ware is heavily potted and roughly finished, with large amounts of sand adhering to the foot ring and base. The decoration usually lacks formal panels, is painted in a darker blue or indigo, and is freely and boldly drawn.

Finally, there are unspecified provincial-ware vessels, including bowls and dishes, that are neither as fine as Kraak porcelain nor as coarse as Swatow ware.

Some researchers contend that some of the porcelain may not be from *San Agustín* after all, but may instead have been left by Sir Francis Drake in 1579. The evidence for this notion is still somewhat controversial; future research may shed more light on this alternative interpretation. In addition to porcelain, numerous iron spikes, likely from *San Agustín* itself, have also been excavated from Coast Miwok sites, as well as a handful of other objects, such as bitumen, wax, and several small metal objects that may include a compass needle and nails.

An interesting set of questions about the intercultural engagement between Europeans from *San Agustín* and Coast Miwok groups in Tamál-Húye revolves around the introduced material culture from the shipwreck, which was evidently salvaged and incorporated into Coast Miwok cultural practice. Archaeologists are interested in how the Coast Miwok may have re-contextualized introduced material culture from *San Agustín* and integrated it into their daily lives, and the long-term implications of an encounter that took place 175 years before Spanish colonialism reached the region.

Although early researchers suggest that California Indian interest in the objects was strictly pragmatic in nature, Lightfoot and Simmons examined protohistoric cultural encounters in California from a more nuanced perspective and offer a different interpretation of Coast Miwok reuse of objects from *San Agustín*. They suggest that because of the ceremonial context of the Coast Miwok's first encounter with Europeans (which likely coincided with the Kuksu ceremony during Drake's visit), they may have collected porcelain shards and iron spikes because they were valued as symbols of previous encounters with Europeans and as objects that signified unknown worlds.

One of the long-term implications of early European voyages to the California coast is the impact of European disease on indigenous populations. This issue has not been thoroughly studied to date, although there has been much speculation about the severity of the impact. It is widely recognized that Old World diseases inadvertently introduced to Native populations by Europeans—diseases against which Native groups had no natural defense—caused severe population decline after European contact. A variety of epidemics are documented during the Spanish Mission period; however, no systematic archaeological evidence has yet been unearthed regarding the period after initial European contact, but before permanent settlement. Some indicators suggest that epidemics in California may have been geographically limited, sporadic, and short-lived. More archaeological evidence needs to be brought to bear, however, to fully answer the question.

Many of the sites preserving the remains of cross-cultural interactions during the pre-colonial era are located in Point Reyes National Seashore, and are part of the Point Reyes Archaeological District. Most of them are not open to the public; however, their story is told in the Kenneth C. Patrick Visitor Center, located on Drakes Beach. The visitor center highlights Coast Miwok culture and early European exploration of the Point Reyes area, especially the voyages of Drake and Cermeño. The Bear Valley Visitor Center, located near Olema, also includes a replica Coast Miwok village from the time of European contact (known as Kule Loklo).

Olompali State Historic Park, overlooking the Petaluma River and San Pablo Bay from the slopes of Mount Burdell, is open to the public and preserves the remains of a variety archaeological sites and historic structures. The most prominent is the adobe house of Camilo Ynitia—the last *hoipu*, or headman, of the Coast Miwok community living at Olompali in the nineteenth century. Coast Miwok groups inhabited sites within the park from as early as 6,000 BC until the early 1850s. The village site at Olompali yielded a 1567 English silver sixpence, one of the oldest European artifacts found in California; therefore the site provides important material evidence of early European visits to northern California. It is not known if villagers from Olompali had direct contact with European explorers, or if Europeans visited the site before Spanish colonization in the late eighteenth century, or if the coin was brought to the site through some other route. However there is no doubt the village was an important regional center for Coast Miwok culture at the time of early contact between California Indians and European voyagers.

Finally, although not an archaeological site, Cabrillo National Monument in San Diego, a unit of the national park system, commemorates Cabrillo's entry into San Diego Bay as the first European visit to the California coast. The monument has a variety of displays documenting the history of the Cabrillo-Ferrelo expedition in 1542–43, including the Age of Exploration exhibit room near the Visitor Center, and exhibits of sixteenth-century armor and navigational instruments.

Further Reading: Bolton, H. E., *Spanish Exploration in the Southwest 1542–1706* (New York: Charles Scribner's Sons, 1916); Erlandson, Jon M., and Kevin Bartoy, "Cabrillo, the Chumash, and Old World Diseases," *Journal of California and Great Basin Anthropology* 17(2) (1995): 153–173; Heizer, Robert F., "Archaeological Evidence of Sebastian Rodriquez Cermeno's California Visit in 1595," *California Historical Society Quarterly* 20(4) (1942): 1–32; Heizer, Robert F., *Elizabethan California* (Ramona, CA: Ballena Press, 1974); Heizer, Robert F., "Francis Drake and the California Indians, 1579," *University of California Publications in American Archaeology and Ethnology* 42(3) (1947): 251–302; Heizer, Robert F., and William W. Elmendorf, "Francis Drake's California Anchorage in the Light of the Indian Language Spoken There," *Pacific Historical Review* 11 (1942): 213–217; Lightfoot,

Kent G., and William S. Simmons, "Culture Contact in Protohistoric California: Social Contexts of Native and European Encounters," *Journal of California and Great Basin Anthropology* 20(2) (1998): 138–170; Meighan, Clement W., *Excavations in Sixteenth Century Shellmounds at Drake's Bay, Marin County*, University of California Archaeological Survey No. 9, Papers on California Archaeology No. 9 (Berkeley, CA: University of California Department of Anthropology, 1950); Meighan, Clement W., "The Stoneware Site, a 16th Century Site on Drakes Bay," in *Essays in California Archaeology: A Memorial to Franklin Fenenga*, edited by William J. Wallace and Francis A. Riddell (Berkeley, CA: University of California, 2002), 62–87; Meighan, Clement W., "'This Is the Way the World Ends': Native Responses to the Age of Exploration in California," in *Early California: Perception and Reality* (Los Angeles: William Andrews Clark Memorial Library, University of California, 1981), 45–74; Meighan, Clement W., and Robert F. Heizer, "Archaeological Exploration of Sixteenth-Century Indian Mounds at Drake's Bay," *California Historical Society Quarterly* 31(2) (1952): 99–108; Nauman, James D., ed., *An Account of the Voyage of Juan Rodriguez Cabrillo* (San Diego, CA: Cabrillo National Monument Foundation, 1999); Oswalt, R. L., *Kashaya Texts*, University of California Publications in Linguistics 36 (Berkeley: University of California Press, 1966); Sanchez, Joseph P., "From the Philippines to the California Coast in 1595: The Last Voyage of San Agustin under Sebastian Rodriquez Cermeno," *Colonial Latin American Historical Review* 10(2) (2001): 223–251; Wagner, Henry R., "The Voyage of Pedro De Unamuno to California in 1587," *California Historical Society Quarterly* 2(2) (1923): 140–160; Wagner, Henry R., *Sir Francis Drake's Voyage around the World: Its Aims and Achievements* (San Francisco: John Howell, 1926); Wagner, Henry R., *Spanish Voyages to the Northwest Coast of America in the Sixteenth Century* (San Francisco: California Historical Society, 1929); Walker, Phillip L., and John R. Johnson, "The Decline of the Chumash Indian Population," in *In the Wake of Contact: Biological Responses to Conquest*, edited by C. S. Larsen and G. Milner (New York: John Wiley and Sons, 1994); Walker, Phillip L., and John R. Johnson, "Effects of Contact on the Chumash Indians," in *Disease and Demography in the Americas*, edited by John W. Verano and Douglas H. Ubelaker (Washington, DC: Smithsonian Institution, 1992), 127–139.

Matthew A. Russell and Kent G. Lightfoot

SPANISH AND MEXICAN COLONIZATION OF ALTA CALIFORNIA

For more than two centuries following the initial voyage of Juan Rodríguez Cabrillo in 1542, occasional visits by maritime explorers resulted in mostly short-term encounters with California Indians. The colonial period of Alta California began in earnest with the founding of Mission San Diego during the expedition led by Gaspar de Portolá in 1769.

Wonderfully detailed, firsthand descriptions of the California Indians come to us from the diaries of expedition members, particularly the journals of Father Juan Crespí, a Franciscan missionary assigned by Father Junípero Serra to accompany the party as it moved northward to locate a route to Monterey Bay.

Over the next seven decades of colonial experience under Spain and Mexico, California Indians in missionized areas

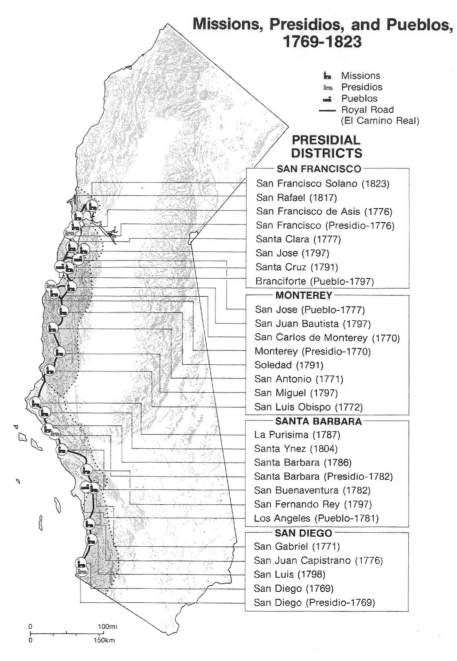

Missions, Presidios, and Pueblos, 1769-1823

- 🏰 Missions
- 🏰 Presidios
- 🏰 Pueblos
- —— Royal Road (El Camino Real)

PRESIDIAL DISTRICTS

SAN FRANCISCO
San Francisco Solano (1823)
San Rafael (1817)
San Francisco de Asis (1776)
San Francisco (Presidio-1776)
Santa Clara (1777)
San Jose (1797)
Santa Cruz (1791)
Branciforte (Pueblo-1797)

MONTEREY
San Jose (Pueblo-1777)
San Juan Bautista (1797)
San Carlos de Monterey (1770)
Monterey (Presidio-1770)
Soledad (1791)
San Antonio (1771)
San Miguel (1797)
San Luis Obispo (1772)

SANTA BARBARA
La Purisima (1787)
Santa Ynez (1804)
Santa Barbara (1786)
Santa Barbara (Presidio-1782)
San Buenaventura (1782)
San Fernando Rey (1797)
Los Angeles (Pueblo-1781)

SAN DIEGO
San Gabriel (1771)
San Juan Capistrano (1776)
San Luis (1798)
San Diego (1769)
San Diego (Presidio-1769)

0   100mi
0   150km

Map of colonial Alta California showing missions, pueblos, and presidios. [Courtesy of the National Park Service]

were to have their lives changed forever as they moved from relatively small, independent tribal groups based on hunting, fishing, and gathering to coalesced, remnant populations concentrated at mission establishments—where cultural ways of life were forever altered, introduced European diseases took a devastating toll, and subsistence based on agriculture and animal husbandry replaced Native economies.

Three Spanish colonial institutions were established in Alta California: missions, presidios, and pueblos. Twenty-one Franciscan missions were eventually established between San

Diego in the south and San Francisco Solano at Sonoma in the north—the latter of which was founded in 1823. Four presidios were built at San Diego, Santa Barbara, Monterey, and San Francisco. These presidios and their accompanying cannon batteries overlooking nearby harbors were intended to guard the colony from hostile Native groups and to give protection from threats that might arise from hostile foreign vessels. Recruiting settlers from Sonora, Sinaloa, and Baja California, three pueblos were founded: San Jose in 1776, Los Angeles in 1781, and the Villa de Branciforte (now Santa

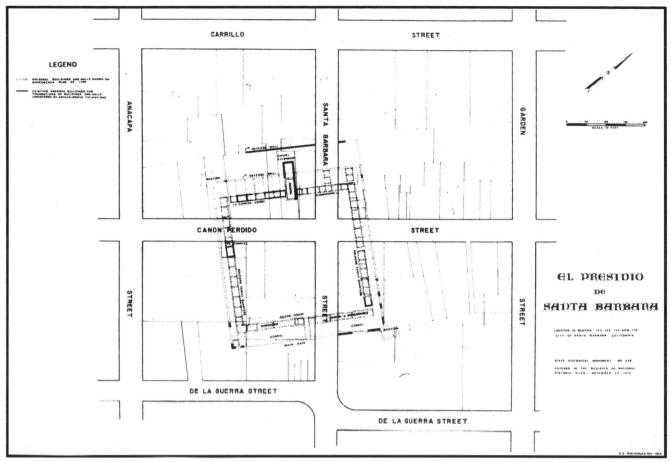

Layout of the Santa Barbara Presidio superimposed on the present street grid, a drawing by Richard S. Whitehead, 1924. [Courtesy of the National Park Service]

Cruz) in 1797. The capital of Alta California was established at Monterey.

So much has been written about the impact of Spanish and Mexican colonization on California Native Americans, and what has been learned from excavations at specific Mission period archaeological sites, that selecting specific references for further reading is a daunting task. The list appended to this entry represents only a small selection of the literature pertaining to Spanish and Mexican Alta California, highlighting some recent scholarship on the subject as well as pointing to specific references pertaining to the sites discussed below. Three Web sites of particular interest are included.

EL PRESIDIO DE SANTA BARBARA STATE HISTORIC PARK

The Presidio of Santa Barbara was founded in 1782 to secure the land supply route connecting the capital of Alta California at Monterey with missions to the south. It was feared that the lifeline linking presidios and missions in the south and north would be severed if the coastal Chumash Indians, who lived in well-populated towns along the Santa Barbara Channel, were to rise in opposition to the Spanish colonial effort. Both the

Spanish governor, Felipe de Neve, and the missionary president, Father Junípero Serra, were desirous that missions and a presidio be established among Chumash peoples as quickly as possible. Neve and Serra differed, however, in their plans for how the Santa Barbara Channel missions were to be organized, and this led to a delay of more than 4 years following the founding of the presidio before Mission Santa Barbara was established.

The major work of constructing the Presidio of Santa Barbara took place between 1782 and 1798, initiated under the first *comandante*, Lt. José Francisco Ortega. During the initial years of construction, Native inhabitants of nearby Chumash towns were hired as laborers and were paid with glass trade beads, which the Spanish soldiers soon learned were highly valued as an addition to the shell bead currency already in use as a medium of exchange.

Once the missions were established, contracted labor between Mission Santa Barbara and the presidio took place, with the proceeds divided between the mission community and the neophyte laborers who undertook the work. The original presidio was designed as a quadrangle with an outer defense wall and two corner bastions. Rebuilding following the severe 1812 earthquake resulted in modifications to the original plan. Following the conquest of California in 1847, those presidio buildings still standing gradually were replaced and built over by the growing city of Santa Barbara. The use of one adobe structure, originally a soldier's family residence (later known as El Cuartel) has continued over more than two centuries.

Through a cooperative arrangement with the state of California's Department of Parks and Recreation, the Santa Barbara Trust for Historic Preservation has gradually acquired more than two-thirds of the property containing the footprint of the original presidio. The trust has undertaken extensive archaeological and documentary research as it has carefully reconstructed much of the original portion of the northern part of the presidio, using original techniques and materials.

The foundations of the original chapel, the adjacent padre's quarters, the *comandancia*, the outer defense wall, the northeast and northwest corners, the soldier's dwellings, and other features have all been studied, along with associated artifacts uncovered in systematic excavations. It is remarkable that intact features, such as an aqueduct bringing water from the vicinity of the mission and the tile floor of a soldier's residence, were preserved to be discovered by archaeologists, despite the creation of streets, homes, and businesses that impacted the foundations of the original presidio.

Because of the trust's reconstruction efforts and well-planned exhibits, visitors to El Presidio State Park can learn much about the history and daily life of a military outpost in the Spanish borderlands.

LA PURÍSIMA MISSION STATE HISTORIC PARK—LOMPOC, CALIFORNIA

In December 1812, a devastating earthquake badly damaged the original Mission La Purísima Concepción, now located within the city limits of Lompoc. Rather than rebuilding the mission where it had existed for 25 years, the Purisimeño Chumash moved it farther up the Santa Ynez Valley to a location less frequented by coastal fogs, at a place called 'Amuwu.

In contrast to the traditional quadrangle used by all other Alta California missions, the principal buildings of the new establishment were aligned parallel to the west side of a well-watered tributary of the Santa Ynez River. The abandonment of the quadrangle plan in 1813 reflects the fact that the Chumash peoples of the surrounding region had already been incorporated into the mission's population, so there was no longer a perceived threat of attack high enough to necessitate a defensive arrangement.

Following the relocation of La Purísima, there were only two significant infusions of new peoples into the mission community: 1) Island Chumash from Santa Rosa and San Miguel islands in 1813–15 and 2) Yokuts tribes of the San Joaquin Valley in 1834–35.

The total numbers of neophytes declined throughout the mission period as the result of introduced diseases, just as they did elsewhere in the Californias. The Chumash uprising of 1824 led briefly to the capture of the mission by the Purisimeños, but was quickly suppressed by the Spanish military. The secularization of the mission in 1834 and exodus of most Yokuts Indians shortly thereafter further depleted the number of neophytes in the mission vicinity. A devastating smallpox epidemic in 1844 left but few survivors. Only one small land grant of the mission orchard was given to two Purisimeño families, and others merged with the Ineseño Chumash community at Zanja de Cota, precursor to the Santa Ynez Indian Reservation.

Extensive archaeological investigations began in 1933–34 prior to the mission's restoration and reconstruction by the Civilian Conservation Corps. Since becoming a state park in 1935, the site has undergone additional archaeological research. Fieldwork at the Mission Indian adobe apartment houses has revealed that Purisimeño Chumash families continued to use traditional ground-stone implements for food processing and cooking, whereas chipped-stone tools were largely replaced by metal knives. Relatively crude brownware pots began to be used, supplementing the large steatite ollas that had been used instead of pottery prior to the historic period. Although shell beads and ornaments remained in use at the missions, glass trade beads replaced types of shell beads that were more difficult to manufacture.

The insights gained from archaeological studies of mission lifeways, reconstruction of buildings on their original foundations, interpretive exhibits, and an active living history program provide park visitors with the best example of what a California mission was like during the colonial period.

MISSION SAN ANTONIO—JOLON, CALIFORNIA

The third mission founded in Alta California, Mission San Antonio de Padua, was established in 1771 and moved to its present location within two years of its founding. Its core population consisted of the peoples known today as Salinan Indians, as well as some of their Esselen neighbors, who lived in the mountains behind Big Sur. In its later years, the mission housed a sizable number of relocated Yokuts Indians from California's Central Valley.

Of all of the California missions, San Antonio is probably the best preserved in its original natural landscape. Surrounded by a military base, the mission has been isolated from nearby development. Most of its archaeological features remain intact for public viewing, including its water system, grist mill, and long mounds, where workshops and neophyte apartments were located.

Beginning in 1976 and lasting for nearly three decades, an archaeological field school was conducted under the direction of Dr. Robert Hoover, resulting in artifact recovery and architectural descriptions of a number of features rarely accessible at other mission sites, including neophyte living quarters, soldiers' barracks, a vineyardist's house, and a brick and tile kiln. The mission remains the property of the Catholic Church, but is open to the public.

MISSION SAN BUENAVENTURA—
VENTURA, CALIFORNIA

Among those missions where considerable archaeological fieldwork has been conducted is Mission San Buenaventura. Established in 1782 (shortly before the nearby Presidio of Santa Barbara was founded), this mission drew its neophyte population from coastal and interior Ventureño Chumash groups, as well as Island Chumash towns. San Buenaventura attained its peak population of 1,328 Mission Indians in 1816, following the incorporation of large numbers of people who migrated from Santa Cruz Island in that year.

The cause of the exodus of the Chumash islanders to the missions on the mainland has been revealed through ethnohistoric sources. An extreme El Niño event of 1815–16 depleted local fisheries, creating famine conditions for the maritime-oriented islanders. The relatively abundant food stores produced by mission agriculture appear to have been a major enticement for hungry islanders. The traditional cross-channel exchange system, whereby shell bead currency produced by the islanders had been traded for mainland resources, had buffered similar crises in the past. The collapse of this trading system—a result of the incorporation of the mainlanders into mission communities—rendered the islanders' situation dire once their fishing livelihood was jeopardized by a severe El Niño.

Two mission complexes were constructed successively at San Buenaventura. The original church was found to be structurally unsound in 1790 and was then demolished while the second church was built. Adjacent to the first church were neophyte residences that had been abandoned by the time the mission reached its final configuration.

The earlier mission complex was thoroughly investigated under the direction of Roberta S. Greenwood in 1974–76, and two extensive archaeological reports describe the findings. The foundations of these early mission buildings have been preserved for public viewing adjacent to the Albinger Archaeological Museum, which is managed by the Ventura Museum of History and Art. The Albinger Museum displays one of the most extensive collections of mission-era artifacts recovered during systematic archaeological investigations, providing a sense of the range and types of material culture used by Mission Indians during colonial times.

AVILA ADOBE, EL PUEBLO DE LOS ANGELES
HISTORICAL MONUMENT—CALIFORNIA

Built by Francisco Avila in about 1818, the oldest standing structure in the city of Los Angeles is located on Olvera Street, near the plaza of the original pueblo. Originally from Sinaloa, Francisco Avila and two of his brothers arrived at the Pueblo de Los Angeles in 1783, two years after its founding. Avila later became the alcalde of the pueblo in 1810.

Like most *pobladores* of Los Angeles, Avila made his living by ranching. Part of his land concession, Rancho Las Cienegas, bordered the famous tar pits at La Brea. There he obtained the asphaltum—which, mixed with animal hair, was used to waterproof the roof of his home. Avila's adobe residence provides a useful example of Spanish-Mexican domestic life in a pueblo setting, as an archaeologically investigated site that is open to the public.

The Avila Adobe was rescued from demolition in 1928 and restored as part of an effort to preserve the old plaza area, which led to the conversion of Olvera Street into a Mexican-style marketplace. The Avila Adobe was badly damaged in the 1971 Sylmar earthquake.

Before further restoration was undertaken, archaeological investigations determined the sequence of construction during the colonial period. The original adobe structure was found to have consisted of three rooms in an L-shaped configuration, with one serving as a kitchen. The floor of these rooms consisted of packed earth. Adobe brick walls were built on stone foundations. Avila added two additional rooms and a ramada to the original structure before his death in 1832, and his widow's next husband expanded and remodeled the residence further in the 1840s, reconfiguring the rooms within the dwelling. Artifacts recovered from the Mexican period occupation are exhibited at the adobe.

PETALUMA ADOBE STATE HISTORIC
PARK—PETALUMA, CALIFORNIA

Following the independence of Mexico from Spain in 1821, the winds of change blew through Alta California, culminating eventually in the secularization of the missions and the breakup of their land holdings. These lands had been intended to be held in trust for the Mission Indians, but the dwindling number of neophytes and demand for agricultural properties to support the families of the growing Spanish-Mexican population led to what is known as the Rancho era of California history. About 800 land grants were allocated by Mexican governors of Alta California between 1822 and 1846, only a fraction of which went to former Mission Indians. California Indians supplied the labor force for most of the Mexican ranchos, having been trained in farming and ranching operations during their experience at the missions.

Located north of San Francisco Bay, the Petaluma Rancho was granted to Mariano Vallejo, one of the prominent citizens of Mexican Alta California. Vallejo employed large numbers of ex-neophytes from Patwin, Pomo, and Coast Miwok tribes on his rancho. A large, two-story adobe ranch house was constructed using Indian labor; these laborers also carried out agricultural operations.

Archaeological research has demonstrated that Vallejo's Native employees were provisioned with beef and lamb, as well as cultivated grains, including wheat, barley, and corn.

These non-Native foods were supplemented with traditional seed and acorn crops gathered from the wild and processed with stone mortars and pestles. In contrast to what was observed archaeologically at Mission La Purísima, there is abundant evidence that Rancho Petaluma's Native laborers continued to rely upon chipped-stone tools within their living areas. Thus archaeological research reveals that there was variability in the ways that different groups of California Indians adapted to particular colonial settings.

Further Reading: Barker, Leo R., Rebecca Allen, and Julia G. Costello, "The Archaeology of Spanish and Mexican Alta California," in *The Archaeology of Spanish and Mexican Colonialism in the American Southwest*, compiled by James E Ayres, Guides to the Archaeological Literature of the Immigrant Experience in American, No. 3 (Rockville, MD: Society for Historical Archaeology, 1995); Butler, William B., "The Avila Adobe: The Determination of Architectural Change," *Historical Archaeology* 7 (1973): 30–45; California Mission Studies Association, http://www.ca-missions.org (online June 2007); Crespí, Juan, *A Description of Distant Roads: Original Journals of the First Expedition into California, 1769–1770*, edited and translated by Alan K. Brown (San Diego: San Diego State University Press, 2001); Deetz, James J. F., "Archaeological Investigations at La Purísima Mission," in *Archaeological Survey Annual Report, 1962–1963* (University of California, Los Angeles, 1963), 162–241; Duggan, Marie Christine, *The Chumash and the Presidio of Santa Barbara: Evolution of a Relationship, 1782–1823* (Santa Barbara, CA: Santa Barbara Trust for Historic Preservation, 2004); Greenwood, Robert S., ed., *The Changing Faces of Main Street: Ventura Mission Plaza Archaeological Project, Ventura, California* (Ventura, CA: Redevelopment Agency of the City of San Buenaventura, 1976); Hackel, Steven W., *Children of Coyote, Missionaries of Saint Francis: Indian-Spanish Relations in Colonial California, 1769–1850* (Chapel Hill: University of North Carolina Press, 2005); Hageman, Fred C., and Russell C. Ewing, *An Archeological and Restoration Study of Mission La Purísima Concepción*, edited by Richard S. Whitehead (Santa Barbara, CA: Santa Barbara Trust for Historic Preservation, 1980); Hoover, Robert L., and Julia G. Costello, eds., *Excavations at Mission San Antonio, 1976–1978*, Monograph 26 (Los Angeles: University of California Institute of Archaeology, 1985); Hornbeck, David, "Hispanic Patterns, 1769–1846," in *California Patterns: A Geographical and Historical Atlas*, edited by David Hornbeck and Phillip Kane, 40–62 (Palo Alto, CA: Mayfield Publishing Company, 1983); Lightfoot, Kent G., *Indians, Missionaries, and Merchants: The Legacy of Colonial Encounters on the California Frontiers* (Berkeley: University of California Press, 2005); Milliken, Randall, *A Time of Little Choice: The Disintegration of Tribal Culture in the San Francisco Bay Area, 1769–1810* (Menlo Park, CA: Ballena Press, 1995); Schuyler, Robert L., "Indian-Euro-American Interaction: Archeological Evidence from Non-Indian Sites," in *Handbook of North American Indians*, Vol. 8: *California*, edited by Robert F. Heizer (Washington, DC: Smithsonian Institution, 1978), 69–79; Silliman, Stephen W., *Lost Laborers In Colonial California: Native Americans and The Archaeology of Rancho Petaluma* (Tucson: University of Arizona Press, 2004); Spanish and Mexican Heritage Sites, State of California Department of Parks and Recreation, http://www.parks.ca.gov (online June 2007); Thomas, David Hurst, ed., "The Californias," in *Columbian Consequences*, Vol. 1: *Archaeological and Historical Perspectives on the Spanish Borderlands West* (Washington, DC, and London: Smithsonian Institution Press, 1989); Web de Anza: Spanish Exploration and Colonization of Alta California, 1774–1776, http://anza.uoregon.edu (online June 2007); Whitehead, Richard S., *Citadel on the Channel: The Royal Presidio of Santa Barbara, Its Founding and Construction, 1782–1798* (Santa Barbara, CA, and Seattle, WA: Santa Barbara Trust for Historic Preservation and Arthur H. Clark Company, 1996).

John R. Johnson

THE RUSSIAN COLONIZATION OF CALIFORNIA

Native Americans have lived on the Sonoma County Coast for perhaps 9,000 years or more. The ethnographic Kashaya Pomo lived in the area of Fort Ross, and the Bodega Miwok people lived in the area of Bodega Bay. These coastal peoples evidently had frequent links with those on the inland side of the coast range. Inland people visited frequently to collect seafood and seashells that were made into beads. The inland Pomo were especially renowned as bead makers; in particular, they used the shells of the clam, olivella, and abalone. An archaeological site at Duncans Point, midway between Bodega Bay and Fort Ross, dates back around 9,000 years before the present.

Bodega Bay was named for the Spanish mariner Bodega y Quadra, who first mapped it in 1775 on an expedition north along the coast of California. Although one researcher, Brian Kelleher, has claimed that Bodega Bay was the real site of Sir Francis Drake's visit to California in 1579, the usually accepted location is on the Point Reyes peninsula. Drake called the area of northern California "New Albion," in honor of his native England.

The Spanish sent land expeditions to settle Alta California (the area of California north of the border with Mexico) in 1769, due in part to worries that the Russians in Alaska might move down along the coast and take over the unprotected coast of California. This region was important to the Spanish; it served as the first American landfall of the returning Manila galleons that annually sailed the Pacific Ocean in their lucrative trading voyages.

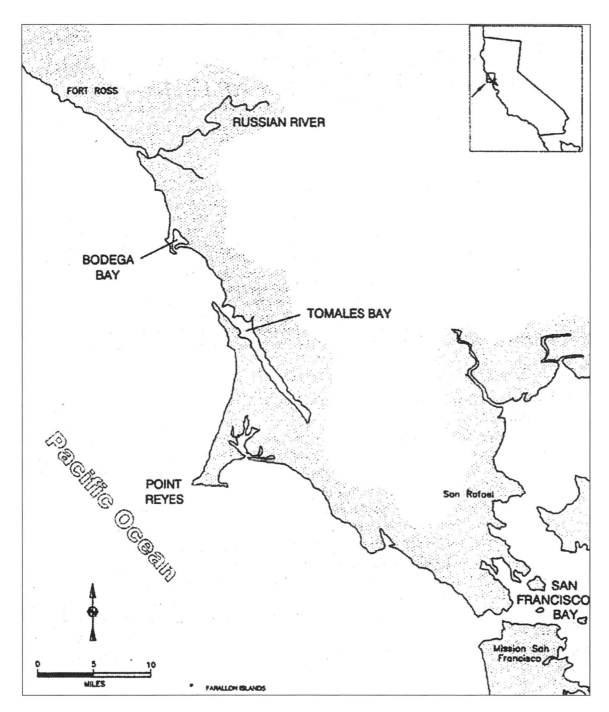

Map of the coast of northern California showing missions, pueblos, and presidios.   [Courtesy of the National Park Service]

However, it was not until 40 years later that a complement of Russians, accompanied by their Aleut sea mammal hunters, arrived at Bodega Bay to set up an establishment. For about six years prior to this, various Alaskan Native sea mammal hunters had been loaned by the Russians to different American sea captains to exploit the lucrative supply of these valuable pelts. On one of these expeditions in 1806, under Captain Oliver Kimball (and aboard the *Peacock*), a Russian named

Timofei Tarakanov, who was in charge of the Alaskan hunters, evidently visited Bodega Bay and made contact with the chiefs of both Bodega and the area that would later be known as Fort Ross. His reports to the governor of Alaska, Alexander Baranov, encouraged the latter to outfit a ship of his own under the leadership of Ivan Kuskov to set up a hunting post.

Early in 1809, Ivan Kuskov led a hunting and exploration party to Bodega Bay, returning in subsequent years. Bodega Bay remained the only viable seaport in Russian California. However, in the spring of 1812, Kuskov directed a group of twenty-five Russians and eighty Alaskan Natives in the construction of a fortified stockade with bastions and warehouses at a point 16 kilometers north of the mouth of the Russian River and 29 kilometers north of Bodega Bay. It was called Fort (*Krepost'*) Ross, although other names—such as Colony (*Selenie*) Ross and Counter (*Kontor*) Ross—were also applied. The Russians renamed Bodega Bay as Port Rumiantsev, in honor of the Russian Foreign minister, Nicolai Rumiantsev.

Another branding technique applied by the Russians was to resurrect the name "New Albion" for the area north of San Francisco Bay—probably to cast doubt on the Spanish ownership of the area. By the early fall of 1812, Kuskov was ready to dedicate Fort Ross as the newest mercantile counter in the Russian American Company system. An *artel* (hunting station) was also established on the Farallon Islands, just outside the Golden Gate. The Spanish authorities, directed by governors Arrillaga and Pablo Vicente de Sola, voiced concern over the Russian colony. The Spanish saw the Russian colony as a potential military and economic threat to their settlements and interests in Alta California immediately to the south. However, Kuskov consistently begged off, saying that any decision to leave would have to be made by authorities who were conveniently many thousands of miles away. The local Indians welcomed the Russians and Alaskans—partly due to their own increasing concern over being forcibly taken to the Spanish missions. Fort Ross never even had a resident priest, much less an active program of proselytizing the local Indians.

Interaction with the local Indians, both the Bodega Bay Miwok and the Fort Ross area Kashaya Pomo, were generally good. In 1817 there was even a treaty of friendship drawn up with several of the local chiefs. The key point of contact was between the Alaskan Native people and the Indians rather than the Russians, although some of the *promyshlenniki* (Russian frontiersmen) also took Indian wives. The colonists were overwhelmingly male, so Indian women were necessary to the development of families.

Kuskov remained in charge at Fort Ross until about the end of the Spanish period (1821) and was replaced by a young man in his early 20s, Karl Schmidt. Schmidt was on hand in October of 1822 to greet the representative of the new emperor of Mexico, Agustin Iturbide. The representative, a cleric named Agustin Fernandez de San Vicente, took a firm line with the Russians but was again told that the decision would have to be made elsewhere.

The twofold purpose of the Russian establishments in California was to hunt fur-bearing sea mammals (mainly sea otters and fur seals) and to provide agricultural goods, ships bricks, and so on to the main Russian American Company bases in the North Pacific. Unlike other visitors to California in the early nineteenth century, the Russians were major pur-

chasers of grain—especially wheat and barley, which were so critical for making bread. Despite the official stance of the Spanish authorities that the Russians should vacate California, numerous occasions of peaceful trade and interaction showed the pragmatic relations between the Californians and Russians. The period of closest political accommodation was probably during the governorship of José Figueroa (1833–35).

After the successful Mexican revolution from Spain, California became open to foreign trade—mainly merchants involved in the hide-and-tallow trade centered in the northeast coast of the United States. The resulting flood of goods were cheaper than those the Russians could provide, cutting back on their trade—although the fact that the Russians were mainly interested in grains as a commodity diminished the direct competition with the American and British companies.

However, in 1833, with the secularization of the California missions, the land shifted to mainly ranching, rather than raising crops. About this time, the Russian authorities promoted the establishment of their own farms and ranches in the area between Fort Ross and Bodega Bay. They even brought in trained agronomist Egor Chernykh in 1836 to introduce improved methods of agriculture. Two windmills were built at Fort Ross related to the milling of the grain—the first windmills in California. Chernykh even built a mechanical thresher, based on plans for a Scottish thresher, to try to improve the processing of the grain.

The inhabitants of Fort Ross also established several light industries, such as boat building, brick making, hide tanning, and the construction of prefabricated wooden houses. Many of the bricks were shipped up to their headquarters in Sitka—called "New Arcangel" by the Russians. In its final years, Fort Ross developed a romantic image—in part because of the last manager, Alexander Rotchev, and his wife, Helena Gagarina, who were probably the most cultured of the Russian inhabitants at Fort Ross. Finally, the Russian American Company decided that the California base was a major money-losing proposition, so once they had contracted with the Hudson's Bay Company to act as the supplier, they put Fort Ross on the market. Eventually a new arrival in California, John A. Sutter, made an offer, and purchased the supposedly movable property in 1841.

Apart from documentary records kept by the Russian American Company, much of our knowledge of Fort Ross and Bodega Bay derives from the accounts of visitors to Fort Ross. These included Spanish and Mexican officials and missionaries, as well as round-the-world travelers of a variety of nationalities (Russian, British, French, and American). Of course, the archaeological record developed over the past half century has added much tangible information to the image of Fort Ross.

STUDYING FORT ROSS

Archaeological and historical research concerning Fort Ross has continued apace over the years. Beginning in the 1940s,

State Parks ranger and curator John McKenzie initiated a variety of systematic attempts to record and investigate areas in and around the stockade. He was primarily interested in the various standing structures (the Rotchev House, the blockhouses, the line of the stockade wall, and the well). In addition, he used historic documents and the recollections of old-timers to map out the locations of a number of archaeological sites in and around Fort Ross.

The first archaeology undertaken by a professional archaeologist was done by Adan Treganza (in 1953), who investigated the remains of the stockade wall. Most of the later excavation projects were generated by plans for the reconstruction of historic buildings inside the fort, such as the officials' quarters (1970, 1972, 1975), the chapel (1972), Kuskov House (1975–76), and the main warehouse (1975–77, 1981, 2003) by archaeologists from State Parks (Glenn Farris) and Cabrillo College (Rob Edwards).

Projects in the 1970s employed a sampling approach based on a model of prehistoric archaeology. However, when it was found that this hopscotch set of units, used at the important site of the officials' quarters, had missed a number of important postholes, State Parks archaeologist Larry Felton recommended a broad exposure technique. This was applied to the 1981 excavation of the old warehouse (or *Magazin*) and proved successful in determining the full outline of the structure, as well as the fact that earlier excavations on the site had actually identified a second warehouse. While trying to marry the historical records with the archaeological finds, Farris discovered that the fathom referred to in the inventory documents was the unusually long (7 ft) Russian fathom. Of particular value was a map, discovered by Russian scholar Svetlana Fedorova, that showed a plan view of the Fort Ross area as of 1817.

Although the initial focus of the work at Fort Ross was on the architecture of the interior of the stockade, interest in the surrounding area drove a number of other projects. Historic Native American village locations were examined both to the north and east of the fort proper, some of which were probably occupied after the Russian period, when William Benitz owned the ranch. However, there were also a number of Native American sites, especially positioned along the coastal bluff and in some protected ravines, that dated to the earlier, pre-Russian Kashaya Pomo period of dominance. Another very important site was the Alaskan Native village on the exposed bluff between the stockade and the sea. Excavations by Kent Lightfoot shed a great deal of light on the lifestyle of the mixed community of Native Alaskan men who had occupied this site, along with their California Native American wives. There was much evidence of the hunting of sea mammals and other foods from the ocean found there.

Other work outside the stockade was intended to mitigate road or sewer line construction. These were the 1972 Highway 1 realignment that touched on the Kashaya village site of *Metini* and the 1984 visitor's center leach line field that identified another Native American site northwest of the fort. Other projects addressing the Native American habitations around Fort Ross were carried out by California State Parks (John White, William Pritchard, Bryn Thomas, and Karl Gurcke), Sonoma State University (David Fredrickson), Santa Rosa Junior College (Ed von der Porten and Thomas Origer) and, most notably, by the University of California at Berkeley (under the direction of Kent Lightfoot). Shipbuilding at Fort Ross was the subject of a doctoral study by James Allan. He did extensive magnetometer studies and some test excavations in the Fort Ross Cove to elicit evidence of this ephemeral activity, which resulted in the construction of four seagoing ships and several launches between about 1816 and 1825.

A most interesting project was an excavation of the Fort Ross cemetery by the University of Wisconsin, led by Lynne Goldstein. She worked in conjunction with a doctoral student, Sannie Kenton Osborn, who examined the archival record to identify people believed to have been buried in the cemetery. Goldstein's work unearthed evidence of 131 graves—about three times as many as had been previously suggested for the cemetery. The cemetery project involved the close collaboration of the Russian Orthodox Church and the Kodiak Area Native Association (KANA), which represented the bulk of the likely non-Russian burials.

In conjunction with these archaeological studies has been a plethora of historical research. These findings have vastly expanded our knowledge of life at Fort Ross during the Native American use of the area, the 30-year Russian occupation (1812–41), and the tenure of ranchers William Benitz (1843–67) and the Call family (1873–1962), as well as the intervening use of the place for milling and shipping lumber by James Dixon (1867–73).

Fortunately, California State Parks has acquired all of the nearby landscape to keep the view-shed around Fort Ross from being spoiled through development. John Foster has focused on the underwater resources of the area with a study of the 1907 wreck of the SS *Pomona*, which lies in Fort Ross Cove. In an effort to embrace the modern computer age, archaeologist Breck Parkman set up a Web site, *Global Village*, to make archaeological work at Fort Ross readily accessible to Russians and Alaskans.

BODEGA BAY

Unfortunately, very little archaeological research has taken place at the site of the Russian port establishment at Bodega Bay. In 1961 David Fredrickson led a dig in advance of the planned construction of a nuclear-energy facility that was eventually abandoned due to environmental protests. In 1999 Roberta Jewett and Kent Lightfoot oversaw a magnetometer survey of the area of Campbell Cove, with mixed results. It is feared that much of the evidence of past use of this site was destroyed during the preparation work for the never-constructed nuclear reactor facility.

FARALLON ISLANDS

Archaeological projects were undertaken at the Farallon Islands in 1949 (Francis Riddell) and in 1998 (Thomas Wake, Anthony Graesch, and Dan Murley) on the site of the sea mammal processing site used by the Russians and their Alaskan Native workers. Definite evidence of the historically recorded *artel* in the form of artifacts and butchered sea mammal remains was found on the site. Because of their sensitive nature as bird and sea mammal habitats, the Farallons are not readily accessible to visitors.

Further Reading: Farris, Glenn J., "The Russian Imprint on the Colonization of California," in *Columbian Consequences,* Vol. 1: *Archaeological and Historical Perspectives on the Spanish Borderlands West,* edited by David Hurst Thomas (Washington, DC: Smithsonian Institution Press, 1989), ch. 30; Farris, Glenn J., "Fort Ross, California: Archaeology of the Old *Magazin,*" in *Russia in North America: Proceedings of the 2nd International Conference on Russian America, Sitka, Alaska, August 19–22, 1987,* edited by Richard A. Pierce (Fairbanks, AK: The Limestone Press, 1990), 475–505; Farris, Glenn J., "The Day of the Tall Strangers and other Events at Fort Ross in 1833," *The Californians* 9(6) (1992):13–19; Farris, Glenn J., "The Bodega Miwok as seen by Mikhail Tikhonovich Tikhanov in 1818," *Journal of California and Great Basin Anthropology* 20(1) (1998): 2–12; Fort Ross Web site, http://www.fortrossinterpretive.org; Kalani, Lyn, Lynn Rudy, and John Sperry, eds., *Fort Ross* (Jenner, CA: Fort Ross Interpretive Association, 1998); Khlebnikov, Kirill T., *The Khlebnikov Archive, Unpublished Journal (1800–1837) and Travel Notes (1820, 1822, and 1824),* edited with introduction and notes by Leonid Shur, translated by John Bisk (Anchorage: University of Alaska Press, 1990); Lightfoot, Kent G., Thomas A. Wake, and Ann M. Schiff, *The Archaeology and Ethnohistory of Fort Ross, California,* Contributions of the University of California Archaeological Research Facility, No. 49 (Berkeley: University of California, Archaeological Research Facility, 1991); Lightfoot, Kent G., Ann M Schiff, and Thomas A. Wake, eds., *The Native Alaskan Neighborhood, A Multiethnic Community at Colony Ross,* Contributions of the University of California Archaeological Research Facility, No. 55 (Berkeley: University of California, Archaeological Research Facility, 1997); Jewett, Roberta, and Kent G. Lightfoot, "Archeology in an Altered Landscape: Topographic and Magnetometer Survey of Campbell Cove, Bodega Head, Bodega Bay, California," manuscript on file (Berkeley: University of California Archaeological Research Facility, 2000); Oswalt, Robert L., *Kashaya Texts,* University of California Publications in Linguistics, Vol. 36 (1964); Riddell, Francis A., "Archaeological Excavation on the Farallon Islands, California," *Reports of the University of California Archaeological Survey* 32 (1955): 1–18; Treganza, Adan E., "Fort Ross: A Study in Historical Archaeology," *Reports of the University of California Archaeological Survey* 23 (1954): 1–26.

Glenn J. Farris

HISTORICAL ARCHAEOLOGY AFTER AMERICAN ANNEXATION

After the 1846–48 Mexican-American War, the United States annexed California. In January 1848, James Marshall discovered gold, greatly affecting the future of the region and the nation. Miners from around the world rushed into California, creating a new landscape of mines, mining camps, and fledgling urban centers. These new cities and towns, often built up from the smaller Mexican towns already in existence, sold food and supplies to miners on their way to the gold fields. The year 1849 was a tumultuous one, with many arrivals from around the world, and on September 9, 1850, California formally entered the Union as a state.

Income from mining and miners dominated the new state's economy throughout the nineteenth century. An increase in agriculture and the construction of railroads expanded the state's economic base. Small, dispersed rural communities grew up around the agricultural fields. Mercantile towns and cities continued to grow, serving as central locations from which to send out products to other parts of the country.

Knowledge of California's settlement history comes from three major sources: the documentary record, oral history, and archaeological remains. These sources of information often complement and expand upon one another.

ARCHAEOLOGY OF CALIFORNIA'S EARLY AMERICAN HISTORY

Archaeologists excavated the Hoff Store site, located in downtown San Francisco, in 1986. W. C. Hoff opened a grocery store near the end of a pier in San Francisco in 1850, and it soon became a full-blown chandlery as well, selling cordage, canvas, anchors, bells, and other ship furnishings.

Fire destroyed the Hoff Store in May 1850. More than 130 years later, excavations encountered thousands of gold rush–period artifacts and well-preserved architectural remnants. Archaeologists studied, cataloged, and interpreted construction hardware, armaments, glass bottles, ceramics, food remains, and clothing fragments. The artifacts helped

Exterior and interior view of the well-preserved Chew Kee Store in Fiddletown, a small California gold rush town. [Rebecca Allen, May 2007]

View of the 1922 turntable and 1910 roundhouse at Railtown 1897 California State Historic Park, Jamestown. [Rebecca Allen, May 2007]

archaeologists to understand the lives of the sailors and miners, but also to tell the story of San Francisco, the new community that would eventually make up one of California's largest population centers.

California did not become Americanized overnight, and its annexation was not without cost: Native Americans and Mexican Americans were displaced, persecuted, and often killed. Many of the state's towns, founded during the Mexican period, retained their Hispanic flavor and influence. The California Department of Parks and Recreation maintains many mid-century adobes and early wooden structures in Monterey.

Excavations at one of these sites, the Cooper-Molera adobe, found a trash deposit associated with the Manuel Diaz family, who purchased part of the adobe building in 1845. The deposit (dating from the late 1840s to early 1850s) prompted archaeologists to interpret the history of the Diaz family in perspective with the rapid social changes occurring after the gold rush, in terms of changing class structures and economic strategies. Diaz lost his ownership of the adobe when it was sold in a sheriff's auction to satisfy his debts in 1855.

Excavators at the McCoy House (built in 1869) in Old Town San Diego Park expected to find artifacts associated with James McCoy, an Irish immigrant who later became the town's sheriff and a state senator. Instead archaeologists discovered foundations of earlier adobe buildings that had housed María Eugenia Silvas and her family, who had sold the property in 1851. Some artifacts, including chipped-stone tools and plain brown pottery, also suggested historic occupation of the area by Native Americans, who worked as servants for the newly arrived families.

INDUSTRIAL AND MINING LANDSCAPES

Almost as early as the gold rush began, large mining corporations took over the operations. Income from mining continued to drive the state's growth and development. Hydraulic mining became the norm, until the Sawyer Decision of 1884 prohibited the dumping of debris into the Sacramento and San Joaquin rivers, as well as their tributaries. Plaintiffs in the court case noted that accumulated mud and gravel from hydraulic mining had clogged rivers and streams, blocked irrigation, choked orchards, flooded towns, and buried agricultural fields.

Some of California's larger mining landscapes have been made into local or state parks. A few of these have been archaeologically investigated, although much of the historical and archaeological record at these parks remains untapped. Malakoff Diggins State Historic Park, located in the Sierra Nevada mountains 26 miles from Nevada City, California (about a 1.5-hour drive northeast of Sacramento), is the site of California's largest hydraulic-mine site. In the 1880s, Malakoff Diggins was also the most productive hydraulic mine in the world. Stark cliffs at the park bear testimony to the physical scarring of landscape caused by the hydraulic water cannons (known as monitors). Here entire mountains were washed away to recover gold; the human-created canyon is about 2,133 meters (7,000 ft) long, as much as 914 meters (3,000 ft) wide, and nearly 182 meters (600 ft) deep in some areas.

Archaeological study of the area has focused on differentiating mining technologies—both large- and small-scale—and the scars left behind on the physical landscape. Archaeologists have catalogued many kinds of historic features at Malakoff Diggins, including standing structures, walls, wells, water-conveyance systems, evidence of former residences and commercial sites (like a blacksmith's shop, a slaughterhouse, and stores), as well as evidence of the mining itself—tunnels, adits, pits, ditches, and more. The historic town of North Bloomfield, which supplied the miners, is nearby.

Native Americans first discovered cinnabar at what is today encompassed by the lands of Almaden Quicksilver County Park, in Santa Clara County. Cinnabar is the more common name for mercuric sulfide, the most productive type of mercury ore. In 1845 Mexican Army officer Andreas Castillero discovered the area's cinnabar deposits, and mining of the ore began. California's forty-niners found mercury, or quicksilver, to be indispensable for recovering gold. Mercury's bonding qualities made the sometimes-elusive gold flakes much easier to recover. At first miners imported mercury from Europe, but as the deposit in Santa Clara became better known, it fed much of the gold country's demands.

Without mercury from New Almaden, the gold rush would have not been economically feasible, and California may have stayed an agricultural backwater. In 1865, at its height, New Almaden had more than 700 buildings and 1,800 miners and town residents. Mining continued in the area until 1972, when it was no longer economically feasible to run the mines.

The county of Santa Clara and the federal government spent two decades and millions of dollars closing tunnels and cleaning up the hazardous mercury waste, and the Almaden Quicksilver County Park opened in the 1990s. The New Almaden National Historic Landmark District encompasses about 960 hectares (2,400 acres) and includes remnants of mines, tunnels, furnaces, and miners' settlements in areas once known as Englishtown and Spanishtown. Casa Grande, constructed in 1854 as the residence of the mine manager, still stands in the area known as the Hacienda.

The nearby town of New Almaden still exists as well; it includes many small houses formerly occupied by mine workers. Historical and archaeological surveys of the area catalogued more than a dozen structures, more than two dozen roads and trails, eight shafts, seventeen tunnels, and more than fifty archaeological features and foundations. Although several New Almaden mining histories have been documented, much of the miners' histories remains untold, both in the archaeological and documentary record. But they survive in the living memories of many of the area's longtime residents.

The study of mining landscapes and associated residential areas holds much promise for historical and archaeological research. Archaeologists study the evolution of the technology itself. Although many changes are noted in the documentary record, individual and region-specific adaptations and innovations rarely appear in the documentary record. These adaptations tell the story of success, but just as often, they speak of the dismal failure that occurred when miners could not innovate or adapt quickly enough. The lives and stories of miners and their families, except for the more prominent and wealthy ones, is also overlooked by history. Archaeological evidence of day-to-day life—the trash and debris left behind—round out the historical picture of changes in California's social and cultural climate, adaptations to environments that were often harsh and challenging, and the social interactions of the many ethnic groups that were drawn to the mining fields. Archaeological evidence of the mines themselves, coupled with historical texts and maps, help to describe and document the environmental consequences of mining, for better or for worse.

ARCHAEOLOGY OF LATE-NINETEENTH- AND EARLY-TWENTIETH-CENTURY SITES

To connect with the rest of the United States, California needed transportation routes. Transcontinental railroad lines permanently linked the state to the rest of the country. This far-reaching transportation system contributed to California's social, political, and economic development. During a ceremony on May 10, 1869, a golden spike was driven into the ground at Promontory Summit, Utah. This event signaled the joining of the West with the East via railroad lines. This meant the arrival of more people, and more goods from the East Coast.

As more immigrants arrived in California, the majority settled into larger cities and towns. Urban historical archaeology has now occurred in most major California cities—San Francisco, Oakland, Sacramento, San Jose, Stockton, San Diego, and Los Angeles—as well as in smaller towns such as Riverside, San Bernardino, San Luis Obispo, and Santa Clara. One of the challenges of urban excavation is to decipher the many layers of occupation that can occur in one area. As a result, most urban excavations have large open areas of excavation, so that archaeologists can understand the complex stratigraphy, the layers of cultural occupation, and the features that are encountered.

Research on these urban sites has in part focused on the study of the growth of a new consumer society. The four decades between 1876 and 1915 are often collectively referred to as the Victorian period in the United States. Local, regional, and national economies were shifting from an agricultural base to one that emphasized manufacturing and industry. Urban settings and industries brought standardization and increasing specialization in occupations.

It also meant that an increasing amount and variety of consumer goods became readily available—especially to city dwellers, but soon to rural areas as well. One historian, Thomas Schlereth, concisely summarized the effect on inhabitants of the United States: the "good life" came to mean the "goods life." This was in part made possible by improved techniques in canning, glass manufacturing, and bottling. Newspapers, magazines, and mail-order catalogues bombarded the consumer population with advertisements touting everything from canned foods to patent medicines to personal goods.

With increased job opportunities, and more choices in where to live and work, mobility between economic classes blurred as the middle class grew. At the same time, though, many American Victorians were acutely class-conscious, and those who claimed the upper class believed that they possessed a moral superiority over the lower classes. Consumer behavior became a way for the emerging urban middle class to assert its closeness—and moral equivalency—to the elite upper class. That is, the more things one could buy and display in one's house, the more important one became. *Things* became symbols of increased status and achievement. The effect on the urban archaeological record in California was immediate and is very noticeable.

This consumer behavior was also marked with a desire for orderliness and cleanliness that in some ways was meant to counteract the effects of mobility and its resulting instability. Orderliness through organization of space, combined with cleanliness, became intertwined with the dominant Christian morality. "Cleanliness is next to godliness" became a national byword. Advances in medicine and the awareness of the importance of cleanliness corresponded with this new morality. Innovations and improvements in household technologies,

especially in the kitchen, accompanied the desire for tidiness. Sewing machines, coffee mills, washing machines, improved coal and gas ranges, apple corers, lard presses, eggbeaters, cabbage borers, butter molds, sausage stuffers, lemon squeezers, and can openers were all designed to help structure domestic life, improve efficiency and orderliness, and help maintain a tidy environment where everything had its place. Urban archaeological records reflect all of these manifestations of Victorian values and behavioral patterns.

Archaeological studies demonstrate that small-town inhabitants and farmers often had the same goals and ambitions as their urban counterparts. The 1862 Homestead Act was a U.S. federal law that gave freehold title to 64 hectares (160 acres) of land in the undeveloped West, providing that the person who claimed the land was at least 21 years of age, had built a structure on the property with dimensions of at least 3.6 meters by 4.2 meters (12 by 14 ft), and had lived there for at least five years. Settlement under the Homestead Act was widespread, and the remains of settler communities are common throughout rural lands in California. At first glance, many small farms and ranches appear to be isolated, but in fact are indicative of larger settlement patterns and communities. The development and demise of many areas of agriculture and ranching was closely tied to irrigation and advances in agriculture. Climate and water availability had tremendous effects on the settlement, growth, and subsequent decline of many rural communities.

While the railroad immediately connected many California towns to each other, in some of the more rural areas, archaeological study has found a different trend. Residents in Likely and Termo, in the most northeast corner of California, purchased goods mainly from East Coast and Midwestern manufacturers, as these were the consumer items brought by the linkage of railroads. As the system of railroads within California grew, linking the state's rural areas to one another, more local goods and industries could fill the consumer demands.

As the twentieth century progressed, local manufacturing capabilities grew, and local markets expanded. Ranchers and farmers were savvy enough to purchase whatever was most convenient and least expensive. Homesteaders in rural places like Termo and Likely soon created their own regional brand of purchasing behavior. Rural industries grew as Californians could ship out their manufactured goods to the rest of the country, using the same system of rail lines.

THE STUDY OF CALIFORNIA'S IMMIGRANTS

From the state's inception, California's rural and urban populations have been some of the most ethnically diverse in the United States. Spaniards and Mexicans began to settle in the area during the Spanish colonization of California; the gold rush and later industrial-agricultural development brought more Hispanic, French, German, Chinese, Slavic, Italian,

Swedish, Japanese, English, and other settlers. California's Native Americans continued to live in the state as well—sometimes maintaining their own cultural identity, especially in rural areas, but in some cases intermarrying with the new arrivals.

Historical archaeologists often study enclaves of these groups in order to understand regional differences, along with the creation and dissolution of cultural boundaries. In studying the history and material culture of a particular group, such as the Market Street Chinatown in San Jose, archaeologists ask questions about how immigrant groups maintain their own identity in a new setting. Archaeological evidence often provides evidence of different religions, foods, economic values, and social relationships. Much work has been conducted on Chinese sites because the artifacts of daily life—such as ceramic bowls, smoking pipes, and coins—are visibly distinct (that is, noticeably unlike artifacts found in a town inhabited by European immigrants). Here too, though, there are differences; archaeologists are discovering the nuances of the variation in goods and food remains between English and German households, for example.

Discovering the differences between groups also helps researchers to understand the commonalities that exist. Understanding cultural patterns can often lead to a better understanding of economic patterns, settlement models, and means and mechanisms of survival and subsistence. In turn, this helps researchers understand how humans inhabit and adapt to their surroundings. Artifacts—the things from everyday life—hold information about the historic past in California, prompt researchers to ask new questions of old documents, and provide three-dimensional illustration of what life was like for all of California's population.

FINDING HISTORY AND ARCHAEOLOGY ALONG THE HIGHWAY 49 CORRIDOR (AN ARCHAEOLOGICAL ROAD TRIP)

Much of California's historical archaeological projects occur prior to the development of rural areas (or redevelopment of urban areas). Archaeological excavation often occurs when new roads are created or when older roads are expanded. As a result, archaeological remains are preserved and interpreted in only a few places, such as museums and parks. The best places to understand the intersection of history and archaeology are those sites with archaeological potential—places that have not been excavated—or historic parks that preserve history in a way that can be used to interpret archaeological findings.

The Marshall Gold Discovery State Historic Park in Coloma, along Highway 49, is intended to illustrate what life was like in the period from 1847 to 1852. It also shows examples of buildings that represent California's original gold town, Coloma, as it developed. A replica of the sawmill where James Marshall was working when he discovered gold has

been erected at the park; nearby are some of the archaeological remains of the sawmill. More than twenty buildings illustrate residences, shops, and community buildings; although all are historic buildings, many of the structures were brought to the park from elsewhere to help interpret the past. Among and between the standing structures are foundations of other buildings, illustrating the archaeological potential of the park. Careful visitors can also look around at nearby landscapes and see evidence of mining in the shape of flat areas and carved-out hillsides.

Southbound from there, several historic towns sit along Highway 49, including Placerville and Diamond Springs. The small gold-rush town of Fiddletown is 9.6 kilometers (6 mi) east of Plymouth (on the Highway 49 corridor). In Fiddletown the Chew Kee Store is one of the best-preserved historic sites in California. Maintained by the active Fiddletown Preservation Society, the store allows visitors to step back in time by entering a small rammed-earth adobe building to find a Chinese herb shop built in 1850. Dr. Yee Fong Cheung operated the store in its early years, and Chew Kee, a man known only by the name of the store he operated, ran the herbal shop and grocery store from the 1880s until 1913. The shop, filled with herbs, bottles, patent medicines, pottery, baskets, and a corner for visitors to play games and sit for a while, served the needs of not only local Chinese miners and railroad workers, but also those of any of the other community members who came into the shop.

Chew Kee's adopted son lived here until 1965, when the building was deeded to the local community. Area residents have preserved the building and its contents, preserving an incredible wealth of information for historical archaeologists. Visitors can see the blending of the familiar—Chinese ceramics, bottles, and advertisements—with the new offerings of the West: European furniture, cabinetry, business ads, and Western medicines. The contents and history of the Chew Kee pharmacy addresses one of the most basic questions for immigrants—how to stay healthy in a new environment.

Farther south, about another hour and a half along Highway 49, is an example of California's rich railroad and industrial history. Railtown 1897 State Historic Park in Jamestown houses the historic headquarters and some of the general shops of the Sierra Railway (later called the Sierra Railroad). Most of the structures at the State Historic Park were built between 1897 and 1922. Although the headquarters were not much used after 1922, the site's structures were preserved—mostly to serve the needs of movie productions, another of California's growing industries. The State Historic Park illustrates the connection of railways, communication, and transportation of goods and peoples.

Technological innovations are also on display here, and highlights include a 1910 roundhouse, a 1922 turntable servicing the roundhouse's six engine stalls, and a machine shop with overhead, belt-driven tools operated by a Pelton water wheel. Electricity was introduced in 1912, and for a time, electrical and water-driven technologies co-existed at this steam-era railroad facility. The change to diesel power was soon to come. The study of adaptation to new technologies is one of the hallmarks of historical and industrial archaeology.

Further Reading: Baxter, R. Scott, and Rebecca Allen, "Mining the West," in *Unlocking the Past: Celebrating Historical Archaeology in North America*, edited by Lu Ann De Cunzo and John H. Jameson Jr. (Gainesville: University Press of Florida and the Society for Historical Archaeology, 2005); California State Parks Web site, www.parks.ca.gov (online May 2007); De Cunzo, Lu Ann, and Mary Praetzellis, "'A Place to Start From': West Oakland, California," in *Unlocking the Past: Celebrating Historical Archaeology in North America*, edited by Lu Ann De Cunzo and John H. Jameson Jr. (Gainesville: University Press of Florida and the Society for Historical Archaeology, 2005); Felton, Larry, "A Pueblo's Past." *Dig* 4(3) (2002): 6–10; Layton, Milton, and Laurence Bulmore, *Cinnabar Hills: The Quicksilver Days of New Almaden*, 5th ed. (Los Gatos, CA: Village Printers, 1991); Greenwood, Roberta S., "The Chinese in the Cities of the West," in *Unlocking the Past: Celebrating Historical Archaeology in North America*, edited by Lu Ann De Cunzo and John H. Jameson Jr. (Gainesville: University Press of Florida and the Society for Historical Archaeology, 2005); National Park Service, *A History of Chinese Americans in California: Fiddletown's Chinese American Community*, Park Net, National Park Service, http://www.cr.nps.gov/history/online_books/5views/5views3h34.htm (online November 2004); Pastron, Allen G., and Eugene M. Hattori, eds., *The Hoff Store Site and Gold Rush Merchandise from San Francisco, California*, Special Publications Series, No. 7 (Ann Arbor: The Society for Historical Archaeology, 1990), available online at http://www.sha.org/ publications/ha-sha/default.htm; Market Street Chinatown Archaeological Project, http://www.marketstreet.stanford.edu (online beginning January 2003).

Rebecca Allen

SHIPWRECKS AND SUBMERGED SITES OF CALIFORNIA AND THE NORTHWEST COAST

Humankind's relationship with the sea extends back in time for tens, if not hundreds, of thousands of years. We have lived beside the oceans, taken nourishment from them, communicated across them, and harnessed their energy. On their floors lie the records of humanity's unrelenting attempts to master them. The ocean bottoms chronicle the trade that has taken place across their surfaces, holding the evidence of the wars waged upon them.

Charles Lyell recognized this wealth of history in *The Principles of Geology* (1832): "It is probable that a greater number of monuments of the skill and industry of 'man' will in the course of ages be collected together in the bed of the ocean, than will exist at any one time on the surface of the Continents."

The boats and ships people have used in their efforts to exploit the oceans have often failed or betrayed them, creating the record today's maritime archaeologists seek to locate and interpret. This submerged—and sometimes buried—record of lost vessels can tell different stories of the ship as machine, as a component of an economic or military system, and as a closed social community (Muckelroy 1978).

While the comparatively mild environments of the eastern seaboard and the Caribbean provide fair to good preservation characteristics, the high-energy environment found along the West Coast of the North American continent does not afford the same long-term preservation qualities for these submerged resources. Similarly, the western slope of the continent has not been endowed with the intricate network of inland rivers and waterways that in the eastern, southeastern, and southern areas have long formed vital corridors of transportation and communication—with the concomitant trove of submerged resources dating from the colonial era through modern day. California in particular can point to only two inland waterways of major historical importance: the lower Sacramento and the San Joaquin rivers.

Despite these comparative limitations, numerous maritime-related cultural resources are located in California and along the northwest coast. These are found in the form of submerged shipwreck sites; remnants of historic shipyards; intact ships and boats preserved in maritime museums; and historic sites in which the associated ships, archaeological features, and artifacts are still being sought.

Although significant evidence exists that Native peoples exploited the resources of the Pacific coast in ancient times through their mastery of boats and navigation, evidence of their watercraft at underwater sites has yet to be found. Archaeological deposits in the form of pottery, mortars, milling stones, and grooved stones have been found off the California coast in waters as deep as 30 meters, but the source of these artifacts is still the subject of speculation, and no definitive proof of their origin has been discovered.

The bulk of cultural material related to the West Coast's maritime heritage dates from the mid-nineteenth century forward, as it was the discovery of gold in January 1848 that sparked the California gold rush, bringing thousands of optimistic argonauts to the western shores of North America. They

View of the wrecked SS *Pomona* (left) in 1908 hung up on rocks in Fort Ross cove. On the right is Whitelaw's salvage vessel, the steam schooner *Greenwood*.   [San Francisco Maritime National Historical Park]

arrived overland and in hundreds of ships; within a period of a year or two, they had dispersed to the north and south, establishing settlements along the way and creating the archaeological record we seek to study today.

Prior to the gold rush, California and the northwest coast were distant outposts—visited only by the early Spanish explorers, missionaries, and military men, and then later by Russian fur hunters, along with settlers and traders from other parts of Europe, the United States, and Canada. California's earliest known shipwreck site is associated with this early period.

SAN AGUSTIN: DRAKES BAY, NORTHERN CALIFORNIA COAST

The site of California's earliest known shipwreck, Drakes Bay is located approximately 80 kilometers north of San Francisco, within the confines of the Point Reyes National Seashore and the Gulf of the Farallones National Marine Sanctuary. Along the shores of Drakes Bay, evidence of the wreck of the Manila galleon *San Agustin* has been found in archaeological investigations of prehistoric sites that date to the era of the galleon's loss. These sites are associated with the Native Coast Miwok people. While the remains of the ship have yet to be located, the nearby terrestrial archaeological sites have yielded evidence of the vessel in the form of iron spikes and drift bolts, as well as shards of Ming dynasty white-on-blue porcelain and fragments of stoneware. Hundreds of ceramic fragments from the ship's

cargo have also been collected after washing up on the beach.

Beginning in 1565 and continuing for nearly 250 years, Spanish galleons sailed on trading voyages between Acapulco in New Spain (now Mexico) and Manila. Once or twice each year, these galleons carried Spanish gold and silver to traders in the Philippines and brought back to New Spain the riches of the Far East, which were then trans-shipped to Spain and other parts of Europe. In November 1597, while returning to Acapulco from that year's trading voyage, Captain Sebastian Rodriguez Cermeño lost his galleon *San Agustin* in the waters of Drakes Bay.

Having been ordered to survey parts of the coast to find a suitable haven for future voyages, Cermeño had anchored the *San Agustin* off the beach in this relatively well-protected harbor and gone ashore. A sudden winter storm arose, and the vessel was pushed into the heavy surf, where it broke up, taking with it the lives of sixteen crewmen. In a remarkable feat, Cermeño managed to salvage the ship's boat—and in that small, frail vessel, he, the remaining crew, and the ship's dog sailed safely back to Acapulco. The *San Agustin* and her cargo of porcelain, spices, silk, and other treasures of the Far East were complete losses.

Remote-sensing surveys and underwater investigations in search of the wreck's remains have been conducted several times, beginning in the mid-1960s. In 1982 the National Park Service (NPS) conducted a comprehensive side scan sonar and magnetometer survey of the suspected wreck site. In 1997 and

1998, the NPS, in conjunction with the National Oceanic and Atmospheric Administration (NOAA) and the California State Lands Commission, conducted additional remote-sensing surveys and underwater investigations of several anomalies identified in the remote-sensing data. The results of these investigations suggest that the remains of the *San Agustin* lie deeply buried under many feet of sand in the high-energy, nearshore surf zone.

To date, that environment and the likely presence of great white sharks, which breed in the waters surrounding Point Reyes, have precluded implementation of a comprehensive, controlled testing program to positively identify the wreck's location and condition, although plans to conduct such investigations are under consideration.

The Kenneth C. Patrick Visitor Center at the Point Reyes National Seashore offers interpretive exhibits on the *San Agustin*, the sixteenth-century maritime exploration of the area, and the area's marine environment and resources.

FORT ROSS/SS *POMONA*: SONOMA COUNTY, NORTHERN CALIFORNIA COAST

In 1811, the Russian-American Company, a nineteenth-century quasi-governmental mercantile company engaged in the sea mammal fur trade, established Colony Ross on a coastal plateau of Spain's Alta California—approximately 145 kilometers north of modern-day San Francisco.

This southernmost company outpost was primarily intended to provide agricultural products for the company's Alaskan settlements. Colony Ross's multi-ethnic workforce of Russians, Native Alaskans, Hawai'ians, and Native Californians also built and operated a tannery, brickyard, and cooperage, as well as the first shipyard on the west coast of what is today the continental United States. From 1816 to 1827, the shipyard produced four brigs for the company's fleet, and two barques for sale to the Spanish—one for Mission St. Francis de Asis at San Francisco, and one for Mission San Jose.

Evidence of the shipyard was discovered during archaeological investigations conducted at Fort Ross State Historic Park in 1996, 1997, and 1998. Several discoveries came along with the identification of the location and orientation of the workshop associated with the shipyard: the remains of a platform likely associated with either the shipyard or the fleet of skin boats (baidaras and baidarkas) used by the colonists, evidence of the yard's shipways, and the remains of the yard's stoving oven.[1]

---

[1]   Prior to the introduction of steam chests, stoving ovens were used to soften hull planking so that it would bend around the frames of a ship. In a stoving oven, a fire of some magnitude was built on a bed of stones to make them red-hot. A layer of wet sand was then spread over the stones and allowed to warm. When the sand was sufficiently heated, the wood hull planks, which had been soaked in water, were buried in the hot sand, where they remained until they were suitably softened.

Although these archaeological features have been reburied, information on the history of Colony Ross and the multi-ethnic population that built and operated the shipyard and the colony's other economic enterprises is presented in the Fort Ross State Historic Park's visitors' center, as well as on panels that can be found along the park's Interpretive Trail, which winds through the grounds of the former Russian-American Company colony and guides visitors to locations pertinent to the colony's history.

The Interpretive Trail also brings visitors to a point overlooking Fort Ross Cove, where the remains of the SS *Pomona* lie submerged in depths of 9 to 12 meters. Built in 1888 by San Francisco's Union Iron Works, the 1,264-ton, steel-hulled coastal steamer *Pomona* was 225 feet (68 m) in length, with a beam of 33.5 feet (10.2 m) and a draft of 16 feet (4.87 m). *Pomona* plied the coastal waters of northern California, serving ports from San Francisco to Vancouver. In 1897 the Pacific Coast Steamship Company (later the Pacific Steamship Company) purchased the steamer and put her into service carrying freight and passengers between ports along the northwest coast. The steamer's reliability and classical design soon earned her the sobriquet "Pride of the Coastal Fleet."

On March 17, 1908, while steaming north to Eureka, *Pomona* struck an uncharted rock some 3.2 kilometers south of Fort Ross. Taking on water through the hole rent in her hull, the steamer's situation quickly became untenable, and the captain decided to steam for Fort Ross, where he planned to save the ship by beaching her at Fort Ross Cove. As the steamer neared the cove, a wash rock appeared in her path. Foundering and unresponsive, the ship would not answer to the helm, and *Pomona* rode over the rock, which punched through her keel and steel hull, impaling the ship and insuring its demise. Passengers and crew were safely evacuated to shore, and the ship subsequently was partially salvaged. Her triple-expansion steam engine and single brass propeller were removed, but she was bound fast to the wash rock and could never be refloated. Eventually, dynamite was used to blow her remains off the rock and send them to the bottom of the cove, where they remain to this day.

The first systematic archaeological investigation of the wreck site occurred in 1981, when an archaeologist from the California Department of Parks and Recreation (DPR) conducted magnetometer and underwater swim surveys to begin documenting the *Pomona*'s remains. Subsequent investigations were conducted by park volunteers in 1988. In 1998 and again in 2000, additional site surveys and documentation of the wreck's remains were conducted on behalf of DPR by researchers from Indian University.

The park's boundaries have been extended to incorporate the *Pomona*'s remains into the Fort Ross Underwater Preserve, and the site is being nominated to the National Register of Historic Places in anticipation of the centennial commemoration of the ship's loss in 1908. The *Pomona's* remains represent one of the best examples of nineteenth-century Pacific coast steam transportation, and they may be viewed by divers who visit the park. Interpretive materials on the ship and her history are available in the park's visitors' center.

FROLIC: MENDOCINO COUNTY, NORTHERN CALIFORNIA COAST

In 1984 Dr. Thomas Layton of San Jose State University was directing an archaeological field school at the site of a pre-contact Mitom Pomo village site in the rugged coastal mountains of Mendocino County. Excavations at the site, known as Three-Chop Village, revealed the expected assemblage of flaked-stone tools and other Native California cultural material. But surprisingly, excavations also included shards of Chinese porcelain.

The discovery of these porcelain fragments in a context that had clearly not been disturbed since the site had been abandoned in the mid-nineteenth century led Layton to an investigation that would take eight years to complete and that would ultimately link the story of the nineteenth-century opium trader *Frolic* with Boston merchants, Baltimore shipbuilders, opium brokers in India, businessmen in gold rush–era San Francisco, artisans of Canton, and the native Mitom Pomo of the Mendocino coast.

The *Frolic* was a Baltimore clipper built in 1844. Rigged as a brig, *Frolic* was 212 tons, with an overall length of 99 feet (30.17 m), a beam of 24 feet (7.31 m), and a depth of hold of over 9 feet (2.74 m). Built for the opium trade between Indian and China, the *Frolic* had become obsolete by 1850. Its owners arranged for one last trading voyage, carrying merchandise from China to the burgeoning gold-rush market of San Francisco. Laden with a cargo of Chinese porcelain, silks, a prefabricated house, decorated camphor trunks, lacquered ware, jewelry, and numerous other consumer goods, the clipper made the 9,660-kilometer crossing between China and California in forty-four days, reaching the Mendocino coast on July 25, 1850. Mistaking their distance from shore, the crew steered the ship too near the reef north of Point Cabrillo, and the *Frolic* struck and grounded in what today is Caspar Cove. The captain and crew abandoned the ship and made it safely to shore in the lifeboats, but the ship and cargo were total losses.

Archaeological investigation of the wreck site began with Layton's research into the pottery recovered from Three-Chop Village and his subsequent linkage of the shards to the *Frolic.* In 2003 and again in 2004, the California Department of Parks and Recreation, Napa Valley College, East Carolina University, and Indiana University joined Layton to form a collaborative team that investigated and documented the wreck's remains. Today the *Frolic* is listed on the National Register of Historic Places and is a central component of the

Point Cabrillo Preserve, one of the newest units in the California parks system.

Interpretation of the wreck site and the history of the *Frolic* are available at the Point Cabrillo visitors' center. Divers can visit the site to examine the *Frolic's* remains, and artifacts from the wreck are displayed and interpreted in the Kelley House Museum in Mendocino, California, and the Mendocino County Museum in Willits, California.

CANDACE: SAN FRANCISCO, CALIFORNIA

The 303-ton ship *Candace* was built in 1818 in Boston and spent many years sailing in the South American and Pacific trade. It was re-rigged as a barque in 1849 and entered the Pacific whale fishery, where it was successfully engaged as a whaler until its demise in 1855. On July 4, 1855, while attempting to return to its homeport of New London, Connecticut, from an Arctic whaling voyage, *Candace* limped into San Francisco Bay, leaking badly and seeking safe haven. Its condition was so poor that it was quickly condemned; it never sailed again.

In an Admiralty court proceeding in San Francisco brought soon thereafter by the crew, Charles Hare, a local ship breaker and chandler, purchased the condemned vessel. Apparently unable to repair it, Hare broke it up in 1857, shortly before abandoning the ship-breaking business.

Hare conducted his ship-breaking operation on the southeast shore of San Francisco's Yerba Buena Cove, in the lee of Rincon Point. Buried when Yerba Buena Cove was filled in the mid- to late nineteenth century, that location today forms the edge of San Francisco's financial district in an area known as South of Market.

In 2005 excavations associated with construction of a condominium complex encountered the intact remains of the *Candace's* hull. William Self Associates Inc. (WSA), the project's archaeological consultant, excavated and documented the hull as construction proceeded around it. WSA discovered that before abandoning the effort, Hare had removed the hull planking, decks, masts, and timbers from amidships forward, but the aft portion of the vessel was still relatively intact. Although Hare had removed the deck, he had left the frames, ceiling planking, and hull planking in place, from approximately the turn of the bilge to the keel in this, the last vessel Charles Hare salvaged in his yard.

Unlike the few nineteenth-century sailing ships that previously have been encountered in San Francisco—the *William Gray,* the *Lydia,* the *Rome,* the *General Harrison,* and the *Niantic,* which have either been destroyed or still lie entombed beneath the developments that first exposed them—the remains of the *Candace* were recovered intact. It is the only early-nineteenth-century barque to have been recovered intact on the Pacific coast. *Candace* is presently undergoing stabilization and conservation and in 2009 will be moved to the Old Mint Building, where she will form the centerpiece of the new San Francisco Museum.

BEAVER: VANCOUVER, BRITISH COLUMBIA

The first steamship to operate on the Pacific coast, the *Beaver* was built in London in 1835 for the Hudson Bay Company (HBC), one of the early fur-trading companies on the northwest coast. Twin side-lever engines powered the 101-foot-long (30.78 m) sidewheeler, which also carried two masts and was rigged as a brigantine. With a beam of 20 feet (6 m) and a draft of 6.5 feet (2 m), the sturdily built *Beaver* was long-lived and versatile. From 1836, when it arrived on the north Pacific coast, until 1853, *Beaver* was used in the HBC's fur-trading operations. For a short while after, it served as a passenger steamer, carrying cargo and travelers between the various HBC outposts. In 1862 the Royal Navy chartered *Beaver* and put it to work as a survey vessel until 1870, when the HBC retired it. Four years later, *Beaver* was sold to a transportation company that used it as a towboat and freighter. On July 26, 1888, it ran aground at Prospect Point in Vancouver, B.C. *Beaver's* owners left it to disintegrate on the rocks, and for the next four years it was picked over by souvenir hunters. Its boilers and paddle wheel shafts were eventually salvaged, and in 1892, the *Beaver's* remains finally broke apart and slipped to the bottom.

Aside from occasional visits to the site by looters and so-called treasure hunters, the *Beaver* remained largely ignored until 1991, when the Vancouver Maritime Museum and the Underwater Archaeological Society of British Columbia conducted the first intensive archaeological survey of the wreck site. That and subsequent efforts to record the wreck have resulted in a remarkably thorough documentation of the first steamship on the Pacific coast. Today the site can be visited by divers and is frequently used to train divers in the techniques of underwater archaeology.

The Vancouver Maritime Museum has an interpretive exhibit of the *Beaver*, illustrating its history and its importance to the development of the Pacific coast through exhibition of artifacts such as its anchor, paddle wheel shaft, and boiler.

Further Reading: Aker, Raymond, *The Cermeno Expedition at Drakes Bay, 1595*, research report of the Drake Navigators Guild (Point Reyes, CA: Drake Navigators Guild, 1973); Allan, James M., "Forge and Falseworks: An Archaeological Investigation of the Russian American Company's Industrial Complex at Colony Ross," Ph.D. diss. (University of California, 2001); Delgado, James P., *To California by Sea: A Maritime History of the California Gold Rush* (Columbia: University of South Carolina Press, 1990); Delgado, James P., *Beaver: First Steamship on the West Coast* (Victoria, BC: Horsdal and Schubart, 1993); Dmytryshyn, Basil, E.A.P. Crownhart-Vaughan, and Thomas Vaughan, *The Russian American Colonies: A Documentary Record, 1798–1867* (Oregon Historical Society, 1989); Everett, Richard, *Found! The Wreck of the Frolic: A Gold Rush Cargo For San Francisco*, electronic document hosted by the San Francisco Maritime National Historical Park, National Park Service, http://www.nps.gov/archive/safr/local/frolic.html (online May 2008); Foster, John W., *Devil-Fish To Archaeology: Overview of Diving and Research at the Site of the S.S. Pomona*, electronic document hosted by California State Parks, http://www.parks.ca.gov/?page_id=23572 (online February 2007); Layton, Thomas N., *The Voyage of the Frolic: New England Merchants and the Opium Trade* (Palo Alto, CA: Stanford University Press, 1997); Layton, Thomas N., *Gifts from the Celestial Kingdom: A Shipwrecked Cargo for Gold Rush California* (Palo Alto, CA: Stanford University Press, 2002); Muckelroy, K., *Maritime Archaeology* (Cambridge: Cambridge University Press, 1978); Office of Underwater Science, Indiana University, *S.S. Pomona Shipwreck Project, Fort Ross State Historic Park, California*, electronic document, http://www.indiana.edu/~e472/pomona/pomona.html (online January 29, 2007); Pethick, Derek, *S.S. Beaver: The Ship that Saved the West* (Vancouver, BC: Mitchell Press, 1970); Shangraw, Clarence F., and Edward P. Von der Porten, *The Drake and Cermeno Expeditions' Chinese Porcelains at Drakes Bay, California 1579 and 1595* (Palo Alto, CA: Drake Navigators Guild, 1981); Tikhmenev, P.A., *A History of the Russian-American Company* (Seattle: University of Washington Press, 1978); Vancouver Maritime Museum, *Beaver*, http://vmmuseum.xplorex.com/page212.htm (online March 2007); Von der Porten, Edward P., *Drake and Cermeno in California: Sixteenth Century Chinese Ceramics* (Point Reyes, CA: Drake Navigators Guild, 1973); Wagner, Henry Raup, "The Voyage to California of Sebastian Rodriguez Cermeno in 1595," *California Historical Society Quarterly* 3(1) (1924): 3–24; William Self Associates Inc., *Final Archaeological Resources Report, 300 Spear Street Project, San Francisco, CA*, submitted to Major Environmental Analysis, Planning Department, San Francisco (copies available from William Self Associates Inc., Orinda, CA, and on file at the San Francisco Public Library).

Information on the following shipwrecks and archaeological sites may also be of interest:

Br. Jonathan (Crescent City)
Canada (Alaska)
City of Ainesworth (British Columbia)
Dimon (Sacramento River)
Emerald Bay Barges (Lake Tahoe)
Ericsson (Vancouver Island)
Il'men (Point Arena, CA)
Isabella (Columbia River)
King Phillip (San Francisco)
LaGrange (Sacramento River)
Lord Western (Vancouver Island)
Lydia (San Francisco)
Montebello (San Luis Obispo County)
Neptune (San Francisco)
Niantic (San Francisco)
Ning Po (Catalina Harbor)
Ninus (Sacramento River)
Reporter (San Francisco)
Rome (San Francisco)
San Francisco Xavier (Nehalem, Oregon)
Sterling (Sacramento River)
Tennessee (San Francisco)
Turner Shipyard (Benicia)
William Gray (San Francisco)
Winfield Scott (Anacapa Island)

James M. Allan

POINT ST. GEORGE, TSURAI (PATRICK'S POINT STATE PARK), AND OTHER SITES

Northwest California Coast

Ancient and Historic Native American Sites Along a Rugged Coast

Northwest California is a rugged region composed of several mountain ranges and deep, elongated valleys. Annual rainfall is high, creating numerous, salmon-bearing streams that were an important source of food for local Native American people. Multiple vegetation communities exist in this area, including conifer forest, open prairie, and mixed hardwood forest. These habitats yielded additional food sources, such as Roosevelt elk, black-tailed deer, and acorns. Coastal environments include offshore rocks and islands, where seals and sea lions could be hunted, as well as sandy beaches and estuaries, where a variety of fish and birds were captured.

High densities of Native American peoples occupied this region at the time of European contact, and many of their descendants live in the area today. Languages spoken include those of the Athabascan, Algic, and Hokan families, representing some of the highest linguistic diversity ever recorded on earth. Many archaeological sites have been discovered, revealing a rich prehistoric record extending back at least 8,000 years. Some of these sites have been excavated, allowing the public to learn about the ancient cultures of this region.

Three main prehistoric patterns are recognized in northwest California: Borax Lake Pattern (8,000–4,000 years ago), Mendocino Pattern (4,000–1,500 years ago), and Gunther Pattern (less than 1,500 years ago). Most Borax Pattern sites are located on the interior and appear to represent the encampments of small groups who used a highly mobile settlement system.

These ancient peoples harvested a wide range of both plant and animal foods, but placed little emphasis on the storage of subsistence resources. A little less than 3,500 years ago, Mendocino Pattern villages were established along rivers. These lowland settlements were supported by the intensive use of salmon and acorn, an adaptive shift later made possible by the development of sophisticated fish weirs and traps, along with the establishment of permanent storage facilities (for example, redwood plank structures).

In contrast to the interior, archaeological data from coastal settings reveal only a few marginal sites pre-dating 1,500 years ago. After this time, large coastal villages were established, and usually contain a rich array of artifacts used to construct houses and redwood dugout canoes (for examples, antler wedges and stone mauls), harvest a wide range of

marine foods (bone harpoons, fishhooks made of shell, stone net sinkers, and so on), and signal wealth and power among high-ranking members of the community (shell beads and large obsidian blades). Excavations at these villages also reveal a high degree of spatial organization, including the remains of houses with stone patios and walkways, cemetery areas, and various storage facilities.

GUNTHER (INDIAN) ISLAND

The earliest professional archaeological investigation in northwest California was conducted by Llewellyn Loud at the Gunther Island site in 1913. Later, H. H. Stuart, a local dentist, excavated 382 burials from the deposit. The site represents the Wiyot village of Tolowot and is located in the tidal flat marshland of Humboldt Bay, near the modern city of Eureka.

Most of the recovered artifacts were used by historic Indian groups, giving archaeologists insight into the use and meaning of such items. These include a variety of antler and stone woodworking tools, such as adzes, mauls, wedges, steatite vessels, net weights, harpoons, shell ornaments, head scratchers, and hairpins. Wealth- or status-related items include dentalium shell bead money, carved-slate quadruped zoomorphs, and large obsidian bifaces.

Historic Indians participated in a series of ceremonial dances, including the famous White Deerskin Dance, which featured dramatic displays of treasures owned by wealthy headmen. Items indicating the wealth of the owner include red-headed woodpecker pelt headdresses; sea lion tooth and flicker quill headbands; albino deerskin pelts; dentalium shell bead money necklaces; and large (30 to 90 cm [1 to 3 ft] long) obsidian blades. The value of the blades was particularly high, as obsidian was transported from great distances to northwest California, and the skill and time required to manufacture the finely chipped-stone items was considerable. Richard Hughes conducted a study of the blades using X-ray fluorescence, a technique that analyzes the chemical constituents of obsidian artifacts and matches them to the volcanic flows the material originally came from. He found that the blades were made of obsidian that was transported from very distant sources, some up to 480 kilometers (300 mi) away.

Gunther Island was inhabited for 1,000 years, until 1860, when local businessmen and landowners slaughtered

Hupa Fish-weir across Trinity River, about 1923. Photo by Edward S. Curtis.   [Library of Congress]

approximately 180 people gathered for the annual World Renewal Ceremony. Since the massacre, the site fell into private ownership, and the Wiyot have not had access to it, even though the site is regarded as the center of their universe. Recently, however, they have reacquired portions of the island (referred to now as Indian Island) and intend to resume the World Renewal Ceremony there, restore the native habitat, and protect the island's cultural resources.

Artifacts from Gunther Island and other local sites, along with baskets and ceremonial regalia, can be viewed in the Native American wing at the Clarke Historical Museum in Eureka.

PATRICK'S POINT
The Patrick's Point site is located on a rugged coastal bluff north of Eureka, in ancestral Yurok territory. The site was first occupied 500–600 years ago and was abandoned sometime before 1850. During an excavation conducted in 1948, Robert F. Heizer encountered two house floors, a hearth, and an artifact assemblage similar to that of the Gunther Island site. The site had a high incidence of artifacts recognized as marine mammal hunting gear, indicating that sea lion hunting was of primary importance at Patrick's Point.

Harpoon hunting is a highly effective technique that was used throughout the northern Pacific Rim. Bone and antler harpoons fit into a slotted wooden shaft and are connected by a line. Once the hunter hits his prey, the harpoon separates from the shaft and remains in the animal. James A. Bennyhoff analyzed harpoons at a variety of sites, including Patrick's Point, and was able to show how the technology improved over time.

A notable discovery at Patrick's Point was a group of miniature obsidian bifaces and slate zoomorphs found in non-mortuary contexts, similar to the large bifaces and zoomorphs from Gunther Island burials. Loud called the large zoomorphs from Gunther Island "slave killers," and hypothesized that they were used to club people to death. However, the presence of the miniature forms led Heizer and Elsasser to conclude that the zoomorphs were probably treasure or wealth items, not weapons used in such a violent manner.

Sumeg is a reconstructed Yurok village that can be visited in Patrick's Point State Park, offering visitors a unique opportunity to explore traditional wood plank houses.

TSURAI
The Yurok village of Tsurai at Trinidad Bay (occupied between AD 1620 and 1916) was visited numerous times by explorers and traders—beginning with Bodega and Vancouver, who landed at the village in 1775 and 1793, respectively.

Yurok houses at Pekwan. Photo by Augustus William Ericson.   [The Ericson Collection, Humboldt State University Library]

Ships also landed at Tsurai during the northwest coast fur trade of the early 1800s, when American- and Russian-sponsored ships provided European goods to trade for sea otter pelts. The seafarers' diary entries, compiled in *The Four Ages of Tsurai*, are some of the earliest descriptions of local Native Americans on record.

Heizer's 1949 excavations at Tsurai revealed evidence of these early encounters. Euro-American trade items, such as iron swords, copper bracelets, and glass beads were found in the historic component of the site. There is evidence that historic contact changed the subsistence patterns of Tsurai villagers. An increase in elk and deer bone suggests that hunting of these animals became more important—a development likely related to the introduction of guns, which would have been more effective in hunting of large land mammals than the bow and arrow.

STONE LAGOON

Problems with erosion and vandalism brought archaeologist David Fredrickson to the Stone Lagoon site, once the Yurok village of Tsahpekw. Salvage excavations at the site revealed stone pavements associated with redwood plank houses, as well as a rich assortment of artifacts. The analysis of butchered animal bone indicates that marine mammal hunting was an important economic activity. Yurok consultants stated that Redding Rock, an island located several miles out to sea, was an important sea mammal hunting place. A lagoon focus at Stone Lagoon is also exemplified by the thousands of net sinkers discovered at the site, which were used to weigh down nets for capture of fish and waterfowl.

Visitors to the Thomas H. Kuchel Visitor Center in Redwood National and State Park, 1.6 kilometers (1 mile) south of Orick, can view a Yurok canoe and many interesting displays about local Indians.

POINT ST. GEORGE

During the summer of 1964, Richard Gould conducted excavations at the Point St. George site, which corresponds to the ethnographic Tolowa village of *Taiga'n*, north of Crescent City. Gould identified three separate activity areas: a habitation area, a workshop area, and a cemetery. His excavations focused on the habitation and workshop areas.

Gould worked closely with Tolowa consultants to interpret the archaeological findings. During the excavations, Gould wondered why he had not encountered houses in what appeared to be a rich part of the midden deposit and spoke with local Tolowa people regarding the lack of such evidence. They laughed and told him that "them old-timers never put their houses in the garbage-dump" and directed him to dig on a steep slope nearby, where surface evidence of archaeological material was not observed. Within minutes, the remains of a redwood plank house with a blue clay floor and a central hearth were discovered.

Gould identified two occupations in the workshop area of Point St. George: one dating between 600 and 175 years ago, and the other to about 2,300 years ago. The more recent deposit was quite rich in artifacts and faunal remains, reflecting a variety of tasks—such as flaked-stone tool production, manufacturing of antler and bone implements, cleaning of fish, and heavy-duty butchering of sea lions. The earlier occupation, which consisted mostly of flaked-stone manufacturing debris and a few fish bones, represented a temporary camp of people who came from the interior to collect and knap local sources of tool stone.

White Deerskin Dance. Photo by Augustus William Ericson.   [The Ericson Collection, Humboldt State University Library]

Based on Tolowa oral testimony, Gould concluded that the village at Point St. George was abandoned due to a cholera epidemic in the 1700s to early 1800s. His consultants told him that many people died of a painful stomach sickness that caused them to "pass blood," symptoms characteristic of cholera.

Local Native American culture can be explored at the Del Norte County Historical Society Museum in Crescent City, which has two rooms devoted to the artifacts, photographs, and baskets of the Tolowa and Yurok people. The End of the Trail Museum, at the Trees of Mystery in Klamath, has an impressive collection of Native American baskets, photographs, and artifacts, including a room devoted to northwest California Native Americans.

RED ELDERBERRY PLACE

In 2003 Shannon Tushingham began fieldwork at interior sites along the Smith River, including the ethnographic Tolowa village of TcuncuLtun, Athabascan for "Red Elderberry Place." Tushingham worked closely with the Tolowa people, many of whom are the descendants of Gould's consultants at Point St. George. The site was occupied beginning around 7,000 years ago until the historic period, repre-

senting the longest continuous chronological sequence of any site yet investigated in northwest California.

The site was used occasionally by mobile hunter-gatherers until around 3,200 years ago, when people began settling down at river sites on a semi-permanent basis, relying heavily on elk, salmon and (to a lesser extent) acorns. Archaeological findings at the site include the earliest semi-subterranean house pit recorded in the region (ca. 2,325 years ago) and a 3,200-year-old hearth.

Beginning around 1,300 years ago, many changes took place at the site. The discovery of residential features, including semi-subterranean redwood plank houses, food caches, and slab-lined hearths, suggest that Red Elderberry Place became a home base for people who invested more time and energy in making specialized tools and equipment geared toward the procurement and processing of salmon and acorns. Artifacts that were absent or rare in earlier contexts, such as net sinkers, stone harpoon tips, and formal ground-stone tools (including flanged pestles, hopper mortars, and mortar bowls) are abundant after approximately 1,300 years ago. Seal and sea lion bone, ocean shellfish, and marine mammal hunting gear were discovered in the recent deposits, suggesting that

Sam Lopez (Tolowa) in ceremonial regalia. Note the large obsidian blade in the foreground. Photo by Edward S. Curtis.   [Library of Congress]

local people obtained these foods at the coast and returned with them, perhaps by canoe, to the site. Additionally, there is the first evidence of luxury items, including steatite pipes and pendants, decorated bone, and a miniature obsidian blade.

Despite the great social upheaval and loss of life during the gold-rush era, people persisted in living at Red Elderberry Place into the historic period. Their presence is reflected by the discovery of a heavily burned, semi-subterranean sweathouse with remarkably well-preserved redwood plank floors, an internal area paved with stones, and a slab-lined hearth. The associated assemblage consists of a diverse array of Euro-American-introduced materials and artifacts that bear similarities to the site's Native American assemblage. This indicates that site inhabitants employed similar subsistence activities during the contact period while incorporating new

(historic period) materials and technology into their cultural system. Such evidence sends a strong message of cultural survival and continuity with an earlier way of life, despite the tragic historical events of the time.

Visitors to the Hoopa Tribal Museum, located in the Hoopa Valley Indian Reservation east of Eureka, can get a taste of what life may have been like at inland river sites. Most of the items on display are loaned to the museum by local Hupa, Yurok, and Karuk people. The artifacts, baskets, and ceremonial regalia are part of a living culture and are removed from the museum for use during traditional ceremonies. Guided tours can be arranged to historical sites, including a visit to the village of Takimildiñ, which features traditional plank houses. As is clear at Hoopa Valley, California Native Americans are not an artifact of the past. Many continue traditional practices while living in the modern world and feel connected to the remarkable archaeological and cultural sites of the region.

Further Reading: Gould, Richard A., *Archaeology of the Point St. George Site and Tolowa Prehistory*, Publications in Anthropology No. 4 (Berkeley: University of California, 1966); Heizer, Robert F., and

John E. Mills, *The Four Ages of Tsurai: A Documentary History of the Indian Village on Trinidad Bay* (Berkeley: University of California, 1952); Hildebrandt, William R., and Valerie A. Levulett, "Late Holocene Emergence of Marine Focused Economies in Northwest California," in *Archaeology of the California Coast during the Late Holocene*, edited by Jon Erlandson and Terry Jones (Los Angeles: University of California Institute of Archaeology, 2003), 300–316.

Shannon Tushingham and William Hildebrandt

LAVA BED NATIONAL MONUMENT, TULE LAKE AREA, AND OTHER SITES

Northeast California

Ancient and Historic Native Sites in a Diverse Environment

The volcanoes, deserts, rivers, and mountains of the northeastern California landscape remind us of the dramatic forces of creation in this part of the world. On the western boundary, the volcanic Mount Shasta and Lassen Peak are 4,316 meters (14,162 ft) and 3,190 meters (10,466 ft), respectively. The Warner Range on the east contains several peaks reaching between 2,390 and 3,028 meters (7,843 and 9,934 ft), and twenty more peaks reaching over 1,830 meters (6,000 ft) in height are scattered throughout the interior. This volcanic landscape makes obsidian and basalt important elements of prehistory, and northeastern California surfaces often glisten with a seemingly endless number of flakes.

The Great Basin ignores our political boundaries and reaches into parts of California, creating the diverse landscape that influenced the adaptations of prehistoric populations. The ancient cultures inhabiting this region include Modoc, Pit River, Yana, Maidu, and Northern Paiute. The archaeological sites associated with these cultures are important because of issues regarding prehistoric adaptation and migration, research in the contact and historic periods, and for acknowledgment of the continuing influence of Native peoples on the cultural and physical texture of the northeastern California landscape. The following includes a brief discussion of sites associated with the Modoc, Yana, Maidu, and Paiute.

MODOC SITES

Lava Beds National Monument was home to the Modoc. They occupied a territory from Mount Shasta to Goose Lake in the north, and Lost River in the south. Their villages clustered around the Tule and Lower Klamath lakes and along Lost River. Major studies conducted within

this area include those by Cressman (1940, 1942), Squier (1956), and Sampson (1985).

Cressman proposed three cultural phases, or horizons, for the Lower Klamath Lake area. His Early Horizon dates to about 5500 BC. The assemblage—apparently associated with fossilized mammal bones—included fossilized bone points, weathered hand stones, and large willow leaf and side-notched projectile points. The Middle Horizon, dating to about 2000 BC, included bone awls, worked antler, hand stones, and large side and corner-notched points. Dating to approximately AD 500, the Historic Horizon assemblage included ground-stone pipes, special *Wokas* mullers and grinding slabs, mortars and pestles, shell beads, and small side-notched and corner-notched points. This later period was thought to be characteristic of Klamath-Modoc material culture documented ethnographically.

One of the most significant investigations for the area involves excavations of the rich Nightfire Island site on Lower Klamath Lake (Sampson 1985). Stratigraphic data from twenty-five excavation units were correlated based on sedimentary descriptions, radiocarbon and obsidian hydration dates, avifaunal remains, projectile points, and flake sizes. Fifteen distinct occupation layers were identified, dating from approximately 5000 BC to AD 1300 or later, but before Euro-American contact. More recently the completion of the PGT-PG&E and Tuscarora pipeline archaeological investigations has provided information regarding a large number of archaeological sites adjacent to Lava Beds National Monument.

EARLY EXPLORATION AND TRADE

A number of trapping parties scouted the Lava Beds and Tule Lake area in the 1820s. Trading companies, including the

Hudson's Bay Company, sent trappers to the unknown lands beyond the Columbia River in search of beaver pelts. By 1840 the fur trade was in decline.

Kit Carson guided Second Lieutenant John Charles Fremont's army expedition from California to Klamath Marsh in 1843. Worried about attacks from the Natives, when Fremont saw smoke from campfires on the far side of the lake, he had his men shoot off their Howitzer in that direction. In retaliation, in 1846, when Fremont again entered the Klamath Lake territory, the Klamaths raided his camp for horses and killed four men. Kit Carson, attempting to retaliate, mistakenly attacked a village of innocent Natives. These types of encounters, as well as the introduction of disease, led to mutual suspicion and hostility between the Native populations and Euro-American explorers and early settlers.

With the establishment of the Bear Flag Republic in California and the ceding of Oregon to the United States in 1846, the Pacific Northwest opened to a flood of new emigrants. Many of these newcomers came via the Applegate Cutoff, which passed by Tule Lake. At first the Modoc allowed the settlers' wagons to pass through the Applegate Cutoff, but after observing the increasing trespassing and disturbance of wild game by the newcomers, the Natives were outraged. In 1850, at a place now known as Bloody Point, a band of more than ninety emigrants were attacked by the Modoc, and all except one were killed.

MODOC WARS
In 1863 Euro-American settlers staked claims around the Lower Klamath and Clear lakes. The Modoc and other Native groups appealed to the U.S. government for land, and the resulting treaty placed the Modoc, Klamath, and Paiute on a reservation on former Klamath land. Corruption was prevalent, and the Modoc, who were forced to live on their former enemies' land, were not happy with their situation. Captain Jack and his followers left the reservation and went back to their former territory on Lost River, north of Tule Lake. With the imposition of drastic reforms at the reservation, Captain Jack was persuaded to return; however, the Modoc were treated as outsiders in what was Klamath territory. In 1870 Captain Jack and his group left again. They moved back to their villages and began to treat the settlers as trespassers on their former territory.

On November 29, 1872, forty mounted cavalrymen arrived to round up the Modoc from their villages on Lost River. The Modoc escaped and paddled across Tule Lake to what is now known as Captain Jack's Stronghold. Another Modoc band, led by Hooker Jim, fled around the lake and killed every male settler they could find, then joined in with Captain Jack's group at the stronghold. The Modoc camp was a natural fortress made up of the walls and trenches of several schollen-domes, which can now be visited at the Lava Beds National Monument.

Despite many parleys between the Modoc and the U.S. Army, Captain Jack continued to insist on a reservation on Lost River, but was refused. Finally, President Grant appointed a peace commission under Alfred B. Meacham, reformer of the Klamath Reservation. The commission, under General Canby, arranged another series of parleys. At the peace talks, Meacham and Canby reiterated that they had no authority to grant Captain Jack's request for land on Lost River. At that point, Captain Jack shot Canby. News of the battle hit the newspapers, and the American public was mesmerized. Many put pressure on President Grant to call off the war, while others insisted that all the Modoc be executed.

EURO-AMERICAN SETTLEMENT
Modoc County was an important link in the overland supply route for the gold rush in southwestern Idaho, resulting in the establishment of Fort Bidwell in the 1860s and the settlement of Alturas in 1872. The Applegate Trail, blazed in 1851, passed by the area, and trading posts were established to serve incoming immigrants and miners bound for southern Idaho.

Because the Lava Beds and Tule Lake area is extremely arid, most forms of agriculture were impossible without irrigation. The Klamath Project, one of the earliest major projects undertaken by the Federal Reclamation Service, proposed to drain Tule and Lower Klamath lakes to expose arable farmland, diverting the lake water to irrigate fields in the Modoc basin. The project involved land in both Klamath County, Oregon, and Modoc County, California. In 1917, thirty-five 32-hectare (80-acre) parcels were opened for settlement within the lakebed of Tule Lake. Additional hectares were permitted in 1922 and 1927, with the final group of allotments made in the 1940s. At that time, the government also made available to World War II veterans thousands of barracks associated with the Tule Lake War Relocation Center; these barracks still dot the Tule Lake Basin.

YANA SITES
It is not until the period between 3000 BC and AD 500 that population developments become evident in the southern Cascade foothills, the Lake Oroville region (in Plumas County), the Lake Tahoe region, and the foothills of Tehama County. A well-known figure in the ethnographic Yana context is Ishi. When Ishi was found in 1911 in Oroville, California, he was known as the last Yahi; some of the sites being investigated by the Lassen National Forest may be directly related to his tragic story.

Kingsley Cave was excavated by a crew from the California Archaeological Survey (from the University of California at Berkeley) beginning in the spring of 1953. Archaeologists James Bennyhoff, Albert Elsasser, W. Atkinson, R. Brooks, L. Burton, D. Pendergast, R. Thomssen, B. Weissberg, and M. A.

Baumhoff conducted the excavation (Baumhoff 1955). The assemblage was subsequently curated at what is now the Phoebe Hearst Museum of Anthropology. The site is on the southeastern slope of the Cascade Mountains, to the east of Red Bluff and Chico, California.

MAIDU SITES

As the state site numbers Ca-Las-1 and Ca-Las-7 suggest, the Tommy Tucker and Karlo sites are important because they were recorded early in the history of California archaeology. The Karlo site is about 32 kilometers (20 mi) northeast of Susanville in Lassen County, California. It is situated in the western Great Basin, near a section of the northeastern California juniper-sage ecozone that includes Secret Valley. The site was excavated in 1955 by Fritz Riddell.

Although refined chronometric relationships were elusive, the large midden deposit appeared to be between 2,000–4,000 years old. Tommy Tucker Cave, about 60 meters (200 ft) above the valley floor, is a fissure on a fault line near the foot of this peak. It is 3 kilometers (2 mi) east of the present lakeshore, the closest permanent water. Perhaps more accessible than the lakeshore is a group of active hot springs at Amadee, 4 kilometers (2.5 miles) to the southwest—or a similar group, near Wendel, 5 kilometers (3 mi) to the northwest. The site is in territory occupied within historic times by a Northern Paiute band called the Wadadökadö.

PAIUTE SITES

At the time of European contact, the people to whom we refer as the Northern Paiute occupied portions of the Great Basin. Many Northern Paiute bands had been interacting with peoples of other cultures in various ways long before the arrival of Europeans.

Surprise Valley is about 97 kilometers (60 mi) long, north to south, and 16 to 24 kilometers (10 to 15 mi) wide. It lies along the California-Nevada border, with most of its area being in California. The valley is bounded on the west by the Warner Mountains and on the east by the Hays Canyon Range. Elevation of the valley floor is about 1,432 meters (4,700 ft). Research has shown that the valley has been continuously occupied by humans for over 6,000 years. James O'Connell has done considerable archaeological investigation of the valley and its surrounding resource areas, with a focus on human-environment relationships and their changes over time. Three sites can be visited on request: King's Dog, Menlo Baths, and Rodriguez.

Further Reading: Baumhoff, M. A., *Excavations of The-1 (Kingsley Cave)*, University of California Archaeological Survey Reports No. 30 (Berkeley: University of California Department of Anthropology, 1955); Bettinger, R., and M. Baumhoff, "The Numic Spread: Great Basin Cultures in Competition," *American Antiquity* 47 (1982): 485–503; Fenenga, F., and F. A. Riddell, "Excavation of Tommy Tucker Cave, Lassen County, California," *American Antiquity* 3 (1949): 203–214; Hughes, Richard E., "Exploring Diachronic Variability in Obsidian Procurement Patterns in Northeast California and South Central Oregon: Geochemical Characterization of Obsidian Sources and Projectile Points by Energy Dispersive X-Ray Fluorescence," Ph.D. diss. (University of California, 1982); Johnson, Jim, with Chris O'Brien, Michael Dugas, Diane Watts, Jamie Moore, and Wally Woolfenden, *Ishi Wilderness Area: Archaeological Test Excavations* (Helena, MT: Mountain Heritage Associates and Lassen National Forest, 2001); Kowta, M., *The Archaeology and Prehistory of Plumas and Butte Counties, California: An Introduction and Interpretive Model*, California Archaeological Site Inventory, Northeast Information Center (Chico: California State University, 1988); Lamb, Susan, *Lava Beds National Monument* (Tulelake, CA: Lava Beds Natural History Association, 1991); Moratto, M. J., *California Archaeology* (New York: Academic Press, 1984); O'Connell, J. F., "The Prehistory of Surprise Valley," Anthropological Papers No. 4 (Ramona, CA: Ballena Press, 1975), 1–57; Ritter, E. W., "Northern Sierra Foothill Archaeology: Culture History and Culture Process," in *Papers on California and Great Basin Prehistory*, edited by E. Ritter, P. Schulz, and R. Kautz (Davis: University of California, Center for Archaeological Research, 1970), 171–184; Sampson, C. Garth, *Nightfire Island: Later Holocene Lake-Marsh Adaptation on the Western Edge of the Great Basin*, Anthropological Papers No. 33 (Eugene: University of Oregon, 1985).

Antoinette Martinez

CLEAR LAKE BASIN AND THE BORAX LAKE SITE

North Coast Ranges, California
One of the Most Important Paleoindian Sites in the West

ENVIRONMENT AND CULTURE

The basin that drains into Clear Lake in the North Coast ranges of California has a deep prehistoric record, with archaeological evidence for human occupation dating back 13,000 years or more. A visit to the region will leave little doubt why ancient people gravitated to this environment.

Clear Lake basin is ecologically productive and diverse, and enjoys a Mediterranean climate with a mean annual temperature of 57 degrees Fahrenheit, alternating between a long, hot, dry summer and a cool, moist winter. Precipitation averages 24 inches annually and occurs almost exclusively between the months of October and April. Winter freezes are rare, and annual snowfall averages just 0.5 inches. This wet/very dry climate cycle produced definite pulses of plant and animal resource surfeit and deficit, which configured prehistoric adaptations in pervasive and fundamental ways.

A LONG ARCHAEOLOGICAL RECORD

Clear Lake basin has produced one of California's most significant records of ancient occupation, anchored by the Borax Lake site (described in the next section). For a time, the Mostin site also received considerable attention as a potential Paleoindian village and cemetery marked by some of the oldest examples of obsidian use in North America (e.g., Moratto 1984). For a while, the Mostin site also bore the additional distinction of being home to North America's largest suite of human bone collagen radiocarbon dates exceeding 8,000 years old. However, subsequent analysis dismissed the oldest age estimates, despite supporting dates of 7,000–9,000 years old.

Middle and Upper Archaic occupation has been documented at many sites in the basin. Such occupation has been especially well studied at the Houx site (Fredrickson 1973) and at excavations in Anderson Marsh State Historic Park (White 2002)—the latter representing the only state park in California established primarily to preserve and protect prehistoric archaeological sites.

The late prehistoric period is still best known via the Pomo ethnographic record, which is one of the best ethnographic records in the continental United States. The late prehistoric site located on Rattlesnake Island was sampled by Harrington (1943), but this research, like that of other late sites, was poorly reported.

A recent synthetic study (White et al. 2002) established that the region supported more and more people over time—living in larger communities; trading at longer distances; making and using more elaborate tools; fabricating and donning more distinctive material culture; and practicing more elaborate ceremonies. All these factors were especially pronounced in the final 450 years before European and Euro-American contact. However, the archaeological record is very specific: hunter-gatherer adaptations predominated in the region and varied only by degree, rather than kind, throughout time and across space. No doubt due in part to the seasonal resource pulses characterizing the region, adaptations were more or less mobile throughout the prehistoric period. To date, no archaeological evidence for sedentism or agriculture has been identified. Although populations were probably unusually dense, they were grouped into small-scale societies that rarely participated in cooperative relationships or recognized political authority outside the immediate village community (Beaton 1991).

Thus the unique property of archaeological research here—and this is really a microcosm of interior California prehistory—is the potential for researchers to study hunter-gatherer adaptations that have a long history and stability, and are spread over a broad region. Such a research framework makes it possible to identify, track, and understand the interplay of potential causes and consequences of culture change contained entirely within a range of hunter-gatherer variation.

THE BORAX LAKE SITE AND IMPLICATIONS FOR PALEOINDIAN OCCUPATION IN CALIFORNIA

Outside California, Clear Lake Basin is best known as the location of one of the most important Paleoindian sites in the far West: the Borax Lake site (Ca-Lak-36). In September 2006, this site was given National Landmark status. The site is located alongside the Borax Lake obsidian flow, between the eastern arms of Clear Lake, on lands owned and managed by the Archaeological Conservancy.

The site was first discovered in the late 1920s by avocationalist Wiley Post, who attracted the attention of M. R. Harrington of the Southwest Museum in Los Angeles. Harrington recognized eighteen fluted projectile points in Post's collection that were similar to points previously observed in association with extinct Pleistocene animals at Clovis New Mexico and elsewhere in North America. Between 1936 and 1946, Harrington dug a number of test pits and trenches at the site. In all this work, however, Harrington recovered just two more fluted point fragments, generating instead a large assemblage of more common forms of chipped-stone and ground stone tools (Harrington 1938a, 1938b, 1939, 1942, 1945, 1946, 1948).

Post's and Harrington's fluted-point discoveries were surface or near-surface finds. Excavations up to 8 feet deep produced more varied artifacts, including notched and leaf-shaped dart points, chipped-stone crescents, large-stemmed points (which Harrington identified as "wide stemmed Borax Lake points"), carved stone plummets, milling stones and manos, mortars and pestles, flake tools, and bifaces.

Convinced of the site's stratigraphic integrity, Harrington advanced the notion that the superposition of the fluted points meant that sub-surface finds were indicative of "Pre-Folsom Man" (Harrington 1938b). He drew tenuous comparison to Great Basin and Mojave Desert artifact types—which, he claimed, must also be "pre-Folsom" (Harrington 1948). This touched off a flurry of dispute from California archaeologists, who cited local comparative evidence indicating that the majority of Borax Lake site artifacts were actually less than 5,000 years old (Heizer 1952; Meighan 1955). Unfortunately, Harrington's chatty reporting style and poor substantive presentation buttressed the criticism. Many overlooked the obvious clues to Paleoindian presence at the site, along with some of Harrington's more insightful ruminations. Many archaeologists branded Harrington a dilettante and dismissed his reports.

Others, however, concluded there was more to the story. Intent on exploring these ambiguities, C. W. Meighan and C. V. Haynes conducted a new investigation of the site in 1968 (Meighan and Haynes 1968, 1970). Haynes excavated backhoe trenches flanking Harrington's excavations. He concluded that

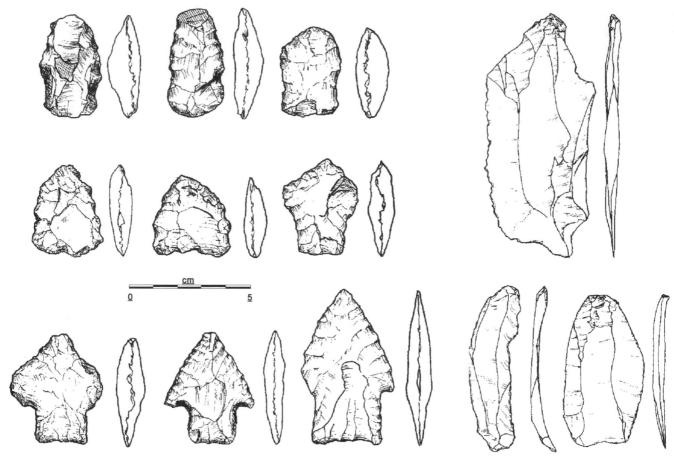

Examples of various arrowheads found in the region.   [Gregory G. White]

the site, formed on an alluvial fan, was in part deposited via a Holocene mudslide, which had incorporated the Paleoindian materials. The deposit had subsequently been mixed by Holocene soil building and historic agriculture. Meighan and Haynes concluded that the site was thoroughly stratigraphically mixed, undermining a centerpiece of Harrington's argument.

It was clear to Meighan and Haynes that a temporal series could not be obtained by traditional stratigraphic analysis, and no sufficient materials or contexts were observed adequate for radiocarbon assay. The investigators then turned to the relatively new technique of obsidian hydration dating to produce a sequence whose results supported both Harrington and his detractors. The surface of obsidian begins to form a distinctive thin layer when exposed to air—for example, when a piece of obsidian is shaped into a tool. The obsidian hydration technique measures the thickness of the outer surface layer of obsidian artifacts to gauge how long the surface has been exposed to air.

The obsidian hydration study by Meighan and Haynes focused on four time-marking artifact forms: fluted points, chipped-stone crescents, "wide stemmed Borax Lake points," and dart-sized, nonfluted, concave-based points. They

identified three distinct phases of occupation marked by (oldest) fluted points and chipped-stone crescents (obsidian hydration rim values of 8.3–9.7 microns), followed by the "wide stemmed Borax Lake points" (rim values of 7.0–7.4 microns), and then by (latest) dart-sized, nonfluted, concave-based points (rim values of 3.7–6.5 microns). They also noted that some of Harrington's finds suggested further, and as yet unrecognized, complexity.

No additional artifacts or residues could be assigned to the Paleoindian assemblage. However, it should be noted that Harrington's reports illustrate bifaces, preforms, and unifaces that are consistent with Paleoindian technology (Collins 1999).

Meighan's and Haynes's (1970) pioneering obsidian hydration work has led to more extensive and productive recent studies, and obsidian hydration is the primary means used by archaeologists for establishing the relative age of artifacts, sites, and cultural complexes found in the Clear Lake region (for example, Origer 1987; Parker 1994; White 2002). Recent obsidian hydration sampling of manufacturing debris from the Borax Lake obsidian quarry and other sites in eastern Clear Lake basin has demonstrated the beginning of apparent cultural activity in the basin at around 10.4 microns (White 2002, 449).

To date, no pre-Clovis cultural assemblages have been identified in the study area. Even after accumulating an obsidian hydration sample of more than 3,000 specimens from more than 70 sites, it is still the case that of all artifact forms found in Clear Lake Basin, only the Clovis points and chipped-stone crescents from the Borax Lake site are firmly tied to the 8.5–10.0 micron range.

The reader may consult Fredrickson and White (1988) for a more inclusive summary of regional Paleoindian finds.

Further Reading: Beaton, J. M., "Extensification and Intensification in Central California Prehistory," *American Antiquity* 65 (1991): 946–952; Collins, M. B., *Clovis Blade Technology* (Austin: University of Texas Press, 1999); Fredrickson, D. A., "Early Cultures of the North Coast Ranges, California," Ph.D. diss. (University of California, 1973); Fredrickson, D. A., "Cultural Diversity in Early Central California: A View from the North Coast Ranges," *Journal of California Anthropology* 1(1) (1974): 41–53; Fredrickson, D. A., and G. White, "The Clear Lake Basin and Early Complexes in California's North Coast Ranges," in *Early Human Occupation in Far Western North America: The Clovis-Archaic Interface*, edited by J. A. Willig, C. M. Aikens, and J. L. Fagan, Anthropological Papers No. 21 (Carson City: Nevada State Museum, 1988), 75–86; Harrington, M. R., "Folsom Man in California," *The Masterkey* XII(4) (1938a): 133–137; Harrington, M. R., "Pre-Folsom Man in California," *The Masterkey* XII(5) (1938b): 173–175; Harrington, M. R., "The Age of the Borax Lake Finds," *The Masterkey* XIII(6) (1939): 208–209; Harrington, M. R., "Return to Borax Lake," *The Masterkey* XVI(6) (1942): 214–215; Harrington, M. R., "A Glimpse of Pomo Archaeology," *The Masterkey* XVII(1) (1943): 9–12; Harrington, M. R., "Farewell to Borax Lake," *The Masterkey* XIX(6) (1945): 81–184; Harrington, M. R., "New Work at Borax Lake," *The Masterkey* XX(6) (1946): 189–190; Harrington, M. R., "An Ancient Site at Borax Lake, California," Southwest Museum Papers No. 16 (Los Angeles: Southwest Museum, 1948); Heizer, R. F., "A Review of Problems in the Antiquity of Man in California," in *Symposium of the Antiquity of Man in California*, Annual Reports No. 16 (Berkeley: University of California Archaeological Survey, 1952), 3–17; Kaufman, T. S., "Early Prehistory of the Clear Lake Area, Lake County, California," Ph.D. diss. (University of California, 1980); Meighan, C. W., and C. V. Haynes, "New Studies on the Age of the Borax Lake Site," *The Masterkey* 42(1) (1968); Meighan, C. W., and C. V. Haynes, "The Borax Lake Site Revisited," *Science* 167 (1970): 1213–1221; Meighan, C. W., "The Archaeology of the North Coast Ranges," Annual Reports No. 30 (Berkeley: University of California Archaeological Survey, 1955), 1–39; Moratto, M. J., *California Archaeology* (New York: Academic Press, 1984); Origer, T. M., "Temporal Control in the Southern North Coast Ranges of California: The Application of Obsidian Hydration Analysis," Papers in Northern California Anthropology No. 1 (Berkeley: University of California, Northern California Anthropology Group, 1987); Parker, J. W., "Dots on a Map: Using Cultural Resource Management Data to Reconstruct Prehistoric Settlement Patterns in Clear Lake Basin, California," Ph.D. diss. (University of California, 1994); White G., D. A. Fredrickson, L. Hager, J. Meyer, J. Rosenthal, M. Waters, J. West, and E. Wohlgemuth, "Culture History and Culture Change in Prehistoric Clear Lake Basin: Final Report of the Anderson Flat Project," Publication No. 13 (Davis: University of California Center for Archaeological Research, 2002).

Gregory G. White

POINT REYES NATIONAL SEASHORE SITES, OLOMPALI AND McCLURE SITES

San Francisco Bay Area, Coastal California

Historic Encounters with Francis Drake and Sebastian Cermeño

Point Reyes National Seashore is located in west Marin County, California. The Point Reyes peninsula is representative of over 34 million years of geologic activity—the result of two massive tectonic plates, the Pacific and North American plates, grinding against one another and carrying rock northward from as far away as southern California. Periodic earthquakes along the infamous San Andreas Fault serve as uncomfortable reminders that California is in constant formation. A stroll along the Earthquake Trail, which begins near the Bear Valley visitors' center and enters the San Andreas rift zone, offers additional information on the geology of Point Reyes.

Eustatic changes, or changes in the global sea level, also shape the Bay Area landscape. For example, 10,000 years ago, the sea level was much lower. San Francisco Bay was a valley, the Golden Gate was a waterfall, and the Farallon Islands—now 43 kilometers (27 mi) off the California coast—marked the late Pleistocene coastline. The past 10,000 years have also seen alterations in plant and animal communities. Saltwater and freshwater marshes, oak forests, redwood forests, coastal scrub, and rocky intertidal habitats once contributed to a veritable cornucopia of resources that attracted Native Americans to this area thousands of years ago.

Kenneth C. Patrick Visitor Center and Drakes Beach.   [Courtesy of KNP Enterprises]

Penutian-speaking peoples migrated into the San Francisco Bay Area as early as 5,000 years ago. Groups like the Coast Miwok, who settled in Point Reyes and the present-day Marin and southern Sonoma counties, established villages, maintaining settlement and subsistence patterns that lasted into the early twentieth century. The Federated Indians of Graton Rancheria represent the federally recognized descendants of the Coast Miwok and Southern Pomo. They maintain an active tribal government, part of which protects and mitigates damage to Coast Miwok and southern Pomo archaeological sites, including those in Point Reyes National Seashore.

DRAKES ESTERO, POINT REYES NATIONAL SEASHORE, CALIFORNIA

Point Reyes National Seashore is the focus of ongoing prehistoric and historic archaeological research. Shell mounds—or

consecutive deposits of soil, shell, bone, food remains, stone tools, and other artifacts in a semi-circular mound—are the most conspicuous archaeological features along the shores and various inlets of Point Reyes. Their complex stratigraphies continue to hold tremendous research potential. Archaeologists working in the 1950s used organized groupings of projectile points, ground stone, bone tools, and shell ornaments found in these mounds to create a central California chronological sequence. These items were also used to establish connections between archaeological sites at Point Reyes to those in other areas of the San Francisco Bay Area.

Iron spikes, Chinese porcelain, and other sixteenth-century artifacts found within shell mounds around Drakes Estero have also attracted the attention of those interested in proving whether Francis Drake careened his ship, the *Golden Hind*, in Drakes Bay for thirty-six days in the summer of 1579. How-

Indian Beach, Tomales Bay State Park.   [Tsim D. Schneider]

ever, other locations for Drake's landing have been proposed—and the famed plate of brass, supposedly left by Drake to mark possession of "Nova Albion" for England, was found to be a hoax in the 1970s.

Although ruse and conjecture hinder the Drake quest, sixteenth-century artifacts excavated from Point Reyes sites also receive careful study by archaeologists interested in locating the wreck of Sebastian Cermeño's ship, the *San Agustin*, which sank in Drakes Bay in 1595. Archaeologists from the University of California in Berkeley excavated numerous sites at Point Reyes from the 1930s to the 1950s. These sites include the Mendoza, Cauley, and Estero sites near Drakes Estero and around the white cliffs that embrace Drakes Bay.

In addition to locating the wreckage of the *San Agustin* in Drakes Bay, archaeologists today are also revisiting museum collections from earlier excavations at Point Reyes archaeological sites. Artifacts like Wan Li period (1573 to 1619) porcelain provide information on European trade and material culture, as well as important information about the Coast Miwok use of such artifacts in daily life.

Edge wear on some porcelain fragments, for example, may indicate use in various Coast Miwok processing activities. Obsidian tools, mortars and pestles, bone tools, and various shell and animal remains from sites near Drakes Estero suggest that the Coast Miwok practiced a form of subsistence that drew on marine animals, terrestrial animals, and a variety of plants. Interviews with Coast Miwok descendants in the early 1930s supplement archaeological data but also offer valuable information on village life, ideology, and the uses of certain resources and processing methods.

Drakes Estero is accessible by several trails. The Estero Trail leads hikers along the east side of the estero toward Drakes Bay. The Mendoza, Cauley, and Estero archaeological sites, like most sites at Point Reyes National Seashore, are not visible from this trail, as they are inaccessible or hidden by soil and dense brush. However, visitors tracing well-worn paths around Drakes Estero can easily imagine Coast Miwok villages and conical bark houses lining the shore, or even the *Golden Hind* or *San Agustin* anchored in the bay.

Interpretive displays at the Kenneth C. Patrick visitor center at Drakes Beach provide further information on the Coast Miwok and the Drake and Cermeño voyages. Additional displays allow visitors a chance to view Chinese porcelain recovered from Point Reyes archaeological sites, as well as information on the natural history of Point Reyes. Panoramic views of Drakes Bay and the distant Farrallon Islands are easily had on the short, paved Peter Behr Overlook Trail, which starts at the Drakes Beach parking lot.

The Bear Valley visitors' center also displays Coast Miwok artifacts, while a short trail leads from the visitor center parking lot to Kule Loklo, a replica Coast Miwok village complete with bark houses, a round house, a dance area, acorn granaries, and a sweat house. The Miwok Archaeological Preserve of Marin (MAPOM) offers classes on Native skills at Kule Loklo, including courses in flint knapping, cordage and net manufacture, basketry, and clamshell disk bead manufacture.

TOMALES BAY STATE PARK, CALIFORNIA

Tomales Bay stretches along the San Andreas Fault line to the east of Point Reyes National Seashore. Visitors to Tomales Bay State Park enjoy warmer temperatures and warmer waters compared to the often frigid Pacific waters at Point Reyes. Tomales Bay State Park also boasts a rich prehistoric and historic archaeological history.

The McClure site is a shell mound located on Tomales Bay. Excavated in the 1950s, prehistoric and historic artifacts unearthed from the McClure site reveal a deeply stratified site, suggesting continual occupation for at least 3,000 years. Other shell mounds along the Tomales Bay shoreline follow a similar pattern in their location near freshwater marshes. For this reason, shell mounds within Tomales Bay State Park are easily identified, but coastal erosion and human disturbances threaten their stability, and they should be left undisturbed.

Park trails within Tomales Bay State Park connect sand beaches and hidden bay coves. The Indian Nature Trail starts at Heart's Desire Beach and weaves through the forest to Indian Beach, where a replica Coast Miwok village—complete with two conical bark houses and a ramada—promises a commanding view of Tomales Bay and the Marin mainland. Signs along the trail identify native plant and animal species and their importance to the Coast Miwok.

OLOMPALI STATE PARK, CA

Just east of Point Reyes National Seashore, numerous state and regional parks offer elegant hikes and unmatched opportunities to experience the cultural and natural diversity of Marin County. Located off Highway 101 and just south of Petaluma, California, Olompali State Park gives visitors a truly unique view of California history. Before the Grateful Dead lived at Olompali in 1966, and before Mariano Vallejo owned the property in the 1830s, Olompali was the largest known Coast Miwok village site continuously occupied since at least 6000 BC.

Excavations at Olompali in the 1970s revealed prehistoric obsidian, ground stone, and bone and shell artifacts—in addition to historic bottle glass, metal, Chinese porcelain, and an English sixpence struck in 1567. The porcelain and English coin have led some to believe that Francis Drake landed near Olompali, while other archaeologists view the unique blend of prehistoric and historic artifacts as an unrivaled opportunity to study colonial encounters between the Coast Miwok and European interlopers.

Interpretive footpaths encircle the Olompali visitor center, meandering through Victorian gardens and around the 170-year-old adobe home of Camilo Ynitia, a Coast Miwok who once owned Olompali. Another trail leads from the visitor center into an oak forest, and eventually up Mount Burdell. Along the way, visitors can see Kitchen Rock, a large boulder with cupules that the Coast Miwok used to process acorns and seeds into flour. This trail also passes through a replica Coast Miwok village and native-plant garden, which detail Coast Miwok lifeways.

Further Reading: Heizer, Robert F., "Francis Drake and the California Indians, 1579," *University of California Publications in American Archaeology and Ethnology* 42(3) (1947): 251–302; Heizer, Robert F., and William W. Elmendorf, "Francis Drake's California Anchorage in the Light of the Indian Language Spoken There," *Pacific Historical Review* 11 (1942): 213–217; Lightfoot, Kent G., and William S. Simmons, "Culture Contact in Protohistoric California: Social Contexts of Native and European Encounters," *Journal of California and Great Basin Anthropology* 20(2) (1998): 138–170; Meighan, Clement W., *Excavations in Sixteenth Century Shellmounds at Drake's Bay, Marin County*, University of California Archaeological Survey No. 9, Papers on California Archaeology No. 9 (Berkeley: University of California, Department of Anthropology, 1950); Meighan, Clement W., "The Stoneware Site, a 16th Century Site on Drakes Bay," in *Essays in California Archaeology: A Memorial to Franklin Fenenga*, edited by William J. Wallace and Francis A. Riddell (Berkeley: University of California, 2002), 62–87; Meighan, Clement W., and Robert F. Heizer, "Archaeological Exploration of Sixteenth-Century Indian Mounds at Drake's Bay," *California Historical Society Quarterly* 31(2) (1952): 99–108; Moratto, Michael, *California Archaeology* (New York: Academic Press, 1984); National Park Service, Point Reyes National Seashore, www.nps.gov/pore (online December 2006).

Tsim D. Schneider

PATTERSON, EMERYVILLE, WEST BERKELEY, AND OTHER SHELL MOUND SITES

San Francisco Bay Area, California

A 5,000-Year History of Shell Mound Construction and Use

The best-known archaeological sites in the San Francisco Bay area are undoubtedly the large shell mounds that once lined the shores of the bay. Archaeologists and the public alike have long been fascinated by these impressive sites, some nearly two football fields long and rising almost 9 meters (30 ft) above the ground.

First investigated by the pioneering archaeologists Max Uhle and Nels Nelson in the early 1900s, the largest shell mounds, such as those at Emeryville, West Berkeley, and Ellis Landing, revealed a wide array of artifacts, hundreds of human burials, and scattered architectural features. Composed of a mixture of soil, ash, and rock, these oval-shaped sites contained many artifacts interspersed throughout complex lenses of sediment, finely crushed shell, and numerous animal bones. Many of these artifacts, including bone tools and implements and stone objects, may have been used to acquire and process food. Shell beads likely served a ceremonial function.

Shell mound studies were advanced considerably by Nelson's 1908 survey of shell mound locations along the bay shore. Nelson recorded more than 400 mounds of varying sizes and supplied a snapshot of the archaeological landscape that is invaluable today. Since that survey, virtually all of the larger shell mounds have been destroyed by development or agricultural activities. Consequently, opportunities for the public to view intact shell mounds are extremely limited, although many collections from these sites are preserved in area museums.

Although shell mounds loom large in the history of local archaeology and play a prominent role in interpretation aimed at the public, they are not the only sites in the area. In fact, over the past forty years, archaeological work has revealed new types of sites and more observations of previously overlooked sites. For example, sites known as petroglyphs, where artistic designs have been carved or etched into rock outcroppings, have been newly identified, as have bedrock mortars—places where acorns and seeds are thought to have been processed. Nevertheless, San Francisco Bay Area archaeology is perhaps best characterized as a "landscape of mounds," due to the great numbers of mounded sites, which vary in terms of their size and the amount of shell. In the northern part of the bay area, for instance, many small- and medium-sized mounds are composed of a high percentage of finely ground shell, whereas comparably sized mounds in the south contain relatively little shell and more soil.

Mounded sites have traditionally been viewed by archaeologists as vast repositories of information on the diet, ecology, and cultural practices of the Native people who inhabited the area in precontact times, primarily the Ohlone, Coast Miwok, and Bay Miwok. After nearly a century of research, it is now known that these sites first appeared between 5,000 and 4,000 years ago, during the Early period (ca. 3000–500 BC) when the bay's estuary system expanded to reach its current state. Although mounds were first occupied during this period, it was not until the subsequent Middle period, from about 500 BC to AD 900, that they were the most numerous. Indeed, some researchers have characterized this period as a "golden age of shell mound communities," recognizing that mounds were likely grouped together and were places where activities involving food processing and ritual took place throughout much of the year. After this golden age, during the Late period (AD 900–1700), many mounds appear to have been abandoned or reoccupied in different ways. Researchers continue to examine why this might have been happened, concluding that climate change or drought may have been responsible, or that increasing population density in the area led to a move away from the mounds to pursue food sources.

Recent investigations of mounded sites suggest that some were specialized places for harvesting specific resources, such as fish, and others were intentionally built. Some researchers characterize shell mounds as specialized cemeteries. Others have argued that they served both as burial areas and as ceremonial places, where activities such as remembrance of the dead, feasts, and dance took place. The idea that shell mounds may have been vacant most of the year, perhaps used only during key ceremonial periods, is also being explored.

Archaeological understanding about the placement of burials into mounds has shifted considerably since Nelson's time. Earlier researchers often characterized shell mounds as "trash heaps," where remnants of meals and food processing accumulated to form mounds. Today, archaeologists agree that the presence of so many burials in the mounds suggests that they played a powerful role in the symbolic world of the Native peoples who created them.

Despite nearly 100 years of research, many questions remain about shell mounds and the types of activities that took place on them. This is often surprising to the public because virtually all museum interpretations and related educational material rely on the interpretation of shell mounds as "mounded villages." In this scenario, traceable to Nelson's work at Ellis Landing, a village sits atop a shell mound, with areas for tule-thatched houses, storage, and trash. Over time, villages grew as houses were modified and rebuilt, as food was processed, and as the dead were buried. Although most archaeologists would agree that this is still the most compelling interpretation of shell mounds, mounded villages like this are not found elsewhere in North America.

Across the Bay Area, interpretative centers, trails, and museums contain excellent displays that emphasize the past and present culture of local tribes. For example, the interpretative center at Coyote Hills Regional Park in Fremont includes displays of artifacts from nearby sites and is situated within a restored wetlands system that is evocative of the pre-contact environment. A short walk away is the Paterson Mound, one of the few places where the public can view a shell mound, albeit on a restricted basis, along with reconstructed tule reed dwellings that are incorporated into regularly scheduled cultural demonstrations, often lead by Ohlone people. At the Chitactac Adams Heritage County Park, near Gilroy in Santa Clara County, a new interpretive trail includes displays that focus on Ohlone history, pre-contact village life, and archaeological site preservation, with access to an extensive series of bedrock mortars and petroglyphs. Two parks in Marin County—Olompali, near

Novato, and Kule Loklo in Point Reyes—focus on Coast Miwok culture.

Most archaeological sites in the San Francisco Bay area are not accessible to the public, and the largest shell mounds have either been destroyed or their deposits lie buried deep beneath parking lots or structures. As a result, education about site preservation and the cultures that produced these sites is more important than ever, because even buried sites continue to be impacted by development. New interpretations of the once highly visible shell mound, including those that emphasize their ceremonial and sacred importance, promise to maintain interest in a feature that has long fascinated much of the public.

Further Reading: Chartkoff, Joseph L., and Kerry Kona Chartkoff, *The Archaeology of California* (Palo Alto, CA: Stanford University Press, 1984); Chitactac-Adams County Park, Santa Clara County Parks Web site, http://www.sccgov.org/portal/site/parks/ (online May 2006); Coyote Hills Regional Park, East Bay Regional Park District Web site, http://www.ebparks.org/parks/coyote.htm (online May 2006); Fagan, Brian, *Before California: An Archaeologist Looks at Our Earliest Inhabitants* (Lanham, MD: Rowman & Littlefield Publishers, 2003); Lightfoot, Kent G., and Edward M. Luby, "Late Holocene in the San Francisco Bay Area: Temporal Trends in the Use and Abandonment of Shell Mounds in the East Bay," in *Catalysts to Complexity: Late Holocene Societies of the California Coast*, edited by Jon M. Erlandson and Terry L. Jones (Los Angeles: Cotsen Institute of Archaeology, University of California, 2002), 263–281; Luby, Edward M., and Mark F. Gruber, "The Dead Must Be Fed," *Cambridge Archaeological Journal* 9 (1999): 95–108; Moratto, Michael J., *California Archaeology* (New York: Academic Press, 1984).

Edward M. Luby

THE BLOSSOM MOUND, BRAZIL MOUND, AND HOTCHKISS SITES

Sacramento Area, Central Valley, California

Sacramento River Delta Archaeology

The Central Valley of California was among the most densely populated regions of North America when Spanish explorers entered the basin between AD 1722 and 1821. Native people of the valley were living in large villages, often in excess of several hundred residents. They ate only wild foods such as deer, fish, and acorns, which they harvested in large quantities and stored for winter use. When archaeologists first began to study this region at the turn of the last century, prehistoric village sites were found every 3–5 kilometers (2–3 mi) along the major rivers

and around the extensive marshlands of the central and southern basin. These mounded settlements were built by generations of Native people, sometimes purposefully to avoid seasonal flooding, but more commonly from the regular accumulation of dietary debris, wood ash, charcoal, and cooking stones. Unfortunately, most of the valley's large village mounds have been destroyed by more than a century of agricultural leveling, urban development, and construction of flood-control levees. However, scientific study of village remnants and earlier settlements has provided an important glimpse of central California's prehistoric past.

Evidence for the valley's earliest human inhabitants is found along the edges of now-dry lakes, which flourished in the southern portion of the basin at the end of the last Ice Age. Projectile points left by Paleoindian hunters more than 11,000 years ago litter these former shorelines, often found near the skeletal remains of extinct camels, horses, bison, and mammoth. Elsewhere in the basin, Paleoindian artifacts are found on ancient weathered piedmonts and other remnants of the Ice Age landscape that survived eons of erosion and flooding. Some of the oldest, well-preserved sites from the valley—dating between 8,000 and 10,000 years old—are found deeply buried in the massive floodplains that now line the major rivers and tributary streams. Dietary remains from these sites include the bones of fish and birds, revealing that California's early inhabitants were not simply big-game hunters. Many archaeologists believe that these human groups moved seasonally from place to place, following the ripening of different plant foods and the migration of elk and pronghorn herds that once occupied the broad oak savanna and grasslands of the valley bottom.

The first substantial village settlements in the Central Valley were established about 5,000 years ago, around the marshes and sloughs of the delta region. This important habitat developed relatively recently—just 6,000 years ago—as rising sea levels caused the Sacramento and San Joaquin rivers to back up behind a narrow exit through the coastal mountain range, creating more than one-half a million acres of wetlands.

BLOSSOM MOUND, CA-SJO-68, THORNTON, CALIFORNIA

The southern delta region was home to the Windmiller people, one of the earliest settled cultures in central California. Their village sites and cemeteries can be found on old levee ridges that mark the former course of the Mokelumne River and on other high spots on the valley bottom near the delta. Windmiller people also established large villages on the lower reaches of major rivers and streams that exited the foothills of the Sierra Nevada and Coast ranges.

Archaeologists working in the Central Valley during the 1920s and 1930s first recognized the Windmiller culture at a series of sites near the confluence of the Mokelumne and Cosumnes rivers, including the Blossom Mound. This important site is one of the earliest known villages in the Central Valley, occupied nearly 5,000 years ago. Residents of the Blossom Mound made a living by hunting, fishing, and collecting plant foods from the nearby marshlands, riparian forest, and oak woodland. Mortars and pestles found at the site were used to pulverize acorns, leading many archaeologists to believe that Windmiller people were among the first to take full advantage of this abundant and important nut crop—a staple food for all subsequent Native groups in the valley. Fishing also appears to have been an important part of village life,

because the bones of salmon and other freshwater fish are common, along with bone fishhooks, harpoons, and net sinkers.

Mortuary practices at the Blossom Mound and other Windmiller sites were among the most elaborate and unique recorded for any time period in the valley. Deceased members of the community were buried in a fully extended position with the head and long axis of the body oriented westward. Graves were often furnished with offerings, including shell beads and well-made, highly polished stone plummets of marble, granite, alabaster, and other exotic materials. Archaeologist Peter Schulz discovered that Windmiller people purposefully oriented their burials toward the setting sun. From this alignment, he found that the season of death could be inferred from the sun's position between the winter and summer solstice. Not surprisingly, it appears that most people died during the winter, when food was scarce in the Central Valley.

People living at the Blossom Mound were also among the earliest to engage in regular exchange with their neighbors. They were important consumers of obsidian quarried in Napa Valley and on the eastern side of the Sierra Nevada, and they obtained shell beads and ornaments from people on the southern and central California coast. Unfortunately, the Blossom Mound remains in private ownership and may be largely destroyed by modern agriculture

BRAZIL MOUND, CA-SAC-43, SACRAMENTO, CALIFORNIA

More common than Windmiller villages are the mounded settlements of later cultures. Sites from the Central Valley's prehistoric Middle period—dating between 900 and 2,500 years old—are found throughout the delta region and along the major rivers and streams. The Brazil Mound is one of these sites, situated on the banks of the Sacramento River, just north of the city of Sacramento. It has been studied several times by archaeologists since the 1930s.

Like many other Middle period villages in the valley, the Brazil Mound was occupied year-round, judging by the remains of migratory birds, anadromous fish, and plant foods from different seasons. Cemeteries found at the Brazil Mound and other Middle period settlements include human burial remains that appear to have been bound, with the knees and upper legs pulled tightly to the chest. These graves often contain bone implements, large obsidian knives, and thousands of shell beads. Change over time in the style of the beads allows archaeologists to precisely date the occupation of these villages.

The bones of water birds and slow-water fishes are abundant at the Brazil site, along with the tools used in their capture. In the cemetery, fish hooks and harpoons were found only with men, suggesting that they did most of the fishing. The butchered remains of deer, elk, pronghorn, and many smaller mammals and birds are common in the Brazil Mound and other village trash heaps from the Middle period. Abundant remains of acorn reveal that stored nuts were important during winter months when plant foods were rare. These nuts were pounded into fine flour using mortars and pestles. Ethnographic observations indicate that acorn flour was made into bread or a thick soup.

Like many of the most important village sites from the Middle period, the Brazil Mound now lies beneath a flood-control levee, built to protect the city of Sacramento and neighboring communities from natural flooding.

HOTCHKISS SITE, BYRON, CALIFORNIA

Many things changed in the Central Valley about 900 years ago with the beginning of the late prehistoric period. It was about this time that the bow and arrow became widely used throughout the California Delta region, replacing the dart and dart thrower. Food gathering became a corporate activity, and entire communities invested in the construction of fishing weirs along the Sacramento River. The use of small seeds increased substantially during the Late period, and some archaeologists believe a simple form of agriculture may have been practiced, judging by an increase in the size of these seeds. Cremation became a way of treating the dead, an honor that may have been reserved for wealthy and important political leaders. It was also at the end of this period that beads made from clam shell served as a form of money and were widely used by Central Valley people to obtain food and other commodities from their neighbors.

Among the most important Late period village sites in the Central Valley is the Hotchkiss Mound, first excavated in the 1930s. Located on the western edge of the delta, this mound covers several acres and appears to have been an important center of trade. At this site, obsidian cobbles and large flake blanks obtained from quarries in Napa Valley were made into finely worked, serrated arrow points by specialist stone workers. Shell beads from coastal California, common in

Hotchkiss graves, were often found in shingled arrangements around the torso and head. These beads were probably sewn to cloaks and basketry hats. Shell ornaments from the site were made into distinctive human forms. Some archaeologists speculate that these represent "big-head" dancers related to the Kuksu Cult, an important religious institution among historic period Native groups in the valley. Animal ceremonialism at the Hotchkiss Mound is represented by the intentional burial of raptorial birds, dogs, and grizzly bear, sometimes accompanied by offerings.

Like most of the Central Valley's archaeological record, the Hotchkiss site is currently threatened by development from several large housing tracts that now surround the site.

Further Reading: Bennyhoff, James A., *The Ethnogeography of the Plains Miwok*, Center for Archaeological Research at Davis Publication No. 5 (Davis: University of California, Department of Anthropology, 1977); Bouey, Paul D., *Final Report on the Archaeological Analysis of CA-SAC-43, Cultural Resources Mitigation for the Sacramento Urban Area Levee Reconstruction Project, Sacramento County, California* (Davis, CA: Far Western Anthropological Research Group, 1996); Heizer, Robert, F., *The Archaeology of Central California, I: The Early Horizon*, University of California Anthropological Records, Vol. 12(1) (Berkeley: University of California, 1949); Moratto, Michael J., "The Central Valley Region," in *California Archaeology* (New York: Academic Press, 1984), 167–284; Ragir, Sonia R., *The Early Horizon in Central California Prehistory*, Contributions of the University of California Archaeological Research Facility, No. 15 (Berkeley: University of California, 1972); Rosenthal, Jeffrey S., Gregory G. White, and Mark Q. Sutton, "The Central Valley: A View from the Catbird's Seat," in *California Prehistory: Colonization, Culture, and Complexity*, edited by Terry L. Jones and Kathryn A. Klar (Walnut Creek, CA: Alta Mira Press, 2007), 147–163; Schulz, Peter, *Solar Burial Orientation and Paleodemography in the Central California Windmiller Tradition*, Center for Archaeological Research at Davis Publication No. 2 (Davis: University of California, 1970), 185–198.

Jeffrey S. Rosenthal

YOSEMITE NATIONAL PARK, INDIAN GRINDING ROCK STATE HISTORIC PARK, AND SEQUOIA AND KINGS CANYON NATIONAL PARKS

Sierra Nevada Mountains, Eastern California

Ancient and Historic Sites in the Sierra Nevada

California's Sierra Nevada lies between the Central Valley to the west and the high desert of the Great Basin of the east. The archaeological record here and in the adjoining foothills documents use by Native people since at least 7500 BC in

lower elevation zones and significant use in higher areas only after 3000 BC. Throughout the millennia, however, the Indian people of the Sierra Nevada lived in relatively small village or family groups, hunted large and small game, gathered a variety of seasonally available plants for food and medicine, and engaged in trade with neighbors to the east and west. They also often moved their residences between the high Sierra areas in the summer and the lower valleys and foothills to the west during the winter to facilitate trade and access to food resources. By the time of European colonization within California in the 1770s, the Sierra Nevada was occupied by numerous Native communities of people speaking Maiduan, Washoe, Miwok, Numic, Yokuts, or Tubatlabal languages.

Interest in the archaeological evidence of Native occupation in the Sierra Nevada dates back to the mid-1800s. Miners drawn to the area by the gold rush in 1849 soon discovered human skeletal remains, stone tools, and shell beads in deep caverns and gold-bearing gravels of the central Sierra Nevada foothills. Systematic archaeological investigations in the region, however, were not undertaken until the 1950s. Since then, excavation of hundreds of archaeological sites and documentation of thousands more from surface evidence has provided a general outline of cultural history. Tool assemblages are dominated by flaked and ground stone implements, while the remains of dwellings, communal ceremonial structures, hearths, roasting pits, hunting blinds, and rock art have also been discovered. Tools include milling implements such as milling stones, mortars, and pestles used primarily to process plant foods, as well as projectile points, drills, scrapers, and flakes from the manufacture of stone tools. Stationary milling features with mortars are the most visible aspect of the archaeological record, and these are very common in all but the highest elevations of the range. Other features such as house floors and hearths are relatively rare due to disturbance of soils by burrowing animals or the relatively ephemeral use in upper elevation zones. Organic materials including animal bone, plant remains, basketry, and shell beads are also infrequent. This is likely due to the coarse, acidic soils typical of the region. Preservation of such remains is enhanced, however, if deposits are in protected areas such as rock shelters and caves, which were rare but present in various areas of the Sierra.

Initial native use of the high Sierra and foothills is demonstrated by large stemmed or corner-notched dart points and portable milling stones on which vegetal foods were ground in a back-and-forth motion with a hand stone. Basalt served as the dominant material used for flaked stone tools in the northern Sierra where such stone was locally available. Use of obsidian—volcanic glass imported from east or north of the Sierra—was prevalent in most other high-elevation areas, and use of local chert was common in the foothills. The bow and arrow replaced *atl atl* dart technology after about AD 500, as indicated by use of smaller corner-notched projectile points. Introduction of bedrock mortars to pound acorns also occurred sometime between AD 500 and 1250, with this technology taking advantage of the large rock outcrops common in the mountains. Use of obsidian became dominant throughout the entire range, and geochemical

study of trace elements in the tool stone documents reliance on the nearest high-quality obsidian.

Severe drought struck between around AD 892 and 1112 and again from about AD 1210 to 1350. These droughts contributed to turmoil and even violence in the region that may have begun a few hundred years earlier. People shifted to a less sedentary mode of settlement, and villages became smaller after AD 500. Populations also declined in much of the mountain range, as Native people either relocated elsewhere or struggled to survive in the face of deteriorating environmental conditions. After around AD 1250, use of small side-notched or contracting-stem arrow points, ground stone ornaments, and bedrock mortar technology became common. Much rock art—both painted pictographs and pecked petroglyphs—also probably dates to this time, although determining the precise age is often difficult. Eventually, populations began to rebound, and settlements became more substantial once again. The manufacture of small arrow points permitted scavenging of obsidian from habitation sites on the western slope of the Sierra rather than requiring acquisition from quarries to the east either through trade or travel. At the same time, the reliance on stationary, rather than portable, milling tools may have brought about changes in social relations within communities. Women's work began to play a larger role in daily life than men's hunting, and the location of large rock outcrops dictated where large villages and small camps were established.

CHAW'SE, INDIAN GRINDING ROCK STATE HISTORIC PARK, CALIFORNIA

The site of *Chaw'se* (CA-AMA-14) contains the largest number of bedrock mortars of any site in the Sierra Nevada or, for that matter, all of North America. Located on a ridge above the North Fork of the Mokelumne River, the huge limestone outcrop that is the centerpiece of the site contains 1,185 mortars and more than 350 petroglyphs, some of which incorporate mortar holes into the design. Archaeological study was initiated by the California Department of Parks and Recreation in the early 1960s, when *Chaw'se* was being considered for inclusion in the state parks system. Detailed recording of the petroglyphs documented fifteen categories of motifs and numerous specific forms, ranging from simple dots to linear geometric and representational elements such as human and animal tracks. The time of initial site use is unknown, but *Chaw'se* continued to be used by local native people into the late 1800s. This site is located within Indian Grinding Rock State Historic Park near Pine Grove, California.

Short, paved trails encircle the mortar outcrop and lead visitors to the community roundhouse—called a *hun'ge* in the local Miwok dialect—as well as several cedar bark houses known as *o'-chum* and acorn granaries known as *chuk-a*. These reconstructed structures provide a sense of what the village was like in the past, and the roundhouse is used today for various annual gatherings of local Native people. In addition, the *Chaw'se* Regional Indian Museum displays artifacts and other items of material culture typical of traditional native life throughout the Sierra Nevada, including flaked and ground stone tools, wooden implements, and baskets.

INDIAN VILLAGE OF *AHWAHNEE*, YOSEMITE NATIONAL PARK, CALIFORNIA

The village of Ahwahnee (CA-MRP-56) is situated in the north central portion of Yosemite Valley on a fan-like geological debris flow emanating from Indian Canyon. This area was the site of multiple episodes of occupation over several thousand years, due in part to the sunny southern exposure and slight elevation of the landform above seasonal floods of the Merced River. Geological evidence indicates that this debris flow was created approximately 4,000 years ago, so evidence of occupation prior to that time, if present, is deeply buried beneath tons of soil and rock. Naturalist C. Hart Merriam noted the village name in the early 1900s, but it was not until the 1950s that archaeologists recorded the archaeological remains of this village and conducted initial excavations. Additional archaeological excavations occurred in the 1960s, when the current National Park Service (NPS) visitors' center was constructed on the site, and several other studies have been undertaken since 1980s as part of planning for additional development within the area.

These archaeological studies have revealed that the village of Ahwahnee is, in fact, a large complex of partially overlapping occupations, each representing approximately 50–200 years of use. Together, they define a huge site that was occupied more or less continuously from around 2000 BC to the late AD 1800s. Because of the poor preservation of organic remains suitable for radiocarbon dating, the history of use has been revealed by obsidian hydration dating. This technique is based on the fact that obsidian absorbs water from the surrounding environment to build up a visually distinct layer on the outer surface of an artifact through time. The thickness of this layer provides an estimate of how much time has elapsed since the obsidian tool or flake was manufactured. Obsidian flakes from the manufacture of tools are common at Ahwahnee, although whole and fragmentary projectile points, scrapers, soapstone vessel fragments and beads, glass beads, and other items lost or discarded by the Native residents have also be recovered through archaeological studies.

Bedrock mortars can be seen behind the Yosemite Valley visitors' center in the reconstructed Indian village, which also contains reconstructed cedar bark houses, acorn granaries, and a ceremonial sweat lodge and semi-subterranean roundhouse used by the local Native community. This village depicts life as it was in the late 1800s, and the adjacent cemetery includes graves of local Indians and non-Native settlers who lived in Yosemite Valley at this time. The bedrock mortars at *Ahwahnee* are still used today by NPS cultural demonstrators, some of whom trace their ancestry to Indian people living in Yosemite Valley before the gold rush. The adjacent Indian Museum houses an impressive collection of Yosemite Indian baskets and other items of material culture, and native basket weavers are also present during the summer months to demonstrate their craft.

HOSPITAL ROCK, SEQUOIA AND KINGS CANYON NATIONAL PARKS, CALIFORNIA

Hospital Rock (CA-TUL-24), which takes its name from events following the accidental shooting of a local trapper in 1873, is located along the Generals Highway on a terrace above the Middle Fork of the Kaweah River approximately 24 kilometers northeast of the town of Three Rivers. This site, known as *pahdin* ("place to go under") by the Potwisha, was occupied by Native people until the 1860s and thus has been well known since that time. It was not subject to archaeological investigation until the 1960s, however, and additional archaeological excavations were completed by the NPS in the 1980s as part of planning for highway reconstruction. These studies have documented the presence of two rock shelters, several panels of linear representational pictographs, boulders with pecked cupules, stationary milling features with both mortars and milling slicks, projectile points, scrapers, milling stones, pestles, soapstone vessels and beads, marine shell ornaments, dietary animal bone, and a few ceramic vessel fragments. The latter were likely brought or traded in from east of the Sierra Nevada, and the shell ornaments reflect trade connections with the coast. In addition, more than 100 burials were discovered at this site. Ethnographic sources suggest that the rock art also held sacred or supernatural significance to the Indian people. Obsidian hydration dating and flaked artifact types document repeated use of the site for thousands of years, although predominant use occurred during the last 700 years.

Further Reading: California State Parks, Indian Grinding Rock State Historic Park Web site, http://www.parks.ca.gov/?page_id=553 (online January 2007); Elsasser, A. B., *Indians of Sequoia and Kings Canyon National Parks* (Three Rivers, CA: Sequoia Natural History Association, 1972); Hull, Kathleen L., "The Sierra Nevada: Archaeology in the Range of Light," in *California Prehistory: Colonization, Culture, and Complexity*, edited by Terry Jones and Kathryn Klar (Walnut Creek, CA: AltaMira Press, 2007), 177–190; Hull, Kathleen L., and Michael J. Moratto, *Archaeological Synthesis and Research Design, Yosemite National Park California*, Yosemite Research Center Publications in Anthropology No. 21 (Yosemite, CA: Yosemite National Park, 1999); Moratto, Michael J., "The Sierra Nevada," in *California Archaeology*, by Michael J. Moratto (Salinas, CA: Coyote Press, 2004), 285–338.

Kathleen L. Hull

ANCIENT AND HISTORIC COAST SITES FROM SANTA CRUZ TO SAN LUIS OBISPO

Southern Coast Ranges, California
Archaeology of the Central California Coast

Bounded to the east by the vast San Joaquin valley plain and to the west by the Pacific Ocean, the southern Coast Ranges are composed of numerous complex steep ridge systems and valley lowlands that fostered a variety of distinctive local culture histories. Spanning a length of approximately 290 kilometers (150 mi.), the northwest by southeast trending southern Coast Ranges are still being shaped by tectonic forces such as the active San Andreas and Calaveras fault systems. Rising sea levels occurring during the Late Pleistocene through the Middle Holocene submerged vast sections of coastal lowlands and former river valleys, and exceeded our current sea level by approximately 1 meter. Sea level reached relative stability after 4300 BC, and the archaeological record became much more pronounced after the regional ecology reached a measure of relative equilibrium. Throughout the Middle and Late Holocene, the northern ranges received considerably more precipitation than the southern ranges, and there has long been a gradation in flora and fauna from one end to the other. To the north, San Francisco Bay and Santa Clara valley formed a productive mosaic of habitats dominated by tidal marsh, mixed hardwood forest, chaparral, and vernal pools among grassland savannah, along with various other micro-habitats, while the Santa Cruz Mountains are the southern reach of the great redwood forests that stretch north to the state of Washington.

Monterey Bay separates the moister Santa Cruz Mountain range from the more xeric Santa Lucia Ranges, and the surrounding bay from Santa Cruz to the Monterey Peninsula is characterized by a long stretch of sandy beach and broad grassland plains. The Monterey Peninsula itself is characterized by a very localized forest of Monterey cypress growing over an intrusive granitic geologic base. A deep marine canyon reaches just off shore from Carmel, and many pelagic open marine species were available to prehistoric hunters. Leading southeastward from Monterey Bay, the Gabilan Range and eastern slope of the Santa Lucia Ranges become separated by the long and narrow Salinas River valley, a semi-level grassland savannah and oak woodland habitat. Also, progressively further inland from the coast and paralleling it, the interior Diablo Range becomes more arid than the coastal ranges, despite much higher elevations. This range is dominated by grassland, poison oak, manzanita and toyon shrub thickets, and chaparral, with oaks and lodge pole pine scattered along ridges and ravines. Occasional stands of juniper and yew trees were favored for the manufacturing of bows.

South of Monterey Bay, along the Big Sur coast the Santa Lucia Ranges terminate abruptly as eroded coastal cliffs and rocky headlands along the Pacific Ocean shore. Much of the uplands are covered by poison oak, sagebrush, stands of lodge pole pine, and scrub oak with occasional yucca cactus clinging to the steep serpentine, and the terrain consists of sandstone and granitic slopes. A few struggling redwood trees can still be seen in steep, well-watered ravines along the Big Sur coast and among the mixed hardwood forests of the upper Carmel River watershed. Despite the rugged conditions, numerous shell middens have been recorded along the mouths of drainages and on the remnant coastal terraces. The great numbers of shell midden sites on top of very steep ridgelines attest to the value of marine foods to the ancestral Esselen- and Salinan-speaking villagers who occupied these ranges.

OVERVIEW OF CULTURE CHRONOLOGY

A generalized culture chronology for the Southern Coast Ranges includes six prehistoric periods and subsequent post-contact historic periods (see Table 1). Nonetheless, the timing of these periods varies slightly among a variety of distinctive archaeologically defined localities throughout the southern Coast Ranges.

Although only tantalizingly few finds of pre-Archaic age have been reported, expressions of the early Milling Stone

Table 1 Generalized Culture Chronology for the Southern Coast Ranges

Cultural Periods	Temporal Periods and Calendar Dates
Historical	Spanish, Mexican, and American (AD 1769–present)
Emergent: Ohlone, Yokuts, Esselen, Salinan	Late (AD 1200–1769)
	Middle/Late transition (AD 1000–1200)
Hunting culture	Middle (1000 BC–AD 1000)
	Early (3500–1000 BC)
Milling Stone culture	Archaic (8000–3500 BC)
Paleoindian	Pre-Archaic (before 8000 BC)

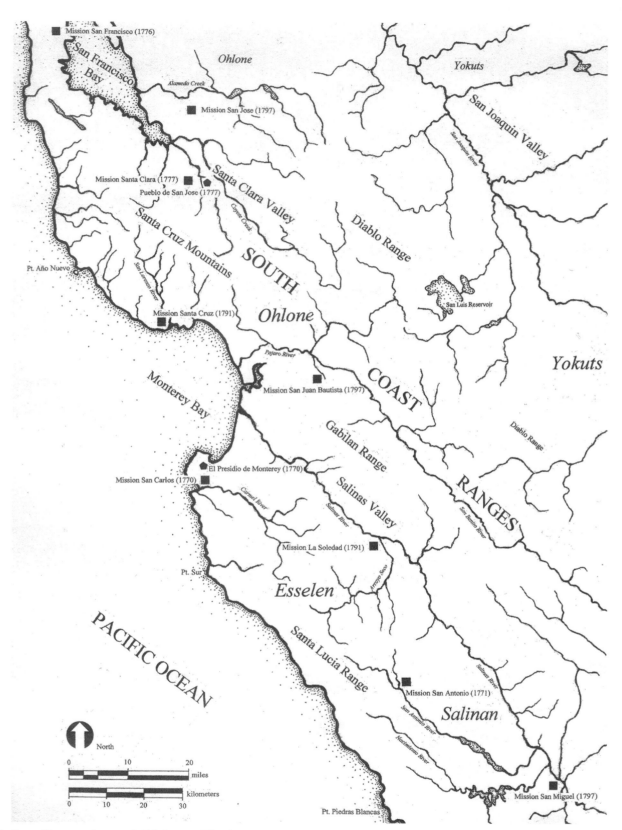

Mission San Francisco (1776)

Ohlone

Yokuts

San Francisco Bay

Alameda Creek

San Joaquin Valley

Mission San Jose (1797)

San Joaquin River

Mission Santa Clara (1777)

Santa Clara Valley

Pueblo de San Jose (1777)

Coyote Creek

Diablo Range

Santa Cruz Mountains

SOUTH

Pt. Año Nuevo

San Lorenzo River

Ohlone

San Luis Reservoir

Mission Santa Cruz (1791)

Pajaro River

COAST

Yokuts

Mission San Juan Bautista (1797)

Gabilan Range

Diablo Range

Monterey Bay

RANGES

San Benito River

El Presidio de Monterey (1770)

Salinas Valley

Mission San Carlos (1770)

Carmel River

Salinas River

Mission La Soledad (1791)

Arroyo Seco

Pt. Sur

Esselen

PACIFIC OCEAN

Santa Lucia Range

Mission San Antonio (1771)

Salinas River

Salinan

San Antonio River

Nacimiento River

North

0   10   20   miles

0   10   20   30   kilometers

Mission San Miguel (1797)

Pt. Piedras Blancas

South Coast Ranges of central California. The distributions of Native American linguistic families have been italicized, and also depicted are the locations and establishment dates of the early Spanish colonial missions.   [Mark G. Hylkema]

Point Año Nuevo above Monterey Bay was the principal source for Monterey chert used to make chipped-stone tools throughout the Middle and Late Holocene.   [Mark G. Hylkema]

culture have been identified at several sites throughout the southern Coast Ranges with dates as old as 7600 BC. Most Milling Stone sites occur within 25 kilometers (15 mi.) of the shore, and even interior sites contain marine shell indicating an early and continued reliance on marine resources. Faunal remains from sites tested in Santa Clara valley and San Luis Obispo County reflect a broad-spectrum hunting focus; however, well-developed faunal assemblages are lacking. Dietary emphasis was on hard seed milling, as indicated by the large numbers of well-shaped hand stones, and hunting deer and rabbits. Chipped-stone projectile points such as willow-leaf-shaped lanceolates and large side-notched chert forms are associated with this time period but are not as common as milling tools. The uniquely shaped eccentric crescent form, generally found in Archaic age contexts throughout western North America, seems to persist on the coast until as late as 4500 BC. There is little archaeological evidence of fishing during Milling Stone times; however, stable isotope analysis of human bone from one Milling Stone site around Monterey Bay revealed a diet of 70–84 percent marine food.

Considerable variations in diet and tool assemblages are evident during the Early period from 3000–3500 to 1000 BC. This temporal period is referred to locally as the Hunting culture because of the great increase in projectile point frequency, increased site distribution, and generally greater density of occupational materials at individual sites. Characterized by both large and small side- and corner-notched dart

tips, lanceolate-shaped spear and knife blades, and a variety of contracting-stemmed forms, the greatly increased number and distribution of sites containing these tools also exhibit marked increases in volumes of chipping debris. The generally robust nature of the predominantly Monterey and Franciscan chert points were used to acquire larger game animals such as tule elk, grizzly bear, brown bear, pronghorn, and mule deer. For coastal populations where oak woodland and grasslands were less developed than in the interior, hunting was augmented by marine mammals including California sea lion, Stellar sea lion, northern and southern fur seals, harbor seals, otters, and occasionally gray whales when they washed ashore. Fish bone becomes more abundant in archaeological deposits, with bone fishing gorges and stone sinkers comprising the fishing gear. Bi-pitted cobbles and other pebble tools increased, but the principal change was in the milling tool assemblages. Around 2000 BC, hand stone and milling slab assemblages were increasingly augmented with stone bowls and shaped stone pestles used to process acorns into food. Despite the high handling costs associated with harvesting, storage, and preparation, acorn-based economies became progressively important and effectively reduced subsistence catchment areas into a mosaic of resource stations. Cupule rock art of unknown purpose, which was found scattered throughout the Diablo Range uplands and Santa Lucia Ranges, may have had its origin at this time.

Visitors to Mission San Antonio de Padua (established 1771) can still see many archaeological features surrounding the main mission complex. [Mark G. Hylkema]

From 1000 BC to AD 1000–1250, Middle period coastal archaeological sites continued to manifest features of the Hunting culture and maintained a foraging adaptive mode. But in contrast to the coast, interior sites began to show a greater preference for residence in semi-sedentary villages that developed around their acorn granaries, and in the Santa Clara valley expressions of greater cultural complexity begin to appear in mortuary contexts. Larger aggregates of flexed burials with a variety of grave associated artifacts such as *Olivella* (Olive snail) saucer shell beads, *Haliotis* (abalone) shell ornaments, stone projectile points, bone tools and flutes, and milling tools occurred; however, these are found among just a few individuals in a given site. Diablo Range settlements in the uplands shifted to lower valley areas and marshland habitats, with interior sites showing a nearly singular focus on harvesting acorns and hunting deer, rabbits, and waterfowl and little reliance on marine invertebrates. Conversely, coastal adaptive modes became increasingly reliant on marine invertebrates—the ocean-dwelling California mussels, in particular, and circular fish hooks made from these shells appear mostly in sites from the Monterey Peninsula southward. Both grooved and notched stones in coastal middens reflect hook-and-line fishing as well as net fishing technology. Greater numbers of bone awl tips imply an increasing reliance on basketry. Hand stones and milling slabs continue to be found along with mortars and pestles among coastal populations because of the dispersed distribution of oak

woodlands scattered along the steep ridge systems. However, in places like Santa Clara valley, where vast stands of oak woodlands existed, an acorn-reliant tradition emerged and became the precursor to greater social complexity that developed during the Late period. Indeed, the people of the adjacent coast near Año Nuevo maintained an older foraging adaptive mode while coexisting with their neighbors in Santa Clara valley who were becoming increasingly more stratified and followed a collector adaptive mode. Many of the coastal foraging middens can still be seen among the drifting sand dunes at Point Año Nuevo State Reserve, which was also the principal source for Monterey chert—the dominant chipped-stone tool material on the coast above Monterey Bay. Although it had a high handling cost since it needed to be heat altered prior to reduction, the substantial volumes of Monterey chert chipping debris and the associated cooking stones still visible throughout the reserve attest to the value of this resource to the coastal economy.

Late period assemblages (ca. AD 1000–1250 to 1769) are readily distinguished from the Early period Milling Stone culture and Middle period Hunting culture by the introduction of bow and arrow technology and an increase in shell bead and ornament wealth in mortuary contexts. The smaller and lighter-weight Desert side-notched and Cottonwood triangular arrow point types became widely represented throughout the Monterey Bay area and the Santa Lucia and Diablo ranges. They bordered the northern Santa Cruz

Mountains and San Francisco Bay area, where contemporaneous serrated obsidian lanceolate arrow tips were found in great numbers. There is also a division in the distribution of exotic obsidian sources represented by tools deposited in both Middle and Late period archaeological sites. Sourced obsidian projectile points from San Francisco Bay and the region north of the Pajaro River, which bisects the Monterey Bay and continues inland to the eastern Diablo Range, are dominated by northern Coast Ranges glass. South of the Pajaro River, obsidian points are nearly all from the eastern Sierra flows.

Fishing from rocky shorelines, sheltered estuaries, and the numerous creeks and rivers became of greater importance in the Late period while intensive harvesting of shellfish continued among coastal residents; however, their villages began to be located further inland to take advantage of oak woodland habitats. Many Late period coastal middens reflect task-specific activities with a return to an inland residential base. This collector-based economic mode facilitated the aggregation of larger populations, which ultimately developed into the ranked societies described in the ethnographic literature. Countless village communities emerged, each with its own leadership and member societies. Expressions of pictographic (painted) rock art became prevalent over petroglyph (incised or pecked) forms, particularly in the Santa Lucia Ranges in the vicinity of Mission San Antonio and in the northern Diablo Range. Along the Monterey Peninsula, interior groups collected massive quantities of abalone, and the remains of these shells are still visible as a pavement along much of the coastal edge. Hunting sea otters and harbor seals, the exploitation of deer and rabbit, the harvesting of great numbers of waterfowl, and gathering the rich variety of seasonally abundant bulbs, berries seeds, and nuts led to a population growth that established residential communities at virtually every valley and stream terrace throughout the southern Coast Ranges. On the other hand, in stark contrast to the Middle period, very few Late period archaeological sites have been recorded in the upland valleys of the interior Diablo Range.

DISTRIBUTION OF NATIVE AMERICAN LINGUISTIC FAMILIES

At the time of the first European land expedition in 1769, the southern Coast Ranges were occupied by large numbers of politically autonomous villages distributed among three language families: Ohlonean (also known as Costanoan), Esselen, and Salinan. Each of these linguistic groups was in turn composed of numerous dialects, creating a cultural mosaic over the landscape that attests to the overall complexity of the archaeological record in this region.

The Ohlone (also known as Costanoan) were members of the larger Penutian language stock. It has been proposed that their expansion into central California from the Modoc Plateau and western Oregon occurred sometime around 2500–2000 BC, and they either merged with or displaced earlier populations, particularly members of the Hokan linguistic stock within the Central Valley and San Francisco Bay region (although the timing of this proposed displacement is still under investigation). The Ohlone were one of two Yokutian language sub-branches that ultimately became composed of some fifty individual tribelets that spread throughout the San Francisco and Monterey Bay regions, even as far down as the Big Sur coast.

From Soledad in the Salinas valley and westward along the upper Carmel valley and over to the coast below Big Sur, the Hokan-speaking Esselen were in frequent conflict with the expanding Ohlonean people. The Monterey Peninsula was referred to as "the place of the enemies" in the Runsien Ohlone dialect, in reference to conflicts over shellfish gathering rights along the productive rocky shore. The scattered bands of Esselen (also noted as Ecclemach) are among the least known of the many ethnographic cultures of California. Their neighbors to the south, the Salinan, were also Hokan speakers but controlled a larger area and were themselves bordered further south by the culturally complex Chumash societies of the Santa Barbara region.

All of these cultures relied on both terrestrial and marine resources, and they developed an interactive economy through the use of shell bead money, marriage alliance networks, and social hierarchies where dynamic leaders would hold several villages together to compose what has come to be called a tribelet. The diffusion of commodities via kinship, wealth, and reciprocal ceremonial obligations between neighboring tribelets served as a method of circulating resources between coastal people and the more distant interior Penutian-speaking Yokuts people of the San Joaquin valley and the Miwok of the Sacramento River delta. The Yokuts in turn were trading with eastern Sierran and western Great Basin Mono and Paiutes, while the more northerly Miwok traded with the Washoe and Paiutes and others as well. This created a much extended trading network that moved obsidian tools, pine nuts, and other items from the eastern Sierra Nevada and Great Basin cultures to the coastal villages. Obsidian from the northern Coast Ranges was also traded into the region via the Marin Miwok and Wappo of the northern San Francisco Bay to the Ohlone of the southern San Francisco Bay. Concurrently, as interior tribelets developed ranked societies, the demand for shell beads and ornaments gave the coastal villagers an economic advantage. Of the various tribal affiliations in the southern Coast Ranges, the Ohlone maintained the larger population centers, probably a result of their control of the best oak woodland settings and ready access to open coastal and estuarine resources. Numerous large Middle and Late period cemeteries throughout the Bay Area contain vast quantities of shell beads and ornaments, bone tools, milling tools, and a variety of exotic goods, such as obsidian points. A progressive emphasis on wealth and social ascription was abruptly truncated with the advent of European contact.

HISTORIC PERIOD

In 1542 Captain Juan Rodriguez Cabrillo became the first European to sail along the California coast, and he named many geographic features along the way. The first documented contact with the Ohlone and Esselen did not occur until 1602, when Captain Sebastian Vizcaino sailed into the harbor Cabrillo had previously named *el Bahia de los Piños* and spent eighteen days there. Vizcaino renamed the harbor Monterey in honor of the then viceroy of Mexico. Amazingly, it was not until 147 years after Vizcaino that a land expedition was sent northward from Baja California to explore the coast and find the harbor of Monterey. In the fall of 1769, a Spanish expedition left lower (Baja) California under the command of Don Gaspar de Portola with orders from the king of Spain to locate Vizcaino's Monterey Bay, and establish a colony at a place called San Francisco (which for them was Point Reyes, north of today's Golden Gate). The expedition reached Monterey Bay and, not recognizing it, continued northward only to inadvertently discover the fabulous harbor that is now called San Francisco Bay. By 1770, the Royal Presidio of Monterey was founded and nearby Mission San Carlos de Borromeo, the first of upper California's twenty-one missions was established.

Monterey became the administrative capitol of Alta (upper) California and functioned as such throughout the Spanish and subsequent Mexican periods. Soon after Mission San Carlos was founded, Mission San Antonio de Padua was established in 1771. This latter mission has been the subject of archaeological investigation, and the mission complex along with many other features can still be seen. In all, nine missions were founded within the southern Coast Ranges between 1770 and 1797, and each can still be visited today. Only Mission Soledad is in ruins, but nonetheless it presents a very fascinating view of California frontier mission architecture because most of the wall alignments are still discernible. The extensive mission landholdings around Monterey Bay and the Salinas valley became a source of aggravation to the newly established civilian pueblos whose agrarian-based economies could not successfully compete with the massive landholdings and Indian labor force of the missions.

Regardless, subsequent Spanish colonial settlement was itself overhauled after 1822 with the advent of the newly formed Mexican Republic and development of "Californio" traditions. Monterey continued to be the seat of government in California, and among many new regulations, the reduction or secularization of the missions became law in 1832. This regulation was decreed in an effort to redistribute mission lands to private ownership and encourage cattle ranching for the increasingly lucrative hide and tallow trade that had developed with American and British traders. Indian neophytes still associated with the missions were forced to choose between working as laborers on the new cattle ranches and retreating to the less settled interior of California. In fact, they did both, but some communities of former neophytes continued to live around and worship at the chapels of Missions San Carlos, San Antonio, San Juan Bautista, Santa Clara, and San Jose (even as late as the 1920s). However, in 1847, within seven days of the end of the United States' war with Mexico and the signing of the Treaty of Guadalupe de Hidalgo, gold was discovered in the Sierra Foothills. This in turn led to a massive population influx that brought with it a diversity of cultures from all over the world. The Mexican government capitulated in 1848, and the American flag was first raised in Monterey. California's statehood was later achieved in 1850, and the state's constitution was drafted and signed at Colton Hall, which still stands along with many other historic buildings in the Monterey Historic District. Inland from Monterey about 48 kilometers to the northeast, the town of San Juan Bautista still evokes a sense of the transition between Mexico and the early American periods since many of the structures from those times still exist and retain much of their earlier appearance. These buildings include the mission, livery stables, hotels, and several homes. Archaeological investigations at that mission are currently underway.

Further Reading: Breschini, Gary S., and Trudy Haversat, *The Esselen Indians of the Big Sur Country* (Salinas, CA: Coyote Press, 2004); Erlandson, Jon M., and Terry L. Jones, eds., *Perspectives in California Archaeology*, Vol. 4: *Archaeology of the California Coast during the Middle Holocene* (Los Angeles: Cotsen Institute of Archaeology, University of California, 2007); Hylkema, Mark G., "Tidal Marsh, Oak Woodlands and Cultural Florescence in the Southern San Francisco Bay Region," in *Perspectives in California Archaeology*, Vol. 6: *Catalysts to Complexity: Late Holocene Societies of the California Coast*, edited by J. M. Erlandson and T. L. Jones (Los Angeles: Cotsen Institute of Archaeology, University of California, 2003), 233–262; Hylkema, Mark G., ed., *Santa Clara Valley Prehistory: Archaeological Investigations at CA-SCL-690, the Tamien Station Site, San Jose, California*, Center for Archaeological Research at Davis Publication No. 15 (Davis: University of California, 2007); Jones, Terry, Nathan E. Stevens, Deborah Jones, Richard T. Fitzgerald, and Mark G. Hylkema, "The Central Coast: A Midlatitude Mileu," in *California Prehistory: Colonization, Culture and Complexity*, edited by Terry L. Jones and Kathryn Klar (Plymouth, UK: AltaMira Press, 2007), 125–146; Margolin, Malcolm, ed., *Monterey in 1786: The Journals of Jean Francois de la Perouse* (Berkeley, CA: Heyday Books, 1989); Milliken, Randall, Richard Fitzgerald, Mark G. Hylkema, Randy Groza, Tom Origer, David G. Bieling, Alan Leventhal, Randy S. Wiberg, Andrew Gottsfield, Donna Gillette, Vivianna Bellifemine, Eric Strother, Robert Cartier, and David S. Fredrickson, "Punctuated Culture Change in the San Francisco Bay Area," in *California Prehistory: Colonization, Culture and Complexity*, edited by Terry L. Jones and Kathryn Klar (Plymouth, UK: AltaMira Press, 2007), 99–124.

Mark G. Hylkema

THE CROSS CREEK SITE

San Luis Obispo County, Coastal California
The Milling Stone Culture: Early Maritime Collectors

The Cross Creek site is one of the most significant prehistoric deposits in coastal California. The site is situated 9 kilometers (5 mi.) from the present shoreline in a valley that lies south of the town of San Luis Obispo and east of Pismo Beach, California. The importance of this site is derived from its antiquity, its unique artifact assemblage, its dietary constituents, and the lifeway they represent. Cross Creek was occupied as early as 8350 BC, making it one of the oldest well-dated deposits in all of California. More importantly, it documents the occupation and exploitation of the mainland coast by a people whose economy is conspicuously reliant upon the gathering and processing of plants and the collection of shellfish rather than the hunting of large animals. It is this unusual combination of great time depth and the inferred gathering lifeway that suggests the people of Cross Creek represent a distinctive maritime/gathering culture that may be an out growth of an earlier coastal migration into the New World.

The culture represented at Cross Creek, known in the literature as the "Milling Stone Horizon" or Milling Stone culture, was thought by scholars to date between 5500 and 3500 BC, a time period occupying the middle ground between the earliest Paleoindians and the later cultures of the California coast (the Chumash, Salinan, etc.). The Milling Stone culture is well documented over a wide area of southern and central California. As the name implies, the Milling Stone sites are distinguished by their great abundance of milling equipment (hand stones and milling slabs) assumed to be used for the processing of plant resources, including small seeds, tubers, roots, berries, and nut crops. Projectile points are relatively scarce in Milling Stone sites, implying a lifeway not focused on hunting. It is thought that a vegetable-based diet was augmented with shellfish, including open water and bay species, the hunting of small game such as rabbits and rodents, and the relatively rare large mammal. The Milling Stone lifeway persisted for as long as 5,000 years in some areas of southern California but eventually was replaced by an adaptation that emphasized hunting of large game, including marine mammals, and intensive acorn collection.

In previous studies, the point of origin of the Milling Stone people was thought to be the interior areas of southern California. Their appearance on the coast was attributed to the ever-increasing arid conditions of southeast California that induced a general population movement to the west around 7,000 years ago. Upon arrival at the coast, these new people soon became proficient collectors of coastal plants and shellfish.

These ideas were pervasive until the excavation of Diablo Canyon (CA-SLO-2) in the late 1960s by Roberta Greenwood (1972), who challenged the prevailing ideas. Diablo Canyon is located about 25 kilometers (15 mi.) northwest of Cross Creek on a peninsula 20 kilometers (12 mi.) long that extends between Morro and San Luis Obispo bays. SLO-2 is the largest of nearly fifty middens in the area. It is situated on a coastal terrace along a stream that empties directly in to the Pacific Ocean. The unusually deep deposit contained evidence of Milling Stone people that dated between 8000 and 6400 BC. These dates were comparable to, if not older than, most of the known sites on interior of California. At the time of the excavation, it represented one of the oldest coastal occupations in North America. Greenwood's finding advanced the idea that over 9,000 years ago there existed cultures on the central California coast that subsisted chiefly on shellfish, ocean fish, and plant foods. However, Greenwood's recognition of the "Milling Stone Horizon" at the bottom of SLO-2 was not widely accepted by the archaeological community, largely because the dates were considered too old. It was argued that some other as yet unidentified Paleo-Coastal tradition was represented at the site and was related to the Paleo-hunting cultures of the interior. This reinterpretation of Greenwood's findings at Diablo Canyon remained in place for over two decades. It was not until the work at Cross Creek and a few recently discovered sites in the central coast region that these ideas began to change. Greenwood now appears to have been correct in promoting the notion that a broad-spectrum plant- and shellfish-gathering way of life was in place throughout much of central and southern California by at least 8000 BC.

The Cross Creek site was fortuitously discovered in the mid 1990s during monitoring activities associated with a water pipeline project 160 kilometers (100 mi) long. The site was not visible from the surface but was found after a large trench exposed a layer of the shell midden. Salvage excavations revealed a well-preserved midden located on an ancient stream terrace. The site had been hidden by recent flood deposits. Sixteen radiocarbon dates, all from shellfish, were obtained from Cross Creek, twelve of which range from 7500 to 8350 BC. Associated artifacts included numerous hand stones, milling slabs, and cobble-based choppers and scrapers. Only four projectile points were recovered, all large side-notched types, the dominant type found in the lowest levels of Diablo Canyon. One enigmatic artifact recovered from deep within the midden is a palm-sized quartzite pebble delicately shaped to resemble a fish. Only

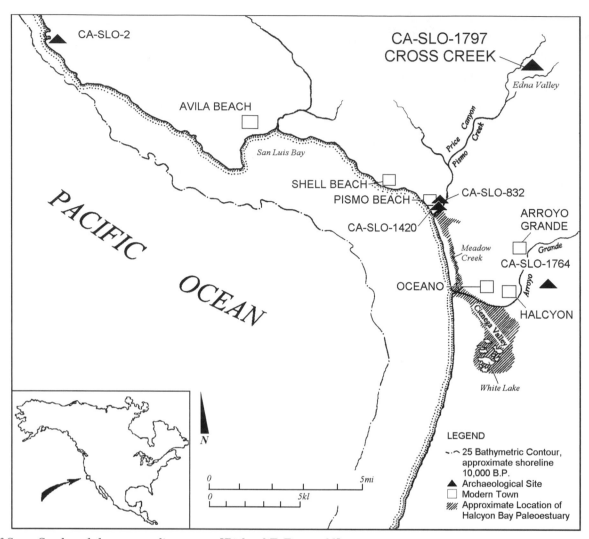

A map of Cross Creek and the surrounding area.   [Richard T. Fitzgerald]

a small quantity of dietary bone was collected, including marine fish and deer bone. Charred seeds of seven edible plants and fragments of yucca heart were also found, indicating that plant foods were an important part of the diet.

Shellfish from Cross Creek included both open coast and shallow bay (estuarine) species. Three types of clams were most abundant at the site, and there were only small amounts of mussels and other open water shellfish. The dominance of estuarine clam suggests they were collected from a nearby bay that no longer exists. One plausible location for this bay is the low-lying areas south of Pismo Beach near the town of Halcyon. Diaries of the eighteenth-century Spanish travelers who passed through the area make mention of a remnant estuary. Corroborating evidence of the extinct "Halcyon Bay" was documented at another nearby site located on a hill that would have overlooked the estuary (CA-SLO-1764). At this site shell including oysters and clams were radiocarbon dated between 7960 and 6990 BC.

These dates are just slightly younger than the oldest dates from Cross Creek.

Taken as a whole, the contents of Cross Creek readily conform to a regional variant of the California Milling Stone culture. The cobble tools found at Cross Creek suggest a possible connection to the Pebble Tool tradition, an artifact assemblage associated with early coastal occupation of British Columbia and southern Alaska. The large side-notched points found both at Cross Creek and Diablo Canyon bear comparisons to specimens found along the north Pacific Rim (Kamchatka Peninsula) dated between 11,500 and 11,000 BC. Together the contemporaneously occupied sites of Cross Creek and SLO-2 at Diablo Canyon suggest that by 10,000 years ago central California was occupied by people who exploited a wide range of marine and terrestrial resources. This broad-based adaptation may have originated with a maritime population that migrated along the coast from the north Pacific. It remains unclear whether the Cross Creek–Diablo Canyon inhabitants are an outgrowth of an even earlier people living on the Santa Barbara Islands (ca. 9500 BC) or mark the arrival of a later southward-moving coastal mainland population.

Further Reading: Fitzgerald, Richard, *Cross Creek: An Early Holocene Millingstone Site*, California State Water Project, Coastal Branch Series Paper No. 12 (San Luis Obispo, CA: San Luis Obispo

County Archaeological Society, 2000); Greenwood, Roberta, *9000 Years of Prehistory Diablo Canyon, San Luis Obispo County, California*, Occasional Paper No. 7 (San Luis Obispo, CA: San Luis Obispo County Archaeological Society, 1972); Jones, Terry, R. T. Fitzgerald, D. L. Kennett, C. H. Miksicek, J. L. Fagan, J. Sharp, and J. M. Erlandson, "The Cross Creek Site (CA-SLO-1797) and Its Implications for New World Colonization," *American Antiquity* 67 (2002): 213–230.

Richard T. Fitzgerald

ARLINGTON SPRINGS, DAISY CAVE, SANTA CRUZ QUARRIES, AND OTHER SITES

Southern California Coast

Northern Channel Islands Archaeology

The northern Channel Islands of Santa Cruz, Santa Rosa, San Miguel, and Anacapa are located 30–40 kilometers (19–25 mi.) off the southern California coast. They were occupied for more than 13,000 years by the Chumash and their ancestors. At the close of the last Ice Age, low sea levels exposed a single ancient mega-island (Santarosea), which was nonetheless still 15–20 kilometers (9–12 mi.) from the mainland. The exceptional time depth of humans on these islands provides the potential to explore important questions about the peopling of America, long-term adaptations to shifting climates, and, late in the sequence, the emergence of some of the most complex hunter-gatherers in world prehistory. Major sites on the islands reflect important long-term cultural developments including very high populations, year-round permanent villages, and some of the most intensive craft production sites in North America. Federal (Channel Islands National Park) and private (Nature Conservancy) stewardship of the islands has protected them from development; sites are extraordinarily well preserved.

Pygmy mammoths roamed the islands for millennia prior to the arrival of humans. Sometime before 13,200 years ago, just about the time of the last known mammoths, the first human populations arrived by boat. The Arlington Springs skeleton from the north shore of Santa Rosa Island establishes this early date. Islanders likely lived at protected near-shore locations and harvested an array of resources such as shellfish and fish from the sea. Through the course of the next several thousand years, as sea levels rose and the climate warmed, populations stayed small and the focus remained on marine resources, including fish, shellfish, marine mammals, and birds, along with carbohydrate-rich plant foods such as seeds and nuts. Early (5500–600 BC) and Middle (600 BC–AD 1150) period adaptations reflected changing technologies, diet, and

settlement locations. Many highland interior sites were occupied then abandoned, and people established large villages at the shores during the Middle phase. They added new fishing technologies and invented a much more seaworthy boat, the plank canoe (*tomol*). These changes allowed them to intensify fishing and engage in more frequent maritime trade.

At the onset of the Transitional period (AD 1150–1300), people began to specialize in the manufacturing of great numbers of stone microdrills and shell beads, reflecting an important change in political and economic organization for the region. This era marked the beginning of chiefdoms with hereditary leaders who controlled production systems and trade routes, with ownership of tomols playing a prominent role in rising inequalities. This complex hunter-gatherer society thrived for the next 500 years, through the Late period (AD 1300–1770s) and into the early historic era. Historic island villages typically consisted of a few hundred people living in up to twenty circular pole-and-thatch houses. The islands were abandoned as people gradually moved to the mainland missions between the 1790s and 1810s.

ARLINGTON SPRINGS (SANTA ROSA ISLAND)

First excavated in 1960 by Phil Orr, the Arlington Springs skeleton is dated to between 13,200 and 13,500 years ago. The remains are not currently known to be associated with other burials, tools, or residential debris, but the surrounding soil layers have been examined meticulously since the mid-1990s by a team of archaeologists and geologists, and both the bones themselves and the soil layers and other soil contents have been dated. Researchers were able to identify the original location of the block of soil containing the bones within the complex stratigraphic sequence in the canyon walls by

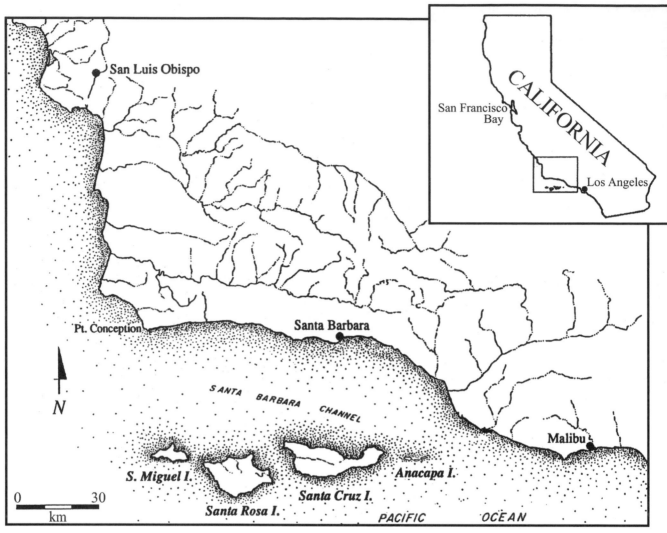

The northern Channel Islands of California and adjacent territory of the Chumash.   [Jeanne E. Arnold]

comparing concentrations of bones of an extinct species of mouse (*Peromyscus nesodytes*) in the block and in the undisturbed strata, and by comparing old photographs and maps with new digitally mapped plans of the canyon wall. Such a date places this among the earliest human remains in North America and raises interesting questions about the pathway of the peopling of North America. Perhaps the first people to reach California arrived by boat rather than trekking by foot from the ice-free corridor and the continental interior. Otherwise, how did someone live and die at such an early date miles off the California coast?

The antiquity of the Arlington Springs skeleton places humans on the island at about the same time that pygmy mammoths (*Mammuthus exilis*) were becoming extinct on this landmass. Although Orr suggested that people hunted the mammoths, for the past thirty years it has been considered more likely that they died off (due to disease or shifting climate) well before humans reached the islands. But a new date for a *Mammuthus* vertebra discovered nearby is about 11,030 ± 50 rcybp (radiocarbon years). Converting from radiocarbon to calendar years, this specimen is within decades (roughly 70–200 years, or statistically contemporaneous at one standard deviation) of the human bones, potentially indicating that humans and these Pleistocene animals coexisted for a short span. If so, it again raises the possibility that humans were partially responsible for the mammoths' demise.

DAISY CAVE (SAN MIGUEL ISLAND)

The Daisy Cave site represents the earliest known residential locus on the Channel Islands, and it remained a productive place to live over the course of thousands of years. The first short-term occupation in this small cave above the north shore of San Miguel Island dates to about 11,600 years ago, making it the oldest coastal shell midden in North America. The assem-

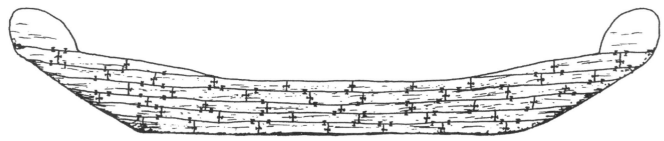

The Chumash plank canoe, typical length about 6 to 7 m.   [Jeanne E. Arnold]

blages demonstrate that Paleoindians in the Americas were using boats on ocean waters for exploration and for gathering food. Slightly later and more substantial Early Holocene occupational strata range between about 8,500 and 10,000 calendar years in age. Excavations in these layers have revealed large faunal assemblages with tens of thousands of fish bones and shellfish specimens representing at least thirty-eight different taxa, clear evidence of a strong orientation to the sea using diverse capture tactics, likely including shore-based collecting, hook-and-line fishing, and the use of simple boats to reach kelp beds. Also found are stone tools, shell beads, bone fishing gear, and woven sea grass artifacts. The assemblage is significant because these are the oldest fishhooks in North America, and the sea grass cordage and other woven fragments constitute one of the largest and best-preserved sets of such objects in the U.S. West (and the oldest from the Pacific Coast). Dense midden layers dating to the Middle and Late Holocene cap the site; these were extensively excavated during the 1960s by the Los Angeles County Museum of Natural History. Among the important findings was a late (ca. AD 1300) bead-maker's kit in a reed container complete with beads, shells, and microdrills. All told, more than fifty radiocarbon dates anchor this important multi-component site firmly in time.

PRISONERS HARBOR (SANTA CRUZ ISLAND)

The Prisoners Harbor village site, also known by its Historic Chumash name *Xaxas*, was among the most important trade centers in Chumash territory. This village of 200–250 people was also home to a chief and other elites during the contact period, and it was a notable manufacturing center for both microdrills and shell beads for centuries. This well-watered location was first occupied at least 5,000 years ago, but its Early period deposits are its least known because they are deeply buried. The dense shell midden left by countless residents over the course of millennia is more than 5 meters deep, and few early strata have been excavated. Archaeologists know more about the extensive Middle (600 BC–AD 1150), Transitional (AD 1150–1300), Late (AD 1300–1782), and Historic period (AD 1782–1819) deposits. Early explorations at the site in search of burials and museum pieces wrought damage, but the worst loss at the site came from an Army Corps of Engineers

earth-moving effort during the 1920s. One third of the village was destroyed at that time. More recent scientific excavations, however, have revealed a superbly preserved record of the last few thousand years of life in the substantial intact parts of the site. Among the significant discoveries is evidence for a deeply buried elite house with a redwood pole framework, the first redwood-supported structure found in this part of California. This household, and presumably others like it, enjoyed elevated social status and wealth. Such high rank allowed them to accumulate valued beads and ornaments, soapstone vessels from the southern Channel Islands, prized food items such as swordfish, and metal tools and colorful glass beads during the early Historic era. They also participated in the production of microlithic tools and the shell bead currency that was a Channel Islands hallmark after about AD 1100. Evidence from the intact house floor reveals great numbers of bead-making byproducts, marine faunal remains, and other materials of daily life. Recent analyses indicate the remains of a great feast near this house that took place shortly before the Chumash abandoned the island in the AD 1810s. Many goods from both the islands and the mainland likely passed through the hands of elites and specialized traders at this important village.

SANTA CRUZ ISLAND QUARRY DISTRICT

Near the El Montañon highlands that divide the eastern tip of Santa Cruz Island from the rest of its landmass were found more than a dozen large outcroppings of chert (flint) that were used for millennia to make various kinds of stone tools. This zone constituted the sole large, concentrated source of chert on the islands or nearby mainland shore, making it a significant resource. Early exploitation of the quarries focused on the acquisition of large cores to make bifacial tools. This pattern shifted notably at about AD 800–900, when the local Chumash began to make drilled shell-disk beads that required strong, narrow stone-drilling implements. The Santa Cruz Island chert was ideal for this task. Small cores were made by the thousands, and diminutive microblades were detached from these cores to produce microdrills. By AD 1150, local and regional demand for beads had accelerated significantly, and people began to specialize in making the drills on eastern Santa Cruz Island, fairly near the quarry sites. Others began to specialize in making beads at various coastal villages, especially those near good sources of shell on Santa Cruz, Santa Rosa, and San Miguel islands. After AD 1150, eastern Santa Cruz Islanders controlled access to this important quarry zone. The numbers of drills and beads manufactured peaked throughout the period from AD 1200 to about AD 1800, and literally millions were made at the most active village sites. The islands were the exclusive "mint" for this important shell-bead money used throughout southern California.

CHRISTY RANCH SITES (SANTA CRUZ ISLAND)

Several large village sites are located near Christy Ranch on western Santa Cruz Island. The ranch house itself is a historically significant building associated with the ranching period, dating to the late 1880s. Nearby, a series of Chumash residential locales represents the typically high density of sites characteristic of these islands wherever reliable fresh water co-occurs with rich marine and plant resources. Included in this set of sites are two important villages: one with Late and Historic components (*Ch'oloshush*) marked by fifteen large house depressions, and the other with Middle through Late components. The latter site was abandoned before the historic era, but it is most important for its well-preserved Transitional component, which reveals critical changes in the island's specialized bead-making industry during the AD 1150–1300 era. Paleoclimatic records indicate that this period was marked by severe droughts and unsettled sea-surface temperature conditions that generated stresses for people living in large communities. Many places on the islands were abandoned due to shrinking fresh water supplies, but the Christy stream still flowed. Meanwhile, major changes in social relationships were occurring, including the emergence of hereditary chiefs and other elites and the conversion of bead making into a true

occupational specialization practiced by many islanders. The archaeological record at Christy captures many of the changes in the ancient politics and economy. The sites chronicle an increasing intensity of bead making, subtle shifts in demand for different bead types, shifts in fishing strategies, and adoptions of new technology. Roughly twenty-five to thirty such village sites of Late and Historic age are found around the islands. More than 2,200 sites have been recorded in total.

ACCESS

The sensitive archaeological sites of the islands are not open to public visitation, but those interested in Chumash archaeology can view cultural, historical, and ecological interpretive exhibits at Channel Islands National Park headquarters in Ventura. To hike in the park, visitors may make arrangements with park-approved vendors for cross-channel transportation.

Further Reading: Agenbroad, Larry D., John R. Johnson, Don Morris, and Thomas W. Stafford Jr., "Mammoths and Humans as Late Pleistocene Contemporaries on Santa Rosa Island," Proceedings of the Sixth California Islands Conference, Arcata, California, 2005; Arnold, Jeanne E., ed., *The Origins of a Pacific Coast Chiefdom: The Chumash of the Channel Islands* (Salt Lake City: University of Utah Press, 2001); Glassow, Michael A., "Identifying Complexity during the Early Prehistory of Santa Cruz Island," in *Foundations of Chumash Complexity*, edited by Jeanne E. Arnold (Los Angeles: Cotsen Institute of Archaeology, 2004), 17–24; Kennett, Douglas J., *The Island Chumash: Behavioral Ecology of a Maritime Society* (Berkeley: University of California Press, 2005); Rick, Torben C., Jon M. Erlandson, and Rene Vellanoweth, "Paleocoastal Marine Fishing on the Pacific Coast of the Americas: Perspectives from Daisy Cave, California," *American Antiquity* 66 (2001): 595–613.

Jeanne E. Arnold

EEL POINT, LITTLE HARBOR, SOAPSTONE QUARRIES, AND OTHER SITES

Southern Channel Islands, Southern California Coast

10,000 Years of Human Occupation and Marine Adaptation

The southern Channel Islands—Santa Catalina, San Clemente, Santa Barbara, and San Nicolas—are home to a rich marine environment that has supported human occupation for thousands of years. Each island offers unique testimonies to the distant and more recent past, but they are linked by common historical trends. They are as exciting as they are exotic, and they hold important clues about the

history and ecology of southern California. In terms of archaeology, little would be known about southern California's past were it not for the thousands of archaeological sites that dot the Channel Islands today. These sites are like treasure troves of information about past human settlement and land use. They document the unwritten stories about how people lived on the islands, how they overcame natural obstacles and

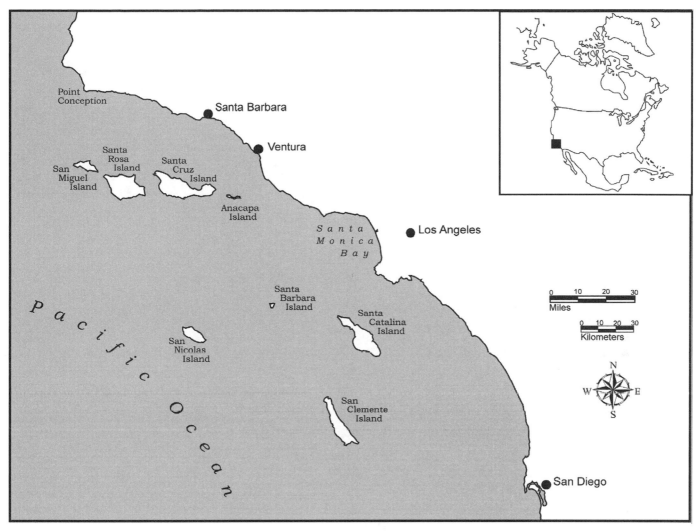

Map of southern California showing the Channel Islands.   [Patricia A. Martz]

barriers, and how they persevered for countless generations. This discussion provides a brief overview of the archaeology of the southern Channel Islands, beginning with the largest island (Santa Catalina) and working down in size to include San Clemente, San Nicolas, and Santa Barbara islands.

ENVIRONMENT AND CULTURE

The southern Channel Islands are a widely dispersed archipelago located off the coast of southern California. They range in size from 2.6 to 195 square kilometers (1–75 mi²), with maximum elevations of over 610 meters (2,000 ft) for Santa Catalina and 180 meters (600 ft) for Santa Barbara Island. Vegetation on the islands consists of low-lying bushes and shrubs interspersed with grasslands and, for Santa Catalina and San Clemente islands, stands of oak and other trees. Land animals include island foxes (except for Santa Barbara Island), rodents, squirrels, and lizards, as well as numerous species of terrestrial and marine birds, many of which breed

on the islands today. The islands are ringed by lush kelp forests that support a variety of marine shellfish, fish, sea mammals, and birds. The island's earliest human inhabitants relied on these resources for survival.

The southern islands contain numerous archaeological sites that offer testimony to the richness of the marine environment and the diversity of past human cultures. Archaeologists have reconstructed an elaborate history of human settlement that stretches back at least 10,000 years. This time period saw the initial colonization and use of the islands by Native Americans. For example, archaeologists working at the Eel Point site on San Clemente Island have uncovered some of the earliest evidence for human occupation. They have shown how the earliest settlers lived off the sea, taking advantages of a bountiful supply of marine plants and animals for food and for making an incredible variety of tools, weapons, ornaments, and other artifacts.

About 5,000 years ago marine environments in general were particularly rich. Sea-level rise that began after the last Ice Age

Field school students excavating on San Nicolas Island.   [Patricia A. Martz]

stabilized around this time, and people started to hunt more sea mammals, including seals, sea lions, and dolphins. Bead styles during this period also began to change, going from simple to more complex designs. For example, *Olivella* Grooved Rectangle beads, made from the wall portion of purple olive shell and commonly found on the sandy beaches of the islands today, have been found in archaeological sites 5,000 years old on the three largest southern islands. Surprisingly, this rare bead type has also been found in western Nevada and central Oregon, showing that Native American trade networks were well established many thousands of years ago. Roughly 3,000 years ago the circular shell fishhook replaced the bone gorge as the hook of choice for hook-and-line fishing, although nets and spears were also important. Shortly thereafter, the plank canoe was invented, which increased travel to and from the islands. The flow of trade goods also increased, as obsidian, soapstone, chert, shell beads, and other trade goods formed the basis of a complex exchange network that bonded people across the islands, the mainland coast, and beyond.

Spanish explorers arrived in the area in the late sixteenth and early seventeenth centuries, bringing with them a different way of life. These new settlers started the Mission system and introduced domesticated crops and animals from their homelands in the Old World. Many of the Native Islanders were sent to the missions or were put on reservations that transformed their lives forever. When missionaries, anthropologists, and early historians first described the languages and customs of American Indians, they suggested that people living on the islands were closely related to the Gabrielino or *Tongva* of the Los Angeles area. Subsequent work indicated that the distribution of ethnic groups on the islands was more complex in the past and included groups such as the Chumash to the north and the Luiseño to the south.

Although the exact timing is unclear, there appears to have been a gradual population replacement on the islands. Before 5,000 years ago people likely related to the Island Chumash, who inhabited the northern islands off the coast of Santa Barbara, appeared to have also lived on the southern islands.

The Jane Russell soapstone quarry on Santa Catalina Island.   [Patricia A. Martz]

Based on skeletal differences, burial practices, and artifact styles, archaeologists have shown that by 3,000 years ago this population replacement was complete. The new arrivals were probably Uto-Aztecan speakers related to the present-day Gabrielino and Luiseño Indians of Los Angeles, Orange, and San Diego counties.

Beginning in the late 1700s Mexican, European, and other settlers began an era of ranching and military activity on the islands that has resulted in a mixture of private and public ownership, including the U.S. Armed Forces (San Clemente, San Nicolas), the Catalina Island Conservancy (Santa Catalina), and Channel Islands National Park (Santa Barbara).

Santa Catalina and Santa Barbara islands are relatively easy to get to by boat or plane. Various options out of Long Beach or Ventura harbors offer day tours or overnight stays on these islands. San Clemente and San Nicolas islands are owned by the U.S. Navy. Although access to the public is restricted, the navy has supported archaeological work on these islands for over fifty years. This research has contributed greatly to archaeologists' understanding of the past and the rich archaeological resources that document it.

SANTA CATALINA ISLAND, CALIFORNIA

Santa Catalina Island is located 43 kilometers (27 mi) west of Los Angeles and is the best known of the southern Channel Islands. It is the only one of the islands with a regular town (Avalon) and for years was owned by the Wriggly family. Today the interior of the island is managed by the Island Conservancy.

The largest of the southern Channel Islands, Santa Catalina is 32 kilometers (20 mi) long with a maximum width of 13 kilometers (8 mi). Mountain peaks reach an elevation of 610 meters (2,000 ft) above sea level. The steep and rugged topography leaves only a few sheltered bays and level areas for settlements. In the past, Indian villages occupied these optimum spaces. Today they are replaced by modern settlements. Although sparse by mainland standards, the island had the greatest variety of plants and land animals of the four southern Channel Islands. Water, although not abundant, was present in springs and small streams. Marine mammals, fish, and shellfish were abundant.

Santa Catalina Island was settled at least 7,000 years ago by seafaring people who relied on fishing, sea mammal hunting, and shellfish collecting for the greater part of their diet. Plants such as roots, bulbs, acorns, and prickly pears supplemented the abundant marine resources. The islanders present at the time of European contact have been identified as Gabrielino (also known as the *Tongva*). The Gabrielino occupied a major portion of present-day Los Angeles and Orange counties and spoke a Cupan language of the Takic family of the Uto-Aztecan (Shoshonean) linguistic stock. They were named Gabrielino after San Gabriel Mission.

The size of the population has been estimated at anywhere between 200 and 3,000, but data to substantiate these estimates is not available. In 1542 the Spanish mariner Rodriguez Cabrillo reported that he was met by a great number of Indians. When the Vizcaino expedition landed at the Isthmus of Catalina in 1602, they found a settlement of more than 300 people. The Spanish described the Catalina Indian men as well built and the women as good featured. They admired their swift canoes and remarked on their friendliness and fondness for barter.

The date and circumstances of the departure of the Catalina Indians from their island is lost in time. It is assumed that the Indians went or were taken to the missions of San Gabriel and San Fernando sometime in the early 1800s. Mission records show fewer than three dozen baptisms of Indians from Catalina, so either the population was greatly reduced by disease, or they settled outside the mission system.

With the Indians gone, looters and antiquarians began collecting and digging for relics, and white settlers built over the remains of the villages. Although the sites received archaeological attention since the 1880s, the emphasis of the early investigators was on the collection of museum-quality artifacts. The contextual information needed to understand the part they played in the lives of the Catalina Indians was rarely noted. It was not until 1959 that modern scientific excavations were conducted and the results published. The good news is that many of the artifacts were donated to the Catalina Museum and can be seen on exhibit today.

The Catalina Museum

The Catalina Island Museum is located on the ground floor of the landmark Casino Building. Its mission is to collect, preserve, and share the cultural heritage of Santa Catalina Island from over 7,000 years ago to the present. The Museum curates one of the most complete and significant collections of Gabrielino/Tongva material in the world. With over 100,000 items the collection represents dozens of archaeological sites with attendant files and reports. The museum's research center houses records, reports, and books on the subject. A small exhibit in the galleries tells the stories of the island's Native people. More information may be obtained by contacting the curator of the Catalina Island Museum by mail at P.O. Box 366, Avalon, CA 90704; by phone at (310) 510-4650, or by e-mail at curator@catalinamuseum.org. The Web site is also a good source for information: http://www.catalinamuseum.org. The museum is open daily from 10:00 am to 4:00 pm; it is closed on Thursdays from January through March as well as on Christmas and Thanksgiving.

The Little Harbor Site

The ancient village at Little Harbor is situated near the edge of a cliff overlooking the ocean on the seaward side of Catalina. Radiocarbon dates indicate that the village was occupied for nearly 7,000 years. The site consists of a dark ashy midden containing abundant marine shell as well as sea mammal and fish bones. Smaller quantities of chipped and ground stone tools and implements, soapstone objects, bone tools, shell beads, fishhooks, tools, and ornaments are also present.

Excavations were conducted between 1953 and 1955 by Clement Meighan. His 1959 publication is considered to be a pioneering study of coastal human ecology and established the site as a marker for the emergence of maritime cultures on the Pacific Coast. The archaeological deposits reveal a great deal about the way the people of the Little Harbor village reacted to the constraints and opportunities of their environment. There was a heavy dependence on marine resources with a specialized maritime economy that exploited dolphins and porpoises and large schooling fish such as tuna. The presence of so many large dolphins and porpoises is remarkable. They are open ocean species, and spearing them from a canoe would require considerable skill and courage.

Shellfish were a staple, and plants seem to have been of minor importance. A shift in shellfish species from abalone in the deeper levels to mussel in the upper levels is attributed to over-exploitation of the favored abalone species and the substitution of mussel in the diet. This suggests that prehistoric humans were not always good managers of their environment. Sometimes they worked the environment for all it was worth until they were forced to use less desirable resources or move somewhere else.

Soapstone Quarries

Soapstone outcrops are numerous on the island, and through time the quarrying, manufacturing, and exchange of soapstone objects, such as bowls and effigies (figurines), became an important economic activity. The success of this enterprise can be seen in the numerous beads, effigies, ornaments, and implements of Catalina soapstone that have been recovered from archaeological sites throughout southern California. The manufacture and use of the plank canoe is further evidence of the skill of coastal and island Indians of southern California.

Soapstone outcrops exhibit considerable variability in mineralogical composition ranging from coarse-grained material that was used for bowls, comals (frying slabs), and other implements to fine-grained steatite and serpentine that was used for effigies, pipes, net weights, pendants, and beads. The soapstone quarries exhibit bowl scars and cavities where large bowl-sized nodules were removed. Slate and schist picks, unfinished bowls, and waste fragments are often present. An example can be seen on the grounds of the Casino building and museum at Avalon.

SAN CLEMENTE ISLAND, CALIFORNIA

San Clemente Island is the southernmost of the California Channel Islands and is situated approximately 60 kilometers (38 mi) southwest of the mainland. The island is about 34 kilometers (21 mi) long and ranges in width between 2.4 and 6 kilometers (1.5 and 4.0 mi). Despite this relatively small size, thousands of archaeological sites have been discovered. The island is a naval installation, and the large number of surviving archaeological sites can be attributed in part to the lack of commercial development. For the past twenty years, archaeological research has been conducted as a result of cooperative research agreements between the U.S. Navy and academic institutions.

For its size, the island provides a significant degree of environmental diversity. The topography consists of coastal marine terraces, upland marine terraces, sand dune fields, an upper plateau, a steep and highly dissected eastern escarpment, and major canyons that dissect the marine terraces on the southwestern slope of the island.

With an average of slightly over 15 centimeters (6 in) of rain per year, the island receives less precipitation than a number of regions of California classified as deserts. The arid conditions are relieved by moderate air temperatures and frequent cloud cover. However, the lack of rain and the unfavorable geological conditions for the formation of aquifers (largely impermeable basalt) significantly limit the availability of surface water. In spite of this limitation, large numbers of archaeological sites suggests that prehistoric mariners found the island to be a favorable place to settle.

Much of the native vegetation has been destroyed or replaced by non-native plants due to grazing of sheep and goats that were introduced by Euro-Americans. Remnant oak tree stands and native shrubs and grasses provide clues to the potential productivity of terrestrial plant resources for the prehistoric island population. As with the other southern Channel Islands, terrestrial game animals were not present.

The earliest settlement on San Clemente Island has been dated to 10,000 years ago and represents some of the earliest evidence for the presence of marine-oriented populations on the California coast. There is evidence to suggest that the early occupants were related to the Chumash peoples to the north and that this genetically distinct population was replaced by later Uto-Aztecan (also known as Shoshonean) peoples who entered California from the eastern deserts. At the time of European contact in the sixteenth century, the island was inhabited by a small, ethnically distinct population with close ties to the Indians of Santa Catalina Island and other Gabrielino Indian communities on the mainland. The San Clemente Indians were relocated to the mainland in 1829.

Archaeological work on the island began during the 1870s with excavations centered on the recovery of museum-quality artifacts. This was followed by recreational relic collecting and looting by professional pot hunters. By 1934, the island came under U.S. Navy jurisdiction and restricted civilian access helped to protect the sites. Early scientific investigations began in 1939, and studies using modern scientific goals and methods began in the mid 1950s. Investigations conducted under cooperative research agreements with academic institutions began in 1983 and continue into the present. Over 5,000 sites have been recorded and more are expected to be located.

The Eel Point Site

The Eel Point site is located on the west coast of the island. Archaeological investigations produced important new data on the maritime economy of the Native inhabitants. In addition, with radiocarbon dates placing initial occupation between 9,000 and 10,000 years ago, the Eel Point site is the oldest confirmed occupation of the southern Channel Islands. This and a number of coastal settlements of similar age on the Channel Islands and mainland have caused archaeologists to rethink the viability and antiquity of a maritime adaptation and to discard the ideas that the earliest settlers of coastal California were terrestrial hunter-gatherers and that an emphasis on marine resources was a late development caused by population pressure.

The Nursery Site

The Nursery site is a large, complex site with deep shell midden (garbage) deposits, burials, and pit houses constructed of whale bones. It is situated along the base of a large sand dune in the inland portion of the western coastal terrace. Radiocarbon dates suggest a range of occupation from approximately 1,400 to 6,400 years ago. The site is important because it contains one of the best preserved and archaeologically studied prehistoric house structures in California. The structure represents the remains of a semi-subterranean pit house where whale ribs were used to form a conical house frame and then covered with skins or sea grass mats. The smooth polished floor covered an area of 4.6 × 4 meters (15.25 × 13 ft). Other features include post holes, hearths, and storage pits. Nearly 1,000 cultural items including seed- and acorn-grinding implements, stone artifacts, and food remains such as carbonized seeds, shellfish, and animal bone were recovered.

The Lemon Tank Site

The Lemon Tank site is situated near the midpoint of San Clemente Island on the upper plateau. It is notable because of the excellent preservation of basketry, cordage, and floral remains. More important, however, are the numerous cache pits and artifacts that provide evidence of ritual activities that have been reported in the ethnographic data. The cache pits contain seeds and animal burials, including a dog, fox, a red-tailed hawk, and another bird of prey. Grave goods were placed with the dog and hawk. Other artifacts found at the site, such as flowerpot-shaped mortars, appear to have been ritually broken. The caches, animal burials, and "killed" artifacts appear to represent the archaeological remains of ceremonial activities associated with the Gabrielino mourning ceremony and the eagle killing ritual held in conjunction with the harvest celebration.

SAN NICOLAS ISLAND, CALIFORNIA

San Nicolas Island, the outermost of all the California Channel Islands, is located about 120 kilometers (75 mi) southwest of Los Angeles and about 97 kilometers (60 mi) from the nearest point on the mainland. The island is about 13 kilometers (8 mi) long and about 5.6 kilometers (3.5 mi) wide, with an overall area of about 57 square kilometers (22 mi²). It is composed primarily of sandstone and shale with some volcanic rock intrusions. The island is dominated by a central plateau that reaches a height of slightly over 275 meters (900 ft). The south side of the island is made up of steep and deeply dissected badlands that plummet hundreds of feet from the plateau to the coast below. The northwest region is low and full of highly active dunes that are constantly in flux because of the prevailing winds that buffet this part of the island.

Vegetation on the island consists mostly of small bushes and grasses. No native trees exist on the island, although some introduced species are present today. The largest land mammal is the island fox. Sea lions, seals, and birds use the island for breeding grounds and rookeries. Nearshore and offshore fisheries are very productive with common species including rock fish, cod, grouper, and halibut. Rocky intertidal zones support a vast array of shellfish and crustaceans, including abalone, mussel, lobster, and crab. Clumps of sea grass, used by the Native islanders for cordage and basket making, cling to the rocks and at low tide are accessible. The island is currently owned and administered by the U.S. Navy, and access is generally restricted.

The earliest dates for the island suggest people had settled there by at least 8,000 years ago. Their arrival marked a period of continuous occupation by Native Americans up to the time of European contact. Although the ethnic makeup of the people changed through time and their population numbers fluctuated, they all lived off food taken from the sea as well as seeds, bulbs, and fruits from plants on land. Fresh water on the island is relatively reliable and comes to the surface in the form of seeps and springs, especially on the northwest coast where the largest sites are located.

Very little is known historically about the Native islanders. Only four words were recorded from Juana Maria, the last Indian inhabitant of the island. Juana Maria's family was taken off the island in 1835, but she was left behind. She lived by herself for 18 years and was taken to the mainland in 1853, where she died a few weeks later. She was buried at the Santa Barbara Mission cemetery where she remains today. Her story was made famous by Scott O'Dell in his children's novel, *Island of the Blue Dolphins*. But long before this book came out in 1960, scores of newspaper and magazine articles about Juana Maria captured the attention of the American public. Her story continues to fascinate people as it is read widely by school children all over the world. Recent investigations on San Nicolas Island are aimed at understanding what the archaeological record has to say about Juana Maria and her ancestors.

The Thousand Springs Site

The Thousand Springs site sits on a rocky headland located on the northernmost reaches of San Nicolas Island. It consists of a series of sand dunes with archaeological deposits embedded in them, representing at least four distinct time periods. The deposits contain artifacts and food remains left behind by people who used the site for hunting, fishing, and shellfish gathering and include evidence that people processed food, made tools and ornaments for use and trade, cooked with fire, and performed other daily activities.

Archaeological studies at the site have shown that early on people mostly hunted sea lions and seals but later focused on sea otters and fish. At deposits dated to 1,000 years ago, archaeologists have found evidence that people intensively fished, hauling in catches of nearby rock fish and perch as well as deepwater fish, dolphins, and whales. People used locally available cobbles and pebbles to make stone tools and process the food remains. People also collected sea grass to twine into string and make nets, bags, and baskets.

The Thousand Springs site has allowed archaeologists to reconstruct past human activities over a 5,000-year period. Archaeologists have recorded past environmental changes at the site and have shown how people adapted to different circumstances through time. In some cases people relied on alternative food sources, and in other cases they changed the nature in which the site was used. In general, people came to Thousand Springs to collect fresh water, hunt and fish, and gather colorful shellfish by the basket load as they left behind faint clues as to what life was like in the past.

Upper Tule Creek Village

The upper Tule Creek Village site is located about 3.2 kilometers (2 mi) southeast of Thousand Springs. It is situated on the northern edge of the upper plateau overlooking Corral Harbor. With incredible views to all directions, the site is one of the largest on San Nicolas and contains evidence that people lived there between about AD 1200 and European contact. This site was probably one of the last villages occupied by Native Americans and may have been home to Juana Maria and her people. Most scholars believe that the last Native inhabitants taken off the island boarded ships at Corral Harbor and likely lived at Tule Creek Village. This site has attracted the attention of archaeologist for decades and remains one of the most important on the island.

Excavations at the site have found the remains of living areas, including house floors, storage pits, and trash heaps. Early investigators found a cemetery and numerous house pits. Archaeological evidence suggests that people extensively used the marine environment to obtain food and other resources. Artifacts include shell fishhooks, beads, and ornaments; bone awls, whistles, and hairpins; and stone drills, arrow points, pendants, bowls, and cooking plates. Obsidian from eastern California, soapstone from Santa Catalina Island, and chert from the northern Channel Islands provide information about past trade networks in the region. Evidence for religious activities at the site include east-west trending hearth alignments, ceremonial trash pits, dog and fox burials, animal and plant offerings, and abundant shaman's paraphernalia, such as ochre, crystals, incised bone, and iron stones found in discrete caches.

SANTA BARBARA ISLAND, CALIFORNIA

Santa Barbara Island is located 61 kilometers (38 mi) off the mainland coast and about 43 kilometers (27 mi) northeast of San Nicolas Island. The island is primarily volcanic rock and encompasses only 2.6 square kilometers (1 mi^2) in area. It contains no surface water and has a relatively impoverished suite of terrestrial plants and animals. Unlike the other southern islands, Santa Barbara Island lacks island foxes and is home to only two small land mammals: the deer mouse and California bat. Plants are small and include prickly pear, rattlesnake weed, wild cucumbers, and yarrow. Marine resources surrounding the island are fairly productive, but few beaches exist for landing boats or canoes.

Very little is known about the archaeology of Santa Barbara Island. Only nineteen sites have been recorded, and of these only a handful has been excavated. Dated sites range from about 1,500 to 4,000 years old. Rocky intertidal shellfish species and nearshore fish dominate the food remains found in these sites. Few formal artifacts have been uncovered, although some mortars and pestles, beads, and numerous pebbles tools have been found on the island. Recent excavations have focused on a small cave that may contain deeply buried deposits, yet this work is ongoing and results have not been reported.

Although small in size and lacking sufficient resources for long-term settlement by humans, many archaeologists have indicated that Santa Barbara Island was probably important as a way station for people traveling to and from the islands and mainland. Particularly for people voyaging out to San Nicolas Island, stopping over on Santa Barbara Island would mean a safe place to land and rest or to gather additional resources or weather out a storm. Future research will undoubtedly begin to fill in the data gaps for this small but important island.

Further Reading: Bolton, Herbert E., *Spanish Explorations in the Southwest, 1542–1702* (New York: Barnes and Noble, 1946); Cameron, Connie, ed., "Archaeology of San Clemente Island, Parts 1–4," *Pacific Coast Archaeological Society Quarterly* 36 (1–4) (2000); Heizer, Robert F., and Albert B. Elsasser, eds., *Original Accounts of the Lone Woman of San Nicolas Island,* Archaeological Survey Report No. 55 (Berkeley: University of California, 1961), 1–55; Martz, Patricia, "Prehistoric Settlement and Subsistence on San Nicolas Island," in *Proceedings of the Sixth California Islands Symposium,* edited by David K. Garcelon and Catherin A. Schwemm (Arcata, CA: Institute for Wildlife Studies, 2005), 65–84; Martz, Patricia, Donn R. Grenda, and Jane Rosenthal, *Marine Exploitation at the Thousand Springs Site, San Nicolas Island: A Reinvestigation of CA-SNI-11,* Technical Report No. 99-10 (Redlands, CA: Statistical Research, 1999); McCawley, William, *The First Angelinos: The Gabrielino Indians of Los Angeles* (Banning, CA: Malki Museum Press, 1996); Meighan, Clement W., "The Little Harbor Site, Catalina Island: An Example of Ecological Interpretation in Archaeology," *American Antiquity* 24(4) (1959): 383–405; O'Dell, Scott, *Island of the Blue Dolphins* (New York: Houghton Mifflin, 1960); Rick, Torben C., Jon M. Erlandson, René L. Vellanoweth, and Todd J. Braje, "From Pleistocene Mariners to Complex Hunter-Gatherers: The Archaeology of the California Channel Islands," *Journal of World Prehistory* 19 (2006): 169–228; Vellanoweth, Rene L., Patricia Martz, and Steven J. Schwartz, "Complexity and the Late Holocene Archaeology of San Nicolas Island," in *Perspectives in California Archaeology,* Vol. 6: *Catalysts to Complexity: Late Holocene Societies of the California Coast,* edited by Jon M. Erlandson and Terry L. Jones (Los Angeles: Cotsen Institute of Archaeology, University of California, 2002); Woldarski, Robert J., "Catalina Island Soapstone Manufacture," *Journal of California and Great Basin Anthropology* 1(2) (1979): 331–355.

René L. Vellanoweth and Patricia A. Martz

GOLETA SLOUGH AREA SITES, PITAS POINT SITE, AND CHUMASH PAINTED CAVE STATE HISTORIC PARK

Southern California Coast

Archaeology of the Santa Barbara Channel and the Ventura Coast

At the time of European contact, the Chumash Indians along the Santa Barbara Channel coast lived in large, permanent villages organized into simple chiefdoms that were governed by a hierarchy of chiefs and other elites. This unusual level of social complexity for a nonagricultural society was made possible by long-term food storage, intensive marine resource exploitation, shell bead money, and extensive intervillage exchange. Chumash society was characterized by a population of greater density than that found in many other areas of prehistoric North America, including those in which agriculture was practiced.

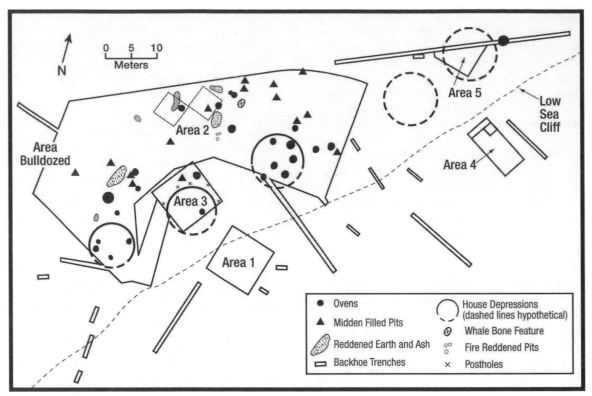

A diagram of the Pitas Point site.   [Lynn H. Gamble]

The Chumash Indians lived along the Pacific coast of California from Topanga Canyon in the south to the Monterey County line in the north, and eastward to the San Joaquin valley. They also occupied the northern Channel Islands of Santa Cruz, Santa Rosa, San Miguel, and Anacapa. There is strong archaeological evidence that the Chumash have lived in the region for approximately 12,000–13,000 years, with some of the earliest radiocarbon dates on the northern Channel Islands. Recent mitochondrial and linguistic data confirm the archaeological evidence for these early dates.

The Chumash subsisted by hunting, gathering, and fishing. The Santa Barbara Channel is one of the most productive fisheries in the world because of its geographic position and the phenomenon of localized upwelling of nutrient-rich deep waters and cold California currents. The many kelp beds in the region attract fish and sea mammals, both of which were important in the Chumash diet. Plant foods, such as yucca buds, were harvested between January and May. Other important sources of food found in the early spring were shellfish and bulbs. Sage, red maids, grass seeds, and other small seeds ripened in the later spring and summer. Acorns, which were a staple food among the Chumash, were most commonly collected in October and November. Many of the plants used by the Chumash required intensive processing; for example, tannins in acorns had to be repeatedly leached out before they were edible, as did toxic substances in other plant foods. Acorns were processed using the mortar and the pestle and could be stored for several

years. After living in the Santa Barbara Channel region for thousands of years, the Chumash had developed adaptive strategies to minimize risks associated with cyclical droughts, wet El Niño events, and other environmental stresses. These mechanisms included storage, exchange, use of money, environmental modifications, and periodic feasts.

The climate in the Chumash region is Mediterranean, with cool and wet winters and hot and dry summers. In the past, larger and more expansive estuaries were found along the mainland coast, remnants of which can still be seen in Goleta and Carpinteria. The one at Goleta was so large that an island was in the middle of it, called Mescalititlan, where about 800 Chumash people lived in 1769 when the region was investigated by the Portola expedition. Here and at some of the other large Chumash settlements, houses were clustered together in rows with walkways between them.

The houses were shaped like domes and were usually made from a frame of bent willow wood that was covered with thatch from tule reeds. The Chumash had a hearth in the middle of the houses that they used for warmth and for cooking. They also processed foods, cooked, and conducted other activities outside of the houses. Some of the houses were quite large, about 6 or 7 meters in diameter, and had room for about eight to ten people. Most large Chumash settlements also had an area that was cleared and used for dancing, a cemetery, sacred enclosures, playing fields, storage structures, and at least one sweat lodge. The larger sweat lodges were about the

Some of the multicolor paintings found on the walls and ceiling at Chumash Painted Cave State Historic Park.   [Lynne H. Gamble]

size of a large house but were semi-subterranean and covered with dirt so they resembled a small hill or knoll. Primarily men took ceremonial sweats inside of these, using direct fires to get the sweat lodges very hot. After they sweated in the lodge, they would dive into a nearby creek, purified and cleansed from the experience. The men also socialized in sweat lodges during the day and often slept in them at night.

A person's status in Chumash society was usually an inherited position that was well defined. There were substantial differences in wealth and social privileges among the Chumash. Social ranks recognized by the Chumash included chiefs, elites, and commoners. High-ranked people had special rights that others lacked. The more common person had to defer to chiefs and other elite individuals in public. Shell beads served as social markers as well as money and were used, in part, to distinguish the wealthy from the poor.

The Chumash had a highly developed economic system that relied in part on an elaborate exchange system. They had mastered the art of building plank boats (*tomols*) that allowed them to safely and swiftly cross the channel to the offshore islands and return laden with large stone bowls, shell beads,

and other trade goods. Canoes also enabled fishermen to venture into deep waters to catch large fish such as swordfish weighing as much as 270 kilograms (600 lb).

The inhabitants of villages on Santa Cruz and the other Channel Islands specialized in producing goods such as bead money as a way of gaining access to resources not available on the islands. In return for bead money, the Chumash on the mainland coast and in the interior of the Santa Barbara coast region traded subsistence and status items to the islanders. The Chumash were similar to other California Indians, such as the Pomo, Patwin, Yokuts, and Yurok, in their reliance on shell beads. Shell beads were used and buried with the dead in the Chumash region for over 5,000 years. Although shell beads have been found in many other parts of the world, the amount of energy invested in their manufacture and use in California was probably greater than that expended by any other hunter-gatherers in the world. The time and energy spent in the production and pursuit of beads could have been invested in other activities, such as the construction of monumental architecture. Instead, extensive trade networks were developed among the Chumash, as well as other California Indian groups.

There are a number of significant archaeological sites located along the Santa Barbara Channel coast. The most populous region, the Goleta Slough area where approximately 2,000 people lived in 1769, caught the eye of several early explorers. At that time, three very large village sites were situated around the Goleta Slough, including the town of *Helo'* (CA-SBa-46) on Mescalititlan Island. Other areas that were heavily populated during the early historic period include Dos Pueblos, to the west of the Goleta Slough, and the area now near Santa Barbara. At Dos Pueblos two large towns, *Mikiw* and *Cuyamu* (CA-SBa-78 and CA-SBa-77), were situated on either side of the creek. There were probably about 1,000 people living in these settlements in 1769. The Smithsonian Institution sponsored excavations in the late 1800s and collected numerous artifacts in the large cemeteries at Dos Pueblos and at Helo'. *Syuxtun* (CA-SBa-27 and CA-SBa-28), situated to the west of the mouth of Mission Creek, was the main historic period settlement in Santa Barbara. The earliest written record about Syuxtun is from 1542, when Juan Rodríguez Cabrillo noted that the settlement was a regional capital and had a female chief. When Cabrillo spent three days at Syuxtun, during which time the Chumash helped supply his ship with wood and water, the old female chief slept on board with some other villagers and told Cabrillo that she was chief of a province between Point Conception and Syuxtun.

The Pitas Point site (CA-Ven-27), northwest of Ventura on Highway 101, was occupied before these later historic settlements, from about AD 1000 to 1550. Several house pits, in addition to numerous rock ovens, hearths, and storage pits, were excavated at the site in 1969 and 1970. There was also an unusual whale-bone shrine at Pitas Point and one of the only archaeological examples of a basket-making area in California. Ethnographic and ethnohistoric data indicate that it was women who made baskets in Chumash society.

Although there are few archaeological sites in the region that are open to the public, there is spectacular rock art that can be seen at Chumash Painted Cave State Historic Park. The sandstone cave is situated in the foothills near Santa Barbara, about 4.8 kilometers south of San Marcos Pass. Its back wall and ceiling are covered with multicolor paintings made by Chumash hundreds of years ago. Although archaeologists are not absolutely sure how these rock art sites were used, there is some consensus that they were associated with spiritual beliefs. Painted Cave is one of the few Chumash rock art sites that have been so well preserved. Human-like figures, animals, and elaborate design elements that suggest sun disks can all be seen at this significant site.

Further Reading: Blackburn, Thomas C., *December's Child: A Book of Chumash Oral Narratives* (Berkeley: University of California Press, 1975); Gamble, Lynn H., *The Chumash World at Historic Contact: Power, Trade, and Feasting among Complex Hunter-Gatherers* (Berkeley: University of California Press, 2008); Gamble, Lynn H., P. L. Walker, and G. S. Russell, "An Integrative Approach to Mortuary Analysis: Social and Symbolic Dimensions of Chumash Burial Practices," *American Antiquity* 66 (2001): 185–212; Gibson, Robert O., *The Chumash* (New York: Chelsea House, 1991); Grant, Campbell, *The Rock Paintings of the Chumash* (Santa Barbara, CA: Santa Barbara Museum of Natural History, 1993); Johnson, John R., "Social Responses to Climate Change among the Chumash Indians of South-Central California," in *The Way the Wind Blows: Climate, History, and Human Action*, edited by R. J. McIntosh, J. A. Tainter, and S. K. McIntosh (New York: Columbia University Press, 2000); 301–327; King, Chester D., *Evolution of Chumash Society: A Comparative Study of Artifacts Used for Social System Maintenance in the Santa Barbara Channel Region before AD 1804* (New York: Garland, 1990).

Lynn H. Gamble

TOPANGA CANYON, MALAGA COVE, SERRA SPRINGS, AND OTHER SITES

Los Angeles Basin, Coastal Southern California

The Archaeological Record in a Modern Metropolis

The Los Angeles basin is generally understood as the plain bounded by the Peninsular and Transverse Ranges in southern California, which contains the city of Los Angeles and its southern and southeastern suburbs extending into Orange County. Bounded and thus limited by the Santa Monica and Santa Ana mountains and the Puente Hills, it measures approximately

35 miles (56 km) long by 15 miles (24 km) wide. The deep sediments of the uplifted province, once under water, have yielded petroleum resources and fossil deposits, some potentially associated with an ancient human presence. Despite all the effects of population growth and physical development, evidence survives of human occupation for tens of thousands of years. While

traces of prehistoric activity are rarely evident on the surface, it is actually the process of construction that continues to reveal many archaeological sites through application of environmental laws such as the California Environmental Quality Act (CEQA) that mandate archival research and physical survey prior to major undertakings.

The earliest documented human remains are those of "Los Angeles Man," recovered in southeast Los Angeles along Ballona Creek and dated to approximately 22,000 years, although this date is questioned by many archaeologists. At the Rancho La Brea tar pits, a female skeleton has been demonstrated to be about 9,000 years old, although animal bones from the same deposit show unmistakable signs of human modification going back some 15,000 years. Little is known about the cultural materials or subsistence practices of these early people. It is assumed that the settlement pattern and way of life reflected a generalized hunter-gatherer culture.

By about 9,300 years ago, evidence is more abundant and demonstrates ways of life that were adapted to the specific natural resources of differing environments. In Topanga Canyon, for example, where grasses and other vegetation producing hard seeds are abundant, people prepared these resources with milling stones, which are large slabs or cobbles, most often of sandstone, with basins formed by grinding with a hand stone, or *mano*. With this tool kit, they were able to establish a fairly sedentary lifestyle. Nearer to the coast, as at Malaga Cove, a broader range of resources was exploited. The lower levels of that deep deposit yielded not only the same types of milling stones but also the remains of marine mammals, sea birds, fish, thousands of mollusks, and tools made from their shells. Other tools characteristic of this period include scrapers, choppers, hammerstones, and a small number of relatively large projectile points or blades. Burials frequently occurred under cairns of milling stones. One such site has been investigated on a bluff in Topanga Canyon, and others are recorded on the flat, undeveloped lands east of the city.

Changes were taking place by about 5,000 years ago, although scholars still debate whether the new traits were brought in by waves of new settlers or evolved from the older pattern. The milling stones were giving way to mortars and pestles, probably used to pound or pulverize acorns or small animals rather than grind hard seeds. The smaller and more numerous flaked projectile points signified greater reliance on hunting; other characteristic cultural materials included sandstone bowls, shell ornaments, small scrapers, stone blades, and flexed burials. Fewer of these intermediate period sites are known, but the middle levels at Malaga Cove are typical. In the final phase before the historical period began, early Hispanic explorers have left written descriptions of villages with as many as thirty domed and thatched pole houses, and swift ocean-going plank canoes that were faster than their own long boats. These *tomols*, or canoes, were as much as 9 meters (30 ft) long and carried trade items back and forth to the Channel Islands. Excavations have revealed elaborate industries in shell and steatite, extensive social and ritual interactions with other groups, flexed burials and some cremations, and the small, finely flaked projectile points that point to utilization of the bow and arrow. Such sites were once numerous along the southern California coast. Trade networks were extensive, as beads came from the Channel Islands in exchange for mainland food products, and the obsidian used for finely flaked tools originated from sources in central California. The local seashells were traded as far as the pueblos of Arizona.

The Native Americans present when the first Hispanic explorers arrived are now known as the Gabrielino. They are said to have been one of the wealthiest, most populous, and most powerful groups in aboriginal southern California. Their territory encompassed not only the Los Angeles basin but included the watersheds of the Los Angeles, San Gabriel, and Santa Ana rivers, the coastline from Laguna Beach in the south to Malibu in the north, the inland ranges as far as San Bernardino, and the offshore islands of San Clemente, San Nicolas, and Santa Catalina. Their settlement pattern included both sedentary villages and temporary camps for the procurement of seasonal foods. They exploited such subsistence resources as small mammals, deer, acorns, sage, yucca, fish, shellfish, other maritime species, and a variety of other plant and animal foods.

The Gabrielino were in contact with the Spanish as early as Juan Cabrillo's voyage in 1542, and they were visited by later expeditions by sea and overland. However, the historic period is usually said to begin with the founding of the Franciscan missions, San Fernando in 1797 and San Gabriel in 1771. Those who lived in the village of *YangNa*, in what is now downtown Los Angeles, were said to number more than 200. The Native Americans were gathered from their ancestral lands to live at the mission complexes and learn a new language, religion, and many new skills such as agriculture, weaving, herding, and making bricks and tile for new constructions. Most of those in the basin were associated with Mission San Gabriel and are now known as the Gabrielino.

They were also employed as laborers on many of the ranchos granted to private owners by the Spanish beginning in 1786, and later under Mexican rule beginning in 1821. The new ways of life upset many cultural traditions, such as marriage patterns, and introduced new diseases; and by the time the missions were secularized in 1834, the Native American population was decimated.

Although the exact location of the Native American village of *YangNa* that was described by early explorers, in what is now downtown Los Angeles, has never been precisely identified, evidence of its presence both before and after the arrival of the mission padres has been found. Among the first endeavors of the padres was construction of an aqueduct, or *zanja*, to provide water for both irrigation and domestic use. Indian labor was used in the construction as well as in the fields and making adobes for the early buildings. Archaeological remains of the system of branching aqueducts are regularly encountered during any current construction down-town that penetrates the existing pavements, and examples are displayed at El Pueblo de Los Angeles historical park.

Another site associated with the Gabrielino survives on the grounds of University High School in West Los Angeles. Frey Juan Crespi, who accompanied the expedition of Don Gaspar de Portolá in 1769, wrote that the explorers camped at springs where the Indians gave them watercress, chia, and fresh water. The location is currently known as Serra Springs, which still flow, and many artifacts have been recovered from the vicinity.

The historic Gabrielino are also represented at the Campo de Cahuenga, a commemorative park in Studio City. This was the location of an early adobe where the signing of the Articles of Capitulation took place in 1847, ending hostilities of the Mexican-American War in California. The stone foundations and tile floors of the structure were exposed by archaeologists, together with associated artifacts, and the outlines of the structure have been recreated at the surface in a City of Los Angeles historical park open to the public.

Another distinctive culture well represented in the Los Angeles basin is that of the Chinese who settled in a flood-prone area of downtown Los Angeles after the gold rush and completion of the railroads they helped to build. The untold and unwritten history of Chinatown was unearthed archaeologically when the location was to be disturbed by a new subway system. The artifacts are on display, and the full research collection curated, at the Chinese Historical Society of Southern California.

Further Reading: Chartkoff, Joseph L., and Kerry Kona Chartkoff, *The Archaeology of California* (Palo Alto, CA: Stanford University Press, 1984); Fagan, Brian, *Before California: An Archaeologist Looks at Our Earliest Inhabitants* (Walnut Creek, CA: Rowman and Littlefield, 2003); Greenwood, Roberta S., *Down by the Station: Los Angeles Chinatown 1880–1933* (Los Angeles: University of California, Institute of Archaeology, 1996); Heizer, Robert F., ed., *Handbook of North American Indians*, Vol. 8: *California* (Washington, DC: Smithsonian Institution, 1978); Moratto, Michael J., *California Archaeology* (Orlando, FL: Academic Press, 1984).

Roberta S. Greenwood

WINDSONG SHORES AND OTHER SITES

San Diego Area, Coastal Southern California

Ancient Coastal Sites

INTRODUCTION

The initial occupation of the San Diego region began over 9,000 years ago and continues today with Native Americans living on eighteen reservations in San Diego County, as well as in nearby communities. Archaeologists have used terms such as San Dieguito, La Jolla, and Yuman to identify selected groups of artifacts within specific time periods, as well as to identify the people who made these tools. This discussion addresses the environmental setting, archaeological sites, and artifacts and provides a general chronology for San Diego County for the past 10,000 years.

ENVIRONMENTAL SETTING

Much can be said about San Diego County's temperate climate, low rainfall, and proximity to the beach and mountains. However, the environmental setting of today was not the same as that of 10,000 years ago, when it was cooler and wetter. The rising sea level flooded coastal valleys and created San Diego County's ten estuaries/lagoons and two bays. The ocean and coastal lagoons provided shellfish and fish, and the valleys provided a wide range of land mammals and plants for food, medicine, and building materials. Stone tools needed to acquire and process these resources were made from local beach cobbles and mountain fine-grained metavolcanic quarry

material. In most cases, the stone tools and debitage represent the bulk of the archaeological record for the past 10,000 years. Around 3,500 years ago, the sea level stabilized and siltation filled in a number of coastal lagoons, therein causing the loss of lagoonal resources and depopulation of the lagoon regions. San Diego Bay was created with the rise in sea level, and because it did not silt in, a continuous record of occupation is demonstrated in the archaeological record from San Diego Bay to the mountains. The environment was warming from the Middle to Late Holocene, and the wooded coastal plain was changed to the drought-tolerant coastal sage scrub and chaparral plant communities. Oak woodland can be found above 900 meters (3,000 ft), and riparian vegetation follows the river valleys from the mountains to the coast. Given the low rainfall during the Late Holocene, the river valleys were the focus of occupation providing the resources needed for daily life. The lagoons reopened around 1,500 years ago; however, the shellfish were smaller, and the species were not as diverse as the shellfish recovered from Early to Middle Holocene archaeological sites.

CHRONOLOGY

The earliest people who lived in this area have been called San Dieguito; they were followed by other groups referred to as the La Jolla Culture and Yuman. Additional terms have been used

Table 1 Terminology for Culture History in the San Diego Area

Geologic Time	Period	Years Before Present	Other Names	Diagnostic Cultural Material
Late Holocene	Late Period	Present ... 1,300	Historic/Contact Precontact/Yuman Kumeyaay/Luiseno Cuyamaca Complex San Luis Rey I,II	Bow and arrow, small triangular and side-notched points, fish hooks, ceramics, Obsidian Butte obsidian, cremations
Late Holocene	Early Period (Archaic)	2,000 ... 3,000		Stone bowls, triangular points, fishing gorges, burials
Middle Holocene	Early Period (Archaic)	4,000 ... 5,000 ... 6,000		Atlatl (dart) points, cogged stones, plummet stones, leaf-shaped points/knives, corner-notched and stemmed points, Coso Obsidian, burials
Early Holocene	Early Period (Archaic)	7,000 ... 8,000 ... 9,000 ... 10,000	Pauma Complex Encinitas Tradition La Jolla Complex ... San Dieguito Tradition/Complex	Spear, crescents, lanceolate and leaf-shaped points, leaf-shaped knives, adze/SEUTs, Casa Diablo and Coso obsidian, burials

Adapted from Gallegos (2002).

to identify and classify past cultures and peoples of San Diego County. These terms include San Dieguito tradition or complex, La Jolla complex, Encinitas tradition, Pauma complex, San Luis Rey I and II, Cuyamaca complex, and late prehistoric. This terminology has been simplified as shown in Table 1, which divides the Holocene into Early, Middle, and Late periods and provides chronology terms (e.g., Early period/Archaic and Late period) based on artifact type and continuity or lack thereof, and cultural material within these periods.

The earliest occupation sites, dated around 9,000 years ago, have been found adjacent to lagoons and along coastal river valleys. These sites include Agua Hedionda sites; Windsong Shores (CA-SDI-10695 and CA-SDI-210/UCLJ-M-15); Rancho Park North (CA-SDI-4392); Kelly Site (CA-SDI-9649), where the state artifact [crescentic (a crescent-shaped chipped-stone tool) in the shape of a bear] was recovered (see Table 1); Harris Site (SDI-149); San Dieguito Estates (CA-SDI-194, CA-SDI-5119, and CA-SDI-5369); and Remington Hills (CA-SDI-11079), located near the Tijuana estuary and the U.S.-Mexico border. The oldest archaeological site is

Windsong Shores, located near Agua Hedionda Lagoon and dated to about 9,450 to 9,910 years ago (using two-sigma calibrated results). Artifacts recovered from the Windsong Shores site include a few large bifaces (knives and points), crescentics, scrapers/adzes, cobble tools, obsidian from Casa Diablo, large quantities of shell, fish bone, and small to large mammal bone, including rabbit and deer. Bird bone from *Chendytes lawi*, an extinct flightless sea duck, was also recovered from Windsong Shores. This collection of cultural material is somewhat consistent for artifacts from Early Holocene archaeological sites; however, milling tools present in the Early Holocene increase through time to the Late period, where bedrock milling features are common, especially where grantic rock, oaks, and water are present. Obsidian was imported over 483 kilometers (300 mi) from both Coso and Casa Diablo (north of San Diego). Burials continued from the Early Holocene to the Late Holocene; however, during the Late period, cremation of the dead became the common practice. Faunal remains from Early and Middle Holocene sites include a range of terrestrial mammal bone (especially rabbit and deer), some marine mammal bone, bird bone, a wide range of fish bone representing both deep- and shallow-water species, and a high amount of shell. The shell from Early and Middle Holocene archaeological middens is representative of a healthy flushing lagoon system open to the ocean. Dominant shellfish lagoon species include *Chione* spp. and *Argopecten* spp. The initial occupation was thought to represent big game hunting, given the large bifaces recovered from the Harris site (CA-SDI-149). However, more recent radiocarbon dating of a number of Early Holocene coastal archaeological sites document the use of plants, ocean and lagoon resources, and small to large mammals, providing a more balanced view of Early Holocene occupation in San Diego County.

During the Middle Holocene, the lagoons, terraces, foothills, and river valleys show evidence of occupation. Artifacts recovered from habitation sites include large bifaces; *atl atl* (dart) points; adzes for woodworking; beads made from shell, stone, and bone; discoidals; cogged stones; donut stones; plummet stones; milling tools such as manos, metates, mortars, and pestles; hearths for cooking; and large amounts of fire-affected rock, suggesting that the rock was heated and used in sweat lodges. Faunal resources sought, collected, hunted, and gathered included a diverse range of plant and terrestrial and marine animals.

Late period occupation is represented by archaeological sites dated from around 1,300 years ago to historic contact with Spanish explorers and early settlers. Late period cultural material and features include small triangular and side-notched arrow points (Cottonwood and Desert Side-notched point types) representing bow and arrow technology; pottery for the storage of seeds and water; beads; fishhooks of shell; cremation of the dead; and obsidian from Obsidian Butte, located approximately 130 kilometers (80 mi) east of San Diego. Structures were small, circular in shape, and made of brush. The Spanish named the people of southern San Diego County "Diegueño," after Mission San Diego, and the native inhabitants of northern San Diego County "Luiseño," after the Mission San Luis Rey.

The term "Diegueño" has been replaced by "Kumeyaay," and this has been refined by the terms "Tipai" and "Ipai" for southern and northern Kumeyaay, respectively.

The archaeology of San Diego County is patterned by landform and environmental setting: Early period/Archaic sites were located near the lagoons, on the terraces, and along the river valleys, whereas Late period occupation was more focused on freshwater sources found at the heads of river valleys and along river valley corridors, which were also used for travel from the ocean to the desert. Pleistocene marine terraces provided the source material (cobbles) used throughout the roughly 10,000 years of occupation to make cutting, chopping, and battering tools and to make cores for flake tools, or to be later worked into arrow points or other formed tools. The best local tool stone was the fine-grained metavolcanic quarry material found in the mountains within 16 kilometers (10 mi) of the coast. Both large and small bifaces, used for knives, dart points, and arrow points, were made from this quarry block core material.

San Diego County's archaeological collections are housed at the San Diego Archaeological Center. The center, a nonprofit facility located at 16666 San Pasqual Valley Road, Escondido, is an excellent source for archaeological information and is dedicated to the preservation of archaeological collections and to promote their educational, scientific, and cultural use to benefit a diverse public. This facility curates thousands of artifacts from hundreds of San Diego County's archaeological sites.

Further Reading: Chartkoff, Joseph L., and Kerry Kona Chartkoff, *The Archaeology of California* (Palo Alto, CA: Stanford University Press, 1984); Fagan, Brian, *Before California: An Archaeologist Looks at Our Earliest Inhabitants* (Walnut Creek, CA: Rowman and Littlefield, 2003); Heizer, Robert F., ed., *Handbook of North American Indians*, Vol. 8: *California* (Washington, DC: Smithsonian Institution, 1978); Moratto, Michael J., *California Archaeology* (Orlando, FL: Academic Press, 1984); San Diego Archaeological Center Web site, www.sandiegoarchaeology.org.

Dennis R. Gallegos

COSO ROCK ART, CHINA LAKE, AND SITES IN JOSHUA TREE NATIONAL PARK

Southeast California

Sites in the California Desert

The arid lands of southeastern California contain hundreds of thousands of archaeological sites. This essay describes some of the kinds of archaeological sites found in this region—rock art sites, sites buried by alluvial actions thousands of years ago when the environment was wetter, and surface archaeological sites.

COSO ROCK ART NATIONAL HISTORIC LANDMARK, INYO COUNTY, CALIFORNIA
This greatly expanded National Historic Landmark (NHL) is situated in Inyo County, California, in the middle of the North Range of China Lake Naval Air Weapons Station. Originally

Petroglyphs found in Joshua Tree.   [Courtesy of Joshua Tree National Park]

320 acres (129 hectares) and encompassing only Big and Little Petroglyph Canyon, additional parts of China Lake were inventoried by archaeologists from the Far Western Anthropological Research Group and the boundaries redrawn to more closely resemble the distribution of archaeological resources. Hence, the new NHL consists of 36,000 acres (14,500 hectares) of archaeological sites and literally millions of uncounted petroglyphs, primarily on the black, highly patinated basalt flows that dominate this portion of the Great Basin.

The petroglyph styles include Great Basin abstract forms; curvilinear, rectilinear, and scratched elements; and animals, many at Little Petroglyph Canyon in the shape of bighorn sheep known as the "Coso style," which is essentially a sheep with a boat-shaped torso. Medicine bags, anthropomorphs, and shaman-like figures cover the rocks, some appearing as if they are coming out of the ground.

Archaeologists debate the age of the petroglyphs. Some believe that they represent the art and communication of Native peoples beginning at the first settlement 11,000 years ago, but most feel that the majority of the petroglyphs are 3,000–5,000 years old. Native peoples who live in the area today sometimes share information about what their ancestors told them about the meaning and use of the petroglyphs. Research is ongoing with the older members of local tribes.

Pictographs (painted art) represent a minor variation of the aboriginal art in the NHL but are found throughout the area,

as are stacked stone enclosures, which could be hunting blinds or "medicine doctor" prayer circles; lines and stacks of rocks; and rock circles. Habitation sites range in age from early antiquity to about the middle 1940s, when the station was designated for military use and the general public excluded from the area.

Today the site is managed by the Department of the Navy. Native peoples continue to use the resources on a limited basis through agreements with the Navy. Members of several tribes collect pine nuts, perform ceremonies at the nearby Coso Hot Springs, collect obsidian at the Sugarloaf Quarry, and use the petroglyphs for cultural experiences.

The public is welcome on a limited basis. Tours to one site, Little Petroglyph Canyon, are allowed on weekends as long as they do not interfere with the operation and mission of the base. Private tours are allowed through the Maturango Museum in Ridgecrest. Volunteers are trained as petroglyph guides, primarily in safety and other procedures required by the U.S. Navy. The NHL is accessed through the main gate at China Lake. Ridgecrest, California, is the closest community to the station. Accommodations such as motels and camping can be found in Ridgecrest or nearby communities. The Bureau of Land Management has a campground approximately one hour's drive north, at Fossil Falls, which is available on a first-come, first-served basis. Public camping is not permitted on the station grounds.

CALICO HILLS ARCHAEOLOGICAL DISTRICT, SAN BERNARDINO COUNTY, CALIFORNIA

One of the first archaeological areas to be listed in the National Register of Historic Places was the Calico Hills Archaeological District. This series of over fifty archaeological sites was made famous by the British paleoanthropologist Louis S. B. Leakey. This was the only North American archaeological location visited by Leakey. From 1963 to the present, archaeologists such as the late Ruth "Dee" Simpson from the San Bernardino County Museum have dedicated themselves based on the notion that these sites can tell a story previously untold in the American West, one of greater antiquity than is generally postulated in standard archaeological interpretations. The sites have been the testing ground for hypotheses about the peopling of the Americas.

The archaeological sites within the district consist of a broad range of lithic pieces scattered over approximately one square mile of alluvium known as the Calico Hills. These are interpreted by the excavators of the sites as the result of stone tool manufacturing. During the Pleistocene era and into the Early Holocene these sites could have been shoreline lithic work stations associated with the remnants of ancient Lake Manix. The Mojave River flowed into Lake Manix from the San Bernardino Mountains, eventually being trapped in Silver Lake, near the present town of Baker, California.

Even today, if there are heavy snow packs in the local mountains or if there is episodic rainfall, the Mojave flows bank to bank through towns such as Victorville and Barstow, on the high desert, a flow that can easily be seen from the Calico Hills Archaeological District.

Excavations at several locations in the Calico Hills have reached depths of over 20 feet (6 meters). Carefully excavated and well-documented archaeological units reveal chalcedony and cherts in the alluvium that some believe to be artifacts, while others disagree and point to the susceptibility of the stone to natural flaking. In a major text about California archaeology, Michael J. Morratto (1984, 40–48) reviews the debate about whether the lithics excavated at the Calico Hills sites were made by humans or are the result of natural geological processes. He concludes that other expert studies of the Calico lithics correctly interpret these pieces as the result of natural processes rather than human manufacture.

On the other hand, artifacts found on surfaces throughout the area seem clearly to be related to human production and use. Scattered throughout the desert pavement and hills, these are rocks that have been reduced by human manufacturing to expended cores, prospected raw materials, and debitage resulting from flaking bifaces and other crude chopping and cutting implements. Excavations have revealed that the chalcedony was heat-treated to make the hard stone easier to manipulate into an acceptable form for lithic work.

The site is situated along Interstate 15, approximately 15 miles (25 km.) east of Barstow, California, on the route to Las Vegas. Signs are posted that say "Calico Early Man Site." One should take the Minneola exit from Interstate 15. Camping is available at the nearby Calico Ghost Town County Park or at the KOA.

The Friends of the Calico Early Man Site excavate, map, and catalogue the materials from the site and work toward the discovery of more substantive remains to help solve the mystery of the peopling of the Americas. Additional information may be obtained from the Barstow Bureau of Land Management office or the San Bernardino County Museum, Redlands, California.

JOSHUA TREE NATIONAL PARK, RIVERSIDE AND SAN BERNARDINO COUNTIES, SOUTHERN CALIFORNIA

Joshua Tree National Park lies at the junction of the Mojave and Sonoran deserts of southern California, immediately east of Palm Springs and north of the Salton Sea. The park (formerly a National Monument) contains a wealth of desert animals and plants—including extensive stands of the unusual tree for which it is named. Among its other attractions are some 240 species of migratory or resident birds, spectacular granite formations, and one of the oldest archaeological records in the state.

Some 10,000 years ago, at the end of the Pleistocene era, much of the western United States was cooler and wetter than today. The Great Basin and southern California were dotted with lakes and marshes where today there are only large expanses of desert playa. These ancient wetlands supported marshland plants, waterfowl, large mammals, and fish, as well as human hunter-gatherers whose broken tools and other refuse can still be found around the shores of these now-dry lakes.

Gradually the climate changed, and by about 7,000–8,000 years ago the West was suffering the major droughts of the Middle Holocene era. It was sometime in this period that the first known human groups lived in what is now Joshua Tree National Park. Their scant remains include flaked-stone scrapers, knives, and a distinctive style of dart or spear point that archaeologists call Pinto points, after the Pinto Basin in the eastern part of the park. Evidence suggests that these early people were nomadic hunters who followed herds of large game animals, based at small campsites rather than larger, more permanent villages.

Archaeologists Elizabeth and William Campbell carried out the first scientific study of these early desert peoples, and their collection of prehistoric ceramics, stone tools, and ollas are among the important collections housed at Joshua Tree National Park. Their work in southern California and Nevada in the 1920s, 1930s, and 1940s yielded detailed field records and photographs that are still valuable to archaeologists working in the area today. It was the Campbells who first discovered remains of the mid-Holocene Pinto culture.

Since that time, archaeologists have identified a great many prehistoric and historic period cultural sites within the park, including rock art sites, camps, homesteads and ranches, remains of mines, and desert oases. Today more than 600 archaeological sites, historic structures, and cultural landscapes are protected within the boundaries of Joshua Tree National Park.

When the first Euro-Americans entered the area in the nineteenth century, there were four distinct groups of Native people living there: the Serrano, whose traditional territory included the Oasis of Mara, the current location of the park headquarters; the Cahuilla, who inhabited the western and southern areas of the park; the Chemehuevi, who periodically occupied the eastern portion and later, the Oasis of Mara; and the Mojave, who likely used the area seasonally while traveling to the coast to trade and visit with other groups. These groups thrived on acorns, pinyon nuts, manzanita berries, cactus fruits, bighorn sheep, deer, rabbits, birds, amphibians, and reptiles. They fashioned bows from hickory and mesquite and often tipped their arrows with obsidian from sources located hundreds of miles away. They used fibers from yucca, agave, and other plants to weave baskets, nets, and cordage. Some groups made pottery by coiling clay and smoothing it with a paddle, often decorating the vessels with yellow or black designs. Rock surfaces were used as the medium for artistic and perhaps ritual expression, as evidenced by the many pecked-stone designs (petroglyphs) and red, black, and white painted stone (pictographs) found throughout the park.

For more than 9,000 years, the cool waters and shade from fan palms attracted people to the Oasis of Mara, including Native people and early prospectors, cattlemen, and health seekers. Prospectors arrived in the area in the mid-nineteenth century in search of gold, silver, copper, and turquoise. Of the 140 or so mines in the park, the most successful was the Lost Horse Mine, which produced gold and silver worth a total of roughly $5 million in today's dollars. Beginning in the 1870s, many of those who did not succeed at mining turned to cattle ranching. Cattlemen built rock and cement dams and developed natural springs to water their cattle. Many of these developed water sources remain today, including Barker Dam. Just west of Barker Dam lies the Desert Queen Ranch, which is now open to the public for guided walking tours.

General information about the park and its many attractions is available on the National Park Service Web site at www.nps.gov/jotr/. The site also has links to information on local archaeology, history, and Native American groups. Photographs, visitor information, and a detailed map of the park (in .PDF format) can be seen at www.americansouthwest. net/california/joshua_tree/national_park.

Further Reading: Budinger, Fred E., "The Lake Manix Lithic Industry and Associated Technologies at the Calico Site, San Bernardino County, California," in *The Human Journey and Ancient Life in California's Deserts*, edited by Mark W. Allen and Judyth Reed, Publication No. 15 (Ridgecrest, CA: Maturango Museum, 2004); California Desert Web site, www.californiadesert.gov; Grant, Campbell, J. W. Baird, and J. Kenneth Pringle, *Rock Drawings of the Coso Range, Inyo County, California,* Publication No. 4 (China Lake, CA: Maturango Museum, 1968); Maturango Museum Web site, www.maturango.org; Moratto, Michael J., *California Archaeology* (Orlando, FL: Academic Library Press, 1984); Simpson, Ruth DeEtte, "An Introduction of the Calico Early Man Lithic Assemblage," *San Bernardino County Museum Association Quarterly* 46(4) (1998); Whitley, David S., *The Art of the Shaman: Rock Art of California,* (Salt Lake City: University of Utah Press, 2000).

Russell L. Kaldenberg, Judyth E. Reed,
Sharon A. Waechter, and Amanda Cannon

SONOMA, PETALUMA ADOBE, AND OLOMPALI STATE HISTORIC PARKS

Northern San Francisco Bay Area, California

The Northern Frontier of Historic Alta California

During the Mexican Republic era (1822–46), the "Northern Frontier" of Alta California encompassed the northern San Francisco Bay area, including the areas now designated Sonoma, Petaluma Adobe, and Olompali State Historic Parks. Today, these three parks help capture a time in California's past when great changes were underway as the Native American control of the area gave way to Mexican rule and later to American conquest.

Prior to the arrival of Spanish explorers in the late eighteenth century, the northern San Francisco Bay area was home to the numerous small nations of the Coast Miwok, Pomo, Wappo, and Patwin tribes. The Coast Miwok and Patwin had lived in the area for about 4,000 years, and the Pomo and Wappo for even longer. The different tribal groups lived beside one another long enough for their cultures to take on numerous similarities.

The arrival of the Spaniards resulted in a rapid and massive change for the Bay Area's Native American cultures. The effects in the North Bay were measured at first but increased dramatically during the early nineteenth century. Perhaps most significant were the events that transpired during California's Mexican Republic era. It was during this time that the foreign conquest of Native land played out in earnest in the North Bay. The coming of the American era was a continuation of this same pattern. Today, the following units of the California State Park system preserve the remnants and story of this important period of California history.

SONOMA STATE HISTORIC PARK

Measuring 20 hectares (50 acres), Sonoma State Historic Park is situated immediately north of the historic Sonoma Plaza in the town of Sonoma in Sonoma County. The park encompasses numerous historic structures, including Mission San Francisco Solano (ca. 1823), the northernmost of California's Franciscan missions and the only mission founded under Mexican rule. The park also contains the Soldiers Barracks (ca. 1834), Servants Quarters (ca. 1834), Blue Wing Inn (ca. 1840s), and Vallejo Home and Carriage House (ca. 1850s). The park's historic structures and the associated cultural landscape are contributing elements to the Sonoma Plaza National Landmark. There are small museums located within the Mission, Barracks, and Carriage House, and a house museum is located at the Vallejo Home.

In 1823 Father Jose Altamira visited the Sonoma valley in order to establish Mission San Francisco Solano. Prior to that time, the site of the future mission was home to a Coast Miwok village known as *Huchi*. By the time Altamira arrived, however, Sonoma valley was likely devoid of inhabitants. The residents had been taken earlier to the missions at San Rafael and San Francisco, or had otherwise fled in advance of the Christian missionaries.

Mariano Vallejo arrived in the area in 1834, tasked with the secularization of Mission San Francisco Solano and the creation of a pueblo that would come to be called Sonoma. Vallejo oversaw a garrison of soldiers who were involved in periodic military engagements against local Native people deemed to be hostile toward the Californios. In the mid-1830s, Mariano began construction of a barracks for his troops and a residence for himself, both made of adobe. The residence, which Vallejo called the Casa Grande, was largely destroyed in the 1860s. Today, only a single wing (known as the Servants Quarters) of Vallejo's adobe home survives. The Soldiers Barracks also survives, as does a portion of the mission.

California's famous Bear Flag Revolt began on the Sonoma Plaza in 1846. The consequences of this action resulted in California's eventual annexation by the United States government. Following a three-month imprisonment by the Bear Flag revolutionaries, Vallejo returned home to discover that he had lost most of his fortune. A few years later, he built the American-style home known today as the Vallejo Home on a small plot at the outskirts of Sonoma.

The archaeological research that has been conducted in Sonoma over the past fifty years has helped to delineate the various structures and their associated features. In the 1950s, extensive archaeological work was conducted in the mission's courtyard by archaeologists associated with the University of California at Berkeley. Archaeology also played a prominent role in the 1970s restoration of the Soldiers Barracks. The mission's museum makes use of some of the information derived from the earlier archaeological investigations. The Sonoma Mission Indian Memorial, located on the west side of the mission, memorializes the names of the almost 900 Native Americans buried in the unmarked cemetery.

PETALUMA ADOBE STATE HISTORIC PARK

Petaluma Adobe State Historic Park measures 18 hectares (45 acres) and is located 4.8 kilometers (3 mi) east of the town of Petaluma in Sonoma County. The Petaluma Adobe is recorded as a national landmark and includes archaeological sites dating back about 5,000 years. Part of Mariano Vallejo's vast holdings, the Petaluma Rancho was the largest rancho in California during the Mexican Republic era. There is a visitors' center inside the adobe and a house museum as well. The adobe contains authentic furniture and exhibits depicting early rancho life. About half of the original two-story adobe is still standing.

Archaeological work conducted by Adan Treganza in the 1950s helped to identify the remainder of the adobe's foundations. More recently, archaeologist Stephen Silliman has identified a significant residential site (CA-SON-2294/H) utilized by Vallejo's Native American work force. Although the remains of residential structures have yet to be identified, Silliman's excavations documented various cooking features and an artifact-rich midden associated with the living site. Various tools of both aboriginal and Western manufacture were recovered, including glass and shell beads; bone, shell, and metal buttons; ceramics including English earthenware and Chinese porcelain; chipped-stone tools as well as tools chipped from broken bottle glass; cut nails; fragments of metal containers; and various other items suggesting a ranching lifestyle.

OLOMPALI STATE HISTORIC PARK

Measuring 304 hectares (760 acres), Olompali State Historic Park is located 1.6 kilometers (1 mi) north of the town of Novato in Marin County. The park is characterized by numerous archaeological sites, some of which date back at least 8,000 years. The archaeological inventory includes an important archaeological site, CA-MRN-193, that marks the ethnographic Coast Miwok village known as *Olompali*. The park also includes the Ynitia Adobe (ca. 1834) and the Burdell Garden (ca. 1870s). Along with CA-MRN-193, these two cultural features are contributing elements to Olompali's listing on the National Register of Historic Places. A visitors' center is located inside the historic Burdell House (ca. 1870s). The park's colorful history is interpreted with selected images and artifacts.

For the past fifty years, Olompali has been the scene of extensive archaeological research. Beginning in the 1950s, Adan Treganza tested the site in search of Elizabethan evidence that might link Olompali to the 1579 landfall of Sir Francis Drake. In the 1970s, archaeologist Charles Slaymaker recovered a silver sixpence from Olompali. The coin, minted in the Tower of London in 1567, was found along with two glass paste beads typical of the Elizabethan era. It is unknown whether these artifacts are associated with Drake's visit.

The research conducted by Slaymaker and others has revealed that Olompali was a major Coast Miwok trading center during the late prehistoric period. The Coast Miwok still make use of the site today, as several reconstructed family houses and other village structures will attest.

In 1834 Chief Camillo Ynitia was granted title to the Rancho Olompali land grant by the Mexican government. Ynitia was a friend and ally of General Vallejo, and was the only Native Californian to be given a land grant and succeed in maintaining ownership.

Further Reading: Carlson, Pamela McGuire, and E. Breck Parkman, "Exceptional Adaptation: Camillo Ynitia, the Last Headman of the Olompalis," *California History* 65(4) (1986): 238–247, 309–310; Kelly, Isabel, *Interviews with Tom Smith and Maria Copa: Isabel Kelly's Ethnographic Notes on the Coast Miwok Indians of Marin and Sonoma Counties, California*, edited by Sylvia B. Thalman and Mary Collier (San Rafael, CA: Miwok Archaeological Preserve of Marin, 1991); Silliman, Stephen W., *Lost Laborers in Colonial California: Native Americans and the Archaeology of Rancho Petaluma* (Tucson: University of Arizona Press, 2004); Smilie, Robert S., *The Sonoma Mission, San Francisco Solano de Sonoma: The Founding, Ruin, and Restoration of California's 21st Mission* (Fresno, CA: Valley Publishers, 1975).

E. Breck Parkman

PRESIDIO DE SAN FRANCISCO PARK, GOLDEN GATE NATIONAL RECREATION AREA

San Francisco, California

Native, Spanish, and Mexican Period Archaeology

The Presidio of San Francisco is a national park site measuring 596 hectares (1,491 acres). The Presidio was in continuous use as a military post from 1776 to 1994, serving under the flags of Spain, Mexico, and the United States. During the transition from an active army post to a national park, an update to the Presidio's National Historic Landmark designation was undertaken. This effort documented nearly 4,000 sites, buildings, structures, and objects as contributing features to the landmark, and the Presidio was reclassified as a National Historic Landmark District—the highest designation. Included were fifty-four locations of predicted archaeological significance, including forgotten cemeteries, shipwrecks, native shell mounds, coastal fortifications, and the cornerstone of the archaeology program, the Spanish colonial site El Presidio de San Francisco. Due to the Presidio's long continuum of history from colonialism until the Cold War, there is an array of important sites beyond the temporal and spatial boundaries of El Presidio, which make this park exceptional as an archaeological resource.

NATIVE CALIFORNIAN (OHLONE) SHELL MOUNDS

Before the arrival of colonists in 1776, the native population of the San Francisco Bay area was between 15,000 and 20,000 people. This population was not homogenous; they were divided into approximately fifty-five independent tribes who spoke at least five mutually unintelligible languages, including Ohlone, Coast Miwok, Bay Miwok, Patwin, and Wappo. Ethnographers estimate that the large villages in the area contained between 200 and 400 residents. The southern reaches of the Bay Area, including the San Francisco peninsula, is the traditional home of the Ohlone.

There have been three Ohlone sites documented at the Presidio. All of these were found along the edges of a historic marsh at the bay shore of the Presidio. University of California at Berkeley archaeologists E. W. Gifford and L. Loud documented the "Presidio Mound" in 1912 as the marsh was being filled in to prepare the ground for the Panama Pacific International Exposition. The exact location of this shell mound remained elusive until it was rediscovered in

Louis Choris's vision of the Presidio from a nearby hill in 1816.   [Courtesy of The Bancroft Library, University of California–Berkeley]

2002. Through radiocarbon, obsidian hydration, and shell bead dating the site is considered to have been occupied between AD 750 and 1350. In 1972 the remains of an isolated individual was discovered during construction in the same area; although not located within the mound, the radiocarbon dates conform with the early occupation of the site. More recently during a project to excavate and re-establish portions of the historic marsh in 1999, archaeologists uncovered a third site. In consultation with Ohlone descendant groups, the design of the new marsh was changed to preserve the site and incorporate the findings into trailside interpretation and education programs. This last shell midden had a date range of AD 1310–1795, prior to and potentially overlapping with the Spanish colonial period.

EL PRESIDIO DE SAN FRANCISCO

El Presidio de San Francisco was established in 1776 as the northernmost outpost of colonial New Spain to act as a defensive check against British, Russian, and French incursions into Alta California. El Presidio was the administrative center of a large colonial district stretching from the northern reaches of the San Francisco Bay, eastward into the Central Valley of California, and south along the Pacific coast to Monterey Bay. It was responsible for the defense of six missions, two civil communities, military and mission ranches, agricultural outposts, and land-grant ranchos.

The Presidio's recruited population did not come from Spain but from Mexico, predominately from the western regions of Sinaloa and Sonora. Soldiers with families were the premium recruits, consequently women and children constituted the majority of the colonial party. Many of these families inherited centuries of mixed ancestry and ascribed themselves to *castas* (racial/ethnic classes) including *español*, *mestizo*, *indio*, or *mulatto* according to a 1790 census. The influence of the enlightenment had some effect on this frontier, and the *castas* system was replaced with a basic two-class society of *gente de razón* (literally, "people of reason") and California Indians. Numbering less than 200, the colonial party would not meet the ethnographic criteria for a "large village" in the area, yet the soldiers dominated the region through fear, firepower, and bloodshed. By 1810 there would be over 11,000 Native people representing forty-five tribes from the region converted by the missionaries.

When colonists first arrived they laid out a fortified quadrangle measuring approximately 90 *varas* (1 vara ~ 33 in.) on each side; their construction plan conformed to prescriptions for presidios in the *Provincias Internas*. The early accounts describe dilapidated structures, inadequate materials, and the lack of skilled labor. Earthquakes and winter storms off the Pacific exacerbated these problems and debilitated the adobe walls yearly. In 1792 British Captain George Vancouver visited and noted that the Presidio was "ill accorded with the ideas we had conceived of the sumptuous manner in which the Spaniards live on this side of the globe." Within the same year Presidio Commandant Hermenegildo Sal submitted a report documenting the decrepit situation and indicted the negligence of government officials. He concluded with "All this that I manifest and expose is notorious and therefore I sign it." Submitted with Sal's diatribe was a plan drawing of the Presidio showing only three of the four defensive walls standing. Conditions improved and eventually there was a major reconstruction effort around 1815. This reconstruction was undertaken in response to major earthquakes in 1808 and 1812, the new Russian presence 100 kilometers (60 mi) north at Fort Ross, and the growing population's desire for better accommodations.

During this period, regular supply ships from Mexico were interrupted because of the ongoing War of Independence (1810–21), and the colonial population became more economically autonomous. Foreign ships such as Vancouver's often stopped in San Francisco Bay, gaining entrance by passing the strategically placed Presidio. Many captains sought to engage the Presidio and associated missions in trade to provision their ships, a common but nonetheless illicit activity under Spain's rule. A Russian scientific expedition in 1816 docked at San Francisco, collected plants, named species, and compiled a robust record of their observations. On board was a young artist named Louis Choris, who painted the Presidio from a nearby hill. At the conclusion of the war in Mexico priorities shifted; afterward the Presidio operated under a Mexican flag, and trade with foreign ships was liberalized.

The strategic importance of the Presidio at the Golden Gate declined during the Mexican Republican era. Eventually the garrison was moved north to Sonoma in 1835 by Mariano Vallejo to be closer to the Russians at Fort Ross. A detachment of artillerymen were left to man the post, but El Presidio was effectively abandoned and partially ruined when the U.S. Army arrived in 1846.

Archaeological research at the site began in the 1990s. As the U.S. Army was preparing to leave the Presidio, utility workers exposed substantial stone foundations behind the Civil War–era officers' quarters. The U.S. Army had not built anything prior to these quarters, yet undoubtedly a massive structure once stood there. Archaeologists excavated at intervals along the foundation's alignment to reveal an expansive fortified structure measuring approximately 152 meters (500 ft) on each of four sides—El Presidio. Research focused first on understanding the general form and composition of the structural remains, which included multiple periods of construction. This identification was followed by detailed work on selected parts of the southern and eastern room blocks to develop further detail on the chapel and residential barracks. El Presidio's 1815 layout is clearly recognizable through excavation, although earlier phases of construction remain difficult to identify. The structure revealed through excavation is approximately 2.5 times larger than the plan submitted by Commandant Sal in 1792.

Aside from architectural remains, field investigations at the site have generated a robust collection of artifacts. By far the most concentrated samples have come from middens, although smaller samples of materials have been recovered from room floors, hearths, and artifact scatters across the site. The faunal remains (animal bones) recovered have provided a rich body of data for analysis of dietary practices. Cattle provided the majority of meat eaten. Domesticated fowl, especially chicken, are plentiful. Midden deposits formed during the first decades of the settlement's history also have significant remains of wild species. Deer and rabbit are the most common, but coyote, wolf, gray fox, grizzly bear, and bobcat have also been identified. Wild birds include quail, ducks, geese, and murre. Despite the abundance of local shellfish and the contribution it made to Ohlone diets, shell has not been found in significant numbers in colonial deposits.

There is little archaeological evidence of trade between Spanish colonists and Native Californian groups at El Presidio. There are only two areas at the settlement that have yielded substantial numbers of artifacts usually associated with Native traditions. Both of these lie outside the walls of the main quadrangle. The first feature is a large deposit, located immediately north of the main quadrangle, that contains several indicators of a Native American presence, including shellfish remains, lithic tools, and several hand-formed conical clay pipes. This deposit yields considerable information about the Native laborers who were documented to have worked at the Presidio. The second site is located in an area known as El Polín Springs (discussed later).

One extant colonial structure remains in use at the Presidio: the Officers' Club. Although masked beneath several U.S. period facades and a restoration attempt in the 1930s, it is an essential part of the modern landscape overlooking the plaza de armas. The standing building offers opportunity for clarification of architectural style and techniques often left unresolved through subsurface archaeology. The Officers' Club is one of the centers of engagement for archaeology at the Presidio and is open to the public. The entrance is flanked with two of the oldest cannons in the country, which were already over a century old when they arrived at El Presidio in the late 1700s. Inside is the Mesa Room, partially deconstructed to expose the multiple interior facades and different building episodes they reflect—from 1960s drywall to colonial era adobe—for public interpretation. Outside, adjacent to the standing structure, is an interpretive landscape representing the subsurface foundations of the 1780 chapel and sacristy.

El Presidio is remarkably well preserved despite the nearby urban environment. Consequently, many of the deposits encountered through excavation can be securely dated to discrete time periods and in some cases can be linked to specific segments of the settlement's population. Although the general dimensions of the site are understood, and archaeologists are repeatedly surprised by its rich contents, the majority of the site remains unknown and unexcavated.

EL POLÍN SPRINGS IN TENNESSEE HOLLOW

Daily life at the settlement of El Presidio de San Francisco extended far beyond the walls of the quadrangle, and colonists and Native Californians established residences, small farms, and work camps in the surrounding landscape. Archaeological research in the valley located immediately to the east of the colonial quadrangle has uncovered evidence of at least three colonial-era residential sites, each located along the streams collectively known today as the Tennessee Hollow Watershed. The southernmost of these, El Polín Springs, was excavated in 1998 and in 2003–04. The area is known to have been the home of a large colonial family that included Juana Briones, who has gained historic notice because of her prominence as a healer, agriculturalist, and businesswoman in Spanish-colonial and Mexican-era San Francisco. Excavations of the Briones home site revealed the remains of an adobe house along with associated refuse deposits and evidence of substantial landform modifications such as cuts into the valley hillsides and water impoundments. The deposits at El Polín Springs and other sites along the valley floor are especially significant in that they contain a mixture of colonial material culture (imported and locally produced ceramics, glass bottle fragments, metal hardware) and Native Californian material culture (worked shell, flaked stone artifacts and debitage, and ground stone artifacts). Although the main quadrangle of the Presidio was largely deserted after 1837, both archaeological and historical evidence indicate that this extramural neighborhood thrived well into the American period, its occupants departing only after the U.S. Army seized control of the area in 1849–50.

EARLY U.S. ARMY AT THE MAIN POST

The U.S. Army reused the derelict adobe structures they seized at El Presidio and spent much of the early years rehabilitating those structures while endeavoring to maintain their numbers and discipline during the gold rush. At least one old Mexican artilleryman refused to relinquish buildings that he claimed as payment for many years of service otherwise unpaid. Little else changed on the Presidio landscape until the beginning of the Civil War, when new barracks for the soldiers, a powder magazine, officers' quarters, a hospital, and housing for the laundresses were constructed. Examples of many of these buildings still remain throughout the main post.

The population at the post was stratified between officers and their families and enlisted soldiers, laundresses, and their families. The annual report in 1857 described one old adobe (the future Officers' Club) to be "objectionable as Officers' Quarters, being dark, badly ventilated, damp and muddy in winter, dusty in summer, and in disagreeable proximity to the barracks of the enlisted men." It was, however, recommended for use as quarters for the laundresses.

Officers at the Presidio enjoyed a relatively privileged lifestyle, often owning side businesses and engaging socially with San Francisco elites. Complaints were made routinely to the War Department regarding their substandard adobe dwellings. In 1862 twelve identical cottages were constructed for officers; six of these were constructed on top of the eastern facade of El Presidio. These were designed as single-family homes that faced westward onto the parade ground. The rear yards of these cottages contained all the trappings of mid-nineteenth-century domestic life—outhouses, chicken coops, gardens, trash pits, and other such remains. As the burgeoning city of San Francisco expanded to the west, ever closer to the Presidio, the U.S. Army decided to reorient these prominent buildings so they fronted the encroaching city. By 1879 the cottages had a new orientation, and by 1884 indoor water closets were installed. These buildings remain today along Funston Avenue and create the oldest streetscape in San Francisco.

Due to the reorientation of the twelve officers' cottages, there are a variety of archaeological features in what were the rear yards (now the front yards) dating from a discrete sixteen-year time period during the Civil War and Reconstruction. In 1999 and 2000 archaeologists began excavations into these yard features based on ground-penetrating radar and gradiometer surveys of the area. Rich deposits of artifacts were uncovered from each of these sites that document the domestic life of officers and their families.

During much of the nineteenth century the U.S. Army employed female civilians as laundresses; these women were responsible for washing linens as well as performing a variety of other tasks, which may have included working as hospital matrons, cooks, maids, or seamstresses. Although they held official positions with the army, laundresses were a socially marginalized group. Laundresses were often housed in derelict adobe buildings at the Presidio or located at a distance from the developing center of the post. In 1876 the post quartermaster in his annual summary to the War Department described the laundresses quarters as "mere shells at best." Most of these quarters were removed during episodes of post beautification.

There is little historic documentation about the laundresses, but the archaeological signature of these poorly understood women is the focus of continuing investigation. In 2005 several privies associated with the laundresses were identified and excavated along Taylor Road behind the stately Montgomery Street barracks (1895). Analysis has provided information about the laundresses' livelihood, diet, consumer profile, and sanitation practices.

Developing robust datasets from these excavated sites allows researchers to begin to compare the lives and routines of the officers and their families with those of the laundresses and their families at the same frontier post during the same time period. This research provides insight into the class and gender divisions that shaped these military communities and structured society in the American West. Literally by digging deeper in some areas, further cross-cultural comparisons can be made between both of these groups and the Spanish colonial and Mexican families that preceded them.

COAST FORTIFICATIONS AND BATTERIES

The coast of the Presidio has been described as an outdoor museum of coastal fortifications through time. Throughout the colonial and post-colonial periods the strategic imperative for the Presidio was to protect the valuable harbor of San Francisco Bay. When the original colonizing expedition, led by Juan Bautista de Anza, reached the area in 1776, Father Pedro Font (whose diary of the expedition is a rich source of information) immediately recognized the value of the bay, which he called "a marvel of nature, and . . . a harbor of harbors, because of its great capacity." Font continued by describing a point of land that created the narrow entrance later called the Golden Gate as "being on a height, it is so commanding that with muskets it can defend the entrance." Soon thereafter the colonial soldiers established the Castillo de San Joaquin at this point, built of adobe ramparts with mounted cannons to guard the entrance. Lieutenant John Fremont and his cohort scaled this point and spiked the old Spanish cannons at the Castillo during the Bear Flag Revolt in 1846. The strategic importance of this point was immediately apparent to the U.S. commanders, and construction began on a brick fortress in 1853, called Fort Point, to protect gold supplies and commerce. Fort Point was nearly obsolete soon after completion with the advent of rifled cannon and ironside ships. Earthwork fortifications with concealed gun emplacements were developed in 1876 to counter the new naval technology and were constructed further up the bluff flanking Fort Point. Later, in 1895, a new series of massive and in some cases experimental weapons systems were developed to defend the coast. This system of batteries could launch projectiles up to 22 kilometers (14 mi) into the Pacific. The advancement of technology and investment in these fortifications freed the U.S. Navy from their defensive mission and allowed U.S. ships to venture further into the Pacific.

MARINE HOSPITAL CEMETERY

The Presidio is home to a national cemetery but also contains a long-forgotten Merchant Marine cemetery at the site of a former Marine Hospital. The cemetery was never widely known,

although the *San Francisco Call* described it in 1896 as "in a valley dreary with stunted growths and hummocks of half-tamed sand dunes, long rows of white posts bearing names and dates . . . intrude upon the landscape." The cemetery remained in use from 1881 to 1912. It was abandoned and in ruins by the 1930s and finally covered by construction fill and a parking lot by the 1970s. The cemetery's history lay hidden almost entirely in secret until research recovered evidence of the historic cemetery in 1989 during the closure of the post. Since that time, archival research and limited archaeological testing have revealed additional information about this lost resting place. Archival research has focused on understanding the cemetery's history and identifying as many of its occupants as possible. It is estimated that 838 individuals are likely interred there from thirty U.S. states or territories and forty-two different foreign countries. Incidental knowledge about the lives and deaths of seafarers at the turn of the twentieth century has also been recorded, from common causes of death to shipping routes to the importance of personal effects, as well as information about the Marine Hospital itself.

Further Reading: *Archaeology at the Presidio,* http://www.presidio.gov/history/archaeology; Blind, E. B., B. L. Voss, S. K. Osborn, and L. R. Barker, "El Presidio de San Francisco: At the Edge of Empire," *Historical Archaeology* 38(3) (2004): 135–149; Langellier, John, and Daniel Rosen, *El Presidio de San Francisco: A History under Spain and Mexico 1776–1846* (Spokane, WA: Arthur H. Clark, 1996); Milliken, Randall, *A Time of Little Choice: The Disintegration of Tribal Culture in the San Francisco Bay Area 1769–1810* (Menlo Park, CA: Ballena Press, 1995); Osio, Antonio, *The History of Alta California: A Memoir of Mexican California,* translated by Rose Marie Beebe and Robert M. Senkewicz (Madison: University of Wisconsin Press, 1996); *Presidio of San Francisco,* National Park Service Web site, http://www.nps.gov/archive/prsf/history/hrs/thompson/thompson.htm; Voss, B. L. *The Archaeology of Ethnogenesis: Race and Sexuality in Colonial San Francisco* (Berkeley: University of California Press, 2008).

Eric Brandan Blind, Sannie Kenton Osborn,
Barbara L. Voss, and Liz N. Clevenger

MISSION SAN DIEGO DE ALCALA, LA PURISIMA STATE HISTORIC PARK, AND OTHER HISTORIC SITES

Los Angeles and San Diego Areas, Coastal Southern California

Spanish and Mexican Missions, Presidios, and Ranchos

Coastal southern California, the western areas of Santa Barbara, Ventura, Los Angeles, Orange, and San Diego Counties, boasts a rich cultural history. The region has a dynamic multiethnic past that includes marked historical

shifts of power from Native American to Spanish to Mexican to U.S. American governance. However, its historical diversity is currently challenged by rampant development. Many of the region's unique and nonrenewable historic resources face an intense struggle to remain part of the local landscape.

Home to numerous distinct indigenous tribes for nearly 10,000 years, coastal southern California was first explored by Europeans in 1542 by Juan Rodriguez Cabrillo, a Portuguese navigator sailing for the Spanish crown. Historical records indicate that no other Westerners investigated the region until Sebastian Vizcaino's 1602 landing, which preceded another lengthy hiatus. The first substantive European presence in coastal southern California began with the northward expansion of Spain's mission system in 1769. For the next fifty-two years, clerics and soldiers established a series of missions and presidio military compounds. Mexico's independence from Spain in 1821 started a twenty-seven-year period of local governance, typified by the secularization of the missions and the creation of numerous ranchos through extensive land grants. Mexican control of the region ended with the Mexican-American War (1846–48) and the consequent U.S. acquisition of California in 1848. Although the early U.S. American period (1848–80) witnessed little growth, it led to the late nineteenth- and early twentieth-century development golden age for the region that burgeoned with railroads, business centers, and international expositions.

Historical sites in coastal southern California have witnessed extensive archaeological excavations. The missions in particular have been repeatedly investigated by archaeologists, and as a result many of these sites are open to the public and have associated museum displays. The following historical sites are discussed temporally and include examples from each of the aforementioned historical periods. They are all open to the public.

Cabrillo National Monument is located at the southern tip of San Diego's Point Loma; it commemorates Cabrillo's 1542 exploration of the southern Californian coastline and includes the 1854 Old Point Loma lighthouse as part of its interpretive exhibits. Although little archaeological work has been conducted in the area, there is great potential for significant underwater finds.

The Royal Presidio of San Diego, established in 1769, was the Pacific Coast's first permanent European settlement and Spain's colonial base of operations for California. When the Mexican army took possession of the Presidio in 1822, it soon became the Mexican governor's residence. In 1929 Presidio Hill was established as a park. A series of extensive excavations at the Presidio over the last four decades located the chapel complex and tens of thousands of artifacts. The Serra Museum is located next to the park; it includes a wide array of archaeological finds from Native American, Spanish, Mexican, and U.S. American periods.

Mission San Diego de Alcala was the first of the twenty-one Franciscan Alta California missions. Founded in 1769, the mission was burned during an indigenous attack in 1775, reconstructed in 1776, expanded in 1780, damaged by an earthquake in 1803, and reconstructed in its current form in

1808. The mission was gradually abandoned during the Mexican period and subsequently occupied by the U.S. cavalry. President Lincoln returned the mission to church ownership in 1862. Excavations at this "Mother of the Missions" have detailed the site's architectural sequence and uncovered numerous artifacts, many of which are showcased in the visitors' center museum.

Father Junipero Serra dedicated the adobe chapel of Mission San Juan Capistrano in 1778. The mission complex included a variety of buildings, gardens, and walkways and was completed in 1812. Archaeological, historical, and architectural investigations have been critical in reconstructing various living quarters and storehouses. Known for its Great Stone Church, scenic gardens, and migratory swallows, Mission San Juan Capistrano also has an active museum.

The Los Angeles Plaza Historic District was the center of activity in Los Angeles during the Spanish, Mexican, and U.S. American periods. Bounded by Spring, Macy, Alameda, and Arcadia Streets, it includes the 1781 Pueblo de Los Angeles, the 1818 Avile Adobe, the 1858 Masonic Hall, the 1869 Merced Theater, and many other significant nineteenth-century structures. Four of the plaza's twenty-seven historic buildings have been restored as museums, some of which have extensive archaeological displays based on decades of excavation.

Established in 1787, the Mission de la Purisima Concepcion de Maria Santisima was once an elaborate complex with military buildings outside of the large quadrangle that enclosed the chapel. An earthquake leveled the mission in 1812, and it was abandoned. In 1874 the Lompoc Temperance colony acquired the land; their township slowly grew to cover almost the entire original mission site. The only remaining ruins of the original mission are between E and G streets in the block south of Locust Avenue.

A second La Purisima mission, known today simply as "La Purisima Mission," was completed in 1818 to service the inhabitants of the first La Purisima mission following the earthquake. It fell into disrepair during the Mexican period. In the 1930s, the Civilian Conservation Corps reconstructed many of the mission buildings. Archaeological investigations during the 1960s added additional insight into the material past. Today, La Purisima Mission is a State Historic Park that has just finished building a new visitors' center complex, which is now open to the public.

Old Town San Diego State Historic Park is the center of an active living history program that includes multiple original structures and a museum. Drawing on history, archaeology, architectural history, and anthropology, the park re-creates daily life in San Diego during the Mexican and early U.S. American periods (1821–80). It contains five original adobes and an assortment of dwellings, offices, and shops, many of which showcase artifacts from past archaeological excavations in the area. Located on San Diego Avenue and Twiggs Street, Old Town San Diego State Historic Park is in the heart of Old Town and just down the street from El Campo Santo, an historic and publicly accessible cemetery that saw extensive activity from 1849 to 1890.

Sepulveda Adobe is a rural adobe in the middle of the Santa Monica Mountain range that was built in 1863. Located near numerous prehistoric, protohistoric, and historical Chumash Indian archaeological sites, Pedro Sepulveda built the adobe after his previous home adjacent to nearby Las Virgenes Creek was destroyed by a flood. The Sepulvedas raised a dozen children in the adobe during the late nineteenth century, farming the nearby land and selling firewood. Located on Mulholland Highway, a block west of Las Virgenes Road in Malibu Creek State Park, the adobe was restored in 2003 and is now open to the public.

Balboa Park's California Quadrangle was the main entrance to San Diego's 1915 Panama-California International Exposition. Held in conjunction with San Francisco's Panama-Pacific Exposition to honor the completion of the Panama Canal, San Diego's exposition celebrated its own Spanish heritage. Architect Bertram Goodhue designed buildings for the exhibition that were heavily influenced by colonial Spanish architecture. As a result, the park's landscape is dominated by stark white buildings with ornate sculptural relief, colorful roof tiles, elaborate towers, and imposing domes. Although Balboa Park did not have an active archaeological program that influenced these structures, the California Quadrangle houses the Museum of Man, which boasts an extensive archaeological archive and numerous exhibits.

El Camino Real is not a site, a mission, an adobe, or a park, but it is a most important part of historical California's cultural landscape that started at the Royal Presidio of San Diego. Originally a footpath to connect the Spanish missions, El Camino Real became a roadway for horses and wagons when the last mission in Sonoma was completed in 1823. Translated as "The King's Highway," El Camino Real was slowly replaced by increasingly advanced roads over time; U.S. 101 is situated on much of the original route. As parts of repeated preservation movements, an extensive series of hundreds of cast-iron bells hung from guideposts have been erected along the historic route.

Further Reading: Ezell, Paul, "The Excavation Program at San Diego Presidio," *Journal of San Diego History* 16(4) (1976): 1–20; Deetz, James, "Archaeological Investigations at La Purisima Mission," *Archaeological Survey Annual Report* 5 (1963): 161–241; Farnsworth, Paul, "Missions, Indians, and Cultural Continuity," *Historical Archaeology* 26(1) (1992): 22–36; Lightfoot, Kent G., *Indians, Missionaries, and Merchants: The Legacy of Colonial Encounters on the California Frontiers* (Berkeley: University of California Press, 2005); Mallios, Seth, and David M. Caterino, *Cemeteries of San Diego* (Charleston, SC: Arcadia, 2007).

Seth Mallios

OLD SACRAMENTO, SUTTER'S FORT, AND WALNUT GROVE/LOCKE SITES

Sacramento Area, Central Valley, California

The Gold Rush and Chinese Immigrants

Historical occupation of California's Central Valley began in the 1830s, when the Mexican government awarded title to vast acres of land to those with proven loyalty to the Mexican government. These ranchos were separated by many miles and often included a central ranch compound, hide and tallow processing areas, grist mills, sawmills, dairies, and other activity areas necessary to sustain a ranch operation. Men such as John Marsh, Johann A. Sutter, John Bidwell, and William B. Ides raised cattle and planted grains and crops on their ranchos, aided by local Native American laborers and workers imported from other countries.

In January 1848 an employee of Sutter's, James Wilson Marshall, found traces of gold in Sutter's sawmill, triggering an international phenomena that continued for over a decade. In the wake of Marshall's discovery thousands of people flowed into California, towns sprang up and disappeared in a blink of an eye, and the rancho way of life gave way to a fast-paced profiteering society. Sacramento, a hub for river traffic from San Francisco, was formed during the gold rush.

As readily available gold disappeared, many of the miners remained in California, lured by rich soils, wide-open spaces, and agricultural potential. In the 1860s and 1870s railroads were built and islands were reclaimed by a large Chinese immigrant work force. The reclaimed islands were planted with fruits and vegetables. Large ranches, many thousands of acres in size, gave way to small homesteads of 8–64 hectares (20–160 acres) by the 1920s.

Initial historical archaeology studies in the Central Valley concentrated on places associated with pivotal events or figures in California history. The few adobes that dotted the interior in the 1830s and 1840s often were abandoned and in ruins by 1900. Although Central Valley archaeology of historic sites started with a "famous places in history" perspective, it has evolved to include studies of the day-to-day lives and living sites of farmers, merchants, loggers, immigrants, and many others who came to California after 1850. Archaeologists working in the Sacramento River delta, for example, have studied the labor camps that ringed the reclaimed islands as well as the towns, such as Locke and Walnut Grove, that served as hubs for the workers.

SUTTER'S FORT

Archaeologists began to study historic-era sites in the Central Valley in the 1950s, drawn by the mystique and romance of the gold rush era. One of the key sites in this early work was the fort built by Johann August Sutter in 1841. Sutter traveled up the Sacramento River from San Francisco in 1839 with the hope of establishing a ranch in the largely uninhabited country. Within two years he applied for, and was granted, Mexican citizenship and a Mexican land grant entitling him to 22,000 leagues or 19,532 hectares (48,830 acres or about 75 mi²) in the middle of the Central Valley.

Sutter built a small, three-room adobe house on a slight rise, eventually surrounding the house with adobe walls 18 feet (5.5 meters [m]) high. Sutter's Fort became the symbol of a journey's end to immigrants traveling over the Sierra Nevada range in the mid- to late 1840s, representing a sanctuary and place to heal after a grueling journey. When gold was discovered in Sutter's sawmill in 1848, his land and home was overrun by thousands of miners with no regard for property rights or legal claims. He sold the fort in 1849 and eventually returned to Europe with little to show for his California adventure. By 1857 the fort was partially in ruins in the center of Sacramento. Recognizing its significance in California history, the state took steps to purchase and preserve this important symbol of early California and obtained title in the 1890s.

Initial attempts to reconstruct the fort were based on written descriptions and a few sketches made by travelers passing through during the gold rush. In 1888 the exterior walls were low mounds and the house was dilapidated. Excavations occurred in that year to locate the southwest corner of the original fort and the colliery (coal and charcoal storage area). Archaeological excavations started in earnest in 1955 to determine the architectural extent, layout and design of the site. This work established the original position of a number of adobe walls and determined the locations of two wells and the shoemaker shop. Subsequent research has identified the work space of a blanket maker, the blacksmith, a brewery, other work areas, and the barracks.

Today the focal point of the fort is Sutter's 1841 adobe house. Walls 15 feet high (4.6 m) surround the house and fort compound. The California State Park system has used archaeological results, extensive archival research, and maps to recreate and interpret the 1846 atmosphere of the site. Visitors experience living history exhibits and can question working blacksmiths, bakers, and candle, shoe, and blanket makers. Activity areas within the fort, based on archaeological results and research, are amply illustrated through actual or replicated artifacts. Archaeologists monitoring development project and road work in the immediate vicinity of the fort often expose random interments from Sutter's era, such as musket balls and 1840s trash deposits, continuing to add to Sutter's rich archaeological and historical legacy.

OLD SACRAMENTO

In January 1848 James Marshall found gold at Sutter's mill, setting off a worldwide race for riches. The quickest way to the mines was sailing upriver from San Francisco to Sutter's embarcadero and then striking out overland into the Sierra Nevada foothills. Sacramento was laid out at the embarcadero in December of 1848. A year later over 9,000 people lived in the city. Journal entries of miners passing through in 1850 describe a riverfront clogged with abandoned ships, a few wood-frame buildings, and makeshift structures and tents stretching east toward the gold county.

The first twelve years of Sacramento's history was marked by a series of fires and floods. After every fire and flood, rebuilding began immediately, with new buildings thrown up virtually overnight on the ruins of the old structures. This rebuilding created layers of occupation, separated by silt deposits from floods. The burned strata—layers of ash and charcoal—contained collections of artifacts with closely dated information on Sacramento's early history, a treasure trove for archaeologists working in the historic district.

The sixth flood in ten years hit in 1862 and flattened the city. The early city planners of Sacramento built brick buttresses and raised the streets up to 12 feet (3.6 m) above the original ground level, filling in the spaces between the brick walls with sand. In response to the raised streets, land owners jacked up or added onto the top floors of their buildings, abandoning the lower levels. This action protected Sacramento from rising river waters in winter and sealed evidence of the pre-1862 past below the newly raised city landscape.

Archaeologists have been exploring these deeply buried and sealed deposits since 1966. Initially work focused on defining architectural remains as an aid to reconstruction or renovation of mid-nineteenth-century buildings on site. The early excavations exposed parts of seven buildings, including the Carroll and the Cothrin and Potter sites, both stores burned with all the merchandise in 1852. Work at the Carroll site recovered a large collection of clay smoking pipes, buttons, and other goods and allowed for a reconstruction of the store interior. Archaeologists recovered thousands of identifiable seeds, clay pipes, hoes, shovels, pickle, ale bottles, and other goods from the Cothrin and Potter store.

Additional excavations occurred every year between 1970 and 1979 and uncovered many intact sealed deposits rich in artifacts from the Hastings Store, the Eagle Theater, Golden Eagle and City hotel, Hannan's Saloon, the Central Pacific Railroad depot, and other commercial ventures. Recovered collections represented by coins, bottled products, dishes and other artifacts from around the world illustrate the international flavor of gold rush–era Sacramento. Remote sensing and underwater reconnaissance undertaken in the 1980s identified several shipwrecks at the foot of Old Sacramento that also reflect the gold rush history of the city.

Many of the artifacts uncovered in Old Sacramento, as well as representations of Sacramento's unique fire and flood strata, are used in exhibits within the Discovery Museum and the State Railroad Museum. The facilities anchor the north side of the three-block-square Old Sacramento district. The restoration and reconstruction work in the 1970s has resulted in a vibrant historic district with the feel of the mid-nineteenth century, although merchants, restaurants, bars, and novelty shops are modern. The district fronts on the Sacramento River as well as the cobblestone streets, horse and buggy rides, and steam-train excursions along the waterfront contribute to the historic atmosphere. Underground walking tours of Old Sacramento (available as of summer 2007) afford an opportunity for visitors to descend beneath the modern city and walk the sidewalks of 1850s Sacramento, view the original store fronts abandoned in the 1860s, and experience firsthand the historical archaeology that lies 12 feet (3.6 m) below the streets of Old Sacramento.

LOCKE/WALNUT GROVE

From the 1850s into the twentieth century Chinese immigrants formed the backbone of California's labor force. Like their international counterparts, Chinese men were drawn to "Gum Shan" (Gold Mountain) by the promise of riches. As the gold rush waned, the Chinese miners, joined by 10,000 new immigrants from China, found work building a railroad to connect the new state to the eastern United States. After the railroad was completed reclamation began, and the Chinese work force turned their skills to levee building, reclamation, and finally to agriculture, becoming experts in the fruit industry.

Archaeologists began digging Chinese sites in the 1970s, drawn by the exotic artifacts and rich material culture. Initial work focused on railroad construction camps and urban community centers. Dozens of sites have been explored over the past thirty years, including mining camps, laundries, stores, social halls, cemeteries, and a wide range of commercial and residential sites occupied by Chinese.

Chinese settled along the Sacramento and San Joaquin rivers by 1870, building levees and clearing land for farming. By the early 1900s small delta towns often included a Chinese district that housed a core population of merchants, barbers, doctors, and others who provided services to a labor force numbering in the thousands. On Sundays these towns were packed with workers who came for supplies, haircuts, conversation, gaming, and food. One of these Chinese communities, Walnut Grove, burned in 1915. During rebuilding efforts a group of Heungshan Chinese from Kwangtung Province moved 1 mile (1.6 km) north, building their own town—Locke—the only all-Chinese community in California.

In 1984 historical archaeologists working in Walnut Grove uncovered over forty deposits under the streets of the old Chinese district. Many of these trash deposits represented cleanup activities from the 1915 fire. Among the rich assortment of ceramics, bottles, and brass artifacts were nine floor safes recovered in various alcoves and tunnels that ran under the main street of the district. These tunnels appeared to connect various buildings by underground passages. Excavations also occurred in Locke. The varied deposits of ceramics, faunal material, and glass that were unearthed indicate the retention of a rich traditional cultural heritage.

Today the narrow streets, closely spaced false front wood buildings, and Chinese signage in the three-block town of Locke draw visitors from around the world. Artifacts from Walnut Grove and Locke are displayed at the local Dai Loy Museum, a 1920s gambling hall abandoned with all its furnishings in place and preserved. The 1920s and 1930s Joe Soon Chinese Language School and a nearly completed state-run museum highlight the Chinese experience in the delta and the traditional culture that perseveres in Locke.

Further Reading: California State Department of Parks and Recreation, Marshall Gold Discovery State Historic Park, California State Parks Web site, http://www.parks.ca.gov/?page_id=23741 (online April 2007); Costello, Julia, and Mary L. Maniery, *Rice Bowls in the Delta: Artifacts Recovered from the 1915 Asian Community of Walnut Grove, California*, Occasional Paper No. 16, Institute of Archaeology (Los Angeles: University of California, 1986); Foster, John W., "The Sterling: A Lost But Not forgotten Gold Rush Shipwreck on the Sacramento Riverfront" (1986), California State Parks Web site, http://www.parks.ca.gov/?page_id=23523 (online April 2007); Kelly, John, and George Stammerjohan, *John Sutter and His Fort*, special Sutter's Fort Issue, *Dogtown Territorial Quarterly* 19 (1994); Leung, Peter, *One Day One Dollar* (El Cerrito, CA: Chinese/Chinese American History Project, 1984); McHenry, Rosanne Smith, *From Ruins to Renown: The Story of Old Sacramento's Restoration*, special Sutter's Fort Issue, *Dogtown Territorial Quarterly* 19 (1994); Schultz, Peter, and Betty J. Rivers, eds., *Papers on Old Sacramento Archaeology*, California Archaeological Reports No. 19 (Sacramento: State of California Department of Parks and Recreation, 1980).

Mary L. Maniery

BODIE STATE HISTORIC PARK, WILDROSE KILNS, AND MANZANAR NATIONAL HISTORIC SITE

Mono County and Owens Valley, Eastern California
Historic Mining Sites and World War II Internment Camp

This essay describes three relatively late (nineteenth- and twentieth-century) historic period archaeological sites on the eastern boundary of the West Coast region. In the arid foothills and valleys of eastern California, gold and silver deposits drew people and companies intent upon extracting these precious and valuable minerals. The town of Bodie and the kilns of Wildrose Canyon represent the archaeological remains of this historic mining enterprise. In the twentieth century the dry, remote landscape was the scene of a dark chapter in the story of American democracy. Early during World War II, communities of Japanese Americans were relocated from homes along the West Coast to internment camps inland. History proved the fear-driven hysteria that led to these relocations to be unjustified. Manzanar National Historic Site recognizes these wartime excesses and commemorates the heroic endurance of the Americans imprisoned unconstitutionally by their own government at a time of war.

BODIE STATE HISTORIC PARK (CALIFORNIA STATE HISTORIC LANDMARK NO. 341), MONO COUNTY, EASTERN CALIFORNIA

For many visitors, Bodie is the quintessential Wild West ghost town, with its silent wooden buildings clustered on a high, wind-swept ridge in the Bodie Hills of eastern California. But in its brief heyday, from 1877 to 1888, Bodie was a mining boomtown—the site of one of the biggest gold and silver strikes in California history.

In the spring of 1874, as nearby mining camps in Nevada were beginning to fade, a cave-in at the Bunker Hill Mine exposed a rich vein of ore that triggered a rush to Bodie. People poured in from Virginia City and Gold Hill, from Sacramento, even from San Francisco. Chinese and Irishmen who had built the Transcontinental Railroad, veterans of the American Civil War, miners who had failed to strike it rich on the Comstock or the Mother Lode, all headed to Bodie. By 1879 the little mountain town of two dozen people had grown to some 8,000 residents.

In those days Bodie had a well-earned reputation for rowdiness: the local "sports" were drinking, gambling, claim jumping, and fistfighting. Shootings were daily events. But this "City in the Sky," so named for its elevation of 8,400 feet, also boasted four newspapers, two banks, several hotels, eating houses, breweries, general stores, barber shops, a volunteer fire brigade, a post office, an opera house, and a school. The residents formed many social and fraternal organizations, established a miners

union, and held public dances and Fourth of July parades complete with music, flags, and bunting.

Wages in the Bodie mines were high by nineteenth-century standards: $4 for a twelve-hour shift, six days a week. For a time, the stamp mills ran twenty-four hours a day. Freight wagons traveled up Bodie Canyon bringing food, lumber, dry goods, and machinery; stages rolled in full of passengers and left full of bullion. Main Street was a mile-long artery in the summer, and during the spring thaw it became a river of mud that trapped wagons and pack mules. Behind Main Street ran Bonanza Street, with the mining-town requisite red-light district. Along King Street on the northeast edge of town, the residents of California's second-largest nineteenth-century Chinatown sold vegetables, chicken, pork, and fish.

But Bodie also had its hardships. Winter nighttime temperatures often fell to 20° F below zero, and many people died of pneumonia. Mine cave-ins were a real danger. And like every western frontier town, where most of the buildings were made of wood or canvas, Bodie faced the constant threat of fire. On July 25, 1892, a kitchen fire escaped and spread quickly through town, destroying some sixty buildings. Although the town survived, it had already begun to decline, and by the turn of the century the population had shrunk to 500. In 1917 the Bodie Railroad was sold for scrap. Another fire, this one in 1932, destroyed much of the remaining town.

In 1961 Bodie was designated a National Historic Landmark, and in 1962 a State Historic Park. In 2002 it was designated California's official State Gold Rush Ghost Town. Only a small vestige of the town still stands, preserved in what historians and archaeologists call a "state of arrested decay." Several of the surviving structures were private homes, and in some of them are original furnishings, dishes, even canned goods, just as they were left when the residents departed. Bodie State Historic Park is open to visitors for most of the year, although deep winter snows make it inaccessible to all but snowmobile traffic. The Park is located on State Route 270, 12.8 miles east of SR 395 and roughly 20 miles southeast of Bridgeport.

WILDROSE CHARCOAL KILNS, DEATH VALLEY NATIONAL PARK, INYO COUNTY, EASTERN CALIFORNIA

Ten large beehive-shaped stone kilns line a narrow canyon in the pinyon woodlands of the Panamint Range high up above Death Valley. Pinyon pine and juniper wood was converted into charcoal in these kilns during a brief period between 1877 and 1878 and then hauled to silver mining camps some 25 miles west in the Argus Range. There, the charcoal fueled furnaces that produced the precious metal. Similar kilns are found in other wooded areas in the western United States, but the Wildrose kilns are remarkably well preserved. They help to evoke the operations of this lost industrial art, which was critical to the success of mining in the nineteenth century.

The kilns were funded and operated by the Modock Consolidated Mining Company; Senator George Hearst, the father of newspaper magnate and San Simeon builder William Randolph Hearst, was one of the directors of this company. About forty woodcutters and burners labored at the kilns. Many of the workers probably came from Mexico, and there are indications that there were also Native American and Chinese laborers. They sawed felled logs into 4-foot lengths and stacked them up inside the ovens up to the ceilings. The doorways were then blocked with metal doors and the wood inside was subjected to a slow cooking process that typically lasted for a week. The charcoal burners could manipulate the temperature of the kilns by blocking or unblocking air vents in the sides of the ovens. The kilns were abruptly abandoned in the summer of 1878, when declining ore quality forced the closure of the furnaces.

The kilns are built of local quarried stone held together by a strong mortar of lime, sand, and gravel. Each stands about 25 feet tall and 35 feet in diameter and has a large arched entryway and a smaller opening high up on the backside. They were coated with plaster, but the exterior coatings have since weathered away. The interior walls retain their plaster finish and are thickly coated with soot that gives off a smoky odor. Each kiln could hold 42 cords of cut wood, from which 2,000 bushels of charcoal could be produced. There are numerous sawed stumps in the area that attest to the hard labor performed by the woodcutters.

In 1971 National Park Service archaeologists surveyed the area and excavated potions of three of the kilns. They found that one was used to bake limestone into lime, and probably supplied the mortar used during construction of the charcoal kilns. This lime kiln is smaller than the other ten ovens, and is built into the hillside behind the ten charcoal ovens. They also found the remains of a small settlement nearby, which was likely the workers' camp. Tree ring studies have been conducted on several pinyon stumps in the area, and they confirm that the trees were cut during the very brief period during which the kilns operated.

The kilns have been repaired and stabilized, first by Civilian Conservation Corps workers in the 1930s and later by a National Park Service stabilization team in 1971.

The kilns are within Death Valley National Monument next to a gravel road on the northeast slope of Wildrose Canyon. From California Highway 190, go south on Emigrant Canyon Road to the turnoff up Wildrose Canyon. The use of large vehicles and motor homes is not recommended. The last 3 miles of the road are unpaved and the road is subject to storm closures.

MANZANAR NATIONAL HISTORIC SITE, OWENS VALLEY, INYO COUNTY, EASTERN CALIFORNIA

At the foot of the Sierra Nevada, in Owens Valley, lies Manzanar National Historic Site, a unit of the National Park Service designated to protect and interpret features associated with the internment of Japanese Americans during World War II. Manzanar was one of ten" relocation centers" at which Japanese Americans, most of them U.S. citizens, were imprisoned. Opened in March 1942, the relocation center remained in operation until late in 1945. At its peak, Manzanar held more than 10,000 men, women, and children; not one had been convicted of any crime.

Although surrounded by a barbed-wire fence, sentry posts, and guard towers, Manzanar was designed to be a self-sufficient town. Families lived in stark barracks, ate in mess halls, and shared latrines and shower buildings; but Manzanar also included schools, an orphanage, a hospital, factories, warehouses, and farms.

After the camp was closed, the barracks and other buildings were removed. Decades later, a government commission determined that the imprisonment of Japanese Americans was not a military necessity, as it had been deemed during World War II, but rather a product of racial prejudice, wartime hysteria, and a lack of political leadership. Today the public can see a reconstructed guard tower, the remains of buildings, gardens, and ponds, and they can visit the Manzanar cemetery. An auditorium built by the internees is now a visitors' center, with exhibits about the daily life of the internees and the political and economic forces that led our country to abandon its Constitution in a time of crisis.

Although the relocation-era remains are most salient, Manzanar also holds traces of earlier displacements of peoples for racial or economic reasons. Paiute and Shoshone people and their predecessors lived in the Manzanar area from at least 3500 BC; a Paiute village, Tupüzi Witu, was in the vicinity. The Paiutes were seen as an impediment to the Euro-American immigrants who arrived in Owens Valley in the nineteenth century. In 1863 the U.S. Army forcefully removed the Paiutes to a reservation at Fort Tejon, north of Los Angeles. Most of the Paiutes returned to their homeland within a few years, but their land had been usurped and their economy shattered.

The remains of one of those early Euro-American settlements can be found at Manzanar. In the 1860s John Shepherd began a cattle operation to supply mining communities in the nearby Inyo Mountains. By the late 1800s the Shepherd ranch had grown to some 2,000 acres. In 1910 the ranch was subdivided as the townsite of Manzanar. By 1912 an innovative cement-pipe irrigation

A marble memorial obelisk in the center of the cemetery at Manzanar Historical Site. Inscription is translated as: "Monument for the Pacification of Spirits." In the distance is Mount Williamson and the eastern front of the Sierra Nevada. [Jeff Burton]

system watered over 20,000 apple and pear trees. The town boasted a general store with a post office, a community hall, a service station, an ice cream stand, a cannery, a lumberyard, a two-room schoolhouse, and over twenty-five homes. Soon, however, Los Angeles came to view the Sierran streams used by the Manzanar community as essential to the aqueduct the city was constructing for its own development. By 1927 Los Angeles had bought most of the Manzanar properties, and by the 1930s all the town buildings had been removed or torn down.

Further Reading: Bodie, California, Web site, http://www.americanwest.com/pages/bodie.htm; Bodie State Historic Park Web site, http://www.parks.ca.gov/?page_id=509; Bodie.com Web site, http://www.bodie.com/; Burton, Jeffery F., Mary M. Farrell, Florence B. Lord, Richard W. Lord, Tetsudan Kashima, and Irene J. Cohen, *Confinement and Ethnicity: An Overview of World War II Japanese American Relocation Sites.* (Seattle: University of Washington Press, 2002); Manzanar Relocation Camp Web site, www.manzanar.com; Manzanar Web site, National Park Service, www.nps.gov/manz; Mattes, Merrill J., and Robert V. Simmonds, *Charcoal Kilns: Wildrose Canyon, Death Valley National Monument, California; Historic Structures Report,* Office of History and Historic Architecture (San Francisco: National Park Service, United States Department of the Interior, 1970); Wallace, William J., and Edith Wallace, *Digging into Death Valley's History: Three Studies in Historic Archaeology* (Ramona, CA: Acoma Books, 1981).

Jeff Burton, Allika Ruby, and Sharon Waechter

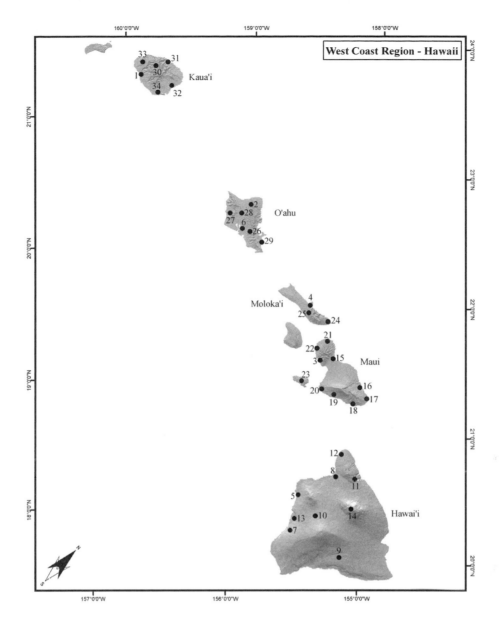

KEY FOR WEST COAST—HAWAI'I REGIONAL MAP

1. Russian Fort Elisabeth (Pa'ula'ula, or "Red Enclosure"), Kaua'i
2. Pu`uomahuka Heiau, O'ahu
3. Petroglyphs at Olowalu, Maui
4. Kalaupapa National Historical Park, Moloka'i
5. Kaloko-Honokōhau National Historical Park, Hawai'i
6. USS *Arizona* Memorial, O'ahu
7. Pu'uhonua o Hōnaunau National Historical Park, Hawai'i
8. Pu'ukoholā Heiau National Historic Site, Hawai'i
9. Hawai'i Volcanoes National Park, Hawai'i
10. Pohakulao Chill Glass Quarry Complex, Hawai'i
11. Waipi'o Valley, Hawai'i
12. Lapakahi, Hawai'i
13. Kealakekua Bay State Historical Park, Hawai'i
14. Mauna Kea Adz Quarry, Hawai'i
15. Haleki'i and Pihana Heiau, Wailuku, Maui
16. Ke'anae Peninsula, Maui
17. Pi'ilanihale Heiau, Hana, Maui
18. Schoolhouse and Church Ruins, Kaupō, Maui
19. Kahikinui, Maui
20. Keone'ō'io Archaeological District, La Pérouse Bay, Maui
21. Honokahua, Maui
22. Lahaina, Maui
23. Kaho'olawe Island
24. Hālawa Valley, Moloka'i
25. Kauleonanahoa, Moloka'i
26. Hālawa and Haiku Valley, H-3 Freeway, O'ahu
27. Kāne'Ākī Heiau, Mākaha Ahupua'a, O'ahu
28. Līhu'e Royal Center, O'ahu
29. Kailua Royal Center and Heiau, O'ahu
30. Hanalei Valley, Kaua'i
31. Heiau Complex at Ha'ena, Kaua'i
32. Heiau Complex at Wailua, Kaua'i
33. Ki'ki'a'ola Aqueduct ("Menehune Ditch"), Waimea, Kaua'i
34. 'Alekoko Fishpond ("Menehune Fishpond"), Kaua'i

HAWAI'I

Ancient house sites, sites associated with quarrying for tools and building materials, economic sites such as artificially created fishponds and agricultural terraces, and ritual sites are found in the archaeological record of Hawai'i. Human modification of the rich natural environments here began as soon as human colonists arrived by sea between 2,000 and 1,500 years ago. The Polynesian colonizers who settled Hawai'i brought with them knowledge of dryland and irrigation farming, as well as crops that included taro, breadfruit, bananas, and sweet potatoes. They also were familiar with animal husbandry and brought along chickens, dogs, and pigs. A wide range of archaeological sites are described in the essays in this section. Hawai'i also has a rich record of historic period archaeological sites, some of which are discussed in the essays on the development of Hawai'ian villages and communities, European exploration and colonization, Moloka'i, and the World War II memorial to the USS *Arizona* at Pearl Harbor.

ENTRIES FOR THE HAWAI'I REGION

THE ANTHROPOGENIC NATIVE HAWAI'IAN LANDSCAPE: FISHPONDS, AGRICULTURE, AND QUARRIES

"Anthropogenic" means "of human origin" or the result of human activities, and "anthropogenic modifications" are what archaeologists call the changes people make to a landscape, whether to improve the land for agriculture, flood control, or building sites. In the Hawai'ian Islands, understanding prehistoric modifications to the landscape is crucial to understanding how the Hawai'ian culture evolved from the common cultural base it shares with other Polynesian groups into the unique Hawai'ian culture reported by early European and American explorers. Native Hawai'ians modified the landscape in substantial ways prior to European contact, primarily for the large-scale agricultural systems that supported the upper levels of the social system: the chiefs, or *ali'i* as they are called in Hawai'ian, and their retainers. Other anthropogenic modifications to the landscape included the construction of large saltwater fishponds on the shore to raise fish for aquaculture food production. Many of these features are preserved and can still be visited in state parks, hotel grounds, or county lands. The scale and extent of these anthropogenic modifications to the landscape provide clues to archaeologists to understand the organization of labor, political structure, and population of Hawai'i prior to contact with Euro-Americans and the resulting changes to the culture that occurred afterward.

The Hawai'ian Islands were first settled sometime between AD 600 and 1000 by people from islands to the south, with the Marquesas Islands being the most likely homeland for the original Hawai'ian colonizers. Traveling the Pacific in large double-hulled voyaging canoes, the first settlers brought with them a well-developed farming and animal husbandry system that included taro, bananas, sweet potatoes, breadfruit, pigs, chickens, dogs, and a host of other useful plants. Agricultural techniques included knowledge of irrigation systems to grow wetland taro, as well as crops adapted to a variety of growing conditions such dryland (non-irrigated) taro and sweet potatoes that could grow in a variety of environments. The material culture included a variety of wooden and stone agricultural implements and tools, such as stone adzes for wood working and tree falling, wooden digging sticks for planting and harvesting, and ground stone pounders for processing taro corms into *poi*, a food staple. Round-trip voyaging between Hawai'i, the Mar-

quesas, and the Society Islands continued for some time after the initial colonization of the Hawai'ian Islands.

The Hawai'ian Islands are located above 16 degrees latitude in the subtropical zone, and the original colonizers from the tropical south had to adapt some of their crops and agricultural techniques to unfamiliar environmental conditions. Over time, as the Hawai'ian culture changed and the population grew, these adaptations resulted in a unique culture with its associated earthworks, stone architecture, and landscape modifications.

FISHPONDS: AQUACULTURE ON A GRAND SCALE

One innovation unique to Hawai'i was the development of large saltwater fishponds, known as *loko* in Hawai'ian and constructed with stone walls built from shore onto reef flats or shallow bay bottoms. The fishponds had wooden gates that allowed sea water and juvenile fish to enter and leave the ponds but did not allow larger fish to escape. The fishponds were built at the direction of a chief or one of their overseers (called *konohiki*) and were maintained and guarded by a caretaker. Certain amounts of the fish or certain species were reserved for the chief, and the rest could be used by the caretaker and the local people. Fishponds ranged in size from a few acres to over 100 acres, with sea walls built of basalt stone or coral rocks. These walls were large enough to walk on, so that the wooden gates could be tended and maintained. Freshwater fishponds were also built on O'ahu and Kaua'i, taking advantage of large marshes or river systems.

Fishponds were especially common on O'ahu and Moloka'i but were present on most of the main islands. They provided a ready source of easily harvested protein, and the surplus food they generated was one factor in the production system that allowed Hawai'i to develop into a near state-like political structure prior to Euro-American contact. Although many fishponds have been filled and lost to development, many others remain and some still function under the care of local communities. Such fishponds provide a tangible link to ancient Hawai'ian culture, and fishponds are considered a culturally important site class in Hawai'i today.

IRRIGATED TARO FIELDS: *LO'I*

Taro, a plant native to Southeast Asia with a large, starchy corm (an underground plant stem), was a staple food plant throughout much of Polynesia, and Hawai'i was no exception. There are several varieties of taro adapted to grow in different conditions. These can be divided into two main types: irrigated (or wet) taro, and non-irrigated (or dryland) taro. Irrigated taro requires constantly running fresh water to grow, and the Hawai'ians constructed large, stone-faced earth terrace systems in wet valleys. These systems, called *lo'i* in Hawai'ian, were irrigated by complex systems of irrigation ditches and terrace-to-terrace flow systems, where water would flow from one taro terrace to the next in small spillways. The flow of this water was politically controlled, with higher-status or favored individuals getting better access to the freshest, coolest water.

Early European explorers were amazed at the complexity and productivity of Hawai'ian irrigation systems, which often had crops of sugar cane or bananas growing on the terrace walls. Taro (called *kalo* in Hawai'ian) and the *poi* or paste made from it are considered delicacies to this day, and many ancient Hawai'ian irrigated terraces are still in use for commercial and private taro growing. The Hanalei valley on Kaua'i is one of the largest taro growing areas in the state and is an excellent place to see taro pond fields in operation.

DRYLAND AGRICULTURAL SYSTEMS

Another large-scale anthropogenic modification to the landscape common to the drier (leeward, or west) parts of the Hawai'ian Islands are non-irrigated field systems, often called dryland systems. These occur in several forms, depending on location, and include either individual clearing mounds or long, linear mounds of stones that defined specific fields. These linear stone piles, called *kuaiwi* in Hawai'ian, meaning "backbone," were the result of clearing stones from the adjacent growing areas.

One of the largest areas of landscape modification for dryland agriculture is known as the Kona Field System, located on the west side of Hawai'i Island in the District of Kona on the volcanic slopes above the town of Kona. Many features of the Kona Field System are still used today by coffee growers. Archaeological features in the Kona Field System include long kuaiwi walls, planting mounds of piled stone, small temporary shelter structures built of low-level stacked rock walls in the shape of a "C" or "U," more permanent house structures, and field shrines dedicated to agriculture. Many of the earliest visitors to Hawai'i Island, including the crews of Captain James Cook and Captain George Vancouver, remarked on the "plantation-like" appearance of the volcanic slopes above the coastal villages they visited on Hawai'i Island. Despite a century or more of abandonment and the near smothering of them by non-native plants, remains of these large-scale dryland agricultural field systems can still be seen while flying over western Hawai'i.

In addition to the large Kona Field System, there are similar large systems on Hawai'i Island in Lalamilo and Waimea that date to either the late pre-contact period, which is the name archaeologists in Hawai'i give to the period before European contact in 1778, or to the early post-contact period when the Hawai'ian Islands were the center of the Pacific whaling trade. These field systems were used during the first half of the nineteenth century, both to supply whaling ships and later to supply the California gold-rush market.

One of the more unique agricultural landscapes anywhere in the Pacific occurs on the dry (or leeward) side of Hawai'i Island in the barren lava fields near the coast. Here ancient Hawai'ian planters excavated shallow pits into the barren lava fields and mulched them with whatever material they could find, including seaweed, plant remains, and animal and human manure. In these pits they would plant sweet potatoes and dryland taro, and William Ellis, an early missionary who traveled the island, marveled that anything would grow in such desolate areas. Similar pits have been found high in the central plateau of Hawai'i Island, and their function there remains a mystery. Experimental archaeology conducted by staff from the U.S. Army Pohakuloa Training Center showed that sweet potatoes could grow at such an elevation, but whether the pits were an attempt to grow a high-elevation crop or were related to hunting the abundant seabirds that nested in the area is unknown.

LARGE STONE QUARRIES OF HAWAI'I ISLAND

One other category of prehistoric Hawai'ian activity that left its mark as an anthropogenic landscape feature is the large stone quarries of Hawai'i Island. Although not as obvious in scale as the agricultural modifications to the landscape or as immediately impressive as the fishponds, three stone quarrying areas of Hawai'i Island are extensive enough to be easily seen while hiking or low-level flying. The largest and most obvious of these quarries is the Pohakuloa Chill Glass Quarry complex, located on the central plateau or "Saddle Region" of the island between the volcanoes of Mauna Loa, Mauna Kea, and Hualalai. Located within the confines of the U.S. Army Pohakuloa Training Center, this extensive complex of quarry areas was not discovered until the 1990s. Within the quarry complex, Hawai'ians quarried the glassy surface of a fresh lava flow that erupted sometime after AD 1600 and used the glassy basalt to make sharp cutting flakes to butcher the abundant seabirds that nested in the area. Two particularly unique qualities about the chill glass quarry complex are both its large size (over 800 acres) and the fact that it developed in a relatively short period of time. The lava flow that is the source of the glassy basalt material did not erupt until sometime after AD 1600 and possibly as late as AD 1700, and use of the quarry probably ended by approximately AD 1800 when metal tools began to flood the islands and the use of stone tools probably declined. There is no historic account of use of the quarry complex, and it must certainly have been abandoned by AD 1825.

Two other large quarry areas are present on Hawai'i Island. These are the Mauna Kea Adze Quarry complex, located on summit plateau of Mauna Kea volcano, and the stone abrader quarries of the leeward coast in the region of Anaehoomalu and Waikoloa. The Mauna Kea adze quarry is the largest stone adze quarry in the Pacific basin, covering an area of over 12 square miles on the south flank and summit of Mauna Kea. Here ancient Hawai'ian craftsmen came to quarry stone from a lava flow that had erupted under a glacier during one of the ice ages, producing hard, dense stone in large quantities. Much of the quarry complex is located above the tree line and at an elevation where temperatures can drop below freezing, and so working at this elevation must have required groups well-supplied with food, water, and firewood. In addition to the quarry features, numerous stone shrines dot the mountain, testament to the reverence in which this wild and isolated place, home to the snow goddess Poliahu, was held.

The stone abrader quarries of the leeward coast stretch for many acres over barren pahoehoe lava, and the pits where scoriaceous lava blocks were quarried and shaped by rubbing them against the surrounding lava can still be seen. The old pahoehoe lava in this area is perfect for making grinding and abrading tools due to its vesicular, scoria surface and the fact that it is already weathered into many fragments. The stone abraders obtained from these quarries were used to shape wood and bone implements, and the abundance of them suggests that the area was either used for many centuries for source material or that many of the features were created when King Kamehameha created his large fleet of war canoes in the area to invade the neighboring island of Maui.

Further Reading: Kirch, Patrick V., *Feathered Gods and Fishhooks: An Introduction to Hawaiian Archaeology and Prehistory* (Honolulu: University of Hawai'i Press, 1985); Kirch, Patrick V., and Marshall Sahlins, *Anahulu: The Anthropology of History in the Kingdom of Hawaii* (Chicago: University of Chicago Press, 1992); He'eia Fishpond Web site, http://ksdl.ksbe.edu/heeia/pages/history.html (online May 2007); Kaloko-Honokahau National Park Web site, http://www.nps.gov/kaho (online May 2007).

Scott S. Williams

DEVELOPMENT OF HAWAI'IAN VILLAGES AND COMMUNITIES

Located in the north Pacific near the Tropic of Cancer, the eight principal islands of Hawai'i have been home to some of the world's most naturally isolated communities. All evidence suggests the island group was first discovered and colonized by Polynesians around AD 700. Founding communities likely consisted of small, nucleated settlements in prime coastal locations with access to fresh water, marine resources, and good farming land. By AD 1450, following a dramatic growth in population, a new type of community was created that centered on territories that crosscut concentric island ecozones from the shore to the mountainous uplands. The development of these communities is closely tied to the rise of powerful chiefdoms in Hawai'i.

In the sixteenth century, following contact with European explorers, the Hawai'i Island chief Kamehameha consolidated politically independent chiefdoms and established the historic Kingdom of Hawai'i. As the kingdom became drawn into the nineteenth-century global economy, the traditional community pattern was abandoned for nucleated villages, plantations, and ranches. These new historic communities would eventually give rise to Hawai'i's unique modern society.

FOUNDING COMMUNITIES (AD 700–1450)
While archaeologists are continually searching for direct material evidence of Hawai'i's earliest founding communities,

two factors have presented major challenges to this work—the rarity of early sites and poor preservation. First, both the total population of the Hawai'ian Islands and the density of settlements on individual islands would have been low following colonization, making it difficult to detect the presence of people from the remnants of their daily lives. In addition, given the small labor pool available and, presumably, the lack of a hierarchy of powerful elites to underwrite large construction projects, it is unlikely these founding groups built massive structures, such as large temples or intensive agricultural fields.

Second, there are major preservation issues to contend with when investigating Hawai'i's earliest occupation phase. An estimated 80 percent of artifacts were made out of wood and other plant materials that survive in tropical environments only under special conditions, such as in dry caves or wet marshes. However, perhaps more important, those artifacts and sites that have been preserved are subject to centuries of modification from natural and human action. This is especially problematic in island contexts where land is limited and the chances of the reoccupation and reuse of a site is high.

Since it is unlikely that archaeologists will ever find direct evidence of Hawai'i's very first communities, they have used existing evidence from early sites and indirect indicators of human presence to date the colonization of the islands and reconstruct the development of a uniquely Hawai'ian culture. Currently, the best proxy indicators of the first presence of people are non-native plants and animals. The ancestors of Hawai'ians brought with them a number of species not naturally found in Hawai'i, including domesticates such as dogs, chickens, pigs, taro, and other crops as well as non-domesticate "hitchhikers" such as rats and land snails. Thus, when evidence of these plants or animals is uncovered in old deposits, archaeologists consider it strong evidence for the presence of early peoples. Indeed, because this is the case on many Pacific islands, recent genetic analyses of modern species and DNA from remains found in archaeological sites have represented a major advance in writing the prehistory of the entire region.

A more commonplace indicator of the presence of people comes from studying environmental change. An increase in charcoal fragments in pollen cores, shifts in the dominant species of plants on islands, and the large-scale demise of birds with few naturally evolved defenses against predators are all considered good indicators of the presence of people. In some cases, species naturally found in Hawai'i were exterminated from individual islands while others have gone extinct. Nonetheless, it is important to keep in mind that these trends in environmental change, while dramatic, should not be viewed as an indicator that the ancestors of Hawai'ians had little regard for their new island home. Similar patterns can be found in the history of islands worldwide and other cases of human colonization of new ecosystems.

As small settlements were established and the overall population grew, the island's founding groups began to diverge culturally from their neighbors in the region. Archaeologists have interpreted stylistic changes in the form of sites and artifacts—including fishhooks, stone tools, and house architecture—as material markers of the evolution of a uniquely Hawai'ian culture by at least AD 1200. In addition, the analysis of modern languages shows that over time the words spoken by these founding groups drifted away from those of their ancestors and related groups. In fact, it was through the construction of "family trees" of Oceanic languages that anthropologists devised some of the first, and most enduring, histories of the larger Polynesian region.

TRADITIONAL COMMUNITIES (AD 1450–1795)

The later prehistoric and early post-European contact periods are marked by the development of hundreds of individual community territories subsumed under a hierarchy of chiefs, as well as other major social, economic, and religious changes. These changes are evident in both the archaeological record and in rich oral traditions handed down over centuries. Anthropological archaeologists take special interest in the development of traditional Hawai'ian society and culture

since it represents a rare case of the evolution of a complex, hierarchical social system under relatively isolated conditions. Thus, as archaeologists learn more about the history of traditional Hawai'ian communities, they increase the chances of understanding a major part of humanity's ancient history in general.

The most immediately striking aspect of traditional Hawai'ian communities that date to between AD 1450 and 1795 is how well adapted each was to local environmental conditions while elegantly fitted into a larger, complex system of land tenure and chiefly power. Ideally speaking, each community occupied a sliver of territory that crosscut an island's concentric environmental zones from the mountains to the sea. This territory was controlled by a low-level elite who employed a land manager to watch over the collection of commoner tribute in the form of agricultural goods, animals, and labor. On the large island of Hawai'i, there were as many as 600 such communities. At one level above the community, island districts had their own chief. Further up the hierarchy, powerful chiefs dominated multiple districts or whole islands. These chiefs were of the highest elite class and would at times move their courts from community to community to collect tribute. Oral traditions suggest these movements were dictated in part by the ritual calendar and in part by the relative abundance of food in different areas at different times.

Methodologically speaking, the introduction of the "settlement pattern approach"—a type of archaeology that attempts to reconstruct the nature of human habitation and land use as an avenue for tracking major social changes—was a key advancement in the study of the establishment of community territories. This approach has led archaeologists to uncover evidence for the development of traditional communities in different environments as seen in case studies of two Hawai'i Island communities: Waipi'o and Lapakahi.

Waipi'o and Lapakahi Communities

Located on the rainy, windward east coast of Hawai'i Island, the Waipi'o valley is oriented perpendicular to the shore and situated between the Kohala Mountains and a sheltered bay. The valley has a permanent freshwater stream and, although archaeologists currently lack direct evidence of early occupation, many of the island's oral traditions are rooted here. Irrigated pondfields, like those used for rice cultivation elsewhere, appear to have been built in the mid-valley floor by around AD 1400 with side-valley fields constructed much later after AD 1650. Archaeologists have also found evidence of the intensification of marine resources with the construction of large ponds for raising fish at the mouth of the valley, although they have yet to securely date these features. This expansion and intensification of agriculture and aquaculture is precisely the kind of material signal of cross-ecozone community territories that archaeologists regularly find in valley environments in Hawai'i.

In a neighboring district on the opposite side of the island, the narrow community territory of Lapakahi is situated on the dry, western, leeward slopes of the Kohala Mountains. Currently a state park, in 1968 the area was home to the first archaeological project that took an entire community territory as its unit of analysis. By surveying and excavating in each of the territory's three ecozones—a densely occupied coastal zone, an inland, dry barren zone, and an upland rain-fed agricultural zone—researchers discovered that founding communities had occupied the coast remarkably later in time than expected and archaeological indicators of the use of the entire range of ecozones dated to soon afterward, around AD 1450. In an upland environment that lacked permanent streams, non-irrigated farming was expanded and intensified to create a large system of fields. Visitors to the park can take a self-guided tour of the coastal habitation zone, which appears to have been occupied right through the historic era. Some distance away in the island's Kona district, now famous for its coffee farms, the Amy Greenwell Ethnobotanical Gardens contain preserved portions of a field system similar to the fields that dominate the uplands of Lapakahi.

Waipi'o and Lapakahi communities, although located less than 35 kilometers (22 mi) from one another, were not equals in terms of the natural productivity of agricultural land. This fundamental difference is often described in terms of "wet" island districts with productive irrigated fields and "dry" districts with non-irrigated fields that were more vulnerable to periodic short fall in times of drought. However, in turning to the island's political history, researchers find that although the most productive districts dominated the landscape at first, it was actually chiefs from the least productive lands that finally came to rule the island. This reversal of the expected relationship between resources and power is best seen in the movement of Hawai'i Island's royal center of power from Waipi'o to a place on the coast of the Kona district called Hōnaunau.

Hōnaunau

Pu'uhonua o Hōnaunau served several different roles in ancient Hawai'ian society up until the nineteenth century. In addition to being the home and burial grounds of generations for high-ranking chiefs and their families, Hōnaunau was known as a "city of refuge" for people who had broken kapu— a religion-based system of law. Also, those who were fleeing battle could be afforded protection by the priests responsible for the refuge. Today, Hōnaunau is a national historical park and has been reconstructed based upon early maps and sketches as well as careful archaeological excavations undertaken to preserve this important site.

Beyond the impressive temples and other structures of Hōnaunau and other highly visible ritual centers, archaeological evidence of traditional Hawai'ian religion and ritual on Hawai'i Island may be found across the landscape. Indeed, from the first surveys of ritual sites by Bishop Museum archaeologist John F. G. Stokes at the end of the nineteenth and beginning of the twentieth century through to today, researchers continue to be overwhelmed by the number, variety, and wide distribution of shrines and temples. For example, shrines have been recorded ringing the coastline as well as at the crest of Mauna Kea, a volcanic peak 13,796 feet (4,205 m) above sea level. In addition, thanks in part to the abundance of exposed, smooth lava stone formations, Hawai'i Island is home to over seventy sites with petroglyphs (rock art), including around 22,600 individual images. Overall, it is clear that both daily and ritual life in traditional Hawai'ian communities spanned the entire landscape.

HISTORIC COMMUNITIES (AD 1795–1900)

Although there is strong evidence for prehistoric long-distance voyaging to and from the Hawai'ian Islands, in January 1778 ships under the command of British Captain James Cook represented the first recorded contact between Hawai'ians and Europeans. By 1795, Kamehameha, a chief from Hawai'i Island, united nearly all of the archipelago's independent chiefdoms and soon after became Hawai'i's first king. However, the unfortunate transmission of diseases, for which Hawai'ians had no immunity, that came with outside contact decimated the Native population. While scholars debate the total number of people who died due to epidemics, the death toll has been estimated to include a staggering 50–90 percent of the population.

In parallel to this horrific and tragic depopulation, both daily and ritual life changed dramatically in the new kingdom of Hawai'i. To a large extent, the traditional community pattern was abandoned for nucleated villages as a formal cash economy developed and Hawai'i was drawn into the nineteenth-century global economy, especially through the trans-Pacific trade in sandalwood and whaling. In addition, Hawai'ian religion was banned by royal decree in 1819 just one year prior to the first arrival of Christian missionaries. Eventually, much of the island's rural landscape became divided into cattle ranches and plantations for crops such as sugar cane and pineapples. In turn, unique historic period communities formed that were made up of a mix of Native Hawai'ians and newcomers.

There are local museums and historic archaeological sites across the Hawai'ian Islands. These sites range from the unique, such as Russian Fort Elizabeth, to more common sites that represent the development of modern Hawai'ian life out of historic communities, such as those associated with paniolo ranching culture. However, one of the most remarkably complete collections of artifacts associated with historic period groups can be found at the Bishop Museum in Honolulu. As one travels from the ground floor to the uppermost levels of Hawai'ian Hall, itself a major historic landmark, one is drawn through the history of the creation of a multicultural society in Hawai'i, with displays dedicated to the many ethnic groups that came to reside in the islands.

Finally, although leprosy—now properly referred to as Hansen's disease—has been treatable for over six decades, much about the disease and the historic settlement at Kalaupapa, Moloka'i Island, continues to be poorly understood. In 1866 the Kingdom of Hawai'i expelled the local population of a small portion of Moloka'i Island and established a settlement for people diagnosed with Hansen's disease. Over the next century, an official quarantine was enforced that, with rare exceptions, imprisoned thousands of people of all ages for the remainder of their lives. Because Hansen's disease is not fatal, this meant decades of forced separation from one's family and the creation of a local patient community. Today, a small group of patients still occupy their home in Kalaupapa settlement by choice. Visitation to the area, now a national historical park, is tightly restricted out of respect for the community rather than due to health concerns. Guided tours are available that include visits to preserved historic buildings such as St. Philomena's church, built by the famous missionary priest Father Damien DeVeuster, who died at Kalaupapa.

Further Reading: Cordy, Ross, *Exalted Sits the Chief: The Ancient History of Hawai'i Island* (Honolulu, HI: Mutual Publishing, 2000); Cordy, Ross, Eric Komori, and Kanalei Shun, "Archaeological Work in Waipi'o Valley, Hāmākua District, Hawai'i Island," *Hawaiian Archaeology* 10 (2005): 70–95; Kirch, Patrick V., *Feathered Gods and Fishhooks: An Introduction to Hawaiian Archaeology and Prehistory* (Honolulu: University of Hawai'i Press, 1985); Kirch, Patrick V., *The Wet and the Dry* (Chicago: University of Chicago Press, 1994); McCoy, Patrick C., "Neither Here Nor There: A Rites of Passage Site on the Eastern Fringes of the Mauna Kea Adze Quarry, Hawai'i," *Hawaiian Archaeology* 7 (1999): 11–34; Mills, Peter R., *Hawai'i's Russian Adventure: A New Look at Old History* (Honolulu: University of Hawai'i Press, 2002); Stannard, David E., *Before the Horror: The Population of Hawai'i on the Eve of Western Contact* (Honolulu: University of Hawai'i Press, 1989); Tuggle, H. David, and P. Bion Griffin, eds., *Lapakahi, Hawaii Archaeological Studies*, Asian and Pacific Archaeology Series No. 5 (Honolulu: University of Hawai'i, 1973); Vitousek, Peter M., Thegn N. Ladefoged, Patrick V. Kirch, Anthony S. Hartshorn, Michael W. Graves, Sara C. Hotchkiss, Shripad Tuljapurkar, and Oliver A. Chadwick, "Soils, Agriculture, and Society in Precontact Hawai'i," *Science* 304 (2004): 1665–1669.

Mark D. McCoy

HAWAI'IAN COMPLEX SOCIETIES IN LATE PRE-CONTACT TIMES

People have lived in the Hawai'ian Islands for almost 1,500 years. The Native people of these islands are the Hawai'ians, with different origins from the Native populations of the other forty-nine states. Hawai'ians are Polynesians. Their immediate ancestors sailed north out of central Polynesia, and their original ancestral line entered Oceania about 3,500–4,000 years ago from Island Southeast Asia (the Austronesian language family). The Hawai'ian Islands were solely a Polynesian and an Austronesian land for all but the last 200 years of their history. Within these islands, stratified kingdoms formed 600 years ago in the AD 1400s, and by the 1700s they had populations ranging from 30,000 to 120,000 people. These kingdoms were similar in size to Mayan, Greek, and early Near Eastern city-states. The last of the Hawai'ian kingdoms, the Kingdom of Hawai'i, which once had a population of 300,000, was overthrown in 1893, just over 100 years ago, by a small number of resident American businessmen with the aid of the U.S. minister.

In 1778, when the first Europeans reached the Hawai'ian Islands (Captain James Cook's third Pacific expedition), four kingdoms were present: the Kingdom of Hawai'i, controlling Hawai'i Island and two eastern districts on Maui Island (Hāna and Kipahulu); the Kingdom of Maui, encompassing the rest of Maui and the small islands of Lāna'i and Kaho'olawe; the

Kingdom of O'ahu, including the islands of O'ahu and Moloka'i; and the Kingdom of Kaua'i, centered on Kaua'i and containing the small islands of Ni'ihau, Lehua, and Ka'ula. The population of these kingdoms ranged from 30,000 (Kaua'i) to 120,000 (Hawai'i). Each kingdom had three chiefly administrative strata—the *mō'ī* or king, fifteen to twenty *ali'i nui* (high chiefs), and several hundred lesser *ali'i* (chiefs)—and thousands of commoners (*maka'āinana*).

The ruler and high chiefs were the elite of the kingdoms, the *haku 'āina*, or lords of the land. When a ruler came to power, he or she redistributed the community lands (*ahupua'a*) of the kingdom. On Hawai'i Island, there were 600 or so such lands. The ruler kept some communities and gave others to powerful high chiefs. These lords then appointed low chiefs (junior kinsmen, renowned warriors, etc.) to manage one or two communities. Commoners had to pay annual tribute (i.e., clothing, feathers, cloth, mats, pigs, dogs, and other foods) to their lord and the ruler and supply them with food, labor on public works projects, and serve in the military. In return, their lords and the ruler were expected to provide the protection of their gods and safety from enemies.

The ruler and high chiefs lived in their most bountiful lands. The ruler moved among several spots during the course of the year—the kingdom's different royal centers. These royal centers were where the court and retinue of the king and the high chiefs resided. Several thousand people were at these locales. The ruler's and high chiefs' dwelling compounds each had ten to fifteen thatched houses: sleeping houses for the lord and each of his wives, a large meeting and leisure house (men's house), a cook house, eating houses for women, storehouses for tribute items, and a small temple house (which had images of the lord's family gods).

The lords and king also had retainers, which included servants: bearers of their clothes and food, holders of feathered standards called *kāhili*, keepers of spittoons and food scrap bowls, and others. Many of these servants were their junior kinsmen who had chosen to serve their ranking relative. Also, the retinue included elite warriors who constantly trained on open grounds in the royal center. There, they practiced throwing, catching, and parrying spears along with coordinated maneuvers. Craftsmen and craftswomen were part of these courts: canoe makers, religious image carvers, weapon makers, and feather cloak and helmet manufacturers. Genealogists, composers, chanters, choreographers, and dancers were also attached to the courts. The nobility had genealogies that extended back to the gods. Honorific chants, songs, and hula dances were composed for feasts, births and deaths, and special events. The ruler and high chiefs supported these artists. Dances and chants were performed at the open grounds of the royal centers or at large thatched houses.

Key elements of elite life at royal centers were religious activities, notably those at the national temple. There were many kinds of temples (*heiau*), but the national temples (*luakini* or *po'o kanaka*) could be built only with the permission of the king. These temples were huge structures, often with rectangular courtyard areas over 2,000 square meters. The courtyard was frequently raised up on a stone platform or terrace foundation. It was enclosed with a stone wall or a wooden fence. Within the courtyard at one end were thatched structures (for storing temple items, e.g.). At the other end were a set of wooden images of gods 2 meters in height and a narrow scaffolding 6–9 meters tall, covered with cloth (the *'anu'u* tower). Here offerings were given and strict prayers were performed by priests, often with the ruler and high-ranking male chiefs in attendance. The luakini was the center for prayer for the kingdom's success in war, for bountiful crops for the entire kingdom, and for long life of the ruler. These luakini were often adjacent to the king's house yard. The luakini dominated the landscape as the king's temple where his family gods were worshipped.

A refuge area (*pu'uhonua*) was often present around the grounds of these large heiau. Any violator of laws or warrior from the side defeated in battle who could reach this refuge area could remain there for a period of days and then depart, absolved and protected from punishment.

The precursors of this political system of kingdoms arose in the AD 1300s. In that century, oral histories describe political units forming with larger territories that were portions of the major islands with multiple communities. These had two administrative strata (ruler and local chiefs) above commoners and populations of perhaps 1,000–9,000. Then, in the 1400s, entire major islands—Kaua'i, O'ahu, Moloka'i, and Hawai'i—became unified, each as a single kingdom. (Two large political units formed on Maui, unifying in the late 1500s.) These developments of the AD 1300s–1400s mark the start of the kingdoms of the contact era. Huge public works projects, many of which have survived as well-known archaeological sites, date from these times on. These include large temples, stone slides over 100 meters long used for *hōlua* sled competitions, fishponds 40–80 hectares in size that walled in areas of shallow reef, vast irrigated taro field systems, and major coastal trails linking the kingdoms' communities.

In the late 1600s, conquest warfare began among the kingdoms. In the early 1700s, the O'ahu Kingdom under its famed kings Kūali'i and Pelei'ōhōlani gained control of Kaua'i and conquered Moloka'i, becoming the first superpower of the islands. In 1783 Kahekili, ruler of the Maui Kingdom, conquered the O'ahu Kingdom and took control of Moloka'i and O'ahu. (Kaua'i had already regained its independence.) A decade later, in 1795, the Maui Kingdom fell in war to Kamehameha's Kingdom of Hawai'i. And in 1810 Kaumuali'i, the last king of Kaua'i, ceded ultimate control of Kaua'i to Kamehameha. One kingdom then ruled all the islands—the Kingdom of Hawai'i—with nearly 300,000 residents. It lasted another eighty-three years, until 1893, when it was overthrown.

Archaeological ruins of these kingdoms still cover the landscape—in pieces where modern urbanization, sugarcane cultivation, and ranching have altered the land, and intact where such impacts have not occurred. The sites often contain surface architecture. They range from houses of commoners to vast irrigated and dryland field systems, to fishponds, to the royal centers themselves. A look at the royal centers will give the best introductory feel for the kingdoms and their archaeological remains. The Bishop Museum in Honolulu should also be visited to see valued perishable objects from the kingdoms (e.g., feathered cloaks, feathered kāhili standards, wooden temple images).

ROYAL CENTER OF HŌNAUNAU, CENTRAL KONA COAST, HAWAI'I ISLAND

On Hawai'i Island many former royal centers of the Kingdom of Hawai'i contain some archaeological remnants: Waipi'o, Hilo, Punalu'u, Hōnaunau, Kealakekua, Kahalu'u, Hōlualoa, Kailua, Kawaihae, and Pu'uepa. Hōnaunau in central Kona on the west side of Hawai'i Island was one of these royal centers. Hōnaunau was a fertile area with a high population density. It started to be prominently mentioned in the oral histories during the reign of Keawe (1720–40). Today, key ruins of this royal center are on the coast within the Pu'uhonua o Hōnaunau National Historical Park, along the

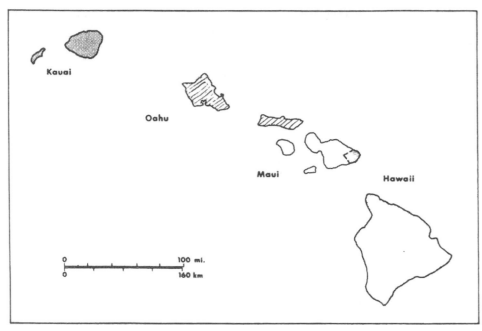

A map showing the four kingdoms (indicated by different fill types) in the Hawai'ian Islands in 1778.   [Ross Cordy]

south side of the small bay at Hōnaunau. The park's interpretation is focused on the pu'uhonua—the royal center's refuge area and its large temples.

At Hōnaunau, the pu'uhonua is on the flat point at the south side of the bay, set off by a huge wall, known as the great wall. Oral histories state that this wall was built in the reign of Keakealanikane (1660–80). Seaward of this wall are the ruins of two luakini heiau (national temples): 'Āle'ale'a and another, whose name is forgotten. 'Āle'ale'a today is a stone platform 2.4 meters high and 39 × 18 meters in area. When in use, this foundation would have supported thatched houses and an altar area with wooden images of gods, and it had a wooden fence atop the edges. In 1793 Archibald Menzies of Captain George Vancouver's expedition spent the night nearby and heard the temple drums and priests' chants. Archaeological work has shown that this temple was built in phases, probably with different rulers adding to its architecture (lengthening it, raising the foundation platform higher, etc.).

Another striking feature of this center is the reconstruction of a small thatched structure at one end of the great wall, right on the edge of the bay. This reconstruction is based on illustrations from the early 1800s, when the structure was still standing. It includes a small fenced yard with a thatched house and a low platform with tall wooden images. This was the Hale o Keawe (House of Keawe), one of two royal mausoleums within the Kingdom of Hawai'i. It was built in the early 1700s, shortly after the ruler Keawe's death. The bones of Keawe were inside within a woven, figure-like casket

(kā'ai). His kā'ai and those of several related high chiefs stood within, near the entry way, wrapped in meters of kapa cloth and capped with feather-covered heads (fiber frame with tied-on feathers) that were deity images. Two human-like wooden images 1.5 meters high (now at the Bishop Museum and Chicago's Field Museum) flanked the altar within this house. Smaller images, calabashes and bowls, and wrapped long bones of related retainers of the rulers were also within the Hale o Keawe.

Additionally, at Hōnaunau, one walks through the king's residential yard when passing from the visitors' center to the great wall and temples. All archaeological remains here are subsurface and have not been extensively studied. To the south along the beach are walled house yards, apparently of high chiefs and their retinue. Nearby are several long slides built of stone, where hōlua sledding competitions were held.

Access to the Pu'uhonua o Hōnaunau National Historical Park is off Māmalahoa Highway (Hawai'i Belt Road), which runs through the uplands of Kona. Signs are highly visible, directing travelers down a well-paved road to the shore. A parking lot and the small visitors' area are at the park's entrance.

THE ROYAL CENTER AT KEALAKEKUA, CENTRAL KONA COAST, HAWAI'I ISLAND

When Captain Cook returned from the northwest coast in 1779, he anchored at Kealakekua Bay, another royal center of the Kingdom of Hawai'i. The ruler, Kalani'ōpu'u, broke off his war with Maui and returned to the bay, with over 100 double-

Photo of a reconstructed Native Hawai'ian temple Hale o Keawe (original structure built about AD 1650), Pu'uhonua o Hōnaunau National Historical Park, Hawai'i. [Ross Cordy]

hulled sailing canoes and over 6,000 warriors arriving over several days. About 2,500 people lived in the immediate area of the bay in normal situations (or peaceful times).

Today, the south side of the bay (Nāpō'opo'o) is easily accessible by Nāpō'opo'o Road, descending from Māmalahoa Highway, the main upper Kona road. The road ends at the bay, at the foundation of the luakini heiau of this center, Hikiau Heiau. This is a large stone platform, 4 meters high, and 49 × 34 meters in area. In Cook's day, the heiau had a wooden fence along its edges mounted with skulls of defeated Maui warriors. In an open area nearby, Cook watched boxing performances and hula dances on different occasions. In 1793 Vancouver observed the kingdom's warriors practicing battle maneuvers on this field.

Across the bay on the north side is Ka'awaloa, a flat area. In 1779 this was the location of most of the high chiefs' house yards, small temples of these chiefs, and the house yard occupied by Kalani'ōpu'u. The ruins of walled house yards and platforms still survive here.

At the head of the bay, separating Nāpō'opo'o and Ka'awaloa, are high cliffs—Pali o Keōua. Above the cliffs began the rich fields of the lands of the bays. Walled fields survive as archaeological sites, once planted in dryland taro, sweet potatoes, and breadfruit.

Today the coastal areas of Ka'awaloa and Nāpō'opo'o around Hikiau Heiau are part of Kealakekua Bay State Historical Park, but this park is not yet developed. One can only easily reach the shoreline near Nāpō'opo'o and see Hikiau Heiau. Hopefully, before long the park will be fully developed with controlled access to the Ka'awaloa side and with full interpretation. The Bishop Museum has an ethnobotanical garden in the former fields above the cliffs of Kealekekua, the Amy Greenwell Ethnobotanical Garden. This garden is on Māmalahoa Highway,

south 0.8 kilometers (0.5 mi) beyond the Nāpō'opo'o Road junction. Here one can walk through the ruins of some of the walled fields that fed the court that lived below on the shore. Varieties of native plants and cultigens are planted in these gardens.

REMNANTS OF ROYAL CENTERS ON O'AHU ISLAND

Līhu'e Royal Center, Wahiawa/Schofield Barracks Area, Island of O'ahu

The first royal center of the O'ahu Kingdom was located at Līhu'e in the Schofield Barracks and Wahiawa area at the center of the island. This was O'ahu's only royal center until the mid-1500s, when Waikīkī, places along Pu'uloa (Pearl Harbor), and Kailua began to be rotating centers. The only accessible remnant of Līhu'e is the Kūkaniloko Birthing Stones near Wahiawa. Today this is a state historical park in a small grove of trees that shade a number of fairly flat stones lying on the ground surface. Visitors can reach this park by driving north through Wahiawa on Kamehameha Highway (HI-80) and turning left at the traffic light just north of Wahiawa (right leads to Whitmore village). Turn off onto a dirt road in the fields, and the grove of trees is immediately visible.

Oral accounts indicate that Kūkaniloko began to be used just prior to AD 1300. Here the O'ahu kings and high chiefs came to have their children born. The nobility witnessed the birth, seated on stones. The child was born at the stone Kūkaniloko, with the mother leaning against the stone supported by retainers, and with others cushioning the child with kapa cloth. Kūkaniloko was one of the most sacred spots for the O'ahu Kingdom throughout its 400-year history. The housing areas of the nobility were nearby and to the west on the flat lands of Wahiawa and Schofield Barracks—all are gone today. Ruins of commoners' houses, farms, and smaller temples have

Photo of birthing stones at Kūkaniloko.   [Ross Cordy]

Two large luakini temples survive today along the edge of Kawainui. One, Ulupō Heiau, is a huge platform (the heiau foundation) capping a bluff edge. The marsh side of this bluff is faced with stone, giving the appearance of a structure 9 meters high. Ulupō is a state historical park and is easily accessible. It lies along the entry road from the Pali Highway into Kailua, right behind the YMCA. The other Kailua luakini heiau that survives is Pahukini. It is protected and fenced off on the edge of the former main dump. It is difficult to get to this site.

The king's and high chiefs' residences, the houses of their retinues, and open grounds for war practices and dances were all on the flat sandy lands where Kailua town sits today. No visible ruins survive in this area. However, subsurface habitation deposits with occasional burials (once small cemeteries in house yards) are frequently found by those building houses or small businesses or even digging in backyards. The collective information from these deposits will be extremely important in telling researchers more about the life in the royal center of Kailua—reputedly the favorite residence of the famed kings Kākuhihewa (1640–60) and Kūali'i (1720–40).

REMNANTS OF THE ROYAL CENTERS OF MAUI
The Wailuku Royal Center, Wailuku, Maui

Maui's kingdom had three famous royal centers: Hāna, Wailuku, and Lahaina. Wailuku was focused around the 'Īao River, and today's towns of Wailuku and Kahului occupy parts of this old ahupua'a. Large, high sand dunes flank 'Īao's sides as it approaches the sea, with a wide valley floor between. Houses once fringed the base of these dunes and the shore, and the alluvial floor of the stream was covered by irrigated taro fields. Construction crews for modern businesses along lower Main Street at the dune's base are constantly finding habitation deposits and house yard burials, but none of the habitation areas have been preserved or interpreted. The alluvial flats have succumbed to development, also with no preservation. However, on the seaward tip of the northern high dune, an important part of this royal center is still present in Pihana-Haleki'i Heiau State Historical Park. Pihana was the main luakini temple of Wailuku from the AD 1400s, and archaeological work shows it was built and enlarged in phases over the centuries. Today, stone facing of the foundation terraces are visible at the top of the dune. Haleki'i, right next to Pihana, has been called a heiau, but it appears from archaeological and oral historical research to actually have been the king's residential area. This is a large, rectangular area on the flattened crest of the dune, with stone terrace faces lining the side toward the stream. From both of these structures, visitors can look over the mouth of the valley. This was a dominant spot for viewing the daily activities of farmers and household dwellers and for identifying the occupants of incoming canoes at the shore.

been found in recent years up almost every stream gulch within Schofield Barracks. Currently, they are inaccessible to the general public.

The Kailua Royal Center, Kailua Town, O'ahu Island

The royal center of Kailua was on the northeast side of O'ahu. A few ruins survive today. Two large ponds and marshlands are in Kailua: Kawainui (between the mountains and Kailua town) and Ka'elepulu (surrounded by today's Enchanted Lakes subdivisions). Today these ponds look like natural features. But both were active, famed fishponds in traditional times with irrigated taro fields along their edges and scattered houses on adjacent dry ground. The fish and taro fed the court at Kailua. Natives believed the goddess Hauwahine protected these ponds and ensured their productiveness. Kawainui is marshland today, but ruins of its taro fields and fishpond (walls and archaeological soils) still are present under the grass and reeds.

Further Reading: Cordy, Ross, *Exalted Sits the Chief: The Ancient History of Hawai'i Island* (Honolulu, HI: Mutual Publishing, 2000); Cordy, Ross, *The Rise and Fall of the O'ahu Kingdom* (Honolulu, HI: Mutual Publishing, 2002); Fornander, Abraham, *An Account of the Polynesian Race: Its Origins and Migrations and the Ancient History of the Hawaiian People to the Times of Kamehameha I*, vol. 2 (London: Trubner, 1880); Hommon, Robert, "Social Evolution in Ancient Hawai'i," in *Island Societies: Archaeological Approaches to Evolution and Transformation*, edited by Patrick Kirch (Cambridge: Cambridge University Press, 1986), 55–68; Kamakau, Samuel, *Ruling Chiefs of Hawai'i* (Honolulu, HI: Kamehameha Schools Press, 1961); Kolb, Michael, "Monumentality and the Rise of Religious Authority in Precontact Hawai'i," *Current Anthropology* 34 (1994): 521–547; Sahlins, Marshall, *Anahulu: The Anthropology of History in the Kingdom of Hawaii*, Vol. 1: *Historical Ethnography* (Chicago: University of Chicago Press, 1992).

Ross Cordy

EUROPEAN EXPLORATION AND COLONIZATION OF THE HAWAI'IAN ISLANDS

CAPTAIN COOK'S "DISCOVERY" IN 1778

The Hawai'ian Islands became famous in the Western world following Captain James Cook's third and final expedition to the Pacific (1776–80). Cook's crew first came ashore on the island of Kaua'i on January 20, 1778, and Cook named the archipelago the Sandwich Islands, in honor of John Montagu, fourth Earl of Sandwich and first lord of the British admiralty. Although he is regularly credited with the discovery of the Hawai'ian Islands, Cook had great respect for the navigational skills of the original Polynesian discoverers and noted the highly similar languages spoken by Hawai'ians, Tahitians, the Cook Islanders, the Maori of New Zealand, and Easter Islanders. In fact, he referred to these native Polynesian peoples as a "nation." One of Cook's lieutenants, James King, calculated that there were 400,000 people living in the Hawai'ian Islands based on observations of houses in shoreline villages. Some more recent research suggests that there were as many as 800,000–1,000,000 people living in the Hawai'ian Islands at the time of Cook's arrival.

Whether or not Cook was, in fact, the first Westerner to reach Hawai'i is unclear. Cook's crew observed several old iron artifacts in the possession of Hawai'ians that apparently did not come from Cook's own ships. These observations, in combination with pre-Cook Spanish maps showing volcanic islands near the latitude of the Hawai'ian Islands (but at varying longitudes), and other such circumstantial evidence, have been employed to support the theory that a Manila galleon had reached the islands before Cook. However, there are other scenarios that might explain the Hawai'ians' possession of iron, including floating debris from shipwrecks, drifting Japanese or Chinese fishing junks, or the acquisition of iron by Polynesian voyagers who had themselves made contact with American or Asian continents. So far, archaeological and genetic evidence has not confirmed any particular scenario for pre-Cook European contact with Hawai'i, although a good possibility exists that such an event did occur.

News of Cook's final expedition became all the more sensational because Cook himself was killed on February 14, 1779, by Hawai'ians at Kealakekua Bay on the "Big Island" of Hawai'i, after he had spent the summer of 1778 exploring in the Gulf of Alaska and the Bering Sea. Cook's party had been welcomed with great hospitality and apparent reverence in 1778 and 1779, but tensions grew as the expedition's visit extended into February. When one of Cook's small boats was commandeered by the Hawai'ians, Cook proposed taking the paramount chief of the island, Kalani'ōpu'u, as a hostage until the boat was returned. Although Kalani'ōpu'u originally agreed to the plan, a skirmish ensued as the party approached the shore, and Cook was killed before he could reach his vessels *HMS Resolution* and *Discovery*.

A heated anthropological debate has ensued regarding whether Hawai'ians considered Cook as a figuration of Lono, one of the four main Hawai'ian *akua* (usually translated as "gods"). Akua are considered deified ancestors of the Hawai'ian chiefs, and genealogical chants related each chief's ancestry back to the akua. Hawai'ians regularly referred to Cook as "Lono" during his sojourn in the islands (the term often transcribed in the Cook journals was actually "Rono," but 1820s missionary orthographies adopted an "L" instead of an "R"); however, there were chiefs who were not akua with that name. One objection raised in response to the idea that Hawai'ians viewed Cook as the god Lono, and forwarded by anthropologist Gananath Obeyesekere, is that it makes the Hawai'ians appear overly naive and irrational. The counterpoint championed by Marshall Sahlins is that the very concept of rationality needs to be considered in the cultural conceptions of the time. Instead of definitively answering the artificially dichotomized question of whether Hawai'ians viewed Cook as a god or a man, this debate has vividly demonstrated the structural complexities and potential cultural biases that underlie our attempts to accurately describe and explain history. Despite such challenges, the Hawai'ian

Islands offer a spectacular opportunity to consider what can happen when powerful indigenous and Western cultures, having vastly different world views, enter into an era of sustained interaction.

HAWAI'IAN POLITICAL TRANSFORMATIONS

Despite the capacity of the Hawai'ian chiefs to amass large armies by the late 1700s, there was never a major military battle between Hawai'ians and foreign powers. Instead, Hawai'ian chiefs in the late 1700s and early 1800s often used foreign alliances to forward their own ambitions. As Western vessels arrived in the Hawai'ian Islands, an evolutionary change in Hawai'ian political control was under way, fueled by the appropriation of Western materials and concepts. By 1778, Hawai'ian chiefs were regularly battling rival chiefdoms. Traditional chiefly polities often controlled only portions of islands, but between 1782 and 1795 one chief, Kamehameha I, engaged in a series of battles that united the entire island of Hawai'i with all of the other main Hawai'ian islands, except Kaua'i and Ni'ihau. The latter two islands remained under the direct control of paramount chief Kaumuali'i until his death in 1824. Kaumuali'i did, in fact, begin paying tribute to Kamehameha in 1810 but then reneged on that agreement more than once. Following the death of Kamehameha in 1819, Kaumuali'i married Ka'ahumanu, Kamehameha's favorite wife in 1821. Although Kamehameha I's kingdom was nominally under the control of his son Liholiho (Kamehemeha II), it was Ka'ahumanu who appears to have wielded the most political clout, and it was her marriage to Kaumuali'i that finally united the islands. Thus, between 1782 and 1821, the Hawai'ian Islands had been transformed from a number of independent chiefdoms into a single Hawai'ian Kingdom modeled after British monarchial rule.

Within six months of Kamehameha I's death, Liholiho, Ka'ahumanu, and most other leading chiefs of the era orchestrated the demise of the Hawai'ian *kapu* (taboo) system. This ritual complex was manifested in virtually every aspect of Hawai'ian life, from sacrifices offered at monumental ritual temples to strict rules governing what kinds of food men and women could eat. The end of this system was undoubtedly related to the influences of foreign commodities and ideas, but it also allowed the chiefs more freedom in their secular pursuits of wealth and power. Within another five months, in April of 1820, the first Protestant missionaries arrived in the Hawai'ian Islands, sent out by the American Board of Commissioners for Foreign Missions (ABCFM) in Boston. As Protestant troupes from the ABCFM continued to arrive in Hawai'i, they slowly gained influence with the chiefly class. Among other things, the missionaries taught the chiefs and their children how to read and write. Over 150 missionaries from the ABCFM arrived in Hawai'i between 1820 and 1853. The first Catholic missionaries arrived in Hawai'i in 1827, meeting great initial resistance, and the first Mormon missionaries arrived in 1850.

Liholiho's reign was short-lived. He left to visit England in 1823 and died there in 1824 along with his favorite wife, Kamamalu. He was succeeded by Kauikeaouli (Kamehameha III), but because Kauikeaouli was still a child at the time, governance fell mostly to several of his relatives. Nevertheless, Kamehameha III held his throne longer than any other Hawai'ian monarch (1825–54) and oversaw the creation of a Hawai'ian constitution and legislative branch, among other elements that established Hawai'i as a "civilized" nation in the eyes of the West. During the Great Mahele beginning in 1848, the Hawai'ian government changed land rights from a usufruct system to a fee-simple system, which allowed entrepreneurs such as sugar planters and ranchers to make capital improvements to land without having to fear loss of ownership of their investments. Between the death of Kamehameha II and 1891, five Hawai'ian monarchs took the throne: Alexander Liholiho (Kamehameha IV) in 1854, Lot Kamehameha (Kamehameha V) in 1863, William Charles Lunalilo in 1873, David Kalākaua in 1874, and Queen Liliu'okalani in 1891.

THE ECONOMY OF COLONIALISM IN HAWAI'I

The political transformations that took place in Hawai'i were heavily influenced by a series of boom-and-bust economic factors that drew foreigners to the islands and brought Hawai'ians to many foreign shores. Following Cook, the next four documented foreign ships reached the Hawai'ian Islands in 1786—two ships led by the French explorer Jean-Francois de la Perouse, and two British merchant vessels commanded by Nathaniel Portlock and George Dixon. From then onward, foreign vessels arrived in the Hawai'ian Islands with ever-increasing frequency. Particularly well-documented exploratory voyages include those of George Vancouver (1792–94); Russian voyages in 1804, 1817, and 1818; and the U.S. Exploring Expedition in 1840–41, led by Charles Wilkes. Interspersed between such extensively documented expeditions were thousands of less thoroughly described merchant and whaling voyages that brought tens of thousands of foreigners to Hawai'i. By the late 1700s, New England merchant fleets headed to the Pacific in droves to make profits from the sale of sea-otter skins and seal furs in the Chinese market. For fur traders in the north Pacific, the Hawai'ian Islands were an essential locality for provisioning their vessels on the way to Canton. The fur trade came to a near end by the 1820s due to overhunting, but by the early 1800s, merchants began to focus on acquiring sandalwood (*Santalum* spp.), a tree with fragrant heartwood in Hawai'i's forests and highly desired in Canton. This resource was exploited with such voracity that by 1830 virtually no marketable sandalwood could be found in the Hawai'ian Islands.

A Hawai'ian commoner class (*maka'āinana*) capable of producing vast amounts of food surplus, particularly taro

(*Colocasia esculenta*) and sweet potato (*Ipomoea batatas*), supported the chiefly class. Maka'āinana traditionally provided tribute to the chiefs in many forms in addition to food, from labor on public works, to beautiful mats made from the leaves of the *hala* tree (pandanus), to colorful capes made from feathers of endemic birds that lived in the mountain forests. Chiefs employed the products of maka'āinana labor in the demonstration of their status, and as the nineteenth century began, the chiefs were appropriating many foreign commodities for similar purposes. In the early 1800s, those commodities were paid for with sandalwood gathered largely by the maka'āinana. For example, between 1819 and 1830, Hawai'ian chiefs purchased at least twenty-five foreign vessels for which the maka'āinana collected over 2.7 million kilograms (6 million lb) of sandalwood as payment.

Just as the sandalwood trade was collapsing, the Pacific whaling fleet was burgeoning. Whalers would stop in the Hawai'ian Islands both to hunt whales in winter months and to re-provision their vessels for voyages to summer whaling fields in other parts of the Pacific. In the three decades from 1830 to 1860, an average of over 400 vessels stopped in the Hawai'ian Islands each year. Trade for provisions was still managed by chiefs, but in this era, commoner labor again focused on the production of massive food surpluses to support the provisioning of whaling vessels. This pattern continued until the demise of the Pacific whaling fleet in the early 1860s, which was due to factors such as heavily depleted whale populations, development of the petroleum industry, and the beginning of the U.S. Civil War.

As vessels arrived in Hawai'i, a significant number of foreigners left their ships and remained in the islands, giving rise to a class of Hawai'ian residents commonly known as "beachcombers." In addition, several commercial outfits set up warehouses and accounting offices in port towns such as Honolulu and Lahaina. By the mid 1800s, many foreign residents were American and British sailors; others came from the British penal colony at Botany Bay, Australia; some were Spanish settlers from Mexico and Alta California; and still others were Chinese, Africans, Native Alaskans, and a plethora of other ethnicities. Two exceptionally significant early beachcombers were a British boatswain named John Young, who became a regular advisor of the famous chief Kamehameha I beginning in 1790, and Don Francisco de Paula Marin, a Spanish immigrant who became a prominent figure in Honolulu while Kamehameha I was ruler. Both men married Native Hawai'ian women and raised families in the islands. Archaeological excavations have contributed to our understanding of both of their multi-ethnic households.

Hawai'ians themselves were eager to explore the globe. For example, in 1787–88, one Hawai'ian chief named Ka'iana took passage to Canton, the northwest coast, and back to Hawai'i with British merchant John Meares, and in subsequent years countless Hawai'ians (men and women) sailed on Western vessels and established diasporic Hawai'ian communities, such as Kanaka Village at Fort Vancouver on the Columbia River. Some Hawai'ians became exceptionally seasoned explorers, including Naukane (John Coxe), who, beginning in 1811, traveled from Hawai'i to Astoria, thence overland via Lake Superior to Quebec, on to England, and back to Fort George on the Columbia via Cape Horn in November of 1813. In subsequent years, he again visited Hawai'i and England, and eventually died in the 1830s on the northwest coast. The whaling industry most likely resulted in the greatest outward migration of Hawai'ians during the nineteenth century: Hawai'ian historian Ralph Kuykendall estimates that in the three-year period between 1845 and 1847, nearly 2,000 Hawai'ians served as seamen on foreign ships. Many of these sailors returned to Hawai'i, but others ended up in New England, the Pacific Northwest, South America, and other ports of call for the Pacific fleet. The cumulative effects of such out-migration is indicated by the 2000 U.S. census, which identified nearly as many individuals of Hawai'ian ancestry living in the continental United States as can be found today in the Hawai'ian Islands.

Plantation economies and contemporaneous ranching operations provided the next large economic booms in the Hawai'ian Islands, beginning in the mid-nineteenth century. In 1835 resident businessmen established a plantation to grow sugarcane on Kaua'i, and following the Great Mahele in 1848–55, huge tracts of land came under commercial production for sugar. Other portions of the islands (mostly at higher elevations) were fenced for use as cattle and sheep ranches, with the products being exported to foreign markets. Native Hawai'ian populations had been so heavily decimated by foreign diseases and out-migration by 1872 that an official Hawai'ian census counted only 56,900 Native Hawai'ians in the entire archipelago. Consequently, sugar planters and ranchers searched for other sources of cheap labor; Japanese contract laborers, Portuguese immigrants, and Chinese immigrants composed the majority of the new labor pool. Fearing the growing anti-American sentiment in the Hawai'ian monarchy, the sugar planters, led by Sanford Ballard Dole and other businessmen, and assisted by the U.S. Marines, organized a coup d'état of the indigenous monarchy in 1893. The U.S. Congress then annexed Hawai'i in 1898, despite an official investigative report prepared by U.S. Commissioner James H. Blount recommending otherwise and formal pleas by Queen Liliu'okalani, who had traveled to Washington, D.C., to present her case.

Further Reading: Beaglehole, John Cawte, *The Journals of Captain James Cook on his Voyages of Discovery, III: The Voyage of the Resolution and Discovery, 1776–1780*, parts 1 and 2 (Cambridge:

Cambridge University Press, 1967); Kirch, Patrick, and Marshall Sahlins, *Anahulu: The Anthropology of History in the Kingdom of Hawaii*, 2 vols. (Chicago: University of Chicago Press, 1992); Kittelson, David, "John Coxe: Hawaii's First Soldier of Fortune," in *Hawaii Historical Review: Selected Readings*, edited by Richard Greer (Honolulu: Hawaiian Historical Society, 1969), 213–216; Kuykendall, Ralph, *The Hawaiian Kingdom*, 3 vols. (Honolulu: University of Hawai'i Press, 1938–1967); Mills, Peter, "*Neo* in

Oceania: Foreign Vessels Owned by Hawaiian Chiefs before 1830," *Journal of Pacific History* 38(1) (2003): 53–67; Obeyesekere, Gananath, *The Apotheosis of Captain Cook: European Mythmaking in the Pacific* (Princeton, NJ: Princeton University Press, 1992); Sahlins, Marshall, *How "Natives" Think: About Captain Cook, for Example* (Chicago: University of Chicago Press, 1995).

Peter R. Mills

NATIVE HAWAI'IAN PERSPECTIVES ON ARCHAEOLOGY

Native Hawai'ian people, the descendants of the first settlers of Hawai'i, have been the subjects of study since initial European contact. Polynesians settled the Hawai'ian Islands nearly 2,000 years ago, the first people to set foot on these lands. These Polynesians flourished in the islands for centuries, cultivating the rich Hawai'ian culture that European voyagers first encountered in 1778. Archaeological investigations in the archipelago began in the early 1900s but did not flourish until the 1950s. The relationships between Native Hawai'ians and people interested in their culture have changed through time, and modern Native Hawai'ian perspectives regarding the discipline of archaeology are varied and complex.

Native Hawai'ian attitudes toward archaeology range from disdain to appreciation, with many Native Hawai'ians maintaining a reserved distrust of the discipline largely fostered by a disconnect between archaeologists and the descendants of the people they study. Current perspectives on archaeology are based on historical events such as the development of Hawai'ian archaeology, the Hawai'ian cultural renaissance of the 1970s, and other specific politically charged archaeological projects carried out in recent decades. Personal experiences with the discipline and its practitioners also shape Native Hawai'ian perspectives, which can vary by age, area of residence, and engagement with cultural and political issues.

A BRIEF HISTORY OF ANTHROPOLOGY IN THE PACIFIC

Early travelers in the Pacific Ocean were not curious about the lives of the indigenous peoples who lived there. Voyagers such as Ferdinand Magellan (in 1520) and Abel Tasman (in 1642) were solely occupied with commercial and imperial concerns in the Americas and Asia. Securing colonial outposts in the Pacific region and locating safer and quicker ocean passages between the known continents were essential for obtaining resources, such as spices, for nations such as England, France, and Portugal. The limited attention given to the Pacific islands themselves was confined to obtaining car-

tographic information for the development of maps, again related to commercial and imperial concerns.

Until the development of the European Enlightenment in the later half of the eighteenth century, voyagers in the Pacific took little interest in the islands scattered in this vast ocean, and took even less interest in the peoples who inhabited these lands. However, fueled by the intellectual curiosity of the Enlightenment tradition, expeditions in the late 1700s purposefully incorporated investigations of the natural and cultural life of these islands into their previous pursuits. Thus the study of Native Pacific peoples began, initiated by voyagers such as Captain James Cook and Captain George Vancouver, followed closely by travelers such as George W. Bates and missionaries such as William Ellis and Dom Felice Vaggioli.

Inquiries into the lives of Pacific peoples steadily increased over time. A century after initial Enlightenment observations, the academic discipline of anthropology emerged, and the first anthropologists entered the Pacific arena. When anthropologists finally got to the Pacific, they were so impressed with Polynesian oral traditions that, prior to the 1950s, archaeological excavation was largely deemed unnecessary. Researchers, arriving at age determinations based on oral history and ethnography, erroneously concluded that Polynesians had not resided in the Pacific for a significant length of time and reasoned that deep stratigraphic cultural deposits would be absent. Following in this line of thinking, early anthropologists viewed the Native peoples as their most important source of information and dedicated their efforts to carrying out ethnographic studies. This reliance on Native informants would change with the discovery of deep stratigraphic deposits by Edward W. Gifford, Kenneth P. Emory, and Yoshihiko Sinoto in places like Fiji and Hawai'i.

The renewed support for subsurface excavations, Willard F. Libby's newly developed technique of radiocarbon dating, and developments within archaeology that made it a more scientific approach in the mid-twentieth century transformed the practice of archaeology in the Pacific. Archaeologists in the 1950s emphasized hypothesis testing and a search for gen-

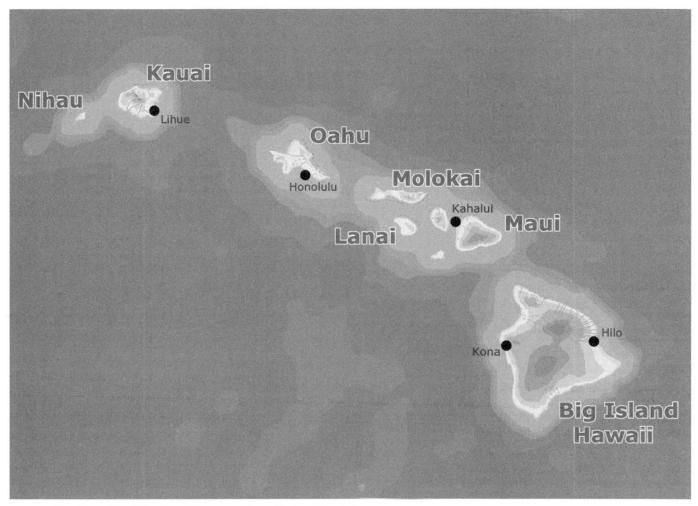

A map of the Hawai'ian Islands.   [Courtesy of the National Park Service]

eral laws of human behavior and turned away from previous culture-historical approaches that focused on specific island peoples. The previous reliance on Native informants was also questioned, such as their reliability for conveying historical information, particularly in light of the expanded time depth revealed by excavations. The skepticism expressed by researchers about the role of oral history in reconstructing the past was a source of tension between archaeologists and Native peoples, and is the basis for ongoing friction in the Pacific. These mid-century developments contributed to distancing Native peoples from the discipline of archaeology by placing artifacts, methods, and theories above Native knowledge.

RECENT SOCIAL AND POLITICAL CONTEXT IN HAWAI'I

Political developments in Hawai'i, most significantly the establishment of statehood in 1959, have also contributed to the changing practice of archaeology in the archipelago. During this time, the rate of economic development in the United States and the Pacific was rapidly increasing, as was the creation of federal and state legislation to protect historical and cultural resources. Historic-preservation-based archaeology, that is, archaeology utilized to mitigate impacts to historical and cultural remains caused by land use and development, part of the broader development of cultural resource management, introduced economic demands to Hawai'ian archaeology. Whereas before the 1960s archaeology had exclusively been pursued for research purposes, the practice was now mandated by government agencies monitoring economic land development in the islands. These new laws further alienated Native Hawai'ians, not only from the discipline but from their cultural roots as well, by taking the stewardship of land and cultural sites from Native Hawai'ians and placing it in the hands of archaeologists. While these mandated laws carried unforeseen consequences, the alternative of having no historic preservation protections in place would have been irreparable, with significantly more cultural sites destroyed by land development.

Socially, the 1950s and 1960s in the United States were a time of political uprising and calls by minority groups for civil rights. In Hawai'i this movement translated into a cultural renaissance, a time when Native Hawai'ians were beginning to shed the burdens of colonial stigmas placed on their culture by Euro-American settlers. Beginning in 1820 with American missionary proselytization, and later through the profit-driven actions of businessmen, Native Hawai'ians and their culture were stifled. Bans were placed on cultural activities such as speaking the Hawai'ian language and dancing hula, while introduced concepts such as individual land ownership radically altered indigenous cultural practices.

The 1970s, however, proved to be the beginning of a time of renewal, overt pride, and eagerness to learn and perpetuate all things Hawai'ian. Cultural knowledge and practices that were commonly observed in the past, but had been relegated to secrecy and silently passed down through generations, were now openly shared. This cultural reawakening fostered a passion for the Hawai'ian language, ocean voyaging, hula, tattooing, and other traditional crafts. Renewed efforts to care for the land and a strong desire for self-governance also characterized this cultural renaissance. Native Hawai'ians were more conscious and protective of their culture and became vocally critical of elements in society that threatened the well-being of Native Hawai'ian people, culture, and land.

Within this context, there are a few crucial events to highlight involving archaeological studies in the last thirty years that shape many current Native Hawai'ian attitudes toward the discipline. These specific events are significant because they embody cultural concerns the people have about the practice of archaeology throughout the Hawai'ian Islands, as well as the policies of the State of Hawai'i regarding land use and development. Native Hawai'ian perspectives on archaeology obviously vary, but the respectful treatment of human remains is one concern shared by all Native Hawai'ians. Other issues of concern to Native Hawai'ians are the privileging of scientific knowledge over Native Hawai'ian knowledge, the problematic link between archaeology and economic development, and the procedures for determining the cultural significance of Native Hawai'ian sites, which are central to decisions of site preservation or destruction.

KAHO'OLAWE ISLAND

One event contributing to current Native Hawai'ian perspectives on archaeology is the grass-roots efforts of a group of individuals, principally made up of Native Hawai'ians, fighting to stop the military bombing of Kaho'olawe Island. After the December 1941 bombing of Pearl Harbor, O'ahu Island martial law was declared in the Territory of Hawai'i, and Kaho'olawe Island was seized by the U.S. Navy for bombing practice. The bombing of the island did not cease at the end of World War II and continued unimpeded until 1976 when a group of people, the Protect Kaho'olawe Ohana (PKO), illegally occupied the island to stop the bombing and heighten

public awareness about access to the land. That same year the PKO filed a suit in federal district court, *Aluli v. Brown*, to seek an end to the U.S. Navy's military activity on the island.

The central issue concerning the Protect Kaho'olawe Ohana was the desecration of the island, both its natural and cultural integrity. The protection of Native Hawai'ian cultural sites from destruction was of utmost importance, because these elements of history, more so than natural resources, could not be regained once damaged. In 1977 a federal judge ordered the U.S. Navy to do an environmental impact statement, which included a survey of the historical sites on the island. Four years later the entire island was placed on the National Register for Historic Places and designated the Kaho'olawe Archaeological District. Former President George H. W. Bush finally ordered his secretary of defense to terminate all weapons training on the island in 1990. The island was transferred to the State of Hawai'i in 1994, the U.S. Navy relinquished control of access to the island in 2003, and all work related to environmental and cultural studies ended in 2004. Today the island is managed by the Kaho'olawe Island Reserve Commission, whose mission is to provide safe and meaningful use of the island for Native Hawai'ian traditional and cultural practices, as well as the restoration of the island and its waters.

The decades-long struggle to restore the integrity of Kaho'olawe Island was a great achievement for Native Hawai'ians, fostering cultural pride, stewardship, and advocacy. The field of archaeology contributed to the goals of the Native Hawai'ian people, in this instance by using scientifically gathered evidence to support Hawai'ian claims of the island's historical significance. Although the benefits of archaeological contributions to the cause are obvious, what is less obvious is the sense that Native Hawai'ian claims about their own culture held less weight than those of Western-trained archaeologists, and what Native Hawai'ians were saying about the island was only found credible after scientific proof was provided.

HONOKAHUA, MAUI ISLAND

In 1987 construction work began at Honokahua for the development of the Ritz-Carlton Kapalua Hotel. A Maui-based community group called Hui Alanui O Makena made attempts to stop the development before construction began, knowing cultural sites, including human graves, existed at the proposed hotel location, but they were unsuccessful. At that time the State of Hawai'i lacked any historic preservation laws associated with the discovery of unmarked graves, and the Department of Health was the only government agency that had regulations pertaining to the treatment of the dead. There were no legal means of barring the development from moving forward. When work commenced, construction crews began to unearth Native Hawai'ian burials, and more than 1,000 human remains would be systematically excavated and removed from the burial site by archaeologists. Individuals of all ages were exposed, and analysis showed the burial site had been used for at least 1,000 years and was probably last used in the early 1800s.

As development for the hotel progressed, and the number of human remains mounted, Native Hawai'ian unease grew exponentially and led to protests at the construction site. Native Hawai'ians from around the islands traveled to Honokahua to voice their outrage at the disrespectful treatment of their ancestors, for the sake of a proposed hotel. The issue was taken to the state capitol on O'ahu Island, where more protests were held to make members of the government aware of the desecration taking place on Maui. More than a year after construction began, former Governor John Waihee ordered a stop to the disinterment process in late 1988. The resulting solution was the purchase of the 5.4-hectare (13.6 acre) sand dune site by the state to be set aside as a preserve, the Honokahua Preservation Site, now a registered State Historic Place. The development project was not abandoned either, as the hotel site was moved uphill away from the preserve.

Not all of the people buried at Honokahua were disturbed in the development process, and estimates of over 2,000 Native Hawai'ians are suggested to have been originally interred there. The individuals whose burials had been excavated were reinterred in designated locations by a small group of Native Hawai'ians, and the cultural site was restored. The events at Honokahua also spurred the formation of Hui Malama I Na Kupuna O Hawai'i Nei, a Native Hawai'ian organization specifically concerned with the care and repatriation of ancient Native Hawai'ian human remains. In the aftermath of this distressing event, several advances were made in state historic preservation law regarding the treatment of Native Hawai'ian remains. Chapter 6E of the Hawai'i Revised Statues was amended to provide greater protection for unmarked burial sites, affording them the same protections given to modern cemeteries. Penalties and procedures were established to deal with circumstances of intentional or inadvertent exposure of human skeletal remains from unmarked burials. Finally the Burial Sites Program was established, as a branch of the State Historic Preservation Division, to regulate the implementation of these laws and to oversee the care, management, protection, and inventory of unmarked burials throughout Hawai'i.

HĀLAWA AND HAIKU VALLEY, H-3 FREEWAY, O'AHU ISLAND

Hawai'i's 1959 Statehood Act secured federal monies for the construction of three interstate and defense freeways on O'ahu Island; H-3 Freeway was the last to be built and was opened in December of 1997. At a cost of $1.3 billion and spanning four decades of work, H-3 Freeway stands as the largest and most expensive public works project in the history of Hawai'i, as well as the most controversial. Along with the other distinctions the freeway holds, it was the first project in

Hawai'i to require an environmental impact statement under the National Environmental Policy Act. Possible cultural impacts caused by freeway construction were included as part of the environmental studies, and archaeological work for the project began in 1970 under the direction of the Bernice Pauahi Bishop Museum.

The historic preservation issues faced by the project were numerous and began at the planning stages, when design and construction of the freeway were initiated prior to the completion of archaeological surveys of the proposed route. Inadequate inventory surveys created difficult situations in which the preservation of Native Hawai'ian cultural sites were pitted against the costly rerouting of the freeway. Department of Transportation officials put themselves in the difficult position of either preserving the cultural sites at an additional cost of millions of dollars or destroying sites to accommodate the planned freeway route. These problems arose because historic preservation was not integrated into the project until 1987, and this created a harried atmosphere where archaeologists were sometimes working literally steps ahead of bulldozers.

Specific conflicts between archaeologists and Native Hawai'ian groups arose over the interpretations of cultural sites. Two sites in Hālawa valley known as Hale O Papa and the Luakini heiau (place of worship and human sacrifice) and the site known as Kukuiokane in Kaneohe stood at the center of these disputes. Controversy over the Hālawa valley sites erupted in a whistle-blowing scandal when a Bishop Museum cultural historian publicly accused the museum of downplaying the cultural significance of the sites. The historian believed the two sites were part of a larger ceremonial complex, an interpretation not shared by the principal Bishop Museum archaeologists or the State Historic Preservation Division's chief archaeologist. Nevertheless, the incident fostered distrust in Native Hawai'ian communities and provoked questions of whether the archaeologists were assigning less significance to sites in order to push the development process forward. Amidst protest marches and prayer vigils the state decided to realign the freeway at a cost of $10 million to avoid the sites.

In another section of the proposed freeway problems emerged around the site of Kukuiokane, which was alternatively interpreted by some Native Hawai'ians as a place of worship and by archaeologists as a series of agricultural terraces. This situation was resolved by carefully covering the site with durable construction textiles and dirt to bury it under the elevated freeway. Mitigating the adverse impacts of development, such as the construction of a freeway, can take many forms, for example, leaving the cultural site undisturbed, recording the information about a site and allowing it to be destroyed, or burying a site to protect it from damage. For many Native Hawai'ians the alternative options, other than leaving a site undisturbed, are simply unacceptable because site destruction provides no real benefit to the people or culture. Despite spending over $22 million for the archaeology work, the survey reports for the project were still not completed by the freeway's opening, in part due to staff turnover at the museum, construction delays, and design changes. To mitigate the cultural impacts of H-3 Freeway, the Federal Highway Administration funded a project in 2000 called Hālawa-Luluku Interpretive Development. The project, which is still in the planning stages, is intended to provide such benefits as educational opportunities about the affected areas, replanting of native vegetation, and restoration and improved access to cultural sites.

Further Reading: Cachola-Abad, C. Kehaunani, and Edward H. Ayau, "He Pane Hoomalamalama: Setting the Record Straight and a Second Call for Partnership," *Hawaiian Archaeology* 7 (1999):

73–81; Cachola-Abad, C. Kehaunani, and Edward H. Ayau, "Approaches to Heritage: Hawaiian and Pacific Perspectives on Preservation," *CRM* 19(8) (1996): 11–16; Dye, Thomas S., *Tales of Two Cultures: Traditional Historical and Archaeological Interpretations of Hawaiian Prehistory*, Bernice P. Bishop Museum Occasional Papers No. 29 (Honolulu: Bernice P. Bishop Museum, 1989), 3–22; Kirch, Patrick V., *On the Road of the Winds: An Archaeological History of the Pacific Islands before European Contact* (Berkeley: University of California Press, 2000); State Historic Preservation Division, State of Hawai'i Department of Land and Natural Resources Web site, http://www.state.hi.us/dlnr/hpd/naiwikupuna.htm (online May 2006); Trask, Haunani-Kay, "What Do You Mean 'We,' White Man?" in *From a Native Daughter*, edited by Haunani-Kay Trask (Honolulu: University of Hawai'i Press, 1999), 123–135.

Kathleen L. Kawelu

PU'UOMAHUKA HEIAU, KEAĪWA HEIAU, ULUPŌ HEIAU, KĀNE'ĀKĪ HEIAU, AND KŪKANILOKO BIRTHING STONES

O'ahu Island, Hawai'i
Native Hawai'ian Temple and Legendary Sites

O'ahu Island is the most developed, populated, and widely visited of the Hawai'ian Islands. The vast development and activity on the island has resulted in the recordation of numerous archaeological sites. Although many have been ultimately destroyed since their initial discovery, some have also been preserved and reconstructed, and are accessible as interpretative centers for the public to learn about ancient and historic Hawai'ian culture. Many of the preserved archaeological sites are *heiau* or religious temples that were constructed and modified during various periods in the prehistory of O'ahu Island. Native Hawai'ians were polytheistic and worshiped many gods, goddesses, and demi-gods, consequently these heiau were dedicated to different deities and for different purposes (e.g., agricultural, war, healing).

Because many of these sites have not only been examined archaeologically but also have been remembered in the oral traditions of Native Hawai'ians, a compelling picture of their ancient uses emerges.

PU'UOMAHUKA HEIAU, PŪPŪKEA AHUPUA'A, O'AHU, HAWAI'I
Pu'uomahuka Heiau is located in Pūpūkea high above Waimea Bay and is the largest heiau on O'ahu Island. Although its function probably evolved over time, it is likely that this site served as a *luakini*, or sacrificial heiau, in the

1700s during a time of fierce political battles between the islands.

Pu'uomahuka means "hill of escape" and is believed to have been initially constructed around AD 1600. The heiau has been associated with the eighteenth-century *kahuna* (priest) Ka'opulupulu, and chief Kahahana. From this structure, it has been said that Ka'opulupulu contacted the god Mahuka and determined that Kekaulike, chief of Kaua'i Island, desired a truce with Kahahana. It is believed to have been connected with the heiau at Wailua on Kaua'i using signal fires that served as a form of communication between the islands.

It is also believed that this may have been where the bodies of three of Captain Vancouver's men were brought to be sacrificed in 1792 when his ship the *Daedalus* anchored in Waimea Bay and the men set forth to acquire fresh water. In 1795, when Kamehameha I took over O'ahu, his high priest Hewahewa was known to conduct religious ceremonies and rituals at Pu'uomahuka up until traditional Hawai'ian religion was outlawed in 1819.

The site covers nearly 0.8 hectares (2 acres) and measures 175 meters (575 ft) by 51. 8 meters (170 ft). The structure consists of three low adjoining enclosures, their walls ranging from 0.9 to 1.8 meters (3–6 ft) high. The interior of the enclosures was paved with large basalt and coral boulders overlain with a

Pu'uomahuka Heiau, Pūpūkea Ahupua'a, O'ahu.   [Lisa Anderson]

surface layer of small waterworn stones. Archaeological investigations at the site indicate that it was constructed in a series of phases, with the upper or eastern enclosure constructed first, and the two lower enclosures added at a later time, probably in the 1700s. The interior of the upper enclosure would have housed wood and thatched structures such as an oracle tower, altar, and various *hale* (houses) that contained sacred and ceremonial objects. Carved wooden images (*ki'i*) of deities would have stood near the altar and entrance to the site.

Visitors can access the site by traveling north on Kamehameha Highway, turning right at Pūpūkea Road and traveling uphill until reaching the site entrance. It is open daily during daylight hours and offers interpretative signage and informational brochures.

KEAĪWA HEIAU, AIEA AHUPUA'A, O'AHU, HAWAI'I

Keīawa Heiau is a medicinal or healing heiau located in Aiea Heights. The temple would have been overseen by a kahuna that specialized in diagnosing and healing those who were wounded or ill. The art of healing in Hawai'i was intricately tied into religious ritual and involved the use of medicinal plants, fasting, and prayers. The kahuna would also train students at this heiau in the arts of healing.

Keaīwa has been translated as meaning either "incomprehensible," or a "period of fasting and meditation." Both translations

are traced to the usage of the heiau as an ancient medical center. The first translation attests to the idea that no one could comprehend the powers of the kahuna, who used plants to heal people. The second translation was associated with the conduct of the initiates in the arts of healing during their study.

The construction date for this temple is unknown; however, one source indicates that it was built in the sixteenth century by an O'ahu chief Kakuhihewa and his kahuna named Keaīwa. The heiau consists of a small rectangular enclosure that measures 30.48 × 48.8 meters (100 × 160 ft) and is composed of low stacked stone walls. It would have contained one or more thatched structures in the interior for storage of medicinal items and implements.

During World War II the structure was badly damaged by soldiers who removed many of the large basalt stones that made up its enclosure wall in order to construct a road. However, the site was restored in 1951 and has since been accessible to the public. Located at the end of Aiea Heights Drive, the site is open daily to visitors during sunlight hours and offers interpretative signage and informational brochures.

ULUPŌ HEIAU, KAILUA AHUPUA'A, O'AHU, HAWAI'I

Ulupō Heiau is a large platform structure located on the edge of Kawai Nui Marsh, a former 160-hectare fishpond that was surrounded by an expansive irrigated and dryland agricultural

Keaīwa Heiau, Aiea Ahupua'a, O'ahu.   [Lisa Anderson]

field system. Because of its proximity to such fertile lands, Ulupō is believed to have been initially constructed as an agricultural heiau. Later, when the islands were locked in battle, it is possible that its function may have changed to a luakini or sacrificial heiau dedicated to ensuring success in war.

Ulupō means "night inspiration," and this name reflects the belief that the heiau was built by the legendary Menehune. The Menehune are little people of Hawai'ian legend that were capable of great construction feats. According to legend, the heiau platform was constructed by passing large rocks across a distance of more than 16.1 kilometers (10 mi), hand by hand, in a single night.

Although the construction date of the heiau is uncertain, its association in legend to the Menehune suggests it is quite ancient. Use of the heiau has also been associated with various chiefs, which provide the site with a timeline, including Kukuhihewa in the 1400s, Kūali'i in the late 1600s, and the Maui chief Kahekili in the late 1700s. However, it is believed to have fallen into disuse by the time Kamehameha I conquered O'ahu in 1795.

The platform of the heiau measures 42.7 × 54.9 meters (140 × 180 ft) and is nearly 9.1 meters (30 ft) high. There is a stone pathway across the center of the platform that is said to have led to a house site that is now destroyed. There is also a natural spring on the site that would have served in religious rituals.

Ulupō Heiau is located behind the YMCA building at 1200 Kailua Road. The heiau site is accessible to the public during daylight hours and offers informational signage and brochures.

KĀNE'ĀKĪ HEIAU, MĀKAHA AHUPUA'A, O'AHU, HAWAI'I

Kāne'ākī Heiau is perhaps one of the best-preserved heiau on O'ahu. The structure is believed to have initially served as an agricultural heiau but later was rededicated as a luakini or war temple. *Kāne'ākī* means "hair-switch-man" in literal translation and may be a reference to Kane, the god of fresh water. However, *ki* is the Hawai'ian word for the ti plant, so another possible translation is "man of the ti," which would honor the god Ku and his association with agriculture. According to oral tradition, in 1795 Kamehameha I ordered that Kāne'ākī be transformed into a war heiau to coincide with his plans to conquer the island of Kaua'i.

The initial construction of the heiau dates back to the fifteenth century and began as a two-terrace structure. Additional construction phases followed, until the largest platform was erected under the power of the paramount chief of Mākaha valley. During this time the size of the heiau nearly doubled. The site consists of two main enclosed platforms with numerous associated terraces and enclosures.

The site has been completely restored with reconstructed altars and thatched structures based upon the locations of

Ulupō Heiau, Kailua Ahupua'a, O'ahu. [Lisa Anderson]

posthole features encountered during archaeological investigations. Interpretative signs throughout the site clearly outline each of the significant features and their uses. Although the site is located on private property, it is open to the public, weather permitting, Tuesday through Sunday from 10:00 am to 2:00 pm.

KŪKANILOKO BIRTHING STONES, WAHIAWĀ AHUPUA'A, O'AHU, HAWAI'I

Unlike the previous sites, Kūkaniloko is not a heiau structure but instead is represented by a series of smooth, worn boulders located in the center of the island. It is at this site that tradition holds the royal class (ali'i) children were born.

Sacred stones (pōhaku) form an important part of traditional Hawai'ian religion. The stones of Kūkaniloko are one such dramatic example. The earliest known reference of a birth at the site is believed to have been sometime between AD 1100 and 1400 (although it could have been earlier) with the birth of Kapawa. The site continued to play a role in the birthplace of important royal personages up until the late 1700s, when Kamehameha I made plans (unsuccessfully) for his heir Liholiho to be born there in 1797.

According to legend, the birth of a royal infant was attended by thirty-six chiefs, and the site was said to have maintained two rows of eighteen stones where these chiefs would stand during the ceremony. The stone against which the chiefess would lean during birth was called Kūkaniloko, and

is said to have relieved the pains of labor. Following the birth the infant was taken to a nearby heiau (now destroyed) for the ceremonial cutting of the umbilical cord and from whence the sacred drums would beat to announce the birth.

Today, the site consists of 180 semi-embedded stones covering an area of approximately 0.2 hectare (half an acre). Many of the stones have smooth bowl-like depressions or fluted edges that are believed to be the result of a combination of human modification and natural weathering. The stones are covered in the natural red pigments of the surrounding iron-rich soil.

The site can be found in the midst of pineapple fields at the intersection of Kamehameha Highway and Whitmore Avenue. Interpretative signs are present at the site, which is open daily during daylight hours.

INTERPRETIVE CENTERS

O'ahu Island is also home to several excellent public interpretation centers housed in significant historic structures where information on the culture and history of the Hawai'ian Islands can be found. The Bishop Museum located on Bernice Street in Honolulu maintains excellent displays and collections of both pre-contact and post-contact Hawai'ian material culture. The Mission Houses Museum, located on South King Street in Honolulu, provides information on the missionary era of Hawai'ian history. The museum is composed of three original historic structures dating back to the 1830s. Finally,

Kūkaniloko birthing stones, Wahiawā Ahupua'a, O'ahu.   [Lisa Anderson]

'Iolani Palace, the only royal palace in the United States, on South King Street, provides visitors with an in-depth look at the monarchy era of Hawai'ian history.

Further Reading: James, Van, *Ancient Sites of O'ahu* (Honolulu, HI: Bishop Museum Press, 1991); Kirch, Patrick Vinton, *Feathered Gods and Fishhooks* (Honolulu: University of Hawai'i Press, 1985); McAllister, J. Gilbert, *Archaeology of Oahu* (Honolulu, HI: Bishop Museum Press, 1933); O'ahu State Parks, Hawai'i State Parks Web site, http://hawaiistateparks.org/parks/oahu/ (online March 2007); Sterling, Elizabeth, and Catherine Summers, *Sites of Oahu* (Honolulu, HI: Bishop Museum Press, 1978).

Lisa Anderson

HEIAU COMPLEXES AT WAILUA AND HA'ENA, RUSSIAN FORT ELISABETH, AND OTHER SITES

Kaua'i Island, Hawai'i

Ancient and Historic Native Hawai'ian Sites

Kaua'i and the smaller adjacent island of Ni'ihau (now privately owned) are the two northwestern-most islands in the Hawai'ian chain that were occupied at the time of Western contact in 1778, although other Hawai'ian islands further to the northwest contain evidence of prehistoric occupation and use (particularly Nihoa and Necker). Kaua'i and Ni'ihau are separated from the other main Hawai'ian Islands by the Ka'ie'ie Waho Channel, which is 103 kilometers (64 mi) wide, and the largest channel between any of the main islands. Although oral histories and early observations by

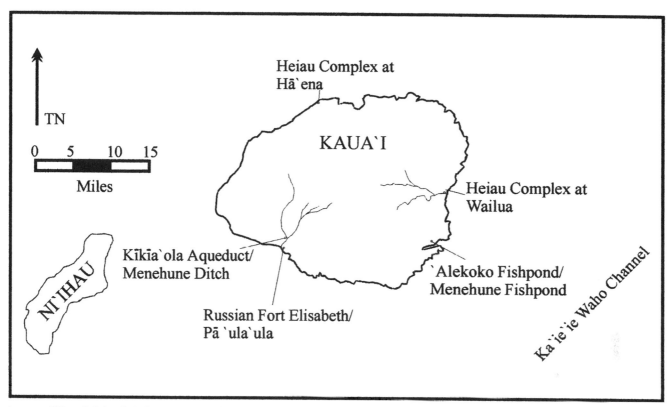

A map of Kaua'i Island, indicating several important archaeological sites.   [Peter R. Mills]

foreigners show that Hawai'ians regularly voyaged across the channel, the distance and difficulty of the crossing may have added to the relative cultural isolation of Kaua'i and Ni'ihau from the other islands. Oral histories show that Kaua'i and Ni'ihau were often controlled by the same chiefly lines. Several aspects of Kaua'i's material culture differed, however, from the cultural patterns observed on the other main islands, including the styles of wooden images in ritual temples, or *heiau*, and the forms of stone pounding tools used to transform taro tubers (*Colocasia esculenta*) into the highly savored staple of the traditional Hawai'ian diet, *poi*. Kaua'i also has rich folklore pertaining to the "Menehune," who are thought to be a small and industrious people who lived in the uplands.

As of 2005, paleoenvironmental studies and archaeological investigations have generated almost 300 radiocarbon dates associated with human activity on the island of Kaua'i. These dates provide good evidence that there were human-induced modifications of Kaua'i's ecosystem by AD 800–1000, and less-substantiated evidence of such activity as much as 500 years earlier. By the time Captain Cook's expedition first arrived at Waimea Bay on the southwest shore of Kaua'i in 1778, over 2,000 people met the British explorers there.

HEIAU COMPLEX AT WAILUA

The Wailua River watershed begins near the center of Kaua'i at Mount Wai'ale'ale—one of the wettest spots on earth, with a thirty-two-year average of 1,168 centimeters (460 in) of rainfall per year—and flows eastward through lowlands that were well suited to taro cultivation. Oral traditions indicate that the Wailua River valley was renowned throughout the Hawai'ian Islands as a chiefly center. This single watershed contains various large heiau still visible along the river.

The ruins of Hikinaakala' Heiau are on the south bank of the Wailua River near the shorefront in Lydgate State Park. Although much of the stone has been removed, its walls were formerly about 3.3 meters (11 ft) thick and 1.8 meters (6 feet) high, with overall dimensions of 120 × 24 meters (395 × 80 ft). Remnants of the stone walls of Malae Heiau are slightly inland on the south side of the Wailua River, and are 83 × 99 meters (273 × 324 ft) in outline. This site has been surrounded by sugarcane fields for years but is currently undergoing restoration. Malae Heiau is reported to be ritually linked to Poli'ahu Heiau, which is about another 1.6 kilometers (1 mi) inland from Malae, and situated on a high bluff on the north bank of the Wailua River. Poli'ahu Heiau is in the best state of preservation of the Wailua River Heiau complex and has interpretive signage available at a roadside parking area. Below it, on the north bank of the Wailua River, is a sacred coconut grove and Holoholoku' Heiau. There are several large stones associated with this complex where high chiefesses gave birth to their children, adding to the *mana* of chiefs who were born there. Some traditions also state that the first Polynesian drum introduced to Hawai'i was brought to this site.

HEIAU COMPLEX AT HA'ENA

At the northern extent of the coastal highway lie Ha'ena and the beginning of the Na' Pali coast hiking trail. This location is most famous for its association with Lohi'au, who studied under a hula master named Paoa and who inspired a rivalry between the goddess of hula, Laka, and her sister Pele, the volcano goddess. Near the base of the cliffs in Ha'ena, above Ke'e' beach, there are the remains of a house platform or heiau associated with Lohi'au and a dancing pavilion and shrine often referred to as "Ka ulu o Paoa" or "Ka ulu o Laka" ("the inspiration of Paoa," or "the inspiration of Laka"). Interpretive signage at this location is limited due to the fragile nature of the sites and their continued ritual significance to Native Hawai'ian cultural practitioners. Many current hula dancers still make pilgrimages to this location, which is managed by Hawai'i State Parks.

KI'KI'A'OLA AQUEDUCT ("MENEHUNE DITCH"), WAIMEA

This prehistoric aqueduct system was first described in detail by Captain George Vancouver in 1792. Irregularly sized but beautifully dressed rectangular slabs of basalt were used to build this aqueduct that carried water out of Waimea Canyon, on the southwest side of Kaua'i, onto the surrounding plains. Oral traditions suggest that Menehune built this structure. Today, very little of the former aqueduct remains visible, but portions of the stonework can still be seen along the side of Menehune Road approximately 2 kilometers (1.3 mi) behind the main shopping complex in the town of Waimea. A bronze plaque is placed in the cliff to commemorate the feature, but there is little other interpretive signage at the site. Further information is available at the West Hawai'i Visitor Center in the town of Waimea.

'ALEKOKO FISHPOND ("MENEHUNE FISHPOND")

This is one of the largest Hawai'ian fishponds, and unlike many of the other large fishponds, which were built along ocean reefs, 'Alekoko pond is built in freshwater along the Hule'ia River in Niumalu. An 850-meter wall, variably built of stone and earth, separates the pond from the river; all the other boundaries are formed by natural topography. Radiocarbon dates from cores taken of the pond deposits suggest that the wall was built in the AD 1300s–1400s, which coincides with an era of rapid population expansion in the region. According to oral traditions, Menehune built the pond for a chief named 'Alekoko and his wife Kala'la'lehua. Today, the pond is located on private property approximately 0.8 kilometers (0.5 mi) from Kaua'i's main port in Na'wiliwili on Hulemalu Road, and is adjacent to the Huleia National Wildlife Refuge. An interpretive sign is placed at an overlook on Hulemalu Road.

RUSSIAN FORT ELISABETH (PA'ULA'ULA, OR "RED ENCLOSURE")

The Russian Fort Elisabeth National Historic Landmark is on Kaua'i's west side near the town of Waimea at the mouth of the Waimea River, where Captain Cook first set foot in the Hawai'ian Islands in 1778. The fort was built in 1816 when Kaumuali'i, paramount chief of Kaua'i, formed an alliance with fur traders from the Russian-American Company. The official name for the fort emphasizes its Western characteristics, but recent research has revealed that many Hawai'ian elements exist within this site. The fort was situated within Kaumuali'i's residential compound, and Hawai'ians built most of it. Archaeological surveys and excavations show that interior structures are in many ways similar to those of Hawai'ian heiau. The walls are over 3 meters (10 ft) thick and enclose more than 6,000 square meters. The monumental size of this fort stands in stark contrast to another smaller fort that the Russians built on the north side of the island without Kaumuali'i's direct assistance. Kaumuali'i evicted the Russian-American Company employees from the island by 1817, but Hawai'ian chiefs continued to use the fort in Waimea (which they called Pa'ula'ula) through 1854. This site demonstrates the fundamental complexities of interpreting multicultural sites in the contact era. Although Kaumuali'i's residential compound surrounding Pa'ula'ula has been destroyed by sugarcane cultivation, the crumbling stone and earth walls of the fort are easily accessible from a parking area where there is an interpretive display maintained by Hawai'i State Parks. Portions of the second fort on the north shore, called Fort Alexander, can still be seen adjacent to the valet parking at the Princeville Hotel.

Further Reading: Bennett, Wendell Clark, *Archaeology of Kauai*, Bernice Pauahi Bishop Museum Bulletin No. 80 (Honolulu, HI: Bishop Museum Press, 1931); Burney, L. P, and David A. Burney, "Charcoal Stratigraphies for Kaua'i and the Timing of Human Arrival," *Pacific Science* 57 (2003): 211, 226; Carson, Mike, and Michael Graves, *Na Mea Kahiko o Kaua'i: Archaeological Studies in Kaua'i*, Special Publication No. 2 (Honolulu: Society for Hawaiian Archaeology, 2005); Joesting, Edward, *Kaua'i: The Separate Kingdom* (Honolulu: University of Hawaii Press, 1984); Mills, Peter R., *Hawai'i's Russian Adventure: A New Look at Old History* (Honolulu: University of Hawai'i Press, 2002); Wichman, Frederick B., *Na'Pua Ali'i o Kaua'i: Ruling Chiefs of Kaua'i* (Honolulu: University of Hawai'i Press, 2003).

Peter R. Mills

THE PETROGLYPHS AT OLOWALU, THE KEONE'Ō'IO ARCHAEOLOGICAL DISTRICT (LA PÉROUSE BAY), AND OTHER SITES

Maui Island, Hawai'i

Ancient and Historical Sites

Sometime between AD 300 and 750, Polynesian voyagers colonized the island of Maui, the second largest landmass in the Hawai'ian archipelago. By the time of European contact in 1778, Maui had become an important center of ancient Hawai'ian culture and political development, serving as the seat for ruling chiefs such as Pi'ilani, Kekaulike, and Kahekili. Throughout its history, it has also been a land of contrasts: between commoners and the ruling class, between "wet" and "dry" environmental regimes, and between Native practices and foreign influences. These contrasts have long fascinated Maui residents and visitors, although it is only within the last few decades that archaeologists have begun to study the island in earnest.

Although Maui is a single island, it was formed from the eruptions of two separate shield volcanoes that coalesced to form a broad isthmus joining West and East Maui. West Maui is considerably older and exhibits deeply dissected valleys with highly weathered soils. East Maui, formed by the now-dormant Haleakalā volcano, lacks the large, deep valleys of West Maui but constitutes the larger part of the island.

The archaeological landscape of Maui is dominated by unmortared stone architecture constructed in a wide array of styles and configurations that range from simple linear shelters to elaborate temple complexes. The timber and thatch superstructures of these sites have long since disappeared, although the foundations that remain provide clues about religious worship, the structure of households, and agricultural practices in the centuries before contact. Archaeologists group these centuries into four main phases: the Colonization period (AD 300–600), which remains little understood; the Developmental period (AD 600–1100), during which distinctly Hawai'ian forms of material culture emerged; the Expansion period (AD 1100–1650), a time of rapid population growth, political change, and agricultural intensification; and the protohistoric period (AD 1650–1795), when the archipelago was divided into four major chiefdoms centered on the islands of Hawai'i, O'ahu, Maui, and Kauai'i.

Many archaeological sites on Maui have been preserved and remain accessible to those who wish to learn more about the ancient and historic Hawai'ian past. The most formidable of these consist of *heiau*, or temple sites, which were dedicated to various gods in the Hawai'ian pantheon. Other sites include habitation structures, which were widely dispersed across the landscape and consisted of functionally discrete structures that were clustered to form a single household complex (*kauhale*). The structures within these kauhale are represented archaeologically by rectangular or circular enclosures; C-, L-, or U-shaped walls; terraces; platforms; rockshelters; and even lava tubes. Native Hawai'ians were also ingenious farmers, and the remains of irrigated or dry terraces that would have supported the growth of staple crops such as taro (*kalo*) or sweet potato (*'uala*) are widespread. Many resources exist for those who wish to visit these sites or learn more about them, and readers are directed to begin with the "Further Reading" section outlined at the end of this contribution.

PETROGLYPHS AT OLOWALU

Before the arrival of European missionaries, the Native Hawai'ian language had never been transcribed; traditions and oral histories were passed on verbally and were communicated *non-verbally* through architecture, design motifs on portable goods, and through markings on immovable rock faces. These markings, known as petroglyphs, have long fascinated scholars and the public alike. Among the most accessible petroglyphs on West Maui that may be visited today are those at Olowalu, south of Lahina. Carved into the cliff face at Olowalu are human figures depicted either as stick figures or as figures with triangular torsos, which may be an attempt to represent both the ruling and commoner classes. Also pecked into the rock are canoe sails, dog figures, and letters, indicating that at least some of these marking were made after the arrival of European missionaries.

HALEKI'I AND PIHANA HEIAU

On the north side of West Maui is the ancient district of Wailuku. During the expansion and protohistoric periods, it served as a seat of power for chiefs such as Pi'ilani, Kekaulike, and Kahekili and was the largest continuous area of wet taro cultivation in the archipelago. Of the many sites that have been preserved in Wailuku, perhaps the most accessible are Haleki'i and Pihana Heiau. First recorded by John Stokes in 1916, the Pihana Heiau is a substantial enclosure with an attached open court. It would have functioned as a *luakini heiau*, or a temple in which human sacrifices were performed in honor of particularly significant events. Historic accounts note that in 1790 Kamehameha I offered sacrifices

Coastal view on Maui.   [Lisa Holm]

at this heiau and that Keopuolani, the wife of Kamehameha I and mother of Liholiho (Kamehameha II) and Kauikeaouli (Kamehameha III), was also born there.

Located just to the northwest of Pihana Heiau is Haleki'i Heiau, a similar structure measuring 91 × 45 meters (300 × 150 ft). It is built of massive waterworn boulders and features a series of four terraces along its south side. It too may have functioned as a luakini heiau, or it may have served as a chiefly compound with timber and thatch houses built atop the stone platform accompanied by family shrines in which the family gods might be honored. Carved images (ki'i) representing the gods would have adorned the heiau, and may have given Haleki'i ("house of images") its name. Excavations of both structures by Michael Kolb in 1989–90 revealed that Pihana was built sometime between AD 1260 and 1400 and that it was expanded between AD 1410 and 1640. It was during this later period that Haleki'i was built, and both were further elaborated between AD 1662 and 1705 and then again between AD 1748 and 1786, when Maui chiefs were engaged in interisland conflict with their rivals on Hawai'i.

KE'ANAE PENINSULA

The Ke'anae Peninsula, located in the district of Ko'olau, is a broad, flat expanse that projects nearly 1.6 kilometers (1 mi) into the sea beyond the Ke'anae valley. Formed by late eruptions from Haleakalā, the peninsula receives its water supply from the Polaukulu Stream, which flows from the northwest corner of the valley to feed irrigated fields (lo'i) of taro (kalo). Although the construction of these fields dates to pre-contact times, taro continues to be cultivated there today using traditional ancient Hawai'ian methods. No archaeological excavations have taken place on the Ke'anae Peninsula, so the age of the irrigation system is unknown, although it remains a living exhibit of past agricultural practices that visitors may enjoy today.

Dog and anthropomorph petroglyphs found at Olowalu.   [Lisa Holm]

PI'ILANIHALE HEIAU

East of Ko'olau and the Ke'anac Peninsula is the district of Hāna, where abundant rainfall supported ancient historic crops of dryland and irrigated taro, sweet potato, and breadfruit. According to Native Hawai'ian oral tradition, a West Maui high chief named Pi'ilani brought the independent chiefdoms of Maui under his control and united them within a single polity (ca. AD 1570). The heiau of Pi'ilanihale may have been dedicated to honor that achievement, and it stands today as perhaps the largest temple site within the entire Hawai'ian chain. Consisting of two platforms joined by a large central terrace, the heiau covers nearly 1.4 hectares (3 acres). It features five levels of terraces, and its imposing height of 12 meters (40 ft) is enhanced by its position on a broad ridge. Excavated in 1989–90 by Michael Kolb, the earliest radiocarbon age determination indicated that construction may have begun in the late twelfth century. It was determined that further phases of building occurred during the sixteenth century and again during the late eighteenth century. Like many Native Hawai'ian temple sites that have been subject to archaeological excavation, the sequences of construction and elaboration evident at Pi'ilani Heiau reflect a complex history of religious belief and sociopolitical power.

SCHOOLHOUSE RUINS AT KAUPŌ

Proceeding clockwise around the island from Hāna, visitors come to the Kaupō District and the coastal flat of Mokulau. There on a broad windswept plain are the remains of the Hawai'ian Congregationalist Huialoha Church (ca. AD 1859), the remnants of a former schoolhouse, a small graveyard, and other ancillary buildings. The most intact of these structures is the old schoolhouse, which was constructed of blocks of cut lava rock held in place with coral-lime mortar. During the mid-nineteenth century, European missionaries used such schools to teach Native Hawai'ians to read and write in their own language, using the Bible or basic primers as instructional material. Scholars such as Samuel Kamakau and David Malo were educated in similar missionary schools; they went on to record histories of the Native Hawai'ian people, and their contributions are invaluable records of Native Hawai'ian lifeways before, during, and after European contact.

KAHIKINUI

To the immediate west of Kaupō on the largely undissected southern slopes of Haleakalā is the district of Kahikinui. The first "settlement pattern survey" in the Hawai'ian archipelago was conducted in Kahikinui in 1966–67 by Stanford graduate student Peter Chapman. Such surveys marked a departure from the way archaeology was conducted previously because they focused not only on major sites such as temples (heiau), but on *all* sites within a given region. Although Chapman was unable to complete his work, it was later taken up in the mid-1990s by Patrick Kirch, who had accompanied Chapman during his 1966 expedition. Since that time, Kahikinui has been the focus of intense archaeological scrutiny, which has contributed much to an understanding of dryland agricultural practices, household

---

A shot of Manawainui Valley.   [Lisa Holm]

organization, district-wide settlement, religious observance, and Native Hawai'ian interactions with the environment.

Within an area of 13 square kilometers, more than 2,200 sites have been mapped and recorded. These range from simple C-shaped shelters to household complexes (*kauhale*) to elaborate temple sites. A large proportion of these have been excavated, and their material remains have been analyzed. These remains include archaeobotanical specimens such as seeds or charcoal; stone tools and tool-making debris; immovable features such as hearths, depressions, and earth ovens (*imu*); the remnants of food items, including shells, bones, and eating implements; and personal items such as dog-tooth pendants, shell bead ornaments, and small rounded stones used in the game *kōnane*. More than any other district on the island of Maui, Kahikinui has remained largely undeveloped and unaffected by time, allowing archaeologists and

visitors alike to better understand what life may have been like for the Native Hawai'ians who made it their home.

KEONE'Ō'IO ARCHAEOLOGICAL DISTRICT, LA PÉROUSE BAY

Although Captain James Cook was the first European to discover the Hawai'ian archipelago in 1778, it was not until 1796 that a foreigner actually set foot on the island of Maui. On May 29 of that year, French explorer Francois Galaup de la Pérouse sailed past the districts of Hāna, Kaupō, and Kahikinui to Honuaula with his two ships, *La Boussole* and *L'Astrolabe*. He weighed anchor at Keone'ō'io Bay on the southwestern shore of Haleakalā; today it has simply become known as La Pérouse Bay. On May 30, 1796, Pérouse and a small landing party ventured ashore, where they were warmly received after trading axes and iron including habitation features, temples (heiau), fishing shrines (ko'a), trails, canoe sheds (hālau), and even grinding depressions worn into the pahoehoe lava. These depressions were likely created by Native Hawai'ian craftsmen during the production of stone or coral files and abraders—implements crucial to making bone or shell fishhooks. When the Keone'ō'io District was first settled remains unclear, although excavations at similar coastal settlements on East Maui have revealed dates as early as AD 1100. Visitors may tour the Keone'ō'io Archaeological District today, and members of the volunteer organization Friends of Keone'ō'io will likely be on-hand to discuss the area's cultural heritage and the precautions that must be taken to ensure its preservation.

Ruins of a Pohaku o Kane.   [Lisa Holm]

implements for taro, bananas, barkcloth (tapa), and other indigenous goods.

The remains of the houses and villages that Pérouse observed on his arrival today make up the Keone'ō'io Archaeological District. The district includes over seventy-five sites

Further Reading: Bernice Pauahi Bishop Museum Web site, http://www.bishopmuseum.org/; Cox, J. Halley, and Edward Stasack, *Hawaiian Petroglyphs* (Honolulu, HI: Bernice P. Bishop Museum, 1970); Daws, Gavan, *Shoal of Time: A History of the Hawaiian Islands* (Honolulu: University of Hawaii Press, 1968); Handy, E. S. Craighill, Elizabeth Green Handy, and Mary Kawena Pukui, *Native Planters in Old Hawaii: Their Life, Lore, and Environment* (Honolulu, HI: Bishop Museum Press, 1972); Hiroa, Te Rangi, *Arts and Crafts of Hawai'i* (Honolulu, HI: Bishop Museum Press, 1957); Ii, John Papa, *Fragments of Hawaiian History*, translated by Mary Pukui (Honolulu, HI: Bishop Museum Press, 1963); Kamakau, Samuel M., *Ka Po'e Kahiko: The People of Old*, translated by Mary Kawena Pukui (Honolulu, HI: Bishop Museum Press, 1964); Kamakau, Samuel M., *Na Hana a ka Po'e Kahiko: The Works of the People of Old*, translated by Mary Pukui (Honolulu: Bishop Museum Press, 1976); Kirch, Patrick Vinton, *Feathered Gods and Fishhooks: An Introduction to Hawaiian Archaeology and Prehistory* (Honolulu: University of Hawai'i Press, 1985); Kirch, Patrick Vinton, ed., *Na Mea Kahiko O Kahikinui: Studies in the Archaeology of Kahikinui, Maui*, Oceanic Archaeology Laboratory, Special Publication No. 1 (Berkeley: Archaeological Research Facility, University of California, 1997); Maui Historical Society and Bailey House Museum Web site, "Let's Talk Story," http://www.mauimuseum.org/talkstory.html; Sterling, Elspeth P. *Sites of Maui* (Honolulu, HI: Bishop Museum Press. 1998).

Lisa Holm

HĀLAWA VALLEY, KALAUPAPA NATIONAL HISTORICAL PARK, AND OTHER SITES

Moloka'i Island, Hawai'i

The Breadbasket of Moloka'i and Father Damien's Leprosy Settlement

The island of Moloka'i is located in the center of the main Hawai'ian chain. Only 679 square kilometers (261 mi²) in area, Moloka'i is one of the smaller Hawai'ian Islands. The island is characterized by striking environmental contrasts.

On the north shore, majestic sea cliffs are cut by deep valleys, and rough seas crash upon the rocky windward coast; on the south side of the island, smaller streams have cut shallow valleys, and a wide coastal plain meets a calmer

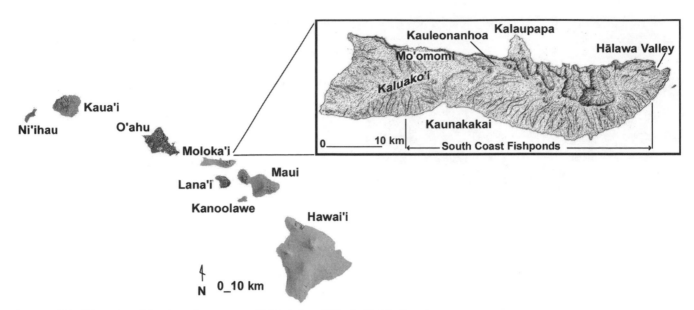

A map of the Hawai'ian Islands with an inset of Moloka'i.   [Windy K. McElroy]

sea; the west end of the island is arid and rocky but offers prime deep-sea fishing grounds. Moloka'i is thought to have been settled as early as AD 650, with the wet, windward valleys occupied first. Population has always centered on the east end of the island, and the dry west end is more sparsely inhabited.

HĀLAWA VALLEY, MOLOKA'I, HAWAI'I

The fertile Hālawa valley, on the east end of Moloka'i, was a major agricultural zone in traditional Hawai'i. Twin waterfalls descend Hālawa's western cliffs and feed a stream that meanders through the valley 3.2 kilometers (2 mi) long and empties into a crescent-shaped bay on the coast. Hālawa and the other windward valleys on Moloka'i produced the bulk of the island's staple crop *kalo*, or taro, which was made into *poi* and other delicacies. Kalo grows in both dryland and irrigated settings, but Hālawa valley is best known for its extensive irrigated pond-field complexes, or *lo'i*, the remains of which run almost continuously from the waterfalls to the seashore.

Lo'i are typically laid out in a series of adjacent stone-faced terraces that step down a slope. Plots are watered by an irrigation canal that leads from the stream to the uppermost fields, and water spills from one terrace to the next down the slope, so that fresh water is continually circulated through each field. Hālawa's lo'i are among the best-preserved examples in the islands, and many are being cleared of a hundred years of overgrowth and replanted by people returning to the valley.

As a major population center, Hālawa also was home to a variety of other archaeological sites, including ceremonial structures and habitation areas. The coastal habitation zone is notable because a buried cultural deposit on one of the sand dunes dates to AD 650. This is one of the earliest radiocarbon dates in all of Hawai'i, and today it is a source of controversy, with recent research suggesting that the area was not occupied until AD 1300 at the earliest.

Hālawa valley is a one-hour drive from the main town of Kaunakakai. Approaching the valley, the road twists and turns above the sea cliffs, providing stunning views of the seascape and nearby islands of Maui and Lāna'i. Nothing remains of the coastal sites, although the inland lo'i and other structures can be accessed by a moderate hike that terminates at the base of the twin waterfalls that mark the head of the valley. Permission must be obtained before embarking on the hike, and guided tours are available though local tour companies.

SOUTH COAST FISHPONDS, MOLOKA'I, HAWAI'I

Fishponds, or *loko i'a*, are unique to the Hawai'ian Islands. These stone structures were constructed to raise fish for consumption, as opposed to catching them in the wild. Both shore ponds and inland ponds were built, although the shore ponds are more common. Two varieties of shore ponds were used: some were completely enclosed, while others exhibited breaks in the walls with wooden gates employed to keep large fish from escaping. The shore ponds are usually semicircular in plan and vary in size from 1 acre to more than 200 hectares (500 acres). Walls are usually 0.9–1.5 meters (3–5 ft) tall, depending on the depth of the water, because walls could not be completely submerged at high tide. Nearly 500 fishponds are known to exist in the Hawai'ian Islands, and the south

Photo of Hālawa valley.   [Windy K. McElroy]

coast of Moloka'i exhibits the largest number of ponds per area of land in the state.

Fishponds were the property of chiefs, and the consumption of their products was limited to the upper echelons of society. Milkfish and mullet were the main species raised in the ponds, and it has been estimated that 2 million pounds of fish were harvested each year from ponds in ancient Hawai'i. The ponds provided a clever alternative to sea fishing, because the imprisoned fish were easier to catch and could be harvested year-round, regardless of weather conditions.

Archaeologists have not been able to precisely date the construction of the first fishponds, although most are thought to date from the thirteenth to sixteenth centuries AD, and a few were built as late as the nineteenth century. Only twenty-three fishponds are documented as having been built by

humans, with the construction of most ponds attributed to the *menehune*, a legendary band of "little people" who completed building projects in the span of a single night.

Fishponds are so numerous on the south coast of Moloka'i because the shoreline possesses the ideal environmental qualities needed for fishpond aquaculture. The coastline is relatively straight, inshore waters are shallow, and a protective fringing reef shields the stone walls from high surf. Many of the island's seventy-four fishponds are accessible and can be easily seen from the main highway.

KAULEONANAHOA, MOLOKA'I, HAWAI'I
The phallic stone Kauleonanahoa is located in Pala'au State Park of north central Moloka'i. Stone phalli are found throughout the Hawai'ian Islands, but none are as large or as

Example of South Coast fishpond, Moloka'i.   [Windy K. McElroy]

realistic as Kauleonanahoa. The stone is thought to have been formed through a combination of natural weathering and subtle hand carving by the ancient Hawai'ians. It stands roughly 1.5 meters (5 ft) tall, but appears larger as it rests on a steep slope. Petroglyphs adorn the surrounding boulders, many of which are anthropomorphs, or human figures.

According to Hawai'ian tradition, the stone called Kauleonanahoa was once a man named Nanahoa, who lived where the rock now stands. His wife, Kawahuna, was enraged when she caught Nanahoa admiring a beautiful woman. In a fit of jealousy, Kawahuna took hold of the woman's hair, and in the struggle that ensued, Nanahoa pushed his wife down the cliff. They both turned to stone and remain separated for eternity.

In ancient times, infertile women would bring an offering to the Kauleonanahoa stone, spend the night there, and become pregnant. Even today, the stone is renowned for its fertility power. One or more female stones occupy the hillsides of Pala'au State Park as well, although they are not as famous as Kauleonanahoa. The site is easily accessed through a short, scenic hike at the apex of the state park. The park also offers a breathtaking overlook of the Kalaupapa Peninsula below.

KALAUPAPA PENINSULA, MOLOKA'I, HAWAI'I

The Kalaupapa Peninsula was formed by late-phase volcanic rejuvenation that produced a low flatland along the central portion of Molokai's north shore. The peninsula protrudes from the base of cliffs 914 meters (3,000 ft) high, creating an isolated landscape, roughly 26 square kilometers (10 mi²) in area. Although Kalaupapa lies within the

Photo of phallic stone, Kauleonanahoa, Pala'au State Park, Moloka'i. [Windy K. McElroy]

wet windward region of the island, rainfall is light because of the peninsula's low elevation. Kalaupapa was originally an area of traditional Hawai'ian habitation, although it is most widely known for its historic-era use as a leprosarium.

Kalaupapa is thought to have been first settled around AD 1300. Dryland crops, such as sweet potato, were the main food source on the peninsula, although taro was grown in irrigated pond fields in the adjacent wet valleys. Remnants of the extensive dryland cultivation system can still be seen today in the form of low rock walls that intersect and abut to create rectangular field plots. Other vestiges of early occupation include *heiau*, or places of ceremony and worship, and habitation remains. The heiau are typically large and imposing stone platforms and enclosures, while habitation structures take the form of simple L-shaped or C-shaped stone walls and small square or rectangular enclosures.

Land use changed dramatically in the 1860s when Kalaupapa was transformed into a leprosarium. The original inhabitants of the area were relocated, and patients with Hansen's disease (formerly known as leprosy) were sent by boat to live in forced isolation on the peninsula. Through the years more than 8,000 patients have lived and died at Kalaupapa, including Father Damien (Joseph DeVeuster), a Belgian Catholic priest who contracted the disease while serving those abandoned there. Father Damien's heroism has been retold in popular books and movies, and his statue graces the entrance of Hawai'i's state capitol. An identical statue stands in Statuary Hall in Washington, D.C.

In the mid-1940s sulfone antibiotics were discovered as a treatment for Hansen's disease, and the practice of isolating

Kalaupapa Peninsula.   [Windy K. McElroy]

patients ceased soon after. Nevertheless, many of the residents continue to live on the peninsula, in a small community of roughly 100 patients and employees. The settlement is part of the Kalaupapa National Historical Park, which includes many of the early buildings of the leprosarium, Father Damien's church, multiethnic cemeteries, the historic Kalaupapa Lighthouse, two offshore islets, and the numerous archaeological features that dot the landscape. Although the settlement is run as a national park and is open to visitors, access is controlled to ensure the privacy of the patients. Visitors must be sixteen years of age or older, must obtain an entry permit, and generally may not stay overnight. The peninsula can be reached by small aircraft or by a steep trail 4.8 kilometers (3 mi) long that begins at Pala'au State Park.

Further Reading: Kalaupapa, National Park Service Web site, http://www.nps.gov/kala (online January 2007); Kirch, Patrick Vinton, *Feathered Gods and Fishhooks* (Honolulu: University of Hawai'i Press, 1985); Kirch, Patrick Vinton, and Marion Kelly, eds., *Prehistory and Ecology in a Windward Hawaiian Valley: Halawa Valley, Moloka'i* (Honolulu, HI: Department of Anthropology, Bernice Pauahi Bishop Museum, 1975); McCoy, Mark, *The Lands of Hina: An Archaeological Overview and Assessment of Kalaupapa National Historical Park, Moloka'i*, edited by David Duffy (Honolulu: Pacific Cooperative Studies Unit, University of Hawai'i at Mānoa, 2005); Summers, Catherine, *Hawaiian Fishponds* (Honolulu, HI: Bishop Museum Press, 1964); Summers, Catherine, *Molokai: A Site Survey* (Honolulu, HI: Department of Anthropology, Bernice P. Bishop Museum, 1971).

*Windy K. McElroy and
Steven Eminger*

KALOKO-HONOKŌHAU, PU'UHONUA O HŌNAUNAU, PU'UKOHOLA HEIAU, AND HAWAI'I VOLCANOES NATIONAL PARK SITES

Hawai'i Island, Hawai'i

Archaeological Landscapes and Ancient and Historic Native Architecture

Archaeology in the Hawai'ian Islands differs from that of most other states in two important respects, and the discussions of sites in this section should be read reflecting these characteristics. First, the intensive occupation of the pre-contact era involved construction of enormous numbers of stone features for habitation and agriculture, seen today as vast cultural-archaeological landscapes. Thus "sites" have to be understood as often somewhat arbitrarily defined segments of very large expanses of architectural remains. Second, there was no writing in pre-contact Hawai'i, but there was an enormous accumulation of historical and legendary knowledge in oral traditions. This knowledge was recorded in great detail after contact, providing a rich traditional cultural-historical record that augments archaeological research.

The island of Hawai'i has five National Park Service units, of which four are complex archaeological landscapes. Three of these parks are located on the western (leeward) side of the island, and include Kaloko-Honokōhau National Historic Park, Pu'uhonua o Hōnaunau National Historic Park, and Pu'ukohola Heiau National Historic Site. The fourth is Hawai'i Volcanoes National Park, covering a large portion of the southern end of the island. The fifth unit is an island-encircling traditional trail, called Ala Kahakai National Historic Trail, which is still in the development stages but when completed will provide access to many archaeological sites.

ARCHAEOLOGICAL AND CULTURAL SITES OF WEST HAWAI'I

At the time of Western contact in 1778, the island societies were complex systems organized into kingships, each controlling large populations and economic resources, and frequently at war with one another. The economic base for these societies was root crop cultivation, collection of ocean resources, and aquaculture (raising and harvesting fish for food). In west Hawai'i there were two extensive regions of agricultural fields dependent on rainfall and good soils. One of these was in the central region (Kona), and the other was in the northern region (Kohala). Most of the people lived in settlements along the coast, with the density of population dependent on the regional agricultural productivity. Scattered among the villages of commoners were residential areas of the elite, as well as great temples that were presided over by the ruling class and their priests.

The present-day town of Kailua-Kona is located in an area that provides a fortuitous combination of natural conditions that favor dense settlement. There are many sand beaches and small inlets that make ocean access easy; there are rich natural ocean resources along this coast; and the soils and rainfall are ideal for dryland agriculture. (Irrigation agriculture was practiced in windward valleys that had permanent streams.) These features that make Kailua-Kona a population center today (via tourism, fishing, and coffee cultivation) are the same conditions that made this the center of pre-contact Hawai'ian population on leeward Hawai'i. There are archaeological remains in Kailua-Kona that can be visited, and a trip to the Kona Historical Society will provide information on these. But, of course, much has been destroyed by development, and the best-preserved areas of the archaeological landscape are found in the national parks to the north and south of Kailua-Kona.

Kaloko-Honokōhau National Historical Park

This park, named for the two Hawai'ian land units that it covers, is located along an arid coastline. Most archaeological features are structures of dry masonry and include house platforms and enclosures as well as temples of various sizes and functions. There are also trails, petroglyphs, and cemeteries. The architectural site that dominates the area is a great sea wall built across a bay forming a large salt-brackish water fishpond named Kaloko. Hawai'ian fishpond construction and aquaculture (raising and harvesting fish for food) were unique in Polynesia, and there were approximately 300 fishponds built throughout the Hawai'ian chain in the pre-contact era. Kaloko is the best example in Hawai'i of a fishpond created by walling the entrance of a bay, and the seawall itself is one the most massive in the islands.

Limited archaeological information suggests that the original occupation of the area occurred around AD 1200, when small fishing communities were established. Population growth did not occur until the AD 1400s, when upland

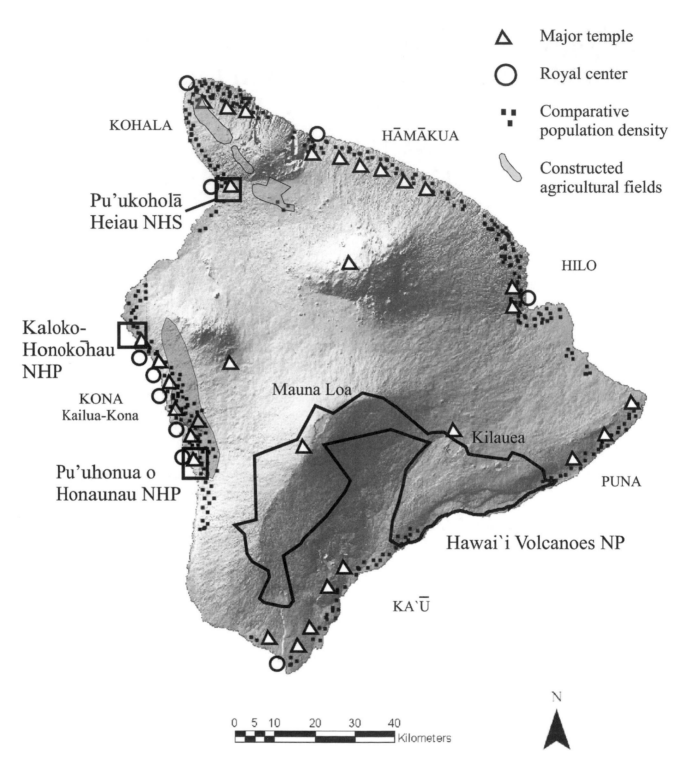

Major temple

Royal center

Comparative population density

Constructed agricultural fields

KOHALA

HĀMĀKUA

Puʻukoholā Heiau NHS

HILO

Kaloko-Honokōhau NHP

KONA
Kailua-Kona

Mauna Loa

Kilauea

Puʻuhonua o Honaunau NHP

PUNA

Hawaiʻi Volcanoes NP

KAʻŪ

0 5 10   20   30   40
Kilometers

N

HAWAIʻI ISLAND

Map of the island of Hawaiʻi, showing national parks and major pre-contact settlement features: population, royal centers, temples, and dryland agricultural complexes.   [David Tuggle]

Kaloko Fishpond, Kona Coast, Hawai'i: Aerial view showing how constructed wall closes off natural embayment (top); Fishpond wall before modern reconstruction (middle); Fishpond wall as reconstructed (bottom).   [Aerial photo courtesy of United States Geological Survey, other photos by David Tuggle]

dryland agriculture efforts became increasingly productive. In the Kaloko region the zone of rainfall sufficient for agriculture is over 1 mile (1.6 km) inland, so coastal dwellers followed long trails to the uplands (well outside the limits of the present park) to tend sweet potato fields or to exchange produce with community members who lived at higher elevations on a semi-permanent basis.

Had there been no bay suitable for the fishpond construction, the villages on the coast would have remained of low social and economic importance. But Hawai'ian traditions relate that sometime in the AD 1500s a ruler mobilized the great amount of labor needed to build and maintain the Kaloko fishpond wall and organized a local system of pond maintenance and the harvesting of fish for the consumption of the elite. With this great fishpond as a resource base, the area became one of the centers of residence for a lineage of elite priests, known as the 'Ehu line, and the fishpond and the associated lands acquired a religious importance as a place of sacred power. Traditions indicate that the pond also had supernatural beings who protected it. These were known as *akua mo'o* (i.e., royal, deified female ancestors), who took a lizard form, one of whom was also a deity in the pantheon of kings. The power of this place was also a source of protection, and Hawai'ian traditions say that the fishpond is the burial place of the most important person in Hawai'ian history, the great King Kamehameha, who died in 1819, and whose remains were placed in a cave hidden somewhere under the waters of Kaloko fishpond.

The seawall of Kaloko creates a fishpond of some 4.4 hectares (11 acres). The wall had been damaged over the years by the battering of the ocean and by use of it as a ranch road to cross the front of the pond, but it is now undergoing reconstruction. The reconstruction research shows that the pond wall was modified several times, and in its final form it was about 240 meters

Pu'uhonua o Honaunau National Historical Park, Kona Coast, Hawai'i: Modern replicas of wooden images of Native Hawai'ian deities (top); Reconstructed Native Hawai'ian temple, Hale o Keawe (middle); Reconstructed wall at the park (bottom).   [Photos by David Tuggle]

(262 yd.) long, varying from 5 to 24 meters in width, and from 1.5 to 3 meters in height (from base below water), about some 4,500 cubic meters of rock. There is no protective fringing reef, so the wall had to be designed to absorb the full force of the ocean surge, and it was constructed with sluice gates for pond and fish maintenance, engineered for perfect water circulation that prevented stagnation. The ongoing reconstruction is a time-consuming process, involving dry-laying of rock by hand following traditional building methods, and it is expected to be completed by about the end of 2009.

The park is located along the main road leading from the Kona International Airport into the nearby town of Kailua-Kona.

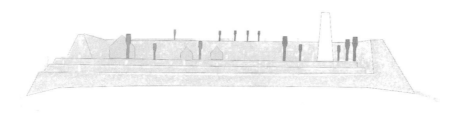

Pu'ukohola Heiau National Historic Site, Kona Coast, Hawai'i: View of heiau walls and coast in the distance (top); Sketch of heiau showing possible placement of ancient images within it (middle); Heiau from below (bottom).   [Photos and drawing by David Tuggle]

Kaloko fishpond is readily accessible via a graded road in the park. Other sites at the park can be reached by walking trails, and a number of interpretive trails and sites are being developed. The visitors' center provides extensive background information on Hawai'ian land use, place names, and history so that the meaning of these names can be understood as part of the experience of viewing this remarkable cultural-archaeological landscape.

Pu'uhonua o Hōnaunau National Historical Park

Located on a basalt flat at the point of a small bay and extending along a rocky shoreline, Pu'uhonua o Hōnaunau is a cultural-archaeological landscape with numerous stone house platforms and enclosures, temples, petroglyphs, trails,

burials, and agricultural features. Like Kaloko-Honokōhau, this park has an unusual archaeological complex, but in this case it is the special religious center, not a fishpond. This was a traditional Hawai'ian place of social refuge. Many cultures have special places of refuge where people can find safety from conflicts and pardon for their social transgressions, and in Hawai'i these were known as *pu'uhonua*. There were several pu'uhonua in the Hawai'ian islands, but the one at the place called Hōnaunau became the best known, was perhaps the most powerful, and has the most dramatic and well-preserved archaeological remains.

Pu'uhonua o Hōnaunau is located toward the southern end of the populated area of the leeward Hawai'i coast. Settlement began in this area in the AD 1300s, but it is not certain when

Photos of Hawai'ian house sites within present-day Hawai'i Volcanoes National Park: House site with recent lava flows over the cliff in background (top); House site with coast in the distance (bottom).   [Photos by David Tuggle]

Pu'uola petroglyph complex. Note steam in background from lava flow entering the ocean. (Wooden walkway for viewing petroglyphs seen at left and upper portion of photograph.)   [Photo by David Tuggle]

this became a sacred place. Hawai'ian traditions suggest that many sacred sites were established on the island at an early date as part of the development of regional power centers and related efforts to establish political and religious authority over the entire island. One such place was at the southeastern end of the island, the temple of Waha'ula (discussed in the section on Hawai'i Volcanoes National Park). Pu'uhonua o Hōnaunau may have been another of these early sacred sites. By about AD 1500 it was a complex of major temples, and at least by the early 1600s it had been sanctified as a pu'uhonua.

The pu'uhonua is only a small part of the entire national park, but it has a unique set of archaeological structures, dominated by a massive stone wall that bounds the point of land of about 2 hectares (5 acres) that is the sacred area. The pu'uhonua wall is about 350 meters (383 yd.) long, 5 meters wide, and 3.5 meters high, built with an engineered rock core and faced with huge angular rocks.

Within the area of the pu'uhonua are remains of temples and the residences of priests, some of which pre-date the wall. The largest of these is a stone platform 40 meters (44 yd.) long, 20 meters wide, and 3 meters high. Excavations of this and other structures within the pu'uhonua indicate multiple phases of building that occurred when new rulers came to power and rededicated the temples.

The most striking temple in the pu'uhonua is known as Hale o Keawe ("house of the King Keawe"), which once contained the skeletal remains of twenty-three chiefs, one of whom had been the king of the island around AD 1700. These individuals were deified ancestors whose physical remains were part of the sanctification of the pu'uhonua. The temple has been reconstructed, including the wooden images of deities, based on drawings made during the early period of Western contact.

Pu'uhonua o Hōnaunau National Historic Park can be reached by a paved road off the main road leading south from Kailua-Kona. The area of the great enclosing wall of the pu'uhonua is an easy walk from the visitors' center. There is also a hiking trail that runs south from the center that takes visitors to many other archaeological structures.

Pu'ukoholā Heiau National Historic Site

The massive structure of Pu'ukoholā Heiau ("temple") stands on a low hill overlooking the bay of Kawaihae. It was built by the king Kamehameha in 1790–91 as a war temple. Its association with Kamehameha and his unification of the islands makes it one of the most important archaeological sites in Hawai'i. Also included in the park are another large temple (Mailekini), an area of a royal residence, and the ruins of the house of John Young, one of the principal English advisors to Kamehameha. The John Young Homestead is one of the earliest Western structures to survive in Hawai'i. Pu'ukoholā is named for the place where it was built, one translation of which is "hill of the whale."

When Captain James Cook made the first Western contact with the Hawai'ian Islands in 1778–79, the island of Hawai'i was ruled by the king Kalaniōpu'u. After his death in 1782, there was a struggle for power, which by 1790 had become a military impasse between two chiefs: Kamehameha, who controlled much of the leeward part of the island, and Keōua, who controlled the windward and southern area. By this time Kamehameha had acquired guns, probably from ships stopping at Kawaihae, and he had the military council of John Young. But Kamehameha decided that he needed the assistance of a Hawai'ian seer to help him break the impasse. That seer told him to build a great temple at Kawaihae dedicated to the war god Kū-kāili-moku ("Kū island snatcher"). This was an enormous undertaking, and when this temple called Pu'ukoholā was completed in 1791, his rival Keōua was asked to attend the consecration ceremony. In one of those historic mysteries of decision making, Keōua did so and was killed, and then his body was offered as the principal sacrifice in the dedication of Pu'ukoholā. Kamehameha thus assumed control of the island, and through conquest and diplomacy united all of the islands into one kingdom. As the nineteenth-century Hawai'ian historian Kamakau wrote (1996, 113), "By the death of Keōua . . . and the placing of his body on the heiau of Pu'ukoholā, the whole of Hawai'i became Kamehameha's."

The temple of Pu'ukoholā has never been excavated in any detail. The construction of Pu'ukoholā was an enormous undertaking, requiring great quantities of stone for the rubble fill and thousands of waterworn cobbles used for its carefully laid facings. Built on a low knoll, it covers an area of about 73 × 42 meters. From its lower edge to the top of the wall at the rear, it is 12 meters high. The architectural details are complicated, but in essence its surface is a large stone-paved platform on which various wooden structures were built that were dedicated to various religious functions. This was a temple of war and human sacrifice, which involved extraordinarily elaborate ceremonies. However, these were intended for the gods, not for public observation, and thus a huge wall was constructed on the inland sides blocking the activities from general view. The wall stands 4.5 meters high and 9 meters wide at the base. The open side is toward the ocean, looking west to the setting sun, the realm of the ancestors.

The remains of the homestead of John Young are near the temple of Pu'ukoholā. John Young lived at Kawaihae from 1793 until his death in 1835, and the homestead was the second house he built there. Extensive excavations have been conducted at the site. Eight structures remain, including those with traditional Hawai'ian features, traditional features that have been modified into a Western (European) style, and some that are entirely Western. The main house was built of stone laid in mud mortar and was surfaced with coral lime plaster.

Pu'ukoholā National Historic Site is located at Kawaihae Harbor, north of the resort area of the south Kohala coast. In 2006 a major earthquake occurred just offshore, resulting in significant damage to the temple and, unfortunately, reducing much of the John Young house to irreparable rubble.

ARCHAEOLOGICAL SITES OF HAWAI'I VOLCANOES NATIONAL PARK

Hawai'i Volcanoes National Park, at the southern end of the island, was established as an area of natural environment preservation, but it includes many archaeological remains. Most of the area in the park has severe limitations for human occupation. It is an arid land extending from the coast to the high elevation of the mountain named Mauna Loa. But more than that, this is an active landscape, a threatening landscape, and the home of Pele-ai-honua ("Pele eater of land"), goddess of the volcano. There are two volcanic mountains in the park: Kilauea, one of the most active volcanoes in the world, and Mauna Loa, which still erupts on occasion. Priests devoted to Pele lived in this region, and temples dedicated to the deity were built around the summit of Kilauea. Despite the harshness of the environment, commoners lived along the coast and journeyed inland to collect natural resources, so that the archaeological sites in the park include shoreline habitation, trails, petroglyph fields, resource collection areas, and temples. There are three sets of archaeological sites in the park that visitors can walk to: a set of coastal villages, a large petroglyph complex, and a unique place known as Keonehelele'i.

The coastal village sites, such as Apua and Keauhou, can be reached by an ancient coastal trail that is open to the public. The coast was occupied from the AD 1500s until the late nineteenth century. The people depended heavily on fishing for subsistence, but in places where there was sufficient rainfall, they created agricultural fields by mounding rocks so that moisture could be preserved with mulching for growing sweet potatoes. Remnants of the hard life in these villages are low stone walls, platforms, shelter caves, fishing shrines, and petroglyphs.

The petroglyph complex, named for the local landmark Pu'uloa, can be reached by a short hiking trail from a parking area. Petroglyphs are images pecked on exposed rock surfaces, and there are more than 23,000 of these images in the Pu'uloa complex. They include human figures, objects such as sails, numerous geometric forms, and simple depressions. The images in this site are predominantly pre-contact forms and, based on the age of the rock, were created after AD 1400. This place had a tradition of religious power, a place where one could obtain the blessing of long life. Creating an image in the rock was part of the ritual to obtain that blessing. The depressions were pecked in order to place the umbilical cords of newborns to assure long life for them.

The site of Keonehelele'i ("falling sands") on the upper slope of the mountain of Kilauea consists of human footprints "fossilized" in an area of some 2,000 hectares (5,000 acres) of volcanic ash deposited from about AD 1500 to 1790. At one time it was thought that all of these footprints were from a

Hawai'ian army that was trapped in an ash eruption in 1790, but it is now known that they were made at many different times as people followed trails that were periodically covered in ash falls. Nearly 2,000 footprints have been recorded, and these represent at least 440 individuals.

The extreme geological activity of this area was the source of the traditions of Pele, but that activity is also one of destruction. Archaeological sites along the coast are damaged or destroyed by earthquakes and tidal waves. Land shelves crumble into the ocean. But the great power of destruction is the lava flow of the volcano itself. Vast areas are periodically covered by lava, and sites in those areas will never be seen again.

One of the most important sites on the island was a temple complex known as Waha'ula, located on the eastern coastline of the park. Hawai'ian traditions identify this as a place representing a revolution in ancient religion and society. This was a temple said to have been built by a priest who came from distant islands and who instituted a new social order in Hawai'i, one that created the class system and the structure of religious prohibitions and ceremonies, including human sacrifice. Waha'ula was the first temple of human sacrifice, perhaps built as early as AD 1300, and continually rededicated over the centuries, the last of which was by Kamehameha in 1817. The temple complex covered an area of about 500 × 600 meters and consisted of multiple structures of platforms and enclosures, and numerous places where wooden images of gods had been placed. Waha'ula was buried under molten rock from a Kilauea lava flow in 1997.

Further Reading: Ala Kahakai National Historical Trail, National Park Service Web site, http://www.nps.gov/alka; Greene, Linda Wedel, *A Cultural History of Three Traditional Hawaiian Sites on the West Coast of Hawai'i Island* (Denver: National Park Service, 1993), http://www.cr.nps.gov/history/online_books/kona/history.htm; Hawai'i Volcanoes National Park, National Park Service Web site, http://www.nps.gov/havo/; Kaloko-Honokōhau National Historic Park, National Park Service Web site, http://www.nps.gov/puhe; Kamakau, Samuel Mānaiakalani, *Ke Kumu Aupuni* (Honolulu: Native Books, 1996; originally published 1867); Kane, Herb Kawainui, *Ancient Hawai'i* (Captain Cook, HI: Kawainui Press, 1997); Lee, Georgia, and Edward Stasack, *Spirit of Place: Petroglyphs of Hawai'i* (Los Osos, CA: Easter Island Foundation, 1999); Masse, W. Bruce, Laura A. Carter, and Gary F. Somers, "Waha'ula Heiau: The Regional and Symbolic Context of Hawai'i Island's 'Red Mouth Temple,'" *Asian Perspectives* 30(1) (1991): 19–56; Pu'uhonua o Hōnaunau National Historic Park, National Park Service Web site, http://www.nps.gov/puho; Pu'ukoholā Heiau National Historic Site, National Park Service Web site, http://www.nps.gov/puhe; Swanson, Donald, "Hawaiian Oral Tradition Describes 400 Years of Volcanic Activity at Kilauea," *Journal of Volcanology and Geothermal Research* (available online, April 17, 2008); Tomonari-Tuggle, M. J., and H. David Tuggle, *Archaeological Overview and Assessment for the Three West Hawai'i Island Parks, National Park Service* (Honolulu, HI: International Archaeological Research Institute, 2006); Valeri, Valerio, *Kingship and Sacrifice: Ritual and Society in Ancient Hawaii* (Chicago: University of Chicago Press, 1985).

David Tuggle

USS *ARIZONA* MEMORIAL

O'ahu Island, Hawai'i

Documenting and Preserving a World War II Icon

USS *Arizona*, sunk in Pearl Harbor, Hawai'i, is a National Historic Landmark that has been part of the National Park System as the USS *Arizona* Memorial since 1980. The site is among the most recognized war memorials in the United States and internationally, and with about 1.3 million visitors annually, the most visited shipwreck on the planet.

The *Pennsylvania*-class battleship, completed in 1916, sank December 7, 1941, during the Japanese attack on the U.S. Navy's Pacific Fleet. USS *Arizona*, struck by a 1,760-pound, armor-piercing bomb that detonated the vessel's forward magazine, sank in the first few minutes of the attack. The explosion of an estimated 300 tons of munitions aboard destroyed the hull's forward half, killing 1,177 sailors and marines, 900 of whom still remain aboard. This site remains a national icon that still commands an honor guard from the many capital ships that ply Pearl Harbor today.

Soon after the memorial became a park unit, the National Park Service (NPS) faced its role as steward and tasked its Submerged Resources Center (SRC) with documenting *Arizona* and determining its state of deterioration to inform management decisions regarding long-term preservation. NPS's active management of the site required answers to such basic questions as: What is there? What is the present condition of the wreck? How quickly is it deteriorating? When the NPS underwater archaeologists began their work, there was very little information about the ship after it sank; U.S. Navy salvage operations ceased in 1948. Beyond public interpretation, NPS's other concern was determining proper management of this important shipwreck in the absence of precedent—no one before had attempted to actively manage a publicly visible sunken steel warship that was both a memorial and tomb.

The SRC divers mapped the wreck and began studying its deterioration from 1983 to 1988. Detailed site drawings, published in 1984, led to a scale model of the sunken vessel so visitors could understand what the ship looks like underwater. The 1980s project recorded the largest object ever mapped underwater and initiated interdisciplinary site formation process investigations on in situ steel wrecks.

In 2000 continuing concern about *Arizona's* integrity, prompted by growing concerns about environmental consequences from the release of an estimated half-million gallons of fuel oil remaining in the hull, impelled SRC to began a second research program, dubbed the "USS *Arizona* Preservation Project," directed at understanding the nature and rate of corrosion processes and structural changes taking place in the submerged hull. This interdisciplinary, management-based program was designed to be cumulative, with each element contributing to minimize the environmental hazard from fuel oil release and provide the scientific research required for management decisions.

Oil currently leaks from the hull in drops at a daily rate of about 10 liters, and it has been leaking since it sank in 1941. Because the hull is the containment vessel for the oil, researchers had to understand the complex corrosion processes at work on the sunken ship. SRC scholars proposed establishing a "curve of deterioration," determining where *Arizona* was on that curve, and developing means to monitor the site for changes as they occurred.

Steel corrosion, unlike iron, does not produce a remnant layer that preserves the original surface that allows direct measurement of metal lost over time. For steel vessels, the most accurate measure of metal loss is to determine actual steel thickness and subtract this value from original thickness specified on ship's plans. Once total metal loss over a given time is established, the average corrosion rate can be calculated for hull portions in similar environmental contexts.

In 2002, eight hull samples 4 inches (10 cm) in diameter were collected using a hydraulic-powered hole saw. A water sample was collected from the interior hull; each indicated very low oxygen concentrations. Microscopic and metallographic methods were used to measure coupon thickness, which was compared to the original steel thickness recorded on blueprints. This comparison provided a corrosion rate in mils (thousands of an inch) per year, which is a simplified expression that assumes a constant corrosion rate from the date of sinking. These hull sample thicknesses provide controls for testing sonic thickness gauges and determining corrosion rate by other means than direct measurement of hull steel. Corrosion engineers, metallurgists, and SRC personnel have developed a minimum-impact method for deriving submerged steel-hull corrosion rates through analysis of physical and chemical properties of marine encrustation as a proxy for collecting hull metal samples. The method has general applicability to other submerged steel vessels in similar environments.

Finite element analysis is a principal research method that will produce the primary predictive tool derived from the *Arizona* research. A finite element model (FEM) is a sophisticated computer model that calculates theoretical changes to structures from stresses and changes under load using experimental variables based on observational data collected from the hull. The FEM divides a complex solid into many small components called "elements," each with material properties that describe that element's characteristics and behavior between its end points (e.g., mechanical properties, heat flow, density, etc., which makes them "finite"). The end points of each finite element are called "nodes." Each node has set boundary conditions on how it transmits load stress to other nodes. Results of element changes can be presented and studied as graphics that model structural changes over time and under different variable conditions.

For historical shipwrecks such as USS *Arizona*, FEM allows manipulation of multiple variables, such as corrosion rate and hull thickness, to analyze loads and stresses on hull structure for prediction of collapse rate and the nature, sequence, and consequent impact on interior structures containing fuel oil. The FEM model is able to incorporate the many corrosion and environmental variables that have been isolated and measured for the site. Its strength is its ability to incorporate and manipulate a range of variables derived from both direct observation and experimental analyses.

The as-built *Arizona* FEM, which uses 40 feet (12.1 m) of hull from frame 70 to 90, uses 52,000 elements from the ship's blueprints and took the National Institute of Standards and Technology a year to complete. This as-built FEM is now incorporating recent hull condition, derived corrosion rates, and environmental data to provide researchers and managers a view of the most likely sequence of structural collapse and how long before significant alterations begin to occur. Because of the *Arizona* FEM's complexity, it takes from one to three weeks of supercomputer time to reach a solution and develop a graphic model.

Preliminary results of the USS *Arizona* Preservation Project are encouraging. Corrosion rates are highest on portions of *Arizona* in the shallowest water and lowest in the anaerobic (low oxygen) environment in the interior and below the mud line. All are considerably lower than predictions based on results of laboratory corrosion experiments. A VideoRay ROV equipped with water-quality-monitoring instrumentation allowed interior access and measurement of the interior water conditions. No divers entered the interior of *Arizona*. Dissolved oxygen levels are nearly zero below the second deck, much like the interior water measurements taken when the hull samples were collected.

A monitoring program has been established to track structural changes in the hull. A complete geotechnical characterization of the sediments upon which *Arizona* rests was completed to control for any changes related to sediment compression. Sediment compression appears to approach the maximum predicted, so any changes can be attributed to structural alterations. High-resolution GPS positioning and crack monitors are used to measure minute structural changes.

Inevitably, there is the question of oil removal: should preservation of a naval tomb and national historic landmark take precedence over a potentially invasive environmental remediation? An admiral in Pearl Harbor recently commented that oil removal is not feasible with current technology and, if attempted, would likely destroy the ship. If USS *Arizona* were any other ship in any other harbor, removal might be attempted with destruction of the hull as an acceptable consequence. But USS *Arizona* is not just any ship in any harbor, and loss of the hull for environmental protection is not an acceptable outcome for many. To consider the question of oil removal from *Arizona*, one must weigh the site's current social significance and future value against potential environmental risk. Is the invasive and damaging procedure of oil removal appropriate or acceptable on these hallowed remains? Most, including the NPS, think not, at least not without considerably more information about impact to the ship and the remains of its crew and the real nature of the environmental risk and consideration of mitigation alternatives to that of oil removal.

Besides the question of oil removal, another management question will be whether intervening in *Arizona*'s natural deterioration process is warranted, feasible, or desirable. Before weighing benefits of intervention in natural processes, specific data is needed about cathodic protection systems, their feasibility, and their effectiveness, as well as the effect on interior and unconnected structure and on the protective concretion.

During the course of the archaeological research on *Arizona*, several historical issues were investigated through the material evidence available on the wreck. For example, there is no physical evidence for torpedo damage or a bomb dropping down the stack, as some eyewitnesses reported. This sort of problem solving is common to historical archaeology; however, there are other aspects of archaeology reflected in the USS *Arizona* research that are more distinctive. The development of interpretive exhibits, such as the model of the ship as it is today produced immediately after mapping the site, have the ability to connect people directly with their past. One must reflect on the nature of war and its devastating consequence by observing *Arizona*'s damaged hull, which remains much as it did when it sank, unlike carefully landscaped commemorative battlefields and cemeteries.

Approached with a multidisciplinary research design based on management-derived questions and a concern with both minimum impact to a naval tomb and the goal of preservation, *Arizona* is providing scientific answers about corrosion processes applicable to vessels worldwide. Also evolving is the scientific information necessary to make informed decisions about how this important piece of American and international history can be preserved, again, with global application by others facing similar problems with valued submerged sites. The research on USS *Arizona* has attempted a balance between social significance and environmental threat using many tools of science, which allow sound decisions to be made on facts and not emotions, common sense, fears, or beliefs. This research has not changed history or altered what is known about the Pearl Harbor attack. Instead, it has focused on viewing and understanding the USS *Arizona* through what is immediately important to society now and to those who come after: preservation, education, interpretation, and science-based site management. The focus is on stewardship of the rich heritage that is inherited from the past, managed well, and left as legacy for the future.

Further Reading: Lenihan, Daniel J., ed., *Submerged Cultural Resources Study: USS* Arizona *Memorial and Pearl Harbor National Historic Landmark*, Southwest Cultural Resources Center Professional Papers No. 23, Submerged Resources Center Professional Reports No. 9 (Santa Fe, NM: U.S. National Park Service, 1989); Russell, Matthew A., David L. Conlin, Larry E. Murphy, Donald L. Johnson, Brent M. Wilson, and James D. Carr, "A Minimum-Impact Method for Measuring Corrosion Rate of Steel-Hulled Shipwrecks in Seawater," *International Journal of Nautical Archaeology* 35(2) (2006): 310–318; Vesilind, Priit J., "Oil and Honor at Pearl Harbor," *National Geographic* 199(6) (2001): 84–99.

Larry E. Murphy and Matthew A. Russell

KEY FOR WEST COAST—PACIFIC NORTHWEST AND SOUTHEAST ALASKA REGIONAL MAP

1. Umpqua-Eden
2. Cascadia Cave
3. Meier
4. Cathlapotle Site
5. Fort Vancouver National Historic Site
6. Olympic National Park
7. San Juan Islands National Historical Park
8. Marpole
9. Namu
10. Groundhog Bay
11. Sitka National Historical Park
12. On-Your-Knees-Cave
13. Gwaii Haanas National Park Reserve
14. Old Town, Knight Island
15. The Kennecott Mine National Historical Landmark
16. Hannavan Creek
17. Calapooia Midden
18. Indian Sands
19. Devils Kitchen and Nah-so-mah Village
20. Yaquina Head
21. Seal Rock
22. Cape Blanco and Blackrock Point
23. Palmrose, Avenue Q, and Pas-Tee sites
24. Clahclellah
25. Tsagiglala petroglyph, Columbia Hills State Park
26. Makah Indian Reservation
27. Willapa Bay and Martin
28. Ozette
29. Glenrose and St. Mungo
30. Pender Canal
31. Yuquot
32. Hesquiat Village
33. Prince Rupert Harbour sites
34. Paul Mason (Kitselas)
35. Skidegate
36. Old Bella Bella and Axeti
37. Richardson Ranch
38. Kimsquit
39. Hidden Falls
40. Thorne River
41. Chuck Lake
42. Whales Head Fort and Daax Haat Kanadaa
43. Fort Clatsop, Lewis and Clark National Historical Park
44. Fort Langley
45. Fort Victoria
46. Fort Nisqually

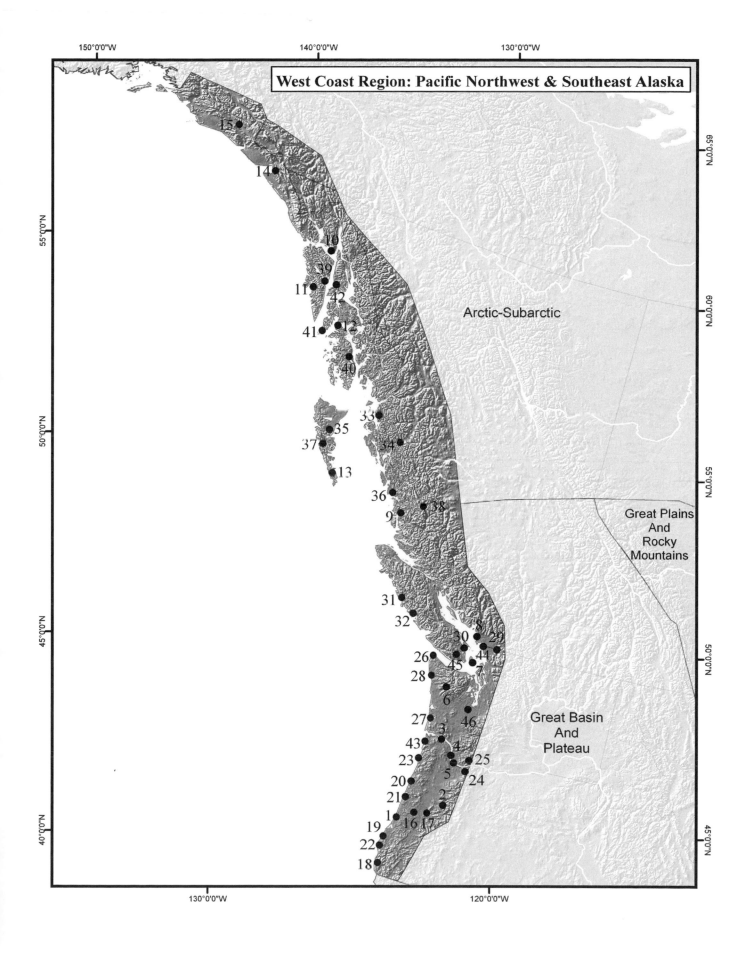

West Coast Region: Pacific Northwest & Southeast Alaska

PACIFIC NORTHWEST AND SOUTHEAST ALASKA

The Pacific Northwest and Southeast Alaska sub-region is characterized by rich, cold marine waters that have provided abundant food for the coastal inhabitants. Along the coast wet, thick forests provide additional natural resources to support and sustain human inhabitants. Like California to the south, early coastal sites are being found along the northwest coast that lend credence to the theory that some of the earliest North American colonists made their way south via a coastal route (see the essays about On Your Knees Cave and the Namu and Prince Rupert Harbor sites). Sites just inland from the coast are included in this section as well because the ways of life followed there were more similar to life along the coast, or involved use of the coast and maritime resources more than the inland resources of the northern Great Basin–Plateau region to the east (see the essays about the Willamette valley sites and sites in the lower Columbia River west of the Dalles).

The late prehistoric and early historic period native cultures along the northwest coast are famous for their material riches. Elaborate ceremonies of feasting and gift-giving fascinated the early anthropologists who observed and reported them. The archaeological record shows the ancient roots of this rich material culture and trading practice where fortuitous preservation has occurred (see the essays about the Ozette site on the Washington coast and Cathlapotle in the lower Columbia River).

During the early historic period furs and other valued raw materials drew European and then Euro-Americans to sites in the region. The English and then American post at Fort Vancouver along the lower Columbia, and Sitka, the capital of Russian America in southeastern Alaska, are prominent locations that were associated with this part of the region's history. A twentieth-century industrial archaeological site is an example of the continuing exploitation of natural resources in this rich region (see the essay about the Kennecott Mine site in Wrangell–St. Elis National Park and Preserve, southeastern Alaska).

ENTRIES FOR THE PACIFIC NORTHWEST AND SOUTHEAST ALASKA REGION

ARCHAEOLOGY OF THE NORTHWEST COAST AND SOUTHEASTERN ALASKA

The ethnographic Northwest Coast culture area is most often defined as extending from the Tolowa and their neighbors in northern California to Yakutat Bay at the northern end of the Alaskan panhandle. It is limited to the coast, except along the major rivers—the Columbia, the Fraser, and the Skeena—where it may run 100 kilometers or more inland. For the Americas, this culture area is seen as unique in terms of the art, social complexity, and the presence of substantial villages of large planked houses, each often containing a number of families. Estimates of the population along this coastal strip range from 100,000 to 200,000, making it one of the more densely settled areas in North America and demonstrating the productivity of the stored salmon economy found here. The central archaeological problem is to understand the development of this uniquely socially stratified (nobles, commoners, and even numerous slaves in some groups) society on a hunting and gathering economic base. Since a wide variety of language families are found in this area, the development of this culture is usually seen as a cultural ecological process, tied to the development of an economy based on procuring, processing for preservation, and storing large amounts of salmon.

In such a sketch important differences among the groups within the region are glossed over. These include the fact that salmon is not always the economic base; that houses vary dramatically in size, from 30 to over 150 square meters; and that winter villages range from being occupied for only a few months (and the houses then denuded of their planks) to much more permanent structures and villages. Generally, however, seasonal moves were common, and house structures were not occupied on a year-round basis.

The earliest archaeological remains are usually chipped-stone assemblages produced by generalized hunters and gatherers, likely descendants of the Clovis culture, and date to about 10,000 years ago. Recently, it has been discovered that the Queen Charlotte Islands were not covered with ice floes at the end of the Pleistocene, as had long been thought, and that neighboring land under the ocean today was above sea level then. This new discovery has led to investigations of the possibility of a pre-Clovis coastwise migration. Although recent discoveries in the Queen Charlotte Islands rival the age of any other known along the northwest coast, they remain several thousand years too recent to be remains of a pre-Clovis migration.

At this point, the earliest material consists of stone tool assemblages with leaf-shaped points and cobble core tools; this is true from the Alaskan panhandle to southern Oregon and includes the recent finds in the Queen Charlotte Islands (or "Haida Gwaii," which is the name preferred by the Haida who live there). On the southern two-thirds of the coast this early material, termed the "Old Cordilleran culture" by many investigators, lasts until 4,000 or 5,000 years ago and shows significant evidence of evolving into the succeeding cultures.

On the northern coast, by about 8,600 years ago, the Old Cordilleran culture is replaced by the "North Coast Microblade tradition," which has abundant stone cobble tools and microblades and very few bifaces. This culture, which continues up until at least 5,000 years ago, is noted for its similarities with the Denali microblade cultures of interior Alaska and the Yukon. Many archaeologists have associated these microblade cultures with Athabascan and related languages (termed *NaDene* by some), and both the ethnographic Tlingit (who live on the Alaskan panhandle) and the Haida are seen by many as members of the NaDene.

Only very limited faunal remains have been recovered from these early cultures, and these remains do not conform to a single pattern. Perhaps most interesting are those from Chuck Lake, a North Coast Microblade tradition site on an island off the Alaskan panhandle. This 7,000–8,000-year-old microblade site has a shell midden up to 30 centimeters thick, showing the use of shellfish along with the remains of a number of fish species, although salmon are not abundant, and sea and land mammal remains. Chuck Lake demonstrates the use of shoreline and coastal resources, apparently in the spring. At the Glenrose site, near Vancouver, along the salmon-bearing Fraser River, the Old Cordilleran culture component shows a more interior adaptation, although salmon are present, along with a fixed barbed antler point. In more interior parts of northwestern North America, artifact assemblages similar to Glenrose are associated with terrestrial adaptations. These scattered early faunal remains show at least a seasonal use of coastal resources and may indicate a much more sophisticated and extensive use of coastal resources in addition to the use of large terrestrial mammals.

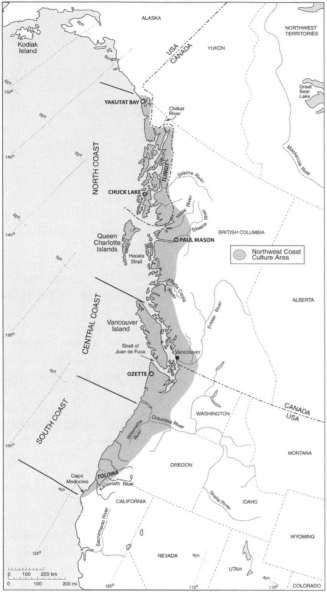

A map of the northwest coast and southeastern Alaska. [R. G. Matson]

Although the first 4,000 years of occupation of the northwest coast can be classified into two cultures, the Old Cordilleran and North Coast Microblade tradition, the next 1,000–2,000 years leads to at least a dozen, and probably many more, cultures. This period is known for the presence of extensive shell middens, many quite large, showing the general use of shellfish. Analyses of these sites also usually show an abundance of fish. Although in the past many archaeologists thought that cultures of this period were similar to those found ethnographically—and a few maintain this today—many key features of the ethnographic pattern have yet to be found at this time. These include the lack of good evidence for plank house villages, hereditary social stratification, and the stored salmon economy.

Many of these cultures in the central and southern coast clearly descended from the Old Cordilleran culture, making the dividing line between these and other distinctive coastal cultures difficult to perceive. Generally, all the archaeological cultures of this period are characterized by the manufacture and use of leaf-shaped points and abundant chipped-stone tools as well as stemmed points, more abundant bone and antler tools, in many sites the first occurrence of ground-stone tools, and often shell and ground-stone beads. The use of fish and shellfish definitely dominated the economy, with mussel usually being the most abundant shellfish.

The best documented of these cultures is the St. Mungo phase, named after the St. Mungo site found around Vancouver. Dating from about 3,300 to 4,500 years ago, this culture had abundant chipped-stone implements, although bone and antler tools as well as some ground-stone ones are present. St. Mungo site shell middens are dominated by bay mussel and a wide variety of fish, with no single species predominant, although salmon and starry flounders are the most abundant. Burial evidence of a hereditary stratified society is absent, as are good indications of large planked houses. The original discoverer of the St. Mungo culture, Gay Frederick, interprets the evidence as that of a foraging adaptation, where a small group utilized a particular area for a range of resources until they were reduced, and then moved on to the next resource locus for a limited time, without large-scale processing of resources for future use. Certainly one of the characteristics of the St. Mungo is that the excavated components are difficult to characterize in terms of seasonality, and all known sites appear to be base camps, unlike the pattern for both earlier and later cultures. Whether other cultures of this period share these characteristics is not yet clear, because they are not as well known.

The next period sees the first clear presence of both the stored salmon economy and villages of large planked houses, but not necessarily the other characteristics of contact times. The Paul Mason site, some 100 kilometers from the coast on the Skeena River in Kitselas Canyon, has remains of ten plank houses in two rows and dates to 3,000 years ago. These houses average about 5 × 10 meters and have two hearths, probably sheltering two families. Kitselas Canyon is the first constriction on the Skeena River and an important salmon fishing location. Even though only a very few salmon remains were recovered from hearth contexts (faunal remains generally were not well preserved at this site), it appears fairly certain that stored salmon were the basis of this economy. The excavator, Gary Coupland, interpreted this site as indicating an "egalitarian cooperate group" as opposed to the ethnographic stratified society. The artifacts associated with this important site are relatively unimpressive chipped- and ground-stone tools; bone and antler did not preserve. Still, the kind of lithic artifacts associated with elites later in time are definitely absent, supporting Coupland's interpretation.

In the Vancouver area, the St. Mungo culture is replaced by the Locarno Beach phase, at about 3,300 years ago. Recent excavations at the Crescent Beach site have confirmed that this phase is based on the stored salmon economy, unlike the earlier St. Mungo component found there. But instead of the remains of large planked house villages, only several very small non-planked winter domestic structures have been found. Along with the stored salmon economy, there is a definite increase in artifacts made of bone, antler, and ground stone, which later dominate central and north coast assemblages. These include decorated objects and such things as labrets (lip plugs), which are associated with high-status individuals in some ethnographic Northwest Coast cultures. Interestingly enough, the most complete analysis of burials indicates the absence of inherited status at this time, in contrast to the next culture.

The Locarno Beach culture also shows fairly large differences in site function, including limited-activity sites with specific seasonality as well as base camps, such as the winter seasonal occupations complete with small domestic structures. This is to be expected from what Lewis Binford termed a logistic economy, to which the stored salmon economy definitely belongs, and contrasts with our current understanding of the preceding St. Mungo. Simulation studies by Dale Croes and Steven Hackenberger indicate that the stored salmon economy may raise the carrying capacity by a factor of 6. This would explain the rapid spread of this economy throughout the northwest coast where salmon is available and the large increase in number of known sites of this age compared to earlier periods.

It is likely that the major features of the Northwest Coast culture did not develop together at one place, but rather that certain characteristics occurred in some areas earlier than in others, and other features now seen as closely connected had very different origins. So such things as the presence of planked house villages along the Skeena and their absence along the Fraser, and good evidence of the stored salmon economy and limited-activity sites along the Fraser and not along the Skeena, are to be expected. Of course, discoveries in the future may change this picture, but currently it does not appear that the full pattern was present anywhere at this time, which is not the case with the subsequent cultures.

The succeeding time period is also best known from evidence in the Vancouver area, where it is known as the Marpole, beginning about 2,400 years ago and lasting until about 1,000 years ago. In this case, not only have archaeologists found the remains of large planked house villages, abundant art, and the stored salmon economy, but the same burial analysis that suggests that the Locarno and St. Mungo cultures are basically egalitarian points to a highly stratified society. Less-documented cultures at about the same time near the mouth of the Skeena River are interpreted in a similar fashion, showing that much of the Northwest Coast culture reached this stage contemporaneously, possibly including groups all the way down to the mouth of the Columbia. Although this has been the conclusion of archaeologists for many years, it is only very recently that the evidence has been produced to substantiate it.

Curiously, the last 1,000 years does not have as impressive an archaeological record. This may be because of the increasing use of artifacts made of wood and other perishable organic material that do not typically preserve in shell middens, and a dramatic decrease in chipped-stone tools north of the Columbia River. In many parts of the coast, burials were no longer placed in middens or in mounds, so this sort of evidence is not available for this period. It is only in the last 1,000 years that the southern coast, between the mouth of the Columbia and northern California, developed its version of the Northwest Coast culture, with small, relatively permanent planked houses and a dense population. Current evidence has the southernmost houses dating to only the last 500–600 years.

Nevertheless, perhaps the most impressive site on the northwest coast is Ozette, in northwest Washington, which was excavated in the early 1970s. This is a waterlogged site, apparently preserved because of a mudslide shortly after AD 1700, where the remains of three large planked houses were discovered. Detailed analysis has revealed status differences between houses, including a differential availability of resources, various functional areas within the structures, as well as abundant baskets and decorated wood objects, showing the full range of Northwest Coast culture as described by the ethnographic accounts.

Further Reading: Ames, Kenneth, and Herbert Mashner, *Peoples of the Northwest Coast: Their Archaeology and Prehistory* (London: Thames and Hudson, 1999); Binford, Lewis R., "Willow-Smoke and Dog's Tails: Hunter-Gathering Settlement Systems and Archaeological Site Formation," *American Antiquity* 45 (1980): 4–20; Croes, Dale, and Steven Hackenberger, "Hoko River Archaeological Complex: Modelling Prehistoric Northwest Coast Economic Evolution," in *Research in Economic Anthropology, Supplement 3: Prehistoric Economies of the Pacific Northwest Coast*, edited by Barry L. Isaac (Greenwich, CT: JAI Press, 1988), 19–85; Fedje, Daryl, and Rolf Mathewes, *Haida Gwaii: Human History and Environment from the Time of the Loon to the Time of the Iron People* (Vancouver: University of British Columbia Press, 2005); Matson, R. G., and Gary Coupland, *The Prehistory of the Northwest Coast* (San Diego, CA: Academic Press, 1995); Matson, R. G., Gary Coupland, and Quentin Mackie, eds., *Emerging from the Mist: Studies in Northwest Coast Culture History* (Vancouver: University of British Columbia Press, 2003).

R. G. Matson

EARLY SITES OF THE NORTHWEST COAST AND ALASKA

Alaska has been the chief, although not the only, focus of interest in the search for archaeological sites with evidence of the earliest ancestors of the Native peoples of the New World. The northwest coast, however, was long viewed as a region occupied rather late in prehistory, after fishing technology had evolved to the point where people could make a living along this rugged conifer-covered coastline of sunken mountaintops. The focus on Alaska has remained much the same despite the absence of sites discovered that date early enough to be ancestral to the earliest known archaeological assemblages from regions to the south. Yet the northwest coast has now become favored by archaeologists as a route by which the earliest ancestors could have spread south from Alaska during the terminal Pleistocene to less frigid lands beyond the glaciers. Current geological evidence indicates that the long-favored route of migration along the eastern flank of the Rocky Mountains, through a corridor that formed as the glaciers parted at the end of the Pleistocene, did not open soon enough for the earliest known peoples to pass through, whereas the northwest coast, a tundra-covered coastal plain at that time, opened several thousand years earlier. The search for the earliest sites in both regions is continuing, and on the northwest coast it includes underwater exploration of drowned coastlines by Parks Canada marine archaeologists.

Stuart Fiedel has summarized the problems encountered in radiocarbon dating of early North American sites. The dating of archaeological sites in the time period between 11,500 and 10,000 radiocarbon years ago is unsatisfactory because of limitations of the technique. The temporal priority of one cultural complex over another cannot be shown consistently on the basis of radiocarbon dating during this period. While it can be shown that sites belong in this period of radiocarbon years, the dates do not accurately show relative ages of sites or complexes within this interval. There is also the problem of converting radiocarbon years to calendar years, but this conversion can be done fairly accurately by comparing the radiocarbon dates with the more accurate tree ring chronology. At this early time period, dates from radiocarbon years are consistently younger than calendar years. To convert the radiocarbon years mentioned in the following discussion to calendar years, approximately 2,000–1,500 years must be added to the given radiocarbon date. In Alaska there are three early stone tool complexes—Nenana, Denali, and Mesa—and because of dating problems, there is debate as to whether they are coeval, sequent, or overlapping.

SITES OF THE NENANA COMPLEX
Along the Nenana and Tanana rivers, tributaries of the Yukon, are a number of campsites in which the earliest components

have radiocarbon dates that average 11,300 years ago. The major sites are Dry Creek, Broken Mammoth, Healey Lake, Moose Creek, Chugwater, and Walker Road. The earliest assemblages of flaked-stone tools at all these sites are similar but differ from those found at other sites in the region, as well as in younger stratigraphic layers at some of these same sites. The following tools are typical: scraper-planes; end, side, and transverse scrapers; small triangular, heart-shaped, and teardrop-shaped bifaces (spear points or knives); drills and perforators; and considerable flaking detritus left from the manufacture of flaked-stone tools. The presence of these types of tools plus the absence of microblade technology are defining characteristics of the Nenana complex (called the Chindadn complex at the Healey Lake site). Tools made of mammoth ivory have also been found but are dated about 2,000–4,000 years earlier. This suggests that ivory was scavenged from remains of mammoth that had become extinct in this region well before the appearance of Nenana. These people were clearly hunters, with their campsites situated on overlooks where game could be spotted. Associated faunal remains include wapiti, bison, caribou, bighorn sheep, and some birds and salmonids. Two sites in the Yukon (Scottie Creek and Moose Lake) and four other sites in central Alaska (Jay Creek Ridge, Carlo Creek, Eroadaway, and Owl Ridge) have non-microblade assemblages resembling the lithics of the core Nenana sites, but date about 1,000 years younger. The earliest sites on the northwest coast also lack microblade technology and contain stone tools similar to those of the Nenana complex.

SITES OF THE DENALI (PALEO-ARCTIC) COMPLEX
There are many sites with tool assemblages that belong to what is called either the Denali complex or the Paleo-Arctic tradition, dating between 11,000 and 8,000 years ago. They are found throughout northern, western, and central Alaska and south into the Yukon Territory. Given space considerations, only the more important ones are considered here. Most of those sites listed earlier with the Nenana complex tool assemblages in their lowermost levels have Denali complex assemblages above them; the exception is the Swan Point site, which has Denali complex artifacts in the lower levels succeeded by Nenana artifacts. In addition to these sites, Denali assemblages are found at Donnelly Ridge, the Campus site at the University of Alaska, Panguingue and Little Panguingue Creek, Nukluk Mountain, the Trail Creek Caves, Bluefish Cave in the Yukon, and the Ugashik Narrows site on the Alaska Peninsula. Many sites containing Denali assemblages are also found on the Teklanika River and on the Tangle Lakes. The site of Anangula in the Aleutian Islands has a

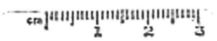

Foliate biface made of quartzite from the 9,000-year-old level at Namu, British Columbia. [Roy L. Carlson]

slightly different blade industry that may be related. It is possible that the Denali complex actually begins as early as or earlier than the Nenana complex since the component at the Swan Point site dates back to 11,660 years ago, well into the time period of Nenana. The way of life of the Denali people was insignificantly different from that of the Nenana people. However, they did differ from Nenana in using microblade technology to make stone cutting and piercing implements. The defining characteristic of the Denali artifact assemblages is the presence of wedge-shaped microblade cores manufactured in a specific manner.

Microblade manufacture is a quite different method of making flaked-stone cutting and piercing tools compared with the techniques employed in making the usual bifacial spear point or knife. The latter involves forming and sharpening a single piece of stone to make a projectile point or knife. In microblade manufacture, a nodule of stone is carefully prepared to form a core so that multiple, small, long, narrow, parallel-sided flakes with very sharp edges can be struck and then broken into segments that can be inserted into slots on the sides of antler or wooden points to form the cutting edges. Knives can also be made this way. The advantage of this technique over biface manufacture is that large cutting and piercing tools can be made using small pieces of stone when large pieces are not available. Bone points slotted for the insertion of microblade segments have been found in both Alaska and northwest coast sites, but they are much more common in Siberia. Denali microblade cores were usually made by truncating a biface and using the truncation as the platform from which to strike blades, whereas northwest coast microblade cores were usually prepared in a different manner.

Microblade technology is very common in northern China, Korea, Japan, and Siberia and was established earlier there than in North America. The Denali complex is probably an extension into Alaska of the Dhuktai culture of Siberia, with which it shares this truncated-biface core technology. It is thought that microblade technology was introduced into North America by the ancestors of the peoples speaking NaDene languages, and from them spread to their neighbors. Microblades are common from Alaska south to the Columbia River in Washington and are found in limited numbers at least as far south as Colorado and at the Eel Point site on San Clemente Island in southern California.

SITES OF THE MESA COMPLEX

Sites of the Mesa complex are found in both northern Alaska and on the Kuskokwim drainage of southwestern Alaska. This complex was first discovered at the Putu and Bedwell sites in the Brooks Range, but is best known from extensive excavations at the Mesa site. As its name implies, this site is situated on an isolated tableland 60 meters high that provides an unobstructed view of the surrounding tundra, a very useful location for hunters. The eleven hearths at the site have provided a series of radiocarbon dates ranging from 9,700 to 11,700 years ago that place it in the same period of radiocarbon time as both the Nenana and Denali assemblages. The stone tools, however, are very different from those found in these other two complexes, and the projectile points in shape and technology more closely resemble those of the Paleoindian cultures south of the glaciated regions than they do any of the local complexes. The points are lanceolate (long and narrow) with parallel flaking, and are not fluted. They more closely resemble the Agate Basin points of the late Paleoindian bison hunters of the plains than other point assemblages, although they are usually smaller in size. Points of this type are also found in southwestern Alaska at the Spein Mountain site.

The Putu site is of interest because in addition to the lanceolate points of the Mesa type, fluted points were also found there. Although the radiocarbon dates are not fully satisfactory, it is reasonably clear that the fluted points appear late in the depositional history of the site and in all probability post-date the artifacts of the Mesa complex. At one time it was thought that the fluted points were associated with a date of 11,470 ± 500 years, but it has since been shown that this date is earlier than any evidence of human occupation at Putu. Other finds of fluted points in Alaska are also undated, although it is probable they post-date their occurrence to the south and represent a late northward swing of people using fluted points as the Pleistocene ended.

EARLY NORTHWEST COAST SITES

In the coastal zones of southeastern Alaska, British Columbia, and Washington there are eleven tested or excavated sites that date between 9,000 and 11,000 radiocarbon years ago, and there are several documented finds of fluted points that because of their specific attributes are known to fall within this period. Stone tools that belong to several different technological and cultural traditions are found in these sites. The earliest artifact assemblages are typified by the presence of bifaces and the absence of microblade technology.

Sites of the Fluted Point Tradition

No fluted points have been found on the coast in British Columbia or southeastern Alaska. On Puget Sound in Washington isolated undated finds of fluted points have been made at Coupeville on Whidbey Island and at other sites near Olympia and Chehalis. At the nearby Manis site on the Olympic Peninsula the remains of mastodon, caribou, and bison have been found and dated to about 11,000 years ago. Although no diagnostic artifactual remains of this period were found at the site, this time period is the same in which fluted points are dated elsewhere on the continent, and further excavation may show this site to belong to that tradition. The closest well-documented site with Clovis fluted points is the Richey-Roberts cache site on the Columbia River east of the Cascade Mountains.

Sites of the Foliate Biface (Pebble Tool or Old Cordilleran) Tradition

All of the earliest known sites on the coasts of British Columbia and southeastern Alaska lack microblades in their earliest assemblages and have "foliate" (leaf-shaped), bifacially flaked spear points and knives. These bifaces lack a base with a flute or a stem for hafting, and thus differ from the points and knives that typify the other early biface traditions. The earliest dated sites are bear dens on the west coast of the

Queen Charlotte Islands, with dates between 10,800 and 10,500 years ago, where leaf-shaped points were found directly associated with bear bones. Early sites with artifact assemblages in the period from 8,500 to 10,000 years ago are Ground Hog Bay 2, On-Your-Knees Cave, Richardson Island, Kilgii Gwaay, TsinniTsinni, Namu, K1 Cave, Bear Cove, and Milliken. Kilgii Gwaay is a waterlogged site at which no actual bifaces were found, although there is evidence of bifacial flaking. More important, a fragment of cordage, probably made of spruce root, and a wooden wedge for splitting wood provide evidence of the early occurrence of these technologies that persist into the historic period on the northwest coast. It is clear from the faunal evidence at Kilgii Gwaay that subsistence centered around fishing and sea mammal hunting, and these people were well adapted to the coastal environment.

Sites of the Microblade Tradition

Microblade technology appeared on the northwest coast between 8,500 and 9,000 years ago, and by 8,000 years ago it was found throughout the coastal region north of the mouth of the Columbia River. Early sites with microblade technology include Namu, Ground Hog Bay 2, On-Your-Knees Cave, Richardson Island, Chuck Lake, TsinniTsinni, South Yale, and Chuck Lake. At Namu and On-Your-Knees Cave and most other sites except in the Queen Charlotte Islands, foliate bifaces continued to be made even after microblade technology was introduced, whereas in the Queen Charlotte Islands bifaces dropped out of use entirely except for ones probably traded from the mainland. Microblade technology persisted in most parts of the coast until 5,000 years ago, and even later in some localities. The earliest human skeletal remains on the coast are associated with both biface and microblade technology at On-Your-Knees Cave, dated about 9,200 years ago. Isotopic analyses of the bones indicate that this individual subsisted almost entirely on protein obtained from the ocean.

Early sites in Alaska and on the northwest coast are remote and not easily accessed. The Manis site near Sequim in Washington is the only one set up for visits by tourists, although museums in all the major cities have exhibits of archaeological material.

Further Reading: Carlson, Roy L., ed., *Archaeology of Coastal British Columbia Essays in Honour of Professor Philip M. Hobler* (Burnaby, BC: Archaeology Press, Simon Fraser University, 2003); Carlson, Roy L., and Luke DallaBona, eds., *Early Human Occupation in British Columbia* (Vancouver: University of British Columbia Press, 1996); Carlson, Roy L., and Martin Magne, eds., *Projectile Point Sequences in Northwestern North America* (Burnaby, BC: Archaeology Press, Simon Fraser University, 2008); Fiedel, Stuart, "Older Than We Thought: Implications of Corrected Dates for Paleoindians," *American Antiquity* 64(1) (1999): 95–115; Hoffecker, John F., and Scott A. Elias, *Human Ecology of Beringia* (New York: Columbia University Press, 2007); Kuzmin, Yaroslav V., Susan G.

Keates, and Chen Shen, eds., *Origin and Spread of Microblade Technology in Northern Asia and North America* (Burnaby, BC: Archaeology Press, Simon Fraser University, 2007); Suttles, Wayne, ed., *Handbook of North American Indians Northwest Coast*, vol. 7

(Washington, DC: Smithsonian Institution, 1990); West, F. H., ed., *American Beginnings: The Prehistory and Paleoecology of Beringia* (Chicago: University of Chicago Press, 1996).

Roy L. Carlson

HUNTER-GATHERERS OF THE NORTHWEST COAST AND SOUTHEASTERN ALASKA

Today archaeological research conservatively confirms the arrival of the earliest humans to the northwest coast at approximately 10,000–12,000 years ago. The complex theories surrounding the habitation and migration to the coast is still open to new research. Geological research suggests that at the end of the Pleistocene and beginning of the Holocene, some 10,000 years ago, the ecology and climate began to gradually stabilize and this likely added to the attractiveness of this region for early human travelers and inhabitants. Recent isotope analysis of human remains from On-Your-Knees Cave on Prince of Wales Island, Alaska, dating to approximately 9,700 years ago suggests that humans were already heavily reliant on a marine diet. Over the course of the next 10,000 years, the Native people of the northwest coast would develop a profound knowledge and relationship with the complex ecology.

The cultural groups of the northwest coast, from Oregon to Alaska, have many ethnographic sociopolitical differences but share many economic similarities. A unifying theme on the coast is the significance of marine resources to these cultures. The harvesting of abundant marine resources has often been suggested as one of the key factors in the population density and frequency of villages prior to Euro-American contact. Classically labeled as hunter-gatherers by early ethnographers, these groups, recent archaeological and ethnographic research suggests, might more appropriately be called gatherer-hunters.

Although this region is well known for its salmon resources, there were many other resources that were gathered and hunted. From Oregon to Alaska, village groups coordinated their movements and harvested their resources based on seasonal cycles. Village settlements were located in close proximity to various marine resources with good sheltered beaches that enabled easy landing of canoes during all seasons of the year. Many of the marine resources required a collective effort to harvest, prepare, and preserve. Groups based on kinship affiliation usually worked together. Labor within each group was often divided along gender and age lines, but as documented throughout the ethnographic literature many individuals transcended these boundaries.

Most of the coastal groups were organized socially and politically into band- or tribal-level groups. Concepts or notions of rank were common, but these groups did not have a socioeconomic class system. An individual's access to resources was determined by his or her kin group affiliation. Each kin or lineage group usually had a leader who led by both ascribed status (born into) and achieved status (earned). Throughout the coast, the political and social authority of leadership varied from centralized to decentralized on the village level. For example, among the Tsimshian, a specific lineage or clan head could emerge as the central leader of the village or area, whereas, among the Tlingit there were many villages in which leadership and authority was specific to a clan and not to the entire village.

In the winter season groups lived in the large settlements that usually comprised several house groups. The winter villages had permanent structures, and these extended family dwellings were constructed primarily out of wood. Each dwelling could house one to several family lineages. Although style of construction of these houses varied along the coast, the most common architectural element was four main house posts with two longitudinal logs placed in notches in the corner post. The longitudinal beams provided the main house beams for the roof. This simple but heavy-duty design required a great deal of human power to erect the four house posts and two longitudinal beams. Therefore, the construction of one of these houses required the congregation of many people and usually was dedicated by a major ceremonial event.

The many different cultural groups of this region had elaborate winter ceremonials. After the culmination of the fall harvesting activities, the family, lineage, and clan groups would return to their winter village. Many groups held what ethnographers have classically called "potlatches." These ceremonies were usually community rites of passage, and the cultural significance and activities were unique to each group. It was during these ceremonies that the kin groups would bring out their regalia, dance, sing their songs, and tell their oral narratives and histories. Most of these ceremonies were usually witnessed by the entire village, and often visitors from other villages or kin groups from distant lands would attend. The sociopolitical importance of these ceremonies was to share resources and to bring people together to reinforce or form new social and political alliances. The winter ceremonies provided an opportunity for reciprocity between kin groups, such as to pay back other groups for services they had provided in the past. The sense of obligation to reciprocate among kin groups along the coast is a universal theme.

Sometimes villages, tribes, or clans would travel great distances for one of these winter ceremonies. Although the cultural groups were well adapted to the sea and they could travel long distances even in stormy, rough conditions, the cold winter weather slowed travel, and many people stayed closer to the main village. During the winter, people gathered clams, cockles, chitons, mussels, sea cucumber, dungeness crab, shrimp, and many other resources from the tidal areas or sea. Recent geoarchaeological and ethnographic work has revealed that many different Native groups actually developed and altered beaches specifically for clam beds and with the intention to increase efficiency of harvesting. All of these resources from the beach helped supplement the winter stores, and the danger of red tides during this season was low.

Some of the men, assisted by members of their immediate family, maintained trap lines during the winter months to harvest mink, otter, beaver, ermine, wolverine, and other fur-bearing animals. The trap lines sometimes stretched far into the interior. Travel along frozen streams and lakes and across drifting snow would require the use of snowshoes and sleds. Furs were important in the making of different parts of winter parkas and ceremonial items. During the historic period, many furs were traded for European goods or were sold for a cash income.

In the spring smaller groups would begin to leave the winter village to go harvest various resources as they became available. Ownership of territories and resource areas were the jurisdiction of the tribe or village, the clan or house group, or sometimes even a specific lineage or family depending on the importance, quantity, and availability of the resource.

In the spring the return of herring (*Clupea harengus*) and eulachon (*Thaleichthys pacificus*) were harvested in large quantities. Among many of the groups along the coast, herring and the roe were a great delicacy and trade item. The eulachon were harvested in large quantities along some of the major rivers of British Columbia and Alaska. The eulachon fish was cooked to draw out the oil, and the oil was traded far into the interior. The oil was used as a food condiment like butter or oil today and was used to preserve other foods. The coastal and interior groups were connected by trade routes referred to as grease trails, named after the eulachon oil or grease that was transported along these corridors.

Marine mammals such as seal could be harvested year-round. Seal meat and oil derived from the fat in addition to the furs were a mainstay of many coastal groups, especially the groups in British Columbia and Alaska. In the late spring, as the birds began to travel north and nest, gathering parties would collect an egg or two from each nest early in the season, leaving some eggs to hatch. This system of harvesting migratory bird eggs conserved the species. In recent years

scientists have studied this method of egg collecting and have confirmed that traditional patterns of harvesting do not have a detrimental impact on bird populations.

In the spring and summer, as the halibut (*Hipploglossus stenolepsis*) moved back into coastal waters, individuals or small groups would go out and jig for the fish by setting individual hooks or lines with multiple hooks, known as skates. Halibut, which range from 18 to 270 kilograms (40 to 600 lb), could provide a large quantity of fresh meat during the lean spring and early summer months.

An additional source of vitamins and minerals, as well as a favorite complement to many meals, was a variety of seaweed and kelp. Seaweed was harvested from rocky exposed areas during the late spring and early summer. Once the seaweed was harvested it was usually sun-dried on the rocks on the beach. Sometimes flavor was added by smoking the seaweed or adding clam juice to it. The seaweed would then be stored and consumed the rest of the year.

In the spring and early summer while the tree sap is still flowing, women would gather red cedar (*Thuja plicata*) or yellow cedar (*Charmaecyparis nootkatensis*) bark and Sitka spruce (*Picea Sitchensis*) roots for the manufacturing of textiles, garments, ropes, nets, hats, baskets, mats, and other containers. First, the bark or roots were collected, and then the tedious and time-consuming process of preparing the inner bark material was necessary. The spring and early summer months were chosen as the optimum time because the sap flowing in the trees added to the ease of preparing the materials and helped the trees heal more quickly. Bark and roots were collected with care and respect for the trees. Although bark stripping left scars on the trees, it was done in such a way as to leave the tree living. In British Columbia and southeastern Alaska today, one can see many of these bark-stripped trees that were used 100 or more years ago.

The harvesting of salmon was scheduled and coordinated along with other summer and fall activities. Once the kin groups traveled to "fish camp" everyone had tasks. The children and elderly would assist the women in large-scale berry harvesting. The berries were picked in the summer and fall as the different species ripened. The berries most frequently collected along the coast were salmonberries (*Rubus spectabilis*), thimbleberries (*Rubus parvis-florus*), blueberries (*Vaccinium ovatum*), huckleberries (*V. parvifolium*), soapberries (*Shepherdia canadensis*), strawberries (*Fragaria chiloensis*), and raspberries (*Robus pedatus*).

The coastal groups had discovered a variety of plants that could be used for all kinds of ailments and illnesses. Different parts of the plants would be gathered depending on the time of year and concentration of active ingredients or potency. Although knowledge about the medicinal applications of different plants was not confined to the shamans, they were usually particularly knowledgeable about the use and efficacy of various plants.

The different groups in this region cultivated and harvested wild plants. At the time of European contact they were cultivating several different types of tobacco (*Nicotiana quadrivalvis*). Recent DNA work on potato cultivars in the northwest coast and Alaska has revealed some ancient varieties that originated from Peru or central Mexico. More research is needed to determine whether those potato cultivars arrived in the northwest coast and Alaska via indigenous trade networks or through trade with early European and American traders.

Economically and ecologically, one of the most dominant resources in the region was salmon. Whether it was coastal groups at the mouths of rivers using fish traps and weirs or the inland cultures who were netting, spearing, or catching the salmon as they migrated upstream, almost all the groups harvested salmon. The techniques used were efficient and effective, epitomizing the idea of an economy of least effort. Simply put, kin groups or villages waited for the salmon to return to the rivers and streams of the coast. The annual runs of five species of salmon—chinooks (*Oncorhynchus tshawytscha*), sockeyes (*Onchorhynchus nerka*), cohoes (*Oncorhynchus kisutch*), pinks (*Oncorhynchus gorbuscha*), and chums (*Oncorhynchus keta*)—return to the rivers and streams at different times during the summer and fall.

Approximately 6,000 years ago geologists hypothesize that the climate and ecology along the coast began to stabilize. The isostactic rebound, or uplift of the land after the glaciers receded, began to slow down and thus the rivers became more stable. It is during this same time period that archaeologists conclude that salmon runs became more consistent as new tools and artifacts emerge at many sites, indicating an emphasis toward salmon. The ecological stability coupled with technological and social changes along the coast enhanced the opportunities to harvest salmon as a primary food source.

The large-scale intense harvesting of resources, such as the salmon, would not have been possible without the development of a sophisticated sociopolitical organization that could mobilize a large group of people to catch, process, and preserve the fish. Thus the idea that the ecology determined the "sophisticated" cultures of the northern Pacific would be a gross oversimplification. Although many marine resources are available in abundant numbers, these resources arrive and must be processed in a very short period of time; even to this day the logistics provide a challenge to large-scale commercial harvesters and processors.

The division of labor and the cooperation of a group of people were necessary to harvest, butcher, and preserve a large quantity of fish. Careful coordination of activities was necessary in order to be able to process and preserve the fish as they were caught. The first activities required preparing the fish weirs or traps. This required the heavy lifting of rocks for the traps or the pounding of stakes for the weirs. The men constructed the frame, while the women made the rope, twine, and netting that were used in the weirs.

While the weirs or traps were being prepared and installed, the women, children, and elderly would be preparing the smokehouses and drying racks and cutting alder and other fresh wood that would produce the proper smoke to cure, dry, and preserve the fish. Smokehouses and drying racks had to be constructed or repaired. Large quantities of wood or containers were needed to store the fish. Knives were made out of stone materials and sharpened. All these steps had to be completed before harvesting could begin.

Once everything was ready for the harvest, the coordination of activities between ritual specialists such as shamans and the kin or village leaders was necessary to have a successful fishing season. Not only were weirs and traps highly effective, but they also provided a sophisticated way to monitor the escapement of salmon upstream. Individuals known as stream guards would study and assist in the fish management by working with the kin leaders in determining and selecting the number of each species and sex of salmon to be harvested. Since the shaman, kin leader, and stream guard were positions that were usually inherited through a particular lineage, the ecological knowledge was transmitted from generation to generation.

Along with the sociopolitical organization, each kin group or village had to maintain well-defined notions of territory and property ownership. Specifically designed weirs, traps, and nets allowed groups from Oregon to Alaska to harvest large numbers of salmon in a small period of time. Due to the efficiency and effectiveness of this technology, local groups developed conservation methods. Without ownership and accountability, the technology was potentially efficient enough to deplete the abundant runs within a few decades. This system of resource management and property ownership provided healthy stocks of salmon for hundreds if not thousands of years. The cultural systems of management and ownership of Native cultures seem more significant in light of the fact that during the historic period (1880s–1940s) commercial fish traps almost entirely decimated the salmon runs in some areas. The absence of management systems and ownership of territories along the coast during the early historic period has been referred to by many historians as the "tragedy of the commons."

In the fall, fishing activities occurred in conjunction with other hunting and gathering activities. Larger animals such as black bear (*Ursus americanus*), brown bear (*Ursus arctos*), deer (*Ocdocoelious*), mountain goat (*Oreamnus americanus*), elk (*Cervus elaphus*) to the south, and moose (*Alces alces*) to the north were harvested. Black bears and brown bears were easily hunted during this time of year as the animals congregated near the streams to eat salmon. Bears were hunted in the fall for their meat and furs, but also for their fat, which was rendered into an oil and used for preserving the fall harvest foods. The last of the fall berries, wild crabapples (*Malus fusca*), plant roots, and other edible plants were collected and stored by the women and children while the men hunted. The animals were butchered, and then the women and children prepared the hides and furs.

The coastal groups also made many articles of clothing, particularly ceremonial robes out of mountain goat fur. The fur from the mountain goat was collected in two different ways. During the summer, the fur was collected from brush in the alpine when the goats were brushing up against and shedding their fur. During the fall and winter as the goats came to lower elevations, the men would hunt these animals for wool as well as meat.

The coastal people also collected alternative sources of wool for weaving from domesticated dogs. Recent archaeological evidence suggests that domesticated dogs may have existed on the coast for at least 2,000 years. Dogs were also used as pack animals and for protection against bears. Many of the oral narratives discuss the use of dogs in hunting bears. Early European explorers in British Columbia included dogs in their paintings, sketches, and written descriptions of Native cultures.

Even though the coastal peoples of the northwest coast had similar strategies for living off the land and sea, their social organization, cultures, and languages were very different and unique. At the core of many of these groups today is still their connection to the land, sea, and resources, an interdependence that gives these people a connection to place that Native elders would express as lasting since "time immemorial."

Further Reading: Ames, Kenneth M., and Herbert D. G. Maschner, *Peoples of the Northwest Coast: Their Archaeology and Prehistory* (London: Thames and Hudson, 1999); Amos, Pamela T., *Coast Salish Spirit Dancing: The Survival of an Ancestral Religion* (Seattle: University of Washington Press, 1978); Dixon, E. James, *Bones, Boats, and Bison: Archeology and the First Colonization of Western North America* (Albuquerque: University of New Mexico Press, 1999); Emmons, George Thornton, *The Tlingit Indians*, edited by Frederica De Laguna (Seattle: University of Washington Press, 1991); Harkin, Michael E., *The Heiltsuks: Dialogues of Culture and History on the Northwest Coast* (Lincoln: University of Nebraska Press, 1997); Hunn, Eugene S., Darryll R. Johnson, Priscilla N. Russell, and Thomas F. Thornton, "The Huna Tlingit People's Traditional Use of Gull Eggs and Establishment of Glacier National Park," National Park Service Technical Report NPS D-121 (2003); Kan, Sergei, *Symbolic Immortality* (Washington, DC: Smithsonian Press, 1989); Matson, R. J., and G. Coupland, *The Prehistory of the Northwest Coast* (London: Academic Press, 1995); Stewart, H., *Indian Fishing: Early Methods on the Northwest Coast* (Seattle: University of Washington Press, 1977); Suttles, Wayne, *Coast Salish Essays* (Seattle: University of Washington Press, 1987); Suttles, Wayne, ed., *Handbook of North American Indians: Northwest Coast*, vol. 7 (Washington, DC: Smithsonian Institution, 1990); Swanton, John R., *Social Conditions, Beliefs, and Linguistic Relationship of the Tlingit Indians*, Bureau of American Ethnology Annual Report No. 26 (Washington, DC: Bureau of American Ethnology, 1908); Turner, Nancy J., *Plant Technology of First Peoples in British Columbia* (Vancouver: University of British Columbia Press, 1998).

Daniel Monteith

BRITISH COLONIZATION OF THE NORTHWEST COAST AND INTERIOR RIVER DRAINAGES

Studies of British colonization of northwestern North America have perhaps been most informed by a rich corpus of historical, ethnographic, and oral historical data. These include the journals of late eighteenth-century European explorers and maritime fur traders, the documented accounts of overland British and American explorers (e.g., Simon Fraser, Meriwether Lewis, and William Clark), and the records kept by early- to mid-nineteenth-century British mercantilists who operated trading posts along drainages connecting the coast to the interior. To these we can add the post-colonial, early twentieth-century ethnographic research of many prominent American anthropologists. This includes the works of Franz Boas, Ruth Benedict, Viola Garfield, Erna Gunther, Homer Barnett, and Wilson Duff, among others. Combined, this corpus of ethnographic data addressing indigenous oral histories, social structures, symbolism, political organization, and material culture is virtually unparalleled in North America.

Northwest coast archaeologists who study the era of encounter between Europeans and indigenous societies enjoy a rare opportunity to examine how historical, ethnographic, and archaeological data articulate. Given that each line of data has inherent biases and limitations, research programs that draw on all three sources of information oftentimes generate fuller reconstructions of past behavior. This approach also permits archaeologists to evaluate how each line of data complements or conflicts with the others. Data generated with high-resolution archaeological investigations is somewhat unique in that it provides glimpses into the everyday experiences of indigenous northwest coast people and early British colonists alike.

Archaeological research addressing the era of European contact and settlement in the northwest coast region has mostly focused on indigenous villages rather than on European outposts. This trend can be contrasted with research traditions in other areas of western North America, such as central and southern coastal California, where until recently most of the post-European contact archaeology addressed life at European institutions, such as Spanish missions and presidios. Thus, northwest coast archaeology has much to offer to the study of European impact on the organization of traditional lifeways, particularly at the community and household levels.

CHRONOLOGY

Archaeologists and historians have traditionally divided the colonial period, or the period of time spanning the earliest arrival of British ships on the northwest coast and the present, into three phases: the northern Pacific maritime fur trade, the land-based fur trade, and the era of intensive British-Canadian settlement. In general, these phases map onto historically documented transitions in intercultural interaction, bracketing periods of time in which the frequency and mode of interaction between Europeans and aboriginal societies differed from preceding and subsequent phases.

However, the wholesale application of this chronology to the varied regions and cultures of the Pacific Northwest can be problematic. For example, some northwest coast communities, particularly those residing along smaller interior drainages, interacted only rarely or never with Europeans in the earlier phases of encounter. Similarly, while some First Nations communities were being displaced during the establishment of large British settlements on the coast (e.g., Vancouver), others were still interacting with the British only in the context of exchange and the land-based fur trade. Also, by using European activities to define the major time phases, this chronology simultaneously ignores and normalizes a period of sometimes subtle and sometimes dramatic changes in indigenous lifeways. In this way, it fails to capture or highlight that which is of interest to anthropological archaeology, including changes in indigenous political organization, shifts in social structure, and the processes by which indigenous ideologies and identities are preserved and transformed.

THE MARITIME FUR TRADE

An era of sporadic contact and interaction between select Pacific Northwest indigenous societies and British mariners began in 1778, only four years after Captain James Cook led the first European expedition to the region. Cook discovered that ample supplies of marine mammal fur pelts could be acquired through exchange with indigenous leaders and households on the northwest coast and sold for handsome profits in Asia. Soon thereafter, British and other European interests made numerous voyages to the coastlines of present-day Oregon, Washington, and British Columbia. The Pacific maritime fur trade was in peak operation between 1792 and 1812. Although Russian and British ships dominated much of the early trade, by 1793 American ships outnumbered British ships in the Northwest, and by 1801 the fur trade was largely controlled by American mercantilists working out of Boston. However, over two decades of intensive trade had a devastating effect on fur-bearing marine mammal populations, and after 1812 the maritime fur trade began to dwindle due to declining supplies of pelts.

Contact with Europeans during the maritime fur trade was typically intermittent and limited to indigenous communities situated on the densely populated outer coast. Owing largely to the variable locations of natural harbors, some stretches of coastline, such as western Vancouver Island, received greater attention by British traders. Interactions between Europeans and indigenous people were primarily economic and focused on the exchange of goods. These episodes of trade, however, were often highly ritualized and almost always structured by long histories of hierarchical social organization on both sides. Much of the direct, face-to-face trading and negotiations occurred between the captains of British vessels and wealthy, high-standing leaders of Pacific Northwest communities. Given the differences in languages on both sides of early interactions, the potential for blunders in social etiquette, misunderstood rituals, and misinterpretations of intentions was particularly high. Furthermore, both British traders and indigenous leaders sometimes used intimidation tactics to manipulate trade in their favor. Historical records reflect occasional skirmishes, some of which resulted in both European and Native casualties.

The cargo holds of British ships carried voluminous supplies of European goods to the northern Pacific to be used in trade for furs. Some classes of goods were stocked in greater quantities than others, and British ships often carried many of the newest trade items as well as blacksmiths that could manufacture items as needed. Although glass beads were among the most valued European trade goods in some areas of western North America, early British fur traders discovered that northwest coast people valued iron knives and several other iron tools more highly than other European objects. To the disappointment of British traders, not all European objects were regarded as valuable by indigenous people, and furs could not be obtained with mere beads, trinkets, or baubles. In fact, British maritime fur traders found that Pacific Northwest people were savvy traders and often drove the exchange value of furs upward by pitting British offers against those made by American traders. In some areas, such as western Vancouver Island, much of the maritime fur trade was controlled by only a few Nuu-chah-nulth leaders and their families.

Distinguishing maritime fur trade activities from those that date to later periods with archaeological data is difficult, at best. Although several British ships were wrecked on the northwest coast, seemingly none were preserved or left intact to constitute an archaeological site. Among indigenous villages, maritime fur trade activities are difficult to discern from the land-based fur trade due to some continuity in the types of European objects circulated in both phases. Furthermore, using known manufacture dates of European objects to determine occupation dates of sites is made problematic by occasional delays in the transport

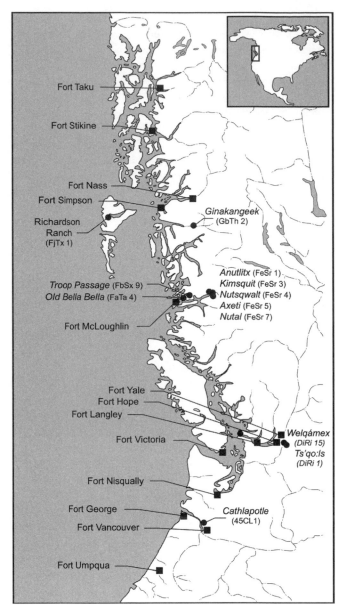

The land-based fur trade in the Pacific Northwest region was largely governed by HBC's Columbia Department, and over a 25-year period the HBC established a chain of thirteen coastal trading posts.　[Anthony P. Graesch]

of goods to western North America, the manufacture of some objects (e.g., iron nails) on British ships, and the fact that people retained and used objects long after they were introduced to local material cultures.

Phil Hobler has argued that further chronological resolution may be gained by also considering the types and quantities of *indigenous* artifacts in post-contact archaeological sites. Working with archaeological collections from the post-contact village sites of Nutal (FeSr 7), Anutlitx (FeSr 1), Nutsquwalt (FeSr 4), Axeti (FeSr 5), Old Bella Bella (FaTa 4), Troop Pas-

sage (FbSx 9), and Richardson Ranch (FjTx 1), Hobler used a Spearman's rank correlation analysis to examine how site assemblages were similar or different with respect to the relative abundance of European and indigenous artifacts. Hobler found that some sites, including Nutal and Nutsquwalt, feature a proportionally greater abundance of traditional flaked stone, ground stone, and bone artifacts and were likely occupied and abandoned in the earlier phases of British activity in the Pacific Northwest.

However, many indigenous villages inhabited during the maritime fur trade were also occupied during the land-based fur trade and up to the era of British-Canadian settlement. Richardson Ranch (FjTx 1), for example, is a Haida village site likely established prior to European contact and abandoned in the 1830s or 1840s. Excavations by Knut Fladmark at FjTx 1 in the 1970s focused on the residence of an elite Haida family. His analysis of excavated house assemblages indicates not only a persistence in the production of traditional tool forms but also an elaboration and innovation of some craft industries (e.g., argillite tobacco pipes) in response to changes in trade networks that began during the maritime fur trade.

The Musqueam village of Stselax (DhRt 2) in the Fraser River delta is another residential site that was likely occupied during and well after the maritime fur trade in the northern Pacific. Michelle Poulsen has worked with artifact assemblages and field notes generated with previous excavations and argues that residents of *Stselax* integrated European material culture into everyday indigenous activities in ways that were consistent with indigenous values, beliefs, and practices.

THE LAND-BASED FUR TRADE

With the decline of the maritime fur trade, British mercantilists shifted operations to rivers and creeks that connected the interior to the outer coast. Here, the fur trade focused on the pelts of beaver, river otter, and mink. European involvement was dominated by trappers and officers working for the Hudson's Bay Company (HBC), a British corporation based in eastern North America on Hudson's Bay. The land-based fur trade in the Pacific Northwest region was largely governed by HBC's Columbia Department, and over a twenty-five-year period the HBC established a chain of thirteen coastal trading posts. The majority of these posts were established and operated in present-day British Columbia, although several existed in the United States and were operated even after the treaty of 1848 and the division of British- and American-controlled North America at the 49th parallel. Trading and other mercantile operations at most of the HBC posts ceased by or before the 1880s. Several HBC posts, including Fort Langley and Fort Vancouver, now feature living museums and visitors' centers that are open to the public.

Among the thirteen HBC trading posts in the northwest coast region, HBC Fort Vancouver has received the most intensive archaeological attention. Excavations have focused on the remains of the chief factor's house, the employee village, the Kanaka village site, and the stockade, among other areas. At the height of its operation, Fort Vancouver was home to English and Scottish HBC administrators who managed a 600-person workforce composed of Native Hawai'ians, Iroquois, and French-Canadian *Métis*. Much of the archaeological research at HBC Fort Vancouver has examined how the hierarchical organization of HBC operations is reflected in the living arrangements, diets, and activities of Fort Vancouver's multiethnic population.

Historical and archaeological data indicate that HBC trading posts were regarded as new resource loci on indigenous landscapes where access to resources had been owned and controlled by northwest coast families for centuries. Although the Columbia Department intended to use HBC outposts to assert control over indigenous exchange networks, they discovered that trade was already controlled by socially prominent families. Existing political privileges, elevated social status, and histories of trade alliances with sources of non-local goods allowed affluent northwest coast families and leaders to differentially establish and benefit from relationships with newly constructed British trading posts. In this way, much of the land-based fur trade occurred only within a long-established indigenous wealth economy.

Archaeologically, the economic significance of HBC trading posts to indigenous wealth economies is evident in the construction and expansion of villages near these outposts. Excavations at one such village in southern British Columbia by Anthony Graesch have generated new data on Stó:lö (Coast Salish) household and community organization during the land-based fur trade. Welqámex (DiRi 15) was an island village situated near HBC Fort Hope and strategically positioned to manipulate and perhaps even control trade between downriver communities and HBC employees. Investigations at this site have revealed that Stó:lö households inhabiting the largest and most architecturally unique residences maintained privileged access to HBC trade goods.

Despite population decline attributable to smallpox and other European diseases, documentary and archaeological data suggest a fluorescence of indigenous political economies during the maritime and land-based fur trades. In part, this is attributable to the infusion of new HBC valuables into local and regional exchange networks. However, the preservation of the traditional lifeways and the fact that indigenous societies were never reliant on HBC food or services are also important factors. Andrew Martindale's investigations at the post-contact Tsimshian village of Ginakangeek (GbTh 2) suggest that the economic autonomy of indigenous households was linked to the maintenance of social relations established well before European arrival on the northwest coast.

Other research addressing indigenous households during the land-based fur trade includes the work of Ken Ames and colleagues at the Chinookan village of Cathlapotle (45CL1)

and that of Jeanne Arnold and David Schaepe at the Stó:lö village of Ts'qo:ls (DiRi 1). Archaeological investigations at Cathlapotle have revealed a large village consisting of at least three large cedar plank structures and strategically located such that village inhabitants could monitor trade up and down the Columbia River. Excavations in several of these structures have recovered over 1,000 glass beads as well as numerous other HBC trade goods, including buttons, ceramic vessels, and iron tools. Research at Ts'qo:ls by Arnold and Schaepe has focused on the house of Captain Charlie. Archaeological data suggest that the structure was occupied in the mid- to late nineteenth century and may reflect a transition from extended family to nuclear family household organization near the end of the land-based fur trade.

BRITISH-CANADIAN SETTLEMENT

In general, the era of intensive and permanent British-Canadian settlement in the northwest coast region post-dates the 1850s gold rush in southern British Columbia and coincides with the arrival of missionaries in the 1860s. This era witnessed the debasement of traditional northwest coast political economies, the suppression of indigenous ideologies, and the displacement of indigenous communities to reservations. In the wake of population decline attributable to smallpox epidemics, many traditional northwest coast lifeways were abandoned or lost, and indigenous people increasingly were assimilated into the British-Canadian economy.

Few studies have addressed the late colonial period with archaeological data. Paul Prince's research at the sites of Kimsquit (FeSr 3) and Anutlitx (FeSr 1) is a notable exception. Prince's analyses of assemblages from both sites demonstrate a persistence of indigenous ideas, innovation, and identity that ran counter to white assimilation efforts and persisted well into the period of white colonization in British Columbia.

Further Reading: Acheson, Steven, and James P. Delgado, "Ships for the Taking: Culture Contact and the Maritime Fur Trade on the Northwest Coast of North America," in *The Archaeology of Contact in Settler Societies*, edited by Tim Murray (Cambridge: Cambridge University Press, 2004), 48–77; Ames, Kenneth M., Cameron M. Smith, William L. Cornett, Elizabeth A. Sobel, Stephen C. Hamilton, John Wolf, and Doria Raetz, *Archaeological Investigations at 45Cl1 Cathlapotle (1991–1996), Ridgefield National Wildlife Refuge, Clark County, Washington: A Preliminary Report* (Portland, Oregon: U.S. Department of the Interior, Fish and Wildlife Service, 1999); Cromwell, Robert J., "Ceramic Analysis at Fort Vancouver NHS," National Park Service Web site, http://www.nps.gov/history/archeology/sites/npSites/FOVACeramics.htm (online 2007); Fladmark, Knut R., "The Richardson Ranch Site: A 19th Century Haida House," in *Historical Archaeology in Northwestern North America*, edited by R. M. Getty and K. R. Fladmark Calgary, AB: University of Calgary Archaeological Association, 1973), 53–96; Graesch, Anthony P., "Archaeological and Ethnoarchaeological Investigations of Households and

Perspectives on a Coast Salish Historic Village in British Columbia," Ph.D. diss. (Department of Anthropology, University of California, Los Angeles, 2006); Hobler, Philip M., "Measures of the Acculturative Response to Trade on the Central Coast of British Columbia," *Historical Archaeology* 20 (1986): 16–26; Martindale, Andrew, "Tsimshian Houses and Households through the Contact Period," in *Household Archaeology on the Northwest Coast*, edited by Elizabeth A. Sobel, D. Ann Trieu Gahr, and Kenneth M. Ames (Ann Arbor, MI: International Monographs in Prehistory, 2006), 140–199; McMillan, Alan D., *Since the Time of the Transformers: The Ancient Heritage of the Nuu-chah-nulth, Ditidaht, and Makah* (Vancouver: University of British Columbia Press, 1999); Poulsen, Michelle D., "Making Choices: Examining Musqueam Agency at Stselax Village during the Post-Contact Period," unpublished master's thesis (Department of Anthropology and Sociology, University of British Columbia, 2005); Prince, Paul, "Culture Coherency and Resistance in Historic-Period Northwest-Coast Mortuary Practices at Kimsquit," *Historical Archaeology* 36 (2002): 50–65.

Anthony P. Graesch

CANADIAN AND AMERICAN SETTLEMENTS OF THE NORTHWEST COAST

Archaeological sites and landscapes from the period of Canadian and American settlement furnish a wealth of information about the history of European and Asian contact with the environment and cultures of the northwest coast. This entry summarizes the history and archaeology of settler societies, before and after the annexation of the region by Canada and the United States in the nineteenth century. The earliest historic settlements on the northwest coast were fur-trading posts, established in early 1800s. As European and Asian migration trickled into the region after the 1840s, a much broader range of settlements, from towns and agricultural communities to lumber camps and salmon canneries, began to conspicuously shape the region. In addition to the archaeology of newcomers, Indigenous cultures were greatly influenced by settler society, and thus significant concentrations of historic artifacts are known from Native settlements.

It is difficult to put a clear number on the quantity of historic sites on the northwest coast because archaeological evidence often goes unrecorded if its historic value is not considered obvious. Moreover, because modern societies continue to create and deposit artifacts or "material culture" throughout the built environment, archaeological records continue to be produced. Although archaeological research on the northwest coast has tended to focus on the prehistory of Indigenous cultures, a significant number of historic sites have also been scientifically studied. Several of these have interpretive centers and offer visitors a view of the history of the early settlement period. Equally, however, because historic artifacts and features are part of the fabric of contemporary settlements and landscapes, with a little knowledge, it is possible to appreciate the meaning of such objects almost anywhere.

THE HISTORY OF SETTLEMENT
Fur Trade Settlements (1811–43)
Following in the wake of international maritime exploration and ensuing territorial disputes in the late eighteenth century, the first sustained non-Indigenous settlements on the northwest coast were established through the activities of the terrestrial fur trade. By the early eighteenth century, fur trade companies based in the relative safety of fortified trading posts were operating west of the Rocky Mountains. Working in the context of the relatively unexplored "Oregon Country," fur traders engaged Indigenous trappers for beaver pelts greatly sought after by Asian and European markets. The Pacific Fur Company was the first to recognize the strategic value of the coast, establishing Fort Astoria at the mouth of the Columbia River in 1811. By 1818, economic control of the trade lay firmly in the hands of the North West Company fur empire. However, in 1821, the British-based Hudson's Bay Company (HBC) absorbed its rival and sought to consolidate its position along the coast. By 1825, the HBC established Fort Vancouver on the lower Columbia River as a new operational hub for the "Columbia District." Less than a decade later, it controlled a string of trading posts along the coast, built as far north as Russian-occupied Alaska. The last major post constructed was Fort Victoria, located on the south coast of Vancouver Island in 1843.

Fur trade posts were sharply hierarchical, largely male, and multicultural settlements, which attracted considerable attention from local Indigenous groups. Although the chief officer or "factor" and head traders were typically educated Scotsmen, company employees—who filled a broad range of functional roles, from coopers and guides to carpenters and laborers—were a multiethnic mix that included among others French Canadians, Hawai'ians (Kanakas), Natives from central and eastern North America as well as employees of mixed descent. Soon after their establishment on the coast, trading posts became important focal points for cultural exchange, and many Indigenous villages relocated to take advantage of direct and indirect trade alliances. In some cases, traders and local Native people developed preferential social and economic alliances through marriage and sexual liaisons. Where contacts fostered longstanding relationships,

Present-day parks and interpretice exhibits at Fort Vancouver, Fort Nisqually, and Fort Langley feature consolidated and reconstructed elements of early nineteenth-century structures and allow the visiting public a view of this fascinating period.   [Jeff Oliver]

the exchange of ideas, material objects, and DNA helped to rework and shape their respective habits, creating new mixed cultural traditions.

Settlement after 1842

By the middle of the nineteenth century, events played out that would ultimately rework the physical and social fabric of the northwest coast. In 1842 word of the rich alluvial soils in the Willamette valley sparked a generation of American settlers to embrace the ideals of "manifest destiny" and stake a claim to the Oregon Country. American migration to the region signaled the demise of HBC preeminence on the coast and prompted the establishment of the 49th parallel as the new international boundary between the westward-looking United States and British North America. On the heels of a few trappers and missionaries, who had already established small farms on the valley prairies, the pioneers founded settlements such as Champoeg, Oregon City, Salem, and other centers along the Willamette River. Other settlers moved north into the more wooded country between the Columbia River and Puget Sound, clearing land for farms and establishing small lumber mills. For pioneers, taking up what they considered to be "empty land" symbolized a new beginning. For Indigenous peoples, in contrast, this process meant the end of traditional freedoms and the beginning of an extended period of persecution.

In 1849 Britain established the colony of Vancouver Island north of the international boundary line as a counterbalance to American expansion. The capital of the new political outpost was established at Fort Victoria. In comparison with American-held lands to the south, settlement in British territory was relatively slow, and it was not until 1858, when gold was discovered on the Fraser River, that there was any impetus for colonization. In that year, over 30,000 miners—chiefly American but also European and Chinese fortune hunters—descended upon the goldfields of the Fraser Canyon, destabilizing the local balance of power and prompting Britain to establish the mainland colony of British Columbia. Nevertheless,

Giant stumps viewed from logging roads are illustrative of the magnitude of the forest industry in the early development of the region. [Jeff Oliver]

because land prices were less expensive south of the border and the gold boom was followed by inevitable bust, settlement to fledgling population centers such as New Westminster slowed to a trickle.

The early history of the northwest coast as a settlement frontier was characterized by growth in spurts and false starts. However, by the later part of the nineteenth century, the hardwiring of transportation networks, including the building of railways and roads and the establishment of regular steamship service ultimately alleviated the coast's isolated position. These changes fueled new economic opportunities, which in turn encouraged migration both within and to the region. With rising settler populations and increased economic ambitions, a new political geography emerged. In 1866 Britain's coastal possessions merged, and in 1871 the enlarged colony of British Columbia joined the Dominion of Canada as a fully fledged province. To the south, American territory was divided between the states of Oregon and Washington, the former joining the Union in 1853 and the latter in 1889. U.S. ambitions on the northwest coast were further enhanced through the purchase of Alaska from Russia in 1867.

The development of "civilized" society on the northwest coast was lauded as "progress" by many newcomers; however, these transformations also contributed to the displacement of Indigenous peoples. Where Native territorial claims caused irritation to settlers, their lands were legally confiscated and they were forcibly removed to Indian reservations. Where hostilities emerged, the new political arbiters could usually count on superior technology and professional soldiers to reinforce their authority. For Indigenous peoples, the emerging geography of the northwest coast in many ways resembled the conditions of South African apartheid. At the same time, while their participation in society was seriously restricted, the colonial landscape also enabled opportunities for cultural change.

The history of interaction between newcomers and the environment varied considerably, but certain patterns can, nevertheless, be identified. In regions with good agricultural potential, such as the Willamette valley and parts of Puget Sound and the lower Fraser valley, land was cleared and small agricultural plots were established by American migrants and settlers of European decent. Hop farms were among the most successful and began to employ seasonal Indigenous labor at harvest times, remapping the traditional pathways of the Native seasonal round. While farmers often considered much of the coast to be an "interminable wilderness," the massive forests of western red cedar, Douglas fir, and Sitka spruce became the focus of major logging activities, attracting an ethnic mix of young itinerant "lumbermen" to its rough and ready lifestyle. Along major rivers, the highly productive seasonal salmon runs provided the impetus for the growth of a commercial fishing industry and the proliferation of salmon canneries, which attracted Chinese, Indigenous, and later Japanese laborers. In the cities, the economic hubs of the unfolding capitalist landscape, the cultural fabric was mixed, but neighborhoods organized themselves along class and ethnic lines.

ARCHAEOLOGICAL SITES AND LANDSCAPES
Fur Trade Sites

The most comprehensively studied settlements from this period include fur trade posts and associated sites such as company-owned farms. Fur-trade sites in this region extend in the south from Fort Astoria (on the estuary of the Columbia River) all the way to Fort Simpson (on the Portland Canal immediately south of Alaska) in the north. Based on predesigned plans, "forts" were enclosed by a rectangular wooden palisade fixed with bastions and made to provide refuge from Native hostilities. Inside the walls were situated sturdy post and beam structures including, principally, the warehouse, where blankets, iron implements, and other goods were exchanged for beaver pelts. The number of buildings in the fort varied with its size but typically included a cooperage, blacksmith, and sleeping quarters for the men. Archaeological evidence combined with the use of written records, such as journals, suggests that class distinctions were strictly marked. The chief officer, or factor, lived and conducted the affairs of the fort in a separate "big house," while company employees slept together in simple bunkhouses. Excavations since the middle of the twentieth century have helped to establish the placement, size, and character of fort architecture. For example, excavations in 1995 at Fort Langley have helped to locate the precise placement of wooden galleries, which would have offered sentries an unobstructed view of activities outside the walls. Using information provided by archaeological and historical evidence, a number of important trading-post sites have been reconstructed. Fort Vancouver, Fort Nisqually, and Fort Langley feature consolidated and reconstructed elements of early nineteenth-century structures and allow the visiting public a view of this fascinating period.

In addition to its fur-trading activities, the HBC established a number of other settlements in the region, which allowed the company to raise alternative lines of capital. Principle among these were company farms that supplied trading posts with mutton and agricultural produce and helped to increase company profits through the private sale of goods to settlers. Important sites were established in the Fraser valley, on San Juan Island, and at Fort Nisqually and consisted of no more than a small collection of expediently erected buildings and garden plots. One of the best places to learn about the history of these sites is at the Belle Vue Sheep Farm, located in the San Juan Island National Historic Park. Related sites include salteries (salmon salting opera-

tions) and sawmills. Like farms, these settlements show how the company diversified when the fur trade became less profitable in the late 1840s and 1850s.

The Archaeology of Settler Societies

Historical settlements from the later part of the nineteenth and early twentieth century are located along the entire length of the northwest coast from southern Oregon to the Alaskan panhandle. However, the majority of early sites tend to cluster along the Willamette valley, the Cowlitz-Chehalis lowland, the Puget Sound lowland, the Fraser valley, and southeast Vancouver Island. Newcomers favored land that was suited to farming, had access to ports or railways, or was adjacent to natural resources such as timber or coal. Archaeological sites range from farmsteads and industrial sites to military fortifications and commercial districts located in modern towns and cites.

Early farmsteads were little more than wooden cabins that were later usually replaced by two-story gabled-roofed structures. The architecture of early farms occasionally survives in the form of dilapidated barns or as renovated farmhouses. Industrial sites include sawmills, lumber camps, mines, and salmon canneries. These were often complex settlements composed of structures with different functions built of wood, steel, or concrete. Economic downturns and structural changes in the resource sector in the last century have meant that many industrial sites have been lost to redevelopment, particularly in urban areas. Sites that survive can sometimes be identified by dilapidated buildings or foundation features. For example, wooden pilings visible at low tide along estuaries may indicate the location of former Salmon Cannery operations, although an excellent example of a reconstructed cannery can be visited at the Gulf of Georgia Cannery National Historic Park of Canada near Vancouver. While a similar fate has befallen many urban sites, a good number of wooden and brick vernacular buildings and facades of the late nineteenth and early twentieth century continue to make up part of the contemporary fabric of modern cities. Places with well-preserved architecture include the important historic settlements of Port Townsend, Victoria, and Portland. Sites that reflect historic political tensions include military forts and encampments established to defend coastal areas and the international boundary. Fine examples include Fort Rodd Hill on Vancouver Island and the twin fortified positions of British Camp and American Camp located at San Juan Island National Historic Park in Washington State.

One unique site that has been excavated and is open to visitors is the historic settlement of Champoeg, located on the south bank of the Willamette River. Although the town was destroyed by a flood recorded in 1861, excavations since 1971 have established important temporal benchmarks in its historical development through the discovery of datable artifact types such as pottery, glass, and cutlery. In particular, without the benefit of historic documents and in opposition to popular perception, recent investigations have revealed that the pioneer settlement was reestablished during the 1880s.

More recently, archaeologists have begun to focus their attention on the settlements of minority ethnic groups, in particular the history of Chinese communities. Chinese migrants were initially attracted to the west coast of North America during the gold rushes of 1849 and 1858, while others came as wage laborers to work on the expanding railroads. Due to serious ethnic and nationalist tensions, most that stayed settled in the squalid Chinatowns that grew up around commercial centers, such as Vancouver, Tacoma, and Cumberland on Vancouver Island. Little was formerly known about the early history of these settlements because records were generally kept by white journalists or officials who were unfamiliar with Chinese culture. However, a new ethos of historical balance offers hope of redressing these issues. For example, in 1996 after breaking through the pavement of a parking lot at "Canton Alley" in Vancouver's Chinatown, archaeologists exposed historic warehouse foundations and artifacts, which are beginning to shed light on the contributions of the Chinese community to the city's development.

In addition, a significant concentration of historic artifacts and features are found at many Indigenous settlements. Although important historic period settlements such as Katzie in the Fraser valley and Skidigate on Haida Gwaii (the Queen Charlotte Islands) are best known from ethnographic records, a number of settlements, including Old Man House on the west side of Puget Sound and Netarts Sand Spit on the Oregon coast, have been revealed through archaeological excavations. An interesting example of the contribution of archaeology is the investigation undertaken at the historic cemetery at Kimsquit on the isolated central coast of British Columbia. At this site, the Indigenous use of tombstones and coffins and the presence of objects such as washbasins and sewing machines appear to reflect Native acculturation (or adoption) of settler society's predominantly European cultural norms and values. However, despite the many European artifacts found at the cemetery, contextual evidence suggests that the Kimsquit people integrated these objects in ways that were consistent with their own culture. For instance, graves are associated with European-style coffins and tombstones, such as Christian settler cemeteries. However, the fact that they deposited Western utilitarian objects such as washbasins and sewing machines as grave goods (reflecting the status of the deceased), clearly shows how outside influences were incorporated into an earlier cultural pattern.

The archaeology of settler communities, however, is not restricted to settlements alone. Historical research shows that as the machinery of capitalism ground into gear, activities such as road building, land survey, and forestry became increasingly important. Roads joined population centers and offered settlers a means to take up land in interior areas. Surveys framed the landscape in a new property grid of boundary markers that separated what Europeans considered wilderness from land that could be bought and sold. One of the best places to view these landscapes is from the air or from mountain tops. Urban and rural landscapes seen from a good height can afford a bird's-eye view of geometric development, roads, suburbs, and agricultural areas, revealing the extent of land surveys of the late nineteenth and early twentieth century. In other areas, giant stands of valuable timber encouraged newcomers to transform vast areas of forest into lumber to feed the growing market in newly established cities and towns. These activities marked the land in conspicuous ways. In many places, signs of past landscape alteration may still be seen. In forested areas away from cities, particularly along the coasts of Alaska and British Columbia, giant stumps viewed from logging roads are illustrative of the magnitude of the forest industry in the early development of the region. For some historians and archaeologists, the remains of logging activity are clear signs of the progress of settler society and show how newcomers "conquered" nature, making it submit to the forces of capitalism. On the other hand, the existence of immature forests of secondary growth on logged-over land also shows how human relationships with the environment can be much more ambiguous. For instance, areas cleared of trees that were abandoned by settlers or loggers quickly returned to a natural state. Due to the vigorous and competitive processes of natural reforestation, in many places this created wildernesses far more tangled and dense than the forests that preceded them.

Further Reading: Harris, Cole, *The Resettlement of British Columbia* (Vancouver: University of British Columbia Press, 1997); Fort Langley National Historic Site of Canada, Parks Canada Web site, http://www.pc.gc.ca/lhn-nhs/bc/langley/index_e.asp (online April 2007); Lim, Imogene L., "China Town Pacific Entry, Pacific Century: Chinatown and Chinese Canadian History," in *Re/collecting Early Asian America: Essays in Cultural History*, edited by Josephine Lee, Imogene L. Lim, and Yuko Matsukawa (Philadelphia: Temple University Press, 2002); Oliver, Jeff, "The Paradox of Progress: Land Survey and the Making of Agrarian Society in Colonial British Columbia," in *Contemporary and Historical Archaeology in Theory*, edited by Laura McAtackney, Mathew Palus, and Angela Piccini (Oxford: BAR International Series, 2007); Prince, Paul, "Cultural Coherency and Resistance in Historic-Period Northwest-Coast Mortuary Practices at Kimsquit," *Historical Archaeology* 36(4) (2002): 50–65; Speulda, L. A., *Champoeg: A Perspective of a Frontier Community in Oregon, 1830–1861*, Anthropology Northwest No. 3 (Corvallis: Oregon State University, 1988); Sprague, R., "The Development of Historical Archaeology in the Pacific Northwest," *Northwest Anthropological Research Notes* 9(1) (1975): 6–19; White, Richard, *Land Use, Environment, and Social Change: The Shaping of Island County, Washington* (Seattle: University of Washington Press, 1980).

Jeff Oliver

NATIVE AMERICAN PERSPECTIVES OF THE ARCHAEOLOGY OF THE NORTHWEST COAST AND SOUTHEASTERN ALASKA[1]

INTRODUCTION

Anthropology is the most humanistic of all the sciences and the most scientific of all the humanities because it employs scientific methods that impact both the living contemporary and those who have passed. The most tangible means by which we can understand the past is primarily through the eyes of archaeological scientists. Archaeologists look at what has been left behind by previous generations and try to assemble a chronological timeline of human and technological development. They do so through excavating prehistoric sites and placing their findings in context with ethnological, linguistic, and biological records. On the northwest coast of North America most of the archaeological sites are villages, cemeteries, and shell middens (garbage dumps), some of which are very ancient—from 6,000 to 11,000 years old.

The northwest coast culture region is a narrow strip, 3,200 kilometers (2,000 mi) long and 240 kilometers (150 mi) wide, extending from southeast Alaska down to the northern California coast. The northwest coast contains some of the most telling of all archaeological sites in North America because it is largely believed that the first inhabitants of North America migrated from Asia across the Bering Strait sometime during the last glacial retreat 10,000 or more years ago or experienced a lengthy occupation spanning at least 1,000 generations. Because it is presumed that Native Americans[2] were the first to inhabit North America, many of the contemporary issues surrounding tribal sovereignty and self-governance come into play whenever ancient sites are discovered. It appears at times that archaeology is at the forefront of challenging Native Americans' claims of being "here first" when in reality archaeological finds continue to support this position. Peopling theories suggest that Native American knowledge about their origins is fractured, flawed, and mythical. Controversies arise in conjunction with ancient finds that may or may not challenge Native American claims to first occupation. Today archaeologists and Native Americans are beginning to work more closely together in providing a clearer picture about the advances of ancient technology and cultural systems, and in the protection of irreplaceable archaeological resources on the northwest coast.

PEOPLING

The issues surrounding the archaeology of the northwest coast are far from simple. Complexities arise when archaeologists debate how and when Native Americans arrived in North America. Many agree that Native Americans arrived from Asia, migrating across the Bering Strait (Beringia), but few can agree on whether the peopling of the Americas took place by land, sea, or a combination of the two. Archaeologists base their arguments on what has been found rather than on the drastic environmental changes known to have occurred during the last glacial retreat, about 10,000 years ago. Therein lies the irony—what might have been evidence of a more lengthy occupation is now submerged 91 meters (300 ft) under the surface of the Pacific Ocean as a result of glacial melting. Simply put, archaeologists cannot be certain as to how or when Native Americans arrived.

American archaeology's goal is ultimately to write the history of the Americas. Volumes of largely descriptive and cultural-historical data have been produced about the northwest coast in attempts to explain the origins of the earliest occupants and of coastal adaptations, the antiquity of various technologies, cultural and ethnographic patterns, sedentism, and social structures. The consensus among the archaeological community is as follows. First, modern Native Americans are the descendents of the first inhabitants. Second, occupation may have begun at least 12,000 years ago. Third, what we know and are unequivocally able to prove pales in comparison to the amount of crucial evidence we know to be misinterpreted, permanently lost, or still undiscovered. Archaeology, in all its conventional wisdom, has developed a history that has led us to exaggerate what we have found and largely ignores what pieces are yet to be discovered.

Many have debated the sources of conflict between Native Americans and archaeologists. It has been argued that the major contested issue is linked to archaeology's systematic disturbance of Native American graves or its ongoing exploitation of cultural and spiritual artifacts. While this is undeniably a source of contention, legislation passed within

---

[1] The content of this article is entirely the opinion of the author and may not reflect the views of the Coquille Indian tribe or the publisher. I am deeply indebted to my tribe, the Coquille Indian tribe, for providing me with great latitude and support in my scholarly pursuits. Also, my sincere appreciation is extended to Dr. Andrew Moore and Dr. William Middleton, who read early drafts of this paper and provided generous editorial comments. This paper is dedicated to all my relations.

[2] Indigenous peoples of Canada are commonly referred to as First Nations and not Native Americans. For convenience only, the author has chosen to refer to all indigenous peoples of North America as Native Americans.

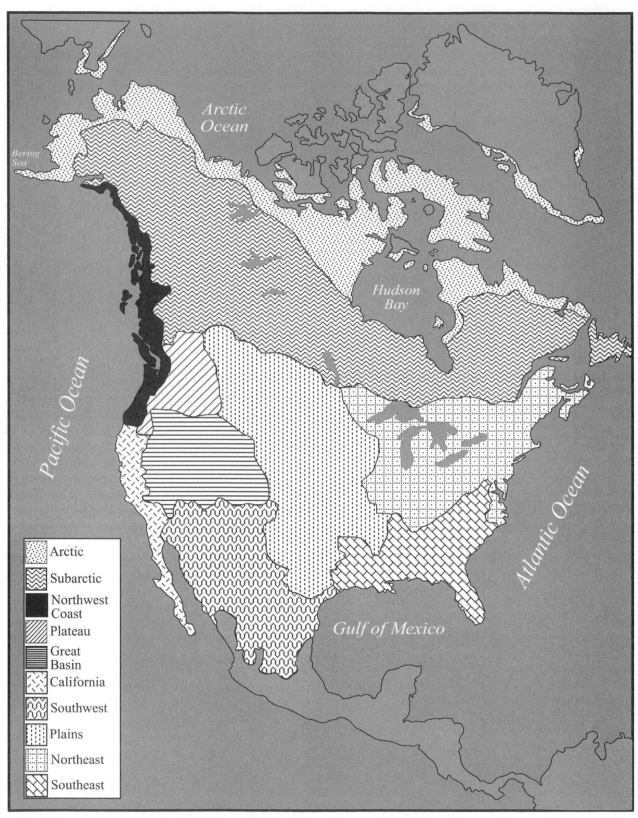

Arctic
Subarctic
Northwest Coast
Plateau
Great Basin
California
Southwest
Plains
Northeast
Southeast

Native North America is sometimes divided into different culture regions. The Northwest Coast culture region is a narrow strip extending from southeast Alaska down to the northern California coast.   [Jason T. Younker]

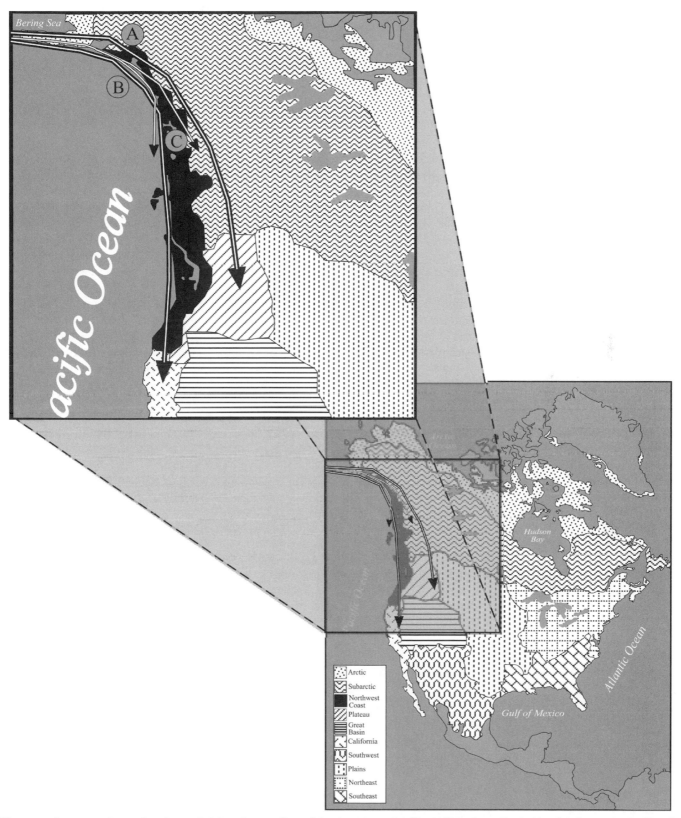

There are three prominent theories explaining the peopling of the Americas: the Clovis First hypothesis (A—land entry), the Pacific Rim hypothesis (B—coastal entry), and the Land and Sea hypothesis (C—combination of the two).   [Jason T. Younker]

the last thirty years, such as the Archaeological Resources Protection Act (ARPA 1979) and the Native American Graves Protection and Repatriation Act (NAGPRA 1990), has facilitated the protection of Native American sites. Consequently, recent cases where Native American graves have been exploited are extremely limited. The real source of rancor, however, is archaeology's often self-serving and selective use of Native knowledge, or in some cases the complete disregard of it. These tendencies emerge more in the discussion of peopling theory than in any other discourse. With all of the reasonable explanations that exist today, the collective Native American oral traditions that maintain local origination are categorically denied consideration.

Archaeology's opening line explaining the peopling of the Americas often denies the validity of Native American knowledge and suggests discontinuity between the living descendents and their ancestors. Imagine the ensuing conflict if for the next 150 years archaeology devoted its time to rewriting the Book of Genesis. Graves would be disturbed, and the people of Vatican City would be displaced and its resources scattered in the wind. Although this scenario is highly unlikely, considering the imperial apparatus in place, a similar response by the affected Native peoples can be inferred.

The three most popular peopling theories today are the Pacific Rim hypothesis (coastal entry), the Clovis First hypothesis (land entry), and the combination Land and Sea hypothesis (combo). The coastal model suggests that during the Late Pleistocene or early Holocene period (12,000–8,000 years ago), people on small watercraft found their way along the ecologically rich Pacific Rim from Asia. Although this model appears plausible, testing has been problematic due to drastic sea level rise, coastal erosion, shifting dune plates, coastal development, and other factors. Western science is very unforgiving when tangible evidence is not available for testing. No matter how reasonable this model appears, the evidence is likely either now covered by the Pacific Ocean, is permanently lost, or remains undiscovered.

The land entry model is possibly the most speculative of the three, but the lion's share of the available evidence remains in its corner. This model suggests entry over Beringia at the end of the last Ice Age through narrow corridors left by retreating glaciers. Migration down the rivers led humans to the coast. By following large terrestrial animals, humans' made a path through the corridors, which is confirmed in the older archaeological sites by telltale projectiles called Clovis points. Although evidence has been heavily scrutinized, there still exists a rather large amount of uncertainty. It is questionable whether the ice corridors were actually open at the time suggested and whether the 3,200-kilometer (2,000-mi) trek could realistically be managed within a single season. This theory also assumes that the Americas were unpopulated prior to 12,500 years ago. Linguistic data, however, suggests that at least 35,000 years would be needed to produce the diversity found in Native American languages. In addition, sites have been discovered that pre-date the 12,500-year benchmark (e.g., Topper Site, South Carolina, 50,000 years ago; Cactus Hill Site, Virginia, 15,050 years ago; Meadowcroft Rockshelter, Pennsylvania, 19,600 years ago). Although this theory makes huge assumptions and posts long odds for plausibility, it has been the primary peopling theory for American archaeologists.

The combo theory occupies the middle ground. It assumes that people arrived from both land and sea and accommodates pre-Holocene arrival. This model assumes that the rising sea has covered the oldest sites and that only this undiscovered evidence can substantiate the model beyond a reasonable doubt. Some believe they may have already found evidence of offshore sites that pre-date Clovis, but neither the combo nor coastal entry theory proponents may ever present enough data to attain an acceptable level of scientific validity.

CONTROVERSY

While peopling hypotheses are based on existing data and assumptions that can be tested by further investigation, it is important to make a clear distinction between theory and fact. In many cases, while archaeologists' theories are being scrutinized, the public often accepts their most recent guesses as factual. Archaeologists need to be aware of this and not misuse the public's ignorance to garner support for their speculations. The Kennewick Man controversy in the lower Plateau culture region bears witness to all that can go wrong when science abuses its position by employing tactics that cater to the public's curiosity and misinformation. Furthermore, it amounts to abuse and questioning of the intention of archaeological preservation laws, and denies authority and credibility to Native American perspectives.

Controversy ensued when an ancient human skeleton was found in shallow water along the shore of the Columbia River in Kennewick, Washington, on July 28, 1996. Dr. James Chatters, a local forensic anthropologist, upon first examination believed the remains to be a nineteenth-century settler. He described the remains as having "Caucasoid" features. When he found a stone projectile point lodged in the hip, he realized the bones might be much older. Chatters was granted an ARPA permit by the Army Corps of Engineers. Among numerous requirements, ARPA permits require the agency to notify Indian tribes if the permitted investigation might affect a site of cultural or religious importance to the tribes. Adequate notification seems highly unlikely, however, when the permit is granted retroactively. Subsequently, the Army Corps ordered the remains to be repatriated under NAGPRA. During his investigation of the human remains, Chatters arranged for destructive radiocarbon testing, which returned an age of 9,400 years. This information found its way to the press. Eight scientists, two from the Smithsonian Institution, sued the Army Corps, blocking repatriation. In addition, a small European religious group, Asatru Folk Assembly, filed a separate lawsuit requesting repatriation of the remains.

While public speculation continued to run wild, the courts ordered the Army Corps and the Department of the Interior to decide who should get the remains. It took almost a decade for the legal case to be resolved. In the end, the federal courts found that NAGPRA did not apply in the Kennewick Man case and that the scientists who sued the government should be allowed to study the Kennewick Man remains.

Possibly the most revealing evidence was the way the remains were found. Scientists were able to confirm that Kennewick Man was 5 feet 9 inches tall, fairly muscularly built, approximately 45 to 55 years old, and very likely to have been purposely buried. The fact that he was carefully buried is quite revealing. Who could have done this? It is safe to assume that Europeans were not in North America but Native Americans were. Can we be certain of its cultural affiliation? Probably not, but reasonable assumptions can be made that the closest possible relatives are from the lower Plateau region—the very tribes who requested that the remains be repatriated.[3]

The controversy surrounding Kennewick Man undermined the thin but slowly developing relationship of trust between archaeologists and Native Americans. In the lawsuit the eight scientists argued that no tribe could prove beyond a reasonable doubt biological or cultural affiliation sufficient to repatriate, as required by NAGPRA. They completely ignored the Umatilla and other tribes' longtime cultural affiliation with the area in question, and also ignored the peopling theories archaeologists had been generating for nearly 150 years. Compounding the scientists' willful ignorance, they completely disregarded the underlying intent of NAGPRA and ARPA, which required meaningful communication with affected Native American tribes.

These laws, especially NAGPRA, which were instituted to rebuild trust and inspire collaboration, require two-way communication to effectively redefine ownership of culturally affiliated artifacts, and to improve the sometimes hostile environment in which archaeologists and Natives Americans coexist. This legislation recognizes that we can learn much more about the prehistory of the Americas with a working relationship than without.

To make matters worse, the print and television media were manipulated into perpetuating Chatters's Caucasoid fantasy. Chatters's reconstruction of the Kennewick Man skull was modeled to look like *Star Trek* actor Patrick Stewart, and these images were widely distributed and made international news headlines. It appears that self-serving tactics were employed that manipulated public opinion, dis-

regarded Native American viewpoints, and undermined the intent of the legislation.

It is certain that modern Native Americans are the descendents of the first inhabitants, and Kennewick Man's discovery changed little of what was known. It did, however, loosen some of the formerly unyielding positions taken with regard to peopling explanations. Although archaeologists don't appear to be ready to assign full validity to Native American oral traditions claiming local origination, they may be closer to admitting uncertainty, confusion, and lack of data about when, where, how, why, and by whom the Americas were peopled. Unfortunately, many archaeologists still largely categorize Native American testimony in the northwest coast as hearsay, myth, legend, and religious or spiritual discourse. This instantly puts archaeological scientists at odds with the Native American communities in which they must work. Now that legislation requires two-way communication and addresses the concerns of these communities, the Kennewick Man controversy gave the impression that archaeologists are looking for loopholes in the legislation as they have done in the past.

It will take many years to overcome the disrepute associated with Kennewick Man and to rebuild the trust that many worked so hard to gain through the passage of NAGPRA and other legislation. Rekindling trust will start with the admission that archaeological science is not infallible, especially with respect to peopling theories. This also means considering the credibility of Native accounts. Archaeologists need to accept Native American perspectives and provide more concerted support for them when controversies such as Kennewick arise. Archaeology will redeem itself when those who have been rigid and unyielding in the past open their minds to all the possibilities, accept that multiple truths may exist, and remember that when science forgets about the people it is supposed to serve, it loses its value. Those who can adopt this perspective will have long and productive careers collaborating with Native Americans.

COLLABORATION LEADS TO EMPOWERMENT

Although the old wounds of archaeology's past have yet to heal, many Native American tribes are working diligently with archaeologists and cultural resource specialists to effect change in the science and to assist in the revitalization of traditional culture and in illuminating our collective past on the northwest coast.

Tlingit, Southeast Alaska

The many clans of the Tlingit of southeast Alaska have a long history of working with archaeologists, most notably with the late Frederica de Laguna in her excavations at Old Town in Yakutat Bay in the 1960s. Her excavations here and elsewhere in southeast Alaska have revealed continuous occupation possibly beginning as early as 1,300 years ago. As

---

[3] Confederated Tribes of the Umatilla Indian Reservation, Confederated Tribes and Bands of the Yakama Nation, Confederated Tribes of the Colville Reservation, and the Nez Perce Tribe.

can be expected, most of the artifacts can be attributed to the fishing and whaling industries. Because of this long history of mutually beneficial and productive collaboration, many southeast Alaska tribal groups encourage archaeological investigation as a way to enrich and support programs of cultural revitalization. Sealaska, a for-profit company formed under the Alaska Native Claims Settlement Act (ANCSA) for the Tlingit, Haida, and Tsimshian, founded the Sealaska Heritage Institute (SHI) in 1981. SHI offers numerous educational scholarships for Native students attending a college, university, vocational, or technical school, including funding for scholars who wish to enter archaeological method training programs.

Makah, Northern Washington Coast

The Makah Nation, located on the Olympic Peninsula of Washington State, has been working with archaeologists for nearly four decades studying the Ozette site near Neah Bay. The Ozette site, discovered in 1970, is one of the most intriguing archaeological sites in North America. Ozette represented about 2,000 years of continuous occupation until it was suddenly covered about 500 years ago by a massive mud slide, which preserved the entire site. After coastal erosion uncovered Ozette, archaeologists and the Makah began excavation and recovered approximately 60,000 artifacts. About 1 percent of these artifacts are on display in the Makah Culture and Research Center in Neah Bay, Washington.

Coquille, Southern Oregon Coast

The Coquille Indian tribe of the southern Oregon coast has been working with archaeologists since the 1980s, first as part of an effort to regain federal recognition and today as a way to preserve and understand their past. In the 1950s the Coquilles were one of 109 Indian tribes nationwide to be included in the Indian Termination Act of 1954. In 1973, however, termination was repealed, and the Coquilles were restored in 1988 with the help of archaeological and ethnographic records. Today the Coquille Cultural Resource Management Program is one of the nation's foremost wet-site archaeological investigation programs.

As with most coastal tribes, many Coquille sites represent advanced fishing technologies. From the mouth of the Coquille River at Bandon to the town of Coquille nearly 32 kilometers (20 mi) upriver, shell middens, fish weirs and traps, and village sites dominate the landscape, some over 3,000 years old. The Coquilles, with the use of a Geographic Information System (GIS), have mapped nearly 150 new archaeological sites on the Coos and Coquille river watersheds since 1996. The Global Positioning System and GIS are used to map site boundaries, track the impact of riverine erosion, and develop predictive landscape models showing the likely location of undiscovered sites. With the assistance of the Coos County government, the Coquille play a significant role in protecting these irreplaceable sites. The Coquille program has been fea-

tured on the cover of the Society of American Archaeology's *SAA Archaeological Record* (2003, Volume 3, Issue 5), and they continue to host the annual Cultural Preservation Conference each May. The conference's proceedings are published in a scholarly journal they established, *Changing Landscapes*.

SUMMARY

Archaeological study on the northwest coast has great potential to further understanding of indigenous peoples' origins, technological development, and cultural adaptations to the environment's drastic changes before, during, and after the last glacial retreat. While peopling theories abound, these often do not take into account the revealing oral traditions of Native Americans or information archaeologists know has yet to be discovered. As archaeologists come to grips with the reality that they might never find conclusive answers to their inquiries, they must be cautious in the ways they share scientific knowledge with the general public, as misleading information can result in stereotypes and misconceptions (as in the case of Kennewick Man).

Today many tribes embrace archaeological investigation and are empowered by the findings. They now collaborate on a regular basis in the preservation and understanding of those things that are ancient and are widely considered part of their living heritage. There is still much to be learned about the northwest coast of North America, and the future is bright for both archaeologists and Native American tribes as each continues to overcome the barriers that divided them in previous generations of archaeological study.

Further Reading: Ames, Kenneth M., and Herbert D. G. Maschner, *Peoples of the Northwest Coast: Their Archaeology and Prehistory* (New York: Thames and Hudson, 1999); Biolsi, Thomas, and Larry J. Zimmerman, eds., *Indians and Anthropologists* (Tucson: University of Arizona Press, 1997); Fedje, Daryl, and Tina Christensen, "Modeling Paleoshorelines and Locating Early Holocene Coastal Sites in Haida Gwaii," *American Antiquity* 64(4) (1999): 635–652: King, Thomas F., *Cultural Resource Laws and Practice*, 2nd ed. (Walnut Creek, CA: AltaMira Press, 2004); Mihesuah, Devon A., ed., *Repatriation Reader: Who Owns American Indian Remains?* (Lincoln: University of Nebraska Press, 2000); National Park Service, *Kennewick Man*, www.nps.gov/archeology/kennewick/ (online May 2007); Nichols, Johanna, *Linguistic Diversity in Space and Time* (Chicago: University of Chicago Press, 1992); Oswalt, Wendell H., *This Land Was Theirs: A Study of Native North Americans*, 8th ed. (New York: Oxford University Press, 2006); Sutton, Mark Q., *An Introduction to Native North America*, 2nd ed. (Boston: Allyn and Bacon, 2004); Swindler, N., Kurt E. Dongoske, Roger Anyon, and Allan S. Downer, eds., *Native Americans and Archaeologists: Stepping Stones to Common Ground* (Walnut Creek, CA: AltaMira Press, 1997); Vitelli, Karen D., ed., *Archaeological Ethics* (Walnut Creek, CA: AltaMira Press, 1996).

Jason T. Younker

INDIAN SANDS, UMPQUA-EDEN, BLACKLOCK POINT, WHALE COVE, AND OTHER SITES

Coastal Oregon

10,000 Years of Human Settlement and Adaptation along the Coast

EARLY PERIOD

Indian Sands (Samuel H. Boardman State Park), Oregon

Indian Sands is located in the Samuel H. Boardman State Park near the town of Brookings and is accessible from a wooded trail originating from a gravel parking lot just off of Highway 101. The Indian Sands site is an open-air archaeological site contained in an ancient soil that lies on a Pleistocene-age (i.e., 10,000 years and earlier) deposit of wind-blown dune sands. Burned mussel shells found on the surface of the site returned three radiocarbon ages ranging from around 8,600 to 9,300 calendar years ago. Excavations led by Loren Davis during 2000 and 2002 revealed that a significant portion of the site remains buried in parts of the site. These excavations revealed a long record of cultural occupation beginning at about 12,300 years ago and extending to about 6,400 years ago. Cultural materials associated with the buried component at Indian Sands are limited to stone tools, stone flakes from tool production, and fire-cracked rocks created in hearths or for cooking in pits. The stone tools included willow-leaf-shaped projectile points, larger bifacial lithic cores, smaller cores made on large flakes of rock from which other flakes could be removed, and flakes that were turned into scraping and cutting tools. Analysis of the lithic toolkit and its manufacturing debris indicates that early occupants of Indian Sands visited the site to access locally available chert deposits. This chert was quarried and used to manufacture a generalized toolkit to be exported elsewhere in order to conduct a wide range of tasks. Several pieces of culturally modified obsidian originating from volcanic sources in southern Oregon and northern California located nearly 300 kilometers away point to the existence of extensive trade routes or to the regional movements of hunter-gatherers.

Blacklock Point Site, Oregon

The Blacklock Point lithic site (35CU75) is located on Blacklock Point in Floras Lake State Park. Archaeological test excavations conducted in 1980 by Richard Ross revealed large numbers of lithic artifacts, but no shell. Ross reports a single radiocarbon age of 2,909 calendar years ago on charcoal collected from a dark sediment exposed in a natural stratigraphic profile. The site was tested again in 1993 by Rick Minor, who produced additional evidence of cultural occupation associated with two radiocarbon ages on charcoal of around 8,400 calendar years ago and 5,100 calendar years ago. Like the Indian Sands site, archaeological investigations at the Blacklock Point site produced only lithic artifacts, which may reflect a generalized economic orientation to the use of terrestrial and marine environments.

Devils Kitchen Site (Bandon Ocean Wayside), Bandon, Oregon

In 2002 archaeologists conducted excavations at the Devils Kitchen site, which is located along on a headland overlooking the Pacific Ocean at Bandon Ocean wayside. The site is largely contained in stream sediments that are buried beneath a sand dune. Below the dune sand deposits, a long record of cultural occupation was found, evidenced by the recovery of flakes of rocks created during stone tool production and formed stone tools. The radiocarbon chronology from the Devils Kitchen site indicates its initial occupation began sometime after 13,000 calendar years ago and extended to about 2,600 calendar years ago. As with Oregon's other early coastal sites, no organic items, including animal remains were found, probably due to poor preservation in coastal soils. After 2,600 years ago, the site appears to have been buried by an eastern movement of dunes, which caused an abandonment of the floodplain at Devils Kitchen. To get to Devils Kitchen from Old Town Bandon, take Ocean Drive SW west where it meets with Beach Loop road. Bandon Ocean wayside is accessed along the west side of Beach Loop road about half a mile (0.8 km) before it turns east back to Highway 101.

DEVELOPMENT OF THE COASTAL ADAPTATION

The way of life associated with Oregon's Native coastal peoples developed over thousands of years, apparently culminating with a more intensive orientation to marine environments. Following the transition from glacial to interglacial environments, melting remnants of continental ice sheets returned water to the world's oceans, causing a rapid rise in global sea levels. From the earliest occupation of Indian Sands at around 10,500 years ago to the arrival of modern sea level around 5,000 years ago, the level of the Pacific Ocean rose about 130 feet (40 m). During this period, prehistoric human occupants of the Oregon coast would have seen sea levels rise about 6 inches (15 cm) during each generation (i.e., twenty-five years). Rising sea levels created significant changes in Oregon's coastal geography, submerging previously dry land, deepening bays, and creating new water bodies through time. Rapid geographic change associated with rising sea levels created relatively unstable living conditions for many marine organisms. Whether these environmental changes were significant enough to have influenced the way in which prehistoric coastal peoples made their living is not clear at this time. Regardless, many of Oregon's coastal sites show how prehistoric peoples lived within this context of changing environmental conditions and ultimately developed an intensive orientation toward marine, riverine, and terrestrial plant and animal resources. The following discussion outlines several of the sites that contribute information on how Native peoples made their living for thousands of years along the Oregon coast. Sites are presented from north to south, beginning at the central coast.

Whale Cove Site (near Rocky Creek State Park), Oregon

The Whale Cove site is located south of Depoe Bay on Oregon's central coast. Archaeological excavations revealed a discontinuous sequence of three occupational layers each dating from 3010 ± 50 to $2,830 \pm 70$ years ago, $610 \pm 40/50$ years ago, and $330 \pm 50/60$ years ago, respectively. The faunal record indicates use of twenty different marine invertebrates, including limpets, barnacles, cockles, chitons, periwinkles, clams, mussels, whelks, and snails, and the exploitation of freshwater mussels from a nearby stream. A wide variety of vertebrate remains were recovered during excavations, including various undifferentiated fin fishes, rabbit, squirrel, beaver, dog, wolf, bear, raccoon, deer, elk, whale, dolphin, sea otter, harbor seal, eared seal, California sea lion, and northern fur seal. Changing patterns of artifact and faunal qualities and quantities are taken to indicate that prehistoric human occupation at Whale Cove became more sedentary through time, with a corresponding intensification of marine mammals during the later period. This pattern is also thought to reflect a shift from a generalized lifeway broadly emphasizing a wide range of resources across large spatial scales, to a specialized lifeway, wherein prehistoric human groups restricted their movements and focused their economic emphasis on a limited set of key marine animals. An overview of Whale Cove can be achieved from Rocky Creek State Scenic Viewpoint, which lies at the north end of Rocky Creek State Park.

Yaquina Head Site (Yaquina Head Outstanding Natural Area), Oregon

Archaeological excavations led by Rick Minor at Yaquina Head, which is located within an interpretive area run by the Bureau of Land Management on the northern edge of Newport, Oregon, and about 7 miles (11 km) south of Whale Cove, recovered a long record of village life on the Oregon coast under changing environmental conditions. Two periods

of site use are described from Yaquina Head. The first period spans the period between 3,300 and 5,000 years ago and is associated with site occupation during a time when the ocean rose from 32 feet (9.75 m) to 12 feet (3.65 m) below modern sea level, and the shoreline would have been farther west than today. Within this environmental context, the prehistoric inhabitants of Yaquina Head exploited a range of terrestrial animals, marine mammals, fish, and birds. There is a notable lack of shell in the early occupation levels; however, this may be due to the site's distance from the ocean. The second period of occupation dates from 2,310 to 3,200 years ago and shows a shift in site activities to the intensive exploitation of molluscan resources and the establishment of semi-subterranean pit house structures, during a time when sea levels rose from 12 feet (3.65 m) to 8 feet (2.43 m) below modern sea level. Study of shell midden deposits show use of twenty-three different shellfish species, as well as fish from rocky intertidal zones and nearshore reef areas. Many different kinds of birds provided an important resource as well. In all, the intensified use of intertidal and nearshore marine species suggests coastal environmental conditions looked similar to modern conditions. Today, rocky sea stacks that lie just offshore of Yaquina Head provide nesting ground for thousands of sea birds, and nearby beaches offer impressive tide pools that can be easily explored during low tides. Yaquina Head is located at the north end of Newport, Oregon, and is accessed from Highway 101.

Seal Rock Site (Seal Rock State Wayside), Oregon

The Seal Rock site is a large shell midden located close to Seal Rock State Park, which lies south of the city of Waldport and contains an extensive late period archaeological site dated between 375 ± 70 and 160 ± 80 years ago. Excavated in the early 1970s under the direction of Richard Ross, the Seal Rock site (35LNC14) produced large quantities of cultural and faunal materials that shed light on littoral and nearshore economic activities of Oregon's prehistoric coastal peoples. A wide range of lithic tools, bone tools, and antler artifacts reflect the pursuit of hunting and resource processing activities. Notably, various types of composite toggling harpoon pieces and fishhooks made on bone were recovered during excavations. Considering their design qualities and the site's environmental context, the presence of numerous triangular lithic projectile points and harpoon pieces are interpreted to reflect an economic emphasis on hunting Steller's sea lions and salmon. Archaeologists interpret the faunal remains as showing a prehistoric economic focus on the local littoral and terrestrial environments, wherein fish, seals, and sea lions were taken from rocky intertidal zones and nearshore rocky reefs and deer and elk were exploited from nearby forests. Seal Rock is easily accessed on the west side of Highway 101, about 10 miles (16 km) south of Newport, Oregon.

Tahkenitch Landing Site (Tahkenitch Lake), Oregon

The Tahkenitch Landing site is located on the west side of Tahkenitch Lake, 7 miles (11.3 km) north of Reedsport. Archaeological excavations led by Rick Minor and Katherine Toepel revealed a long record of maritime adaptation reaching back to 8,000 years ago. The Tahkenitch Landing site provides an important view of human use of changing coastal environments over a long period of time. From 5,200 to 8,000 years ago, the site appears to have been next to an estuary with deep water, offering opportunities to catch different kinds of fish. At this time, Tahkenitch Lake was a free-flowing stream that was affected by rising and lowering ocean tides. From 3,000 to 5,200 years ago, rising sea levels caused the estuary to become shallower, changing its appeal as a fishing site. After 3,000 years ago, migrating sand dunes blocked the drainage of the estuary to the ocean, changing the site from an estuary to the freshwater environment of modern-day Tahkenitch Lake.

Umpqua-Eden Site, Reedsport, Oregon

The Umpqua-Eden site is located on the central Oregon coast near Reedsport and the mouth of the Umpqua River at the transition between the coastal margin, mountainous uplands, and Umpqua River valley. Archaeological excavations at this site uncovered a 3,000-year record of cultural occupation culminating in the establishment of a plank house village. Artifacts recovered from this site indicate a strong orientation toward marine and riverine resources. They include bone harpoons, which were used to hunt sea mammals such as seals, sea lions, and sea otters, as well as bone fishhooks and stone weights used along with nets to capture flatfish, rockfish, salmon, sturgeon, greenling, and sea perch. Occupants of Umpqua-Eden used bone and antler wedges to work wood into various forms. They made stone scrapers, knives, and points for arrows and harpoons to hunt animals on land and sea. A wide variety of animals were exploited by villagers including waterfowl (about 85 percent of all bones come from ducks), harbor seals, stellar sea lions, sea and river otters, blacktail deer, raccoon, bear, beaver, herons, cranes, swans, gulls, murres, and robins. Shellfish species such as bay mussel, bent-nose clam, butterclam, and horse mussel were commonly found in the site.

Cape Blanco Site (Cape Blanco State Park), Oregon

Archaeological excavation of a large shell midden located on the grounds of the Cape Blanco Lighthouse reflects human use of local intertidal resources during a period between 1,270 and 4,370 years ago. From this site, prehistoric peoples accessed local coastal environmental zones and nearby islands to gather mainly California mussels, sea urchin, barnacle, piddock, and clams; to fish for greenlings, lingcod, and cabezon; and to hunt beaver, river otter, seals and sea lions, elk, deer, and sea birds. Cape Blanco is accessed from Highway 101, 9 miles north of Port Orford, Oregon.

Lone Ranch Site (Lone Ranch Beach), Oregon

The Lone Ranch site is located at Lone Ranch Beach, 4.5 miles (7.2 km) north of Brookings, Oregon. Excavated in 1936 by Joel Berreman, this site contains the remains of a large village with several plank house structures buried within an extensive shell midden. The midden is overwhelmingly composed of California mussel shell but also includes a wide range of other intertidal shellfish species and the remains of mammals, mainly including elk, deer, sea lion, seal, and whale. Artifacts include bone and antler harpoons, fishing hooks, needles, sewing awls, pendants, beads, and wedges. Stone arrow points, harpoon tips, knives, pipes, net weights, bowls, mauls, and pestles were also found. The timing of occupation is not clearly known, but the archaeological materials are typical of later period sites.

GREAT EARTHQUAKES AND HUMAN-ENVIRONMENT INTERACTION

Coastal Oregon lies within the central portion of the Cascadia Subduction Zone, which is a large fault that marks the boundary where the Juan de Fuca oceanic plate and the North American continental plate collide and pass each other. At this collision point, the Juan de Fuca plate is slowly pushed beneath the western edge of Oregon; however, for the most part, these two plates are stuck together at a point that geologists call the "locked zone." The physics of this collision of two plates creates incredible strain at the locked zone, the force of which causes gradual uplift of Oregon's coastline a few millimeters each year. Every 500–600 years or so, the strain at the locked zone becomes too great and the plates slide past each other, causing a great earthquake and relaxation of the uplift on Oregon's coast. In addition to the intense ground shaking associated with these periodic earthquake events, earth scientists have observed that great Cascadia Subduction Zone seismic events also caused large tsunamis and lowering of the coastline (called co-seismic subsidence). Co-seismic subsidence is seen to have instantaneously lowered parts of Oregon's coastline 2–3 meters (ca. 6.5–10 ft), causing significant environmental change due to changes in relative sea level. Within a century or so, accumulated strain at the Cascadia Subduction Zone locks the plates together once again, and Oregon's coast begins to slowly uplift once again until another great earthquake causes the plates to slip, triggering a large earthquake, tsunami, and coastal subsidence. Records show that this geologic cycle of strain buildup and release repeated many times over thousands of years and likely produced significant impacts to coastal environments inhabited by Native Americans. Regional patterns of earthquake deformation of the coastal landforms exacerbated tsunami impacts by submerging coastal environments and producing long-term changes in the configuration of the coastline, the salinity of estuaries, and the productivity of coastal environments on which humans depend. Yet human settlement in these locations persisted, apparently involving human resettlement to new locations, adaptation of fishing and foraging patterns to the new environmental conditions, and eventual return to productive sites, as these sites recovered from the immediate and prolonged consequences of the earthquakes.

Geological and archaeological evidence indicates that some Native coastal settlements were repeatedly buried by tsunami deposits, or swallowed by the rising sea level in the aftermath of catastrophic plate-boundary earthquakes that occurred on average every 500–600 years. Archaeological excavations at two notable coastal sites provide insights into the effects these great earthquake events had on native populations.

Palmrose, Avenue Q, and Par-Tee Sites, Seaside, Oregon

Archaeological excavations conducted at the Palmrose, Avenue Q, and Par-Tee sites, located in the city limits of Seaside, Oregon, produced a record of human occupation dating from 4,000 to about 1,000 years ago. Intensive cultural occupation of a large semi-subterranean house begins at the Palmrose site around 2,700 years ago, which is located at the upper end of the Neawanna Creek drainage. This house was rebuilt several times until the site was abandoned about 1,500 years ago. Following abandonment of the Palmrose site, excavations show that dense shell middens began to accumulate at the nearby Avenue Q and Par-Tee sites, both of which are located farther to the west, along the Neacanicum River. The timing of abandonment at Palmrose and start of intensive occupations at the Avenue Q and Par-Tee sites corresponds to a coastal subsidence event associated with a great Cascadia Subduction Zone earthquake about 1,700 years ago, which may have caused significant westward growth of the local beachfront, requiring the reestablishment of villages closer to the ocean. Cultural occupation at the Avenue Q and Par-Tee sites continues to their apparent abandonment around 1,000 years ago. In 1805 explorer William Clark recorded two villages on a beach now located west of the Neacanicum River, suggesting further westward coastal expansion continued during the last 1,000 years.

Nah-so-mah Village Site, Bandon, Oregon

The Nah-so-mah Village site is located beneath the streets of modern-day Old Town Bandon, Oregon, at the mouth of the Coquille River. Archaeological excavation of the historic and prehistoric Nah-so-mah Village site were led by Roberta Hall and Richard Ross and revealed a long sequence of human occupation in the lower Coquille River estuary spanning a period from about 750 to 4,000 years

ago. Prehistoric occupants of the Nah-so-mah Village were strongly oriented to use of the local Pacific coast, Coquille River estuary, and adjacent uplands, as reflected in the large quantities of animal remains recovered from the site. An abundance of waterfowl species, including loon, grebe, albatross, pelican, cormorant, heron, swan, brant, goose, duck, coot, plover, gull, murre, and auklet, signal a strong use of estuarine and nearshore marine environments. Shellfish gathering was another activity, and many different species of barnacle, clam, limpet, mussel, chiton, crab, and snail were also found. The presence of harbor seal, northern fur seal, sea lion, river otter, sea otter, porpoise, and whale remains attests to the importance of hunting nearby marine and freshwater mammals. Terrestrial mammal hunting is indicated by the remains of bear, coyote or wolf, dog, fox, and cougar.

The geologic layering of the site shows that evidence of village occupation was rapidly buried beneath layers of clean water-lain sediment at three different times. The earliest burial event occurred sometime between about 1,845 and 2,295 years ago, and two other burial layers date after this time. Each of these burial events was followed by a period of abandonment, followed by an eventual return to pre-burial levels of occupation. In each case, site burial and abandonment is thought to indicate a cultural response to flooding, probably triggered by earthquake-induced coastal subsidence. In time, as uplift of the coast resumed, the site became available for reoccupation, only to be flooded after the subsequent earthquake event.

Further Reading: Ames, Kenneth M., and Herbert D. G. Maschner, *Peoples of the Northwest Coast: Their Archaeology and Prehistory* (New York: Thames and Hudson., 1999); Atwater, Brian F., "Evidence for Great Holocene Earthquakes along the Outer Coast of Washington State," *Science* 236(4804) (1987): 942–944; Atwater, Brian F., Alan R. Nelson, John J. Clague, Gary A. Carver, David K. Yamaguchi, Peter T. Bobrowsky, Joanne Bourgeois, Mark E. Darienzo, Wendy C. Grant, Eileen Hemphill-Haley, Harvey M. Kelsey, Gordon C. Jacoby, Stuart P. Nishenko, Stephen P. Palmer, Curt D. Peterson, and Mary Ann Reinhart, "Summary of Coastal Geologic Evidence for Past Great Earthquakes at the Cascadia Subduction Zone," *Earthquake Spectra* 11(1) (1995): 1–18; Berreman, Joel V., *Chetco Archaeology: A Report on the Lone Ranch Creek Shell Mound on the Coast of Southern Oregon*, no. 11, *General Series in Anthropology* (Menasha, WI: George Banta Publishing Company, 1944); Connolly, Thomas J., *Human Responses to Change in Coastal Geomorphology and Fauna on the Southern Northwest Coast: Archaeological Investigations at Seaside, Oregon*, University of Oregon Anthropological Papers No. 45 (Eugene: Department of Anthropology and Oregon State Museum of Anthropology, 1992); Coues, Elliot, ed., *The History of the Lewis and Clark Expedition*, vol. 2 (New York: Dover Publications, 1987; reprint of 1893 Francis P. Harper 4-vol. ed.); Darienzo, M. E., and C. D. Peterson, "Episodic Tectonic Subsidence of Late Holocene Salt Marshes, Northern Oregon Central Cascadia Margin," *Tectonics* 9 (1990): 1–22; Davis, Loren G., Michele L. Punke, Roberta L. Hall,

Matthew Fillmore, and Samuel C. Willis, "Evidence for Late Pleistocene Occupation on the Southern Northwest Coast," *Journal of Field Archaeology* 29 (2004): 7–16; Hall, Roberta L., *People of the Coquille Estuary: Native Use of Resources on the Oregon Coast* (Corvallis, OR: Words and Pictures Unlimited, 1995); Hall, Roberta L., "The Earthquake Hypothesis applied to the Coquille: Beginnings," in *Changing Landscapes: Proceedings of the 3rd Annual Coquille Cultural Preservation Conference, 1999*, edited by R. J. Losey (North Bend, OR: Coquille Indian Tribe, 2000), 33–42; Hall, Roberta L., and Stefan Radosevich, "Geoarchaeological Analysis of a Site in the Cascadia Subduction Zone on the Southern Oregon Coast," *Northwest Archaeological Research Notes* 29 (1995): 123–140; Hall, Roberta, L. Lee Lindsay, and Betty Vogel, "Southern Oregon Prehistory: Excavations at 35CS43, Bandon, Oregon," *Pacific Coast Archaeological Society Quarterly* 26(1) (1990): 60–79; Hall, Roberta, Loren G. Davis, Samuel C. Willis, and Matthew Fillmore, "Radiocarbon, Soil, and Artifact Chronologies for an Early Southern Oregon Coastal Site," *Radiocarbon* 47(3) (2005): 1–11; Kelsey, H. M., R. C. Witter, and E. Hemphill-Haley, "Plate Boundary Earthquakes and Tsunamis of the Past 5,500 Yr, Sixes River Estuary, Southern Oregon," *Geological Society of America Bulletin* 114(3) (2002): 298–314; Kelsey, H. M., R. L. Ticknor, J. G. Bockheim, and C. E. Mitchell, "Quaternary Upper Plate Deformation in Coastal Oregon," *Geological Society of America Bulletin* 108(7) (1995): 843–860; Kelsey, Harvey M., Alan R. Nelson, Eileen Hemphill-Haley, and Robert C. Witter, "Tsunami History of an Oregon Coastal Lake Reveals a 4600 Yr Record of Great Earthquakes on the Cascadia Subduction Zone," *Geological Society of America Bulletin* 117(7–8) (2005): 1009–1032; Lyman, R. Lee, *Prehistory of the Oregon Coast: The Effects of Excavation Strategies and Assemblage Size on Archaeological Inquiry* (New York: Academic Press, 1991); McNeill, L. C., C. Goldfinger, R. S. Yeats, and L. D. Kulm, "The Effects of Upper-Plate Deformation on Records of Prehistoric Cascadia Subduction Zone Earthquakes," in *Coastal Tectonics: Geological Society of London*, edited by I. Stewart and C. Vita Finzi, Special Publication Vol. 146 (1998); Minor, Rick, and Ruth L. Greenspan, *Archaeological Test at the Cape Blanco Lighthouse Shell Midden, Southern Oregon Coast*, Heritage Research Associates Report No. 216 (North Bend, OR: Coos Bay District Bureau of Land Management, 1998); Minor, Rick, and Kathryn A. Toepel, *The Archaeology of the Tahkenitch Landing Site: Early Prehistoric Occupation on the Oregon Coast*, Heritage Research Associates Report No. 46 (Corvallis, OR: Siuslaw National Forest, 1986); Minor, Rick, Kathryn A. Toepel, and Ruth L. Greenspan, *Archaeological Investigations at Yaquina Head, Central Oregon Coast*, Heritage Research Associates Report No. 59 (Salem, OR: Bureau of Land Management, Salem District, 1987); Mitchell, C. E., P. Vincent, R. J. Weldon II, and M. A. Richards, "Present-Day Vertical Deformation of the Cascadia Margin, Pacific Northwest, U.S.A.," *Journal of Geophysical Research* 99 (1994): 12,257–12,277; Moss, Madonna L., and Jon M. Erlandson, "Early Holocene Adaptations on the Southern Northwest Coast," *Journal of California and Great Basin Anthropology* 20(1) (1998): 13–25; Nelson, A. R., A. C. Asquith, and W. C. Grant, "Great Earthquakes and Tsunamis of the Past 2000 Years at the Salmon River Estuary, Central Oregon Coast, USA," *Bulletin of the Seismological Society of America* 94(4) (2004): 1276–1292; Nelson, A. R., H. M. Kelsey, E. Hemphill-Haley, and R. C. Witter, "A Potential Record of Tsunamis Generated by Great Earthquakes along the Southern Cascadia Subduction Zone," Open-File Report, U.S. Geological Survey 94-0568 (1994): 134–136; Ross, Richard, "Prehistory of the Oregon Coast," in *Handbook of North American Indians*, edited by W. Suttles, vol. 7, *Northwest Coast* (Washington, DC: Smithsonian Institutions, 1990), 554–559; Witter, Robert C., "Great Cascadia Earthquakes and Tsunamis of the Past 6700 Years, Coquille River Estuary, Southern Coastal Oregon," *Geological Society of America Bulletin* 115(10) (2003): 1289–1306.

Loren G. Davis

CASCADIA CAVE, HANNAVAN CREEK, CALAPOOIA MIDDEN, AND OTHER SITES

Willamette Valley, Western Oregon

The Long History of Settlements in an Interior Valley

The plain of Oregon's Willamette Valley was formed by sediment deposited at the end of the Pleistocene, when catastrophic floods originating at glacial Lake Missoula swept down the Columbia Gorge and backed up into the valley. The Missoula flood sediment formed an undulating plain of pothole lakes, marshes, and bogs; the modern Willamette River and its tributaries negotiated their courses across this new surface.

TERMINAL PLEISTOCENE/EARLY HOLOCENE

The earliest cultural record is sparse. Several Clovis projectile points have been found in the valley, all from undated contexts. These distinctive artifacts consistently date to around 12,000 years ago throughout North America. There is also trace evidence of a human presence associated with terminal Pleistocene peat deposits that formed in depressions on the Missoula flood silt, including animal bone fragments (primarily bison) that exhibit possible butchering marks and stone fragments that appear to be flaking debris from stone tools.

Few Willamette Valley sites have produced early Holocene dates; among the most significant are Cascadia Cave, a rock shelter in the foothills of the western Cascades, and several sites in the Long Tom River basin on the valley floor. Faunal remains from Cascadia Cave indicate that hunting was a focus, with prey that included deer, elk, rabbit, weasel, and grouse. A hearth near the base of the deposit produced an age of about 8,800 years ago. Common tools include laurel-leaf-shaped "Cascade" projectile points, edge-ground cobbles, and end scrapers, an assemblage that suggests hide processing and wood working. Several sites are known from the valley with similar tool assemblages, including the Geertz site in the Portland Basin at the north end of the valley.

The early sites in the Long Tom River basin are generally small, with simple tool assemblages: at site 35LA861 a small lens of charcoal and fire-cracked rock dating to 10,500 years ago is associated with cultural flakes of chert and basalt; at site 35LA658 a small lens of charcoal and burned earth dating to 10,900 years ago is associated with obsidian flakes and several charred hazelnut meats; a lens of charcoal and burned earth dating to about 8,480 years ago is associated with an obsidian scraper at site 35LA860; a cluster of fire-cracked rock, charcoal, and burned earth associated with obsidian chips and a formed obsidian scraping tool dates to 9,910 years ago at site 35LA439. The Hannavan Creek site, located on the floor of the Fern Ridge Reservoir downstream from the other sites, contains the earliest clear example of a food-processing oven from the valley. Camas bulbs charred in the stone-lined pit oven were dated to about 8,500 years ago. At the nearby Ralston site, a similar oven feature eroding from a stream bank dates to around 7,500 years ago. Camas was an important staple food in the valley during the Middle and Late Holocene, and these sites provide the earliest evidence for systematic camas processing.

MIDDLE HOLOCENE (ABOUT 3,000–7,500 YEARS AGO)

The Middle Holocene (ca. 3,000–7,500 years ago) is best known from excavations along Mill Creek in the central part of the valley, and on the Long Tom River in the upper valley. The Mill Creek cultural record, based on work at ten sites, is fixed with over sixty radiocarbon determinations, nearly all from cultural features; most are rock-lined pit ovens dating between about 3,000 and 5,500 years old, many of which produced charred camas bulbs. Chipped and ground stone tools are present, but in relatively low frequencies.

The Long Tom cultural record echoes that from Mill Creek, with frequent camas ovens, typically containing charred camas bulbs and occasional charred hazelnut shells and acorn meats. Modest portable artifact assemblages are dominated by flaked cobble choppers, expedient flake tools, and dart-sized corner-notched projectile points. A probable residential area at the Long Tom site produced stone bowls, a hopper mortar base, pestles, and cobble-sized hammer

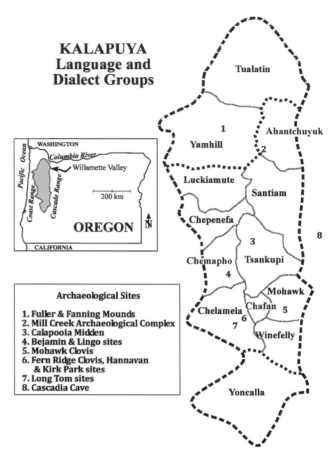

KALAPUYA Language and Dialect Groups

Archaeological Sites
1. Fuller & Fanning Mounds
2. Mill Creek Archaeological Complex
3. Calapooia Midden
4. Bejamin & Lingo sites
5. Mohawk Clovis
6. Fern Ridge Clovis, Hannavan & Kirk Park sites
7. Long Tom sites
8. Cascadia Cave

Map of the Willamette Valley showing historic Kalapuya language groups, and locations of key archaeological sites. [Thomas J. Connolly]

stones. Other representative Middle Holocene sites, including the Lingo, Flanagan, and Chalker sites, produced similar evidence.

Camas processing is a dominant theme in Middle Holocene sites; some camas ovens are more than 2 meters in diameter, suggesting the bulk processing of foods for deferred consumption or trade. All investigated sites suggest occupations of limited duration, indicating a relatively mobile population.

LATE HOLOCENE (3,000 YEARS AGO TO THE CONTACT ERA)

Many sites with a record of intermittent occupation during the Middle Holocene—including the Benjamin, Lingo, Lynch, Hurd, Flanagan, Chalker, Calapooia[1] Midden, and other

---

[1] The people of the Willamette Valley are collectively known as "Kalapuya," for the language family represented by three languages and more than a dozen dialects. Variations in spelling for this name are numerous, as well as for modern landmarks such as the Calapooia River and the Calapooya Mountains.

Excavation of a camas baking oven, approximately 4,700 years old (Chalker site, Long Tom site complex).   [Thomas J. Connolly]

sites—appear to have seen continuous or near-continuous occupation during the last 3,000 years or so, and particularly within the last 2,000 years. Hundreds of mound sites, the product of accumulated midden debris, line major tributary rivers of the Willamette. Although many sites were in use earlier, all radiocarbon dates from mounded midden deposits fall within the last 3,000 years. The number of mound sites attests to a large and increasingly sedentary population.

Initial occupations at the Calapooia Midden site were intermittent and focused on the seasonal processing of vegetable foods, primarily camas. During about the last 1,200 years, and into the nineteenth century (confirmed by the presence of glass trade beads), the site was occupied on a more or less continual basis, and it is during this time that the midden deposits accumulated. Pit features, most interpreted as storage facilities, were common. Fifteen burials were also exposed; the presence of midden fill in the burial pits indicates that all date to within the last 1,200 years. Burials were found in two areas of the site; the earliest appear more haphazard in arrangement, and the latter appear to be organized in a formal burial area. Most interments did not have associated grave goods, but one female was buried with a stone mortar, and two males were buried together with a whalebone club and twenty-five arrow points. It is not clear whether the arrows reflect grave goods or cause of death, or both. Evidence of traumatic death has been reported for burials from other similar Willamette Valley mound sites.

During the last 1,200 years the Calapooia Midden site probably served as a family residential center, which was part of a larger village community. Evidence suggests that the resident group may have used a set of similar sites to occasionally shift the focus of primary residence. Based on interpretations derived from the ethnographic record, it is thought that this small corporate group probably had exclusive rights over specific resource areas, and the presence of an organized burial ground suggests strong ritual ties to the locality.

Excavations at midden sites in Kirk Park, located at the north end of the Fern Ridge Reservoir on the Long Tom River, suggest a comparable homestead set (as opposed to a single homestead site). The sites were occupied during the last 3,000 years, taking on a more settled and residential character over time. The sites are all essentially contemporaneous, but somewhat functionally distinct, and are thought to represent residential sites and seasonal task camps for a single small resident group.

The Fuller and Fanning mounds, at the northern end of the valley, also probably date largely within the last millennium. Excavations in the early 1940s focused on burials, of which sixty-six were removed from the two sites. Cranial shaping, an important mark of high status along the lower Columbia and on the southern Northwest Coast, was present on some of the individuals who were also buried with a disproportionate share of grave goods. Apart from the chipped stone tools, artifacts included bone and abalone shell pendants, bone beads, dentalium and olivella shell beads, tubular stone pipes, antler digging-stick handles, carved bone figurines, and whalebone clubs. Some historic trade goods, including brass buttons and glass trade beads, were present, indicating occupation of the sites into the nineteenth century.

Willamette Valley projectile points: top row, Middle Holocene time period; bottom two rows, Late Holocene time period.   [Thomas J. Connolly]

Bow and arrow technology was introduced to the area within the last 2000 years or so, and sites of this period are dominated by hundreds of arrow points, frequencies that are ten times those found in comparable excavated volumes in Middle Holocene sites. Their dramatic increase likely indicates an increased concern with defense, raiding, and boundary maintenance.

CONTACT PERIOD
At the opening of the nineteenth century, Kalapuyan speakers occupied the entire Willamette Valley above the falls at Oregon City, as well as the northernmost tributary drainages of the Umpqua Basin to the south. Based on texts recorded by linguists between the late 1880s and early 1900s, the Kalapuyan language family comprised three languages and at least thirteen dialects. Each dialect community included a group of villages occupying a major tributary stream; these communities correspond to the commonly identified Kalapuya treaty groups, whose identities survive today in the names of the Willamette River's major tributary rivers (Tualatin, Yamhill, Santiam, Luckiamute, and others).

The valley's poor ethnohistoric record is a legacy of devastating epidemics. The most reliable estimates put the Kalapuya population approaching 20,000 in 1770, but by the mid 1840s (when the Oregon Trail migrations of American settlers began) the total Kalapuya population was estimated at less than 600, greater than 95 percent mortality in fewer than seventy years. Most Kalapuya descendents are now affiliated with the Confederated Tribes of the Grand Ronde and the Confederated Tribes of Siletz reservations of Oregon.

Further Reading: Aikens, C. Melvin, ed., *Archaeological Studies in the Willamette Valley, Oregon*, University of Oregon Anthropological Papers No. 8 (Eugene: University of Oregon, 1975); Aikens, C. Melvin, *Archaeology of Oregon* (Portland, OR: USDI Bureau of Land Management, 1993); Boyd, Robert T., "Strategies of Indian Burning in the Willamette Valley," in *Indians Fire and the Land in the Pacific Northwest*, edited by Robert Boyd (Corvallis: Oregon State University Press, 1999), 94–138; Cheatham, Richard D., *Late Archaic Settlement Pattern in the Long Tom Sub-Basin, Upper Willamette Valley, Oregon*, University of Oregon Anthropological Papers No. 39 (Eugene: University of Oregon, 1988); Mackey, Harold, *The Kalapuyans: A Sourcebook on the Indians of the Willamette Valley* (Salem, OR: Mission Mill Museum Association; Grand Ronde, OR: Confederated Tribes of Grand Ronde, 2004); O'Neill, Brian L., Thomas J. Connolly, and Dorothy E. Freidel, *A Holocene Geoarchaeological Record for the Upper Willamette Valley, Oregon: The Long Tom and Chalker Sites*, University of Oregon Anthropological Papers No. 61 (Eugene: University of Oregon, 2004); Zenk, Henry B., "Kalapuyans," in *Northwest Coast*, edited by Wayne Suttles, vol. 7, *Handbook of North American Indians* (Washington, DC: Smithsonian Institution, 1990), 547–553; Zenk, Henry B., "Tualatin Kalapuyan Villages: The Ethnographic Record," in *Contributions to the Archaeology of Oregon 1989–1994*, edited by Paul W. Baxter, Association of Oregon Archaeologists Occasional Papers No. 5 (Eugene: Association of Oregon Archaeologists, 1994), 147–166.

Thomas J. Connolly

THE MEIER AND CLAHCLELLAH SITES

Lower Columbia River, Oregon and Washington
Trading Center and Gateway to the Interior West

The Columbia is the great river of the American West, flowing 2,100 kilometers from the Canadian Rockies to the Pacific Ocean. The lower Columbia River stretches 275 kilometers from the modern city of The Dalles, Oregon, to the Pacific Ocean. The eastern segment of the lower Columbia River flows through the Columbia River gorge, a steep-sided canyon cutting through the Cascade Mountains. The western segment flows through the Portland Basin and Coast Range, then empties into the Pacific Ocean.

At the time of European contact, Chinookan-speaking people inhabited the land immediately flanking the lower Columbia River. The community in each town was politically independent but linked with other communities by family ties, exchange relationships, and shared social and economic structures. The social structure included a system of rank, with elites holding the most influence and wealth, commoners holding less, and slaves holding none.

In winter, and sometimes all year, lower Columbia people lived in settlements along the Columbia and the lower parts of tributaries. The inhabitants dwelled in large, wooden plank houses. During other seasons, lower Columbia people sometimes traveled elsewhere to harvest resources, trade, and socialize. The Native economy was based on fishing, gathering, and hunting. Important foods included salmon, shellfish, elk, seal, tubers, berries, and nuts. Trading was also significant, as the lower Columbia was the nexus of a vast exchange network extending into the Plains, Great Basin, and sub-Arctic regions of North America. Trade was most intensive around The Dalles, where superb fishing conditions enabled Chinookan residents to trade tons of salmon to thousands of visitors each year.

Land bordering the lower Columbia River contains hundreds of known archaeological sites, including the remains of large towns, small villages, camps, cemeteries, and rock art (engravings and paintings on rock). These sites have yielded artifacts of stone, bone, antler, shell, and plant material. In addition, sites occupied at the time of Euro-American contact have yielded Western manufactures, such as glass beads and brass buttons. Unfortunately many lower Columbia sites have been extensively looted over the last century. Consequently we have lost much evidence of past lifeways. However, some sites have been professionally excavated. These sites provide the most reliable information about ancient human occupation of the lower Columbia River valley.

Evidence gathered primarily during professional projects indicates that most archaeological material from the lower Columbia floodplain dates to the last 3,000 years. Earlier remains are uncommon, because the dynamics of the Columbia River apparently destroyed most archaeological materials preceding that time span—or buried them so deeply that they are rarely found.

However, humans undoubtedly inhabited or visited the lower Columbia area by 13,500 years ago, as artifacts that old have been found in nearby uplands. The oldest archaeological sites along the lower Columbia contain stone artifacts dating to the Early Archaic period, between 13,000 and 9,000 years ago. These rare sites, together with remains from other parts of the northwest coast suggest that Early Archaic people lived in small, extremely mobile groups. They built small, lightweight dwellings and subsisted by hunting, gathering, and fishing. Early Archaic sites appear concentrated in low-elevation areas, whereas Late Archaic sites, dating from 9,000 to 6,400 years ago, occur not only at low elevations, but also on plateaus above the Columbia River and in the Cascade Mountains. This distribution suggests that by the Late Archaic, people had come to use the full range of habitats in the region.

Early Pacific period (6,400 to 2,800 years ago) remains are poorly understood. In contrast, middle and late Pacific period (2,800 to 250 years ago) remains clearly evidence significant economic and social changes: the development of sedentary life in towns, large-scale food storage, more intensive harvesting of wetland resources, the gathering of a diverse range of plant foods, a sophisticated woodworking technology, a distinctive Columbia River art style, expanded long-distance trade, and social ranking. Archaeological evidence of these changes includes remains of big wooden houses, storage pits, diverse plant and animal remains, woodworking tools such as stone mauls, small stone sculptures, nonlocal material such as obsidian,; and inter-household wealth disparities.

Modern-period sites, dating from 250 years ago to the present, shed light on cultural developments after Euro-American products and people entered the region. Euro-Americans first set foot in the lower Columbia River in AD 1792. From that time through the 1840s, interactions between Natives and Euro-Americans occurred largely in the context of the fur trade. This period was also marked by the deaths of more than half of all Chinookan Natives due to infectious diseases introduced by Euro-Americans. Surviving Indians faced large-scale Euro-American settlement along the Columbia River, which began in the 1840s. In the 1850s, the U.S. government forcibly incorporated some Chinookans into tribes and moved them onto reservations, including the Grand Ronde, Quinault, Warm Springs, and Yakama reservations. However, the United States never ratified the 1851 Tansy Point treaty, leaving many Chinookans without a reservation or federally recognized tribal status. Despite these trials, many Chinookans currently inhabit and use their ancestral lands along the Columbia River.

The outstanding rock art of the lower Columbia, created by Pacific and Modern period peoples, merits additional discussion. Hundreds of petroglyphs (engravings) and pictographs (paintings) have been observed on basalt boulders, outcrops, and canyon walls along the Columbia River, mostly around The Dalles. Motifs include human stick figures; animal figures, most often mountain sheep, birds, elk, or deer; hunting scenes, perhaps intended to facilitate successful hunts; rayed arcs and circles, often associated with human faces and fig-

ures, which may symbolize supernatural powers; and stylized anthropomorphic and zoomorphic beings with pronounced eyes, distinctive ribs, and headdresses that may represent supernatural entities. This last motif is exemplified by a well-known Dalles-area petroglyph called Tsagiglalal, which is Chinookan for "She Who Watches." Much lower Columbia rock art has been lost to the ravages of dam construction, looting, and vandalism. However, the public can see a number of outstanding examples, including the Tsagiglalal panel, by appointment at Columbia Hills State Park in Washington.

The public can learn more about lower Columbia River archaeology by visiting sites and museums in Washington, including Ridgefield National Wildlife Refuge, Bonneville Dam Visitor Center North, Columbia Hills State Park in Dallesport, Columbia River Gorge Interpretive Center Museum in Stevenson, Maryhill Museum of Art in Goldendale, and Yakama Nation Museum in Toppenish. Interpretive facilities in Oregon include the Bonneville Dam Visitor Center South, Columbia River Discovery Center in The Dalles, Museum at Warm Springs, Museum of Natural and Cultural History at the University of Oregon in Eugene, and Portland Art Museum.

Museums and publications shed light on two especially significant lower Columbia sites, Clahclellah and Meier, best known for the information they have yielded concerning household and community life among lower Columbia residents.

CLAHCLELLAH SITE (SOUTHWEST WASHINGTON)

Clahclellah was a busy Chinookan town when Lewis and Clark visited it in 1805 and 1806. Archaeological excavation uncovered remains of this Native town, as well as remains of subsequent activity at the site by the U.S. military and by Euro-American settlers, including thousands of Oregon Trail emigrants. The Clahclellah site is significant because it reflects this critical chain of events in Pacific Northwest history. In addition, remains of seven Native plank houses were fully excavated, making Clahclellah the most fully excavated plank house site in the Pacific Northwest.

Clahclellah is located in Washington State, on the north side of the Columbia River, along a series of rapids called the Cascades of the Columbia, 65 kilometers upriver from the modern city of Portland, Oregon. The site was excavated in the late 1970s under the direction of the U.S. Army Corps of Engineers. After the excavation, remaining site deposits were destroyed by construction of a second powerhouse at Bonneville Dam.

The excavation uncovered remains of a Native town established sometime between AD 1400 and AD 1700 and inhabited into the mid-1800s. This town contained at least seven plank houses with floor areas ranging from 65 to 120 square meters. Tools, such as projectile points (arrow points) and net sinkers; plant remains, such as tubers; and animal remains, such as sturgeon, salmon, and elk bones indicate residents subsisted by fishing, hunting, and gathering. Numerous

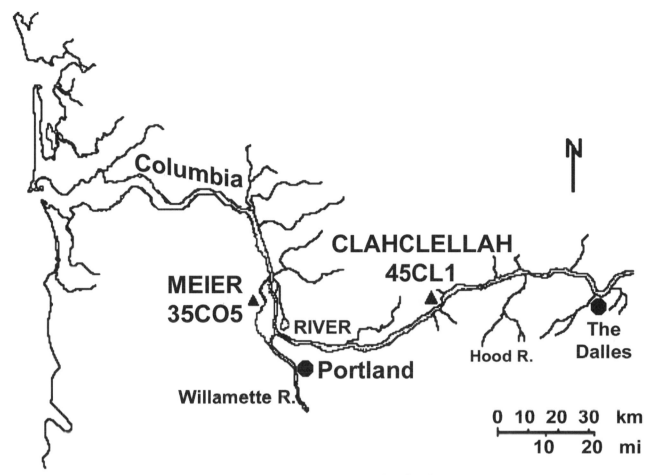

Map of the area, showing major geographic features, modern cities, and archaeological sites mentioned in the text. [Elizabeth Sobel]

hearths, ovens, storage pits, and refuse deposits reflect intensive food processing and tool manufacture.

The archaeological remains indicate that long-distance exchange with other Native communities, as well as trade with Euro-American fur traders and settlers, was important to the Clahclellah economy. A variety of artifacts indicate this trade activity. Exchange with other Native communities is indicated by artifacts made of obsidian, a volcanic rock that does not naturally occur along the lower Columbia. A geochemical analysis revealed that some obsidian artifacts originated as far away as California. Trade with Euro-Americans is indicated by Western manufactures, including glass beads, ceramic dishes, and brass ornaments. Two houses contained especially high quantities of imported goods. These may have been high-status households that dominated long-distance exchange activity by community members.

Historical documents, Native oral testimony, and archaeological deposits suggest Chinookan people continued to inhabit Clahclellah into the 1850s, despite scores of white homesteaders in the area by that time. Indigenous habitation may have lasted until 1856, when conflicts between settlers and Indians led the U.S. military to remove Natives from the area and to execute several Native men, including Tumulth, reportedly a chief at Clahclellah. Several surviving members of the Clahclellah community returned to the area by the late 1800s, and some descendants still live in the area today.

Information and artifacts from Clahclellah are displayed at three facilities in Washington State: Yakama Nation Museum in Toppenish, Columbia River Gorge Interpretive Center in Stevenson, and Bonneville Dam Visitor Center.

MEIER SITE (NORTHWEST OREGON)

The Meier site contains remains of a large wooden plank house inhabited for 400 years, from about AD 1400 to AD 1800. Along with the Cathlapotle site, the Meier site has been studied more extensively than any other Native village site along the Columbia River. Consequently, archaeological research on Meier has contributed significantly to our understanding of ancient household and community life along the lower Columbia River.

The Meier site is located on the south side of the Columbia River about 35 kilometers downriver from the modern city of

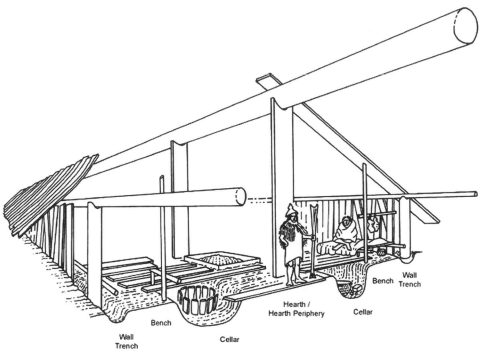

Sketch of a wooden plank house, like the one excavated at the Meier site.   [Elizabeth Sobel]

Portland, Oregon. Richard Pettigrew conducted a small-scale excavation at Meier in 1973. Kenneth Ames of Portland State University directed a large-scale excavation from 1987 to 1991. The excavations unearthed remains of a rectangular house, along with abundant stone, bone, and antler artifacts. Radiocarbon dates and trade goods indicate the Meier house was built around AD 1400 and occupied until roughly AD 1800, several years after Euro-Americans began exploring the lower Columbia River. This termination date may indicate that residents abandoned the house because of factors related to Euro-American arrival—for example, diseases introduced by Euro-Americans.

The Meier house was about 12 meters by 30 meters and consisted of at least 55,000 board feet of lumber at any given time. The large size and 400-year lifespan of the house, along with evidence of burned timbers, rotted posts, and multiple construction episodes, suggests residents had to continually work at maintaining the structure. Interior architectural features included wide benches, sub-floor pits, and large hearths. The pits yielded high artifact densities, reflecting inhabitants' use of these facilities for both storage and garbage disposal. In contrast, the hearth areas yielded low artifact densities, reflecting inhabitants' efforts to keep these high-traffic areas free of debris.

Artifact distributions indicate the Meier household was segregated into higher- and lower-status residents. For example, one end of the Meier house held a concentration of costly objects, including ornately carved stone bowls and exotic imports, such as European trade goods and adze blades made of nephrite (a jade-like stone). This end of the house was likely occupied by elite individuals who controlled household property and monopolized household trade activity. The opposite end of the house contained fewer luxury goods and larger, more intensively used hearths, suggesting that lower-status individuals occupied this end, where they performed much of the food processing for the household.

Ames and colleagues have studied other aspects of the Native community that once lived at Meier, including their subsistence activities, craft production, and responses to Euro-American contact. Several studies compare Meier with the nearby Cathlapotle site, another Chinookan town inhabited at the time of Euro-American contact. Additional information about the Meier site is available in several publications and at http://web.pdx.edu/~b5cs/virtualmeier/virtualmeier.html.

Further Reading: Aikens, C. Melvin, *Archaeology of Oregon* (Portland, OR: U.S. Bureau of Land Management, 1993); Ames, Kenneth M., and Herbert D. Maschner, *Peoples of the Northwest Coast: Their Archaeology and Prehistory* (London: Thames & Hudson, 1999); Butler, Virginia, "Relic Hunting, Archaeology, and Loss of Native American Heritage at The Dalles," *Oregon Historical Quarterly* 107(3) (2007); Keyser, James D., *Indian Rock Art of the Columbia Plateau* (Seattle: University of Washington Press, 1992); Sobel, Elizabeth, D. Ann Trieu Gahr, and Kenneth Ames, *Household Archaeology on the Northwest Coast* (Ann Arbor, MI: International Monographs in Prehistory, 2006); Virtual Meier Site, Cameron Smith Web site, http://web.pdx.edu/~b5cs/virtualmedia/virtualmedia.html (online May 2008).

Elizabeth Sobel

CATHLAPOTLE SITE

Lower Columbia River, Oregon and Washington
Native Trade Center and Intensively Studied Village Site

The Cathlapotle archaeological site is the remains of a large Native American town on the lower Columbia River near Portland, Oregon, and Vancouver, Washington. It was one of the largest Native towns on its stretch of the Columbia River, with perhaps 900 to 1,100 residents.

The people of Cathlapotle played an important role in the fur trade (AD 1792–1845), including hosting Lewis and Clark on March 29, 1806. The expedition spent several hours there and left lengthy descriptions in their journals. The town itself was established at its current location around AD 1450 and abandoned (no doubt as the consequence of epidemic diseases) in the 1830s. It contained six large post-and-beam houses; the largest was 10 meters by 41 meters, and the smallest was 8 meters by 13 meters. These large houses were constructed by placing smaller structures end to end. There are also thirteen to sixteen smaller structures. As an archaeological site, Cathlapotle is important for several reasons: it is extremely well preserved, it is archaeologically very rich (excellent preservation and abundant artifacts), and it spans one of the most important periods in the history of the United States—the arrival of Europeans.

The lower Columbia River encompasses the lowest 200 miles (322 km) of the river before it enters the Pacific Ocean. The area is topographically and ecologically diverse. At its eastern edge, the Columbia gorge breaches the Cascade Mountain Range. West of the gorge, the river passes through the Portland Basin, which Lewis and Clark called the Wapato Valley—the name still used by regional scholars for the area. Here, the river's broad floodplain once contained extensive wetlands, bordered by rolling plateaus with grasslands and groves of oak and pine. Below the lowland, the river penetrates the Coast Range—a long, rugged chain of relatively low, heavily forested mountains—and enters its wide, fjord-like estuary, where it meets the Pacific Ocean. The climate is maritime, with heavy rains and moderate temperatures. The combination of topography and climate made the region ecologically very rich, especially the Wapato Valley.

The region is part of the Northwest Coast culture area, a zone of distinctive Native cultures extending from northern California to southeast Alaska. Several ethnolinguistic groups representing three distinct language families occupied the lower Columbia at contact.

Speakers of Chinookan languages were the most numerous. Populations were large and comparatively dense, ranking twenty-sixth worldwide among 205 documented foraging societies. Pre-contact populations have been conservatively estimated at 34,000 people. They were concentrated on the major rivers and tributaries, particularly in the Wapato Valley. Chinookan social organization and economy shared many similarities with other northwest coast societies. The household was the basic socioeconomic unit, and the village or town the highest unit. Households lived in large post-and-beam plank houses of western red cedar (*Thuja plicata*).

The Chinookan society was divided into two broad classes: free and slave. Free people were subdivided into the commoners and the chiefly elite. Chiefly status was based on heredity, wealth, and widespread social and economic ties. The slave population in the late eighteenth and early nineteenth centuries may have constituted 25 percent of the total.

The storage-based subsistence economy produced large volumes of diverse foods. Subsistence economies were productive, harvesting a wide array of fish, plants, and wetland and upland mammals. Canoes—ranging in size from small, one-person vessels to enormous freight canoes—permitted access to the smallest creek and allowed people to move tons of food and raw materials. Trade and exchange, both along the Columbia River and beyond, were important activities, particularly among Chinookan speakers. Cathlapotle was situated in the most fertile part of the lower Columbia River region, the Wapato Valley—at the heart of the trade and exchange networks.

Contact with Europeans began around 1775, with the first known exploratory voyages along the coast. Ongoing contact began in 1792, with the European discovery of the Columbia River's mouth and the start of the maritime fur trade on the river. Boats from the British Vancouver expedition were the first European vessels to go any distance up the Columbia. In October 1792, these vessels encountered a large flotilla of canoes from a large Chinookan town that was probably Cathlapotle. Though the Native warriors' behavior was at first threatening, they quickly removed their armor when they realized the British wanted to trade with them, not attack them. The fur trade brought the lower Columbia River's people into a European trading and colonial system spanning the globe.

Exploration was fueled by competition among Spain, Great Britain, and Russia. By the 1790s, the United States had replaced Spain. British and Americans directly competed on the lower Columbia. Probably at least one trading vessel each year entered the lower Columbia River after 1792. Vessels trading on the lower Columbia then sailed to

The replica Cathlapotle Plankhouse on Ridgefield National Wildlife Refuge, Washington.   [Courtesy of the U.S. Fish and Wildlife Service]

Canton, South America, Hawai'i, and elsewhere. Before 1811, the fur trade was entirely maritime, or borne by ships. These vessels were wholly dependent on Native people for furs and fresh provisions.

The Lewis and Clark expedition spent the winter of 1805–06 near the Columbia River's mouth. In 1811 Fort Astoria, the first permanent Euro-American base on the lower Columbia, was established. The Hudson's Bay Company (HBC) in 1824 placed the headquarters for its entire Columbia Department at Fort Vancouver in the Wapato Valley, 29 kilometers (about 18 miles) upriver from Cathlapotle. The region became part of United States territory in 1848. By then the lower Columbia River's Native populations had been decimated by epidemics. The effects differed significantly within the region, with the Wapato Valley among the hardest hit. Population decline there probably exceeded 90 percent between 1792 and 1832, when Cathlapotle was probably abandoned as a town.

Cathlapotle was placed very strategically within the Wapato Valley. Among the evidence indicating the importance of its location is data suggesting it was the most recent in a series of towns in this immediate area for perhaps 2,000 years. Additionally Cathlapotle was sometimes the victim of massive flooding, and it was reoccupied and even rebuilt after each flood. It sits on a low ridge facing out toward the confluences

of a small stream and two rivers with the Columbia River. Behind Cathlapotle are extensive wetlands and higher hills and plateaus. Its location gave people easy access to both the full environmental diversity of the Wapato Valley and to traffic on the Columbia River.

Its elevation put it above all but the largest floods and gave its people visual access to sweeping vistas up- and downriver, especially for someone keeping watch from one of the house roofs. However, Cathlapotle was almost invisible to travelers sailing up or down the Columbia, except in one small stretch of the river. It was from this one place that Vancouver's expedition, and Lewis and Clark, first saw Cathlapotle. The visible remains of its six visible houses are aligned in two rows along the ridge, paralleling the small river in front of it. The three largest houses were higher up the ridge, while the three smaller houses were down near the riverfront. The visible house pits today appear as long, deep depressions in the ridge's surface. The site covers 2.8 hectares.

Major excavations were conducted at Cathlapotle between 1991 and 1996, but related laboratory analyses and studies are still continuing as of 2007. House 1, the largest, and House 4, one of the smaller houses, were extensively excavated, while two other houses saw limited study. The associated middens and outdoor activity areas were also explored. The cultural deposits are about 2 meters deep. A seventh house was discovered buried deeply at the base of these deposits, under House 2.

The excavations revealed that the Cathlapotle structures were of two types: the larger four were subdivided into compartments, while the two smaller structures had open interiors. It was noted above that Cathlapotle is extremely well preserved. This is illustrated by the presence of very low ridges crossing the ground surface in the bottoms of the house depressions. These ridges mark the locations of the interior walls separating the compartments. The houses also had cellars used for storage of food, raw materials, and valuables, among other things. The excavations produced very rich and diverse collections of animal and plant remains, tools, and manufacturing debris.

Throughout its history, the people of Cathlapotle were deeply involved in trade and exchange. Obsidian recovered at Cathlapotle indicates the village was part of a web of relationships extending as far south as northern California and eastern Oregon. It was situated so as to monitor and interdict movement along the Columbia River from a protected location. When European traders arrived, Cathlapotle's people actively engaged in the fur trade. Excavations have uncovered copper, iron, and glass trade beads. What was exchanged for these goods is less clear. However, the presence of large numbers of elk bones and stone hide scrapers suggests Cathlapotle's people made clamons (processed elk hides) popular among Native peoples to the north, who used them as armor. European and American traders came to the lower Columbia not so much for fur, but for clamons to take north to trade for furs. It appears hide production expanded rapidly at Cathlapotle after the fur trader arrived. It also appears that the people of Cathlapotle were in the process of successfully adjusting to the presence of European and American traders until that adjustment was cut short by epidemics in the 1830s.

Cathlapotle is located on the U.S. Fish and Wildlife Service's Ridgefield National Wildlife Refuge. Though the archaeological site is not readily accessible, visitors are welcome and encouraged to visit the refuge's Cathlapotle Plankhouse, a full-scale replica of a Chinookan-style post-and-beam house constructed according to archaeological and ethnographic data. Built by volunteers using both modern and traditional tools and methods, the plank house provides an enduring venue not only for telling the story of Lewis and Clark's visit to Cathlapotle, but also for the interpretation of the rich cultural and natural legacy of the Native people who have made their home along the lower Columbia River for thousands of years.

Further Reading: Ames, Kenneth M., and Herbert D. G. Maschner, *Peoples of the Northwest Coast: Their Archaeology and Prehistory* (London: Thames & Hudson, 1999); Ames, Kenneth M., Cameron M. Smith, William L. Cornett, Elizabeth A. Sobel, Stephen C. Hamilton, John Wolf, and Doria Raetz, *Archaeological Investigations at 45CL1 (1991–1996) Ridgefield Wildlife Refuge, Clark County, Washington: A Preliminary Report*, Cultural Resources Series No. 13 (Portland, OR: U.S. Department of the Interior, Fish and Wildlife Service Region 1, 1999); Boyd, Robert T., *The Coming of the Spirit of Pestilence: Introduced Infectious Diseases and Population Decline among Northwest Coast Indians, 1774–1874* (Seattle: University of Washington Press, 1999a); Hajda, Yvonne, "Regional Social Organization in the Greater Lower Columbia, 1792–1830," Ph.D. diss. (University of Washington, 1984); Smith, Cameron M., "The Social Organization of Production in Three Protohistoric Lower-Columbia River Plankhouses," Ph.D. diss. (Simon Fraser University, 2004); Sobel, Elizabeth A., "Social Complexity and Corporate Households on the Southern Northwest Coast, A.D. 1400 1840," Ph.D. diss. (University of Michigan, 2004).

Kenneth M. Ames and Virginia Parks

FORT VANCOUVER NATIONAL HISTORIC SITE

Vancouver, Washington

British and American Trade Center in the Northwest

During the critical period of transition between pre-contact Native American cultures and settlement by American immigrants via the Oregon Trail, Fort Vancouver was the center of the British presence in the Pacific Northwest (ca. 1825–60). In 1849 it also became the first permanent U.S. military post in the region, serving as its departmental headquarters, quartermaster's depot, and arsenal (1849–48). Since 1947 archaeologists have explored the remarkable material record of these two large, overlapping sites, addressing issues of Native American contact, cultural diversity, immigration, economic exchange, medical practices, architecture, and the material culture of the fur trade and U.S. Army periods.

There is a poorly known pre-contact component at Fort Vancouver (from approximately 3,000 years ago to about 1792) demonstrating that American Indians used the Fort Plain prairie next to the Columbia River for hunting, gathering, and probably other activities. Artifacts, including stone projectile points and tools, net weights, and fire-cracked rock, are typical of semi-sedentary villages or fishing campsites of the lower Columbia River.

Fort Vancouver was the headquarters of the Hudson's Bay Company's Columbia Department, which stretched from Russian Alaska to Mexican California and from the Rocky Mountains to the Hawa'ian (Sandwich) Islands. In the 1830s and 1840s, it was the largest and most diverse colonial settlement in the Pacific Northwest, rivaling both San Francisco (Yerba Buena), California, and Sitka (New Archangel), Alaska. The fort was also the supply depot from which the Hudson's Bay Company distributed goods from annual supply ships to other trading posts throughout the region. Company employees—also known as engages—collected, cleaned, and packed furs, especially beaver pelts, at the fort for transport back to England.

Because of the parent company's remoteness, the difficulty of supply from Europe and eastern Canada, and the remarkable set of natural resources of the area, Chief Factor John McLoughlin (who is now revered as the father of the Oregon Territory), diversified the company into a variety of industries. These included lumbering, salmon pickling, shipbuilding, and agriculture. Such pursuits produced food and other products to supply employees, along with surplus to sell to the Russians in Alaska, the Hawai'ians, and the American immigrants. Fort Vancouver supplied European goods, food, and agricultural stock to employees at the fort and the other far-flung posts of the company, and to the missionaries (starting in 1834 with Jason Lee) and the stream of American settlers who flooded the area in the 1840s and 1850s.

Louis Caywood was the first archaeologist to work at Fort Vancouver (1947–55). His excavations relocated the 1829–60 stockade, which enclosed an area of 2.2 hectares (5.4 acres) at its maximum extent. He discovered traces of the site's structures, including the Chief Factor's house (home of John McLoughlin, James Douglas, and other company managers), kitchen, clerk's apartments, offices, warehouses, powder magazine, sale shop, trade store, jail, blacksmith shop, carpenter's shop, bake house, wells, privies, belfry, and bastion. Through the years, other National Park Service, academic, and contract archaeologists have explored architectural and artifact remains of the fur trade post. They have documented distinctive features of French-Canadian styles of architecture and recovered a wealth of fur-trade artifacts.

Outside the stockade, the employees' village was home to an incredible diversity of people thrown together by the fur trade, including Native Hawai'ians, French-Canadians, Scots, Americans, English people, and over thirty-five different Native American tribes.

The village site has yielded hundreds of thousands of artifacts—including transfer print ceramics, Chinese-export porcelain, clay tobacco pipes, glass bottles, window glass, beads, musket balls, and gunflints—deposited by the estimated population of 600 to 1,000 people during peak periods. Archaeologists have typically found traditional American Indian items, including stone projectile points, stone pipes, lithic debitage, and fire-cracked rock features in association with the Euro-American and Chinese manufactured items.

Beginning with Susan Kardas and Edward Larrabee's excavations of 1968 and 1969, explorations of the village have uncovered fifteen of the estimated forty to sixty house sites, as well as roads, fence lines, and other features. Excavations in the 1970s by David and Jennifer Chance and Caroline Carley at the Hudson's Bay Company riverside complex revealed the remains of a hospital and boat works. More recently, Larry Conyers, Kendal McDonald, and Keith Garnett have examined the Hudson's Bay Company cemetery through remote sensing and cartographic studies. Archaeologists are just beginning to address the extensive gardens, fields, and other outbuildings of the Fort Vancouver stockade and village through explorations of the landscape.

Investigations of the U.S. military post have been conducted by a variety of researchers. Excavations have found remains of some of the officers' quarters, barracks, laundress's quarters, corrals, shops, bandstands, warehouses, military hospitals, and the 1850 quartermaster's ranch, at the time known as the finest house in the Pacific Northwest. Captain Ulysses S. Grant stayed with Rufus Ingalls at the quartermaster's ranch during his time at Fort Vancouver before the Civil War. Robert Cromwell and Douglas Wilson have explored the remains of a stockaded sutler's store. The latter contains distinctive French transfer print ceramics and a privy filled with demolition debris and other refuse related to the operation of the first sutler's store. Notably, Captain Ulysses S. Grant was an investor in the store prior to the Civil War.

Archaeologists have uncovered the remains of a large lumber mill from World War I (1917–18) within and outside the stockade site. This U.S. Army mill prepared spruce lumber for transport to aviation factories in Europe and in the eastern United States to support the war effort. It altered the early twentieth-century lumber industry in the Pacific Northwest by modernizing the technologies of harvesting and milling. It also left a lasting impact on labor practices by changing the dynamic between worker and company owner.

Excavations have determined that the army placed about 30 centimeters of fill on top of the nineteenth-century deposits to provide a platform for the railroad lines and buildings, effectively capping and protecting portions of the earlier archaeological record. Remnants of footings, drainage features, the sawdust burner, and other features of the large industrial complex remain below the ground surface.

Archaeologists have uncovered traces of the regional headquarters of the Civilian Conservation Corps (CCC,

Archaeological field school excavations at the powder magazine site inside the reconstructed fort stockade.   [Douglas C. Wilson]

1933–42), revealing footings, roads, and artifacts associated with the facilities that General George C. Marshall commanded as one of his Army postings prior to World War II. Archaeologists have also discovered remains of World War II (1941–45) training facilities. U.S. military artifacts that span the period from the establishment of the post in 1849 to the end of World War II have been collected and analyzed.

Material culture from the site includes the largest excavated collection of mid-nineteenth-century Spode ceramics; over 150 varieties of glass trade beads; British wrought and machine-cut nails; abundant finished iron objects and partially finished iron debitage from the manufacture of a variety of fur trade, agricultural, and utilitarian blacksmith items (including iron trade axes and beaver traps); knives; musket balls; gunflints and military cartridges; uniform parts; and a wealth of other Hudson's Bay Company and U.S. Army items. The collection consists of nearly 2 million artifacts that represent the largest assemblage of excavated Hudson's Bay

Company artifacts in the world and a significant assemblage of U.S. military items.

The site area is located entirely within Fort Vancouver National Historic Site and the Vancouver National Historic Reserve. Visitors can view archaeological artifacts on display in the visitors' center at the eastern edge of the Vancouver Barracks parade ground and in the fur store within the reconstructed Fort Vancouver stockade. A number of interpretive signs display information about the history and archaeology of the fort site and barracks. Visitors can observe archaeologists and museum curators and technicians working on artifacts at the fur store, and an interactive children's exhibit is available inside the counting house. Public access to the collections is available through special programs, exhibits, Web features, and online databases that illustrate the variety of Hudson's Bay Company and U.S. Army artifacts. Exhibits on the Spruce Mill and aviation history are located in Pearson Air Museum, east of the reconstructed fort. Self-guided walking tours and inter-pretive panels discuss facets of the archaeology and history of the site. During summer, field schools from local universities (led by park archaeologists) investigate portions of the site. Digs are open to the public, and students and staff actively share their activities with visitors. Children between the ages of 8 and 12 are encouraged to participate in the periodic Kids Digs programs, where park rangers and archaeologists teach the techniques and preservation ethic of archaeology using a mock dig. There is an avocational program where the interested public can volunteer in the archaeological laboratory and curation facility and participate in the ongoing archaeological investigations.

Further Reading: Johnson, Dennis, "A Stockade of Archaeological Riches," *American Archaeology* 7(1) (2003): 30–37; National Park Service, *Archaeology at Fort Vancouver*, site bulletin (Vancouver, WA: Fort Vancouver National Historic Site, 2003); National Park Service, Fort Vancouver Web site, http://www.nps.gov/fova/planyourvisit/brochures.htm (online May 2008); Ross, Lester A., "Trade Beads from Hudson's Bay Company Fort Vancouver (1829–1860), Vancouver, Washington," *Beads* 2 (1990): 29–67.

Douglas C. Wilson

WILLAPA BAY, OLYMPIC NATIONAL PARK, AND THE MAKAH RESERVATION

The Pacific Coast of Washington State

Outstanding Preservation at the Ozette Site

The outer coast of the state of Washington occupies a prominent position in the southern northwest coast region of North America. In early historic and late prehistoric times, it supported cultures that had sophisticated maritime adaptations and advanced artistic and technological traditions. The antiquity of these cultures is not known.

The outer coast of Washington is an approximately 150-mile coast (241 km) of marked environmental contrasts. The northern half is the Olympic coast—a steep, rugged region of rocky shores and exposed open beaches backed by dense forests and hilly terrain. Much of the area is either within the Olympic National Park, the Olympic Coast National Marine Sanctuary, or six Native American reservations. In contrast, most of the southern Washington coast is a broad, flat plain broken by two large saltwater bays. As such, the southern Washington coast is considerably more developed than areas farther to the north.

All of the early historic Native peoples of the Washington coast expressed the broader Northwest Coast culture of this area. Still, some more localized patterns are apparent. Most of the occupants of the large southern bays—the Willapa, Shoalwater, and lower Chehalis peoples—are Coast Salish speakers who are related to the Native peoples of the nearby Puget Sound basin. The southernmost of the Olympic coast peoples—the Quinault and Queets Indians—are also Coast Salish. The next to the north are the Hoh and Quileute Indians. These closely related groups speak an isolated language that is distinct from any of the large language families on the northwest coast. Finally, the northernmost of the outer Washington coast Native peoples are the Makah. The Makah are closely related to the Nuu-Chah-Nulth (formerly Nootkan) peoples on nearby Vancouver Island.

European and Euro-American interest in this region came relatively late by continental standards. Spanish explorers began to investigate the area in the mid-eighteenth century and even briefly maintained a small fort in 1792 at what is now Neah Bay on the Makah reservation. Shortly afterward, the Pacific Fur Company (and later the Hudson's Bay Company) operated out of the mouth of the Columbia River, just to the south. Despite this, there was no significant non-Native settlement on the Washington coast until after 1850. By this time, British claims to the region had been extinguished, and the area was a part of the Washington Territory. Treaties with the western Washington tribes were signed in 1855–56, and the Washington Territory became a state in 1889. Until recently the major economic activities in the area were logging and fishing. These remain significant today, but recreational interests and eco-tourism are increasingly important.

The first written accounts of archaeological sites in this region date to the 1910s. Despite this early start, however, research efforts lagged until relatively recently, and it is probably the case that more than 80 percent of all the research effort has occurred in the last 35 years or so. Our data from this region is also geographically skewed. An overwhelming majority of the data reflects the northern end of the Olympic coast. Only relatively limited information is available about the archaeology of the southern Washington coast, or even the southern Olympic coast. Finally, while we know that people have been in Washington for at least 12,000 years, nearly all of the known sites reflect occupation during the last 2,000 to 4,000 years.

Slightly more than 100 archaeological sites have been recorded on the outer coast of Washington. This number does not actually represent the total inventory of sites present. Rather, we should consider it a reflection of both the region's difficult environmental conditions and the relatively short period within which active work has occurred. The vast majority of the sites are shell middens—accumulations of marine shell, animal bones, and other occupation refuse that may represent a number of different types of settlements ranging from large, multi-season villages to smaller, more specialized camps and processing locations. Present in much smaller quantities are sites where only chipped-stone artifacts are preserved, where images have been carved into beach rocks, where alignments of rocks have been built, and where stands of old-growth cedar trees show evidence of the collection of bark and or wood. Beyond these, there are also a few sites where waterlogged ground conditions have resulted in the preservation of normally perishable plant fiber artifacts. In contrast, relatively few recorded historical archaeological sites are located here. Most of the latter are built features associated with early historic structures, such as homesteads, railroad grades, and lighthouses.

Only a small number of sites on the southern Washington coast have been studied in detail. The best known of these is the Martin site, a shell midden deposit located on the Long Beach Peninsula, between Willapa Bay and the ocean. This site was first investigated by Robert Kidd in the 1950s, and subsequently by Robert Shaw. The site is thought to contain two prehistoric components representing occupation during the last 2,000 years or so. The deposits are rich in the remains of a wide variety of marine and terrestrial animals. The deposits also contain small, triangular chipped-stone arrowheads and a variety of other ground-stone, bone, and shell artifacts.

The situation is more complex on the northern Washington coast. Many of the sites here are relatively recent late prehistoric shell middens, similar to the Martin site. In contrast to the latter, however, the more northerly late prehistoric sites lack chipped-stone artifacts, and their faunal assemblages are much more heavily dominated by marine animals.

The best-known site in the region is Ozette at Cape Alava. This site, representing one of the traditional villages of the Makah people, is a large shell midden. The village was partially covered by a mudslide about 300 years ago. The portion covered by the slide is waterlogged and contains large number of perishable plant fiber artifacts, including baskets, cordage, fishhooks, harpoons, boxes, bowls, and structural remains. A large-scale effort conducted here in the 1970s by Richard Daugherty of Washington State University, in coordination with the Makah tribe and the Olympic National Park, completely excavated three longhouses, producing one of the largest single collections of prehistoric artifacts from anywhere on the northwest coast. As a wet site, Ozette yielded a collection that includes many types of artifacts that do not occur in most sites in the area. Extensive study of the Ozette materials, combined with traditional knowledge from the Makah people, have offered many important insights into the economy and technology of the late prehistoric Makah people.

Recent archaeological efforts on the northern Washington coast have expanded researchers' focus to investigate older sites. David Conca, Olympic National Park, has investigated chipped-stone sites at Lake Ozette (near Cape Alava); and Gary Wessen, working with the Makah Cultural and Research Center, has been investigating older shell middens on the Makah Indian Reservation that appear to be associated with an earlier sea level stand. Conca's sites have not been dated, but there is reason to suspect that they represent occupation between around 5,000 and 9,000 years ago. The older shell midden sites represent occupation between around 1,500 and 4,500 years ago.

While most of this research has been conducted by university or government-based archaeologists, recent years have seen important changes in this trend. Most notable has been the experience of the Makah tribe. When Daugherty excavated at Ozette in the 1970s, many Makah people were closely involved with the work. The Ozette artifacts were treated and stored in Neah Bay. The Makah tribe eventually developed the Makah Cultural and Research Center (MCRC), which opened in 1979. The MCRC includes extensive visitor galleries, where Ozette artifacts and other important Makah objects are on display. The institution also supports a Makah language program and other cultural activities. Most recently, the MCRC developed a Makah Tribal Historic Preservation Office, which manages cultural resources on the reservation, including archaeological research.

Given the region's environmental conditions and limited development, few opportunities exist for the public to visit archaeological sites on the outer coast of Washington. The principal exception to this is Ozette; both the site and the MCRC are open to the public. The Ozette site may be reached by trail from Lake Ozette in the Olympic National Park. Round trip, the hike to Cape Alava is 8 miles (13 km) long. While the excavations were closed in 1980 and there is minimal interpretive information at the site, the site is still worth the trip. The MCRC in Neah Bay is a spectacular facility that should be visited by everyone, regardless of whether they've been to Cape Alava. The MCRC exhibits show the richness of the Ozette materials and offer large dioramas, including a full-sized longhouse replica that one can enter and explore. Numerous documents describing aspects of Ozette and other regional sites are available at the MCRC gift shop.

Further Reading: Kidd, Robert S., "The Martin Site, Southwestern Washington," *Tebiwa* 10(2): 13–29; Samuels, Stephan R., ed., *Ozette Archaeological Project Research Reports, Volume I* (Pullman: Washington State University Department of Anthropology and the National Park Service, 1991); Wessen, Gary C., "Prehistory of the Ocean Coast of Washington," in *Handbook of North American Indians,* Vol. 7: *Northwest Coast,* edited by Wayne P. Suttles (Washington, DC: Smithsonian Institution, 1990), 412–421; Wessen, Gary C., *An Assessment and Plan for a Program of Studies Addressing Prehistoric Archaeological Sites Associated with Paleoshorelines on the Olympic Coast of Washington* (Neah Bay, WA: Makah Cultural and Research Center, 2003).

Gary C. Wessen

SAN JUAN ISLANDS NATIONAL HISTORICAL PARK

Puget Sound and Juan de Fuca Strait, Coastal Washington State
Shell Midden, Subsistence, and Lithic-Technology Studies

The San Juan Islands are part of an archipelago in the Salish Sea, north of Puget Sound, between Vancouver Island and the Washington coast. Prehistoric peoples inhabited this region by at least 4,000 years ago. They were fishers, hunters, and gatherers who relied on marine mammals, fish, and shellfish, as well as plants and terrestrial animals. The archaeology of the San Juan Islands centers on shell midden sites—piles of refuse that contain shell—because they are the most numerous and visible type of site in this area.

The English Camp shell midden is one of the most extensively studied sites on the islands and is open to the public as part of San Juan Island National Historical Park. Analyses of archaeological materials from this site have provided key insights into prehistoric subsistence and technology.

ENVIRONMENTAL SETTING

The San Juan Islands consist of a concentration of over 400 small islands. They offer a diversity of habitats, including open saltwater, rocky shorelines, sand and gravel shorelines, lagoons, prairies, open woodland areas, dry coniferous forests, and wet coniferous forests. In the nearshore environment, kelp forests and eelgrass beds provide productive habitats for marine plants and animals. Sockeye salmon run through the San Juan Islands each year on their way to spawn in the Fraser River. Sea level in the San Juans has been relatively stable since the Early Holocene. Small changes documented in the Late Holocene are likely attributable to seismic activity associated with earthquakes that originate in the Cascadia subduction zone, where the oceanic Juan de Fuca Plate meets the continental North American Plate.

SETTLEMENT PATTERNS AND SOCIAL SYSTEMS

Archaeologists hypothesize that prehistoric people in the Gulf of Georgia increased their emphasis on marine resources and developed traits associated with more complex sociopolitical organization beginning in the Locarno Beach phase (4,500–2,500 years ago). Such trends as craft specialization; social inequality; and an increase in population density, settlement size, and permanence are thought to have intensified during the Marpole phase (2,500–1,000 years ago). The San Juan period (which followed) was similar, but there may have been changes in technology, including a decrease in emphasis on stone-tool technology. A recent study on settlement patterns in the San Juan Islands indicates a dramatic increase in

number of sites at 1,000–500 years ago, suggesting either an increase in population or a change in settlement patterns in which people established more small campsites for food-procurement activities.

THE HISTORIC PERIOD

First contact between the indigenous inhabitants of the San Juan Islands and Europeans occurred in 1792, during Spanish explorations in search of the Northwest Passage.

The British voyaged in this area throughout the 1790s with the expeditions of Vancouver and Broughton. They reported few encounters with Native peoples, likely due to a smallpox epidemic in the 1780s. Throughout the Puget Sound area, coastal groups were decimated by disease by 1800. A full-scale European settlement in the San Juan Islands did not begin until after the 1840s. At this time, the British Hudson's Bay Company established a farm there, and logging began on Lopez Island.

The 1850s and 1860s were characterized by a boundary dispute between the British and the United States, with military outposts for both groups on San Juan Island. The issue was resolved in favor of the United States in 1871 in an agreement arbitrated by Kaiser Wilhelm I of Germany as part of the Treaty of Washington. Interactions with Europeans altered the lifeways of the Native peoples of the San Juan Islands, but their descendants—known by anthropologists as the Coast Salish—continue marine-oriented subsistence practices and stewardship of the land.

THE ENGLISH CAMP SITE

Recent efforts to understand the subsistence behavior and technology of prehistoric peoples of the San Juan Islands have focused on the English Camp site, a large shell midden site on Garrison Bay that was occupied from approximately 2,000–300 years ago. It consists of a large midden area beneath the historic British parade grounds (Operation A) and a U-shaped ridge made from shell piles in a nearby forested area (Operation D). In total the site is over 300 meters long and over 4 meters deep.

The first excavation of English Camp was a University of Washington field-school project conducted by Adan Treganza in 1950. Throughout the 1970s, Roderick Sprague and Stephen Kenady led National Park Service–funded investigations at English Camp—efforts that were continued by Jim Thomson, Bryn Thomas, and colleagues at San Juan Islands

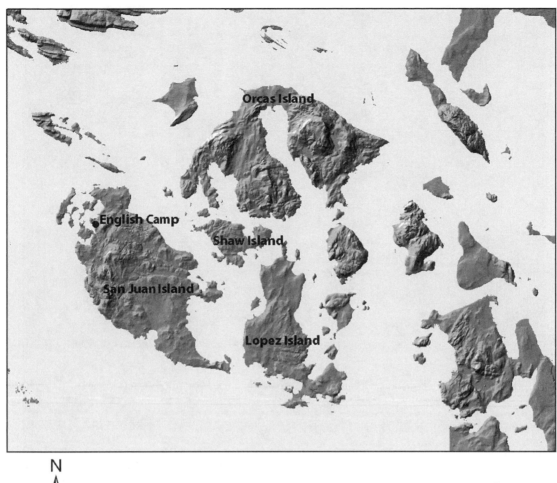

A map of the San Juan Islands, Washington.   [Amanda K. Taylor]

National Historical Park in the 1980s, in order to investigate the historic landscape. Julie Stein conducted the San Juan Island Archaeological Project (SJIAP) from 1983 to 1991 as the University of Washington field school, focusing her research on geo-archaeological and chronological problems.

PREHISTORIC SUBSISTENCE AT ENGLISH CAMP
Based on analyses by University of Washington undergraduate and graduate students, many different taxa of mammals were identified at English Camp, including deer, elk, dogs, wolves, foxes, and rodents. Aquatic and terrestrial birds are also present, although they are rare. An analysis of fish remains suggests that salmon, herring, and dogfish were the dominant taxa, and the shellfish assemblage includes bentnose clam, littleneck clam, and cockle.

Research that focuses specifically on zooarchaeological work has also been conducted by Kristine Bovy at the

Watmough Bay site, on Lopez Island. She finds that between around 1,650–1,250 years ago, people shifted their hunting efforts from juvenile cormorants to diving ducks. This may be because colonies of cormorants moved farther from Watmough Bay to avoid human hunting.

TECHNOLOGY AT ENGLISH CAMP
Prehistoric peoples of the San Juan Islands focused their flint-knapping technology on the manufacture and use of bifacial (flaked on both sides) and flake tools made from fine-grained volcanic rock. A wide range of flaked tools have been found in this area, including flake tools and knives, microblades (blades less than 2 cm long), bifaces, and projectile points. People also manufactured large stone mauls; adzes and wedges thought to be associated with the use of cedar for plank houses and clothing; and celts, labrets, sinkers, antler points, and harpoons. The variety in artifacts present on the San Juan

Excavations at Operation A during the 1984 SJIAP field school.   [Amanda K. Taylor]

Islands attests to a wide range of daily activities, including woodworking and plant and animal resource procurement and processing.

Stone tool assemblages at the English Camp site on San Juan Island include two kinds of diagnostic projectile points: stemmed points, which date to about 4,500–1,500 years ago; and triangular points, which appear around 2,500 years ago. Detailed investigations of the stone tools and debitage (waste product from flint knapping) at this site have provided valuable insights into change over time in manufacturing techniques and daily activities.

Using collections from the SJIAP excavations, University of Washington graduate student Kim Kornbacher analyzed the stone tools and debitage from the Operation A area of the English Camp site and compared lithic artifacts from assemblages before and after 1,000 years ago. She found that at approximately 1,000 years ago, there was a rapid decrease in abundance of flaked-stone tools, an overall increase in tool types and ground-stone tools, and that microblades disappeared from the archaeological record.

A recent study of the flaked-stone tools at Operation D at English Camp by Angela Close presents a chaîne-operatoire approach, where the analyst focuses on the ways of life of prehistoric peoples by studying the life histories of the artifacts. This begins with the procurement of the lithic raw material, continues through the manufacture and use of the tools, and proceeds through the discarding of the tool.

Close suggests that the people at English Camp brought fine-grained volcanic material to English Camp in the form of small, unworked pebbles. Based on spatial patterns in the discard of finished tools and waste products from the manufacturing process, Close makes an interpretation that if men were associated with triangular points while women relied on flake tools and scaled pieces, they worked in different areas of the site, with women doing most of the tool manufacture. She finds some evidence of more experienced flint knappers teaching novices how to make stone tools, and she speculates that the people at English Camp participated in trade relations with other groups.

ENGLISH CAMP TODAY

The English Camp site is part of San Juan Island National Historical Park. Information on archaeology is available to the public at the American Camp Visitors Center, on the southern part of the island. Tours of the site are provided to the public during the summer by National Park archaeologists. Artifacts from English Camp can also be viewed at the Burke Museum of Natural History and Culture, on the University of Washington campus.

ACKNOWLEDGMENTS

We thank Phoebe Anderson, Cristie Boone, Kris Bovy, and Bob Kopperl for information from their research on the zooarchaeology of English Camp, and Adam Freeburg for creating the map of the San Juan Islands.

Further Reading: Bovy, Kristine M., "Effects of Human Hunting, Climate Change and Tectonic Events on Waterbirds along the Pacific Northwest Coast during the Late Holocene," Ph.D. diss. (University of Washington, 2006); Carlson, Roy L., "Chronology and Culture Change in the San Juan Islands, Washington," *American Antiquity* 25(1960): 562–586; Close, Angela E., *Finding the People Who Flaked the Stone at English Camp (San Juan Island)* (Salt Lake City: University of Utah Press, 2006); MacDonald, Lucile S., *Making History: The People Who Shaped the San Juan Islands* (Friday Harbor, WA: Harbor Press, 1990); San Juan Island National Historical Park, National Park Service Web site, http://www.nps.gov/sajh; Stein, Julie K. (ed.), *Deciphering a Shell Midden* (San Diego, CA: Academic Press Inc., 1992); Stein, Julie K., *Exploring Coast Salish Prehistory: The Archaeology of San Juan Island* (Seattle: University of Washington Press, 2000); Vouri, Michael, *The Pig War: Standoff at Griffin Bay* (Friday Harbor, WA: Griffin Bay Bookstore, 1999).

Julie Stein and Amanda K. Taylor

VANCOUVER ISLAND AND LOWER FRASER VALLEY SITES

Southern British Columbia Coast

Abundant Resources and Settled Maritime Hunter-Gatherers

Northwest coast peoples have inhabited the southern coast of British Columbia since the glaciers began to recede during the Quaternary period, over 10,000 years ago. These hunter-gatherers have long maintained a way of life centered around the coast and its rivers. Archaeological sites are found predominantly along the coasts—often in the form of shell middens, which are thick layers of village trash deposits that can be several meters deep. Other settlement sites are located at confluences and turns of the Fraser River at areas near fishing spots and access routes into the mountain forests.

Each year, particularly in late summer and early fall, large salmon runs return and swim hundreds of miles up the river, and northwest coast groups created a variety of methods to rein in catches to dry and store. These preserved fish then were used throughout the rest of the year. The temperate rain-forests contained extensive stands of cedar, which provided the raw material for constructing houses, nets, baskets, and clothing. Chiefs used surpluses generated from the coast and forests to put on great feasts and potlatch ceremonies. Many sites contain items given or traded at such events; trade networks extended from the islands and upriver into the mainland. One should consider northwest coast sites not with a land-based perspective, but with an eye toward the past orientation to the water. The Coast Salish and Nuu-chah-nulth peoples in these territories relied heavily upon the water for subsistence and as their primary mode of travel by canoe.

According to one theory, the first inhabitants of the region are even thought to have arrived thousands of years ago by water—traveling from the north along the coastline. Archaeologists have evidence for early coastal sites that suggest a pattern of island migration from northeastern Asia and down the Alaskan coast into the waters of British Columbia. Glaciers may have covered most of the landscape on the continent—enough to actually lower the sea level. Islands and parts of the coast are thought to have provided refuge along the route. Early sites are documented in the north, in the Queen Charlotte Islands, and in the islands of southeastern Alaska. But in southern British Columbia, the sites are located on the mainland coast and along the lower Fraser River. The subsistence base of the people living at southern sites appears to have been more reliant upon terrestrial rather than marine resources. For this reason, some of the earliest peoples also are thought to have arrived by a land route over the Bering Strait (available due to the lower sea level) and around the Cordilleran ice sheet during the latest years of glaciation, from 13,000 to 11,000 years ago.

In the Fraser River canyon, the Milliken site documents the earliest site in the region, dating to 9,000 years ago. Other early sites include Glenrose, further downriver, and Bear Cove, located on northeast Vancouver Island. These early sites contained large, leaf-shaped knives and spear points, along with a tool kit of large cobble tools. Since the Milliken site was occupied along the narrows of the Fraser River in summer—a peak time for salmon—it appears that fishing for salmon extends back to the site's earliest inhabitants, even if it may not have been a primary focus.

The inhabitants kept small camps, and they appear to have ranged widely, indicating a highly nomadic existence. They lived in small, egalitarian groups that drew upon a wide range of resources, with land mammals outnumbering sources from the sea. Archaeologists refer to these people as belonging to the Old Cordilleran culture of the Archaic period, which lasted for over 4,000 years (9,000 to 4,500 years ago). During the periods that followed, there was an even more intensive orientation to marine sources.

By 4,500 years ago, beaches showed evidence of large shell middens—soils that are black due to organic content and dense with disposed shells from mussels and clams. This is regarded as the beginning of the early Pacific period in many

areas. Shell middens are characterized by excellent preservation, because the calcium in the shells often maintains bone materials in soils that are otherwise quite acidic and destructive to most organic artifacts. Evidence for antler and bone tool use at this time, however, increases and continues to increase with each millennium.

Around 2,000 years ago, large village settlements became common, with cedar-plank houses often 10 by 15 meters in size—and even much larger if associated with individuals of higher social status. Although the settlement inhabitants had large residential villages, their lifestyles were still semi-nomadic at this time, with extended seasonal forays away from the villages for hunting and fishing within various family camps from spring to fall. During winter households gathered in the residential villages. Such large villages are unusual for foragers, whose way of life is typically too nomadic to allow the building of residences in any one location or the storage of surplus foods and resources; this is one of the reasons the Northwest Coast peoples are known as complex hunter-gatherers.

Nearly all the wood for their houses came from one species of wood: western red cedar (*Thuja plicata*). This tree was of such immense utility to these people that it was regarded as sacred. In fact the range of western red cedar approximates the boundary of the Northwest Coast cultural area. In part, the wood of the tree was preferred for its resistance to rain and weathering; also, it split easily along the grain, and planks of wood could be split off from standing trees and used for houses and boxes (for cooking or storage). The straight trunks of felled trees were used for carving canoes, house posts, and roof beams. The tree's bark was used for making baskets and clothing, while roots and withes were used to make ropes and nets for fishing and other uses.

In many cases, the scars from cedar gathering have left their mark on trees that remain alive and standing even hundreds of years later. This has resulted in a relatively new type of archaeological site that has been recorded since the 1990s: culturally modified trees, or CMTs. Pioneered by early studies on Meares Island (on the west coast of Vancouver Island), most of these sites consist of bark-stripped trees. But also found at these locales are felled and planked trees and canoe blanks, among other features that date prior to contact, partly because of the long lifespan of cedar, but also because of its rot-resistant nature.

In rare cases, archaeologists have recovered cedar artifacts, such as baskets, tool handles, nets, and boxes. These artifacts are preserved within waterlogged places, called wet sites, that create anaerobic conditions preventing organic deterioration. In the Gulf of Georgia, archaeologists have excavated wet sites at the Musqueam Northeast site, in southern Vancouver, and at Little Qualicum site, on eastern Vancouver Island, as well as in nearby sites in Washington (for example, Ozette and Hoko River). These wet sites document the heavy use of cedar and other organic items. In fact, the vast majority of artifacts at wet sites (more than 90 percent) were made from wood and plant fibers, while the remaining artifacts (less than 10 percent) were made predominantly from shell, bone, or stone.

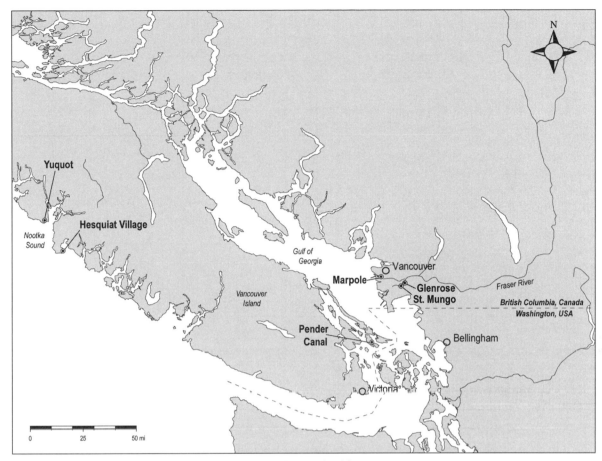

A map of southern British Columbia with sites indicated.   [Bill Angelbeck]

The legacy of archaeological sites on the northwest coast, including middens, wet sites, and culturally modified trees, is important to the descendant First Nation communities, documenting how their ancestors occupied and used traditional territories. In contemporary contexts, the archaeological evidence in the landscape and within the standing forests is especially important for these indigenous groups, since many are still engaged in treaty negotiations with the provincial and federal governments over land claims and use.

Excellent museum exhibits on northwest coast anthropology and archaeology can be seen at the Field Museum in Chicago, the American Museum of Natural History in New York, and the Museum of Civilization near Ottawa. However, museums within the region provide a richer experience. For instance, the Museum of Anthropology at the University of British Columbia in Vancouver is predominantly oriented around Pacific Northwest coastal cultures, including an outdoor exhibit with two plank house structures and numerous memorial and totem poles.

Other cities in southern British Columbia also have regionally focused exhibits, including the Museum of Archaeology and Ethnography at Simon Fraser University and the Royal British Columbia Museum in Victoria. In the Fraser River Valley, near Mission, the Xá:ytem National Historic Site con-

tains a reconstructed pit house, and visitors can walk to a transformer stone called Hatzic Rock, which is sacred to the Coast Salish people for its connection to the mythical time of transformation. Culturally modified tree sites can be viewed in numerous parks in the province and even seen along the trails of Stanley Park in downtown Vancouver.

GLENROSE SITE—SURREY, BRITISH COLUMBIA

The Glenrose site contains the earliest evidence of habitation at a coastal site in the region, dating to about 8,500 years ago. The inhabitants repeatedly used this site from its earliest occupation to about 5,500 years ago, during the Old Cordilleran culture. The Glenrose site appears to be an upriver site, but its situation today (to the southeast of Vancouver) is substantially different from the landscape of 8,000 years ago. The peoples who inhabited Glenrose settled on an overlook above the coast and at the mouth of the Fraser River at a time when sea levels were higher. When the glaciers melted and receded, the Fraser delta filled with sediments that extended the coastline about 19 kilometers westward to where it is today.

The majority of the tool kit is represented by cobble tools—large, water-worn stones that lithic knappers fractured to produce a sharp edge on one side. They also created leaf-shaped

Millennia BP	General Northwest Coast Chronology	Gulf of Georgia Chronology	West Coast Chronology
0	LATE PACIFIC	Historic	Historic
1		Gulf of Georgia	Late West Coast
2		Marpole	
3	MIDDLE PACIFIC	Locarno Beach	Early West Coast
4	EARLY PACIFIC	St. Mungo	
5			
6	ARCHAIC	Old Cordilleran Culture	
7			
8			
9			
10			
11	PALEOINDIAN		
12			

General and regional chronologies for the Gulf of Georgia and the west coast.   [Bill Angelbeck]

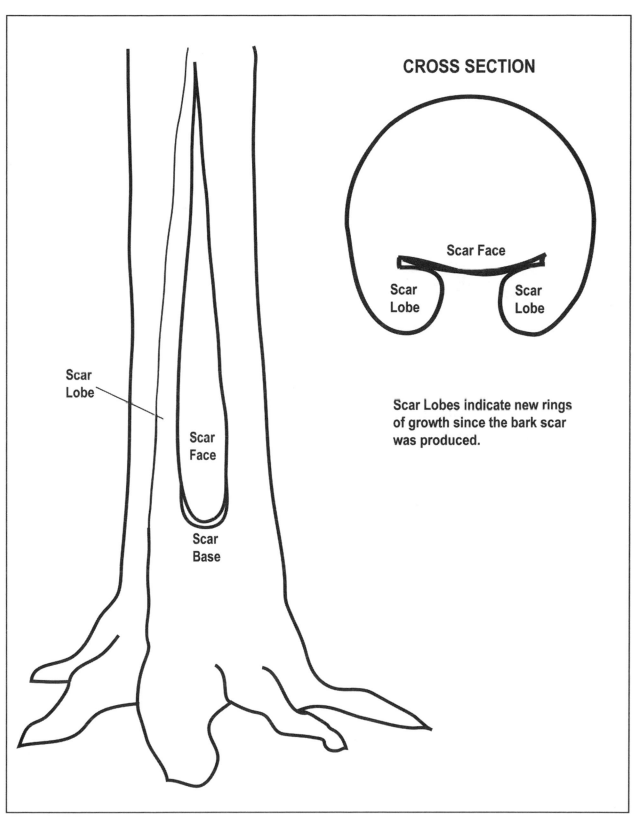

CROSS SECTION

Scar Face

Scar Lobe

Scar Lobe

Scar Lobes indicate new rings of growth since the bark scar was produced.

Scar Lobe

Scar Face

Scar Base

A diagram showing typical features of a standing bark-stripped CMT.   [Bill Angelbeck]

Drawing of a seated-human figurine bowl from the Marpole site. Drawing by Don Welsh.   [Bill Angelbeck]

projectile points and knives, along with smaller contracting-stem points, in addition to a variety of scrapers and flake tools. The faunal remains reveal that the inhabitants occupied the Glenrose site during late spring and early summer as a generalized hunting and fishing camp, with much of the remains coming from land mammals such as elk and deer. Salmon, eulachon (a small fish prized for its high oil content), and bay mussel shells were also used. At other Old Cordilleran sites, such as the Bear Cove site on northeastern Vancouver Island, there is evidence of sea mammal hunting during this period as well. The upper components of the deeply stratified Glenrose site reveal that Salishan peoples occupied the site long after the Old Cordilleran period, which ended around 5,500 years ago.

PENDER CANAL SITE—VANCOUVER, BRITISH COLUMBIA

The earliest indications of a complex hunter-gatherer society in the region began to emerge at the Pender Canal site, located in the southern Gulf Islands between the mainland and Vancouver Island. Elaborate burials are present, including individuals who were treated with greater accord than others—such as those buried with long antler spoons carved with zoomorphic imagery. These burials have been radiocarbon-dated to about 3,600 years ago, during the late Mayne phase.

Burials from a slightly more recent time period, the Locarno Beach phase (which dates from 3,500 to 2,500 years ago), reveal a few individuals buried with a labret, an ornament inserted into a pierced hole in the lower lip. Other individuals reveal wear patterns on the mandible that indicate long-term labret use. Since only a few individuals bear such items, usually in combination with other fine grave goods, some archaeologists have interpreted labrets as symbols of a higher status.

In both components at the site, many features of the Northwest Coast culture of the later historic contact period are present, such as funeral ceremonialism, social ranking, craft specialization, and even sculptural art forms. The Locarno Beach component contained many contracting-stem points, large ground-slate points, bone points for fishing, and toggling harpoon valves. There is evidence of a marked increase in the hunting of sea mammals, in addition to deer, elk, and birds. The initial evidence of social inequality apparent at this time intensified in later periods, particularly during the Marpole phase.

MARPOLE SITE (GREAT FRASER MIDDEN)—VANCOUVER, BRITISH COLUMBIA

The Marpole site contains the remains of a large Salishan village that includes elaborate burials and grave goods. The site is known to the descendant Musqueam community as *cusna'um* (tsis-NAW-im). Strategically situated along the Fraser River confluence on the coast, the people who lived at the Marpole site relied intensively upon the harvesting, drying, and storing of salmon, establishing the practices and way of life that continued into the period of historic contact with Europeans. The storage of salmon undoubtedly contributed to the elaboration of ceremonialism and feasting; in fact, the surpluses allowed people to specialize in crafts and art forms, which at this time appear to foreshadow the distinctive historic Northwest Coast style.

Excavated house floors, village layouts, and arrays of woodworking tools from Marpole and associated sites during that period (about 1,200–2,500 years ago) indicate that the ethnographic Coast Salish plank house has its origins in the building styles of Marpole times. House floors contain large post molds, hearths, and high middens that indicate building outlines often visible today. Typical artifacts included unilaterally barbed harpoons, nipple-topped hand mauls, and chipped-stone points with contracting and expanding stems. Bone artifacts are common: awls, needles, and various points for fishing.

Due to the wide range of unique, stylistic items in the Gulf of Georgia region at this time, it is clear that Marpole peoples participated in a regional exchange network. Items such as seated-figurine bowls (several of which were found at the site), obsidian, dentalia shell beads, and pounded copper items were shared across the region. Some items of high value, such as the carved-stone bowls, appear to have been traded among elites. In fact, the rank of elite individuals appears to have increased at this time. Labrets generally are no longer used; however, cranial deformation—the practice of shaping infants' heads while their skulls are still malleable—became the marker of status. With this symbolic mark permanently applied to infants, some archaeologists interpret the practice as indicative of stratified class.

The site has one of the longest histories of excavation in the province, with collections from the site known in the mid-1880s. In 1938 T. P. O. Menzies (1938, 360) summarized some of the finds from the early excavations, noting that there was a burial of "a man of high rank, and about twenty-two years to twenty-four years of age. The body was encased in sheets of beaten native copper, with a copper crown or band on the head." Menzies also described a Marpole-style seated-human figurine bowl at the apex of a stone cobble pyramid nearly 1.52 meters high—a cairn containing fragments of human bone. In total, over a hundred burials have been excavated from the Marpole site, although mostly from excavations decades ago that do not provide the provenience or context that archaeologists typically record today in their excavations.

Unfortunately the site also has been severely impacted by development associated with the expansion of Vancouver. For this reason, no house depressions are clearly visible today, although such depressions are present at other Marpole phase sites in the region, such as Beach Grove and Dionisio Point (the latter site can be visited at Dionisio Point Provincial Park, a marine access–only park on Galiano Island). The Historic Sites and Monuments Board of Canada declared the Great Fraser Midden a National Historic Site in 1933.

YUQUOT AND HESQUIAT HARBOUR VILLAGE SITES—WEST COAST, VANCOUVER ISLAND, BRITISH COLUMBIA

Yuquot and Hesquiat Harbour Village are two principal sites along the west coast of Vancouver Island. In contrast to the Coast Salish sites discussed above, the cultural emphasis on the west coast centered on the whale instead of salmon in terms of subsistence, economy, and ideology. Among northwest coast groups, whaling was predominantly associated with the Nuu-chah-nulth (formerly known as Nootka). Evidence from these sites indicates that the Nuu-chah-nulth had practiced whaling in their territory for perhaps 3,000 years.

The earliest component in the region was found at the Yuquot site, with dates extending back over 4,200 years ago. Artifact assemblages from West Coast sites are distinctive for the near absence of chipped-stone tools in preference for tools from bone and mussel shell. Ground-stone tools are also rarely found—with the exception of sandstone abraders, which are used to shape bone tools. Artifact assemblages from the early West Coast components (dating to more than 2,000 years ago) include mus-

sel shell knives, a variety of bone points, whalebone harpoon fore-shafts, and unilaterally barbed harpoon heads. The Hesquiat Village site contained materials related to the late West Coast components. The artifacts and features in late components (2,000 to 200 years ago) reveal a high degree of continuity with earlier ones. However, the latter also contain mussel shell celts, bone and stone fishhook shanks, and composite harpoon valves.

Archaeologists have discovered whalebone fragments within the middle component (prior to about 2,000 years ago) at Yuquot, although whether those bones were derived from the hunting of whales or from beached whales is unclear. Large toggling harpoons provide better evidence for whaling, and those are also found at both sites in the later components, which date to the last 1,200 years. One harpoon from Yuquot is decorated with incised motifs that are known ethnographically to spiritually aid the whale hunter.

There are also unique sacred sites to aid whalers in gaining spiritual powers for the hunt. These whaling shrine sites were located near both Yuquot and Hesquiat Village and consisted of a stand of carved wooden human and whale figures, along with human skulls. The shrine at Yuquot was still present in 1904, when it was taken apart and placed in the American Museum of Natural History in New York—a move that remains controversial to Nuu-chah-nulth groups today.

Further Reading: Ames, Kenneth M., and Herbert D. G. Maschner, *Peoples of the Northwest Coast: Their Archaeology and Prehistory* (London: Thames and Hudson, 1999); Burley, David V. Marpole, *Anthropological Reconstructions of a Prehistoric Northwest Coast Culture Type* (Burnaby, BC: Simon Fraser University Department of Archaeology, 1980); Carlson, Keith Thor, ed., *A Sto:lo Coast Salish Historical Atlas* (Vancouver, BC: Douglas and McIntyre, 2001); Carlson, Roy L., and Luke Dalla Bona, eds., *Early Human Occupation in British Columbia* (Vancouver: University of British Columbia Press, 1996); Croes, Dale, "Northwest Coast Wet-Site Artifacts: A Key to Understanding Resource Procurement, Storage, Management, and Exchange," in *Emerging from the Mists: Studies in Northwest Coast Culture History*, edited by R. G. Matson, Gary Coupland, and Quentin Mackie (Vancouver: University of British Columbia Press, 2003), 51–75; Matson, R. G., and Gary Coupland, *The Prehistory of the Northwest Coast* (New York: Academic Press, 1995); McMillan, Alan D., *Since the Time of the Transformers: The Ancient Heritage of the Nuu-chah-nulth, Ditidaht, and Makah* (Vancouver: University of British Columbia Press, 1999); Menzies, T. P. O., "Northwest Coast Middens," *American Antiquity* 3(4) (1938): 359–361; Museum of Anthropology at the University of British Columbia Web site, http://www.moa.ubc.ca (online February 2007); Museum of Archaeology and Ethnography at Simon Fraser University Web site, http://www.sfu.ca/archaeology/museum (online February 2007); Stewart, Hilary, *Stone, Bone, Antler, and Shell: Artifacts of the Northwest Coast*, 2nd ed. (Seattle: University of Washington Press, 1996); Stryd, Arnoud, and Morley Eldridge, "CMT Archaeology in British Columbia: The Meares Island Studies," *BC Studies* 99 (1993): 184–234; Xá:ytem Longhouse Interpretative Centre, Mission, BC, *9,000 Years of History in the Valley of the Stone People*, http://www.xaytem.museum.bc.ca/ancient.htm (online February 2007).

Bill Angelbeck

THE NAMU SITE AND PRINCE RUPERT HARBOR SITE

Northern British Columbia Coast
11,000 Years of Human Adaptation and Settlement

Hundreds of ancient shell midden sites dot the northern British Columbia coast. These sites consist of layers of shell and other occupational debris—often up to several meters deep. Their varied forms and contents tell different stories about the archaeological histories of the indigenous peoples of this region. Some sites, such as Namu, on the central mainland coast, show long-term continuity in settlement. The midden deposits there contain evidence of 11,000 years of culture change and resource use. Others, such as the many large village sites in the vicinity of Prince Rupert Harbor (on the northern mainland coast near the mouth of the Skeena River), show a much more volatile history of village establishment, growth, and abandonment. Their records of house features and village plans tell a story of social change and periodic political turmoil.

NAMU, BRITISH COLUMBIA

Namu, located in the traditional territory of the Heiltsuk Nation, is famous as the oldest continuously occupied site on the coast of British Columbia. It was first settled 11,000 years ago and remained a major settlement up through the time of European contact in the early nineteenth century. Subsequently, the site was a Euro-Canadian settlement established around the operation of a major fish cannery. Now a small remnant of its former size, Namu serves mainly as a stopover for recreational boaters and kayakers and as a base for sport fishing operations.

The extensive shell midden deposits are located on a raised area above the mouth of the small Namu River. The midden deposits once lay partially under a bunkhouse built for cannery workers, which has since been demolished. The site was first excavated in 1968–70 by researchers from the University of Colorado, under the direction of James J. Hester. Subsequent excavations directed by Roy L. Carlson of Simon Fraser University in 1977–78 and 1994 more fully documented the history of culture change and resource use. The Namu site contains a record of flexible and resilient strategies for sustaining settlement through long periods of local cultural development, regional interaction, and environmental change.

The earliest deposits, pre-dating 7,000 years ago, contain no preserved bone or shell, but show ample evidence of stone tool manufacture and a well-developed lithic technology. With increased deposition of shell—and consequently, better preservation—there is evidence of a prevalent bone and antler technology, including small points and a variety of harpoons used for fishing and sea mammal hunting.

Obsidian, a glassy volcanic stone used for making sharp-edged tools, was obtained from as far away as Oregon and the northern and central interior of British Columbia. The consistent presence of small amounts of this material, along with the presence of early stone tool industries initially found farther north, suggest Namu was long a crossroads for the movement of ideas, materials, and people. Its location at the juncture of sheltered passages to the north and south and a long inlet penetrating eastward to the mouth and valley of the Bella Coola River facilitated cultural interaction and exchange.

Continued settlement was also a function of a rich and reliable marine resource base, evident in the preserved shell and bone in deposits dating from 7,000 years ago and onward. The key resources were salmon and herring, supplemented by a wide array of fish, shellfish, and hunted land and sea mammals. Gathered plant foods, including seaweed, roots, and berries, were undoubtedly important as well, though they have left no preserved trace in the midden deposits.

Recent DNA analysis of salmon bone has shown a focus on pink salmon, which is well suited for drying and storage, throughout the last 7,000 years of the site's occupation. Further evidence suggests this fishery may have been subject to periodic shortages in the period after 4,000 years ago. This was a time of increased use of shellfish and various, more marginal resources—and a time when parts of the site were abandoned, and new settlements were established at nearby locations.

The resilience and long-term development of the subsistence economy at Namu and nearby sites is the subject of continuing investigation. Geochemical analysis of shell is being used to detect and to determine the influence of long-term climate change and other environmental shifts. Analysis of shell is also showing evidence for the development of clam resource management strategies.

PRINCE RUPERT HARBOR AND THE LOWER SKEENA RIVER, BRITISH COLUMBIA

Prince Rupert is now an important commercial seaport and fishing center. The protected harbor and nearby highly productive Skeena River salmon fishery were equally important in the past. At the time of European contact, the harbor was the location of a number of major village sites of the Tsimshian Nation, who also seasonally occupied sites on the lower Skeena River.

Sustained archaeological investigations began with a major project initiated in 1966 by the National Museum of Canada (now the Canadian Museum of Civilization) under the direction of George F. MacDonald. Excavations were conducted at several major village sites, including the Boardwalk site in 1968–70. The Prince Rupert project dated the earliest settlements to 5,000 years ago. It documented a rich subsequent archaeological history based on a record of house features, burials, faunal remains, and abundant artifacts, including some elaborate carved objects and rare examples of preserved basketry and wooden items.

Many Prince Rupert Harbor villages were abandoned at some point in their histories—likely, in some cases, the result of conflict with the Tlingit Nation to the north. Oral histories document a series of conflicts between the Tlingit and Tsimshian over control of the rich Skeena and Nass River salmon and eulachon fisheries. A weapons cache and burial evidence of injuries due to interpersonal violence further attest to the scale of conflict. In many cases, village abandonment has left clear impressions of the platforms for ancient houses on the site surface. This unique attribute provides a record of village organization and changes in social inequality over time.

The earliest record of house structures and village organization comes from the Paul Mason site (located at Kitselas Canyon, some 160 kilometers up the Skeena River). Investigations by Gary Coupland in the early 1980s recorded the outlines of ten rectangular houses dating to 3,000 years ago. The relatively small and equal size of the structures suggested that social differences between household groups were not pronounced at this time.

Detailed mapping of the surface features of sites in Prince Rupert Harbor by David J. W. Archer has provided a clear indication of when differences in household rank emerged. He mapped the visible house platforms at eleven sites with final occupations dating to between 2,500 and 1,500 years ago. Archer found an abrupt shift around AD 100 from villages consisting of a single row of equal-size houses to villages more typical of the ethnographic period—consisting of multiple rows of houses, with larger houses fronting the shoreline and smaller houses in one or two rows behind. The implication is a shift from a relatively egalitarian society to one much more highly structured and ranked according to household and individual status. Further understanding of the basis for the emergence of ranked society in the area is the focus of continuing research by Coupland, who has conducted extensive excavations within house platforms at the McNichol Creek site.

Most sites on the northern British Columbia coast are not easily accessible. They also typically show very little to the untrained eye, though eroded foreshore exposures may show layers of shell and other cultural deposits. Namu and the Prince Rupert Harbor sites are the subjects of major museum displays and virtual exhibits accessible through the Internet. An array of artifacts and a reconstructed section of the Namu excavations are on display at the Simon Fraser University Museum of Archaeology and Ethnology in Burnaby, British Columbia. The Canadian Museum of Civilization in Hull, Quebec, has a major exhibit on the Prince Rupert Harbor sites, including a reconstruction of excavations at the Boardwalk site. An exhibit of artifacts from Namu is on display at the Heiltsuk Cultural Education Center in the small Heiltsuk community of Bella Bella, and exhibits of archaeological materials from local excavations are on display at the Museum of Northern British Columbia, in Prince Rupert.

Further Reading: Ames, Kenneth M., and Herbert D. G. Maschner, *Peoples of the Northwest Coast: Their Archaeology and Prehistory* (London: Thames and Hudson, 1999); Canadian Museum of Civilization—Boardwalk Site Excavation, www.civilization.ca/aborig/tsimsian/arcexcae.html; Carlson, Roy L., and Luke Dalla Bona, eds., *Early Human Occupation in British Columbia* (Vancouver: University of British Columbia Press, 1996); Cybulski, Jerome S., ed., *Perspectives on Northern Northwest Coast Prehistory* (Hull, QC: Canadian Museum of Civilization, 2001); Simon Fraser University Museum of Archaeology and Ethnology—Namu, http://www.sfu.ca/archaeology/museum/bc/namu_src/index.htm.

Aubrey Cannon

NORTH POINT, HIDDEN FALLS, GROUNDHOG BAY, AND OTHER SITES

Southeastern Alaska

Earliest Sites to Historic Times on a Rugged, Lush Coast

Southeast Alaska is substantially made up of land managed by federal and state agencies. The largest of these is the 17 million–acre (6.8 million–hectare) Tongass National Forest, which makes up approximately 80 percent of the region. The remainder is a patchwork of lands owned by Native corporations, municipal governments, individuals, and conservation agencies (national parks, monuments, wildlife refuges, and recreation areas). Many tribal governments in southeast Alaska are involved actively with federal and state land managers in cultural research and preservation.

Comprising most of North America's only temperate rainforest, the area has a maritime climate, with heavy precipitation and cool temperatures resulting in thick coastal forests. In many areas, the rugged coastline rises abruptly from sea level to the coastal mountain range. In addition to the resources of the forests, ocean, and tidelands, rivers and smaller drainages support several species of Pacific salmon.

Southeast Alaska is also a geologically active region. Its coastlines have been influenced by several processes relevant to the archaeology of the region, including glacial erosion, deposition of glacial drift, and sea level changes due to glacial withdrawal, tectonic movement, and seismic activity.

One important factor in southeast Alaska archaeology is the fact that parts of the region were either thinly glaciated or continually ice free during the late Pleistocene, forming glacial refugia that could have supported human life. Another is that glacial movements and sea level histories were localized, so archaeologists have no single timeline of glacial advance, glacial retreat, or sea level change. Recent paleontological studies of southeast-Alaska caves have provided archaeologists with important information about southeast Alaska's glacial history and paleo-environments.

Ethnographically, southeast Alaska is at the northern end of the Northwest Coast culture area, which includes several distinct cultures that share a way of life oriented to coastal resources and a complex social organization involving clans and moieties. Today the Tlingit, Haida, Tsimshian, and Eyak claim traditional lands in southeast Alaska. A detailed discussion of the cultures of the region can be found in the Smithsonian Institution's *Handbook of North American Indians* volume on the northwest coast (Suttles 1990).

Southeast Alaska is at the heart of new interpretations of the peopling of the Americas. In the past, the most widely held theories explaining the human settlement of the New World focused on an early west to east Beringian migration, followed by a north to south interior migration. Many archeologists now acknowledge the possibility that migration was more complex and may have included—or even begun—with migration along deglaciated coastlines, perhaps by watercraft.

Compared to other regions, interpretations of southeast Alaska's prehistory are based on relatively few excavated sites and assemblages. Speaking in very general terms, however, the region's culture history can be organized into broad cultural traditions that share a coastal, marine focus. Key is the transition from the microblade and core technology of the earliest components to the technologies associated with ethnographically recognizable Northwest Coast cultures—especially ground-stone tools and bone harpoons and points.

A very general three-part developmental sequence proposed by Moss (1998) for the northern northwest coast consists of an early period (10,000–5,000 years ago), a middle period (5,000–1,500 years ago), and a late period (1,500 years ago to AD 1741). A somewhat different chronological framework proposed by Davis (1990) terms the earliest components the Paleomarine tradition (10,000–7,000 years ago), followed by a less-defined Transitional period (7,000–5,000 years ago), and finally a Developmental Northwest Coast stage, which is further broken into early (5,000–1,000 years ago), middle (1,000–550 years ago), and late (from 550 years ago to contact) phases. With its sharp, efficiently manufactured microblades, the Paleomarine tradition is considered a regional variant of the American Paleoarctic tradition from more northern and interior Alaska, believed to be derived from Asia.

Both frameworks agree that the presence of microblade technology and lack of bifacial stone tools defines many of the region's earliest cultural components. They also agree that a general replacement of chipped-stone technology (including microblades) with ground-stone technology occurs sometime after the Paleomarine/early period, but there is no clear date for that transition. Chipped-stone and ground-stone artifacts have been known to occur together as late as 1,400 years ago. The North Point site, near Petersburg, is one example.

Important sites that illustrate the Paleomarine/early period are Component I at the Hidden Falls site (9,500–8,600 years ago), on the east coast of Baranof Island; the Thorne River site (7,600 years ago), on Prince of Wales Island; and the Chuck Lake site, on Heceta Island. The Chuck Lake site contained a midden dating to about 8,200 years ago that is thought to be the oldest shell midden on the northwest coast. The lowest component of the Groundhog Bay site on Icy Strait has been dated in this same time frame (9,500 years ago), but was found to contain bifacial tools without microblades. A later component at the site, dated from 9,000–4,000 years ago, was found to contain microblades.

The oldest known human remains excavated in Alaska (among the oldest human remains in North America) were found at a site known as On Your Knees Cave, on Prince of Wales Island. The coastal cave was found in 1993 during a survey for a proposed timber sale and first excavated as a paleontological site where the thick sediments coating the cave floor preserved the remains of the flora and fauna of prehistoric southeast Alaska. A stone spear point, the first evidence of human use of the cave, was discovered in 1996, followed by a bone point and human remains, including a mandible with teeth. The remains were radiocarbon-dated at 9,730 years ago and associated with obsidian microblades and bifacial tools of the same age.

Some of the hallmark characteristics of Moss's middle period are an apparent increase in the number and size of archaeological sites (especially shell middens), the appearance of ground-slate industries (slate points, adzes, beads, and labrets), and increasing numbers of various bone tools

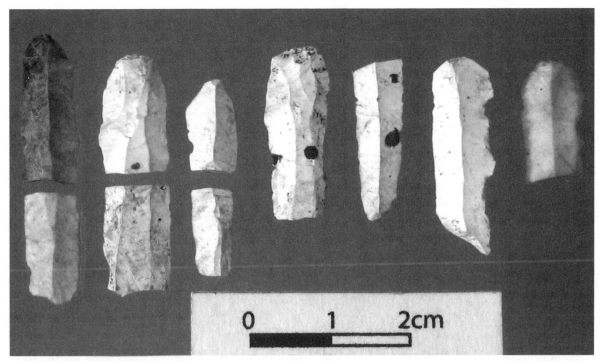

Examples of 9,200-year-old chalcedony (chert) microblades from the main entrance at On Your Knees Cave (49-PET-408). The artic-ulating, broken microblades represent "refits" that link activities at different parts of the site. The breaks likely resulted from their use in composite tools, such as slotted projectile points or knives and end-hatted, scalpel-like knives.   [Photo from (Lee 2007, 116), courtesy of Craig M. Lee and the On Your Knees Cave Archaeological Project]

(unilaterally and bilaterally barbed bone points, harpoon heads, and awls). The region's earliest wood stake fish weirs also are from this period, indicating intensive fish harvesting techniques.

By the end of Moss's middle and late periods and Davis's middle to late Developmental Northwest Coast stage (from 5,000 years ago to historic contact with Europeans), sites have many of the characteristics of the ethnographic cultures observed at the time of contact, such as large coastal settle-ments; a coast-oriented subsistence pattern, shown by the presence of shell middens; decorative objects, such as labrets; and a diversity of specialized artifacts of ground stone and bone, including adzes, chisels, and harpoons with lashing holes. Excavations at a number of important sites by Frederica deLaguna in the 1950s helped establish a late prehistoric cul-tural sequence in southeast Alaska. These include the Whale's Head Fort and Daax Haat Kanadaa sites, near Angoon on Admiralty Island, and the Old Town site on Knight Island, near Yakutat (where deLaguna excavated ten houses). The Hidden Falls and Groundhog Bay sites also have late prehis-toric components.

SUBMERGED, OR WET-SITE, ARCHAEOLOGY

Although southeast Alaska's acidic soils pose a preservation challenge for archaeological remains, its consistently cool, wet climate and extensive wetlands are ideal for the condi-tions that result in water-saturated sites, known as wet sites. These conditions preserve artifacts made from organic mate-rials that are often absent from the archaeological record (wood and plant fiber, for example).

The North Point site, near Petersburg, is an intertidal wet site that has produced ground slate, chipped slate, and microblades, along with spruce root cordage, wooden wedges, and wooden harpoons dated to around 1,400 years ago. Another example is a nearly complete spruce root basket excavated from the Thorne River and dated at 5,360 years ago, making it the oldest example of spruce root basketry on the northwest coast. Similarly well preserved basket frag-ments excavated from an eroding stream bank on southern Baranof Island have been dated to between 4,000 to 5,000 years ago. Tlingit basket weavers who studied the frag-ments noted weaving techniques identical to those used by contemporary weavers.

A wide range of wood and basketry fish traps have been preserved in wet conditions in southeast Alaska, reflecting thousands of years of—and considerable diversity in—fishing technology in the region. A 700-year-old basket-style fish trap was excavated in 1991 by the Alaska State Museum from the banks of Montana Creek near Juneau. An intertidal wooden-stake-style weir found along the Chilkoot River near

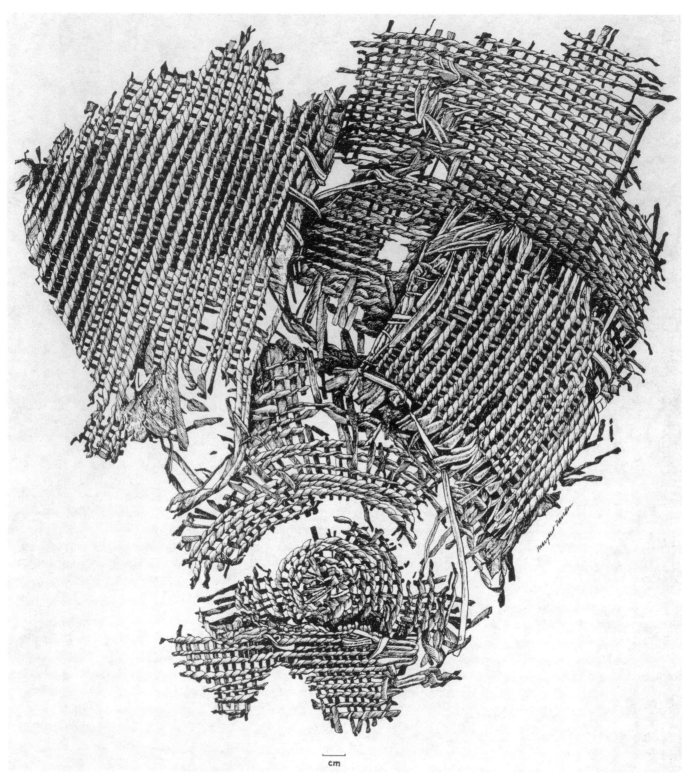

cm

Drawing of approximately 5,300-year-old basket fragment from Thorne River site.   [Drawing provided courtesy of Margaret Davidson, the artist, and the Alaska State Museum]

This numbered metal tablet proclaiming Alaska as Russian territory is one of a series of plaques placed in secret locations by Russian explorers. Thought to have been buried in 1795, it was excavated from the Old Sitka site on Baranof Island in the 1930s. The inscription reads "Land of Russian Possession." [Courtesy of the National Park Service Digital Imaging Team, Brian Sendler Photographer]

Haines in 2002, excavated by the Sheldon Museum in Haines, has been radiocarbon-dated at 2,200 years ago. More than forty intertidal wooden-stake weirs have been recorded on Prince of Wales Island, with the oldest dated at 3,800 years ago. A fish trap near Petersburg, excavated by the USDA Forest Service, has been radiocarbon-dated at 4,900 years ago.

PETROGLYPHS

Petroglyphs are a well-known part of the cultural record of southeast Alaska, but it is difficult to put them in a specific time frame. These designs, pecked onto rock outcrops and boulders, are often found at or near sea level, near major fishing and village sites. Various explanations for the designs have been suggested, ranging from spiritual symbolism to simple displays of art. The ethnographer George Emmons (1991) recorded petroglyphs at some of the best-known Tlingit sites, including those at Petroglyph Beach, a state historical park near Wrangell, which has one of southeast Alaska's most concentrated and accessible collections of petroglyphs.

HISTORICAL ARCHAEOLOGY

Historic era sites have also been the focus of archaeological investigation in southeast Alaska. The first of these was the excavation in the 1930s of the 1799 Russian settlement Redoubt St. Michael (Old Sitka) by Civilian Conservation Corps workers under the direction of the USDA Forest Service.

Artifacts recovered during the excavation included a fragile metal plate that was one of a series of plates with which the Russians proved their claim to Alaska. Another important excavation was the 1958 excavation of the site of the Tlingit fort Shish'k'i Noow and the 1804 Battle of Sitka (now Sitka National Historical Park) by Frederick Hadleigh West. A new archaeological inventory project is following up on West's excavation and will be completed in 2008.

Several historic structures and features associated with the Klondike gold rush have undergone archaeological investigation by the National Park Service in historic Skagway. These include archaeological monitoring of features associated with the Chilkoot Trail and White Pass City, along with excavations of preserved structures, like the Moore House and the Mascot Saloon (within the town of Skagway). Other excavations in Sitka have included the grounds of the 1843 Russian Bishop's House and a circa 1860 Russian hospital trash pit by the National Park Service in the early 1980s, and very productive excavations of the culturally complex Tlingit-Russian site known as Noow Tlein, or Castle Hill, by the Alaska Office of History and Archaeology between 1995 and 1998.

MUSEUMS

Although Alaska's most extensive collections and exhibits of archaeological material are in Fairbanks (the University of Alaska Museum of the North) and Anchorage (Anchorage Museum of History and Art), several of southeast Alaska's museums have collections and exhibit materials that aid the study of prehistoric southeast Alaska.

- The Alaska State Museum, in Juneau, has exhibits on history and ethnology that include a small number of archaeological materials.
- The Juneau–Douglas City Museum, in Juneau, has an exhibit that includes a re-creation of the above-noted fish trap excavated from Montana Creek.
- Collections and museum exhibits at Klondike Gold Rush National Historical Park, in Skagway, illustrate the historical archaeological work that is associated with Skagway and the Chilkoot Trail.
- The Sheldon Museum (Haines), the Wrangell Museum, the Ketchikan Historical Museum, and Totem Heritage Center have collections and exhibits on southeast Alaska cultures and history.
- The Sheldon Jackson Museum in Sitka exhibits artifacts from the ethnographic period across Alaska, including displays that illustrate the art and technology of Northwest Coast culture.
- The visitor center at Sitka National Historical Park has exhibits about the contact history of the Tlingit and Russian fur traders, including the Battle of 1804, which took place at the present location of the park. The

Russian possession plaque excavated from Old Sitka is in the park's museum collection.

For more information, visit the directory of Alaska's museums at http://www.museumsalaska.org/alaskas_museums.html.

SOUTHEAST ALASKA ARCHAEOLOGY IN THE MEDIA
Internet

Both the National Park Service (NPS) and the Tongass National Forest make information about southeast Alaska archaeology available to the public on the Internet. Use the main NPS Web site, http://www.nps.gov, to connect with individual parks in southeast Alaska: Sitka National Historical Park, Klondike Gold Rush National Historical Park, and Glacier Bay National Park and Preserve.

Film

The discovery of human remains at the On Your Knees Cave site brought archaeologists and the region's Native people together for consultation under the Native American Graves Protection and Repatriation Act (NAGPRA). This kind of consultation and communication is critical to the work that modern-day archaeologists do. The outcome is explored in a short film titled *Kuwóot yas.éin: His Spirit is Looking Out from the Cave.* The film was produced in 2005 by Sealaska Heritage Institute and several partners.

Further Reading: Alaska Department of Natural Resources, Office of History and Archaeology, Castle Hill Archaeological Project, http://www.dnr.state.ak.us/parks/oha/castle/castle.htm (online June 2007); Ames, Kenneth M., and Herbert D. G. Mashner, *Peoples of the Northwest Coast: Their Archaeology and Prehistory* (London: Thames and Hudson, 1999); Davis, Stanley D., "Prehistory of Southeast Alaska," in *Handbook of North American Indians*, Vol. 7: *Northwest Coast*, edited by Wayne Suttles (Washington, DC: Smithsonian Institution, 1990); Dixon, E. James, *Quest for the Origins of the First Americans* (Albuquerque: University of New Mexico, 1993); Dixon, E. James, *Bones, Boats and Bison: Archeology and the First Colonization of Western North America* (Albuquerque: University of New Mexico Press, 1999); Emmons, George Thornton, *The Tlingit Indians*, edited and with additions by Frederica deLaguna (Seattle: University of Washington Press; New York: American Museum of Natural History, 1991); Lee, Craig M. *Origin and Function of Early Holocene Microblade Technology in Southeast Alaska*, USA. Ph.D. dissertation, Department of Anthropology, University of Colorado, Boulder, 2007; Moss, Madonna L., "Northern Northwest Coast Regional Overview," *Arctic Anthropology* 35(1) (1998): 88–111; National Park Service, *Prehistory of Southeast Alaska*, http://www.nps.gov/akso/akarc/seast.htm (online June 2007); Olson, Wallace M., "A Prehistory of Southeast Alaska," *Alaska Geographic* 21(4) (1994); Suttles, Wayne P., ed., *Handbook of North American Indians*, Vol. 7: *Northwest Coast* (Washington, DC: Smithsonian Institution, 1990); *Tongass National Forest, History and Archaeology*, http://www.fs.fed.us/r10/tongass/forest_facts /resources/heritage/heritage.shtml (online June 2007).

Kristen Griffin

ON YOUR KNEES CAVE

Prince of Wales Island, Southeastern Alaska

On the Trail of the Earliest Americans

On Your Knees Cave (49-PET-408) is located on a peninsula at the northwest end of Prince of Wales Island in the Alexander Archipelago of southeast Alaska. The cave is located less than a kilometer from the ocean and was used repeatedly by humans for more than 12,000 years. It is best known for its earliest occupations and contains the oldest reliably dated human remains found in Alaska or Canada. The sea level was higher in the region at the time the first people used On Your Knees Cave, and the island could have been reached only by watercraft. The site is significant because it provides evidence suggesting early maritime adaptations in this region of North America at the end of the last Ice Age.

The archaeological research at On Your Knees Cave is also well known for the partnership that developed between Alaska Native tribes, the United States Forest Service, and scientists. This unique relationship brought together parties with diverse interests in a spirit of cooperation and mutual respect. They worked together to learn about the site and the partial remains of an ancient person found in the cave in an era when the interests of scientists often conflicted with those of indigenous people. This exceptional relationship has been documented in the educational video *Kuwóot yas.éin: His Spirit Is Looking Out from the Cave.*

ENVIRONMENTAL CONTEXT

Glacial ice had reached it maximum extent during the last Ice Age by about 21,000 years ago and was melting rapidly by about 17,000 years ago. At this time, sea level was about 100–120 meters lower than it is today. The lower sea level exposed the continental shelf between Alaska and Siberia. It created a land area called the Bering Land Bridge, which was more than 1,000 kilometers wide from north to south. As the massive glaciers melted, vast areas along the northwest coast may have been deglaciated beginning about 19,000 years ago.

This ice-free area provided a coastal corridor for the movement of plants, animals, and possibly humans. With the use of watercraft, it would have been possible for people to move south, gradually colonizing unglaciated refugia on the continental shelf exposed by the lower sea level along the Pacific coasts of the Americas. This route would have been open prior to the melting of the continental glaciers that blocked southward movement in the middle of the continent.

Geological research indicates that, except for a 400-kilometer coastal area between southwest British Columbia and Washington State, the northwest coast of North America was free of ice by about 19,000 years ago. Subsequent melting of the glaciers released water to the oceans, causing the sea level to rise. At the same time, the melting ice removed tremendous weight from the land, causing it to rebound. The timing and scale of these processes largely determined the location of the shoreline and its movement through time on the islands of the Alexander Archipelago. Geological research in this area suggests that glaciation during the peak of the last Ice Age was limited to alpine areas and a few large valley glaciers extending from the Cordilleran Mountains to the outer coast. As a result, the ancient shoreline along the northwest coast was located at the western limit of the continental shelf, and large areas were not covered by glacial ice.

HUMAN REMAINS

A few human bones have been found scattered throughout On Your Knees Cave. They include a jaw, a few ribs, part of the pelvis (hip bone), and several vertebrae. All of the bones appear to be from one individual, a young male in his early twenties. Carbon and nitrogen isotope values derived from chemical analysis of the human bones suggest the individual was raised primarily on a diet of marine foods, largely comprising marine predators—possibly marine mammals, such as seals, and carnivorous fish, such as salmon. Analysis of mtDNA (mitochondrial DNA) may suggest genetic relationships with extant Native American populations primarily (but not exclusively) located along the Pacific coast of the Americas.

Most of the young man's bones have puncture and gnaw marks that suggest they may have been carried into the cave by scavengers. It is unknown how he died; perhaps he passed away in or near the cave, or had been buried somewhere outside the cave, with his remains later dug up and carried into the cave by scavengers. Bear bones were also found in the cave, and perhaps he was killed or dragged into the cave by this creature.

MATERIAL CULTURE

On Your Knees Cave contains artifacts ranging between 12,000 and 1,500 calendar years old, documenting at least four periods of use. The most extensive use of the cave occurred about 10,300 years ago, about the same time the human remains were deposited in the cave.

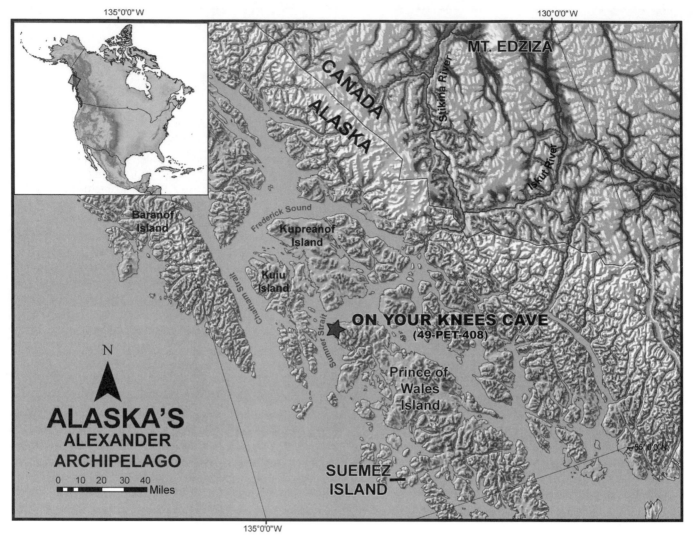

Regional map depicting the location of On Your Knees Cave and Mt. Edziza and Suemez obsidian sources.   [E. James Dixon]

Volcanic glass, or obsidian, dating to the same time as the human remains is from Mount Edziza, in British Columbia, and Suemez Island, Alaska. The location of the obsidian sources indicates that these early people were coastal navigators who probably had established trade networks for obsidian and other types of exotic tool stone, such as the quartz crystal found on nearby Kupreanof Island. Obtaining these types of stone necessitated the use of watercraft to cross bodies of water between islands and the mainland.

Animal bones from the cave indicate that it was situated in what may have been an unglaciated refugium, and was perhaps part of a larger unglaciated area along the continental shelf created by the lower sea level during the last Ice Age glaciation. It is also possible that the site was glaciated very briefly at the height of the last Ice Age, about 21,000 years ago. During the time when humans first used the cave, between about 10,000 and 12,000 years ago, animals such as fox (*Vulpes vulpes*), caribou (*Rangifer tarandus*), brown bear

(*Ursus arctos*), black bear (*Ursus Americanus*), and a variety of fish and sea birds inhabited the island and adjacent ocean.

There is some evidence to suggest the cave was a place where bears hibernated; perhaps early people came to the cave to hunt the bears while they were groggy and safer to kill. However, stone chips and charcoal from fires indicate that people made and repaired tools while camping at the cave for brief periods of time.

Many artifacts were left outside the cave about the same time that the young man died (around 10,500 years ago), but they do not appear to be grave goods. Virtually all of them are made of stone and have been found outside the cave, where no bone is preserved. In addition to the hundreds of stone chips left from making tools, the artifacts include stemmed and leaf-shaped projectile points or knives; scrapers, choppers, and abrading stones possibly used for working wood, animal bone, and antler; tiny slivers of stone called microblades, probably used as razor-like insets in slots carved in

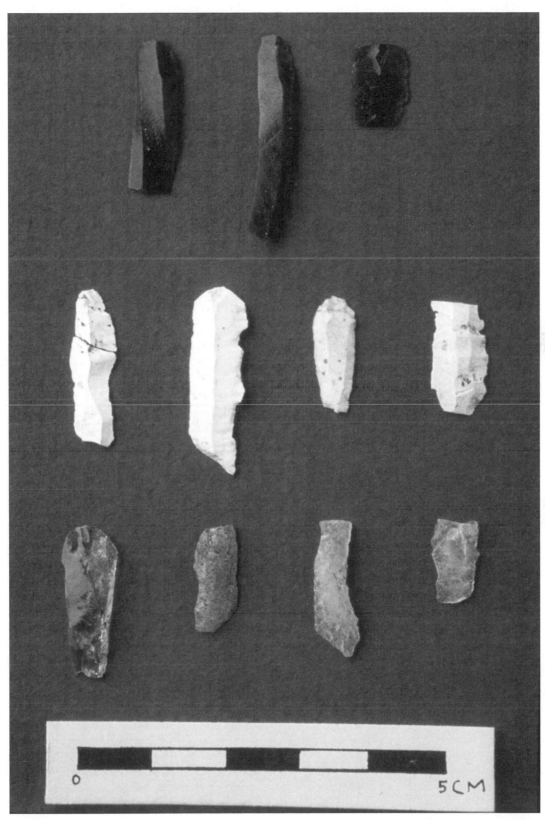

Microblades from On Your Knees Cave: *top*, obsidian; *middle*, chert; *bottom*, quartz and quartz crystal.   [E. James Dixon]

antler or bone projectile points or hafted in handles and used like X-acto knives; stone cores from which larger flakes and microblades were struck; and small pieces of red and orange ocher, which was probably ground for use as pigment to color objects.

This evidence documents very early maritime adaptation on the northwest coast of North America and lends credence to the idea that the Pacific coast was colonized by seafaring people with boats. Coastal migrations to the northwest coast may have enabled people to enter areas of North America south of the continental glaciers earlier than previously believed—and thousands of years earlier than the interior-oriented Clovis culture. Understanding the timing and processes of the colonization of the Americas is important, because the cultural adaptations (either maritime or terrestrial) of the New World's first populations established the foundation for all subsequent cultural development and for the rich and diverse cultures that followed.

On Your Knees Cave is located in a remote area of Prince of Wales Island and is not accessible to the general public. There is no road to the cave, and because it is not located on

the coast, it is not easily reached by boat. In 2005 the Sealaska Heritage Institute of Juneau, Alaska, produced a 30-minute video about the site and the discoveries and investigation there. Interested readers can see the site and its surroundings by viewing the film *Kuwóot yas.éin: His Spirit Is Looking Out from the Cave.*

Further Reading: Dixon, E. James, *Bones, Boats, and Bison: Archeology and the First Colonization of Western North America* (Albuquerque: University of New Mexico Press, 1999); Fedje, Daryl, "The Early Post-Glacial History of the Northwest Coast: A View from Haida Gwaii and Hecate Strait," *Athena Review* 3(2) (2002): 28–30; Fladmark, K., "Routes: Alternative Migration Corridors for Early Man in North America," *American Antiquity* 44(1979): 55–69; Heaton, Timothy H., and F. Grady, "The Late Wisconsin Vertebrate History of Prince of Wales Island, Southeast Alaska," in *Ice Age Cave Faunas of North America*, edited by B. W. Schubert, J. I. Mead, and R. W. Graham (Bloomington: Indiana University Press, 2003), ch. 2; Koppel, Tom, *Rewriting Prehistory—How New Science Is Tracing America's Ice Age Mariners* (New York: Simon & Schuster, 2003).

E. James Dixon

SITKA NATIONAL HISTORIC PARK AND THE CASTLE HILL ARCHAEOLOGICAL PROJECT

Southeastern Alaska

Investigations in the Capital of Russian America

SOUTHEASTERN ALASKA: HISTORICAL OVERVIEW

The southeast Alaska panhandle extends approximately 800 kilometers (500 mi) along America's northern Pacific coast, between British Columbia and Yakutat Bay. It was along this irregular coastline, punctuated by numerous islands and protected passages, that America, Russia, England, and Spain competed for land, resources, and trading rights during the late eighteenth and early nineteenth centuries.

The material evidence of these earliest Euro-American visitors to southeast Alaska, often superimposed over remnants of earlier northwest-coast Native American culture, is now largely hidden by rain forests and coastal waters.

Archaeological evidence of the eighteenth-century English and Spanish voyages in southeast Alaska is virtually nonexistent, as those journeys were dedicated to exploration and trade. More abundant is the material culture of the Russians, whose occupation of southeast Alaska lasted from the late eighteenth century until the sale of Alaska to the United States in 1867. The three decades following the sale of Alaska are known largely from records of U.S. military excursions and intermittent contact by American traders or

whalers. Few archaeological sites are known from this period.

As marine traffic increased, however, so did the number of shipwrecks in the region. It is expected that knowledge and interest in these transient American visitors may expand with the advent of regional underwater archaeological studies. The late nineteenth and early twentieth centuries are known for the discovery of gold in Alaska and the Klondike. During this period, southeast Alaska's inland waterways served as transportation corridors for the sailing ships and steamers that carried fortune seekers north.

It is within the context of intersecting Euro-American and Native cultures that one must interpret the historical archaeology of southeast Alaska. Despite the region's rich history and potential for archaeological research, however, scientific investigations have focused on only a few easily accessible areas. The most prominent of these is Sitka, a picturesque town that was once the capital of Russian America.

SITKA AND RUSSIAN COLONIZATION

The Russian settlement of southeastern Alaska was the culmination of an eastward movement of Russian fur seekers into far

An aerial view of Sitka, looking northwest, around 1945–55. Castle Hill is in the foreground at left.   [J. David McMahan]

eastern Siberia, then along the Aleutian chain and into coastal Alaska. Vitis Bering is given credit for making the first landfall on the Alaska mainland in 1741, although sightings occurred as early as 1732.

Eager to get rich from the fur trade, the Russians first established a settlement on the Aleutian island of Unalaska around 1770, and then on Kodiak Island in 1784. Their colonization of southeastern Alaska began with the establishment of a settlement near Yakutat in 1796. They soon realized, however, that Sitka was a more strategic location due to a year-round ice-free harbor.

In 1799, the Chief Manager of the Russian-American Company, Alexander Baranov, traveled to the site of present-day Sitka with the intention of establishing a fort on the rocky promontory now known as Castle Hill. Because the site was already occupied by the Kiks.ádi Clan of the Sitka Tlingit, however, he initiated construction of the small fort of St. Archangel Mikhail about 9.7 kilometers (6 mi) north of Sitka. Only three years later, while Baranov was in Kodiak, the Tlingit attacked and burned the fort, leaving few survivors. Determined to re-establish a Russian presence at Sitka, Baranov returned in September 1804 with a large force of Aleuts. He occupied Castle Hill, which the Kiks.ádi had abandoned in favor of a nearby location that was better protected from cannon bombardment. Assisted by Captain Iurii Lisiansky on the naval sloop *Neva*, however, the Russians eventually forced the Kiks.ádi to withdraw to the other side of the island.

Baranov immediately constructed a new settlement on and around Castle Hill. He named the settlement Novo-Arkhangel'sk (New Archangel) to commemorate the first Sitka settlement. The years following the founding of New Archangel were plagued by constant fear of Tlingit retribution, difficulties in obtaining supplies, a shortage of ships, and an unsuccessful fur trade. Nevertheless, in 1808 New Archangel succeeded Kodiak as the administrative center of Russian possessions in America. For almost 60 years, southeastern Alaska was dominated by the Russian-American Company (RAC). Through a 1799 decree by Paul I, the newly formed company was granted a monopoly over hunting and mining on the coast of North America, the Aleutian Islands, and the Kurile Islands. The company's economic strategy focused on intensive fur procurement, which was carried out and managed through a hierarchy of outposts, settlements, forts, and administrative centers. Because the maximum number of Russians in Alaska never exceeded approximately 800 people, the company's industries depended on a labor force of Natives and Creoles.

Today, Castle Hill is regarded as one of the most important historical sites in Alaska. From the company headquarters on the hill, Baranov and his successors managed colonies in California, Hawai'i, and throughout Alaska. It was the site of the formal transfer ceremony following the U.S. purchase of Alaska from Russia on October 18, 1867, and the first seat of American military government for Alaska. When Alaska became a U.S. state in 1959, Castle Hill was the site of one of the first official flag raisings of the new forty-nine–star flag. The site has been a territorial and a state historical park since the 1950s and a National Historic Landmark since 1962.

ARCHAEOLOGY AT CASTLE HILL
A major park renovation project during 1997–98 prompted the state of Alaska's Office of History and Archaeology (OHA) to

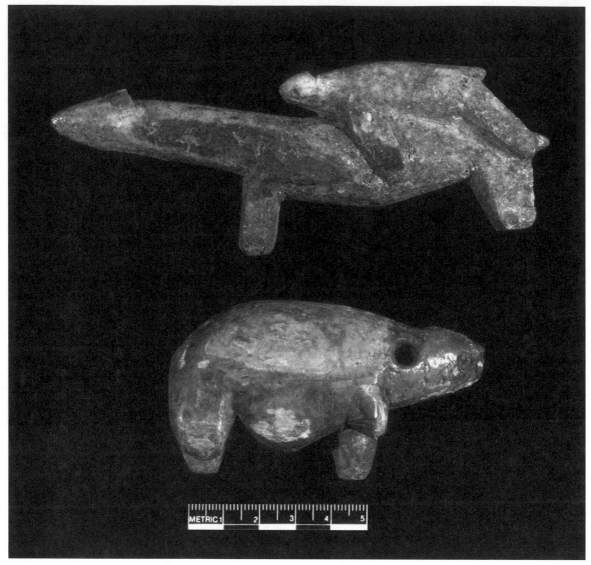

Ivory carvings from the Castle Hill workshop workers' quarters: *top*, polar bear with cub; *bottom*, brown bear.   [J. David McMahan]

conduct archaeological excavations on and around Castle Hill. On a terrace near the base of the hill, the archaeologists uncovered the buried ruins of four Russian buildings from the 1820s and 1830s. These structures, once located within the main fortress, constituted a workshop complex where craftsmen applied the trades of coppersmithing, blacksmithing, shoe manufacture, firearm and instrument repair, coopering, and woodworking. The general sequence and age of the buildings was established from artifact types and soil stratigraphy. Building 1 is believed to have been a bunkhouse for the craftsmen. Building 2 contained the remains of a metalworker's forge constructed of bricks on a stone foundation. Debris from the floors of both buildings 2 and 3 suggest that craftsmen there were working with copper, iron, lead, and precious metals. All three buildings are believed to date from the 1820s and are reminiscent of Siberian architecture. The fourth building ruin (Building

4, post-1830s), largely destroyed by twentieth-century gardening and trail construction, was possibly a bath house.

The approximately 300,000 artifacts from Castle Hill constitute the largest, most diverse collection of nineteenth-century Russian-American materials from any excavated site in North America. The importance of the collection is enhanced by the extraordinary preservation of textiles, hair, and other organic artifacts. This unusual preservation is believed to have been caused by slightly raised soil acidity brought about by an abundance of spruce wood chips—or perhaps by the tannin used in leatherworking. The artifacts have caused archaeologists to reconsider some of their previous ideas regarding trade relations and life in Russian America.

The archaeological record suggests that the material culture of working-class citizens was much more abundant and diverse than previously considered. This is evidenced by children's toys and luxury items, such as jewelry. The collection also contains distinctively Russian items, such as glass bottle seals, uniform parts, Russian coins, samovar parts, and religious items. Surprisingly, a large percentage of the Castle Hill ceramics were also of Russian manufacture, including examples from many well-known factories. Previous interpretations suggested that, due to difficulties in getting shipments from Russia, the colonies were supplied primarily by British and American sources during this time period.

The artifacts also interestingly document Sitka's multi-national and multi-ethnic trade contacts. For example, the collection includes bamboo, coconuts, and coconut husk fibers (coir) that may have originated from the Sandwich Islands (Hawai'i). Six Phoenix buttons, known to have been manufactured in England for Haitian troops prior to 1820, may have derived from Russian trade with the Columbia River region.

The site also produced U.S. and Japanese coins; tobacco pipes from England and the Ottoman Empire; possible southeastern Asian pottery; French and British gunflints; and a broad array of other exotic items. The archaeological data from Castle Hill has provided insights on architecture, trade, industry, food preference, and consumer choice. The result is a better understanding of the day-to-day lives and industries of Russian America.

RESOURCES FOR PUBLIC INTERPRETATION IN SITKA

With more than 200,000 visitors each year, Sitka is one of the most popular cruise ship destinations along the Inside Passage. The community's shops and historical sites still convey a feeling of Russian colonial culture. Sitka's history and cultural heritage are interpreted at Sitka National Historical Park,

operated by the U.S. National Park Service. The park includes a visitor center, interpretive center with museum exhibits, and cultural center with workshops for Native artists. There are regular ranger-led tours of the park and the restored Russian Bishop's House during the summer months—sometimes supplemented by walking tours of the town, Castle Hill, and ongoing archaeological field projects. Self-guided walking trails within the park are lined with historic totem poles that convey a sense of Tlingit culture. On October 18 of each year, a parade, ball, Russian dancing, and other festivities are held to commemorate the 1867 purchase of Alaska.

Further Reading: Arndt, Katherine L., and Richard A. Pierce, *Sitka National Historical Park Historical Context Study: A Construction History of Sitka, Alaska, as Documented in the Records of the Russian-American Company*, 2nd ed. (Sitka and Fairbanks: Sitka National Historical Park, National Park Service, and University of Alaska in Fairbanks, 2003); Black, Lydia T., *Russians in Alaska: 1732–1867* (Fairbanks: University of Alaska Press, 2004); Crowell, Aron L., *Archaeology and the Capitalist World System: A Study from Russian America* (New York and London: Plenum Press, 1997); Khlebnikov, Kyrill T., *Notes on Russian America*, Vol. 1: *Novo-Arkhangel'sk*, translated by Serge LeComte and Richard Pierce (Kingston, ON: Limestone Press, 1994), McMahan, Dave, "Archaeology at Alaska's Castle Hill, the Colonial Capital of Russian America," in *Unseen Treasures: Imperial Russian and the New World* (Arlington, VA: American-Russian Cultural Cooperation Foundation, 1999), 17–22; Olson, Wallace M., *Through Spanish Eyes: Spanish Voyages to Alaska, 1774–1792*, ltd. ed. (Auke Bay, Alaska: Heritage Research, 2002); Castle Hill Archaeological Project, Alaska Office of History and Archaeology Web site, http://www.dnr.state.ak.us/parks/oha/castle/castle.htm (online March 2006); National Park Service, Sitka National Historical Park Web site, http://www.nps.gov/sitk (online March 2006).

J. David McMahan

THE KENNECOTT MINE NATIONAL HISTORICAL LANDMARK

Wrangell–St. Elias National Park, Southeastern Alaska
Twentieth-Century Industrial Archaeology on the Alaskan Frontier

Kennecott, Alaska, is one of the best preserved examples of early-twentieth-century copper-mining operations in North America. The initial discoveries were made in 1898, the mines went into full production in 1912, and the operations finally closed in 1938. The history of the mines demonstrates in detail the intricacies of establishing and operating an industrial enterprise in the Alaskan wilderness. The mines were organized and financed through the Alaska Syndicate, a

cooperation between the Guggenheim family and the House of Morgan. Eventually, the Alaskan operations were incorporated into the broader Kennecott Copper Corporation—at one time among the largest copper producers in the world.

Kennecott is located deep in the Wrangell Mountains of Alaska in the heart of what is now the Wrangell–St. Elias National Park and Preserve. The site is at the end of the 315-kilometer (about 200 mi) Copper River and Northwestern Railway built to connect the mines with Cordova on the coast. Even today the only road to Kennecott follows the right of way of the old railroad.

The site is complex: it encompasses the main mill town; five distinct mines (complete with support facilities); and a network of roads, trails, aerial tramways, and water and power lines. The mine building and structures are organized in interconnected clusters scattered across approximately 1,200 hectares (about 3,000 acres). While the mine buildings located high on Bonanza Ridge—762 meters above the mill town—have not fared too well in the face of extreme winter weather conditions, the mill town contains a substantial number of well-preserved industrial and domestic buildings. Even where most of the structures have collapsed, the component parts of the site remain obvious. The main bunkhouse at the Bonanza mine may have been burned, but the steel shop still contains the tools and machines needed to resharpen drill bits. The upper tramway terminal is also intact. Bunkhouses at the Erie and Jumbo mines, as well as in the mill town, provide details on the general characteristics of the missing Bonanza features.

The overall industrial organization of the Kennecott site is evident on the landscape. The mines were the source of ore, the raw material. The tramways moved the ore to the mill, where it was concentrated to increase the value and decrease the volume. From there the sacked ore was stacked on flat cars for the trip to Cordova, the smelter at Tacoma, and the world markets. At each node of the operation are a number of necessary support structures: shops, warehouses, and bunkhouses. The main receiving and distribution points were located in the mill town, where the mining and milling operations connected with the railway. Power generated in the mill town supplied the entire operation with electricity, while each mine had its own heating plant.

The richness and geologically simple nature of the Kennecott ores permitted the gravity concentrator to be operated successfully over the life of the mine. The primary ore was chalcocite, which contained nearly 80 percent copper. Differences in the specific gravity of the ore and the limestone matrix made separation on the basis of specific gravity practical and economical for most of the ore produced at Kennecott. Secondary ores, such as malachite and azurite, were rich carbonates with low specific gravities. At first they presented a problem, because the limestone waste rock precluded acid leaching—the usual method of recovery at the time. Ammonia leaching, developed for Kennecott and the Michigan copper mines at the same time and installed in 1915, served just as well.

After 1920 the majority of the world's large copper mines abandoned gravity concentration in favor of the flotation process, which was well suited to the low-grade ores that characterized the majority of the mines after 1900. At Kennecott modifications were made to the gravity equipment, and flotation cells were added—but only as a sec-

ondary treatment. As such, Kennecott can be described as the culmination of the nineteenth-century tradition of metallurgical practice, rather than as a leader in twentieth-century innovation.

The gravity concentrator, the centerpiece of the mill town, has most of its equipment intact—crushers, screens, tables, and jigs—as well as the interconnecting lauders and piping that fed ore from process to process. The ammonia-leaching plant is also well preserved. Much of the equipment in the power house was salvaged when the mines closed, but enough was left to ensure power to a small operation if Kennecott ever chooses to re-establish a presence in the area.

The mill building, a towering timber structure, provides copious evidence of how it and the concentrating procedures evolved over the life of the mines. Initially the building was a straight line down the hillside, capable of processing approximately 600 tons of ore per day. As its capacity grew, the building widened to form a delta, and new floors were added between the exiting ones. Little attention was paid to the aesthetics of the building as the mill underwent at least four major—and innumerable minor—reorganizations. Hence, newer additions are obvious where they abut older sections. Red paint on interior walls deep within the mill state unequivocally that they were once exterior walls, exposed to the elements. Machinery no longer in use was not removed unless it was in the way of newer installations. Unused pipes and launders run up to newer walls and are simply cut off. The opportunities to investigate the detailed evolution and interrelationships of structure and process are many.

Much of the research on Kennecott has revolved around the long process of acquiring the site by the National Park Service and includes several private and academic plans to preserve and interpret the landmark. Hazardous-waste mitigation, especially asbestos removal, and efforts to effect a short-term stabilization of the major buildings generated a considerable amount of information prior to acquisition. Fieldwork identified the many mine openings for subsequent securing and confirmed there was a wealth of mining artifacts left underground in the mines.

An overview history of the site written in 1977 was published in the *Western Historical Quarterly* a year later. Kennecott still has its children: the sons and daughters of the managerial and technical staff, who spent parts of their childhoods at the mines. Theirs was a privileged position, since few employees were allowed to have their families with them. Most of the workers were single men, frequently immigrants, who lived in the bunkhouses and rarely stayed more than six months, if that.

Considerably more information has been published in popular works on the Copper River and Northwestern Railway. The railway, built by the same people who constructed the White Pass and Yukon Route across the mountains from Skagway to the Yukon, was an engineering achievement in its own right. It crossed the Copper River delta, squeezed between glaciers, and hugged canyon walls as it penetrated the Chugach Mountains.

Since 1998, when the United States National Park Service acquired the Kennecott site, a long-term stabilization and rehabilitation program has been under way. Historic structures reports describe the nature and evolution of many of the buildings. Compliance archaeology has added considerably to the information available on the day-to-day operations at Kennecott.

In many cases, the unearthed evidence has raised as many questions as it has answered. This is particularly true in the storage areas and dumps—industrial middens—where superseded material and equipment was stored or discarded.

For additional information, see the culture and history entries for the Wrangell-St. Elias National Park and Preserve at http://www.nps.gov/wrst/cultural.htm. These pages expand on the National Historic Landmark and provide information on the wider mining history and other aspects of the Kennecott region.

Published sources useful to the general reader are listed below. Several additional National Park Service studies on the technical and social histories of Kennecott are currently in preparation.

Further Reading: Grauman, Melody Webb, "Kennecott: Alaskan Origins of a Copper Empire," *Western Historical Quarterly* 9(1978): 197–211; Janson, Lone E., *The Copper Spike* (Anchorage: Alaska Northwest, 1975); Kain, Ann, ed., *Kennecott Kids; Interviews with the Children of Kennecott*, 2 vols. (Anchorage, AK: National Park Service, 2001); Gilbert, Cathy, Paul White, and Anne Worthington, *Cultural Landscape Report: Kennecott Mill Town* (Wrangell–St. Elias National Park and Preserve, Alaska: National Park Service, 2001).

Logan W. Hovis

Arctic/Subarctic Region

KEY FOR ARCTIC/SUBARCTIC REGIONAL MAP

1. Round Island
2. Brooks River Archaeological District
3. Mink Island Site and the Amalik Bay Archaeological District
4. Bering Land Bridge National Preserve
5. Tuluaq Hill
6. Mesa
7. Tanana River sites: Dry Creek, Broken Mammoth, Healy Lake, Swan Point
8. Utqiagvik Archaeological Project, Barrow
9. Hamilton Inlet sites
10. Martin Frobisher site
11. Alarnerk
12. Skagway, Klondike Gold Rush National Historical Park, and Chilkoot Trail National Historic Site
13. Onion Portage
14. Cape Krusenstern
15. Point Hope
16. Tuktu, Anaktuvuk Pass
17. Mosquito Lake
18. Tukuto Lake sites
19. Punyik Point
20. Yukon Island-Cook Inlet
21. Bear Cove
22. Palugvik
23. Uqciuvit
24. Tiq'atl'ena Bena
25. Three Saints Harbor, Kodiak
26. Nunakakhnak, Kodiak
27. Reese Bay
28. Tikchik
29. Dutch Harbor and Margaret Bay, Unalaska
30. Zapadni, St Paul Is, Pribilof Islands
31. Kapuivik
32. Hazard Inlet sites, Somerset Island
33. Charley Lake Cave

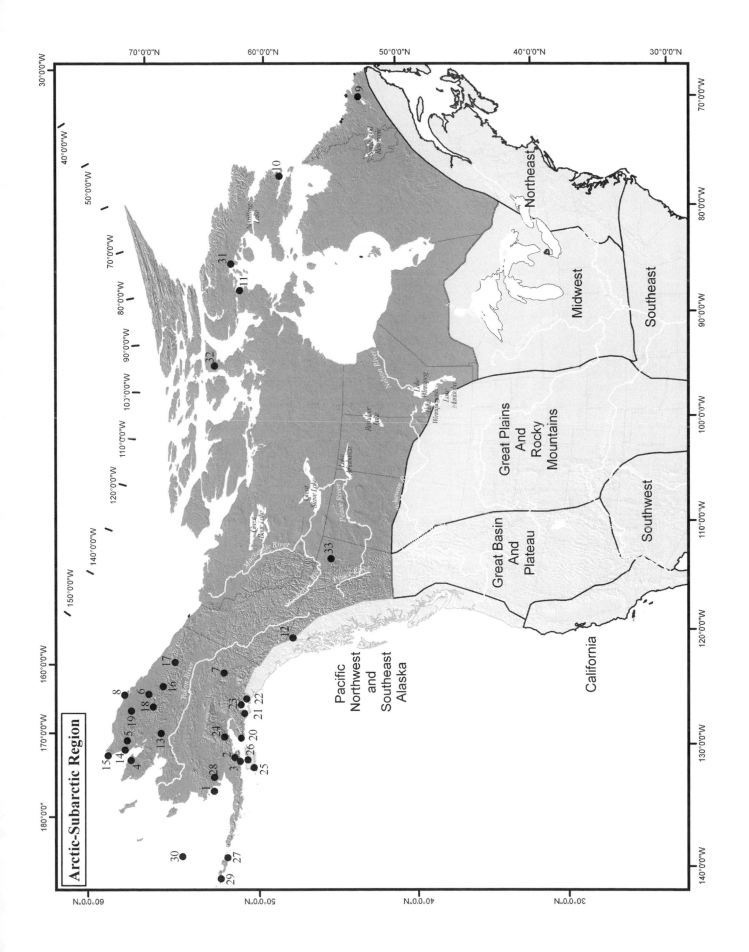

Arctic-Subarctic Region

INTRODUCTION

This section of *Archaeology in America* includes essays about archaeological sites in the vast Arctic and Subarctic region of North America. This region includes most of Canada, with the exception of the Pacific coastal strip, the southern quarter or so of the other provinces, and the Maritime Provinces in eastern Canada. With the exception of its southeastern arm, most of Alaska also is included in this region. The distinction between the Arctic and the Subarctic is based on climate and distance north of the equator, both of which strongly affect vegetation. The Arctic has an extremely cold climate and long winters with limited hours of daylight; summers are short but have very long daylight periods. Low-vegetation tundra underlain by permafrost dominates the landscape. Subarctic vegetation is primarily homogeneous small-needled evergreen forest, often referred to as "boreal forest." The farther north one goes in this zone, the more one encounters areas of low-lying tundra in woodlands. Food resources in the region can be very rich; however, they are quite often concentrated in certain locations. Large game animals, in particular caribou, are found in large migratory herds; certain portions of inland rivers provide rich sources of fish, and certain coastal locations give access to maritime species (see the general essays by Dumond on the Arctic and Subarctic parts of Canada and mainland Alaska for detailed descriptions of the environments and available resources for human populations living there).

Human settlement of this region began at least 12,000 years ago with the first immigrants from northeast Asia, who either walked across the Bering land bridge, or paddled along its coast, or both (see the essays by Dixon about the earliest inhabitants, early settlements, and routes south and the essay by Potter about inland sites in the Tanana River drainage). Settlements throughout the region have been small and generally widely scattered. To the extent that there has been any focus of human settlement, it has been in coastal areas—for example, along the coasts of the Alaskan peninsula, around Norton and Kotzebue sounds, and along the Arctic Ocean coast where maritime resources could be fished for or hunted (see the essays by Anderson, Dekin, Schaaf, Steffian and Saltonstall, and Veltre).

Many of the essays in this section focus on sites of the Alaskan portion of the region; however, sites in the central and eastern parts represent the long human histories in these challenging environments of the Canadian Arctic and Subarctic, and are also covered (see the essays by Savelle, Fitzhugh, and Auger). Many of the essays relate to ancient and Native human adaptation and settlement, but the archaeology of English, Russian, and American exploration, exploitation, and settlement also are described (see the essays by Auger, Crowell, Higgs, and King).

We have targeted these essays on the most important and interesting archaeological sites and topics in the Arctic/Subarctic region. Readers can learn more about these sites, and others as well, by consulting the additional sources of information listed at the end of each essay. Here articles, books, Web sites, museum collections, and other sources are identified to help readers learn more about these fascinating places and subjects. Given the harsh environment of this region, many of these sites are less accessible than other sites described in *Archaeology in America*; however, we have listed those that can be visited as parts of national, state, local, or other public parks.

The articles in the Arctic/Subarctic section of *Archaeology in America* include eleven general essays on various topics that cover ancient or historic time periods. The general essays are followed by thirteen essays on specific archaeological sites or related groups of sites in a particular region. These more specific essays are arranged in roughly chronological order.

ENTRIES FOR THE ARCTIC/SUBARCTIC REGION

ARCHAEOLOGY OF ARCTIC AND SUBARCTIC CANADA

The Subarctic and Arctic regions in Canada discussed here, taken together, cover essentially all of Canada, save for the coastal strip along the Pacific Ocean on the west; the approximate southern one-fourth to one-half of the provinces of British Columbia, Alberta, Saskatchewan, and Manitoba; and the Maritime Provinces of New Brunswick, Newfoundland, and Nova Scotia to the southeast. The Subarctic is the region now dominated by homogeneous small-needled evergreen forest (generally referred to as boreal forest) in a zone east, south, and west of Hudson Bay, plus a narrow strip to the north of the thicker forest, in which trees are interspersed with low-lying tundra. This is a region in which caribou and moose are the largest game, with hares inland and some seals on sea coasts, including those of Hudson Bay. Fish are important in the salmon streams of the far west but less so elsewhere. North of this Subarctic lies the tundra-dominated Arctic of northern Yukon, the northern Northwest Territories, and Nunavut—plus some of northern Quebec and extending eastward into Labrador.

Early explorations of the region coincided generally with the spread through Canada of the Hudson Bay Company, originally chartered in 1670, which by 1800 had established factories as far west as the Pacific coast. In the Subarctic, these revealed Native American people of Algonquian languages in the east, and those of Athabascan speech west of Hudson Bay. Although company representatives encountered speakers of the eastern Eskimoan language (now referred to as Inuit or Inuktitut) around Hudson Bay and at spots in the Arctic, explorations of the latter zone generally occurred later, with some Native peoples not having met Europeans until the twentieth century.

Heavily glaciated during the Pleistocene epoch (Ice Age), the early prehistory of Canada mirrors the withdrawal of the ice. There were two great ice sheets; the larger Laurentide sheet was centered over Hudson Bay, and the smaller Cordilleran ice extended from the Pacific to the eastern slope of the Rocky Mountains. The mass of water locked up in these mountains of ice—and to a somewhat lesser extent in those over northern Europe—was so great that the level of the seas was lowered by nearly 400 feet below today's level, exposing portions of continental shelves worldwide. These included the shallow floors of the Bering and Chukchi seas, west of Alaska, creating a bridge with Asia—a bridge presumed to have provided the dry-land route by which humans first entered the New World.

For several thousand years before about 17,000 BC, the Laurentide ice rose in a major dome above present Hudson Bay and extended southward over the Great Lakes and southwestward to about the modern Canada–United States border; on the northeast, Laurentide ice coalesced with the glacial mass over Greenland; to the northwest, it met Cordilleran ice, leaving exposed only the thin western edge of the modern territory of Yukon—which, like adjacent interior Alaska, was unglaciated. This unglaciated portion of the Yukon and interior Alaska formed the eastern end of a low-lying and tundra-covered peninsula that thrust from northeast Asia to the ice mass of America. The larger area, from northeast Asia to the North American glaciers, is now referred to as Beringia. It was through Beringia, at least in part, that humans moved to begin settlement of the American continents.

In this narrow, unglaciated part of Yukon excitement was aroused several decades ago when apparent artifacts of bone, together with smashed bones of Pleistocene elephants (mammoths), were found displaced on silt banks along the course of the Old Crow River (a tributary of the Porcupine, which in turn feeds into the Yukon River). The bone of one of these implements, an apparent skinning tool or flesher similar to those used historically by Athabascan Indians of the region, was dated earlier than 25,000 BC by radiocarbon.

The conclusion that this was evidence of the first people to enter America led to frenzied research in the region, which revealed neither stone artifacts nor extensive living sites of comparable age. This finally led to a re-dating of the collagen content of the bone flesher by improved technology—yielding a date around AD 300. This brought an end to much research, but it had already resulted in excavations in caves in the nearby Bluefish Hills that produced some evidence of delicate, elongated chips of stone (microblades), a core such as those from which microblades were produced, and radiocarbon evidence of human presence as early as 12,000 BC. This is joined now by evidence from northern Alaska of the presence of microblade-making humans at this time, and it is still probably the earliest direct radiocarbon evidence of humans in Canada.

By 14,000 BC the ice sheets were deteriorating, leaving Laurentide ice domes both northwest and southeast of Hudson Bay, but with contact still between Laurentide and Cordilleran sheets in the west. In the next three millennia or so, further wastage at the glaciers' edges led to the opening of a channel between the two major ice sheets and an expanding strip of tundra over the newly deglaciated zone. At 10,000 BC most of Yukon and the east half of British Columbia were open, and the ice had withdrawn north of the Great Lakes. But the entire Canadian northeast was still covered with ice and would remain so until nearly 6000 BC, with remnant ice both east and west of Hudson Bay, and northward on Baffin Island and the Queen Elizabeth Islands.

The presence of the Canadian ice sheets means that the prehistory of much of Canadian territory is considerably shorter than that of the United States, and when it can be traced, it bears an obvious debt to occurrences in the more southerly regions. Further, the presence or absence of an ice-free corridor between the two North American ice sheets has significant implications for understanding the initial human occupation of the Americas. Such a corridor after 10,000 BC extended from unglaciated western Yukon in the northwest to northern Alberta on the southeast, and it is the supposed ancient existence of just such a corridor that has provided much of the perceived importance of the early archaeology of western Canada.

Over past decades, discussions among archaeologists depended heavily on the expectation that this corridor had existed through all or most of the last great period of glaciations. The discussions also depended on the related supposition that terrestrial hunters of big game—game including Pleistocene period elephants (mammoth and mastodon)—had entered the New World equipped with the hunting implements, skills, and inclinations of people of the Old World Paleolithic age, like those who have long been traced in northern Europe. Although estimated dates for such hypothetical migrations of newcomers have varied, general statements were that it was by 14,000 BC or earlier. This expectation easily matched the earliest radiocarbon dates for the widespread Clovis archaeological horizon of the United States—marked by fluted projectile or spear points, which have been convincingly shown to date from sometime around 11,500 BC. Such expectations fairly easily accommodated arguments—provocative, but less thoroughly convincing to some archaeologists—that occupations within North America preceded 11,500 BC by an unknown number of millennia. These arguments would also accommodate the several sites in South America that have been dated around 11,000 BC, and the one of them that is fairly widely accepted at nearly 13,000 BC.

More recently, however, fairly convincing evidence has been presented that the corridor between the two North American ice sheets was not reasonably passable by humans between about 30,000 and 11,500 BC. Although surface finds and a few excavated examples of fluted projectile points that are at least roughly analogous to artifacts of the Clovis complex have been reported in southern Canada, and although others are known from numerous surface and a very few excavated finds in Alaska to the northwest, there are no such finds, surface or excavated, through the central portion of the supposed corridor. One result is an increased interest in the possibility of other routes of early immigration into the New World, including movement along the west coast (e.g., Dixon 1999; Fedje 2002; Fladmark 1979).

THE SUBARCTIC

Insofar as fluted (that is, Clovis-like) projectile or spear points are concerned, numerous scattered examples have been found in undated contexts in the prairie provinces (Alberta, Saskatchewan, and Manitoba); in southern Ontario and Quebec; and still farther east. In only two cases are these from Canadian archaeological sites convincingly dated by radiocarbon—the Debert site, in Nova Scotia of far southeastern Canada; and Charley Lake Cave, in northeastern British Columbia. In both of these, the calendar dates are about 10,500 BC. In both cases, they are approximately contemporaneous not with the earliest Clovis culture of the southwestern United States, but rather with slightly later North American archaeological cultures thought to be derived from Clovis—cultures such as Folsom and Agate Basin. The points of the former were fluted, and the latter were not fluted, but chipped with impressive skill and beauty and dated about the same. Both are also possibly contemporaneous with at least some of the numerous fluted points recovered from undated contexts in Alaska—at least to judge by what at least hints at an acceptable date of about 10,000 BC from one newly discovered site.

With regard to early fluted-point users in southeastern Canada, and in the absence of numerous sites anywhere in eastern North America yielding evidence of the taking of Pleistocene elephants, the presumption has been that as hunters, the people of deglaciating southeastern Canada were largely in pursuit of caribou, a herd animal found on the tundra and in the tundra forest that moved north as vegetation changed in the wake of the retreating ice. Remains of bone trash in sites are scanty, however, and with the exception of one locale in Ontario, the presence of caribou has not been specifically demonstrated.

In British Columbia, the dated fluted-point site boasts some bone preservation; Charley Lake Cave yielded small amounts of bison bone in association with the tools. As with evidence concerning caribou to the east, it is possible to conceive here of another southern herd animal moving northward as ice receded.

In the east, by about 8500 BC, changes in tool forms—especially in projectile blades— involved the introduction of notching the sides or corners of chipped-stone points. A relationship has been suggested between this and the adoption of a new projectile system derived from the south, as thrusting spears of the fluted-point cultures were replaced by darts propelled with the spear thrower, or *atl atl*. This change, which generally coincides with the northward expansion of the boreal forest treeline, is generally considered to mark the beginning of local Archaic culture, of which several variants have been recorded over the area of the broad Canadian Shield, that ancient (Pre-Cambrian) rock surface that underlies Hudson Bay and extends well to each side of it. On both sides of the bay, people of Archaic culture moved northward into areas freed of ice. On the southeast fringe of the Subarctic, some of these people took up a coastal lifeway by 6000 BC. This included use for ocean-side hunting with the toggling harpoon—an implement whose head was designed to twist securely crosswise to the harpoon line after an animal was struck. By 4000 BC their descendants had moved onto the coast of Labrador. Thereafter these early people east of Hudson Bay developed steadily into the Native American groups met by men of the early Hudson Bay Company.

To the west, and into the so-called Barrenland of southern Nunavut, evolution of the fluted-point cultures was not into what is classed as Archaic, but rather into Plano. The latter term was coined for the plains region of the western United States, and then applied to the nonfluted but well-made lanceolate stone projectile tips that followed after about 10,500 BC. Chief among the major markers is the point type called Agate Basin, named for the type site located in Wyoming, where occupations have been dated to around 10,500 BC. Its inhabitants hunted species of bison in western North America. In the region immediately west of Hudson Bay, this projectile technology of Plano type was succeeded not long after—and apparently as a local development—by an Archaic variant referred to as the Shield Archaic.

Much farther west, such a shift to Archaic modes of weaponry thought to involve the spear-thrower occurred later, and it is presumed that people of Plano culture spread northward through Yukon, although evidence in Yukon itself is poor. Suggestive, however, is the appearance of people of indubitably Agate Basin Plano-like culture around about 10,000 BC in Alaska. These people lived along the northern slope of the Brooks Range, as well as in a few other, scattered regions, not more than a few hundred years after the earliest acceptable date for the Agate Basin people of Wyoming. This appears to be evidence of a northward shift paralleling that of Archaic cultures farther east, in Canada.

In the central Northwest Territories, Agate Basin–like projectiles characterized people around 6000 BC, but as the treeline pressed northward and styles of hunting changed in this large Subarctic region of central Canada, artifact assemblages became more and more like those of the Archaic people of the Canadian Shield—apparently as the result both of contacts and of adaptation to a shifting, warming environment. Some elements partook of so-called Early Plains culture with rather indifferently chipped notched points. These elements presumably involved the local adoption of the spear thrower. In the northwest, some relatively comparable artifact collections also include microblades, in a composite notched-point and microblade industry (the so-called Northwest Microblade culture) reminiscent of contemporary Northern Archaic assemblages of the Alaska interior. On the Barrenland northwest of

Hudson Bay, however, where trees did not expand so readily, remnant Plano people adapted themselves to the local caribou herds—which, in their annual movements, migrated in summer toward the tundra-covered Arctic coast and retreated in winter into the edge of the treeline to the south. This pattern of presumably Native American occupations in the Barrens continued until sometime after 2000 BC.

THE ARCTIC

Northward movements through the Subarctic region generally halted south of the tundra strip, fringing the Arctic coast and covering the islands of the Arctic Archipelago, leaving this region of ice-loving sea mammals, northward-migrating caribou, and resident musk oxen vacant of humans. Change came sometime around 2500 BC, when people of the Arctic Small Tool tradition, first in evidence in Alaska and clearly adapted to ocean-edge tundra, moved rapidly eastward across northern Canada to occupy the region.

These first Arctic people, known most commonly in Canada as Pre-Dorset or early Paleo-Eskimo, were at their Alaskan roots primarily terrestrial hunters armed with the bow and arrow. It is possible that much of their movement was made possible by preying on the non-migratory musk-ox herds. As they moved into the tundra-covered Arctic islands, however, they turned more and more to coastal resources, including sea mammals hunted especially at polynyas (those special and scattered sites where geography and winds act together to minimize the formation of ice, even at the highest latitudes).

By about 2000 BC, these people had arrived in Greenland, and about the same time had moved down the coast of Labrador to the end of the Gulf of St. Lawrence. It is not clear whether it was here that they learned the use of the toggling harpoon from Maritime Archaic people, or whether they had come to Canada already equipped with the knowledge. In any event, armed with harpoons and bows—and apparently living primarily in tents with interior hearths for burning wood or mammal bones—they successfully occupied one of the most demanding climates ever mastered by humans. Within a few hundred years, these versatile people also penetrated into the Barrenland northwest of Hudson Bay in pursuit of caribou, apparently displacing the Indians who had followed the herds from the south.

Sometime after 1000 BC, local changes had been instituted that bring archaeologists to refer to the Dorset culture. These included evolutionary modifications in subsistence technology that fitted the people more and more for life on the coasts. Soapstone vessels were adopted as lamps to burn sea mammal oil; houses were now small, stone-lined, and semi-subterranean; and in later Dorset years, some extremely long stone-rimmed structures were used as either habitations or ceremonial locations. Dorset people are commonly credited with invention of the snow block house and techniques for taking seals through the ice, both of which permitted winter occupation on the sea ice.

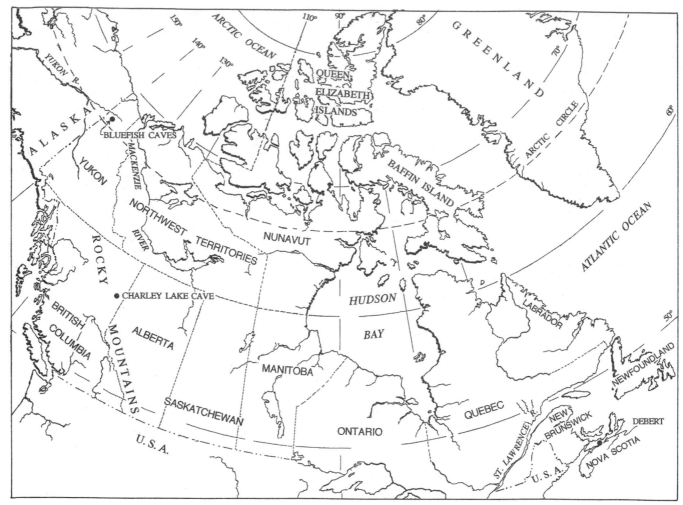

Map of Canada showing the locations of archaeological sites mentioned in the essay.   [Don E. Dumond]

Their territory retracted from the Barrens, which were re-entered by Indians from the south. Dorset occupations extended along the Labrador coast to insular Newfoundland, and people of identifiable Dorset culture were also present on the coasts of Greenland, where early Norse settlers may have made some contact with them. Far to the west, around and west of the outlet of the Mackenzie River, there is evidence of intrusions by, or contacts with, contemporary people of Alaska of the Norton culture or tradition. These contemporary people used pottery adopted under ultimate Asian stimulus near Bering Strait.

Around AD 1100, the Arctic world of Canada was changed again. This time, people of Thule culture, also from Alaska, moved rapidly across the same route taken by their Arctic Small Tool predecessors. Unlike those predecessors, Thule folk were an accomplished maritime people, equipped with skin boats and capable of pursuing the largest sea mammals, including the great whales. They were familiar already with some uses of iron obtained from northeast Asia, and they lived in semi-subterranean houses framed with whale bones and

heated by the oil-burning lamp. Although discussion continues about the motive for the Thule movement, it appears certain that it occurred at a time of warming climate, when ice patterns in the Arctic seas must have changed to the point that migrations of the northern bowhead whale were altered, and whaling improved in the region off the Arctic coasts. One other recent suggestion is that from their Dorset predecessors, they learned of the availability of iron—either traded from the Norse or obtained as the result of an iron-rich meteoric deposit in north Greenland—and pursued it as a treasure.

Moving again through the Arctic islands, into Greenland, and along the Labrador coast as far as the Gulf of St. Lawrence (where they apparently displaced certain coastal groups of Indians), they established themselves in all of the regions in which the peoples speaking Eskimoan languages would be found with the final European expansions of the historic period. Once they arrived, further adaptations were necessary as the somewhat warmer climate gave way to the so-called Little Ice Age that climaxed at AD 1500 or so. Environmental conditions caused the people of the Arctic coast to give up semi-subterranean habitations for tents in the summer caribou areas and snow-block houses on the winter sea ice, which provided fresh seal dinners at their doorstep. Some of them re-entered the Barrenland and again took up movements shadowing the caribou herds, now forced to accommodate themselves to their Indian neighbors, with whom they were largely unfriendly, and who maintained their hold on the territory at the north edge of the treeline to which the caribou retreated in winter.

And so Indian descendants of the Subarctic Archaic peoples on the one hand, and Inuit descendants of Thule Arctic migrants on the other, met arriving Europeans and ultimately were incorporated into Canada.

Further Reading: Dixon, E. James, *Bones, Boats, and Bison: Archeology and the First Colonization of Western North America* (Albuquerque: University of New Mexico Press, 1999); Fedje, Daryl, "The Early Post-Glacial History of the Northwest Coast: A View from Haida Gwaii and Hecate Strait," *Athena Review* 3(2) (2002): 28–30; Fladmark, K., "Routes: Alternative Migration Corridors for Early Man in North America," *American Antiquity* 44 (1979): 55–69; Gordon, Bryan C., *People of Sunlight, People of Starlight: Barrenland Archaeology in the Northwest Territories of Canada* (Hull, QC: Canadian Museum of Civilization, Archaeological Survey of Canada, 1996); Helm, June, *Handbook of North American Indians*, Vol. 6: *Subarctic* (Washington, DC: Smithsonian Institution, 1981); McGhee, Robert, *Ancient People of the Arctic* (Vancouver: University of British Columbia Press, 1996); Mandryk, Carole A. S., and Nat Rutter, eds., "The Ice-Free Corridor Revisited," *Quaternary International* 32 (1996); Storck, Peter L., *Journey to the Ice Age: Discovering an Ancient World* (Vancouver: University of British Columbia Press, 2004); Wright, J. V., *A History of the Native People of Canada*, vols. 1 and 2 (Hull, QC: Canadian Museum of Civilization, Archaeological Survey of Canada, 1995 and 1999).

Don E. Dumond

EARLIEST AMERICAN SITES AND ROUTES SOUTH IN THE ARCTIC AND SUBARCTIC

Archaeological research has demonstrated that humans evolved in the Old World and later migrated to Asia, Europe, Australia, and finally the Americas. The preponderance of linguistic and biological evidence indicates that Native Americans most likely originated somewhere in northeastern Asia. The evidence used to determine when the first human colonization of the Americas occurred includes geological events, human remains, artifacts, and environmental conditions during the last Ice Age.

The first people to arrive in the Americas occupied a vast region known as Beringia, which encompasses the Bering and Chukchi seas and adjacent areas of North America and Asia. Beringia is divided into three provinces: western Beringia, central Beringia, and eastern Beringia. Eastern Beringia includes Alaska and adjacent areas of Canada that were not covered by the massive continental glaciers during the ice ages (called the Pleistocene period). Eastern Beringia is the only area of North America adjacent to Asia and connected to it in the past by a land bridge. Most archaeologists agree that it is through Siberia, the Bering Land Bridge, and Alaska that people first discovered North America, either by crossing the Bering Land Bridge or navigating along the coast using watercraft.

During the height of the last Ice Age (about 18,000 years ago), vast amounts of ice accumulated in polar regions and at high elevations. Water evaporating from the oceans and falling as snow on land formed glaciers and caused the worldwide sea level to drop almost 200 meters (650 ft). Because the Bering and Chukchi seas are shallow (less than 200 m), the continental shelf between Asia and Alaska was exposed as dry land. This created a landmass called the Bering Land Bridge, which connected North America and Asia. When continental glaciers melted at the end of the last Ice Age (beginning about 16,000 years ago), water was transported back to the oceans by the earth's rivers and calving glaciers. This caused the sea level to rise approximately 120 meters, and the land connection between Alaska and Siberia was severed for the last time approximately 10,000 years ago.

At the end of the last Ice Age, several species of large North American mammals became extinct, including mammoths, horses, and camels. But bison, elk, caribou, musk oxen, moose, mountain sheep and goats, bears, and other types of large animals survived. Although marine mammals along the coast of the Arctic Ocean were probably limited to a few species, such as polar bear and ringed seal, the southern Beringian coast probably supported larger numbers of seals, whales, sea cows, fish, and marine birds. This was a period of dramatic environmental change and a difficult time for people to adapt to new environments.

It is still not known when people first came to Beringia. There is circumstantial evidence suggesting people may have inhabited the region prior to 15,000 years ago. However, the first firm evidence is a well-documented camp at Swan Point in Alaska's Tanana River valley dating to about 12,200 years ago. Artifacts found at Swan Point demonstrate that widespread trade in obsidian (volcanic glass) was already established, and this indicates that human occupation of eastern Beringia occurred prior to that time. A number of other sites suggest that humans occupied eastern Beringia near the end of the last Ice Age, when the Bering Land Bridge still existed. In addition to Swan Point, some of the most important sites are Trail Creek Caves 2 and 9; Dry Creek; Broken Mammoth; Anangula; Onion Portage; the Mesa Site; and On Your Knees Cave.

Archaeologists use the term "tradition" to classify and describe archaeological remains reflecting a common way of life that persists for a long period of time throughout a large geographic area. The beginning and end of a tradition is marked by a major change in technology and economic system. Archaeologists also use the term "complex," which is similar to a tradition but is more restricted geographically, and possibly temporally.

The very earliest types of artifacts found in eastern Beringia belong to the American Paleoarctic tradition, which is best known from northwestern Alaska. The stone artifacts that characterize this tradition include wedge-shaped microblade cores, microblades, blades and blade cores, bifaces, burins, grooved-stone abraders, and antler arrow points slotted to receive microblades. Microblades are small, parallel-sided stone artifacts used for a variety of specialized purposes. In central interior Alaska, the American Paleoarctic tradition is called the Denali complex. This way of making stone tools originated in Asia and is typical of artifacts associated with the Upper Paleolithic archaeological sites in the Old World. These people primarily made their living by fishing and hunting caribou and other animals.

However, about 11,300 years ago, some people did not make or use microblades. They relied primarily on bifacially flaked stone knives and projectile points that probably were used to tip light spears, called darts, propelled with a spear thrower (atl atl). These sites belong to the Nenana complex, which appears to have lasted until about 10,500 years ago. The stone tools most characteristic of the Nenana complex are triangular and teardrop-shaped projectile points and knives, and straight or concave-based lanceolate projectile points.

The Northern Paleoindian tradition appears for the first time in eastern Beringia around about 10,500 years ago and may have lasted as late as 8,000 years ago in some areas. This tradition is derived from more southern areas of North America and is best known from the western plains of North America, where it is older. Paleoindian sites on the American plains are most commonly associated with big-game hunting, primarily bison. Like the people of the Nenana complex, Northern Paleoindian hunters did not use microblades. They relied on fluted and concave-based stone projectile points and gravers made on flakes. Northern Paleoindian people probably migrated northward as the continental glaciers melted and as plants and animals colonized recently deglaciated areas.

It is unclear whether these contrasting traditions and complexes (the ones that use microblades and the ones that do not) represent different cultural and historical groups of people (cultures) or whether these differences can be explained based on sampling or functional, ecological, or seasonal differences. If cultural historical factors explain the differences in technology, perhaps the boundaries between these technological traditions shifted repeatedly over time, as reflected in some archaeological sites with repeating sequences of non-microblade versus microblade occupations.

People living in the interior regions of eastern Beringia made their living by focusing on hunting, fishing, and foraging along rivers and lakes. However, people living on the coast made their living primarily from fishing and hunting marine mammals. It is difficult to determine the timing and origins of early maritime adaptations (making a living from the plants and animals of the sea), because the rising sea level flooded the former coastline of Beringia at the end of the last Ice Age, and coastal archaeological sites are now underwater. In the eastern Aleutian Islands and along the northwest coast of North America (southeast Alaska and British Columbia), the earliest coastal sites date to about 10,500–8,000 years ago. However, in most other places, the rising sea level has flooded ancient shorelines, and coastal archaeological sites occupied prior to 8,000 years ago are submerged. There is strong evidence from On Your Knees Cave and other sites along the Alaska coast that suggests people were coastal navigators making their living primarily from the sea prior to 10,000 years ago.

People using microblades made from blocky, irregular microblade cores occupied the northwest coast by about 10,300 years ago. This is called the Northwest Coast Microblade tradition. Although this is the earliest firmly documented tradition from this region, evidence suggests that people who did not use microblades may have occupied the coast prior to this time.

The archaeology of eastern Beringia is complex, because this region linked the early cultural developments in the Old World with those in the Americas. The early settlers of Beringia set the stage for the cultural development that was to follow in the Americas. Once people had colonized eastern Beringia, they moved southward to colonize the rest of the Americas. Some archaeologists believe southward migration from Beringia into the Americas may have begun as early as 50,000 years ago—or possibly earlier—while others suggest it may have been as late as 12,500–13,500 years ago. Geography during the last Ice Age limited possible migration routes available to the first humans to colonize the Americas.

THE CONTINENTAL ROUTE

During the last Ice Age, the climate was much colder, and massive glaciers in eastern and western Canada formed a huge ice sheet covering most of Canada. The ice blocked access between what is today Alaska and the contiguous United States. Because much of the earth's water was

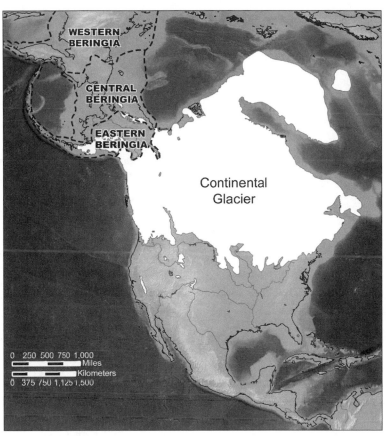

Map of North America depicting unglaciated Beringia and the extent of glacial ice at the height of the last Ice Age, about 21,000 years ago. [E. James Dixon]

trapped in glacial ice, the sea level was lower. The first humans to enter the region would have been confronted by a seemingly endless landscape of ice reaching from Canada's Yukon Territory in the north to the Great Lakes in the south. The continental glaciers would have blocked human migration southward until the ice melted sufficiently to enable plants and animals to colonize the deglaciated land.

Some researchers have hypothesized that an ice-free corridor may have existed in the region of central western Canada. They further theorized that this hypothetical corridor could have provided an avenue through which humans may have passed from Beringia to the more southern regions of the continent prior to the end of the last Ice Age. The concept of an ice-free corridor has been proposed to explain the discovery of archaeological evidence south of the continental glaciers that is believed to be older than about 13,000 years old, predating the melting of the glaciers.

However, recent research demonstrates that glacial ice covered an extensive area in southern Alberta where the corridor was believed to have existed, and that the continental glaciers did not melt in this area until sometime between 12,500 and 13,600 years ago. Consequently, the unglaciated

areas of eastern Beringia and the northern plains of North America remained separated by ice until about 12,500 years ago, when the glaciers had melted enough to enable plants, animals, and people to move into this new territory. Because the ice sheets blocked the way south from eastern Beringia, the North American continent south of the continental glaciers could not have been colonized by humans on foot until sometime around 12,500 years ago. This conclusion is supported by the fact that no animal bones dating between about 21,000 to 13,000 years ago have been found in the region formerly believed to be the ice-free corridor. This demonstrates fairly conclusively that an ice-free corridor did not exist, and that the continental glaciers prevented the area from being inhabited by animals during the last Ice Age. This evidence precludes a mid-continental route for human entry before about 12,500–13,000 years ago.

Several archaeological sites in North and South America are older than 13,000 years. While the age and character of these sites is considered controversial by some researchers, this growing body of data strongly supports the idea that humans were widespread throughout the Americas prior to the melting of the continental glaciers (approximately 12,500–13,000 years ago).

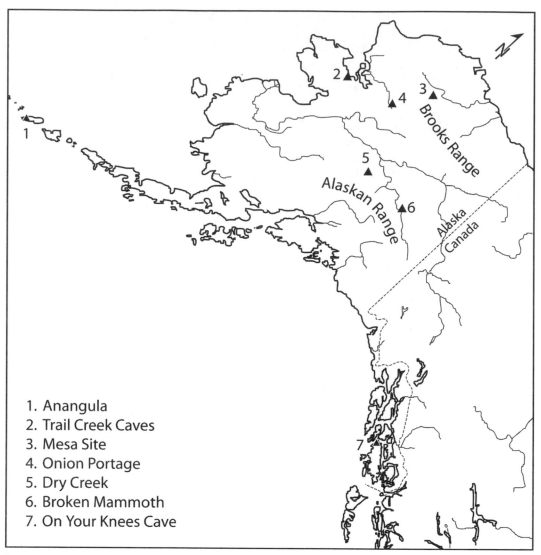

1. Anangula
2. Trail Creek Caves
3. Mesa Site
4. Onion Portage
5. Dry Creek
6. Broken Mammoth
7. On Your Knees Cave

Important early archaeological sites in eastern Beringia. [E. James Dixon]

COASTAL MIGRATION

There is a growing body of evidence suggesting that the most plausible route for the initial colonization of the Americas may have been along the northwest coast, beginning possibly as early as 16,000 years ago. Some researchers suggest that the earliest human migration to North America may have occurred with the use of watercraft along the southern margin of Beringia and then southward along the northwest coast of North America. This would have enabled humans to enter southern areas of the Americas prior to the melting of the mid-continental glaciers.

Prior to the early 1970s, it had been assumed that the continental glaciers of North America extended westward to the Pacific Ocean and margins of the continental shelf. This would have created a barrier to human migration via watercraft from eastern Beringia southward. More recently geologists working in southeast Alaska and British Columbia have discovered that deglaciation along the northwest coast of

North America had begun by about 16,800 years ago and was sufficiently advanced to enable humans using watercraft to colonize coastal areas by about 15,400 years ago.

This research has also documented the existence of ice-free areas, or refugia, throughout major coastal areas along the northwest coast that were never covered by glacial ice during the last Ice Age. It is now clear that some areas of continental shelf and offshore islands were not covered by ice during the last Ice Age, and vast areas along the coast that were glaciated may have been free of ice beginning about 16,000 years ago. Except for a 400-kilometer coastal area between southwest British Columbia and Washington state, the northwest coast of North America was largely free of ice by this time. This evidence indicates that the exposed continental shelf and offshore islands were available as a migration route from eastern Beringia to the rest of the Americas around approximately 15,000 years ago.

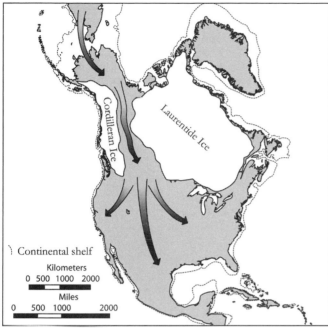

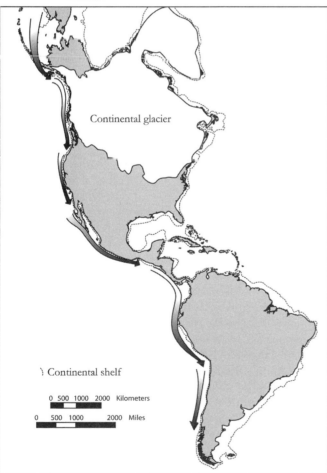

Hypothetical migration routes from Beringia to the southern regions of the Americas. [E. James Dixon]

This hypothesis has gained increased support, because the remains of black and brown bears, caribou, and other land animals dating to the last Ice Age have been found in caves in southeast Alaska and British Columbia. The remains of land and sea mammals (including caribou, seals, birds, and fish) dating to this time have also been discovered in a number of caves along the northwest coast. These discoveries provide additional evidence that there were sufficient plant and animal resources for people to survive. This evidence suggests that people using watercraft were able to colonize ice-free regions along the continental shelf exposed by the lower sea level before the end of the last Ice Age. This would have enabled people to settle south of the continental glaciers before the opening of an ice-free area in western Canada connecting eastern Beringia and the ice-free southern areas of North America. If the theory is correct, the oldest archaeological sites in the Americas should be located along the west coast of the Americas in areas that are underwater today.

The coastal hypothesis suggests an economy based on marine mammal hunting, saltwater fishing and shellfish gathering, and the use of watercraft. By contrast, the interior ice-free corridor model for human colonization requires an economy based on the hunting of terrestrial mammals, freshwater fishing, and pedestrian travel. Each required different types of adaptations by the New World founding population.

SUMMARY

Beringia is the gateway to the Americas. There is little evidence to suggest that people occupied Beringia prior to the last Ice Age. The data indicates that a land route from Beringia to the rest of the Americas was not available until 12,500 years ago. Geologic data indicates that the northwest coast was largely deglaciated possibly as early as 14,000–16,000 years ago, which may have enabled the first people using watercraft to move south of the continental ice along the northwest coast.

The microblade traditions of eastern Beringia clearly have their origins in northeast Asia, where similar ways of making stone tools pre-date them. In contrast the non-microblade industries emphasize the manufacture of bifacially flaked stone projectile points and appear to have originated in the New World. The origins of the Nenana complex remain a mystery, but the Northern Paleoindian tradition appears to have its roots in the southern regions of North America, having moved north sometime around 11,500 years ago, after deglaciation in central Canada

Eastern Beringia is unique in the history of North America. The human history of this vast region reflects the complex push-pull forces at a global scale. The rise in sea level reduced the landmass of central Beringia. At the same time, the melting continental ice created a new habitat in interior Canada and along the northwest coast. The extinction of

Pleistocene fauna reduced large terrestrial mammal resources. At the same time, the opening of the Bering Strait led to the exchange of warm Pacific water with the cooler Arctic Ocean, increasing maritime productivity. These geological and biological forces contributed to the complexity of Beringia as a cultural interface between the Old World and New World.

Further Reading: Burns, J. A., "Vertebrate Paleontology and the Alleged Ice-Free Corridor: The Meat of the Matter," *Quaternary International* 32 (1996): 107–112; Dillehay, T. D., *The Settlement of the Americas: A New Prehistory* (New York: Basic Books, 2000); Dixon, E. James, *Boats, Bones, and Bison: Archeology and the First Colonization of Western North America* (Albuquerque: University of New Mexico Press, 1999); Elias, Scott A., *The Ice-Age History of Alaskan National Parks* (Washington, DC, and London: Smithsonian Institution Press, 1995); Fladmark, K. R., "Routes: Alternative Migration Corridors for Early Man in North America," *American Antiquity* 44 (1979): 55–69; Goebel, Ted, Michael R. Waters, and Dennis H. O'Rourke, "The Late Pleistocene Dispersal of Modern Humans in the Americas," *Science* 319 (March 14, 2008): 1497–1502; Heaton, T. H., S. L. Talbot, and G. F. Shield, "An Ice Age Refugium for Large Mammals in the Alexander Archipelago, Southeastern Alaska," *Quaternary Research* 46(2) (1996): 186–192; Jackson, Lionel E., Jr., and Alexandra Duk-Rodkin, "Quaternary Geology of the Ice-Free Corridor: Glacial Controls on the Peopling of the New World," in *Prehistoric Mongoloid Dispersals*, edited by Takeru Akazawa and Emoke J. E. Szathmary (Oxford, UK: Oxford University Press, 1997); Josenhans, H. W., D. W. Fedje, R. Pienitz, and J. Southon, "Early Humans and Rapidly Changing Holocene Sea Levels in the Queen Charlotte Islands–Hecate Strait, British Columbia, Canada," *Science* 277(1998): 71–74; Parfit, M., "Hunt for the First Americans," *National Geographic* (December 2000); West, F. H., ed., *American Beginnings* (Chicago: University of Chicago Press, 1996).

E. James Dixon

ARCHAEOLOGY OF A BORDERLAND: PRINCE WILLIAM SOUND AND COOK INLET, SOUTHERN ALASKA COAST

INTRODUCTION

The Kenai Peninsula and two adjacent great bays—Prince William Sound to the east and Cook Inlet to the west—constitute a cultural border zone shared by two anciently divided but interactive cultural traditions. The Alutiit (or Sugpiat) are the southernmost division in an arc of Inuit cultures that follows the coastlines of Alaska, northeastern Siberia, Arctic Canada, and Greenland. The Dena'ina are northern Athabascan Indians, the only members of this large cultural family to live on salt water and to include sea mammal hunting in their traditional subsistence economy.

Today both peoples occupy much the same areas that their ancestors did, within territorial boundaries that have been stable for about 1,000 years. Alutiiq villages and archaeological sites are located along the coasts of Prince William Sound, the Kenai Peninsula, lower Cook Inlet, the Alaska Peninsula, and the Kodiak Archipelago. The Dena'ina homeland—past and present—includes the rivers and shores of the vast Cook Inlet drainage, as well as interior areas west of the Alaska Range. Steep mountains, active glaciers, subarctic boreal forest, and richly productive coastal waters characterize these two cultural regions in the heart of south central Alaska.

CULTURAL RELATIONSHIPS

History, archaeology, and oral tradition indicate a high level of interaction between the two groups. Inter-societal warfare, trade, and political alliances figure prominently in oral histories recorded by Dena'ina elder Shem Pete and others. Raiding and trading parties traveled by water or over trails through mountain passes. Close contact led to cultural borrowings, including Dena'ina adoption of the Eskimo kayak, sea mammal harpoon, and waterproof clothing made from sea mammal intestines. The Alutiit traded with the Dena'ina for caribou skins, forest furs, and other products of the interior. At the time of Russian and European contact in the late eighteenth century, both groups occupied permanent villages and had complex, lineage-based societies with divisions between elites, commoners, and slaves. These characteristics—unusual worldwide for non-agricultural peoples—were shared by adjacent coastal populations from the eastern Aleutian Islands to the Canadian northwest coast.

Dena'ina and Alutiit probably had a common foundation in the microblade-using Alaskan Paleoarctic cultural tradition of approximately 10,000–7,500 years ago, a period represented by the small Beluga Point site in the upper Cook Inlet. In the Alutiiq area, the Paleoarctic tradition was followed by the Ocean Bay (7,500–3,500 years ago) and Kachemak/Palugvik (3,500–900 years ago) phases, which show increasing reliance on marine resources, growing populations, new elements of social complexity, and the elaboration of spiritual and artistic traditions. At various times, these cultures expanded into both lower and upper Cook Inlet, as represented by the Yukon Island and Tiq'atl'ena Bena (Hewitt Lake) sites described below and by Riverine Kachemak salmon-fishing camps on the Kenai and Kasilof rivers between 3,400 and 1,000 years ago.

In comparison Dena'ina prehistory prior to 1,000 years ago is poorly known. Through several cultural phases, including the Northern Archaic period (around 5,400–4,200 years ago), ancestral generations seem to have relied primarily on caribou and other game and fish of the forests, tundra, and interior waterways.

Major shifts in culture and territory occurred from about AD 1000 to 1400, coinciding with ecosystem changes during the global Medieval Warm period. Dena'ina groups expanded into the Cook Inlet region, taking over former Kachemak territory; they became sea mammal hunters (for seals, porpoises, and beluga whales) and intensive salmon fishers. A wave of Yup'ik cultural influence, language, and (most likely) people swept into the Alutiiq region, coinciding with an archaeological transition to the late pre-contact Koniag phase on Kodiak Island and the Chugach phase in Prince William Sound. Influences on Alutiiq culture from the Tlingit of southeastern Alaska are also evident at this time.

ARCHAEOLOGICAL SITES

Sites of the early Dena'ina cultural tradition represent a nomadic population that left few detectable traces on the landscape. Artifacts are scant, and bone is rarely preserved in acidic forest soils. Sites dating after AD 1000 are far more visible and include single and multi-roomed houses with sunken floors and earthen wall mounds. Artifacts and faunal remains are still relatively scarce, however, due to the spiritually motivated disposal of these objects away from living areas.

In contrast Alutiiq prehistory for the last 7,000 years is represented by substantial coastal villages; semi-subterranean houses; diverse and abundant artifacts; and deep middens (trash mounds) containing shell and animal bone. Calcium carbonate from seashells reduces soil acidity, so bone artifacts and faunal remains are often well preserved. On the other hand, glacial advances and the sinking of coastal areas during great earthquakes have erased parts of the Alutiiq archaeological record, especially along the outer Kenai coast and inner Prince William Sound.

Palugvik and Uqciuvit Sites—Prince William Sound

Frederica deLaguna (Bryn Mawr College), a major figure in Alaskan anthropology, carried out pioneering archaeological surveys of Cook Inlet and Prince William Sound during the early 1930s. Her excavations at Palugvik, a multi-layered village site, revealed evidence of Chugach (eastern Alutiiq) life from about 2,300 years ago to several centuries before Russian contact. Many Palugvik artifacts resemble Inuit implements from farther north (for example, stone oil lamps, semi-circular knives, ground-slate lance, and arrow points), but others bear the stamp of life on a forested southern coast, where the sea rarely freezes. Darts and harpoons with barbed bone heads were favored for sea mammal hunting—rather than toggling harpoons, which are more suited to securing animals beneath

or among floating sea ice. Chisels, wedges, and other woodworking tools are common at Palugvik and other Alutiiq sites, including heavy northwest coast–style splitting adzes. The latter came into the area about AD 1000, probably from the Tlingit. Copper arrowheads from Palugvik and other sites in Prince William Sound could have been obtained through trade with the Ahtna, Dena'ina, or Tlingit. The excavation also produced objects of personal adornment—labrets (lip plugs), nose pins, bone beads, a copper ring—that functioned in Alutiiq societies as markers of social rank. Animal remains from the site also reflect the southern environment. These included harbor seal, sea lion, sea otter, porpoise, killer whale, sperm whale, abundant shellfish, and diverse fish species.

Data on an earlier part of Prince William Sound prehistory come from the Uqciuvit site, excavated by Michael Yarborough (Cultural Resource Consultants) and Linda Yarborough (U.S. Forest Service) in 1988. The oldest layers date back to 3,800 years ago and show affinities with Ocean Bay culture. At Uqciuvit and throughout Prince William Sound, there is a noticeable gap in occupation that coincides with a period of cold temperatures and glacial advances between 3,200 and 2,500 years ago. Some sites were probably destroyed by the advancing ice.

Bear Cove—Aialik Bay, Outer Kenai Coast

Bear Cove, excavated in 2003 by Aron L. Crowell (Smithsonian Institution) for the Kenai Fjords Oral History and Archaeology Project, illustrates the impact of earthquakes, sinking coastlines, and volcanic eruptions on humans. Radiocarbon dates from this seal-hunting camp indicate several periods of use from about AD 1000–1800, and artifacts (lance blades, knives, splitting adzes) are similar to those found in the upper levels at Palugvik and Uqciuvit. Dwellings at Bear Cove were built partially underground, probably with wooden plank walls and bark-covered roofs, like historically known Chugach houses.

Bear Cove residents were forced to flee their village in about 1170 AD, when a very large earthquake (known from geological studies) caused at least 2 meters of instant subsidence. A layer of beach gravel, washed in by the sea after the earthquake, separates the earliest occupation levels at Bear Cove from deposits laid down about a century later, when people were able to return. Progressive sinking of the outer Kenai coast means that very few sites older than 800 years are known.

Another disruption of life at Bear Cove occurred about 500 years ago, when a volcanic eruption in Cook Inlet or the Alaska Peninsula dropped a layer of ash (tephra) across the region. The site was again temporarily abandoned, perhaps because the tephra disrupted the Aialik Bay ecosystem.

Yukon Island—Kachemak Bay, Lower Cook Inlet

In 1931–32 deLaguna excavated at Cottonwood Creek and at the Great Midden and Fox Farm sites on Yukon

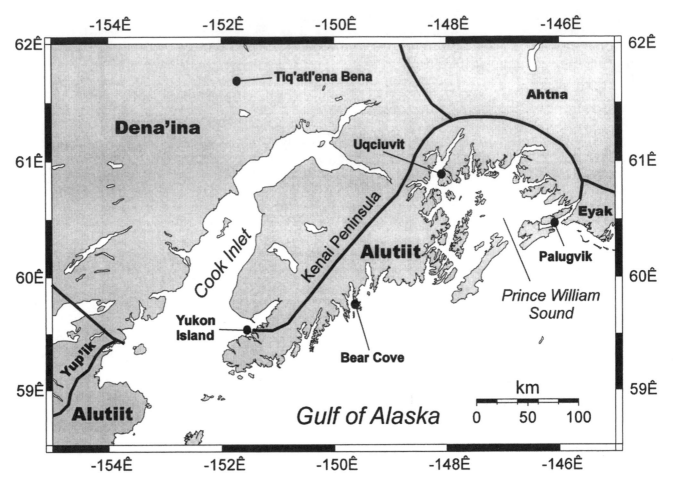

Archaeological sites and cultural tradition boundaries around Cook Inlet and Prince William Sound, south central Alaska.   [Aron L. Crowell]

Island, in Kachemak Bay. DeLaguna used her results to provide the first definition of the Kachemak period and its several phases. Since the 1970s, William and Karen Workman (University of Alaska, Anchorage) have carried out further investigations into the sequence of early Eskimo and later Dena'ina sites in this ecologically rich corner of Cook Inlet. The Great Midden shell mound is some 3.5 meters thick and produced a large inventory of hunting, fishing, and domestic artifacts, as well as decorated stone lamps and carved ivory figures and pendants—types that are artistic hallmarks of Kachemak culture. DeLaguna and the Workmans have also excavated Kachemak burials at Yukon Island, Cottonwood Creek, and other sites that included grave goods (stone and bone tools), personal ornaments (labrets and large numbers of bone beads from necklaces or headdresses), and evidence of elaborate mortuary ritual. Clay masks with ivory eyes and stone labrets covered several skulls.

Small Dena'ina camps and villages, including the upper layer at the great Yukon Island midden, indicate Dena'ina expansion into Kachemak Bay after AD 1000, following

abandonment by Kachemak residents about 500 years earlier.

Tiq'atl'ena Bena (Hewitt Lake)—Skwentna River Drainage, Upper Cook Inlet

R. Greg Dixon (National Park Service) tested cultural deposits at this important Dena'ina location in 1992. Several habitation areas around the lake are collectively remembered in oral tradition as the site of an old permanent village, as well as fishing and hunting camps that were used as recently as the 1930s.

Local resources include salmon, trout, char, moose, black bear, beaver, marten, and ground squirrel. Dixon counted more than twenty surface house depressions and sixty fish storage pits; he selected one of the larger dwellings for excavation. This was a traditional multi-family house (nichił), including a main room with sleeping benches and a back chamber used for steam bathing with heated rocks. Stone tools, chipping debris, and a few bones were found, along with a single blue trade bead and iron knife—artifacts that indicate occupation during the early period of Western contact. Underlying the historic house floor, however, were layers representing use of the location since about 4,500 years ago. The lowest of these levels contained ground-slate projectile points typical of the Ocean Bay culture, indicating that this ancestral Eskimo group once penetrated well into the hinterlands of upper Cook Inlet.

LEARNING MORE

Studies at Palugvik, Uqciuvit, Bear Cove, Yukon Island, and Hewitt Lake represent only a small sample of past and current research in the Dena'ina and Alutiiq regions. The work is conducted by state, federal, and university-affiliated archaeologists, often in collaboration with Alaska Native communities. Visitors to south central Alaska can discover its deep history and contemporary cultures through visits to museums and tribal cultural centers, including the Anchorage Museum, Alaska Native Heritage Center (Anchorage), Alutiiq Museum and Archaeological Repository (Kodiak), Eklutna Historical Park (Eklutna, near Anchorage), the Pratt Museum (Homer), the K'Beq Interpretive Site (Kenai), Kenai Fjords National Park Visitors' Center (Seward), and the Ilanka Cultural Center (Cordova).

Further Reading: Crowell, Aron L., "Connecting with the Past—The Kenai Fjords Oral History and Archaeology Project," *Alaska Park Science* 3(1) (2004): 32–38; Crowell, Aron L., and Daniel H. Mann, *Archaeology and Coastal Dynamics of Kenai Fjords National Park, Alaska* (Anchorage, AK: National Park Service, 1998); Crowell, Aron L., Amy F. Stefian, and Gordon L. Pullar, eds., *Looking Both Ways: Heritage and Identity of the Alutiiq People* (Fairbanks: University of Alaska Press, 2001); DeLaguna, Frederica, *Chugach Prehistory: The Archaeology of Prince William Sound, Alaska* (Seattle and London: University of Washington Press, 1956); De Laguna, Frederica, *The Archaeology of Cook Inlet, Alaska*, 2nd ed. (Anchorage: Alaska Historical Society, 1975); Kari, James, and James A. Fall, *Shem Pete's Alaska: The Territory of the Upper Cook Inlet Dena'ina*, with Shem Pete as principal contributor, 2nd ed. (Fairbanks: University of Alaska Press, 2003); Reger, Douglas R., "Archaeology of the Northern Kenai Peninsula and Upper Cook Inlet," *Arctic Anthropology* 35(1) (1998): 160–171; Workman, William B., "Archaeology of the Southern Kenai Peninsula," *Arctic Anthropology* 35(1) (1998):146–159; Yarborough, Michael R, and Linda Finn Yarborough, "Prehistoric Maritime Adaptations of Prince William Sound and the Pacific Coast of the Kenai Peninsula," *Arctic Anthropology* 35(1) (1998): 132–145.

Aron L. Crowell

THE ARCHAEOLOGY OF KODIAK ISLAND, ALASKA

Perched on the edge of Alaska's continental shelf, the Kodiak Archipelago is an expansive chain of islands. Here, warm north Pacific storms collide with cold mountains, bringing strong winds and rain. Beneath the persistent clouds lies a dramatic landscape formed by the collision of tectonic plates, sculpted by glacial ice, and inundated with ocean water. Fjords lined by steep mountains split Kodiak's granite heart, channeling the sea far inland. No inland area is more than 29 kilometers from the ocean.

This complex shoreline shelters an abundance of life. Sea mammals, fish, shellfish, birds, and bears of legendary size have sustained Native societies for 7,500 years and enticed others to settle. Hundreds of archaeological sites preserve this human history. In addition to abundant natural resources, Kodiak has an unusual wealth of cultural deposits—created by large prehistoric populations, a reliance on maritime resources, and the persistently damp climate. Many prehistoric sites have well-preserved bone, shell, and ivory artifacts, and a few hold spectacular wood and fiber objects. These artifacts occur around the remains of red ochre floors, stone tent rings, and sunken sod houses—features that chronicle the development of Native societies from small, mobile, hunting, fishing, and gathering groups to large, permanent communities led by wealthy families.

The Sugpiaq—known today as the Alutiiq people—occupied the archipelago when Russian traders arrived in the late eighteenth century. Over the past 75 years, archaeological research has revealed the deep history of these Natives. The Alutiiq Museum and Archaeological Repository, a Native-governed culture center where visitors can explore local prehistory, now stores many of the objects and information from this research. The museum preserves and shares Alutiiq heritage through exhibits, programs, research, and publications—including an extensive Web site. Visitors can even sign up to participate in field research as volunteers with the museum's annual community excavation.

More recent sites, many with historic structures, record the history of European settlement: Russian conquest and the development of the north Pacific fur trade; American rule and the rise of the modern fishing industry, and the World War II military buildup. Visitors can experience the last 250 years of Kodiak history at two museums housed in historic sites: the Baranov Museum in the Erskine House, a Russian era magazine; and the Kodiak Military History Museum in the Ready Ammunition Bunker at Fort Abercrombie State Historic Park.

Community volunteers assist with the excavation of Zaimka Mound, 2002.   [Patrick G. Saltonstall]

ZAIMKA MOUND—CLIFF POINT, KODIAK ISLAND

Archaeological research suggests continual occupation of the Kodiak Archipelago for at least 7,500 years. Kodiak's first settlers must have been able mariners, as ocean waters surrounded the region thousands of years before human colonization. Scientists believe people arrived by boat, paddling eastward from the Alaska Peninsula. Evidence of early settlements occurs throughout the region, although the most extensive data comes from sites at the northeastern end of the Kodiak Island. Here tectonic activity and changing sea levels preserved ancient settlements on terraces behind the modern shore.

One of these sites is Zaimka Mound, a 4,000-year-old accumulation of cultural debris that rests on Cliff Point, directly opposite the Kodiak airport. A short drive from the Chiniak Highway, Zaimka lies in a sheltered coastal meadow. Here, researchers found more than 2 meters of cultural deposits. At the bottom of the site, thin, oval layers of ochre-stained soil pockmarked with postholes and littered with microblades—tiny leaves of stone used to arm bone spears—suggest the brief tent camps of sea mammal hunters. A sandstone lamp with a charred lip found at the very base of the site indicates that for light, Kodiak's first residents burned oil rendered from sea mammal blubber. Artifacts from Zaimka Mound can be seen at the Alutiiq Museum.

Through time Zaimka's residents extended their stays and refocused subsistence activities around marine fishing. By 6,000 years ago, residents built substantial tent rings made of stacked slate slabs with permanent slab hearths. By 4,500 years ago, they constructed sod houses—structures dug partially into the ground, fitted with a wooden frame, and covered with a sod roof. And by 3,800 years ago, Zaimka's visitors created a great variety of pits around their sod houses. Layers of charcoal and gravel in these pits, new types of fishing gear (heavy, plummet-style line sinkers and notch cobble net sinkers), and more efficient ground-slate cutting tools suggest that people were catching, drying, and storing quantities of cod and rockfish. Over four millennia, residents switched from harvesting small quantities of food for immediate use to harvesting large quantities of fish for storage.

THE UYAK SITE—LARSEN BAY, KODIAK ISLAND

Evidence of village development continued in succeeding centuries, documented in hundreds of coastal shell middens—like the Uyak site. This massive accumulation of well-preserved faunal materials, artifacts, sod house remains, and burials rests at the entrance to Larsen Bay, a protected fjord on the southwestern coast of Kodiak Island. Here materials spanning the last 2,500 years of Kodiak prehistory cover a low bluff at the northern end of an Alutiiq village (also named Larsen Bay). The community's main road dead-ends on the site. Today private buildings sit on the site, including a hunting and fishing lodge where visitors can stay.

Smithsonian anthropologist Ales Hrdlicka studied the Uyak site in the 1930s, mining its deposits for human remains and artifacts. A 1987 re-study revealed a large cluster of houses and storage structures at the eastern end of the site,

Archaeological remains of a single-room house with a long, sunken entrance tunnel (outlined with white rope) from the Uyak site, Kodiak Island. [Amy F. Steffian]

built about 1,200 years ago. Like earlier structures, these single-roomed dwellings had sunken floors, post-and-beam frameworks, and sod roofs. New facilities included deep entrance tunnels designed to trap warm air in living areas, benches for sleeping and sitting, and cooking features. Clay aprons, clay-lined pits and troughs, and gravel-filled bowls surround slate slab hearths. Studies of discarded clamshells suggest the houses were winter residences, occupied from fall until spring. Sites on nearby salmon streams likely functioned as summer fish camps.

Artifacts from the village reflect long-distance trade with the Alaskan mainland. Caribou antler, walrus ivory, bituminous coal, and basalt—materials not found on Kodiak— appear in large quantities, both as finished objects and as pieces of manufacturing debris. These materials indicate that people of this era interacted regularly with neighboring societies. People fashioned some of these materials into jewelry and artwork. The Uyak site produced a large assemblage of labrets (decorative lip plugs carved in a distinctive set of styles and sizes), perhaps to indicate the family and age of the wearer.

Uyak residents buried their dead around the village, placing people in crypts—facilities that held multiple individuals and from which the living removed bones. Archaeologists believe that the rise in village sites, the expansion of long-distance trade, the production of distinctive jewelry, the use of mortuary crypts, and the manipulation of human remains reflect increasing territoriality.

Kodiak societies of this era appear to have filled the landscape. Rather than moving their settlements to meet economic needs, people managed the resources around their communities and formed alliances to obtain other goods. Artifacts from the Uyak site can be seen at the Alutiiq Museum.

KARLUK LAGOON—KODIAK ISLAND

Archaeological sites spanning Kodiak prehistory ring Karluk Lagoon, a long, narrow waterway where ocean tides meet with the fresh waters of the Karluk River on southwestern Kodiak Island. Large, late prehistoric (900 to 250 years ago) and historic sites are particularly evident on the riverbanks, strategically located to harvest the seasonal surfeit of salmon. Today the lagoon is home to Karluk, a rural Alutiiq village where sport fishermen flock each summer.

Karluk One lies above the river mouth, beneath the ruins of mid-twentieth-century Karluk Village. House depressions line the meadow surrounding the Chapel of the Ascension of our Lord, a Russian Orthodox chapel first built in 1843 and now a National Register site. Karluk One once extended onto the riverbank below the church. Here archaeologists discovered a wet site with deposits stretching back 800 years. Water from the adjacent hillside permeated the remains of sod houses, preserving wood and fiber objects. These objects, many of which are displayed at the Alutiiq Museum, illustrate the continued evolution of Alutiiq societies and the emergence of social inequality.

A Russian Orthodox chapel sits atop the remains of Karluk One, a late prehistoric Alutiiq village at the mouth of Karluk River. [Patrick G. Saltonstall]

Karluk One houses are much larger than their predecessors, with side chambers for sleeping, steam baths, and storage connected by tunnels to a large, central room. Archaeologists believe these were dwellings for groups of related people. Other changes include the adoption of salmon harpoons—presumably used in weir fishing, the development of new and larger containers, and the presence of larger storage features, all of which suggest the accumulation of even greater food surpluses.

Labrets continue to be a popular type of jewelry, but occur in more sizes and with more decoration, reflecting an emphasis on individual display. Evidence of the increasing importance of ritual and feasting appears in the masks, mask attachments, drum parts, rattle part, decorated bowls, and gaming pieces that appear at this time—artifacts historically associated with winter festivals that helped families ratify their social positions. Archaeologists believe that these changes reflect the emergence of new leadership—specifically, the development of wealthy families who controlled community resources in an increasingly competitive environment. These cultural changes coincide with both population increases and a period of colder, stormier weather.

Farther upstream, where the waterway narrows, lies Nunakakhnak, the remains of a nineteenth-century Alutiiq village. People first occupied the site in the 1840s, after a devastating smallpox epidemic that killed a third of Kodiak's Alutiiq people and led to the resettlement of many families. Those who lived here harvested salmon for the Russian-American Company provisioning post at the river's mouth. Collapsed multi-roomed sod houses line the low riverbank. Excavation in the westernmost structure revealed a five-room house. The structure has an Alutiiq floor plan, but it is filled with a mixture of Native and Western goods, indicative of the changing economy. Fragments of transfer-printed European ceramics, Russian axes, and thousands of glass beads occur with stone lamps, adzes, and knives. This structure remains open for visitors to explore. Artifacts from Nunakakhnak can be seen at the Alutiiq Museum.

ERSKINE HOUSE—KODIAK

The more recent history of Kodiak is preserved in a variety of historic sites and structures around the city of Kodiak. Among them is the Erskine House, Alaska's oldest remaining Russian-era building. This three-story log structure, named for a former owner, was originally a Russian-American Company magazine. Built between 1805 and 1808, it is the oldest of only four Russian structures standing in the United States; it is also a National Historic Landmark. The structure represents Kodiak's years as the headquarters of the Russian-American Company—and as the administrative capital of the Russian empire in North America. Here, company officials gathered furs harvested around southwest Alaska for shipment to Russia and the Orient.

The Erskine house is home to the Kodiak Historical Society's Baranov Museum. Visitors can explore the inside of this historic structure, portions of which are furnished in Russian and American styles, and view exhibits of artifacts and photos on many aspects of Kodiak history.

Further Reading: Alutiiq Museum and Archaeological Repository, http://www.alutiiqmuseum.org (online April 2006); Baranov Museum—Kodiak, Alaska, http://www.baranov.us/index.htm (online April 2006); Crowell, A. L., A. F. Steffian, and G. L. Pullar, eds.,

Looking Both Ways: Heritage and Identity of the Alutiiq People (Fairbanks: University of Alaska Press, 2001); Fitzhugh, J. Benjamin, *The Evolution of Complex Hunter-Gatherers: Archaeological Evidence from the North Pacific* (New York: Kluwer Academic/Plenum, 2003); Knecht, Richard A., and Richard H. Jordan, "Nunakakhnak: An

Historic Period Koniag Village in Karluk, Kodiak Island, Alaska," *Arctic Anthropology* 22(2) (1985): 17–35; Kodiak Military History Museum at Miller Point Fort, Abercrombie, http://www.kadiak.org/museum/museum.html (online April 2006).

Amy F. Steffian and Patrick G. Saltonstall

WHERE THE BERING SEA MEETS THE PACIFIC OCEAN: THE ARCHAEOLOGY OF THE ALASKA PENINSULA

The Alaska Peninsula is 420 miles (670 km) in length as measured from Cape Douglas and the mouth of the Kvichak River in the northeast to False Pass in the southwest. It slants southwestward from the Alaska mainland to cross nearly 5 degrees of latitude, or from 59 degrees north to 54 degrees, 40 minutes north. Although located in the nominal subarctic, it forms the boundary between the arctic-trending Bering Sea on the northwest, and the more temperate north Pacific on the southeast. Its backbone is the volcano-studded Aleutian Range of mountains, which rise abruptly from the Pacific edge of the peninsula to provide in effect an ecological barricade between weather systems then march westward into the oceans for more than 1,000 miles (1,600 km) as the peaks form the scattered string of Aleutian Islands. On the Bering Sea side of the peninsula mountains, a glacial outwash plain of varying width (wider at the north) is studded with lakes that remain as relics of Pleistocene glaciers. The half-dozen rivers flowing out of them to the Bering Sea provide highroads for migrating sockeye salmon. On the Pacific side, there is a single sockeye system—the Chignik Lakes and Chignik River—that rival the fish-rich streams of the Bering Sea littoral. Other shorter streams receive much more modest runs of pink or chum salmon. The peninsula is generally unforested: a scattering of spruce have within the past three centuries moved as far down as the Naknek River; for 100 miles (160 km) farther southwest there appear a few cottonwood groves.

The peninsula caribou herd, one of the major herds of Alaska, moves north and south along the plain fronting the Bering Sea. Now the herd gathers in early spring to calve in the vicinity of Port Heiden, moving both north and south from there in regular migrations later in the year. The distance covered depends on the overall size of the herd, which like all caribou herds fluctuates in numbers from decade to decade. When the herd is large, the northern migration in late fall and early winter has been known to reach the extreme northern end of the peninsula, and at times to intermingle with the next major herd to the north.

Lakes and bays along the peninsula, especially the eelgrass-choked lagoons of the southwest end, are summer nesting spots for enormous numbers of migratory waterfowl. Sea mammals are largely resident harbor seals, with some walrus seasonally present on the aptly named Walrus Islands of Bristol Bay. Although most species of large whales do not visit the shallow southeastern Bering Sea, bottom-feeding gray whales move close offshore in the summer, also entering bays and lagoons, and smaller belukhas or white whales pursue salmon into the mouths of major streams. In appropriate seasons, then, the peninsula is rich in salmon, caribou, birds, seals, and even certain species of whales.

The Bering Sea plain of the northeastern half of the peninsula—that is, from Port Heiden north, the area that receives winter ice from the Bering Sea—partakes of the historical sequence of human occupation and cultures of the mainland coast from the Paleoarctic tradition to recent speakers of Eskimoan. In the same northeastern half, on the other hand, the coast of the Pacific marched in historical lockstep with the cultural progression of the Kodiak Island region. The lower portion of the peninsula, especially from Port Moller southwestward, was related more closely to events in the Aleutian Islands.

Although the region is easily accessible by scheduled airlines (towns of Dillingham on Nushagak Bay of Bristol Bay, King Salmon and Cold Bay on the Alaska Peninsula), facilities for visitors are relatively limited, and general information about the region's archaeology even more so. However, tourist facilities are available around King Salmon and especially at Brooks River in Katmai National Park and Preserve, which can be reached either by air or by boat from the limited King Salmon road system. At Brooks River, in an area now known especially for the major volcanic eruption of 1912 and famous as a place to watch Alaska brown bears fishing in the short river (especially in July), a reconstructed aboriginal house dating from about AD 1300 is on exhibit with a very limited display of additional finds.

THE NORTH SHORE OF BRISTOL BAY

River systems emptying into Nushagak Bay have yielded clear evidence of the presence of remains of Norton culture sites, although little has been published. Archaeologist

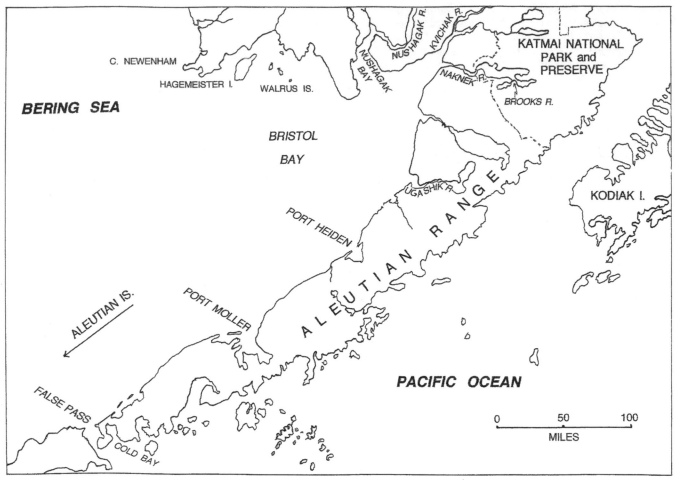

A map of the Alaska Peninsula showing archaeological locations mentioned in the essay.   [Don E. Dumond]

James W. VanStone of the Field Museum of Natural History conducted a major study of nineteenth-century sites of Yupik Eskimos along these rivers, culminating at the now-abandoned trading center of Nushagak, a village on the bay and site of the original Russian outpost (Aleksandrovsk) established in 1819.

Since VanStone's excavations of the 1960s and 1970s, limited work has been undertaken on two of the Walrus Islands off the mouth of the Togiak River by the Alaska State Historic Preservation office and by the National Park Service. This field research has revealed evidence of a particularly rich occupation of Norton culture people beginning some 2,000 years ago and (on Hagemeister) enduring until possibly a century or so after AD 1000. There also is evidence for later systematic exploitation of the islands, especially for walrus and walrus ivory, by Yupik-Eskimo-speaking people of the nearby mainland.

Most recently, tests on a second of the Walrus Islands by the National Park Service have confirmed the Norton occupation and produced radiocarbon dates that suggest earlier occupations. An apparent ancient living floor dated to about 1800 BC

suggests the possible presence of people of the Arctic Small Tool tradition, although artifacts that would be definitively diagnostic of this tradition were not recovered. The lowest level of one test provided a date of about 3800 BC, the charcoal apparently associated with part of a walrus skull. This date is contemporary with Northern Archaic occupations, another site of which is known from 70 miles (113 km) to the west, near Cape Newenham. This early date suggests an occupation during the time when local sea level was low enough that some of the Walrus Islands were still joined with larger Hagemeister Island and thence to the mainland. Again, for the earliest dated occupation, fully diagnostic artifacts were not recovered.

THE NAKNEK RIVER REGION

This vicinity has received by far the greatest attention by archaeologists of any region around the eastern Bering Sea. Work began with the 1930s visit of a Smithsonian Institution physical anthropologist and has continued from the 1950s to the present day with excavations by the University of Oregon and the National Park Service. Many of the sites are located within Katmai National Park and Preserve.

About 10 miles (16 km) north of the mouth of the Naknek River and the present village of Naknek, a site known locally as Graveyard Point (named from a historic cannery cemetery) produced evidence of a late occupation of Paleoarctic people, who camped about 7000 BC in sand dunes that were then 30 miles or so from the (lowered) sea. Presumably interest was centered on caribou crossing the nearby Kvichak River. The caribou crossing was probably also of interest to the people of the Northern Archaic tradition or culture who reoccupied the site around 3500 BC, although by now the sea had risen to about its present level, and the site would have been near the Bristol Bay coast as well as the river.

In the drainage basin of the Naknek River itself, most of the sites explored are located in the Brooks River Archaeological District, so designated because of numerous sites situated along the 1.5-mile (2.4 km) Brooks River, a Naknek system tributary. Here occupation was essentially continuous since about 3000 BC, late in the Northern Archaic period, when people camped at crossings of the river used by the Peninsula caribou herd. In the same approximate period as these scattered Northern Archaic visits, the river was also visited occasionally by people of the Pacific Coast, apparently inland for caribou hunting.

Thereafter, occupations were punctuated by frequent eruptions of the many volcanoes that form the mountainous backbone of the peninsula. Some time after one of these explosive events, at about 1700 BC, Arctic Small Tool people appeared, constructed semi-subterranean houses at productive fishing spots along the river, and returned at least seasonally until shortly before 1000 BC, when there was another massive eruption that blanketed the area with pumice. Like the lower course of the Naknek River, Brooks River was reoccupied about 600 years later by Norton people, who fished along the river and hunted caribou. Their stable occupation and use of small semi-subterranean houses continued until around AD 1100, at which time an intrusion of people from the north brought marked changes in culture, transforming it into one easily recognizable as late prehistoric Eskimo. After only about two centuries, however, another deposit of volcanic ash marks a time in which the upper river drainage was again abandoned, to be reoccupied this time by Yupik-related Pacific Eskimo (or Aluttiq) people who probably migrated from Kodiak Island. Later generations of these people would meet the newly arriving Russians along the Naknek River.

A major late prehistoric site on the lower Naknek River represents this period, located at the mouth of tributary Leader Creek, some 6 miles (10 km) upstream from the modern village of Naknek. At the very mouth of the river is the site of Paguvik, excavated by the University of Oregon and the Field Museum of Chicago in the 1980s. It is of the Russian period, specifically the time between about 1820 and 1870.

UGASHIK RIVER REGION

Some 100 miles (160 km) to the southwest, the Ugashik River drainage system is the site of excavations in the 1970s by the University of Oregon. The culture history sequence from the Naknek vicinity was confirmed there. More notably, however, in the upper drainage system between upper and lower Ugashik Lakes, the site of Ugashik Narrows, still a major caribou crossing, produced substantial evidence of Paleoarctic people dating from 8000 to 7000 BC, as well as of the extensive presence of Northern Archaic people between about 3700 and 3000 BC.

PACIFIC COAST OF THE NORTHERN PENINSULA

Coastal sites in this region have been explored by University of Oregon archaeologists and by the National Park Service. The archaeological sequence, known to begin by about 5000 BC, is closely parallel to that of the Kodiak Islands, with a focus on harvesting of local ocean resources, including some that imply a sophisticated use of watercraft.

LOWER PENINSULA

Both coasts of the lowest third of the Alaska Peninsula—from north of Port Moller to the tip of the Peninsula near the modern village of Cold Bay—were occupied by Aleuts at the time of the Russian arrival. Excavations in the region are still relatively limited, although they began in the 1920s by an archaeologist from the American Museum of Natural History at a major site at Port Moller and were continued there in the 1960s and 1970s in a relatively long-term, if intermittent, Japanese project. After initial and desultory work in the 1970s near the tip of the peninsula, explorations were resumed in the 1990s by Herbert Maschner of Idaho State University. Results indicate occupation beginning as early as 3000 BC. Although there was seemingly an advance of people or influence from farther north on the peninsula around AD 1100 or so, the evidence as a whole apparently relates to direct ancestors of the Aleut people.

Further Reading: Clark, Gerald H., *Archaeology on the Alaska Peninsula: The Coast of Shelikof Strait, 1963–1965*, University of Oregon Anthropological Papers No. 13 (Eugene: University of Oregon, 1977); Dumond, Don E., *A Naknek Chronicle: Ten Thousand Years in a Land of Lakes and Rivers and Mountains of Fire* (King Salmon, AK: National Park Service, Katmai National Park and Preserve, 2005); Henn, Winfield, *Archaeology on the Alaska Peninsula: The Ugashik Drainage, 1973–1975*, University of Oregon Anthropological Papers No. 14 (Eugene: University of Oregon, 1978); Maschner, Herbert D. G., "Prologue to the Prehistory of the Lower Alaska Peninsula," *Arctic Anthropology* 36 (1–2) (1999): 84–102; VanStone, James W., *Eskimos of the Nushagak River: An Ethnographic History* (Seattle: University of Washington Press, 1967); VanStone, James W., *Historic Settlement Patterns in the Nushagak River Region, Alaska*, Fieldiana Anthropology No. 61 (Chicago: Field Museum of Natural History, 1971).

Don E. Dumond

THE MOST ISOLATED PART OF AMERICA: THE ARCHAEOLOGY OF THE ALEUTIAN AND PRIBILOF ISLANDS

Arguably the most isolated region of the United States, the Aleutian Islands of Alaska are the traditional homeland of the Aleut (Unangax, in the Native language) people. Stretching for over 1,000 miles from the southwestern end of the Alaska Peninsula westward toward the Kamchatka Peninsula of Asia, the Aleutian Islands are bounded on the north by the Bering Sea, on the south by the Pacific Ocean, and to the west by several hundred miles of ocean. The islands were created where two great plates of the earth's surface came together, one dipping beneath the other, to produce rugged volcanic landforms. Today the islands form the northern segment of the earthquake-prone and volcanic Pacific known as the Ring of Fire.

To the north of the Aleutian Islands in the central Bering Sea lie the similarly isolated Pribilof Islands. Hundreds of miles from their nearest neighbors, these five islands are Aleutian-like in resources and climate—although, unlike the somewhat warmer Aleutian Islands, every few years the Pribilofs are engulfed in winter sea ice from areas farther north.

At the time of the first foreign contact in 1741, an estimated 12,000–15,000 Aleuts lived throughout the Aleutian Archipelago, although the Pribilof Islands were likely uninhabited. Such a large indigenous population was made possible by the diverse and abundant resources of the Aleutian Islands region. Except for a few land items, all Aleut foods and raw materials came from the oceans, coasts, and streams. These included sea mammals (like harbor seals, sea lions, and whales), birds (like ducks and geese), fish (such as halibut, cod, and several species of salmon), and marine invertebrates (like sea urchins, clams, and mussels).

Because Aleuts focused on the sea for sustenance, it is not surprising that they established almost all of their villages and seasonal hunting camps along the shore. Aleut homes were semi-subterranean, with lower stone- and earth-walled portions roofed with driftwood, whale bone, and an outer layer of sod. Entry and exit was achieved through one or more holes in the roof, from which notched beams descended to the floor.

Throughout the islands, well over a thousand archaeological sites have been identified, although it is assumed that several times this number exist. Many of these reveal their presence today by especially lush vegetation—the product of the deep, nutrient-rich organic deposits that accumulated around former living areas—and by depressions left from former houses. The archaeological record of the Aleut region extends back some 9,000 years, to when the first people entered the area from the east and, over the next several thousand years, migrated westward through the island chain. While the cultural identity of these earliest inhabitants is the subject of some debate, by about 4,000 years ago, the archaeological record provides fairly strong evidence of fundamental cultural continuity to today's Aleut population.

As elsewhere in Alaska, ownership of archaeological sites often rests with the Native village corporations established under provisions of the Alaska Native Claims Settlement Act of 1971. Thus, in the Aleutian and Pribilof regions, each of the eleven Aleut communities owns most of the land, including archaeological sites, in and within several miles of its village.

THE MARGARET BAY SITE, AMAKNAK ISLAND, UNALASKA, ALASKA

Within the limits of the city of Unalaska, the Margaret Bay site, on Amaknak Island, lies on a knoll overlooking a small bay in the larger Unalaska Bay. Although some of the upper portion of the site was disturbed during World War II by intense U.S. military activity in the area, recent archaeological excavations have revealed deeper intact materials dating from about 6,700 to 3,000 years ago.

Because archaeological sites dating older than around 4,000 years are rare in the Aleutian Islands, the Margaret Bay site offers an uncommon glimpse into early Aleut adaptations. For example, faunal remains from the site include polar bear and ringed seal—species that today are found only farther north in Alaska. These findings indicate that the environment was significantly colder at the site in the past than has been the norm in the Aleutian Islands for the past several thousand years. Likewise, stone tools are intriguing, suggesting complex cultural connections between Margaret Bay and areas in Alaska to the east and north.

One of the remarkable findings at Margaret Bay was the remains of several semi-subterranean stone-walled houses dating to about 3,200 years ago. Excavation of one 6-meter-diameter house floor revealed abundant artifacts and animal remains, as well as several sub-floor storage pits, likely for food items.

The Margaret Bay site, accessible from the nearby road system on Amaknak Island, is on land owned by the Ounalashka Corporation (the local Aleut corporation in the city of Unalaska), whose permission must be obtained before going to the site. The nearby Museum of the Aleutians has exhibits concerning the archaeology of the Unalaska area.

Archaeologists excavate a 3,200-year-old stone-walled house at the Margaret Bay site, with more modern housing—a hotel—in the background.   [Douglas W. Veltre]

The excavation of a longhouse at Reese Bay. The central house floor is in the middle of the photograph, with side rooms on both the left and right. On the central floor are large stones (here with short pieces of wood placed on them for emphasis) that served as supports for the main beams holding up the roof.   [Douglas W. Veltre]

THE REESE BAY SITE, UNALASKA ISLAND, ALASKA

Just to the northwest of the city of Unalaska on Unalaska Island lies a large lake separated from the small Reese Bay by a long spit of land. At the western end of this spit, near a small stream that drains the lake, is the Reese Bay site, a former Aleut village occupied from around AD 700 until the early 1800s, or some 30 years after Russians first came to the area. The Reese Bay site, therefore, has offered insights into the response of Aleuts to the arrival of Russians in the early contact period in Alaska.

The Reese Bay site has a number of distinct components. One is a deep midden area located close to the mouth of the stream. Here cultural deposits extend to a depth of approximately 3.5 meters, providing a rich record of Aleut artifacts and foods. Another component, consisting of a number of surface depressions from Aleut houses, lies mostly near the Bering Sea beach.

The third component lies on the spit midway between the ocean and the lake and includes the remains of two Aleut houses, both of which are substantially larger and more complex than those at most other sites throughout the Aleutian Islands.

While most Aleut houses were single-room, semi-subterranean structures some 4 meters by 6 meters in size, the two Reese Bay houses, also semi-subterranean, cover areas of 16 meters by 30 meters and 25 meters by 52 meters, respectively. Each consists of a long, narrow main room about 6 meters wide and up to 45 meters long, connected by wall passages to a series of rooms along each side of the house. Termed "longhouses," structures of this type are known from only about a dozen sites in the entire Aleutian Islands region and are likely a late-prehistoric and early historical type of house built at a time of increasing social ranking and economic complexity. The drawing of the interior of an Aleut house by John Webber, the artist traveling with Captain James Cook to the Aleutians in 1778, may have been of a longhouse of the Reese Bay type.

Because of its isolated location, visiting the Reese Bay site is possible only by boat or floatplane. The site is on land owned by the Ounalashka Corporation (the local Aleut corporation in the city of Unalaska), whose permission must be obtained before going to the site.

THE CHALUKA SITE, UMNAK ISLAND, ALASKA

One of the largest and most important archaeological sites ever excavated in the Aleutian Islands is the Chaluka site, located in a portion of the contemporary village of Nikolski, on southwestern Umnak Island. The site is situated on the Bering Sea coast near the mouth of a very productive salmon stream and close to extensive intertidal rocky flats, from whence abundant invertebrate foods could be obtained.

A low-altitude aerial photograph of the Korovinski site. House depressions are visible on the edge of the bluff overlooking the spit. Boat slips on the shore of the spit and faint traces of sod house walls on the spit are also visible. [Douglas W. Veltre]

Because Chaluka is located at a favorable place for hunting, fishing, and collecting, Aleuts have lived here continuously for the past 4,000 years, as they continue to do today. The site is a large mound—some 60 meters by 200 meters in area and approximately 6 meters deep—created by the slow buildup of the by-products of everyday life: collapsed houses, bone and stone tools, and food refuse. This midden affords excellent preservation for bone and ivory, allowing study of organic artifacts like harpoons and spears, as well as animal bones and shells indicative of past hunting and dietary patterns.

Because Chaluka is on land owned mostly by the Aleut village corporation of Nikolski (the Chalukax Corporation), permission must be obtained before venturing on to the site.

THE KOROVINSKI SITE, ATKA ISLAND, ALASKA

The Korovinski site lies on a hillside and adjacent spit on the northern portion of Atka Island in the central Aleutian Islands. The site's remains include two main components. One is an earlier prehistoric portion dating from 2,000 to 500 years ago—at which time a large volcanic eruption blanketed the area with a 20-centimeter layer of ash, bringing the site's occupation to an abrupt (though not permanent) end. This component of the site is characterized by a 3-meter-deep midden, rich with artifacts and food remains indicative of a large, established Aleut village. On the surface of the site are depressions from semi-subterranean Aleut houses occupied prior to the ash fall.

A second, later component of the Korovinski site is that dating to the Russian occupation of the island, from the late 1700s to the sale of Alaska to the United States in 1867. During this time, the Russian-American Company, which controlled all commercial activities in Alaska during the Russian period, maintained an office at Korovinski to administer company activities in the central Aleutians. Spread out over the Korovinski site are the remains of some 80 Russian period houses and other buildings, potato gardens, a Russian Orthodox church and cemetery, and coastal boat slips. Artifacts from this time period recovered during archaeological research in the 1970s include glass trade beads, iron nails and spikes, bottle and window glass, and other imported materials. By the early 1870s, the Aleut residents of Korovinski had moved their village to its present location on eastern Atka Island.

Access to the Korovinski site is by boat or float plane only, with permission to visit required from the Aleut village corporation of Atka, the Atxam Corporation.

THE ZAPADNI SITE, ST. PAUL ISLAND, ALASKA

Aleut oral tradition holds that the Pribilof Islands had been visited by Aleuts prior to the arrival of Russians in the late 1700s, but it was not until Russians found these islands and began their exploitation of the fur seals that intense settlement took place. Certainly the largest—and probably the first—of four or five Aleut and Russian settlements from this time on St. Paul

Island was the Zapadni site, where depressions and raised sod walls from more than thirty houses and other structures can easily be seen on the heavily vegetated ground surface.

Most of the features at Zapadni date from 1787 to the early 1800s, when Aleuts and Russians lived there to harvest fur seals from the nearby hauling areas. Fur seal pelts, highly valuable because of their soft and especially dense fur, were exported from the Pribilofs to furriers in China, Russia, and elsewhere. By about the 1820s, the several settlements on St. Paul were consolidated at the present village on the island. Until recent decades, Zapadni continued to be used as a temporary seasonal hunting camp by Aleuts of St. Paul.

Zapadni is close to the road system on St. Paul and can easily be visited. However, permission to do so must be obtained from the Tanadgusix (TDX) Corporation, the Aleut village corporation on St. Paul.

Further Reading: Aigner, Jean S., "Bone Tools and Decorative Motifs from Chaluka, Umnak Island," *Arctic Anthropology* 3(2) (1966): 57–83; Denniston, Glenda B., "Cultural Change at Chaluka, Umnak Island: Stone Artifacts and Features," *Arctic Anthropology* 3(2) (1966): 84–124; Knecht, Richard A., Richard S. Davis, and Gary A. Carver, "The Margaret Bay Site and Eastern Aleutian Prehistory," in *Archaeology in the Aleut Zone of Alaska: Some Recent Research*, edited by Don E. Dumond, Anthropological Papers of the University of Oregon No. 58 (Eugene: University of Oregon, 2001), 35–69; Knecht, Rick, and Rick Davis, Margaret Bay Archaeological site, http://www.brynmawr.edu/Acads/Anthro/m-bay/index.html (online April 2006); Lantis, Margaret, "The Aleut Social System, 1750 to 1810, from Early Historical Sources," in *Ethnohistory in Southwestern Alaska and the Southern Yukon: Method and Content*, edited by Margaret Lantis (Lexington: University of Kentucky Press, 1970), 139–301; Veltre, Douglas W., "Korovinski: Archaeological and Ethnohistorical Investigations of a Pre- and Post-Contact Aleut and Russian Settlement on Atka Island," in *Archaeology in the Aleut Zone of Alaska: Some Recent Research*, edited by Don E. Dumond, Anthropological Papers of the University of Oregon No. 58 (Eugene: University of Oregon, 2001), 187–213; Veltre, Douglas W., and Allen P. McCartney, "Ethnohistorical Archaeology at the Reese Bay Site, Unalaska Island, Alaska," in *Archaeology in the Aleut Zone of Alaska: Some Recent Research*, edited by Don E. Dumond, Anthropological Papers of the University of Oregon No. 58(Eugene: University of Oregon, 2001), 87–104; Veltre, Douglas W., and Allen P. McCartney, "Russian Exploitation of Aleuts and Fur Seals: The Archaeology of Eighteenth and Early-Nineteenth-Century Settlements in the Pribilof Islands, Alaska," *Historical Archaeology* 36(2002): 8–17; Veniaminov, Ivan, *Notes on the Islands of the Unalashka District*, translated by Lydia T. Black and R. H. Geoghegan (Kingston, Ontario: Limestone Press, 1984).

Douglas W. Veltre

ARCHAEOLOGY OF THE COAST OF MAINLAND ALASKA

Humans have been present on American lands bordering the Bering and Chukchi seas for at least 12,000 years. By that time the major North American ice masses of the last glacial period (there were no glaciers of comparable size in northeasternmost Asia) were substantially gone, and melt waters had raised sea level to a point ready to flood the Pleistocene-era land bridge to Asia that had existed at the present Bering Strait, which occurred between 10,000 and 11,000 BC.

Inland, major land mammals in the prehistoric period on both sides of the seas were herd animals of the genus *rangifer* (called caribou in America, reindeer in Asia). In the seas whales of differing species migrated through the region, some (the bowhead) moving south from the Arctic Ocean in winter as sea ice expanded, and northward again in summer; herds of walrus moved similarly. Other whales (e.g., the gray whale and right whale) moved north out of the Pacific to summer in the Bering Sea, returning south in winter. In the Bering Sea near the American coast, where water is shallow, only the smaller sea mammals have thrived, but the rivers emptying along this coastline receive major seasonal runs of Pacific salmon. In winter, major coastlines are either frozen fast in sea ice or inundated by drifting ice from the north. Coastal waters freeze in Asia along the entire Bering Sea fringe as well as around the Okhotsk Sea to the southwest. In America, seas may freeze as far south in the Bering Sea as the Pribilof Islands and through Bristol Bay to a point in the vicinity of Port Moller on the Alaska Peninsula. This press of winter ice brings small herds of walrus that haul out in the summer on islands in Bristol Bay.

The first Europeans to view the region were Russians. The two expeditions of Vitus Bering departed from the Okhotsk Sea during the first half of the eighteenth century, the second succeeding in brief landings in America south of the Alaska Peninsula. Bering himself died after his ship was wrecked on one of the Commander Islands, west of the outermost Aleutians, but survivors returned to Kamchatka carrying some furs, inspiring Russian fur hunters to move quickly to the Commander and Aleutian islands in the 1740s. They ventured east to the Kodiak Island group by the 1780s. By AD 1800 they had explored a portion of the region north of the Alaska Peninsula, establishing their first outpost at the mouth of the Nushagak River on an arm of Bristol Bay in 1819.

Within twenty-five years they had established posts on the Kuskokwim and Yukon rivers and on the American seacoast as far north as St. Michael. After 1865, and with the purchase of Alaska two years later, explorations farther north were taken over by Americans, who traversed the interior more frequently than had the Russians before them.

The people the Russians encountered in the Aleutian Islands and at the tip of the Alaska Peninsula, as well as those of Kodiak, they had called "Aleuts." This designation is still current for both people and language of the Aleutians and the southwestern tip of the Alaska Peninsula, whereas Native people of the Kodiak region, speakers of a non-Aleut but Eskimoan language, are today most commonly referred to as Alutiiq. People Russians met around the Bering Sea to the north are now recognized to have been speakers of Eskimoan Yupik, forming with the Alutiiq people the western branch of Eskimos. North of the Bering Strait, the Inupiaq Eskimos form the western end of the eastern language branch of the Eskimoan people. The more forested interior was peopled by various subdivisions of the Athabascan Indian people.

Through ancient times there were complex successions and interactions of peoples. From their initial occupation of the Aleutian Islands around 7000 BC, insular Aleuts subsisted chiefly on ocean products, sea mammals, and fish. Aleuts and Eskimos of the mainland depended heavily on both salmon and seals, plus some land animals such as the caribou. From the Bering Strait north, an area with fewer migrating fish, coastal subsistence was chiefly on sea mammals—including walrus and some whales—and caribou where available. Recent Indians of the interior pursued caribou and moose and fished rivers and lakes. Inhabitants of the mainland before 3000 BC, however, were much more specialized toward hunting land animals, especially the caribou.

ARCHAEOLOGY

In the tundra-covered north interior of mainland Alaska, by 12,000 BC there was a scattering of people archaeologists call Paleoarctic culture, who made use of blade tools, many of them very small. This tool assemblage is reminiscent of the small blades or microblades used even earlier in northeast Asia, apparently holdovers from the first humans known to have entered Alaska across the earlier Bering Strait land bridge, which had flooded by about 11,000 BC. Sites are commonly located at points where migrating caribou could be intercepted. These Paleoarctic people are the earliest known human occupants of Alaska.

Although stone projectile points with carefully thinned, or fluted, channels extending up the sides from the base—to some extent reminiscent of the characteristic artifacts of the famous Clovis hunters of the western United States to the south—have been found plentifully on ground surfaces in northern Alaska, but a lack of context has prevented acceptable dating. A claim was made several years ago of an applicable date of before 11,000 BC, a time contemporary with the southern Clovis hunters. However, a reevaluation of this find has questioned the association with the dated charcoal and suggests a date no earlier than about 9000 BC. One recent discovery, possibly acceptable, now appears to suggest a date of about 10,000 BC, well after both the southern Clovis and the appearance of microblades in Alaska.

In any event, by 8000 BC some microblade-making Paleoarctic representatives can be recognized on the Alaska Peninsula in the south, within only a few kilometers of the seacoast. At almost exactly the same time, the characteristic microblade tools can also be traced in a few early sites along the northwest coast, in what are now southeast Alaska and British Columbia, suggesting a movement of these people and their descendants south along a coastal pathway or immediately east of the coastal mountains. By the time these tools appeared on the central coast of British Columbia (ca. 9000 BC), they were present with other non-blade artifacts more evidently derived from still farther south or from the adjacent interior.

Yet at about 10,000 BC there also appeared in far northern Alaska, especially in the tundra of the north slope of the Brooks Range of mountains, sites yielding artifacts that did not include the small blades but rather lanceolate projectile points. These points are almost identical to those that have been dated to the same time period in what is now the northern Great Plains and Rocky Mountains of the United States, with sites especially in Wyoming where they have been given the name of Agate Basin. In Alaska, as in Wyoming, these assemblages have been referred to as Paleoindian, and they can be taken to suggest that people were moving northward as the major North American glaciers melted, following migrating caribou or early bison along a path east of the Rocky Mountains. Although these sites may also have included some of the fluted points mentioned, possibly dated to the same period, there is no clear demonstration of their association yet. Nevertheless, such evidence as is available suggests that the fluted points and Agate Basin non-fluted points were essentially contemporary within Alaska.

By 7000 BC sites of the earliest people in the eastern Aleutian Islands, with plentiful blade tools, are referred to as the Anangula phase or complex. Although explanations of their presence there have varied, the most straightforward idea is that these people were Paleoarctic descendants who had moved into the treeless islands after mastering techniques for exploiting sea mammals and fish of the maritime Aleutian environment. Thereafter, the evolution of Aleutian Island culture was relatively unbroken. By about 4000 BC ancestral Aleuts had moved westward more than midway through the chain of Aleutian Islands, and by sometime around 1000 BC they had reached the western end at the Near Islands. Here their villages of semi-subterranean houses with the distinctive roof entryway would be contacted by Russians nearly 3,000 years later.

Farther to the east on the Kodiak Island group, some archaeologists propose that people of Anangula-like culture were ancestral to the microblade-using earliest inhabitants known there after 5000 BC, although completely Anangula-like sites have not been located. From that time, the Kodiak people developed along their own lines, emphasizing the use of oceanside products in their own ways. Not long after, there is evidence that their way of life was shared with the Pacific coast and southwestern tip of the Alaska Peninsula. But as time passed, the people of the peninsula tip came to partake more and more in the artifact styles of the eastern Aleutian Islands, probably a reflection of its geographic proximity.

After 5000 BC on the entire Alaska mainland, including much of the Alaska Peninsula, Paleoarctic and Paleoindian people were followed by groups now referred to as Northern Archaic. Like the Alaskan Paleoindians, these Northern Archaic people seem to reflect cultural practices current in mainland America to the southeast. Although they are known to have appeared near Alaska's west coast at a few sites (e.g., Cape Krusenstern, near the village of Platinum, and on the Alaska Peninsula), such visits were apparently incidental to their major interest in terrestrial hunting of caribou and other land animals, with possibly some fishing, which was an activity carried on largely in the evergreen forests that were expanding across the region. In some sites microblades and micro-cores also appear, suggesting some measure of amalgamation, or at least contact, with remnant Paleoarctic people in the interior.

After 3000 BC, in the largely treeless strip of land inside the Alaskan coastline, Northern Archaic people were replaced by people of Arctic Small Tool culture, who are thought to represent a new immigration from Neolithic northeast Asia. By this time hunters who are referred to as Continental Neolithic were to be found in many interior northeast Asian riverine sites, where they made pottery and were apparently semi-sedentary. The immigrants bringing the Arctic Small Tool culture to America evidently did not carry the pottery tradition with them. They did, however, bring use of the bow and arrow, which would subsequently spread to other people of the north. First reported from Cape Denbigh in Norton Sound, where their artifacts were designated the Denbigh Flint complex, Arctic Small Tool sites have apparently been dated earliest on the Seward Peninsula.

The people using the Arctic Small Tool culture in Alaska are thought to have been hunters of caribou and occasionally of seals along the coast. Before 2000 BC they had moved north within Alaska and east across the top of the American continent as far as Greenland. There is plenty of evidence that they migrated south inside the east coast of the Bering Sea to the Alaska Peninsula. Around Bristol Bay and on the peninsula they established themselves along salmon streams in small settlements of semi-subterranean houses with tunnel entrances through the side. These settlements were apparently stable, if only seasonally occupied. Hints of changes at this time in artifact styles suggest the inhabitants also exerted some influence on peoples of both the Kodiak Island region

and the eastern Aleutians, although none of the Arctic Small Tool sites are identified there. Meanwhile, farther into the forested interior of mainland Alaska, mobile Northern Archaic descendants continued to hunt terrestrial animals. The degree to which these archaeologically represented people were directly ancestral to the historically known Athabascan Indians of the forested interior is uncertain, although some archaeologists have made this linkage. By 500 BC the Arctic Small Tool people of treeless coastal Alaska were succeeded by those of the Norton culture, who founded settlements on the coasts, their occupations extending around the Alaskan coast to the north and nearly as far east as the Mackenzie River mouth in Canada. The Norton people were hunters of both sea and land animals, and around the Bering Sea were heavily devoted to fishing. To judge by artifacts, they were in part descended from their Arctic Small Tool predecessors, but the Norton culture also included artifacts and artifact styles from other areas. The Norton people made pottery in styles borrowed from contemporary Asia, and they had oceanside hunting equipment, stone basins used as oil-burning lamps, and ornamental lip plugs or labrets, all reminiscent of their contemporaries of the Aleutian Islands. Their sites are the first to appear in some islands, such as Nunivak, and they are believed to have penetrated well into the swampy delta region between the lower Kuskokwim and Yukon rivers, although only one site, Manokinak, has been more fully documented there. They would endure around the eastern Bering Sea coast until about AD 1000.

In Alaska north of the Bering Strait, however, within a few centuries of their appearance, the Norton people were replaced by those of the Ipiutak culture—similar to Norton in many ways, but lacking both pottery and the use of sea-mammal oil lamps. Ipiutak is famous for its striking cemetery art style in incised and carved ivory and bone, with coastal sites located from Point Hope to the Seward Peninsula, including Cape Krusenstern, and with at least one outlying site on the Seward Peninsula's south coast. The Ipiutak sites are also in the northern Brooks Range, where they may have practiced a terrestrial lifeway similar to that of their Denbigh Flint complex predecessors. At about the same time, in the early centuries AD a third contemporary culture appeared. Known as the Old Bering Sea culture since the 1930s, it is found on the east coast of the Chukchi Peninsula of Asia and on the islands in and about the Bering Strait—St. Lawrence Island and the Diomedes. A pottery-using and walrus-hunting people, with their own spectacular art style that shared a number of motifs with that of Ipiutak, they were the most maritime of the groups north of the Aleut region. Thus, in the middle of the first millennium AD, radiating from Bering Strait, were to be found the threesome of Norton, Ipiutak, and Old Bering Sea cultures, their people evidently engaged in interactions the nature and scope of which are only dimly glimpsed through archaeology.

Before the end of the first millennium AD, the Old Bering Sea culture of the Bering Strait region gave way to the successor

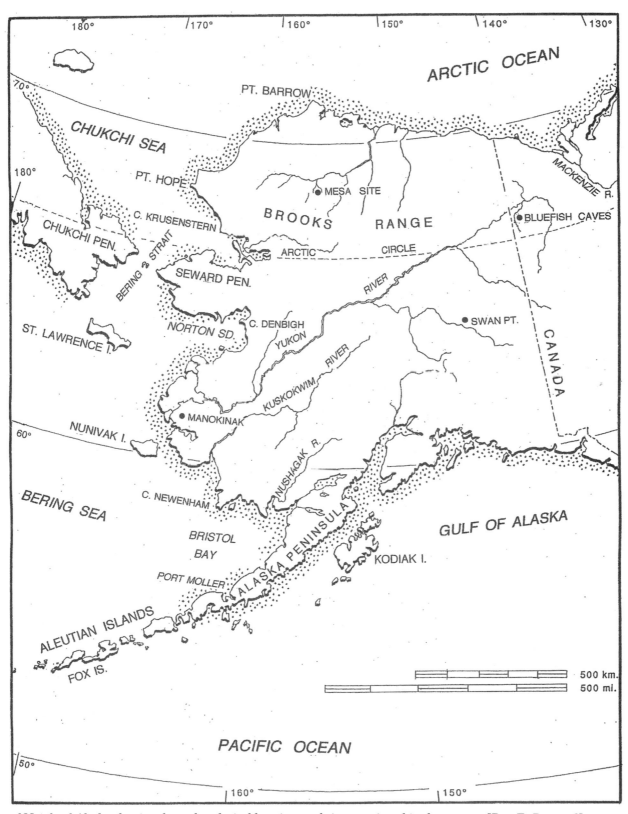

A map of Mainland Alaska showing the archaeological locations and sites mentioned in the essay. [Don E. Dumond]

Punuk culture of whale and walrus hunters, with simpler art but even more effective maritime hunting techniques. These Punuk people apparently expanded onto the northernmost coast of Alaska, living alongside local seal hunters of Birnirk culture, together with whom they eclipsed the earlier Ipiutak culture. By around AD 1000, the Punuk and Birnik people gave way to the Thule culture of able hunters and whalers who within a couple of centuries of their appearance had expanded across northernmost Canada to Greenland, retracing the route taken three millennia earlier by their Arctic Small Tool predecessors.

Around the eastern Bering Sea, the Norton people endured much longer, being succeeded only about AD 1000 when the northern Thule culture appeared. They were a maritime-adapted population, possibly in part Norton descendants, but still more obviously related to their contemporaries of the Punuk and Thule cultures of the Bering Strait, the adjacent Asian coast, and northern Alaska. They appear to have been part of a great wave of maritime-adapted people, or at least part of the spread of groups with increasingly sophisticated maritime abilities. Thus, in the second millennium AD, people of comparable coast-oriented cultures were to be found on the entire littoral from a point north of Port Moller on the Alaska Peninsula—where they maintained often hostile relations with their Aleut neighbors—northward along the coast, upstream along the Yukon and Kuskokwim rivers for 200 miles (322 km) or so, and in the low-lying lands between the river mouths. They were found yet farther north, past the Seward Peninsula to northernmost Alaska and eastward to Greenland, the direct ancestors of historic Eskimoan people. Meanwhile, the people of the more forested interior had become clearly identifiable as ancestral

Athabascan people of various groups between which subsistence practices varied widely from those on major rivers, those approaching the coast as in south-central Alaska, and those next to the territories of the major caribou herds of northern Alaska. These Eskimoan and Athabascan groups would soon enough be encountered by foreigners from Europe and Europeanized America.

Further Reading: Bever, Michael R., and Michael L. Kunz, eds., "Between Two Worlds: Late Pleistocene Cultural and Technological Diversity in Eastern Beringia," *Arctic Anthropology* 38(2) (2001); Damas, David, ed., *Handbook of North American Indians*, Vol. 5: *Arctic* (Washington, DC: Smithsonian Institution, 1984); Dumond, Don E., *The Eskimos and Aleuts* (London and New York: Thames and Hudson, 1987); Ford, James A., *Eskimo Prehistory in the Vicinity of Point Barrow, Alaska*, Anthropological Papers of the American Museum of Natural History No. 41, pt. 1 (New York: American Museum of Natural History, 1959); Giddings, James L., *The Archeology of Cape Denbigh* (Providence, RI: Brown University Press, 1964); Giddings, James L., and Douglas D. Anderson, *Beach Ridge Archeology of Cape Krusenstern*, National Park Service Publications in Archeology No. 20 (Washington, DC: U.S. Department of the Interior, 1986); Griffin, Dennis, *Ellikarrmiut: Changing Lifeways in an Alaskan Community*, Alaska Anthropological Association Monograph Series (Anchorage, AK: Aurora, 2004); Larsen, Helge, and Froelich Rainey, *Ipiutak and the Arctic Whale Hunting Culture*, Anthropological Papers of the American Museum of Natural History No. 42 (New York: American Museum of Natural History, 1948); Mason, Owen K., "The Contest between the Ipiutak, Old Bering Sea, and Birnirk Polities and the Origin of Whaling during the First Millennium A.D. along Bering Strait," *Journal of Anthropological Archaeology* 17 (1998): 240–325.

Don E. Dumond

THE ARCHAEOLOGY OF NORTHWEST ALASKA

Hunting and fishing peoples have lived in the interior of northwest Alaska for more than 11,000 years. About 4,200 years ago, some of these people also began spending late spring and summer along the coast, but it took still another 1,000 years before they occupied the coast year-round. The major land mammal hunted throughout northwest Alaska was the caribou. On the coast, people hunted ringed seals, walrus, beluga (white whales), and—at favored locations—baleen whales. Below about 65 degrees north latitude, the coastal and riverine peoples also obtained large quantities of salmon—and north of that latitude, Arctic char.

Most early interior northwest Alaskan archaeological sites are surface or near-surface lithic scatters situated on high promontories that served as hunting lookouts. Although the sites are difficult to date with certainty, and it's difficult to

know which of the artifacts in the sites were deposited together, several of these sites have produced radiocarbon dates between 10,000 and 12,000 years ago. Of these Early Man sites, the best known are Sluiceways and Mesa (located on the North Slope) and Trail Creek Cave 2 (on the Seward Peninsula).

Sites that were first occupied over 10,000 years ago in the interior frequently contain bifacially flaked projectile points, either notched or lanceolate, and some also contain microblades. The different combinations of artifact styles and types making up the varied artifact assemblages have prompted archaeologists to question whether the artifacts in fact were deposited at the same time—or if they were, whether the different sites and artifact styles reflect different activities, different stages in the manufacture of particular artifact forms, varying accessibility to sources of high quality cherts necessary for the manufacture of microblades and the best-made projectile points; or perhaps the diverse cultural preferences of different groups.

Several archaeologists consider at least some of these sites, such as the Mesa site, as representative of northern extensions—or perhaps even progenitors of Paleoindian culture. Archaeologists have even recovered a few so-called Clovis-like fluted points from some early sites—such as Putu, located on the North Slope—but the historical relationships between Alaska and mid-continent North America Paleoindian culture are still unclear.

More recent interior northwestern Alaskan prehistoric sites are situated along the shores of the larger lakes and the major rivers, where the people were able to intercept north-south migrating caribou and to set up fishing camps. Of these, Onion Portage, located on the middle Kobuk River, is the most deeply stratified, containing more than fifty clearly separated cultural layers dating from 10,000 years ago to the present.

Until recently the post-10,000-year archaeological sequence seemed straightforward in northwestern Alaska. Early microblade-using peoples represented by the American Paleoarctic tradition seemed to have occupied most of the northern tundra regions until about 6,500 years ago, when they began to share the region with a more southerly derived archaeological tradition termed Northern Archaic. This later tradition was characterized by small, stubby, asymmetrical notched points and various implements more in keeping with cultural complexes of the forested regions farther south and east.

But since the mid 1990s, many newly dated surface finds in the interior do not fit this scheme at all. These sites, like the sites that are over 10,000 years old, contain aggregations of artifact types, such as blades, microblades, and notched and lanceolate points, that were once seen to be culturally distinct.

In contrast to the uncertainties of the early prehistory, the cultural historical framework for the past 4,000 years is rather secure. It is from this later period onward that people began to occupy the coast. Here, dozens of archaeological sites—the earliest of which date to about 4,200 years ago—are scattered from the Seward Peninsula to the Arctic Alaskan-Canadian border. The major sites, mostly on barrier beaches, are located at Barrow, Point Hope, Cape Prince of Wales, and Cape Krusenstern, all facing the Chukchi Sea. In some locations, beach deposits have accumulated outward to form undulating series of fossil beach ridges spanning millennia. As each beachfront favored for campsites was superseded by a newer one, the older beach became vegetated with humus mat that then made it attractive for situating sod-covered semi-subterranean winter houses. This succession from sandy seafront campsite locations to near-coast sod-covered winter house sites—and eventually to unoccupied back beaches—is the basis of

beach ridge chronology in northwestern Alaska. The most extensive of these beach ridge series, located at Cape Krusenstern, records nearly the entire Middle and Late Holocene depositional and human occupational history of the coast.

ARCHAEOLOGICAL SEQUENCES IN NORTHWEST ALASKA

The archaeological sequence for northwest Alaska is organized into a series of long-lasting cultural traditions. Some of these traditions appear to signal the introduction of new peoples into the region, but others reflect technological innovations and changed ways of doing things carried out by the same people, who occupied the region for long periods of time.

The traditions include, in overlapping chronological order, the American Paleoarctic, Northern Archaic, Arctic Small Tool, and Northern Maritime traditions, each subdivided into several smaller periods or phases. This scheme does not include the as yet unnamed cultural tradition or traditions dating to more than 10,000 years ago.

The earliest named tradition is the American Paleoarctic (APA), a term employed to indicate an American extension of a Circum-Arctic cultural tradition characterized by prepared core lithic industries generally adapted to a tundra way of life. The typical artifact associated with the APA is referred to as the Akmak complex. This kind of assemblage is found at the Onion Portage site, and several other smaller microblade sites from the region. APA is characterized by large blade tools; core bifaces, some of which were obviously heavy cutting or chopping tools; microblades for the manufacture of small rectangular insets for antler points; and large, bifacially flaked cleavers and knives. APA also contains a burin technology used to produce tools for cutting and scraping hard organic materials, along with grooved shaft smoothers of a size used for arrow shafts.

Around 6,500 years ago, Northern Archaic–tradition (NAT) sites arrived in the region. The assemblages of this tradition are characterized by stubby, rather poorly made notched points, numerous end scrapers, heavy cobble tools, notched net sinkers, and numerous non-diagnostic flake tools. The sites, including the type site at Palisades near Cape Krusenstern, lack all traces of microblade manufacture, the *sine qua non* of the various Arctic traditions in the region. Although the absence of microblades was originally interpreted as culturally significant, many archaeologists now argue that since microblade technology is only used to produce a limited set of specific tools, the presence or absence of microblades in the Northern Archaic sites is simply a reflection of the particular activities carried out there. NAT artifacts are mostly found at lookouts or campsites. Thus far, only two house sites have been located: an early house site from Anaktuvuk Pass, where it is referred to as the Tuktu complex; and a later house site at Onion Portage, where it is referred to as the Portage complex.

About 4,300 years ago, a new archaeological tradition swept across northwest Alaska, and even beyond. This is the Arctic Small Tool tradition (AST), beginning with the Denbigh Flint complex. The type site for Denbigh Flint is Cape Denbigh, located on the northern shores of Norton Sound, but the complex is distributed from Brooks River, southwestern Alaska, to just below Barrow, in Arctic Alaska. Derived complexes also quickly spread across previously unoccupied regions of northern Canada, where it is termed pre-Dorset, and into Greenland, where it is known as Independence I.

Denbigh Flint is characterized by a microblade industry used to manufacture delicate knives, scrapers, and weapon insets, as well as a distinctive form of burin for grooving antlers or working hard materials and burin spalls for incising bone and antler. Other tool types include spear points, knife blades, and tiny, bifacially flaked weapon insets so expertly made that they may have been produced by itinerant craftsmen.

Denbigh peoples wintered along rivers or lakes in the interior. The two major winter house sites are Punyik Point (Itivlik Lake, North Slope) and Onion Portage. The Punyik Point Denbigh houses were small, rectangular, single-roomed structures with short entrance passages, but the earlier Onion Portage house was a sub-rectangular mid-passage form more characteristic of the early eastern Arctic houses, and the later ones hemispherical structures enclosing round floor areas.

Denbigh Flint peoples were the first in northwest Alaska to spend part of the year at the coast, where (especially at Cape Krusenstern) they camped to hunt seals and caribou, and probably also to fish.

After about 1500 BC, Denbigh descendants intensified their use of the coasts of northwest Alaska. Termed Choris complex—and named after its type site on the Choris Peninsula, Kotzebue Sound—it is found at Cape Krusenstern and Walakpa, with the latter situated just below Barrow; and in the interior, at Trail Creek Caves, the Seward Peninsula (called Middle Trail Creek), at Onion Portage, and along the Noatak River.

The Choris period is divided into an early and late phase. The earlier, dated to between around 1,500 and 900 BC, includes small campsites along the coast and in the interior, but the later phase includes more substantial dwelling sites at Onion Portage and the Choris Peninsula.

Early Choris people were the first pottery makers of Alaska, if not all of northern North America, producing small, cord-marked, round-bottomed pots with techniques clearly introduced from Asia. Choris people also began to grind and polish slate using techniques previously employed by coastal peoples south and west of the Bering Strait. These slate-grinding techniques were either introduced along with pottery making from Asia, or—as has been assumed by many—spread northward from southeastern Alaska, where it had become a dominant form of lithic use as many as 1,000 years earlier.

Choris people used stone lamps, ground-slate knife and ulu blades, small weapon insets stylistically derived from Denbigh Flint, large weapon points hafted directly to wooden spears, and decorated organic artifacts (such as ivory labrets, human figurines, and amber beads).

Following several centuries of occupation by the early Choris people, a different group of people, completely unrelated to the Arctic Small Tool tradition, appeared briefly on the coast, perhaps for as little as one or two years. Known only from Cape Krusenstern, these were the Old Whalers, whose origins and descendants remain obscure even after 5 decades of searching. While at Cape Krusenstern during the early eighth or ninth century BC, they established a sizable village of ten large houses—five for winter occupation, and five for summer. The winter houses were deep, multi-roomed, oval structures obviously built for multiple families. They hunted ring seals, caribou, and—most intriguingly—whales, apparently the California Gray.

Following the Old Whaling interlude, late Choris peoples again occupied the coast, this time also wintering there in large, oval, multi-family, semi-subterranean structures of a unique form. In the interior, Choris people lived in small, hemispherical houses and large tents.

Late Choris pottery from the type site, dating to about 650 BC, includes fiber-tempered vessels with round or conical bases and exterior surfaces decorated with linear or check-stamped designs.

Choris is seen by most archaeologists as derived in part from Denbigh Flint and thus as a phase of AST. Others see the introduction of slate and pottery in Choris as signaling the beginning of a new tradition, termed the Norton tradition.

Norton refers to a cultural complex first located at Iyatayet, Norton Sound, but subsequently found to be distributed from the Alaska Peninsula to northwestern Alaska. In northwest Alaska, Norton house sites are found at Point Hope, where the complex was originally referred to as Near-Ipiutak, and on beach ridges along the entire northern shores of the Seward Peninsula. Norton people also camped at Cape Krusenstern and Battle Rock, located about 20 miles north of there.

For the final six centuries BC, Norton residents at Point Hope utilized the coast intensively, for bowhead whaling as well as sealing and walrus hunting. In addition to the chipped-stone technology ultimately derived from Denbigh, the Norton people made ground-slate tools and pottery in styles developed out of Choris.

Although they appeared in the regions north of the Bering Strait 400 years earlier than anywhere else, Norton camp and winter house sites also became numerous south of the Bering Strait after 200 BC, where they evidence sealing and especially salmon fishing.

The evidence that the Point Hope Norton people were whalers was first thought to demonstrate that the historically known northwestern Alaskan Eskimo whaling culture had evolved in an uninterrupted, continuous development directly out of an ancestral base 2,500 years ago. But the discovery of Ipiutak at Point Hope—a culture entirely out of line with this hypothetical evolution—disrupted this scheme by exhibiting none of the traits attributed to whalers. Discovered by

Froelich Rainey and Helge Larsen in 1939, this post-Norton culture not only did not utilize slate implements or pottery—artifacts common in Alaskan whaling cultures—but also did not even hunt whales, despite living at one of Alaska's primary whaling locations.

The material culture of Ipiutak was based on the use of flaked-stone implements, many of which were stylistically derived from Denbigh Flint, that included small, bifacially flaked insets for weapons, spear points, and a wide variety of specialized chert tools for working wood, antler, and ivory.

The Ipiutak people at Point Hope erected well over 100 individual houses within a 200- to 300-year period. At Cape Krusenstern, they lived in small, clustered settlements of single-family houses surrounded by one or two larger houses, which may have served as community centers.

One of the most striking aspects of Ipiutak culture is the elaborate artwork associated with its burial customs. Originally described as an extension of Scytho-Siberian styles, many of the artistic elements clearly originated in Asia. The art includes open latticework carvings in the round, stylized anthropomorphic and zoomorphic figurines— curvilinear designs incised on weapons, death masks, and many other unidentified complexly carved objects often described simply as bizarre.

One explanation for the unusual features of Ipiutak culture is that it represents one of several major military and trading polities competing for resources around the Bering Strait and adjacent islands. With such competition, the groups would have developed an unusual degree of social hierarchy that is represented by the elaborate artwork associated with certain powerful individuals.

With the end of Ipiutak culture early in the first millennium AD, AST passed from the scene. After a brief period of co-existence, a new cultural tradition, termed Northern Maritime, became established along the coast. In northwest Alaska NMT, to which the Inupiat/Inuit Eskimo culture of today clearly belongs, is divided into an earlier Birnirk phase and a later Thule phase.

Birnirk culture, first identified by Vilhjalmur Stefansson from excavations near Point Barrow in 1912, appears at Cape Prince of Wales, Point Hope, Cape Krusenstern, Walakpa, and Kuk (near Nome), as well as along the northern coast of northeastern Asia as far west as the mouth of Kolyma River.

Birnirk origins are still unknown—since, although its flaked-chert tools are derived stylistically from Ipiutak, the organic implements, slate, and pottery bear no relation to Ipiutak or earlier cultures. Birnirk pottery, for example, is quite unlike Norton and Choris pottery in that it is thick walled, poorly fired, and, most significantly, decorated with elaborate curvilinear stamped designs. The organic artifacts include numerous new specialized forms and functions related to ice and open-water seal hunting. These include ice scratchers for attracting seals basking on the ice in spring, wound pins for skewering the incisions of seal carcasses, and open-water seal hunting equipment, such as bladder floats.

An especially important artifact type for understanding NMT culture history is the sealing harpoon head. The characteristic Birnirk harpoon head is self-pointed and open socketed, with a single lateral barb and an opposing chipped-stone side blade inset. The basal toggling spur is usually bifurcated or trifurcated. A second harpoon head form found in Birnirk is the Sicco type, a variant of the unbarbed, end-bladed early Punuk–style harpoon head found on St. Lawrence and the Punuk Islands. This form continued to evolve as a major harpoon head type in the subsequent Thule period.

Birnirk settlements were small, with only one or two houses occupied at any one time. The houses themselves are also small and could not have been occupied by more than single families. Two forms of the houses have been noted: the more common, with a relatively short entrance passage and a single-side bench; and the other, with a long entrance passage and bench along the rear wall. Most of the houses lacked open fireplaces and instead were lit and heated by lamps. The physical type of Birnirk people, described in 1930 by Ales Hrdlicka as typical northern Eskimo, has more recently been linked by Charles Utermohle and Stephen Zegura to some coastal Asian groups.

Birnirk people also hunted baleen whales, though from settlements too small to have permitted the use of the multiple boat crews often deemed prerequisite to successful ice edge whaling. Evidence for whaling is seen in the presence of a whaling harpoon head from Barrow, whaling harpoon end blade insets, baleen, and whale effigies.

The distribution of Birnirk along the coasts of the Chukchi Sea and Arctic Ocean suggests that it represents the emergence of an Eskimo-like ice-hunting culture out of a broader cultural milieu that had been developing for centuries on the islands and adjacent Asian coast of the Bering Strait—where cultures like Okvik, Old Bering Sea, and Punuk exhibit a line of continuous development.

In the last centuries of the first millennium AD, the descendants of Birnirk populations, the Thule people, spread over much of coastal Alaska and simultaneously spread eastward across northern Canada and Greenland and southward in Alaska as far south as Bristol Bay and the northern shores of the Alaska Peninsula. This culture was first identified in the Thule District of northwestern Greenland. By extension, those subsequently discovered in Alaska were classified as Western Thule.

In northwest Alaska, resources seem to have reached a peak during the Western Thule period. Caribou were numerous, both in the interior and along the coast, and bowhead whales—which, since about AD 1400, have been absent from Kotzebue Sound—were near enough to the coast to have been harvested from Cape Krusenstern. This was a warm period that also allowed for salmon to stock the rivers in numbers not previously seen.

The earliest known Western Thule sites in northwestern Alaska are from the shores of Kotzebue Sound and the middle

Kobuk Valley, where they form the foundation for the Arctic Woodland culture that spread throughout the adjacent tundra and forest zones. Dating from between AD 1000 and 1250, these include several sizable village sites along the coasts and up the adjacent rivers. Western Thule sites of comparable age likely existed at the modern whaling villages of Cape Prince of Wales, Point Hope, and Barrow, but since these sites have been continuously occupied since Birnirk times, it has been difficult to locate precisely the earliest Western Thule components there.

Beginning about AD 1400, major changes occurred in the subsistence and settlement patterning around coastal North Alaska. In Kotzebue Sound, whaling was no longer practiced, likely because of changes in spring ice conditions that no longer made it feasible to hunt from there. At the same time, caribou populations declined. This double blow to the food supply resulted in resettlement into areas closer to reliable shee and salmon fishing grounds nearer the mouths of the rivers.

Farther north along the Chukchi Sea coast, whaling continued at the traditional whaling stations of Point Hope and Barrow, and here we see considerable continuity right to the present in artifact styles and subsistence activities that originated during Birnirk times. Especially prominent is the balanced economy incorporating sea mammal hunting, caribou hunting, and fishing that continues to characterize the Inupiat of northwest Alaska.

Further Reading: Alexander, Herbert L., *Putu: A Fluted Point Site in Alaska*, Publication No. 17 (Burnaby, BC: Simon Fraser University, Department of Archaeology, 1987); Anderson, Douglas D., "Onion Portage: The Archaeology of a Stratified Site from the Kobuk River, Northwest Alaska," *Anthropological Papers of the University of Alaska* 22(1–2) (1988); Giddings, J. L., *The Arctic Woodland Culture of the Kobuk River*, Museum Monographs (Philadelphia: University of Pennsylvania, University Museum, 1952); Giddings, J. L., *Ancient Men of the Arctic* (New York: Knopf, 1965); Giddings, J. L., and D. D. Anderson, *Beach Ridge Archeology of Cape Krusenstern* (Washington, DC: Government Printing Office, 1986); Dumond, Don E., *The Eskimos and Aleuts* (London: Thames and Hudson, 1977); Kunz, Michael L., and Richard E. Reanier, "The Mesa Site: A Paleoindian Hunting Lookout in Arctic Alaska," *Arctic Anthropology* 32(1) (1995): 5–30; Larsen, Helge, "Trail Creek: Final Report on the Excavation of Two Caves on Seward Peninsula, Alaska," *Acta Arctica* 15 (1969); Larsen, Helge, and Froelich G. Rainey, "Ipiutak and the Arctic Whale Hunting Culture," *Anthropological Papers of the American Museum of Natural History* 42 (1948); Stanford, Dennis J., "The Walakpa Site, Alaska: Its Place in the Birnirk and Thule Cultures," *Smithsonian Contributions to Anthropology* 20 (1976).

Douglas D. Anderson

A NATIVE AMERICAN PERSPECTIVE ON THE BERING STRAIT AND ITS PEOPLE

The Bering Strait is astounding; it is a body of water of many realities, yet it is submissive to the changes of season in its own reality. A southerly flow of water changes to a northerly flow in the late fall season. It is the seasonal change during the early spring months that pulls boundless numbers of mammals, birds, and fish northward as the ever-rising sun wakens the sea and the land from a winter's slumber.

The Bering Strait is a shallow body of water that separates the North American and Asian continents by less than 52 miles. Three prominent islands with separate international entities rest in the middle of the strait. The sea is "our garden," as expressed in thankful appreciation to the sea by a noble elder[1] from St. Lawrence Island, defining gratitude not only from one person, but on behalf of all people. Such articulation, expressed from the heart, reinforces meaningful testimonies when they are stated by elders regarding issues of importance that infringe upon the lifestyles of the people. Ancient stories of the way of life of the people define periods of time not described anywhere else; these tales are heard by our ancestors only as stories that come from the dawn of time.

Indigenous life follows a very intricate spectrum. The way of life is enhanced by the changes of season, as it is the seasons that bring life, giving gifts to the people from the land and the sea. The way of life of the people is extremely strenuous, as the cold frozen land and severe winter seas allow them only a brief opportunity to replenish food sources that must be gathered during the short lull of the spring.

The Bering Strait region, in its earthly majesty, is a land of many people. In ancient and pre-contact times, the people resided within invisible boundaries that were jealously guarded. Treading into another country uninvited was punishable by very

---

[1] Conrad Oozeva from Gambell, Alaska, on St. Lawrence Island, testified of our relationship with the sea and the gift of life that the sea provides. This information was confirmed through unrecorded telephone correspondence with Branson Tungiyan of Gambell.

brutal means. Land and sea cannot be separated, as they are a part of the reality of completeness, and time has finely woven man with his natural surroundings, attuning him to the qualities of both land and sea.

The people are as diverse as the natural inhabitants of the region, be they mammal, bird, fish, or insect; diverse also are the plants of the land and the sea. The reality is so inspiring that young or old are struck by the beauty of the awesome wonders of nature. A person of place is continually astounded but recognizes quickly that they are but a simple part of an awesome universe.

The former estate of indigenous people is immense within all parts of the earth—equally so in northern regions, where it is understood that vast tracts of land have never felt the footprint of man. Unproven notions such as that may be true, but the hunter-gatherer has been representative of his surroundings throughout ancient times. There are places he no longer goes to, because that part of the land cannot support the people as other places can; the land has always been known by the people for what the land can offer for survival. The land is ancient, and since northern people were found as contributors to survival in a harsh, forbidding land, studies of this population have become intense. The worldview of indigenous people is extremely broad, as the whole spectrum of knowledge related to survival is contained in their learning.

From the onset of contact with whalers, explorers, and missionaries, the lifeways of indigenous people faced a breakdown of cultural values. The ancient traditions of the people and their philosophies of life, which go back thousands and thousands of years, fell under the guise of discovery, religion, and means found very unsuitable today. The loss of the language, ceremonies, and rituals resulted in the loss of cultural formalities; thus began the downward plunge of an intact people into a chasm of helplessness, despair, and cultural loneliness. It is fortunate that the veil of cultural loss is not deep; today the enthusiasm and the willingness of the newest generations to regain the lost relationship the people had with traditional human reality are again unifying the people with a complete heart, mind, and soul.

The first visitors to our land were not the rightful representatives they thought themselves to be when they returned to their places of origin, as many of them corrupted their observations with falsehoods that are still believed as fact by many people throughout the world. The way of life of the Native people represents an understanding of survival found by our ancestors; this lifeway became the time-honored method of survival in a land that can become brutal for ill-prepared people. Research in human studies has seen an ebb-and-flow response from members of the Native community, but now the scientists are interviewing elders in order to probe into the very depths of our relationship with the land. The unwritten record of the people contains exact stories as recited through our ancient narratives. Indigenous cultures are living cultures.

Northern latitudes remain an unlikely place of human habitation to the visitor, as the winters can be cold and the summers extremely short. Yet the land, thought of as uninhabitable and inhospitable, has been a host to noble people since unknown millennia. The land, being outside of the contiguous United States, presents a unique set of difficulties; transportation services can cease because of impassable ice conditions, and traversing great distances between points is just an integral part of the effort to be a member of the world community. The great land is largely understood as a foreign land, but that mentality is slowly waning as the business, finance, and military communities move away from such an attitude. During interviews, researchers gathered crucial points of understanding regarding who the people are. But researchers need not look to interviews to study some century-old customs, as they remain a part of modern life just as they were discovered at the time of initial contact. Indigenous cultures relate to their survival subject to the environment they are in, and people of northern latitudes are no exception.

The way of life—its traditions and its insurmountable magnitude of knowledge—can be traced through our oral history. Its facts, celebrations, rituals, and ceremonies, along with the ancient stories of the people, will bear the truthful evidence of our tenure upon the land. Wholesome research in human studies will probe into the hearts and minds of our ancestors. Studies of northern people are increasing, and ethnographic information is being gathered by dedicated scientists who also aim at interpreting information correctly. Significantly broadened research provides a more accurate interpretation and assigns a proper meaning in understanding the way of life of our ancestors as it was naturally made for them.

The people are hunter-gatherers, and as hunter-gatherers, they are placed by their lifestyles along the sea, the islands, the rivers, or the mountains in quest of survival. Arctic lands are not an oddity, not to the people of the land; the land is an intimate part of their livelihood, and therefore its people have offered their respect in conformity with their survival throughout the ages.

Life intersects with the land very vividly, but it is difficult to define when northern people first became known to the world outside of their own. There is no notion in our ancient stories that we migrated to where we were "found" to be, as we are of the land and always have been of the land. Northern people surfaced recently into the norm of world history, if the timeline of written history is considered; and today, the north and its people are as driven into the computer age as most developed nations. But the land's location outside of the contiguous forty-eight states has some effect on personal comforts and luxuries most newcomers take for granted.

Wholesome research in human studies can produce information that probes into the depths of the traditional knowledge of ancient people. This vast network of knowledge is wedged into the memories of older generations. The opportunity to teach and the opportunity to learn can surface at any moment; thus the system does not perpetuate itself according to a schedule, unlike the learning found in educational systems today. The teaching can occur during a gathering of people through observation; the tradition is transferred through tales related during festivals, hunting expeditions, preparation of food resources, or the creation of clothing, implements of hunting, or weapons.

Teaching and learning are objectives in all societies; in the way of northern people, the young and the newcomers must observe and learn from their elders. Time is never still, and the time shall come when a person must pass on their knowledge to the new generations. The women, as the hunters, are important members of the society; they must define their knowledge to the young, thus guiding the young to membership in a full, successful community. The way of teaching among indigenous communities is articulation; what you are told sends you into deep thought, and what you are taught is embedded into your innermost being until that knowledge must again be presented to the new generations in its full form. It is a system of learning that recognizes that you are a part of the earth, and that the earth itself is crucial to the survival of the earth.

Today the language survives, but among only a few; and the passing of each elder upon whom some form of knowledge rests brings the world of indigenous people nearer to what may be the final disintegration of their way of life. The philosophy of many Native groups is that our ways may be on a decline, but the ways of the people will return to assist the descendants in a new dawn far different to the times today. The people are now witnessing the return of some of our traditions, and this prophecy was told many generations ago by our ancestors as they related what the new generations will experience. The children have been a catalyst in regaining the ancient performances formerly pushed aside by edicts, principles, or circumstances not our own. As the environment is being severely tested with the phenomena of global warming, this prophecy will certainly come to pass.

Further Reading: Burch, Ernest S., Jr., *Social Life in Northwest Alaska: The Structure of Inupiaq Eskimo Nations* (Fairbanks: University of Alaska Press, 2006); McCartney, Allen P., ed., *Hunting the Largest Animals: Native Whaling in the Western Arctic and Subarctic* (Edmonton, AB: Canadian Circumpolar Institute Press, 1995); McCartney, Allen P., ed., *Indigenous Ways to the Present: Native Whaling in the Western Arctic* (Edmonton, AB: Canadian Circumpolar Institute Press, 2003); Nelson, Edward William, *The Eskimos about Bering Strait*, Eighteenth Annual Report of the Bureau of American Ethnology, Smithsonian Institution (Washington, DC: Government Printing Office, 1900); Smith, Kathleen Lopp, ed., *Ice Windows: Letters from a Bering Strait Village: 1892–1902* (Fairbanks: University of Alaska Press, 2001).

Herbert O. Anungazuk

RUSSIAN COLONIZATION OF ALASKA AND THE NORTHWEST COAST

INTRODUCTION

During the sixteenth and seventeenth centuries, Russian fur traders and government forces led the conquest of Siberia, subjugating its indigenous peoples and stripping the vast region of ermine and sable. Following Vitus Bering's voyage across the north Pacific in 1741, armed Russian merchantmen pushed eastward across the Aleutian Island chain, exploiting Alaska Native populations and reaping new sources of wealth— Alaskan sea otters, fur seals, and foxes. Missionaries, administrators, and workers soon followed, transforming southern Alaska into an overseas colony of the Russian Empire. The Russian-American Company (RAC), established in 1799, administered Alaska until the U.S. purchase in 1867.

The historical archaeology of "Russian America" is a record of colonial domination, indigenous struggle, and cultural interchange between immigrants and first peoples. Archaeologists have investigated dozens of sites from this period, including colonial forts, Russian trade outposts, and Alaska Native villages. Researchers interpret colonial artifacts and dwellings in conjunction with historical records and indigenous oral history.

FORCED LABOR, FREE TRADE, AND ARCHAEOLOGY

Russian control was established most forcefully in the Aleutian Islands, home to the Unangan (Aleut) people, and in the Kodiak archipelago, inhabited by the Alutiit. As fur traders (*promyshlenniki*) entered these areas during the 1740s to the 1780s, they sometimes engaged in peaceful barter with aboriginal populations, but frequently they sought to coerce and exploit them by means of armed force, threats, and hostage taking. Native resistance, such as the eastern Unangan uprising of 1763–65, was crushed.

In the Aleutian and Kodiak regions, called "dependent" by the RAC, labor for the company was obligatory. Unangan and Alutiiq men harvested large numbers of sea otters, using kayaks to surround the animals and then killing them with darts and arrows. Some Aleutian Islanders were resettled in the Pribilof Islands to club fur seals that migrated there. Other men and women were ordered to hunt whales, fish, trap foxes, harvest birds, prepare plant foods, make skin clothing, or tan hides for company use. Village chiefs (*toions*) were made responsible for meeting production quotas. Most Alaska Natives received little recompense for their work—perhaps some beads or leaves of tobacco but often only tanned skins or clothing that they themselves had produced. Toions received extra gifts and had greater access to Russian goods.

The obligatory labor system brought hunger and hardship because it undermined the ability of Native communities to provide for their own needs. Indigenous populations declined by as much as 75 percent in some areas due to epidemics, malnutrition, social disruption, and the loss of men on forced sea otter hunts.

Russian dominance over so-called semi-dependent and independent peoples was more limited. These categories included the Alutiiq residents of Prince William Sound and the outer Kenai coast, the Dena'ina of Cook Inlet, the Yup'ik of southwest Alaska, the Ahtna of the Copper River, and the Tlingit of southeast Alaska. Involuntary servitude was far less common in these regions, and Russian fur traders operated more like their French and British counterparts in North America, exchanging beads, metal ornaments, and other imported goods for pelts.

These conditions create unusual archaeological expectations. Native settlements in the areas of most intensive Russian control, such as the Aleutians and Kodiak Island, should contain *fewer* imported trade items than areas where Russian domination was less complete. This is the inverse of what historical archaeologists expect in other parts of North America, where an influx of foreign goods is interpreted as a sign of close contact with the British and French. Moreover, Alaska Native societies in the areas of Russian contact were stratified by class and rank, leading to expectations that scarce trade goods should be unequally distributed within and between Native households.

The Russian fur trade was exceptional in other ways. Supply lines from homeland to colonial frontier were far weaker than those that supported the British and French. Throughout the eighteenth century, agricultural products (e.g., flour, beef) and necessities such as cloth and iron had to be trekked across Siberia to the eastern port of Okhotsk and then shipped to Alaska via a dangerous north Pacific route. Unpaid Native labor was one solution to this unreliable connection, because it reduced the need for manufactured trade items. Among the Russians themselves, all but the highest-status residents of the colony received little from home and had to rely on local foods, clothing, tools, and watercraft; they even built their houses using local materials and designs. The British explorer George Vancouver, visiting a Russian fort in Cook Inlet in 1794, remarked with disdain that the men "appeared to be

perfectly content to live after the manner of the Native Indians of the country; partaking with equal relish and appetite their gross and nauseous food, adopting the same fashion, and using the same materials for their apparel" (Vancouver 1801, 207). Vancouver's insults aside, it is clear that the Russians recognized that indigenous foods and technologies (e.g., the kayak and waterproof clothing made of sea mammal intestines) were highly suited to local conditions and in many cases far superior to what could be imported.

This pattern of colonial dependence on Native production and acculturation to indigenous lifeways was unusually pronounced in Russian America. It was accentuated by intermarriage between Russian and Siberian men (who made up 90 percent of the immigrant population) and Alaska Native women, giving rise to an ethnically mixed, bilingual creole class. Reading the archaeological evidence of colonial technology, diet, and architecture, we can expect to see evidence of this cultural convergence between colonizers and colonized.

RUSSIAN ARCHAEOLOGICAL SITES
Komandorskii Camp, Commander Islands, Russia
In 1741 Bering's Second Kamchatka Expedition explored the Aleutian Islands and Gulf of Alaska. The voyage produced the first reports of southern Alaska geography and Native peoples as well as hundreds of sea otter pelts, treasures that triggered the Russian push into these new lands. One of the expedition's two ships, captained by Aleksei Chirikov, made a safe return to Kamchatka (eastern Siberia), but Bering's *Sv. Petr* wrecked in the Commander Islands only one day's sail from home. Bering died there of scurvy, along with thirteen others. After spending the winter and building a small boat from the wreck of the *Sv. Petr*, the survivors were able to complete the voyage.

In 1979–81, a team led by Russian archaeologist G. L. Silant'ev (Russian Academy of Sciences) excavated huts that sheltered Bering's shipwrecked men at a site called Komandorskii Camp. Artifacts from the dwellings indicate how eighteenth-century voyagers were typically equipped. Sailors carried flintlock muskets, pistols, and swords. Officers wore uniforms, of which stamped bronze buttons and belt buckles remained. Glass and metal containers, coins, personal effects, tools, and navigation instruments were found. Items for Native trade included a Chinese pipe, glass mirrors, metal thimbles, needles, and beads. With the aid of a magnetometer, investigators found seven of the ship's cannons buried in sand at the *Sv. Petr* wreck site. Researchers compared their finds with information from the voyage's logbooks, journals, and equipment inventories, concluding that archaeological and historical data are complementary, each filling gaps in the other to enable scientific synthesis.

Three Saints Harbor, Kodiak Island, Alaska
In 1784, 130 men led by Grigorii Shelikhov massacred Alutiiq villagers on Kodiak Island and built a stronghold at

Three Saints Harbor. This event was a turning point in the Russian expansion and for a brief period (1784–93) Three Saints was the largest settlement and unofficial capital of Russian America. In 1989–91, Aron L. Crowell (Smithsonian Institution) undertook an archaeological and historical study of the site in partnership with the University of California at Berkeley, the Kodiak Area Native Association, and a Russian team led by Valery Shubin (Sakhalin Regional Museum).

The project investigated Three Saints Harbor in the context of the eighteenth-century capitalist world system, examining the flow of materials that linked the distant Russian industrial core with its colonial periphery. Site analysis focused on the ethnic-class divisions of Russian colonial society. Historical sources suggested that low-ranking workers (many of mixed Russian and Siberian Native descent) quickly adapted to local resources and Alaskan indigenous technologies, while the company elite spurned such influences and sought to maintain a purely Russian manner of dress, diet, and housing. Excavation of a workers' barracks—identified from a 1790 depiction of the settlement—provided confirmation. The building was a thatched, earthen lodge, similar to Unangan houses in the Aleutian Islands. Food remains included sea mammals, birds, fish, shellfish, and berries. Strewn on the sand floor were metal tools, gun flints, lead shot, and glass beads as well as Alutiiq stone tools and pottery. The latter may have been used by the workers themselves or by Alutiiq women who served them; Shelikhov reported that hundreds of female hostages were held at Three Saints to ensure the cooperation of island leaders.

In contrast to the workers' dugout, the building that housed Shelikhov and his managers was an expensively furnished log house with a wooden floor, brick stove, glass or mica windows, icons, and mirrors. A garden, bread oven, and bones of cattle, pigs, and goats showed that the occupants dined in Russian style. Part of the investment in the building was ideological—it expressed Shelikhov's conceit that Russia's mission in Alaska was to demonstrate the superiority and benefits of Western civilization.

Castle Hill, New Arkhangel (Present-Day Sitka), Southeast Alaska

New Arkhangel was built in 1799, destroyed by the Tlingit in 1802, and then rebuilt to become the Russian colonial capital in 1808. Over the next decades it grew into the largest and most cosmopolitan port on the north Pacific. The colony's once dire supply problems were alleviated by trade with foreign vessels, round-the-world (rather than trans-Siberian) shipping, food from the RAC's agricultural center in California (Fort Ross, 1812–41), and trade with the British Hudson's Bay Company. New Arkhangel was a hub of colonial industry, from shipbuilding to lumbering, milling, and munitions manufacture.

Alaska state archaeologist J. David McMahan conducted extensive excavations at the Castle Hill site (Tlingit *Noow*

Tlein) in Sika between 1995 and 1998, uncovering a complex of Russian period features that included workers' residences and a metalwork shop dating to the 1830s. About 300,000 artifacts were collected, reflecting a diversity and abundance of goods that is extraordinary in comparison with earlier settlements such as Three Saints Harbor. Broad artifact classes included kitchen items (ceramic tableware in many varieties, glass containers, cooking pots), architectural elements (iron fasteners and hardware, glass), firearms, tools, clothing, tobacco pipes, personal ornaments, game pieces, and children's toys. Russian dependency on local Tlingit food supplies and trade were represented by cedar bark cordage, spruce root baskets for food storage, and parts of arrows. McMahan concluded that the material culture of working class employees of the RAC in New Arkhangel was more varied and abundant than previously thought.

ALASKA NATIVE SITES

Reese Bay Site, Unalaska Island, Eastern Aleutian Islands

Reese Bay is the earliest Russian period Alaska Native village site to have been intensively studied. Unangan people were living in up to four longhouses at Reese Bay during the time of initial Russian contact (1759–66), but abandoned these structures in about 1790. Nineteen village residents were killed in 1765 during a conflict with one of the traders. Archaeologists Douglas W. Veltre (University of Alaska, Anchorage), Allen P. McCartney (University of Arkansas), and Jean S. Aigner (University of Alaska, Fairbanks) excavated a large part of Longhouse 2 in 1986–90. Ethnohistorian Lydia Black (University of Alaska, Fairbanks) gathered data from Russian documents.

Traditional bone and stone tools made up over 80 percent of more than 10,000 artifacts found in the multifamily dwelling, which may have housed 100 people or more. About 90 percent of the Russian-imported artifacts were glass beads, the remainder consisting of curved and flat glass, iron nails, and other metal items. The limited quantity and diversity of imported artifacts is typical of early contact period sites in the Aleutian Islands and Kodiak region, where people were living under the forced labor system. Bead varieties, which changed over time and are used in Alaska to estimate the dates of historic sites, were very similar to those found at Three Saints Harbor. Investigators examined the spatial distribution of beads within the house, finding a concentration in the eastern half where the lineage head and high-ranking families probably resided.

Nunakakhnak Site, Kodiak Island

A smallpox epidemic raged across southern Alaska during 1837–39 and was especially devastating on Kodiak Island. Many Alutiiq villages were abandoned, and Nunakakhnak at the mouth of the Karluk River was one of seven locations where the RAC resettled refugees. In 1984 archaeologists

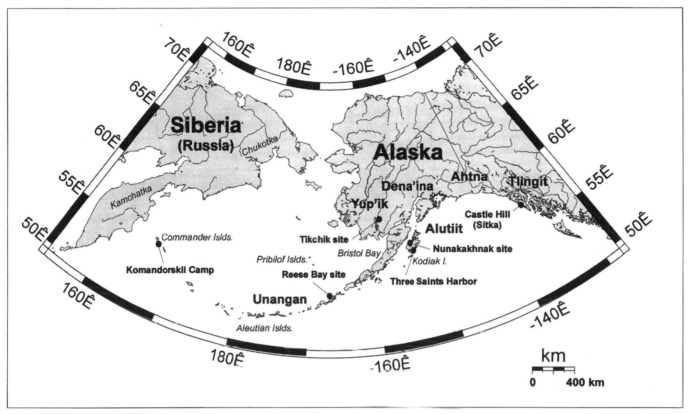

A map of Siberia and Alaska showing archaeological site and cultural tradition locations mentioned in the essay.   [Aron L. Crowell]

Richard Knecht and Richard Jordan, both of Bryn Mawr College, excavated an 1840s semi-subterranean Alutiiq house at the settlement.

Artifacts included over 1,000 shards of imported ceramics, mostly English transfer-printed dishes but including some Chinese porcelains. Several thousand glass beads, iron ax heads, gunflints, musket balls, a Russian Orthodox cross, pieces of cloth, bottle glass, and numerous iron objects were recovered. Ground slate knives and other stone artifacts showed that Alutiiq occupants were still using some traditional tools, but substantial replacement of indigenous material culture by Russian-supplied goods was evident. The late date of this cultural shift—sixty years after the beginning of intensive contact—is significant. Older Alutiiq sites in the Kodiak archipelago contain very few Russian-imported items. For example, Alutiiq middens at the village of Mysovskoe, abandoned a decade or two prior to 1840, contained only 7 percent non-aboriginal items. The increase of imported goods in Alaska Native sites after 1840 reflects better RAC access to foreign supplies as well as amelioration of its Native labor policies.

Tikchik, Tikchik River, Interior Southwest Alaska

The Tikchik village site represents cultural interaction at the margins of Russian influence. Russian explorers Korsakovski, Kolmakov, and Vasiliev penetrated the Yup'ik-speaking region

north of Bristol Bay between 1818 and 1830, seeking RAC access to beaver, muskrat, lynx, and river otter pelts. During the 1960s, archaeologists James Van Stone (Field Museum) and Wendell Oswalt (University of California, Los Angeles) excavated Tikchik, other nineteenth-century Yup'ik sites, and Kolmakovskiy Redoubt, a fortified Russian trading post on the Kuskokwim River.

Trade in this "semi-dependent" region was voluntary, although the Russians encouraged Yup'ik families to incur lifetime debts to the trading posts. The Alaska Commercial Company, an American firm, took over the trade after 1867 and carried out its business in much the same way. At Tikchik (occupied from before 1827 to 1900), VanStone found glass beads, English teacups and saucers, buttons, bottle glass, tin cans, kettle fragments, parts of flintlock and percussion cap guns, iron ax heads, and metal tools. A large part of this collection dates to the Russian period, although indistinguishable American era artifacts are included. Despite this influx of new goods, Yup'ik residents continued to make and use their own implements, weapons, and pottery. They fashioned new materials (metal and glass) into traditional forms such as knives, spearheads, and arrow points. This "conservative" pattern of acculturation, as VanStone called it, may have been related to the remote location of the village and unreliable access to imported supplies (e.g., gunpowder) that encouraged continuation of older technologies for hunting and domestic life.

THE LEGACY OF RUSSIAN COLONIALISM

The historical legacy of Russian colonialism can be seen in southern Alaska's towns and villages today. The blue domes of Russian Orthodox chapels float above Unangan, Alutiiq, Yup'ik, Dena'ina, and Tlingit communities, and the interiors glow with candles, richly painted icons, and the sound of hymns sung in Slavonic. Orthodox missionaries who arrived in the late eighteenth century pressed the RAC for more humane treatment of Alaska Natives, and the church took root. In many areas, Orthodoxy represents an important part of Native identity. Russian heritage is evident in family names, place names, loan words in Native languages, foods (e.g., tea, salmon pie), and customs such as steam bathing. Because Russian interests were in furs, not land, almost all Alaska Native peoples still occupy their ancestral home regions. In some villages, archaeological sites that represent colonial history are directly underfoot. Alaska Native tribes, corporations, and cultural organizations are working with archaeologists to uncover this evidence of the past.

Further Reading: Crowell, Aron L., *Archaeology and the Capitalist World System: A Study from Russian America* (New York: Plenum Press, 1997); Crowell, Aron L., Amy F. Stefian, and Gordon L. Pullar, eds., *Looking Both Ways: Heritage and Identity of the Alutiiq People* (Fairbanks: University of Alaska Press, 2001); Knecht, Richard A., and Richard H. Jordan, "Nunakakhnak: An Historic Period Koniag Village in Karluk, Kodiak Island, Alaska," *Arctic Anthropology* 22(2) (1985): 17–35; Len'Kov, G. L., G. L. Silant'ev, and A. K. Staniukovich, *The Komandorskii Camp of the Bering Expedition (An Experiment in Complex Study)*, translated by Katherine L. Arndt (Anchorage: Alaska Historical Society, 1992); McMahan, J. David, *Archaeological Date Recovery at Baranof Castle State Historical Site, Sitka, Alaska: Final Report of Investigations (ADOT & PF Project No. 71817/TEA-000-3[43])*, Report No. 84 (Anchorage: Alaska Office of History and Archaeology, 2002); VanStone, James W., "Tikchik Village: A Nineteenth Century Riverine Community in Southwestern Alaska," *Fieldiana: Anthropology* 56(3) (1968); Vancouver, George, *A Voyage of Discovery to the North Pacific Ocean and Round the World* (London: John Stockdale, 1801); Veltre, Douglas W., and Allen P. McCartney, "Ethnohistorical Archaeology at the Reese Bay Site, Unalaska Island," in *Archaeology of the Aleut Zone of Alaska: Some Recent Research*, edited by Don E. Dumond, University of Oregon Anthropological Papers No. 58 (Eugene: University of Oregon, 2001).

Aron L. Crowell

EUROPEAN AND AMERICAN EXPLORATION, SCIENTIFIC, AND TRADING SITES IN THE WESTERN ARCTIC AND SUBARCTIC

DISCOVERY OF NORTHWESTERN NORTH AMERICA

In 1741 Vitus Bering and his crew were the first recorded non-Natives to set foot on land that is now part of Alaska. Although this is reminiscent of Christopher Columbus's discovery of the New World, there were many important differences. Columbus, a Portuguese in service of Spain, made landfall in the Caribbean on his first voyage in 1492 and would return for several more trips, surviving until 1506. Also, he was soon followed to the New World by other explorers from other countries eager to stake claims for their own nations. Finding gold and other wealth plus spreading the Catholic faith were major incentives.

Bering, however, was a Dane in service to Russia and was on what would be his final voyage when he and his crew landed on Kayak Island in southeastern Alaska on July 16, 1741. Thirteen years earlier, on his first voyage of discovery in 1728, Bering had seen and named St. Lawrence Island in what was later named the Bering Sea. Yet he had not been able to land. He also discovered the Diomede Islands during that expedition, but fog prevented him from seeing the mainland of North America. Bad weather in 1729 again thwarted follow-up discoveries, yet he kept trying.

Between 1734 and 1743 a series of expeditions, all planned by Bering, but most not under his command, succeeded in charting and exploring land on the western side of the Bering Strait claimed by Russia. But for Bering, although the expedition of 1741 would bring his long-sought triumph, it would also result in his death. Bering, then 60 years old, set sail on one final attempt to find the mainland of northwestern North America and, as before, almost failed due to weather. This time, however, the plan was to sail east assuming that land eventually would be found—and it was. Ironically, he and his crew sailed in an easterly direction roughly parallel to the southern coasts of the Aleutian Islands and Kodiak Island, missing them all. It was only when he saw Mount St. Elias, elevation 18,008 feet (5,489 m) looming out the fog that Bering realized his success. By then, he had traveled to the northern part of southeastern Alaska.

Meanwhile, Bering's lieutenant, Chirikoff, was making further discoveries in another Russian ship sailing in a southeasterly direction. On the day before Bering's landing on Kayak Island, Chirikoff, sighted land at what is now near the southernmost border of Alaska. From there he and his crew sailed northwestward along the coast. Near Sitka they lost a landing party to hostile Tlingit Indians and decided to return to their base at Kamchatka, part of the Russian mainland far to the west.

Unfortunately, Bering's own attempt to return to Kamchatka from Kayak Island was a disaster. He and most of his crew became sick, and their boat wrecked on what is now called Bering Island, part of the Komandorski group in the Russian Far East in the Bering Sea. There, Bering died on December 8, 1741. Eventually, his surviving crew reached Siberia after constructing a vessel from the wreckage.

RUSSIAN EXPANSION AND COMPETITION

Although the ill-fated 1741 expedition did result in significant geographic discoveries, unlike Columbus's discovery, no further official Russian expeditions were undertaken until 1761. Yet some Russian fur traders, hearing of new lands to the east, began their own explorations of Alaska as early as the mid-1740s. The first Russian fur hunters were a rough and rugged lot of men called *promyshienniki*, who left no lasting settlements yet began decades of cruel treatment to the Native people of the region. This included forced labor and enslavement for those not wiped out by disease. Although some trade goods are found in the Aleutian Islands and Kodiak Island in Native sites into the first few decades of the nineteenth century, their numbers are relatively limited with inexpensive, easily transportable goods predominating, such as trade beads. This contrasts to the later Russian period in Alaska after the 1840s when Native sites in other areas contacted show a greater quantity and variety of Russian trade goods. This pattern corresponds to an approach more like free trade by Russians with Natives in the latter period. In effect, the Russians were having to trade more and better goods for the declining numbers of furs—with the continuing decline of fur in Alaska being one of the motivations for the later sale of Russian America.

As for the earliest Russian settlements in Alaska, Russian merchant Gregor Shelikoff established the first permanent trading post at Three Saints Bay on Kodiak Island in 1784. Archaeological work undertaken there in the early 1990s has provided one of the best snapshots of late eighteenth-century Russian material culture in Alaska.

By 1784, however, other nations were also showing interest in northwestern North America and the riches it might contain. Between 1774 and 1794, Spanish explorers sailed into the northern Pacific Ocean and explored southeastern Alaska, although they made no settlements. Today they are remembered for certain place names along the coast of Alaska, including Cordova and Valdez.

Besides the Spanish, the British were also quite active in late eighteenth-century exploration. Captain James Cook in 1778 in search of the Northwest Passage sailed along the coast of Alaska and northward through the Bering Strait into the Arctic Ocean before being halted by ice near Icy Cape, as he named it. His expedition also brought him into Cook Inlet and the Anchorage area before his death on the same voyage in February of 1779 in the Sandwich (now Hawai'ian) Islands.

Following Cook's voyage, the French in 1786 sent their sole expedition to the area under La Pérouse, who retraced much of the same coastline of southeastern Alaska as the Spanish. In the 1790s English Captain George Vancouver, previously on Cook's 1778 voyage, also explored much of the same area, naming Douglas Island across from today's Juneau in 1798 for John Douglas, the bishop of Salisbury. But again, there were no settlements. Various trade goods from this period ended up in a few archaeological sites, although some Western-made items had already entered Alaska for centuries. This includes possibly fifteenth-century artifacts found in northern Alaska at the Punyik site originally excavated by William Irving in 1954 and 1961.

Besides exploration, some of the early expeditions also made important scientific discoveries. The earliest was Bering's 1741 voyage during which Georg Wilhelm Steller, a physician-naturalist, made descriptions of many new types of wildlife including while stranded on Bering Island. Naturalists were also with Cook and Vancouver.

THE RUSSIAN-AMERICAN COMPANY AND ESTABLISHMENT OF SITKA

In the late eighteenth century, Russia's contacts with Alaska intensified. In 1799 Czar Paul I of Russia gave exclusive rights for trade in Russian America to a new trading corporation called the Russian America Company. It was headed by Gregor Shelikoff under the condition that the company would promote further discoveries, commerce, and agriculture. It would also aid in the propagation of the Orthodox faith. Subsequently, from 1799 until 1863, the company virtually ruled Alaska. Alexander Baranov (Baranof), selected in 1799 as first chief director of the company, served as a powerful governor of Alaska for two decades. Despite Native American attacks and challenges by British and American trading vessels in Alaskan waters, Baranov brought steady profits to the company.

One of his biggest challenges came early in his rule when he decided to move his capital from Kodiak to Sitka. The reason for the move was the near exhaustion of the natural resources of the Aleutians, and the need to look elsewhere for revenue. In 1802 Russian-American Company men established a settlement at what is now called Old Sitka, first discovered during Bering's 1741 expedition. Yet most of the original party was massacred in May of 1802 by the local

Tlingits, whose village (called Shee Atika) was in the area. Unlike the more passive Aleuts, the Tlingits would continue their pressure on the Russians even after New Sitka (modern Sitka) was founded and fortified, following a retaliatory strike by the Russians in 1804. This was called the Battle of Sitka and was the last major stand by the Tlingits against the Russians, although for decades the peace would be an uneasy one between them. Until about 1822, the Indians did not return to the immediate Sitka area to live. Meanwhile, by 1808, Sitka became the capital of Russian Alaska. Baranov's impressive wooden residence atop Castle Hill overlooked the harbor. The location was also the site of the home of the last Russian governor, with the final structure on the site (built after Baranov's first residence) burning in 1894.

During 1997–98, the State of Alaska funded an excavation of part of Castle Hill to improve visitor access to the popular town overlook. That work resulted in the recovery of thousands of artifacts from the Russian period, including some that showed the cosmopolitan nature of the settlement. Earlier, another important window into the Russian material culture of Sitka came from the 1981 excavation of the Russian Bishop's House and nearby trash pit at Sitka. Built in 1842 and restored by the National Park Service, the Russian Bishop's House is the most intact structure at Sitka from the Russian period.

During the mid-1800s, Sitka remained the premier port on the north Pacific coast, with ships arriving from many countries. Furs destined for European and Asian markets were the main export, but salmon, lumber, and ice were also shipped to Hawai'i, Mexico, and California. After the purchase of Alaska by the United States in 1867, Sitka remained the capital of the territory until 1906, when the seat of government was moved to Juneau.

In the early 1800s under Baranov, Russian influence slowly spread to more parts of Alaska from Kodiak and Sitka. A prime motivation was to find more furs that otherwise were becoming scarce from over harvest. New Russian settlements or trading posts were established during this time in western, southern, and southeastern Alaska, including in Prince William Sound, Cook Inlet, on five of the Aleutian Islands, on the Pribilofs, at Nushagak in Bristol Bay, and even in California at Fort Ross. Also, Russian exploration parties were sent up the Copper River, along Bristol Bay, and into the southern part of the Arctic Ocean.

Although Baranov had concluded a commercial agreement with the American fur trader John Jacob Astor, members of the Russian navy opposed allowing non-Russians entry into the fur trade. It resulted in Baranov's replacement, and an attempt by the Russian navy to close off the whole coast of western North America north of 51 degrees (at about the northern end of Vancouver Island) to all but Russians. By 1824, Americans had secured an agreement for equal trading privileges for ten years north of 54 degrees, 40 minutes, but by then illegal trading and whaling were occurring, with the

relatively low numbers of Russians unable to do much about it. Also, Russia was involved in the Napoleonic wars in Europe and internal problems from serf uprisings.

LAST YEARS OF RUSSIAN AMERICA

Russian exploration to advance the fur trade continued for several more decades. In 1819 an expedition under Russian explorer Pëtr Korsakovskiy reached the mouth of the Kuskokwim River with coastal exploration of southwestern Alaska commencing the next year. In 1832 the Kolmakov Redoubt was established on the middle Kuskokwim River, which was later excavated in the 1960s by Wendell H. Oswalt. In 1833 the Mikhailovskiy Redoubt was built at what is now St. Michael, Alaska, near the mouth of the Yukon River. And with its establishment, Russia was poised for new explorations. During 1842–44, the most significant of these occurred with the travels of Lieutenant Lavrentii Zagoskin. He was commissioned by the Russian-American Company to determine whether the Russians could capture ongoing Native trade traditionally connecting the Yukon River region to the Seward Peninsula and Chukchi Sea areas through intermediaries. Zagoskin's exploration took him up the Kuskokwim and Koyukuk rivers, and up the Yukon River to near the mouth of the Tanana River in central Alaska.

Yet by this time, Russia's interest in, and ability to govern, far-off Alaska was waning. Significantly, in 1841 Baranov's trading post at Fort Ross, California, was sold to John Sutter. (He was the same man whose mill near Coloma was the later site of a major gold discovery in 1848 that set off the California gold rush.)

One consequence of allowing Americans into the area was their increased contact and trade with Alaska Natives, resulting in more trade goods that would end up in archaeological sites. Yet the Americans were not alone in challenging Russian dominance over Alaska. The British, pressing westward from Canada, also would end up in Alaska by the mid-1800s. For the British, the westward move into the Yukon River region was a continuation of their expansion into northwestern Canada. The British had earlier established Hudson's Bay Company outposts on the Pelly and Mackenzie rivers from which trade goods entered northwestern Canada.

The start of the process was the exploration by Alexander Mackenzie and his 1789 discovery of the river that bears his name. This was followed in the 1820s by Sir John Franklin, who also explored parts of the Mackenzie River system while searching for the Northwest Passage. In July 1825 Franklin encountered a party of Eskimo with iron- or steel-pointed arrows along the Arctic coast. Through an interpreter he learned that they had obtained them in trade from white men to the west, who Franklin assumed were Russian traders along Alaska's coast. This encouraged him to travel westward along the Arctic coast and resulted in his party being the first white people to ever enter what is today the Yukon Territory.

Photo by Edweard Muybridge taken in 1868 during an Army expedition to the newly-purchased American territory of Alaska. The photo is one of the earliest photographs ever made in southeastern Alaska. It shows Tlingit Indians at "Fort Wrangle" (now called just "Wrangell"), in southeastern Alaska. Wrangell began as a Russian trading post several decades prior to the purchase of Alaska by the United States in 1867. The photo indicates the substantial amount of acculturation that had occurred during the Russian period. [Courtesy of the Bureau of Land Management]

Franklin's report of his trip mentioned fur-bearing animals and reindeer. This led the Hudson's Bay Company in the late 1830s to send an exploration party under John Bell to further examine the area. Consequently, Bell explored the Snake River to its headwaters, and in 1840 established the first trading post, Fort Reliance, in the Mackenzie River delta in what is now the northwestern part of the Northwest Territories. In 1846 Lapierre's House, another trading post, was established to the west in the Porcupine River drainage in the northern part of today's Yukon Territory.

Earlier, in 1842, Bell also explored parts of the Porcupine River, and in 1846 he traveled to its confluence with the Yukon River. Encouraged with this news, in 1847, Alexander Murray established a Hudson's Bay Company trading post called Fort Yukon on the Yukon River, about 4 miles (6.4 km) above the mouth of the Porcupine River, which was well over 100 miles (161 km) west of the present Alaska-Canada border. This was an outright invasion of Russian territory, but who was to stop it? The Russians learned of this troubling development soon afterward and sent a note to the manager at Fort Yukon, although it

This photo (ca. 1880s) by Richard Maynard shows part of Sitka, the former Russian capital of what is now Alaska. The structure atop the hill was built in 1837 as the official dwelling for the various chief managers of the Russian-America Company, and it served that purpose for about thirty years. These managers, often called the Russian governors of Alaska, also used the structure for state business and official entertainment such as balls. Consequently, this building is also called the Capitol of Russian America.   [Courtesy of the Bureau of Land Management]

was never answered. Worse still, the British offered better terms for furs than the Russians and traded more modern guns. Soon British rifles were being traded widely, including in the lower Yukon, lower Kuskokwim, and Copper rivers. It was a festering problem for the Russians, and as late as 1862, the Russian manager of the Kolmakov Redoubt on the Kuskokwim River was sent on orders to the upper Yukon River to learn more about British activities in the area.

Yet before that, the Russians had faced another setback. In 1851 several Russian traders were killed at Nulato in hostilities brought on in part by their interference with the local Native trade network. After that encounter, the Russians withdrew to the lower Yukon. There were also challenges before this time to Russian Territory in southeastern Alaska. In 1840 the Hudson's Bay Company had entered what is now Wrangell Harbor and raised its flag over Russian-built Fort St. Dionysius (renamed Fort Stikine) at the mouth of the Stikine River. The same year the company established another trading post on the Alaska mainland at Taku Harbor northwest of Fort Stikine. Although it was abandoned in 1843,

The Last Climb to the Summit of Chilkoot Pass, 1898

Gold rush stampeders climbing up the American side of Chilkoot Pass in 1898, headed for the gold fields of the Klondike. [Courtesy of the Bureau of Land Management]

followed by the Hudson Bay Company's departure from Fort Stikine in 1849, intense trading continued in Alaskan waters, but off the boats of Hudson's Bay Company ships.

Overall, the increasing British presence and expansion into eastern Alaska along the Yukon River were additional factors that led to Russia's sale of Alaska to the United States. From the Russian perspective, it was preferable to have the United States in Alaska as a buffer between Canada and Siberia than to have the British in ownership of Russian America with possible ideas to expand their empire even farther west across the Bering Sea. Ironically, thirty years after the sale of Russian America to the United States, Americans were in effect invading Canada—this time for gold during the Klondike gold rush.

THE AMERICAN PERIOD IN ALASKA

With the purchase of Russian America by the United States in 1867, some trade goods still entered Alaska through northwestern Canada. This included items from an American trading post named Fort Reliance that was operated by the American Commercial Company under François Mercier starting in 1874. Its location was just downstream from what is now Dawson City. This post was in business until the end of the 1885–86 trading season, with archaeological investigations by the Canadian Museum of Civilization occurring there in 1983 and 1991. Goods from this post were obtained by some of the earliest prospectors in the Fortymile-Klondike region before the Klondike gold discovery in 1896.

The lure of gold, something that never drew much Russian interest despite small discoveries, was the next major catalyst for significantly changing Alaska and northwestern Canada. Gold discoveries in the Stikine River near Wrangell in southeastern Alaska had created a rush, but the 1880 gold discovery in the Gastineau Channel brought many more miners northward, leading to the new gold rush city of Juneau. This was followed in 1886 by the first significant gold discoveries in the eastern interior of Alaska in the Fortymile River region. The major Klondike discovery came a decade later just east of Dawson in the Yukon Territory. Between those dates, other important gold discoveries were made near Circle and Rampart in the Yukon River region of Alaska, with prospectors also exploring many parts of Alaska and northwestern Canada for new bonanzas. In 1898 major gold discoveries at Nome and in 1902 in the Fairbanks area were followed by a series of significant discoveries into the early twentieth century, such as in the Iditarod River area in 1909.

Today, archaeological work has been done at several of these sites, including numerous excavations at the gold rush gateway town of Skagway, Alaska.

Further Reading: Antonson, Joan M., and William S. Hanable, *Alaska's Heritage*, 2nd ed., Alaska Historical Commission Studies in History No. 133 (Anchorage: Alaska Historical Society for the Alaska Historical Commission, Department of Education, State of Alaska, 1992); Black, Lydia T., *Russians in Alaska 1732–1867* (Fairbanks: University of Alaska Press, 2004); Blee, Catherine Holder, *Archeological Investigations at the Russian Bishop's House, 1981, Sitka National Historical Park, Sitka, Alaska* (Denver, CO: National Park Service, Denver Service Center, 1985); Blee, Catherine Holder, *Wine, Yaman and Stone: The Archeology of a Russian Hospital Trash Pit, Sitka National Historical Park, Sitka, Alaska* (Washington, DC: National Park Service, 1987); Clark, Donald W., *Fort Reliance,*

Yukon: An Archaeological Assessment, Mercury Series Archaeological Survey of Canada Paper No. 150 (Hull, QC: Canadian Museum of Civilization, 1995); Crowell, Aron L., *Archaeology and the Capitalist World System: A Study from Russian America* (New York: Plenum Press, 1997); Morrison, William R., *True North: The Yukon and Northwest Territories* (Toronto: Oxford University Press, 1998); Office of History and Archaeology, Alaska Department of Natural Resources, Division of Parks and Outdoor Recreation, Castle Hill Archaeological Project, Castle Hill Web site, http://www.dnr.state. ak.us/parks/oha/castle/introd.htm (online April 2007); Oswalt, Wendell H., *Kolmakovskiy Redoubt: The Ethnoarchaeology of a Russian Fort in Alaska*, Monumenta Archaeologica No. 8 (Los Angeles: University of California, Institute of Archaeology, 1980); VanStone, James W., "Exploration and Contact History of Western Alaska," in *Handbook of North American Indians*, Vol. 5: *Arctic*, edited by David Damas (Washington, DC: Smithsonian Institution, 1984), 149–160.

Robert E. King

THE BROOKS RIVER ARCHAEOLOGICAL DISTRICT

Katmai National Park and Preserve, Southern Alaska

10,000 Years in a Land of Lakes, Rivers, and Mountains of Fire

Brooks River, 1.5 miles in length, flows from Brooks Lake to Naknek Lake in the upper portion of the Naknek River drainage system of the northern Alaska Peninsula. Both banks of the river and the immediately adjacent shores of the two lakes were designated an archaeological district in the mid-1970s, by which time seventeen separate sites had been recorded in the area, spanning the period from about 3200 BC to AD 1800. Sites were first reported in 1953 by archaeologists working as part of a multidisciplinary team to inventory the overall resources of what was then Katmai National Monument (now a major part of Katmai National Park and Preserve). Research in the 1960s and 1970s was conducted by the University of Oregon, with projects in the 1980s and after AD 2000 by the National Park Service.

Toward the end of the last major glacial period, 12,000–14,000 BC, both modern lake basins were beneath an ancestral Naknek Lake, the level of which was 85 feet higher than the modern lake of that name. As the bed of the Naknek River—the outlet stream from the lake to Bristol Bay—eroded, lake surface lowered. When it dropped 15 feet (ca. 6000 BC) the modern lakes appeared separated by a constriction. Another 10 feet of lowering produced a short Brooks River, and with another 10 feet (ca. 3000 BC) Brooks Falls began to appear across a stone ledge located about the midpoint of the present river. With continuing decreases, the river below the falls meandered from side to side, with the river

current and waves of Naknek Lake creating a complex set of terraces. Birch and willow were present along the river throughout this time, and within the last 300 years white spruce colonized the area. Meanwhile, volcanic eruptions in the Aleutian Range periodically deposited layer after layer of ashy pumice, creating an acid soil cover that inhibits the preservation of organic materials.

Although human presence on the Alaska Peninsula is known as early as 8000 BC, the earliest recognized sites at Brooks River are short-term camps dating from between 3200 and 2000 BC, located on the major ridges that then flanked the river mouth, providing attractive camping spots. Pulverized mammal bone suggests seasonal camps of caribou hunters. Two separate peoples camped at the river mouth, although no doubt in different years and likely even in different decades. Slightly earlier were people of the Pacific coast of the peninsula, some 50 miles to the southeast, who camped in tents, used spearing lances armed with long blades of polished slate, and burned sea-mammal oil in flat stone lamps. The second, known from slightly later (ca. 2900 BC) but with campsite dates interspersed among those of the coastal people, were late carriers of the Northern Archaic tradition, whose caribou-hunting compatriots were largely of the Alaska interior. Simple campsites yielded chipped-stone projectile points, mostly lance-like in form, and numerous scrapers. Use of the river mouth by both of these peoples ended a little before 2000 BC, when a major volcanic eruption farther southwest along the peninsula deposited a substantial layer of volcanic ash.

Shortly after 2000 BC, the area was entered by very different people of the Arctic Small Tool tradition. People of this tradition made diminutive chipped stone tools, including small leaf-shaped points for tipping arrows, more asymmetric ones hafted with a side projecting outward for use as knives, and small groovers or burins. They people constructed small, partly sod-covered houses, usually square and 13–14 feet on a side and excavated as much as 2 feet below surface, with a central fireplace and an entrance by a sloping passageway. Unlike camps of their predecessors, Small Tool habitations are found the length of the river on essentially every terrace and beach ridge in existence at the time, suggesting their interest was in the river itself as a resource; further, the houses appear suitable for winter occupation. By this time the waterfall was high enough to be a partial barrier to upstream salmon migrations, and Small Tool houses are especially plentiful close by. Fishing is confirmed by fish teeth screened from house floors, and smashed mammal bone suggests caribou as a second resource. Dated nearly 1,000 years later than the earliest Small Tool people on the Seward Peninsula near Bering Strait, these people represent the time when Small Tool folk had become more sedentary, departing from earlier purely hunting habits to live by the streams of southwestern Alaska. However satisfactory life may have been, occupation along Brooks River ended at least a century or two before 1000 BC, and coincided with another massive volcanic eruption and heavy volcanic ash.

It was nearly 1,000 years before the river banks were occupied again. Although there may have been at least one additional volcanic eruption in this period of vacancy, it is hard to imagine that all subsistence resources evaporated. In any event, around 300 BC the river banks were again host to people—this time of the Norton tradition. Although many of the chipped-stone tools from Norton sites bespeak relationship to the earlier Arctic Small Tool tradition, and farther north in Alaska this similarity is enough to suggest that Small Tool people were to some extent Norton ancestors, the hiatus makes it clear that Brooks River was not the place where descent occurred. Among the new possessions of Norton people also was the open lamp of shaped stone for burning sea-mammal oil, a south-Alaskan characteristic. One of the most noticeable new possessions of Norton people was pottery, indicating knowledge derived from northeast Asia. Thus, the cultural parentage of Norton people was multiple and complex.

At Brooks River the Norton period lasted well over a millennium, until AD 1000 or 1100. Archaeologists recognize three sequential Norton phases there, marked by changes in both stone artifacts and pottery, but without any shift in subsistence practices or society. The first phase was short, and was the most like major Norton sites around the Alaska coast of the Bering Sea to the north, which date to 500 BC or so. The second phase was longer, as much as 600 to 700 years, and more widespread along the river. The third was again short, with a

major site located on a high terrace immediately above Brooks Falls. During all of Norton time, houses were similar in plan to those of the Arctic Small Tool predecessors: roughly square, 13–14 feet on a side with a central fireplace, excavated 1 foot or more into the ground, and entered by a simple sloping passage. Tools were largely of chipped stone, including asymmetric side-blades, projectile blades (usually stemmed), and scrapers plus, of course, stone lamps. Clusters of bi-notched pebbles suggest fishing with nets. Pottery was plentiful, although it changed in form and surface decoration over time. By the final phase, polished slate knives were replacing chipped side-blade knives, coinciding with increased contact with slate-using people of the Pacific coast of the peninsula. Salmon fishing was the major subsistence attraction, although some small Norton campsites in surrounding hinterlands suggest that seasonal hunting was still an important occupation.

At AD 1050 or 1100, the latest Norton people were either displaced or heavily infiltrated by a different people, evidently from the north and as a southern echo of the Thule-related expansion of maritime peoples in north Alaska. Two major sites of what is termed the Brooks River Camp phase of culture are on the river's north-bank terraces. Pottery changed in form and paste, finished implements were almost exclusively of polished slate, and stone lamps were replaced by basins of clay, scarcely baked. Houses were still heated by a central fire but were often slightly larger, excavated more deeply in the ground, covered with sod roofs supported by massive posts, and entered by a passageway the floor of that dipped well below the house floor to provide a "cold trap" to lessen drafts in the house. Surviving artifacts from this time include barbed points of caribou antler, and a few scraps of whalebone indicate direct connections with the coast. In addition to similarities in artifacts and houses with more northerly Alaska, at least one comparable and contemporary site is known on the Pacific coast of the peninsula, suggesting that these northern people crossed the mountains to the coast, rich in marine resources, where some archaeologists believe they exerted an influence on people of the Kodiak group of islands.

Again, however, this occupation of Thule-related people ended with a volcanic eruption in the mountains with a heavy deposit of volcanic ash—this time at AD 1300–1350. There was no repeat of a long break in occupations, however, for by AD 1400 Brooks River was in full use again as a fishery resource and post near paths of seasonally migrating caribou, this time with sites scattered along the south bank from the falls to the river mouth. Although the people did not depart entirely from practices and artifact categories of the preceding Camp phase, it appears that the affiliations of these Brooks River Bluffs phase people were across the mountains to the east, toward the Pacific coast of the peninsula and the Kodiak group of islands immediately across the strait. Polished slate projectile blades and knives were altered toward the Kodiak style, clay lamps were replaced by stone, and careful incisions of human-like depictions appeared on small pebbles as are known from Kodiak. Houses were still at least partly sod-covered and excavated into the ground surface, but they included a larger central room with central fireplace, from which radiated smaller rooms: some apparently for sleeping, some with plentiful bone trash and charcoal indicating food preparation, and some with piles of fire-cracked rocks marking sweat baths.

This Kodiak-influenced occupation endured at least until AD 1800, with both constructed houses and more surficial campsites, suggesting year-round use. At about that time the mouth of the Naknek River was invaded by Yupik-speaking Eskimo people from the north, and two decades afterward Russian fur hunters were traversing the region, but no evidence of the period has been found at Brooks River. Although some historical accounts from the late 1800s indicate Native people were making at least summer fishing use of the river, no sites of that period have been explored either. Whatever these cases, any heavy use was interrupted in 1912 when the most massive volcanic eruption of all—from the vicinity of Mt. Katmai in the mountains to the east—deposited nearly 1 foot of volcanic ash over the area, with use to be resumed only a couple of decades afterward. By this time the region was officially a tract under management by the National Park Service with special attention to the results of the 1912 volcanic eruption.

At present, tourist accommodations are available at Brooks Lodge near the mouth of Brooks River, as well as in the local center of King Salmon located along the mid-course of the Naknek River. A partly reconstructed Camp phase house can be viewed as a modest Brooks River archaeological display, together with a small number of artifacts. The area can be reached by way of King Salmon, thence by air or boat across Naknek Lake to Brooks River.

Further Reading: Bundy, Barbara E., Dale M. Vinson, and Don E. Dumond, *Brooks River Cutbank: An Archeological Data Recovery Project in Katmai National Park*, University of Oregon Anthropological Papers No. 64 (Eugene: University of Oregon, 2005); Dumond, Don E., *Archaeology on the Alaska Peninsula: The Naknek Region, 1960–1975*, University of Oregon Anthropological Papers No. 21 (Eugene: University of Oregon, 1981); Dumond, Don E., *A Naknek Chronicle: Ten Thousand Years in a Land of Lakes and Rivers and Mountains of Fire* (King Salmon, AK: National Park Service, Katmai National Park and Preserve, 2005); Harritt, Roger K., *The Late Prehistory of Brooks River, Alaska: A Model for Analysis of Occupations on the Alaska Peninsula*, University of Oregon Anthropological Papers No. 38 (Eugene: University of Oregon, 1988).

Don E. Dumond

MINK ISLAND SITE AND THE AMALIK BAY ARCHAEOLOGICAL DISTRICT

Katmai National Park and Preserve, Pacific Coast of the Alaska Peninsula, Alaska

A High-Resolution, Long-Term Snapshot of Human Maritime Adaptation

The Mink Island site is located on a small, unnamed island along the Pacific coast of the Alaska Peninsula, across Shelikof Strait from the Kodiak archipelago. The site is important regionally for its excellent preservation of several nested occupation floors and associated shell and bone deposits dating between 5500 and 2100 BC and AD 0–1500. The recently excavated site provides a high-resolution, long-term snapshot of human adaptation to a volatile environment from the time the earliest known maritime-based people settled along this coast to site abandonment in the Little Ice Age. In addition, the well-preserved vertebrate and invertebrate assemblages and site stratigraphy are unparalleled records of the area's environmental and natural history over the past 7,000 years.

The discoveries at the Mink Island site led to the designation of the Amalik Bay Archaeological District National His-

toric Landmark, which includes the Takli Island Archaeological District, long recognized as significant based on early research conducted by the University of Oregon. The Takli Island group may have been a single large island when the first marine-focused hunter-gatherers camped there around 5500 BC. Sea levels continued to rise and stabilized at present levels after a high stand around 4,000 years ago, at which time the site was apparently abandoned for the next 2,000 years. Tsunamis generated by earthquakes and volcanic eruptions, high waves and winds from winter storms, and changes in relative sea level over the millennia have erased most of the early archaeological record along the coast. The Mink Island site is a rare occurrence, and although much diminished in size, it retains a remarkable integrity in the remaining deposits. The data from Mink Island confirms a close cultural connection with Kodiak Island after 5500 BC until 1000 BC,

Boat-shaped lamp from the earliest occupation of Mink Island.   [National Park Service photo by Chris Arend]

View across Mink Island to the west-northwest, showing the north shore of Amalik Bay in the background.   [Courtesy of the National Park Service]

The ocher-stained floor of the earliest occupation at Mink Island, 5500 BC.   [National Park Service photo by Jeanne Schaaf]

Immature sea lion scapula and tools from an occupation on the white ash, or tephra, from a volcanic eruption, 4600 BC.   [National Park Service photo by Jeanne Schaaf]

or the beginning of the Kachemak tradition on Kodiak Island (not present at Mink Island). Connections to earlier Paleoarctic sites on the Alaska Peninsula and in the Aleutian Islands are also indicated. The use of non-local basalt for the early large blades found on Kodiak Island suggests an Alaska Peninsula origin for these earliest people.

The first people to leave a trace on Mink Island arrived during a time when summers were warmer and drier than today, with mean July temperatures perhaps 2.5°C warmer (called the Hypsithermal interval). The island vegetation would have been similar to now, with low willow and birch shrubs, grass, lichens, and a multitude of flowering plants, allowing an unobstructed 360-degree view that included the Kodiak Island group 40 miles to the east. Although alder pollen is abundant by 5000 BC in local peat deposits, it is still a rare occurrence in the vegetation on Mink Island. Within the view and soundscape was an important resource— a Steller sea lion rookery—located 3 miles south. Although no faunal material was recovered for this time period, the bones of immature sea lions appear throughout the succeeding occupation levels and likely sustained these earliest people as well. These early occupants constructed a house or

shelter by excavating a basin about 40 centimeters deep and covering its floor with powdered red ochre.

Because the house was partially eroded and only partially excavated, no other architectural details have been documented except for two low perpendicular berms of unknown function on the house floor. In an ochre-stained pit below the house floor, a finely made boat-shaped lamp was found resting on two large basalt blades and mussel shell. Charcoal from the bottom of this basalt lamp yielded the oldest date for the site, predating the radiocarbon dates on the house floor by over 200 years. It and a similar lamp found on a house floor at the Zaimka Mound site on Kodiak Island are believed to be the oldest reported lamps in North America. The discrepancy between the dates from the subfloor pit containing the lamp and the house floor may indicate separate occupations, or it may be due to the use of old driftwood, because the only material available for radiocarbon dating from the bottom of the lamp was unidentified softwood. Driftwood could have been "banked" on the island for quite a long time prior to settlement.

Although no evidence was found in the artifact assemblage, these people undoubtedly used watercraft for travel, for fishing, and for hunting a variety of sea mammals abundant in

Excavated occupation floor of a red ocher–stained shelter occupied around 3400 BC.   [National Park Service photo by Jeanne Schaaf]

the area, such as porpoise, seal, sea otter, and sea lion. Artifacts recovered from the house are dominated by large basalt blades, similar to those found at two earlier sites—one on the Alaska Peninsula (Ugashik Narrows, 8000 BC) and the other in the Aleutian Islands (Anangula, 9000 BC). A few microblades, a broken bifacial point, a grooved ground stone artifact, and some simple flake tools encrusted with ochre and organic residue constitute the small artifact collection from this occupation.

The site stratigraphy records evidence of a turbulent period immediately following the earliest occupation of the site and coincident with the end of the warm period or Hypsithermal interval. The next major occupation closely followed a volcanic eruption, which deposited a blanket of white ash 10 centimeters thick on the site around 4600 BC. The site was reoccupied within years of the ashfall by sea lion hunters using ochre-stained, stemmed chipped points, large basalt blades, whalebone clam-digging tools and expedient objects made from temporarily abundant pumice (such as grooved net floats). A contemporary occupation at the Tanginak Spring site in the Kodiak archipelago similarly occurs just above the white ash, indicating that the volcanic event had widespread but not disastrous effects on local populations.

Around 4000 BC, corresponding with a short-term warm spike in reconstructed mean summer temperature, people may have over-wintered on the island in a substantial house, and did so for many seasons based on the thick, laminated floor sediments. This is a rare example of a mid-Holocene and coastal winter house in Alaska. The builders utilized driftwood logs to support the structure, based on the size of the post holes, and heated it with a large pebble-filled hearth. Stone lamps, pecked from rounded cobbles and microblades are present in the assemblage, whereas large blades are lacking. A brief cold period (with a 2.5°C drop in mean summer temperature) followed this winter occupation and is possibly reflected by light use of the site until a small, temporary shelter was occupied around 3400 BC. This was a shallow oval depression, with a pole-supported hide cover that was, along with the floor, stained with red ochre. By this time, the use of ground slate tools is established, although evidence for the use of ground slate occurs in the preceding occupation. The floor, sealed by a volcanic ash, is exceptionally well preserved, with discreet activity areas such as concentrated ochre grinding and stockpiling, chipped-stone tool manufacture, and bone needle production. The deposit 90 centimeters thick above this floor contains cultural material throughout, including distinct occupation sur-

Upper portion of a thick shell midden deposited between AD 0 and 1500.   [National Park Service photo by Jeanne Schaaf]

faces, yet the dates from twenty-two excavation levels range from 3400 BC to 2100 BC in no particular order, indicating continuous site use during a period of rapid deposition.

Cultural activity abruptly ceased at the site by 2100 BC, a cooler period, and a sand dune 1 meter thick formed on the site. This is consistent with a hiatus in the archaeological record elsewhere in the region. By AD 0, the site was reoccupied and the site occupants began accumulating an extensive shell and bone midden on top of the earlier deposits that eventually became 3 meters thick over the next 1,500 years. As did the earlier site occupants, people continued harvesting a wide variety of intertidal resources, as well as adding whales to the list of sea mammals procured. Several human burials associated with this period of site occupation were removed from the site in the 1960s. In 1997 eroding burials were excavated, consisting of two extended sub-adults with three small children placed between them on planks hewn from driftwood. An older female was buried in a flexed position in a pit placed immediately above the previous burial. Radiocarbon dates corrected for the marine carbon reservoir effect place the interment of the family around AD 1450, contemporaneous with the last occupation of the site, a late prehistoric village of five houses, abandoned at the onset of the Little Ice Age.

Amalik Bay is spectacularly rich in marine resources, with migratory waterfowl and terrestrial resources immediately available as well. The fauna identified from the Mink Island site show that despite severe periodic perturbations in the environment, people kept coming back throughout the known prehistory of the region.

Invertebrate fauna collected from the site number in the thousands, and twenty-eight species have been identified, including large butter clams, mussel, whelks, snails, cockle, chiton, limpet, sea urchin, and razor clam. Vertebrate faunal elements recovered number over 250,000 and consist primarily of sea mammals (whale, harbor and Dall's porpoise, Steller sea lion, walrus, bearded seal, northern fur seal, harbor seal, ribbon seal, spotted seal, ringed seal, and sea otter). Terrestrial mammals present in the collection are few and represent bear, caribou, dog or wolf, unidentified medium and small mammals, and microtines. Fish identified include salmon, halibut, cod, and rockfish.

Excavations were completed at the Mink Island site in 2000, and in 2006 a revetment of gabion baskets filled with local cobbles was emplaced to protect the remaining portion of the site. Analyses of the extensive collections are underway, and the material can be viewed in the Katmai collections housed at the National Park Service Anchorage office. The site is within Katmai National Park and Preserve and access is by float plane or boat only.

Further Reading: Clark, Donald W., *Ocean Bay: An Early North Pacific Maritime Culture*, Archaeological Survey of Canada Paper No. 86 (Ottawa: National Museum of Man, Mercury Series, 1979); Dumond Don E., *A Naknek Chronicle: Ten Thousand Years in a Land of Lakes and Rivers and Mountains of Fire* (Anchorage, AK: National Park Service, Katmai National Park and Preserve, 2005); Fitshugh, Ben, *The Evolution of Complex Hunter-Gatherers: Archaeological Evidence from the North Pacific* (New York: Kluwer Academic/Plenum, 2003); Mann, Daniel H., Aron L. Crowell, Thomas D. Hamilton, and Bruce P. Finney, "Holocene Geologic and Climatic History around the Gulf of Alaska," *Arctic Anthropology* 35(1) (1998): 112–131.

Jeanne Schaaf

ROUND ISLAND SITE

Walrus Islands State Game Sanctuary, Bristol Bay, Western Alaska

Qayassiq, "Place to Go in a Kayak"

The Round Island archaeological site is significant as the oldest dated coastal site, by over 3,000 years, in Alaska north of the Alaska Peninsula. The site has clear evidence of island-based walrus hunting about 5,700 years ago (3790 BC) and again 3,600 years ago (1630 BC). Over 100 mapped prehistoric surface depressions on Round Island represent semi-subterranean houses, cold storage pits, and other activity areas from settlements affiliated with the Norton and Thule cultural traditions spanning the last 2,500 years before contact in the late eighteenth century. Excellent bone preservation in the site's major occupations provides an important opportunity to better understand the prehistoric subsistence economies and their environments as well as the natural history of important marine species from mid-Holocene times.

Round Island, known as *Qayassiq* ("place to go in a kayak") by local Yup'iq speakers, is one of seven islands protected in the Walrus Islands State Game Sanctuary

Male walrus at their summer haulout on Round Island.
[Courtesy of Alaska Department of Fish and Game]

located in northern Bristol Bay, Alaska. The sanctuary was established in 1960 primarily to protect what was then the last remaining terrestrial haul-out for Pacific walrus (*Odobenus rosmarus divergens*) in North America. The sanctuary attained National Natural Landmark status in 1968, adding nationwide recognition to the importance of this area for its concentration of Pacific walrus, with Round Island in particular serving as a summer haul-out for male walrus.

Round Island is the southeasternmost island in the sanctuary, located 63 miles southwest of Dillingham and 35 miles south-southeast of the small villages of Togiak and Twin Hills in Togiak Bay. Sheer-walled, granodiorite cliffs rising to an elevation of 1,400 feet encircle the island, except for a low bench along the northeastern shore, where the site and the only boat landings are located. Only 1.3 square miles in area, Round Island is seasonally home for as many as 14,000 walrus, hundreds of Steller sea lions,

and 250,000 nesting seabirds. Grey, humpback, minke, and orca whales pass by, sometimes feeding offshore in the spring on their migration north. This area is one of Bristol Bay's principal spawning areas of herring and yellowfin sole, and all five species of Pacific salmon are found here. The vegetation is a mosaic of wet and dry tundra, meadow, and herb communities, and the site area is a bluejoint grass meadow.

Although the entire area that is now Bristol Bay was under glacial ice during the maximum extent of Pleistocene glaciations, ice during the last glacial maximum 20,000 years ago was confined in this region to the Ahklun Mountains north of the Walrus Islands and to the Alaska Peninsula. The Walrus Islands were high ground, overlooking part of the vast southern Bering Land Bridge plain, exposed when sea level was 120 meters lower than it is today. As the plain flooded and the land rebounded from the weight of the ice, areas of high ground became increasingly smaller islands, reaching their present configuration by 2,000 years ago, when sea level was within 1 meter of today. The Walrus Islands were still part of the mainland 8,000 years ago, when sea level was about 14 meters below present, but by 6,000 years ago it rose to within 10 meters of present sea level, and Round Island became separated from the other islands and the mainland (12 miles distant at its nearest point). It was around this time that people first camped on the island and hunted walrus with spear-mounted, chipped-stone points.

Two radiocarbon dates, 3680 BC and 3790 BC, and some artifacts from the earliest occupation identified on Round Island indicate that this occupation is contemporaneous with the Northern Archaic tradition. On the north side of Cape Newenham, 70 miles west of Round Island, the earliest coastal sites are recorded in Security Cove and are assigned to the Northern Archaic tradition based only on artifact types. These sites are thought to represent seasonal excursions to the coast by inland-based caribou hunters using spear-mounted and usually side-notched points. Inland Northern Archaic sites are recorded near the mouth of Goodnews River in the Ahklun Mountains and at Kagati Lake where the hunters constructed stone cairn drive lines to channel caribou into a small lake around 2200 BC.

Following the Northern Archaic people, the Arctic Small Tool culture is represented in this region by a few scattered mainland sites. It is securely identified and dated at only one site, located 100 miles northeast in the Wood River chain of lakes draining into Nushagak Bay. Bureau of Indian Affairs archaeologists excavated small shelters with slab-lined hearths at this site dating between 1600 BC and 1500 BC and found small, finely chipped end blades and scrapers, characteristic of Arctic Small Tool assemblages. This culture practiced a mixed-subsistence economy, seasonally balancing terrestrial (caribou and fish) and marine (seal) resource use. On Round Island, there is evidence of a

Broken spear point resting on a walrus skull. The tip of the arrow scale is at the location of the dated charcoal sample (3680 BC). Scale is in 5 cm sections.   [National Park Service photo by Jeanne Schaaf]

localized but substantial occupation occurring 2,100 years after the earliest hunters camped there. Radiocarbon dated to 1630 BC, the occupation is contemporaneous with Arctic Small Tool sites on the mainland and shares some elements in stone tool technology. Both the earliest sites and this component at Round Island were identified in limited test excavations in a very small area of the overall 5.7-acre site. The limited number of artifacts recovered from these occupations at this time does not allow certain identification of cultural affiliation.

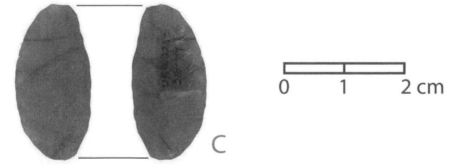

Side blade from the Round Island occupation dated 3790 BC. The small, finely made artifact is 0.28 cm thick banded grey chert. [Courtesy of the National Park Service]

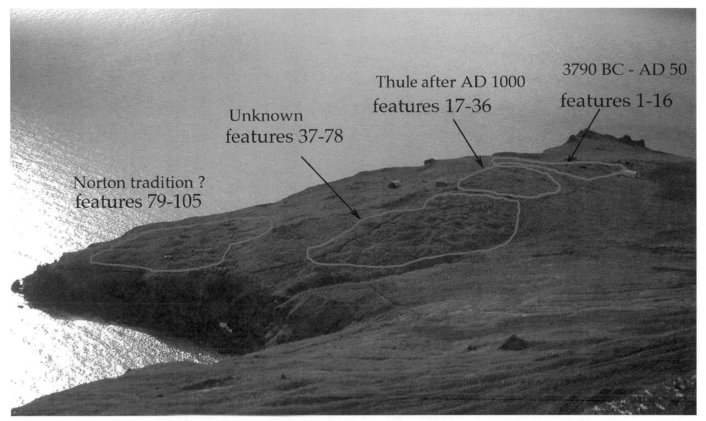

Unknown
features 37-78

Thule after AD 1000
features 17-36

3790 BC - AD 50
features 1-16

Norton tradition ?
features 79-105

The Round Island archaeological site, showing the surface features, estimated time period, and associated cultural tradition. [National Park Service annotated photo by Jeanne Schaaf]

Prior to the recent archaeological discoveries on Round Island, the earliest recorded coastal sites in northwestern Bristol Bay were dated to the Norton tradition, beginning about 500 BC. With about a 600-year gap between dated Arctic Small Tool sites, villages of the related Norton tradition are found along the coast of western Alaska and up major river drainages. Robert Shaw documented five sites dated from 500 BC to AD 1300 on Summit Island, located within the Walrus Island Sanctuary just off the mainland coast and about 19 miles north of Round Island. Summit Island was occupied intermittently beginning 2,500 years ago, during a time when large village sites affiliated with the Norton tradition became widespread in this area. Shaw proposed that this was the result of a population increase and innovations in net fishing and possibly food storage technologies. Several other Norton sites have been studied in this region: in Chagvan Bay just northeast of Security Cove, on nearby Hagemeister Island, in the Wood River/Tikchik Lakes drainage, and on the northern Alaska Peninsula.

The Norton tradition in this region spans about 1,500 years, and traits include thin, well-made ceramics with fiber or sand temper and often decorated with linear or check stamping, square or rectangular houses, notched stone net sinkers, stone lamps, small bifacially flaked side and end blades, and some use of ground slate. The Norton culture on Round Island is represented by several of these artifact types, diagnostic chipped-stone points, and many well-defined single-roomed square houses lacking apparent entries. These houses, associated with cache pits for food storage, occur in at least two distinct clusters that may represent temporally distinct settlements. Two radiocarbon dates from the Norton culture occupations on Round Island are 10 BC and AD 50, and it follows the preceding occupation by about 1,600 years.

Sometime after AD 1000, the Norton culture was replaced or absorbed by a northern maritime-based culture, the Thule tradition, directly ancestral to the historic Yu'pik-speaking people inhabiting the area, including the Tuyuryarmiut of Togiak Bay, at the time of contact. The Thule occupation on Round Island occupies the center and the highest land within the site area, at 132 feet above sea level. It has large, deep house depressions, at least three with storm sheds or entry rooms, and a very large rectangular depression measuring 24 × 48 feet that is probably a men's community house or *qasgik*. The Thule village has several cache depressions and some sod borrow areas are apparent.

The late prehistory and history of this immediate area is best told in the report of the 1960 excavations at Old Togiak on the mainland by Makoto Kowta. Kowta's analysis of the occupations and artifacts dated by typology from AD 1000 to 1700 showed a mixed economy with emphasis on both land and sea hunting and fishing, with shellfish collecting becoming increasingly important through time. Antler armor slats found in the upper levels of the site indicate increasing levels of technological sophistication and warfare. A decrease through time in seal remains at Old Togiak may have resulted from overhunting or environmental change. This may have forced residents to diversify and abandon winter settlements in the summer months for fishing and hunting inland. This is the subsistence pattern practiced by the Tuyuryarmiut at the time of contact.

Round Island was named by Captain James Cook when he sailed across Bristol Bay, briefly stopping at Cape Newenham, in 1778. Togiak Bay was bypassed by most early exploration until 1819, when the Russian Fort Alexandrovsk was established at Nushagak. But even as late as 1890, and despite commercial activities in the Bay, the isolation of the Tuyuryarmiut is evident in travelers' descriptions of them. The transition for Togiak residents from sea-mammal hunting with skin boats and hand-held harpoons to guns, wooden boats, and outboard motors occurred during the 1930s and 1940s. Round Island was a primary walrus-hunting site for them before and after the transition until it was closed to hunting in 1960. Limited walrus hunting by the Togiak residents was resumed in 1995.

Visitor access to Round Island is allowed only by permit and when sanctuary staff are present, usually between May 1 and August 15. Because driving rain, winds, and rough seas are common, visits are extremely weather dependent, and visitors should come well prepared. Several scheduled airlines have daily flights from Anchorage to Dillingham and Togiak throughout the summer. Transportation to Round Island by boat is available through local commercial operators. For detailed information see the Alaska Department of Fish and Game Website, http://www.wc.adfg.state.ak.us/index.cfm?adfg=refuge.rnd_is. The Sam Fox Museum in Dillingham has a library and limited cultural displays (http://www.ci.dillingham.ak.us/museum1.html).

Further Reading: Ackerman, Robert E., "Early Maritime Traditions in the Bering, Chukchi, and East Siberia Seas," *Arctic Anthropology* 35(1) (1998): 247–262; Dumond, Don E., "Maritime Adaptation on the Northern Alaska Peninsula," *Arctic Anthropology* 35(1) (1998): 187–203; Fall, James A., Molly Chythlook, Janet Schichnes, and Rick Sinnott, *Walrus Hunting at Togiak, Bristol Bay, Southwest Alaska*, Alaska Department of Fish and Game, Division of Subsistence, Technical Paper No. 212 (Juneau: Alaska Department of Fish and Game, 1991); Kowta, Makoto, "Old Togiak in Prehistory," Ph.D. diss. (University of California, Los Angeles, 1963); Shaw, Robert D., "An Archeology of the Central Yupik: A Regional Overview for the Yukon-Kuskokwim Delta, Northern Bristol Bay, and Nunivak Island," *Arctic Anthropology* 35(1) (1998): 234–246; VanStone, James W., *Eskimos of the Nushagak River: An Ethnographic History* (Seattle: University of Washington Press, 1967).

Jeanne Schaaf

ICE FIELD ARCHAEOLOGY

Eastern Alaska

Warming Climate Exposes the Archaeological Record

As a result of climate change, rare archaeological materials are being exposed by the melting of ancient glaciers around the world. Spectacular organic artifacts include prehistoric bows and arrows, spears, hunting tools, baskets, clothing, and even human remains. These unusual discoveries—frozen in ice and preserved for thousands of years—provide an unprecedented glimpse into the lives of ancient people. Without the preservation of organic artifacts, archaeological collections consist primarily of stone and ceramic artifacts that represent only a small percentage of the material culture manufactured and used by early people. These finds provide

new insights into cultural development and highlight the exceptional craftsmanship and genius of early people in living in northern North America.

Most discoveries from North America have been reported from the Yukon Territory in Canada and from Alaska. Without the organic artifacts recovered from ice patches, there would be little evidence of the rich material cultural essential for survival in many high-latitude environments. Melting glaciers and small features called "ice patches" are important places for archaeological and paleoecological research associated with climate change. Evidence of recent warming in the North

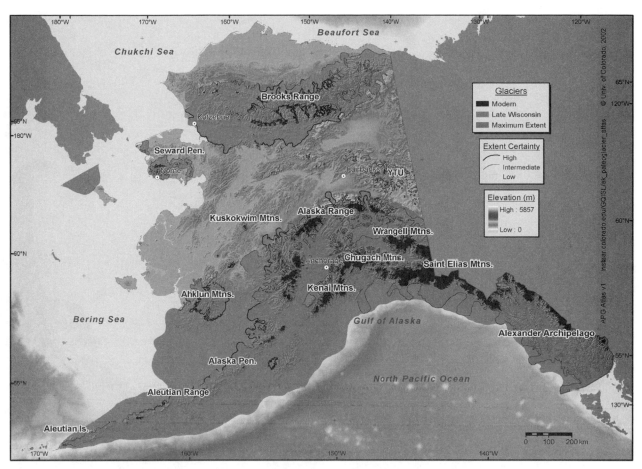

Computer map showing the maximum extent of glacial ice during the last ice age (dark grey) and the extent of modern glaciers (black). [From *Alaska PaleoGlacier Atlas*, volume 1, W. F. Manley and D. S. Kaufman, Institute of Arctic and Alpine Research, University of Colorado, http://instaar.colorado.edu/QGIS/ak_paleoglacier_atlas. Courtesy of W. F. Manley and D. S. Kaufman]

American Arctic includes historic records of increasing temperature, melting glaciers, reductions in the extent and thickness of sea ice, thawing permafrost, modified ecosystems, and rising sea level (Arctic Climate Impact Assessment, http://www.amap.no/acia/). These environmental changes are resulting in the emergence of artifacts from ancient ice. The discovery of ancient artifacts presents clear and compelling evidence that very old ice is melting for the first time, and climate is changing.

Although some of the archaeological discoveries have been made on retreating glaciers, most have come from small features called ice patches, which frequently occur along the margins of high-elevation plateaus and other large, relatively flat, treeless landforms. Most seem to be formed by drifting snow that accumulates to depths sufficient to persist through the entire summer, forming patterns that recur every year. Animal tracks and feces are commonly observed on the surfaces of ice patches.

Ice patches are invisible in the winter when the entire landscape is covered by snow. However, in summer they become conspicuous oasis-like features composed of ice and snow that attract caribou, sheep, and other animals that seek water and relief from heat and insects. Accumulated feces and windblown organic material released from melting ice patches enrich plant growth. The animals that use these microenvironments attracted ancient hunters, who lost weapons, tools, clothing, and other possessions. These artifacts were buried by new snow that eventually became ice that accumulated over millennia—layer upon layer of ice, artifacts, animal remains, and other fossils.

The exceptional preservation of organic artifacts found at these sites can make them appear to be recent, particularly to the untrained eye. As a result, their full significance may be overlooked. For these reasons, it is important for archaeologists to date every artifact and not assume that specimens are recent, or that groups of objects found on the surface are contemporaneous. Once thawed, organic remains and artifacts decompose or are subject to destruction by scavenging animals and soon disappear.

Ice patches are poorly known features of the cryosphere (the part of the world that remains perennially frozen). Part-

A researcher (in center of photo) inspects area for newly exposed artifacts and documents an Alaskan ice patch.   [E. James Dixon]

nerships between scientists and Native people have enhanced understanding of these ecological features by incorporating traditional ecological knowledge of local residents with scientific research. This synergy greatly enhances understanding ice patches and their importance to people.

Ice patch archaeology also presents unique challenges. Because artifacts are covered by accumulated snow for much of the year, archaeological survey is limited to late summer within the ablation zone (i.e., the lower part of a glacier or ice patch where melting and evaporation of ice and snow exceeds accumulation of winter snowfall). Furthermore, it is not feasible or practical to dig test pits in ice, so archaeologists must rely primarily on surface finds. Ice patches exhibiting greater ablation than accumulation over the course of a year provide the best possibilities for finding artifacts. Field research often requires complicated and expensive logistics, including helicopter support. Because most glaciers and ice patches do not contain archaeological remains, archaeologists are developing scientific methods to identify specific glaciers and ice patches that are most likely to contain frozen archaeological remains.

By taking very small (micro) samples from the organic artifacts, they can be radiocarbon dated using accelerator mass spectrometry (AMS), which enables researchers to determine the age of an organic artifact from a very small sample. This method permits scientists to learn how old an artifact is and still preserve virtually the entire original object. The oldest dated artifact recovered from an ice patch is from Canada's Yukon Territory and is dated to about 8,360 radiocarbon years ago. However, there is evidence to suggest that some of the ice at some ice patches may be remnants from the last ice age, possibly more than 10,000 years old.

The archaeology of glaciers and ice patches is yielding significant results. In Canada's southern Yukon Territory near the British Columbia border, hunters found the remains of an "ice man" who was named *Kwaday Dan Ts'inchi*, meaning "Long Ago Person Found" in the Southern Tutchone

A recently exposed arrow shaft at the base of a melting ice patch, Alaska. [E. James Dixon]

(Athabascan) language. The remains of this nearly 500-year-old man were found melting from the edge of a glacier, and artifacts found with him included tools, weapons, clothes, and even trail food.

Ice field archaeology also has provided new insights regarding the origins and antiquity of the bow and arrow in northern North America. The antiquity of the bow and arrow in southern regions of North America has been inferred to be about 1,500 years ago based on the widespread distribution of small stone projectile points that some researchers believe were used to tip arrows. Wooden arrow and light spear shafts propelled with a spear thrower (or *atl atl*) found on melting ice patches in Canada and Alaska have provided radiocarbon dates for these technologies and document that the bow and arrow was adopted about 1,800 years ago in northwest Canada.

The archaeology of glaciers also provides opportunities to better understand ice patch dynamics in relation to climate change and their role in regional ecology. Although difficult to quantify, a variety of methods have been employed to estimate the rate of melting of mountain and subpolar glaciers. Data demonstrates increased glacial melting began in the mid-1960s and dramatically increased beginning in the late 1980s. The increase in glacial melting correlates to increased reports of archaeological discoveries from high-altitude glaciers and ice patches around the world. If this trend continues, it is reasonable to assume that archaeological and paleontological remains will continue to be exposed over the next few decades. It is possible that these ephemeral sites could largely disappear in the near future. Consequently, there is an urgent need to better understand them and collect, study, and preserve the artifacts they contain before they are lost forever.

Artifacts have only been found at a few glaciers and ice patches in Alaska and Canada and most are located on public land in remote areas. They are not accessible to the general public, and artifacts should not be collected without appropriate scientific research and collecting permits. Many glaciers and ice patches are dangerous, and proper equipment and training are required to access them.

Further Reading: "Arctic Climate Impact Assessment" (Cambridge: Cambridge University Press, 2004), http://www.amap.no/acia/; Beattie, O., B. Apland, E. W. Blake, J. A. Cosgrove, S. Gaunt,

S. Greer, A. P. Mackie, K. E. Mackie, D. Straathof, V. Thorp, and P. M. Troffe, "The Kwäday Dän Ts'ínchi Discovery from a Glacier in British Columbia," *Canadian Journal of Archaeology* 24(1&2) (2000): 129–147; Dixon, E. James, William F. Manley, and Craig M. Lee, "The Emerging Archaeology of Glaciers and Ice Patches: Examples from Alaska's Wrangell–St. Elias National Park and Pre-

serve," *American Antiquity* 70(1) (2005): 129–143; Hare, Greg P., Shelia Greer, Ruth Gotthardt, Rick Farnell, Vandy Bowyer, and Charles Schweger, "Ethnographic and Archaeological Investigations of Alpine Ice Patches in Southwest Yukon, Canada," *Arctic* 57(3) (2004): 260–277.

E. James Dixon

SWAN POINT, DRY CREEK, BROKEN MAMMOTH, HEALY LAKE, AND OTHER SITES

Tanana River Drainage, East Central Alaska
Understanding the Colonization of the New World

Important research on the peopling of the New World and later cultural adaptations to changing climates and biodiversity is being conducted in the Tanana River drainage basin, located in central Alaska. With the area encompassing almost 45,000 square miles, archaeologists have investigated relatively few sites to date, and most information on patterning in the archaeological record results from survey or excavations at a few key sites. This review summarizes the setting, general cultural patterns, and significant sites in the region.

Complex geologic processes have shaped the landscape, affecting the three major physiographic regions of the Tanana basin: (1) the foothills of the Alaska Range to the south, with moraines and other glacially derived features extending to the north; (2) the Tanana-Kuskokwim lowland, where large braided glacial rivers cross unglaciated terrain and flow into the Tanana River; and (3) the Yukon-Tanana upland, a hilly country with clearwater streams flowing south into the Tanana River. Thick deposits of windblown sand and silt from outwash fans to the south blanket much of the region, resulting in excellent conditions for buried, stratified sites and organic preservation in some areas. Largely unglaciated with a steppe-tundra vegetation supporting many herbivores such as mammoth and bison during the Late Pleistocene, this region has a complex climatic and biotic history, and numerous projects have used local data to define archaeologists' understanding of the climate, paleontology, and vegetation of the last glacial period. Currently the region is dominated by spruce and hardwood forests, although there are areas of tundra vegetation in the foothills of the Alaska Range.

This region has a long prehistoric record and was inhabited by various cultural traditions from almost 14,000 years ago until the Athabascan tradition, the ancestors of the current native residents. All prehistoric peoples in this region are characterized as mobile foragers with hunting, fishing, and gathering economies. Most prehistoric sites are characterized as ephemeral lithic scatters (stone tools and tool-making debris), typically inferred to be hunting camps or stations, and are located in overlook settings. Stone structures (cairns, hunting blinds, caribou and moose drivelines), rock shelters, and pictograph sites are uncommon. After about AD 1000, other site types like more substantial settlements associated with semi-subterranean house pits and cache pits (for seasonally abundant salmon and caribou) are common.

Archaeological research from the 1930s has resulted in the identification of over 2,000 prehistoric and Native historic sites and about 2,200 Euro-American historic and recent sites. This area is among the most developed in Alaska, and numerous cultural resource management projects have been undertaken; however, several academic research projects (e.g., North Alaska Range Early Man Project) have generated significant amounts of data, although synthetic treatments remain rare. Nevertheless, archaeology in the Tanana basin has driven research problems and defined most of the relevant cultural units for the Alaskan interior (Yukon, Susitna, and Copper watersheds) and played significant roles in discussions of northwest North American prehistory. With some exceptions, the archaeological interpretation is generally site based, with cultural traditions and intersite comparisons based almost exclusively on lithic typology and technology. This summary reflects the current consensus of Tanana basin prehistory.

This region has an important role in understanding the colonization of the New World, with some of the earliest sites in the hemisphere located along the Tanana River. The earliest period of occupation (12,000–10,000 BC) is characterized by considerable variability in technology. The earliest component, Swan Point Cultural Zone 4 (dating around 12,000 BC),

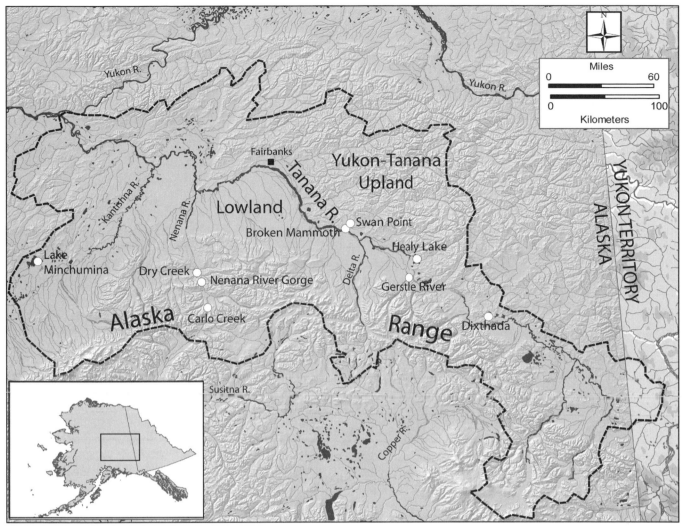

Tanana River Basin, showing major physiographic regions and sites mentioned in the text.   [Courtesy of the United States Geological Survey]

contains technology similar to that of the Siberian Late Upper Paleolithic, with specially prepared microblade cores and multifaceted burins. Microblades were inset into organic implements to form composite tools. This technology is termed the Beringian (or East Beringian) tradition, and is present in related forms from 10,000 to 6000 BC (Denali complex). Small teardrop-shaped bifaces, termed Chindadn points, are key diagnostics of the Nenana complex, originally found without microblade technology in several sites in the Nenana valley dating between 11,500 and 10,500 BC. Association of several of these bifaces with microblade-bearing components in the middle Tanana basin suggests this variant may reflect technological organization rather than a distinct people. Some archaeologists suggest the Nenana complex is related to the contemporaneous Clovis culture from farther south. A wide variety of bifacial projectile-point forms were

used during the Late Pleistocene and Early Holocene (lance-olate, triangular, pentagonal, etc.), and this variability, along with inferred composite points, may reflect seasonal or prey-specific hunting technology. Additionally, preserved mammoth ivory artifacts at Broken Mammoth indicate a well-developed organic industry.

The sequence of excavated components from the Swan Point, Broken Mammoth, and Gerstle River sites provide important data on subsistence and technology from the Late Pleistocene to Middle Holocene in the middle Tanana River region. Well-preserved faunal remains indicate use of a wide range of animals, including bison, wapiti, caribou, small mammals, fish, and possibly mammoth in the earliest components. Sheep, bison, wapiti, and small-mammal hunting in the upper Nenana valley to the south are attested by Dry Creek, Carlo Creek, and other sites.

Relatively little is known about the period from 6000 to 4700 BC, but several new technological elements enter the record after 4700 BC, such as notched bifaces and notched cobbles, collectively defining the Northern Archaic tradition, which is interpreted by some to reflect migration of new populations. However, earlier technologies such as microblade and burin industries are present throughout this period, suggesting diffusion of new elements among local groups and perhaps reflecting adaptation to the spreading boreal forest. The Northern Archaic tradition continued until about AD 1000, with important components found at Lake Minchumina, Healy Lake, Swan Point, Broken Mammoth, and Dry Creek. Faunal remains indicate continued reliance on bison and caribou supplemented with small- and medium-sized mammals. Indeed, the continuity of bison hunting has been linked with microblade technology. Well-preserved organic remains from alpine ice patches in Alaska and the Yukon Territory indicate *atl atl* (spear thrower) and dart-hunting equipment was replaced by bow and arrow technology around AD 700.

A major transformation in technology, settlement, and subsistence occurred around AD 1000, associated with the emergence of the Athabascan tradition, which continued until after Euro-American contact in the mid-nineteenth century. Athabascan tradition sites are characterized by semi-subterranean house pits and cache pits. Flaked-stone technology was greatly reduced and microblade technology disappeared, contrasted with a greater reliance on bone, antler, and copper implements. Faunal remains from important Athabascan tradition components found at Healy Lake, Lake Minchumina, Dixthada, and Nenana River Gorge sites indicate a broad-spectrum hunting and fishing economy (including moose, caribou, sheep, bear, small mammals, fish, terrestrial birds, and waterfowl). Increased reliance on fishing, storage of seasonally abundant resources, and consequent reduced mobility may explain these technological and settlement changes. Settlements were commonly along large rivers and lakeshores, with highland areas used less intensively for seasonal hunting.

During the period of Russian rule (AD 1741–1867), European cultural elements consisted primarily of trade goods obtained through indirect contact related to the fur trade. After the sale of Alaska to the United States in 1867, exploration, missionization, and settlement (especially during and after the gold rush from the beginning of the twentieth century) had increasing impacts on the culture of Native peoples, who were progressively drawn into the American economy. Early Euro-American sites tend to be related to mining, transportation, or communication (telegraph stations, roadhouses, etc.). During World War II, a number of installations and support features were constructed, including the Alaska-Canadian highway. The Tanana basin currently contains two bases and numerous training areas for the U.S. Army and Air Force, including numerous Cold War–related facilities.

Unresolved questions relating to several issues of interior Alaskan archaeology are spurring current research. Many researchers focus on colonization of the New World, especially delineating human relationships with Pleistocene megafauna. Remains of mammoth ivory are dated contemporaneously with occupations at Broken Mammoth and Swan Point, although others are dated to several thousand years earlier, which suggests scavenging. Technological conservatism evident in the presence of microblade technology over almost the entire archaeological record (13,000 years) has lead to a number of recent investigations into technological organization, although few functional/use-wear studies of lithic artifacts have been conducted. Most of the sites identified from the Late Pleistocene to Late Holocene are characterized as temporary camp sites, and no substantial habitation sites have been identified. It is uncertain whether these habitations were (1) located in geologically active environments (e.g., along the edges of braided rivers) and were subsequently destroyed or buried under meters of sediments, or (2) these foragers had very high residential mobility and thus few longer-term habitations.

Another important problem is the nature of the subsistence and technological conservativism in cultures of the Middle to Late Holocene, which has received considerably less attention than the early prehistoric record. Continuity exists in the form of microblade industries, but the processes involved in subsistence technology are clouded by the general lack of preserved fauna. Volcanic eruptions periodically covered portions of the western Subarctic and may have impacted settlement and subsistence. The local extirpation of bison in this period may also have influenced culture change. Overall, the Late Holocene has received relatively little attention, but several ongoing studies relating ethnogeography, oral history, and archaeology are attempting to understand the development of local Athabascan cultures.

Further Reading: Cook, John P., "Historic Archaeology and Ethnohistory at Healy Lake, Alaska," *Arctic* 42(2) (1989): 109–118; Dixon, E. James, Jr., "Cultural Chronology of Central Interior Alaska," *Arctic Anthropology* 22(1) (1985): 47–66; Hadleigh West, Frederick, ed., *American Beginnings: The Prehistory and Palaeoecology of Beringia* (Chicago: University of Chicago Press, 1996); Hoffecker, John F., W. Roger Powers, and T. E. Goebel, "The Colonization of Beringia and the Peopling of the New World," *Science* 259 (1993): 46–53; Holmes, Charles E., "Tanana River Valley Archaeology Circa 14,000 to 9,000 BP," *Arctic Anthropology* 38(2) (2001): 154–170; McKennan, Robert A., *The Upper Tanana Indians*, Yale University Publications in Anthropology No. 55 (New Haven, CT: Yale University, 1959); Shinkwin, Anne D., *Dakah de'nin's Village and the Dixthada Site: A Contribution to Northern Athapaskan Prehistory*, Archaeological Survey of Canada Paper No. 91 (Ottawa, ON: National Museums of Canada, 1979); Yesner, David R., "Human Adaptation at the Pleistocene-Holocene Boundary (Circa 13,000 to 8,000 BP) in Eastern Beringia," in *Humans at the End of the Ice Age: The Archaeology of the Pleistocene-Holocene Transition*, edited by L. G. Straus, B. V. Eriksen, J. M. Erlandson, and D. R. Yesner (New York: Plenum Press, 1996), 255–276.

Ben A. Potter

BERING LAND BRIDGE NATIONAL PRESERVE

Northern Seward Peninsula, Western Alaska

Late Prehistoric Iñupiaq Villages and Monuments: AD 1500–1800

Near the center of what was once a vast ice age land bridge between the Old and New Worlds lies the Seward Peninsula of Alaska. During a series of ice ages beginning 2.3 million years ago, low sea levels exposed the shallow floors of the northern Bering Sea, Bering Strait, and Chukchi Sea. This transformed the shores of the Seward Peninsula into high ground, several hundred kilometers inland from the ice age coasts, rising above an expansive lowland plain dissected by now-submerged river systems. Conversely, melting of continental ice masses during warm climates brought higher sea levels, and during exceptionally warm periods they carved shorelines well inland from today's northern Seward Peninsula coast.

Even after the land bridge was flooded about 9,500 years ago, cultural and biological exchanges between the Old and New Worlds continued. The archaeological record shows that by 2,000 years ago the shores of the Bering Strait area formed less of a gateway, as monikers such as "bridge" and "crossroads" suggest, than a well-established culture center with distinct cultural groups settled in large permanent villages with highly developed marine-based technologies, elaborate art, and extensive trade networks.

Anthropologists Dorothy Jean Ray and Ernest S. Burch have defined the existence of six to seven Iñupiaq and four Yup'ik societies inhabiting the Seward Peninsula by the early 1800s. The nineteenth-century societies are characterized as each having a discrete territory, a distinct dialect or sub-dialect, a distinct seasonal round, and a material culture that was unique in some detail of structure or ornamentation, among other traits. Although the existence of separate dialects and sub-dialects suggests stable development in the area over a long period of time, the oral historical data do not document how long these traditional societies had been in existence prior to their demise, which began in the late 1830s and was complete by the end of the nineteenth century. The original anthropological research identified these societies based on reconstructed ethnographies (ethnographies constructed from the oral traditions remembered by people born after 1860) and historical records. Analysis of material culture patterns in late prehistoric sites has provided insight into the social and economic organization of the late prehistoric Iñupiat (ca. AD 1500–1800) on the northern Seward Peninsula within what is now the Bering Land Bridge National Preserve.

Patterns and the spatial distribution of distinct semi-subterranean house forms identified in the late prehistoric archaeological record correspond with the some of the proposed territories of identified nineteenth-century Iñupiaq societies. House depressions are a very survey-visible record for the late prehistoric period in this region of treeless tundra. Major architectural features such as presence and length of entrance tunnels and presence and location of side rooms and storm-shed entries are easily identified in house depressions and represent the original house layout. House styles are taken to represent the integrated manifestation of long-standing social and cultural templates and relationships to the environment and landscape. This follows anthropologist Amos Rapoport's argument that the basic template or model for house form shows most clearly the link between form and life patterns and provides the "best way of relating the whole system of house, settlement, landscape, and monumental buildings to the way of life" (1969).

The nineteenth-century societies maintained territories centered on the drainage systems of major rivers, and during winter, when warfare and raiding were common, virtually all of a society's members could be found within their own territory at settlements located near the core of the territory relative to fishing inland and sealing at the coast. The archaeological record on the northern Seward Peninsula is dominated by late prehistoric winter settlements, with 493 mapped semi-subterranean house depressions distributed across the 17,500-square-kilometer study area, and therefore is well suited to this study.

The archaeological sites occur primarily in the historic Iñupiaq *Tapqaġmiut* (Serpentine River), *Qaviaraġmiut* (Kuzitrin River), and *Pittaġmiut* (Espenberg and Goodhope rivers) territories and in the region of Kuzitrin and Imuruk lakes, where the Qaviaraġmiut, Pittaġmiut, *Igaḷuiŋmiut* (Fish River), and *Kuuyuŋmiut* (Koyuk River) territories met. The Kuzitrin and Imuruk lakes area is particularly interesting because the nineteenth-century territorial boundaries converged in a very rich resource area, evidenced by fishing and small- to large-scale caribou hunting sites dating from as early as 4,500 years ago to within the last few hundred years. Oral historical records indicate that boundaries were both commonly trespassed and aggressively defended here. A series of atypical sites, unique in the Arctic archaeological record, is located along this convergence of historic boundaries. These sites are substantial villages with as many as twenty-five houses (exceptionally large in a region where villages of seven or more houses are considered large), associated with massive stone monuments,

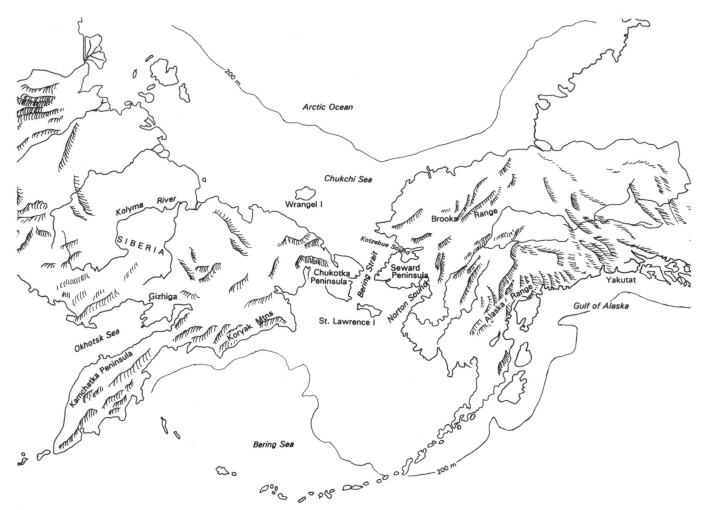

Area map showing the Bering Land Bridge as exposed by 200 meter (650 ft) lower sea level about 16,000 years ago.   [Courtesy of the National Park Service]

and situated atop ancient volcanic cinder cones and lava complexes. The importance of the landforms and cultural features for caribou procurement and meat storage is apparent, but the concentrations of winter houses on lookout promontories, without readily available water and fuel and associated with monumental architectural features, are unexplained. It is possible that they represent a response to boundary perturbations related to population movements or to changes in resource availability due to climatic change. It is also possible that they represent occupation of a strategic area important for controlling a key resource (caribou) or the flow of Native and European trade goods in the eighteenth century.

The distribution of house types classified from survey data and a regional comparison of the house types suggest the presence of distinct material culture traditions dictating house form in the late prehistoric period. There is a pronounced homogeneity in the occurrence of house types within the drainage units and within sites. With the recognition that both environmental and cultural parameters influence house

form, this pattern in the distribution of house types is interpreted as reflecting some degree of material culture disparity between the people occupying the northern Seward Peninsula Chukchi Sea coast and those occupying the shore of Kotzebue Sound and the inland areas.

There is a very marked distinction between the house forms used along the Chukchi Sea coast from Cape Espenberg west to the Bering Strait and the houses built along the shore of Kotzebue Sound and in the inland portions of the study area (Imuruk Lake and Kuzitrin River areas). Houses with long entryways (greater than or equal to 4 m) and storm sheds, some with one or more side rooms attached to the passageway, dominate in late prehistoric sites along the coast from Espenberg southwest to Ikpik. Houses with short entryways, having no storm shed or side rooms, characterize the sites along Kotzebue Sound. This pattern, which appears to have been consistent throughout the examined late prehistoric record in the study area, must have been created by the long-term repetitive ways in which people positioned themselves

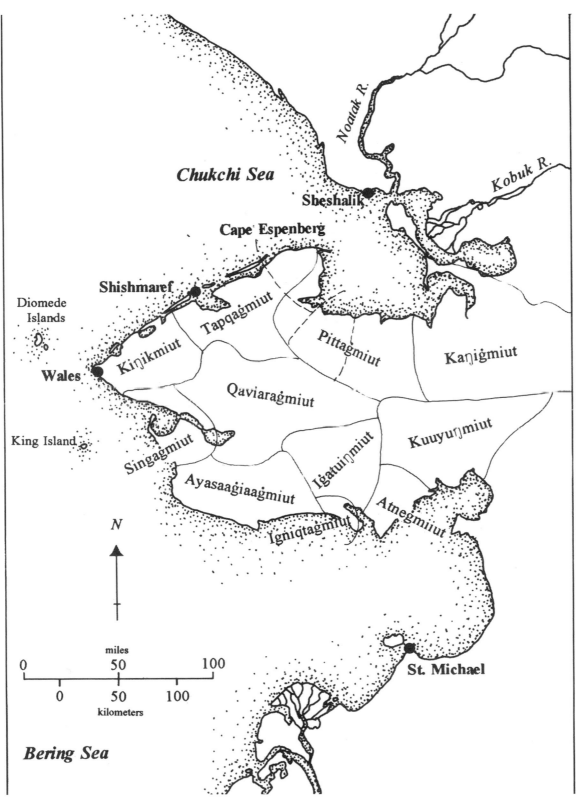

Nineteenth-century Iñupiaq and Yup'ik territories, Seward Peninsula. Adapted from Burch (1994) and Ray (1984). Dashed lines mark Ray's Espenberg and Goodhope territories.   [Jeanne Schaaf]

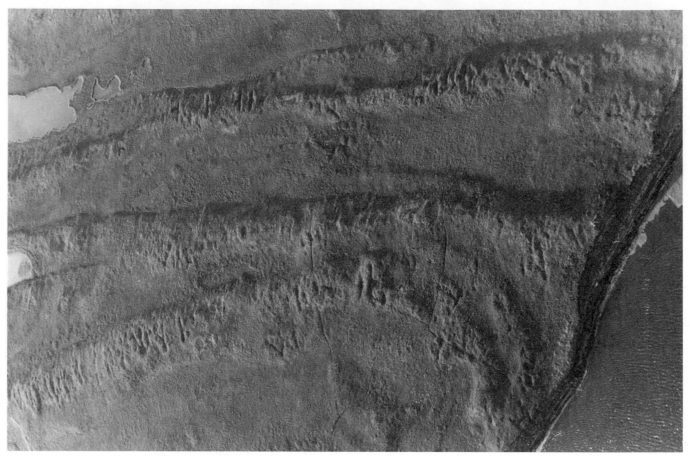

Aerial photo showing late prehistoric house depressions on relict beach ridges at the tip of Cape Espenberg, Bering Land Bridge National Preserve; current coastline is shown in the lower right.   [Photo courtesy of James Magdanz]

on the landscape. A striking discontinuity in the settlement pattern in the Imuruk lava plateau area suggests that here the processes that produced the patterns were disturbed.

The earliest large villages in the study area are located at Cape Espenberg, where they coincide temporally with the Late Western Thule period (AD 1250–1400) as defined at Cape Krusenstern by James L. Giddings and Doug Anderson. Before AD 1400, houses at Cape Krusenstern are like those used at Cape Espenberg, with a slight localized variation regarding the placement of the kitchens. After AD 1400, houses associated with the Kobuk River appear at Cape Krusenstern and seem to replace the earlier house types. A similar displacement is not seen at Cape Espenberg in the late prehistoric record. Although the archaeological data at Cape Espenberg shows a continuity in house form and settlement pattern from the fourteenth century to the nineteenth century (and perhaps as early as the seventh century AD), oral historical and historical census data indicates that early in the nineteenth century occupation of this area was in a state of change, resulting in depopulation of the area or perhaps movement into the area by a people called the Malimiut (or Malemiut, a Yup'ik word used on Norton Sound that refers

to Iñupiaq dialect speakers from northwest Alaska) from the Kobuk and Selawik River areas.

The occupation of large settlements in the study area from the fourteenth to the nineteenth centuries coincides with the Little Ice Age (LIA), a period of generally cooler climate marked by glacier advances in Alaska. More important, the LIA was characterized by drastic weather variability—lower lows and higher highs. These irregularities would have required immediate social and economic responses, especially if sea ice and snow cover conditions or the timing of freeze-up and breakup were to change, thereby changing the availability of key early spring and fall resources. Glacial evidence in the Kigluaik Mountains on the southern Seward Peninsula indicates that a major maximum occurred in the early to mid-1700s. This corresponds roughly with a dramatic increase in the number of interior tundra sites in north Alaska and is coincidental with the large-scale use of dog traction in place by AD 1700.

Little data exists about the actual effects of the LIA on terrestrial and marine resources, and researchers disagree about whether the effects were less severe inland than on the coast. For the Seward Peninsula, where the Iñupiat depended on

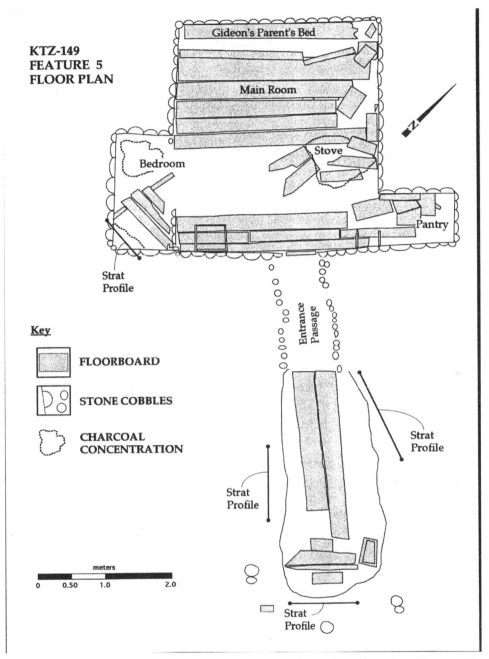

**KTZ-149
FEATURE 5
FLOOR PLAN**

Gideon's Parent's Bed

Main Room

Stove

Bedroom

Pantry

Strat
Profile

Key

FLOORBOARD

STONE COBBLES

CHARCOAL
CONCENTRATION

Entrance
Passage

Strat
Profile

Strat
Profile

meters
0   0.50   1.0   2.0

Strat
Profile

House plan view from the historic village Ublasaun, showing continuity of house form from late Western Thule to historic times (drawing by James Creech).   [Courtesy of the National Park Service]

both coastal and inland resources, whether obtained from within their own territories or through intergroup alliances, this may be a moot point. Certainly the regional and local effects of the LIA were complex, and adverse conditions in one area may have resulted in resource enhancement in another. Elsewhere in Alaska, cultural responses to the effects of the LIA are reflected by sudden and widespread shifts in settlement patterns beginning around AD 1400. On Kodiak Island, Richard Knecht found there was a shift away

from sea mammal hunting to fishing, a dramatic increase in village and house size (multiple-room houses), and an increase in conflict and warfare.

The archaeological evidence indicates that the large villages situated atop volcanic cinder cones in the Kuzitrin and Imuruk lakes area are single component and were occupied for a brief period of time, possibly only a few seasons. Site use may have continued for meat storage or as caribou lookout stations after the habitations were abandoned. Although present data is

Stone monument, 2.4 meters (8 ft) high, on the summit of Twin Calderas, Bering Land Bridge National Preserve. This monument and others like it are part of the late prehistoric settlement pattern and are believed to reflect conflict in a resource-rich boundary zone, possibly dating to the late 1700s and related to control of resources in a time of accelerated trade and climatic deterioration. [National Park Service photo by Jeanne Schaaf]

insufficient to securely date the time of occupation, these sites are thought to pre-date the mid-nineteenth century.

Above- and below-ground stone caches and alignments or drive lines (*inuksuit*) are scattered in this same area on high ground and lava flows. These fit well with the nineteenth-century Pittaġmiut and Qaviaraġmiut pattern of inland late-summer caribou drives at lakes, where meat was dried and stored for retrieval by dogsled after freeze-up. William Oquilluk recounts that a few hunters would stay up to a month after a successful drive while the meat was drying. However, winter villages in this area are anomalous. LIA-induced changes in resource abundances and distribution may have led to different subsistence emphases; yet given the mobility at the time, winter settlements would have been located along water bodies or rivers to maximize access to other resources. On the cinder cones, there was only one primary resource available—migratory caribou. Additionally, Burch's sources never associated the location of nineteenth-century freeze-up sites with caribou procurement.

These out-of-place winter villages may reflect the interactions of distinct societies. The nineteenth-century Iñupiaq and Yup'ik territory boundaries were generally in resource-poor areas, and yet these boundaries were "sharply defined" and "jealously guarded" according to Ray (1984). In the Kuzitrin and Imuruk lakes area, where the cinder cone villages occur, four territory boundaries converged in a very rich

resource area, especially important to the Pittaġmiut, the Qaviaraġmiut, and their allies. Ray states that the Koyuk River people "aggressively coveted" the Kuzitrin Lake area, which was likewise aggressively defended by the Qaviaraġmiut because the lake was the headwaters of the Kuzitrin River and an extremely important place for fish and caribou procurement.

The late prehistoric villages atop the cinder cones and the extensive complexes of caribou drive lines, hunting blinds, meat caches, and monumental architecture are located along the Continental Divide (which at its far western end runs east to west through the Steward Peninsula), separating the drainages defining the territories of four nineteenth-century societies. Twin Calderas most certainly played a key role in large-scale caribou procurement, yet the massive stone monuments at this location are more elaborate than required to encourage directional movements of caribou. In other regions monuments have been interpreted as geographical symbols erected by local competing groups, which may increase in importance in times of economic stress and related conflict.

The tall well-built cairns at Gosling Cone, Skeleton, Butte, Twin Cairns, Rocky Point, Cygnus Cone, Cassiope Cone, and Virginia Butte, among others, all along the Continental Divide in the Imuruk Lake area, may therefore have been territorial symbols. They would have clearly marked ownership of resources and territory in a lowland area where drainage

Stone monuments 3.5 meters (11.5 ft) high on the rim of Twin Calderas, an ancient volcanic caldera in the Bering Land Bridge National Preserve. Stone cairns like these may have marked the boundaries between territories of different ethnic groups who exploited the resources of the interior Steward Peninsula. [National Park Service photo by Jeanne Schaaf]

divides were not obvious. Here the drainages disappear into vast wetlands that drain in two or more directions; therefore if territories were divided according to drainages, there may have been a need to clearly mark boundaries in this area.

Defensive positioning is a second line of evidence that suggests that the cinder cone villages arose during a time of conflict. Occupants of the cinder cone summits would have had the distinct advantage in bow-and-arrow battles with intruders approaching from the surrounding lowlands.

If the large villages and stone monuments along the Continental Divide are indicative of conflict, what might have precipitated and intensified the conflict to the degree that settlement patterns were disrupted and villages were established on the cinder cones?

Burch (1998) has shown that in the 1800s, warfare between traditional societies in northwest Alaska was sophisticated, widespread, and intense. Generally, raids were surprise attacks on villages, carried out on foot after dark, most often in winter after the ground was frozen but before heavy snowfall. A large war party could attack in the open in any season. In open battles, the uphill, upwind position was superior. The location of the cinder cone villages suggests a heightened state of war readiness beyond the general state of watchfulness for sporadic raiders from more typical settlement locations.

LIA climatic fluctuations could have had serious effects on both inland and coastal resources, as discussed earlier. If, for example, sea mammal hunting was greatly curtailed, as

researchers have shown for both Kotzebue Sound and the Gulf of Alaska, greater pressure would be placed on caribou and other inland resources. As it was probably already an area of conflict over abundant resources, the need to defend access to critical resources in the Imuruk and Kuzitrin lakes region would have been intensified by LIA-induced changes in resource availability.

Consideration of other factors influencing intersocietal conflict over the control of resources must include late prehistoric Native trade. The importance of pre-contact Native trade between societies in northwest Alaska and across the Bering Strait has been underscored by several researchers. Clifford Hickey wrote, "This far-reaching trade system was a highly organized massive effort involving thousands of human beings every year, some of whom invested considerable amounts of human energy and capital into resource harvesting, manufacturing, and transportation of surplus goods" (1979).

From the earliest European accounts about the Bering Strait area, archaeologists know that by the beginning of the eighteenth century the Seward Peninsula Iñupiat actively interacted through trade and warfare with the Chukchi. Tobacco, beads, and iron items, especially iron lances, were highly desired by the Alaska Natives in exchange for furs and ready-made clothing, such as vests of young caribou and rabbit skins. Maintaining the structure of this trade network and control of the flow of goods, especially European goods, which were scarce through the eighteenth century, was extremely important, as demonstrated by the 1836 attack on St. Michael, a Russian post established three years earlier in Norton Sound. The Russian post disrupted the established Native trade route south from the Bering Strait to the Yukon River, bringing on a bow-and-arrow attack, which the Russians lost.

Caribou skins and fawn skins were among the most common, although not the most valuable, trade items offered by the northwest Alaska Natives. The archaeological and oral historical data demonstrate the historic and prehistoric focus on caribou procurement in the Imuruk and Kuzitrin lakes area. It is possible that the cinder cone villages and monuments were established to protect boundaries and access to a critical resource in a time of accelerated trade beginning with the Anyui-Kolyma trade fair initiated in 1789. Ray's research shows that Malimiut-dialect speakers began moving south and west onto the Seward Peninsula in the late 1700s, when they became middlemen in the Russian-Native trade market. They undoubtedly moved onto the Seward Peninsula to gain control of an important Native fur trade route from the Yukon to the Buckland River and Kotzebue Sound, as well as control of key points in Norton Sound.

In response to this intrusive population movement, resident groups may have taken measures to protect access to resources and to control trade and travel routes, resulting in the establishment of the "outpost" villages on the cinder cones observed in the archaeological record. The increased trade may have increased demand and therefore led to greater resource stress and scarcity, in turn resulting in greater conflict.

The cinder cone sites are probably related to protection and control of access to caribou and perhaps large supplies of cached meat for the people occupying the Qaviaraġmiut and likely the eastern portion of the Pittaġmiut territories (as defined by Burch) in late prehistoric times. Conflict over this resource in an area that was possibly a calving ground may have been due to climatic pressures, increased demand due to accelerated trade, or even perhaps conflict over accumu-

lated food. If the actual time of occupation of these sites was the late 1700s, their use may have been short-term due to the rapid disruption of Native trade networks by American traders and whalers beginning in the 1840s.

There are regularly scheduled commercial flights from Anchorage, Alaska, to Nome, Alaska, the headquarters for the Bering Land Bridge National Preserve. There is no road access to the preserve. Summer access is by chartered boat or float plane; winter access is by small plane on skis, snow machine, or dogsled.

Further Reading: Burch, Ernest S., Jr., *The Iñupiaq Nations of Northwest Alaska* (Fairbanks: University of Alaska Press, 1998); Giddings, James L., and Doug Anderson, *Beach Ridge Archeology of Cape Krusenstern*, National Park Service Publications in Archeology No. 20 (Washington, DC: National Park Service, 1986); Hickey, Clifford G., "The Historic Beringian Trade Network: Its Nature and Origins," in *Thule Eskimo Culture: An Anthropological Retrospective*, National Museum of Man Mercury Series No. 88 (Ottawa, ON: National Museum of Man, 1979); Oquilluk, William A., *People of Kauwerak: Legends of the Northern Eskimo* (Anchorage: Alaska Pacific University Press, 1981); Powers, William Roger, Jo Anne Adams, Alicia Godfrey, James A. Ketz, David Plaskett, and G. Richard Scott, *The Chukchi-Imuruk Report: Archaeological Investigations in the Bering Land Bridge National Preserve, Seward Peninsula, Alaska, 1974 and 1975*, University of Alaska Cooperative Park Studies Unit Occasional Paper No. 31 (Fairbanks: University of Alaska, 1982); Rapoport, Amos, *House Form and Culture* (Englewood Cliffs, NJ: Prentice-Hall, 1969); Ray, Dorothy Jean, *The Eskimos of Bering Strait, 1650–1898* (Seattle: University of Washington Press, 1975); Ray, Dorothy Jean, "Bering Strait Eskimo," in *Handbook of North American Indians*, Vol. 5: *Arctic*, edited by D. Damas (Washington, DC: Smithsonian Institution, 1984); Schaaf, Jeanne M., "Before Our Father's Time," in *Ublasaun: Iñupiaq Hunters and Herders in the Early Twentieth Century, Northern Seward Peninsula, Alaska*, edited by Jeanne M. Schaaf (Anchorage: Alaska Region National Park Service, 1996), adapted from "Late-Prehistoric Iñupiaq Societies, Northern Seward Peninsula, Alaska: An Archeological Analysis AD 1500–1800," unpublished Ph.D. diss. (University of Minnesota, Minneapolis, 1995).

Jeanne Schaaf

THE TULUAQ HILL, ONION PORTAGE, TUKTU, MOSQUITO LAKE, AND TUKUTO LAKE SITES

Brooks Range, Northern Alaska

A Complex Prehistoric Record of a Variety of Cultural Adaptations

The prehistory of the Brooks Range encompasses over 13,000 years of occupation by peoples with a wide variety of adaptations to changing environments from the end of the last Ice Age to European contact in AD 1741. This review summarizes archaeological research and important cultural patterns of this region. The Brooks Range is a northern extension of the Rocky Mountains, extending from east to west from the Canadian-Alaskan border to the Chukchi Sea. Mountain glaciers covered portions of the range until around 12,000 years ago. Most of the area is currently characterized as alpine tun-

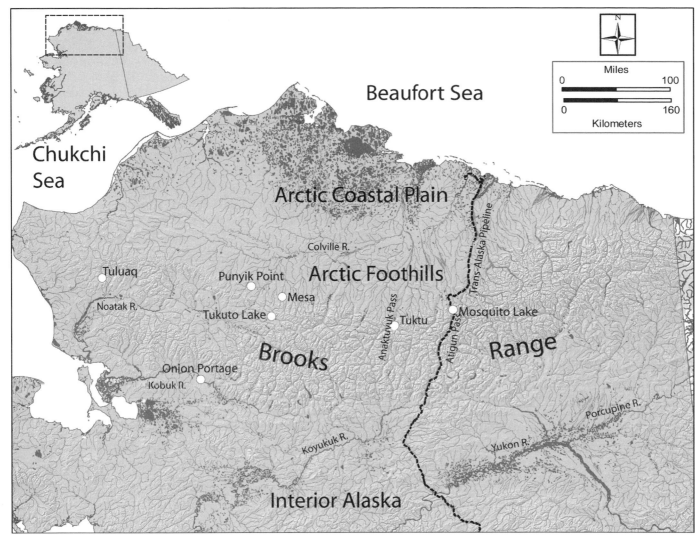

The Brooks Range, showing major physiographic regions and archaeological sites mentioned in the essay.   [Courtesy of the United States Geological Survey]

dra, with boreal forests in the river valleys draining the southern flanks and moist tundra on the northern flanks. Consequently, soil development is limited, and archaeologists are hampered by a relative lack of buried, stratified sites and organic preservation until a few thousand years ago.

This region has a complex prehistory, with evidence of use by various peoples with different cultural adaptations. Currently, Athabascan Indians inhabit the southern flanks, and Nunamiut Eskimo occupy the central Brooks Range. Understanding the history of these two peoples' use of the region has always been an important anthropological question. The biotic and physiographic diversity makes the Brooks Range a fascinating laboratory to investigate high-latitude human ecology. Lewis R. Binford's work on Nunamiut ethnoarchaeology from 1969 to 1976, centered in Anaktuvuk Pass, provided important methods and data for archaeologists around the world to link the dynamic present with the static past. However, the majority of research has been driven by cultural

resource management. As a result, archaeological investigations are typically site-based, with very little landscape or settlement-scale research.

Archaeological survey coverage is limited in this area, generally centered on road or pipeline routes and compliance-driven development projects. Access is limited to a single road adjacent to the Trans-Alaska Pipeline (TAPS); archaeologists typically use helicopters to insert archaeological survey teams into remote locations and pedestrian survey within these investigation areas. Various projects sponsored by the Bureau of Land Management and the National Park Service have identified many sites within their jurisdiction, but there also are many lacunae in this region, particularly east of Atigun Pass. Dissertations and theses from the University of Alaska at Fairbanks and other institutions have been targeted on specific sites or small regions. Over forty years of research has produced numerous survey and site excavation reports, but synthetic regional treatments are rare. Cultural traditions are defined on the basis of stone tool (lithic) typologies, and these are used in a normative cultural historical framework. This strong lithic orientation has resulted in advances in obsidian hydration studies (used to "date" stone tools), geochemical lithic raw material sourcing, and use-wear studies; however, this has limited the development of zooarchaeology, paleoecology, and prehistoric land use studies.

This summary reflects the current consensus of Brooks Range prehistory. Over 3,000 sites have been recorded, but very few have been inventoried or tested, and even fewer have been excavated. All prehistoric peoples in this region are characterized as mobile foragers (with hunting, fishing, and gathering economies). Sites are generally characterized as ephemeral lithic scatters, typically with overlook settings. Tent rings (stones set to anchor hide tents) are found throughout the region and date from the Middle to Late Holocene (3800 BC to recent). Caribou drivelines and corrals are associated with Athabascan and Iñupiaq occupations in the Late Holocene, but villages with substantial semi-subterranean houses are not in evidence until the late prehistoric period. Ethnographic and historical frameworks in combination with archaeological materials suggest that the Brooks Range was used seasonally to extract subsistence resources by Eskimo peoples who primarily occupied the Chukchi and Beaufort Sea coasts and by Athabascans with habitations adjacent to large interior rivers and lakes.

The oldest known occupations in the Brooks Range date from 11,200 to about 7000 BC and are termed the Paleoindian tradition (e.g., Mesa and Sluiceway complexes, named for their type sites), delineated on the basis of conventional lithic typologies. These groups have been linked to Paleoindian complexes (like Clovis) in central North America, although it is debated whether they represent ancestors or descendents of the latter populations. Proposed similarities include lanceolate projectile points and spurred gravers. This region may play an important part in understanding the colonization of the New World; for example, a recently excavated quarry site, Tuluaq Hill, has hearth dates of 11,200 BC. Lack of faunal preservation and recovery limits have hampered archaeological understanding of the lifeways of these earliest peoples, but all were mobile hunters with strong terrestrial mammal emphasis. Paleontological work suggests that mammoth, bison, and other Pleistocene megafauna were present during this time, but no large faunal assemblages have been excavated to date. Future work may enable a better understanding of the Late Pleistocene occupation of this region.

Another technological complex dating to the Late Pleistocene–Early Holocene, the American Paleoarctic tradition is characterized by distinctive wedge-shaped microblade cores, microblades, and burins, part of a widespread lithic tradition from the Siberian Late Upper Paleolithic complexes to those on Holocene complexes on the Northwest Coast of North America. These microblades were inserted into organic implements to form composite tools.

Dates from Onion Portage, a stratified site in the Kobuk River, just south of the Brooks Range, place this tradition from 8000 to 6000 BC, although microblade technology is associated with dates of up to 12,000 BC in interior Alaska. The presence of both industries during the same period suggests that the early prehistory of Alaska was more complex than is widely acknowledged.

Between 7000 and 3800 BC, new artifact types spread throughout Alaska, including side-notched biface forms and microblades struck from tabular cores, which are diagnostics for the Northern Archaic tradition, although microblade technology was still present. This tradition may represent adaptations to the spreading boreal forest or reflect new populations entering Alaska. Tent rings and exploitation of mountain lakes, with abundant waterfowl and fish, may be first associated with the Northern Archaic tradition. Subsistence likely was tied to caribou and possibly sheep. The Tuktu site, in Anaktuvuk Pass, has played an important role in archaeological understanding of this time period through recovery and dating of multiple concentrations of lithic material.

Around 3200 BC, the Arctic Small Tool (AST) tradition, locally expressed as the Denbigh Flint complex, represented Paleoeskimo people who spread from Siberia to Alaska, the Canadian high Arctic, and Greenland. Their technology is characterized by small, delicately flaked tools, very different from earlier traditions. While most of AST tradition sites are on the coast, several sites are present in the Brooks Range, including Punyik Point and Mosquito Lake, the latter excavated during the TAPS survey. Artifacts include small bifaces used as end or side blades, microblades, and particular burin forms. Later, related groups like Choris, Norton, and Ipiutak complexes have representative sites in the Brooks Range, such as the Croxton site at Tukuto Lake, with an Ipiutak component dating to AD 1260. Cord-impressed and check-stamped pottery styles are associated with Choris and Norton, respectively, and microblade use was reduced. Caribou hunting was a primary economic resource, and several sites contain numerous caribou remains, with sheep and small mammals present but generally to a lesser extent.

One interpretation of the Onion Portage record argues for replacement of Northern Archaic populations by AST tradition on the coast, although Northern Archaic continued in the interior until around AD 1000. Understanding the relationships between AST tradition and interior populations in the Late Holocene is an important ongoing research problem. This is complicated in that the Brooks Range likely reflected a seasonal portion of total landscape use, with different cultural traditions incorporating this region in parts of their seasonal rounds. The Kavik complex, characterized by small lozenge-shaped or stemmed projectile points, is present in several sites in the central Brooks Range in the late prehistoric period and may represent Athabascan peoples.

From the late prehistoric up to and after Euro-American

contact, the Brooks Range was contested territory, with Athabascan and coastal and inland Eskimos competing at times for access to subsistence resources and control over the major river valleys and foothills lakes. The later prehistory of the Brooks Range is characterized by developmental and historical complexity that is not captured in the existing culture historical models, in part because relatively few site specific excavations or regional investigations have been conducted.

Several large lakes scattered from east of Anaktuvuk Pass west across the northern foothills of the Brooks Range are known to have rich archaeological records spanning early AST tradition to late prehistoric and historic Eskimo village sites. Although the AST tradition through Ipiutak occupations tend to reflect seasonal use of the area for caribou procurement and other specialized subsistence activities, the late prehistoric and historic Eskimo villages are large, containing in some cases hundreds of semi-subterranean houses and associated features, and reflect year-round occupation of the Brooks Range foothills. Limited archaeological investigations at Tukuto Lake suggest that the initial early late prehistoric occupations began in earnest and then flourished during the little ice age centuries AD 1550–1750, with earlier ephemeral occupations at AD 1410–50, and capped with three brief occupations in the nineteenth and twentieth centuries. For unknown reasons, the large lake foothills villages appear to have been more or less abandoned by about AD 1850. The sheer size of the foothills lakeside villages and length of occupation indicates a successful foraging economy with a stable resource base of caribou.

Further Reading: Anderson, D. D., *Onion Portage: The Archaeology of a Stratified Site from the Kobuk River, Northwest Alaska*, Anthropological Papers of the University of Alaska 22(1–2) (Fairbanks: University of Alaska, 1988); Bever, M. R., "An Overview of Alaskan Late Pleistocene Archaeology: Historical Themes and Current Perspectives," *Journal of World Prehistory* 15(2) (2001): 125–191; Binford, L. R., *Nunamiut Ethnoarchaeology* (New York: Academic Press, 1978); Damas, D., ed., *Handbook of North American Indians*, Vol. 5: *Arctic* (Washington, DC: Smithsonian Institution, 1984); Hall, E. S., Jr., ed., *Contributions to Anthropology: The Interior Peoples of Northern Alaska* (Ottawa, ON: National Museums of Canada, 1976); Mason, O. K., and S. C. Gerlach, "Chukchi Hot Spots, Paleo-Polynyas, and Caribou Crashes: Climatic and Ecological Dimensions of North Alaska Prehistory," *Arctic Anthropology* 32(1) (1995): 101–130; Minc, L. D., and K. P. Smith, "The Spirit of Survival: Cultural Responses to Resource Variability in North Alaska," in *Bad Year Economics: Cultural Responses to Risk and Uncertainty*, edited by P. Halstead and J. O'Shea (Cambridge: Cambridge University Press, 1989), 8–39; Reanier, R. E., "The Antiquity of Paleoindian Materials in Northern Alaska," *Arctic Anthropology* 32(1) (1995): 31–50.

Ben A. Potter and S. Craig Gerlach

THE MESA, LISBURNE, AND PUNYIK POINT SITES

Colville River Drainage, Northern Alaska

The Sequence of Ancient Cultures in the Brooks Range Foothills

The Colville River drains an area of roughly 20,000 square miles, the largest watershed in arctic Alaska. All of the rivers and streams flowing north out of the central Brooks Range empty into the Colville. The river flows 350 miles east-northeast from the Arctic interior to the Arctic coast through a roadless, treeless region of mountains, foothills, ridges, glacial deposits, alpine and tussock tundra, sedge meadows, and numerous lakes and streams. The area can be accessed by watercraft while the bedrock and glacial topography provide reasonable overland travel routes through most of the region. The diverse landscape supports a variety of mammals, fish, and fowl that provided food, clothing, and other materials necessary to the survival of prehistoric peoples. Chert, the rock that stone tools are made from, is abundant throughout the region. Because of its topography, landscape, and natural resources, the region was very attractive to prehistoric peoples, and the density of archaeological sites there is higher than in other regions on Alaska's north slope.

During the last Ice Age (Pleistocene epoch) Alaska and Siberia were connected by dry land. It was across this "land bridge" 15,000–20,000 years ago that humans entered the Western Hemisphere. People have continuously occupied Alaska since that time, and therefore some of the oldest archaeological sites in North America are found in Alaska. Technically, the prehistoric period in Alaska lasted until AD 1741, when Russian explorers made initial contact with Alaska Natives.

Archaeological sites in the Colville River drainage reflect all of arctic Alaska's cultural time periods, beginning with the Paleoindians of 13,500 years ago and up to the historic Nunamiut Eskimo who were living a nomadic lifestyle until the late 1940s. Prehistoric site types include seasonal residence camps composed of semi-subterranean houses, sod houses, and caribou skin tents as well as trading, fishing, and hunting locales. Historic period sites include Euro-American discovery expedition sites, Eskimo contact and

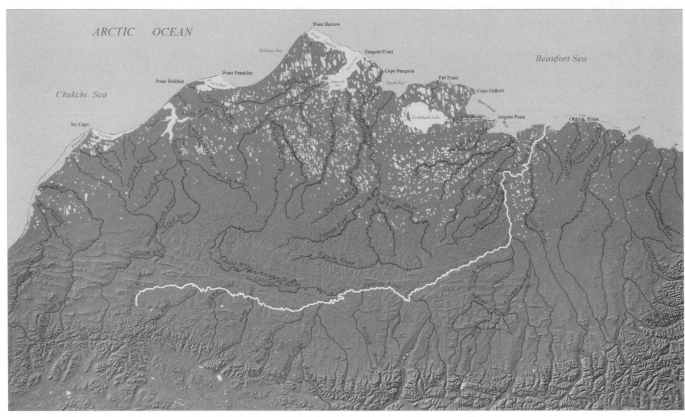

A map showing the drainage from the Colville River.   [Michael Kunz]

The Mesa archaeological site is located atop the mesa-like ridge, in the middle distance of the photo, just north of the Brooks Range front, in the far distance of the photo.   [Michael Kunz]

Although microblade and burin technology disappeared along with the Arctic Small Tool people, the manufacture of small composite tools remained the identifying aspect of the Eskimo cultures through the end of the prehistoric period.   [Michael Kunz]

subsistence camps, and locales of early oil and gas exploration activities.

MESA

The Mesa is a Paleoindian site, one the oldest in North America and the site where the characteristics of the Mesa complex were defined. Although arctic Alaska may be the region where the Paleoindian culture evolved, Paleoindians were first recognized eighty decades ago at a site more than 3,000 miles to the south, near Folsom, New Mexico. Paleoindians are generally considered by most archaeologists to be the first indigenous, geographically widespread North American culture. The Paleoindian sites of arctic Alaska are found primarily in the Brooks Range. Paleoindians occupied the region at the end of the Ice Age, between 11,800 and 13,500 years ago, when Ice Age animals such as mammoth (*Mammuthus primigenius*), bison (*Bison priscus*), and horse (*Equus lambei*) were becoming extinct. The landscape was in transition, changing from a grass-dominated steppe prairie to a moist tussock tundra. Besides being recognized as hunters of now-extinct animals, Paleoindians are known for their excellent stone workmanship, producing distinctive spear and dart points, knives, hide scrapers, and incising tools.

The site is located on a mesa-like ridge surrounded by gently rolling tundra several miles north of the range front. Elevated almost 200 feet above the surrounding landscape, the Mesa provides an excellent 360-degree view encompassing about 40 square miles. This exceptional view is the reason for the site's existence. It was used as a hunting lookout. The hunters who used the Mesa probably had a base camp on a nearby creek and spent much of their time on top of the Mesa scanning the surrounding country for game. While looking for game, the hunters worked on their equipment, removing broken projectile points from dart and spear shafts and replacing them with new ones. This activity was usually conducted next to a small fire, which may have provided heat needed in the hafting process or may have been for personal warmth. Regardless of their purpose, the fires were an integral part of the activities at the Mesa, as indicated by the high density of artifacts that closely surround the remains of these small fires. More than 450 broken and resharpened projectile points and other tools and 130,000 stone chips (the waste material from manufacturing stone tools) were recovered through excavation

An aerial view of the Lisburne archaeological site. Some depressions indicating former semi-subterranean houses can be seen. Iteriak Creek is shown at the top of the photo.   [Michael Kunz]

of the site. The charcoal from these ancient fires is used to radiocarbon date the site. Both bison and caribou (*Rangifer tarandus*) lived in the region when the Mesa site was being used. Archaeologists think that the hunters were probably after bison, because techniques used to hunt caribou do not require an elevated vantage point like the Mesa. It is worth noting that all known Mesa complex sites are located on high promontories. If bison were the target animals, then hunting them must have been quite an adventure because the Ice Age bison were considerably larger than modern bison (*Bison bison*). When the steppe prairie disappeared at the end of the Ice Age, the Paleoindians disappeared too, and due to the changing climate/ecosystem and the extinction of some large game animals, the Colville region appears to have been largely uninhabited for the next 1,500 years. Once the climate stabilized and the modern ecosystem was in place, about 10,000 years ago, people again regularly resided in the region.

LISBURNE

The Lisburne site lies on a low bluff overlooking Iteriak Creek about 10 miles north of the range front. Unlike the Mesa site, which was used intensively only by Paleoindians, the Lisburne site was used by people representing almost all of the subsequent prehistoric cultures of arctic Alaska, making it one of the most important sites in the region. Additionally, the long-term use of the site is a testament to its excellent location and the stability of the climate and ecosystem over the last 10,000 years. The Lisburne site was used primarily as a camp, but its strategic location in the valley made it a good hunting lookout and occasional kill site. Although moose (*Alces alces*) and musk oxen (*Ovibos moschatus*) were occasionally taken, the primary subsistence animal in the region was the caribou, without which the human residents of the area could not have survived.

Although Paleoindians may have briefly and sporadically utilized the Lisburne site, the first true residents were people of the American Paleoarctic tradition. This culture appears to have its roots in Siberia, and its stone tool industry reflects this with its microblade and burin technology. Around 7,500 years ago the people of the Northern Archaic tradition appeared on the scene. Their stone tool industry is much the same as the previous site occupants, but the style of their projectile points is typical of Archaic cultures across North America. Beginning about 5,000 years ago, Eskimos used the

Semi-subterranean house remains found at Punyik Point. [Michael Kunz]

site. Eskimos inhabited both the coastal and interior areas of arctic Alaska, so it is not surprising they were at the Lisburne site 200 miles from the coast. The Arctic Small Tool tradition people were the earliest Eskimos and the first of that cultural tradition to use the site. Arctic Small Tool tradition people used microblade and burin technology and made some large projectile points, but much of their stone tool assemblage was quite different from their predecessors. Many of their projectile points were a composite of several small pieces of flaked stone, called end and side blades, set in an antler or ivory shaft. Although microblade and burin technology disappeared along with the Arctic Small Tool people, the manufacture of small composite tools remained the identifying aspect of the Eskimo cultures through the end of the prehistoric period. With the possible exception of the late prehistoric Eskimo culture, the site was utilized by all the interior arctic Alaska Eskimo groups.

PUNYIK POINT

Located on the shore of Etivlik Lake, the Punyik Point site appears as a large group of semi-subterranean house remains. The lake lies just inside the northern limit of the

Brooks Range. The Punyik Point locale was first used by Arctic Small Tool people about 4,000 years ago, followed by the Norton (about 2,200 years ago) and Ipiutak (about 1,200 years ago) Eskimo cultures. While the Arctic Small Tool, Norton, and Ipiutak people built semi-subterranean houses, most of the houses at Punyik Point are attributable to the late prehistoric Eskimo culture. There appear to have been two periods of late prehistoric Eskimo occupation at the site, the first around AD 1450 and the second about AD 1550. Both of these periods of occupation occurred several centuries before Alaska's historic period began. Some of the most fascinating artifacts at the site are the glass beads and smelted iron pendants recovered through excavation. The artifacts radiocarbon date to about AD 1450, forty years before Columbus discovered America. How this material arrived in North America before AD 1492 is an intriguing story. The beads were probably made in Venice, the Mediterranean city-state that controlled European trade to the Orient. The beads probably traveled across Asia via caravan to the northern edge of civilization and from there moved across Siberia via Native traffic eventually arriving in the Bering Strait region. The beads were then traded across the strait to

Table 1 **Prehistoric Cultures of the Colville River Drainage**

Culture/Tradition	Approximate Age	Representative Material	Representative Sites
Paleoindian	13,500–11,800 years ago	Bifacial lanceolate projectile points, bifacial knives, single & multispured gravers	Mesa, Kuna Bluff
American Paleoarctic	10,300–7,500 years ago	Microblade technology, burins, bifacial projectile points and knives	Lisburne, Kurupa Lake, Kealok Creek
Northern Archaic	7,500–3,000 years ago	Microblade technology, notched and stemmed bifacial projectile points and knives, large scrapers	Kurupa Lake, Lisburne, Tuktu
Denbigh Flint Complex (Arctic Small Tool Tradition)	5,000–2,400 years ago	Microblade technology, stylized burins, diminutive side and end blades, flake knives, discoids composite tools	Punyik Point, Kurupa Lake, Tukuto Lake
Choris	3,800–2,200 years ago	Burins, large bifacial projectile points, pottery, ground stone, bone, antler & ivory implements, semi-subterranean houses	Lisburne (?), Kurupa Lake (?)
Norton	2,600–1,800 years ago	Pentagonal projectile points, end and side blades, flake knives, discoids, ground stone, pottery, composite tools, antler, bone & Ivory implements, semi-subterranean houses	Punyik Point, Kurupa Lake, Tukuto Lake
Ipiutak	1,800–1,200 years ago	End & side blades, flake knives, discoids, (no pottery or ground stone), composite tools, intricate ornamental ivory carvings, burials, semi-subterranean houses	Punyik Point, Kurupa Lake, Tukuto Lake
Birnirk	1,600–1,000 years ago	End & side blades, ground slate tools, ivory and antler harpoon heads, composite tools, pottery, semi-subterranean houses	Niglik
Thule	1,000–400 years ago	End & side blades, ground slate tools, ivory and antler harpoon heads, composite tools, pottery, semi-subterranean houses	Niglik
Late Prehistoric Eskimo	700–400 years ago	End & side blades, long, stemmed projectile points, pottery, bone, antler, ivory implements, ground stone, semi-subterranean houses	Tukuto Lake, Etivlik Lake, Kinyuksugvik, Swayback Lakes
Nunamiut	400 years ago–Historic	Bifacial stone projectile points, bone & antler projectile points, ground stone, sod houses	Colville River, Etivlik River, Nigu River, Anaktuvuk River, Kinyuksugvik

Alaskan Eskimos, who took them up the Noatak River travel route into the Arctic interior. Punyik Point lies at the head of the Noatak drainage. Thus European goods arrived in the New World traveling the same general route as the first immigrants 15,000–20,000 years earlier.

There are several thousand known sites in the Cloville watershed and thousands more not yet discovered. Because of the remoteness of the region, only limited archaeological research has been conducted. As a result, the potential for finding additional sites of significant scientific value, particularly those associated with the initial peopling of the New World, is high.

Further Reading: Bowers, P. M., *The Lisburne Site: Analysis and Cultural History of a Multi-component Lithic Workshop in the Iteriak Valley, Arctic Foothills, Northern Alaska*, Anthropological Papers of the University of Alaska 20(1–2) (Fairbanks: University of Alaska, 1982), 79–112; Kunz, M. L., M. R. Bever, and C. M. Adkins, *The Mesa Site: Paleoindians above the Arctic Circle*, BLM-Alaska Open File Report No. 86 (Anchorage, AK: U.S. Department of the Interior, Bureau of Land Management, 2003); Kunz, Michael L., and Richard E. Reanier, "Paleoindians in Beringia: Evidence from Arctic Alaska," *Science* 263(5147) (1994): 660–664; Schoenberg, K. M., "The Post-Paleoarctic Interval in the Central Brooks Range," *Arctic Anthropology* 32(1) (1995): 51–62.

Michael Kunz

THE UTQIAGVIK ARCHAEOLOGICAL PROJECT

Barrow, Coast of the Arctic Ocean, Alaska

The Historic and Recent Archaeology of a Native Community

The Arctic coasts of the Beaufort Sea and Arctic Ocean are carved by along-shore currents, storm-tossed seas, ice movements, and land erosion. Where the coast has been stable, evidence of human land use dates back several thousand years. Until the Bering Strait was inundated by rising sea levels as the Late Pleistocene ice sheets melted and Holocene currents of the Bering Sea exchanged waters through the strait and the Chukchi Sea, the northern Arctic Ocean coast seems to have been largely untouched by the cultural and technological developments occurring in more southern areas of both coastal and interior Alaska. Extensive archaeological remains of the activities or settlements of maritime-oriented people seem to be limited to an Arctic Small Tool cultural tradition of about 2500 BC followed by a Thule cultural tradition (and descendants) beginning about AD 1000.

From a recent review of the broad patterns of Arctic prehistory, and the attempt to make general sense of them for undergraduate archaeology students, one of the most striking patterns seemed to be these two later cultural traditions of successful maritime hunters of frozen coasts, emanating through northern Alaska and moving eastward in time, experiencing changing environmental conditions with new technologies and practices that were revolutionary and extraordinarily successful. Although the tundra and the coast had been reached by people with primarily land-based subsistence patterns numerous times in the past, the earlier cultures remained focused on interior resources of the rivers, lakes, and land. Whereas the northern interior Alaskan archaeological record shows successions of Paleoarctic, Paleoindian, and Archaic hunters and gatherers (see Anderson 1968), the early coastal archaeological record seems to indicate only occasional (and perhaps seasonal) forays from the interior. It is not until relatively late in the prehistoric period (about 5,000 years ago) that the evidence of migration, site frequencies, site settings, faunal materials, and cold-adapted strategies and facilities becomes substantial. From this time onward, archaeological evidence of human occupation mounts, and the Arctic coast develops its own distinctive cultural characteristics, including year-round habitations along the coasts and the immediately adjacent interior.

Prior to about 13,000 years ago, this portion of the Arctic Ocean was dominated by a coastwise circulation of cold, Arctic waters, with relatively low marine productivity and unknown levels of migratory fish, birds, and sea mammals. However, this situation changed markedly with the opening of the Bering Strait as sea levels rose following the glacial maximum. This change was caused by the spilling of warmer Bering Sea waters northward along the Alaskan coastline, where upwelling and admixture increased the productivity of marine resources and the carrying capacity for human groups exploiting these resources along the coast and in adjacent seas. The timing and extent of these events are emerging from the study of marine sediments, but it is difficult to reconstruct precisely environmental conditions during the Younger Dryas, a time of colder climate that lasted for several thousand years (approximately 10,000–13,000 years ago and corresponding with a number of glacial and oceanic events).

Notwithstanding the speculative nature of interpretations based on negative data, it appears that thousands of years passed after initial human settlement of interior Alaska before people with a successful maritime adaptation (and a balanced coastal/inland economy) occupied this northern coast in any numbers. The ample evidence of Arctic Small Tool tradition sites in coastal, riverine, and inland settings stands in marked contrast to earlier times, when coastal sites seem to be confined to the west and south along Bering Sea beaches and farther south.

THE PALEOESKIMO (ARCTIC SMALL TOOL) TRADITION

Investigations by Dennis Stanford (1976) and others (see especially articles in Damas 1984) demonstrated the presence of Arctic Small Tool tradition sites along the north Alaskan coast and adjacent interior. Archaeological surveys in advance of oil and coastal development projects continue to reveal sites from this period. About 2500 BC, people of the Arctic Small Tool tradition initiated a pattern of coastal/inland exploitation that continued through the historic period. The Arctic Small Tool tradition is widely regarded as the most widespread technological horizon across the Arctic and Subarctic coasts and adjacent interior; similar technological adaptations by human groups are sometimes described as extending throughout the expanse of seasonally frozen coastlines in North America, from the Alaska Peninsula to Labrador and Greenland. These adaptive technologies included kayak transport, harpoon/float hunting, extensive ivory carving (mostly for tools), burins and other small stone tools, and arguably the bow and arrow. There is strong evidence from sites located along the coast at freshwater sources of exploitation of sea mammals and birds, along with caribou and other land mammals.

This widely successful cultural tradition possessed the technology and skills that supported this extensive geographic extent and the movement of people as early as 4,000 years ago. Some archaeologists interpret that the Arctic Small Tool tradition represents the initial occupation of the Arctic coast by people whose descendants were known as Eskimos (Inuit, Inupiat, and Yupik). However, this identification is based largely on three notions: balanced subsistence—sea mammal hunting, fishing, and land mammal hunting—geographic congruence, and developmental continuity, all of which are subject to criticism. This tradition (and its descendants in the eastern Arctic) also has been termed "Paleoeskimo" by most archaeologists, building on this notion of cultural continuity.

In coastal Alaska, the widespread Arctic Small Tool tradition was soon part of the threads of population movement, cultural change, and cultural interaction that were evident from Prince William Sound across the Kodiak and Aleutian archipelagos and northward through the Bering Strait to Alaska's northern coast. This ancient cultural phenomenon was a very complicated mixture of cultural preferences, influences, and peoples. One might describe the cultural mixing during this period as a "Bering interaction sphere" wherein developmental influences were more multilineal than unilineal. In such a historical pattern, ethnicity and other cultural differences are not always clearly defined by distinctions in the technology that are typically recognized in archaeological tool assemblages. In addition, the movement of peoples with different cultural traditions can result in archaeological site intrusions into otherwise gradual cultural developmental sequences.

The coastal region had numerous peoples and cultures during this early time, each with an awareness of the others and an engagement with each other that fostered complex social relations that did not involve a common sense of ethnicity or a common language. The lines on historic interpretive maps that purport to show historic territories of defined and distinctive social groups may have no relationship to a complex prehistoric past and population movements and cultural developments spanning several thousand years. Some distinctive cultural traditions may be represented in the archaeological record by many sites and others by one or a few. Contemporary archaeologists need to recognize that the Bering Strait region (and environs) was attractive to a variety of seafaring peoples, some of whom visited and others of whom stayed and joined the throng.

NEOESKIMO TRADITION

From this diverse cultural cauldron emerged a sequence of influential, distinguishable cultural developments in northwest Alaska, from Ipiutak through Birnirk to Thule cultural periods. These involved major technical changes, made possible by environmental and cultural developments, that spawned another extensive horizon, this time from the Bering Strait north and east, extending almost as far as the earlier Arctic Small Tool tradition. This change involved a technology and social organization characterized by open-water whale hunting, based on development of whaling technologies and consequent changes in the nature of hunting and social organization, logistics, religion, and perhaps transportation.

Although it is possible to distinguish changes and trends through this cultural sequence, the overall pattern has emerged from previous studies. And although this process of development of Thule culture is eventful, the source and course seem clear. Along the northwest Alaska coast, both the technology and artistic embellishment support a developing cultural trajectory. Cultural developments resulted in an emergence of successful coastwise whaling that spread eastward from an area of which Barrow was a part. The cultural developments included religious and social characteristics that converted, enveloped, and/or replaced existing late Dorset populations whose cultural traditions had developed as the "terminal" Paleoeskimo, broad-spectrum maritime adaptation.

The spread of the Thule cultural tradition (as an expansive adaptation) undoubtedly occurred at the expense of earlier approaches to technology, subsistence, and other aspects of culture. Much scholarly debate has focused on the dichotomous interpretations between population replacement and population mixture. But recent histories of cultural interactions clearly demonstrate that some people are replaced, others mingle, others adapt, and still others persist. Absent evidence of population or site destruction—for example, burials indicating wounds from warfare, hastily abandoned villages, or burned houses—archaeologists can infer that the eastward wave of technological, subsistence, and social change that the Thule cultural tradition represents invoked a complex set of responses by both the colonists and residents.

Research by Dennis Stanford (e.g., 1976), Allen McCartney (1977, 1979), and others has synthesized the origin, nature, spread, and extent of Thule culture tradition sites across the northern Arctic. Whatever the relationship between the resident Dorset peoples and the spreading Thule peoples (especially in terms of genetic patterns), it is clear that there were many changes taking place. There are discussions about the "Eskimo" nature of these peoples, but it seems likely that each represents a movement of people from a biological and social population of several thousand years ago, with biological, social, and cultural roots in an Arctic Small Tool tradition.

INUPIAT TRADITION

Research conducted in northern Alaska, especially that of the Utqiagvik Archaeology Project in Barrow, managed and directed by Albert A. Dekin Jr. along with colleagues Raymond Newell and Edwin Hall, confirmed the geographic and cultural connections between the Birnirk culture (as a regional antecedent to the Thule cultural tradition in coastal northwest Alaska) in this vicinity, the early occupations of

Utqiagvik about AD 1500, and more recent historic events as reflected in the traditional history and oral historical stories of the Inupiat residents of the region. The latter have been recorded in a series of reports and publications (see articles in Dekin 1984, 1987).

This work was significant for several reasons. Perhaps most important, it represents extensive cooperation and involvement, under the glare of public scrutiny, by several public/governmental agencies, the Public Archaeology Facility at Binghamton University, State University of New York, the community of Barrow, Native corporations and municipalities, all of which (though not without some bumpy times) resulted in creation of an archaeological collection and substantial knowledge of the ancient and historic past for Barrow. This outcome has served the community well. Specific results included interpretations and new knowledge from the archaeological studies of winter village sites; cooperative study of 500-year-old frozen bodies; repatriation for burial of these bodies following autopsy; repatriation to the community museum of all artifacts from these excavations; and, similar preservation of excavation records and publications to the community. The demonstration that cooperative relations could benefit many constituencies, and especially the present community, led to the incorporation of archaeological expertise into the planning and preservations processes. Perhaps of major significance was the notion that these human remains should be reburied with appropriate reverence, following a period of respective study and analysis. In accordance with the expressed wishes of the descendant community, while some tissue samples remained archived, the remains of five Inupiat individuals were reburied in consecrated ground in Barrow in the summer of 1984. These are among the first respectful reburials of aboriginal human remains consecrated in accordance with the desires of a descendant community prior to the formal requirements of the Native American Graves Protection and Repatriation Act of 1990. Researchers at Barrow were privileged to be respectful of descendant concerns in these matters, in the face of criticism from some sectors of the archaeological discipline.

The analysis of the archaeological materials included the extensive involvement of the elders of the North Slope region, for which researchers were exceptionally grateful. The results demonstrated not only the overall continuity of the Birnirk–Utqiagvik–Pignik–Barrow cultural traditions (see Ford 1959), but its similarity with pieces of this ancient and historical sequence in adjacent regions. The integrity of the past cultural tradition through time (since approximately AD 1500) is clear, as are its roots and its similarities with such traditions in other regions.

The exceptional opportunity to study the human remains of five individuals from the same event in a rich archaeological context was appreciated by everyone who became aware of these finds. It was a privilege to be allowed to remove the several bodies and skeletons from this remarkable find to be autopsied and studied (through the efforts of Jack Lobdell to obtain financial sponsorship from the ARCO foundation). These results are reported in a volume of *Arctic Anthropology* (see Dekin 1984) and shed light on the health of these five individuals from five centuries ago. Archaeologists cannot accurately extrapolate the implications from these few individuals to the aboriginal population in Barrow (or elsewhere, for that matter) at that time. The information is but a small sample, yet informative in limited ways.

Researchers were able, with the support of the Barrow descendant community, to learn more of the health of these representatives of the population through a medical autopsy of the two well-preserved bodies and a radiographic examination of the skeletal materials from the house on Mound 44. There had been periods of nutritional stress (through the evidence of Harris lines on bones; Lobdell 1984), and there was evidence of disease and infection (anthracosis, atherosclerosis, arthritis, lice infestation, and trichinosis) as well as the trauma causing death by crushing (Zimmerman and Aufderheide 1984).

Archaeologists were prepared to study artifacts left by people now dead, but whose evidence had been left for 500 years in the place that they last left them. Since most of the artifacts were apparently left at nightfall storage while occupants were sleeping and then redeposited as a result of a middle-of-the-night house destruction, much of it reflected the act of storage (e.g., where the laundry was stored, where clean dishes were stored, where tools were put away for use the next day) rather than the location of tool use. Thus archaeologists learned a lot about storage, organization of materials, sorting and storing into bags or bunches, and so forth. Although this was unique and extremely valuable, it was not exactly what was expected. From unique events, unique things are learned (Dekin 1987, 1996).

It is also important to note that research in the Barrow area was expanded to include the entire range of behavioral evidence of what people did at sites of this nature. Previous investigations focused on the excavation of winter house interiors, paying little attention to the exterior land uses and deposits and concentrating on a narrow range of evidence. Archaeologists' approach was to understand the range of land uses (and deposits) at this locale (and others) in order to expand the understanding of what people were doing and where. This approach opened up a new dimension that related directly to ethnohistoric and descendant knowledge and allowed researchers to apply linguistic, historic, ethnohistoric, and archaeological knowledge (cf. de Laguna et al. 1964) to enhance a holistic understanding of the past.

Probably the best result of the Utqiagvik excavations (apart from the information recovered before it was destroyed) was the attitude of the community to work with archaeologists to preserve the evidence of the past. Recent *ivu* (ice override events) have shown the ability of storm events to push ice over (and destructively) onshore facilities, hence in these cases to preserve and present evidence of past peoples and behaviors. Archaeologists in Barrow (especially Anne Jensen and Glenn Sheehan) have been able to work with local schools and governmental agencies to protect, preserve, and understand the relevance of these threatened resources to modern concerns and interests and to interpret the past in the interest of those who bear the future.

Archaeological understandings of the past are seen through the framework of the present in anticipation of the future. The importance of the past cannot be separated from the present experience and these expectations.

Further Reading: Anderson, Douglas D., "A Stone Age Campsite at the Gateway to America," *Scientific American* 218(6) (1968): 24–33; Damas, David, ed., *Handbook of North American Indians*, Vol. 5: *Arctic* (Washington, DC: Smithsonian Institution, 1984); Dekin, Albert A., Jr., ed., "The Frozen Family from the Utqiagvik Site, Barrow, Alaska: Papers from a Symposium," *Arctic Anthropology* 21(1) (1984); Dekin, Albert A., Jr., "Tragedy at Utqiagvik," in *Eyewitness to Discovery*, edited by Brian M. Fagan (Oxford: Oxford University Press, 1996), 314–323; Dekin, Albert A., Jr., ed., *The 1981 Excavations at the Utqiagvik Archaeological Site, Barrow Alaska*, Vols. I–III (Barrow, AK: North Slope Borough Commission on Inupia History, Language, and Culture, 1987); De Laguna, Frederica, et al., *Archeology of the Yakutat Bay Area, Alaska*, Bulletin No. 192 (Washington, DC: Bureau of American Ethnology, 1964); Ford, James A., *Eskimo Prehistory in the Vicinity of Point Barrow, Alaska*, Anthropological Papers of the American Museum of Natural History 47(1) (New York: American Museum of Natural History, 1959); Lobdell, Jack, "Harris Lines: Markers of Nutrition and Disease at Prehistoric Utqiagvik Village," *Arctic Anthropology* 21(1) (1984): 109–116; McCartney, Allen P., *Thule Eskimo Prehistory along Northwestern Hudson Bay*, Archaeological Survey Paper No. 70, Mercury Series (Ottawa, ON: National Museum of Man, 1977); McCartney, Allen P., *Thule Eskimo Culture: An Anthropological Perspective*, Archaeological Survey Paper No. 88, Mercury Series (Ottawa, ON: National Museum of Man, 1979); Stanford, Dennis J., *The Walakpa Site, Alaska: Its Place in the Birnirk and Thule Cultures*, Smithsonian Contributions to Anthropology No. 20 (Washington, DC: Smithsonian Institution, 1976); Zimmerman, Michael R., and Arthur C. Aufderheide, "The Frozen Family of Utqiagvik: The Autopsy Findings," *Arctic Anthropology* 21(1) (1984): 53–64.

Albert A. Dekin, Jr.

THE KAPUIVIK, ALARNERK, AND HAZARD INLET SITES

Foxe Basin, Melville Peninsula, and Somerset Island, Central Canadian Arctic, Nunavut

The Paleoeskimo, Dorset, and Thule Cultures in the Canadian Arctic

Much of the Canadian Arctic was covered with glacial ice and permanent snow fields until approximately 6,500 years ago, and the first humans arrived in the area between approximately 4,200 and 4,000 years ago. These earliest inhabitants were the first people to cope and successfully adapt to the harsh climate of the Canadian Arctic. The period of occupation of the Canadian Arctic encompasses two major cultural traditions: Paleoeskimo (approximately 4,200–800 years ago) and Neoeskimo (approximately 1,000 years ago to historic times). Although both of these cultural traditions were Arctic adapted, it was only during the latest Neoeskimo occupations that seal-hunting, igloo-dwelling, dogsled driving, highly nomadic Inuit cultures, as popularized in early Arctic exploration narratives and modern media, developed. Prior to that time, Canadian Arctic cultures would have been largely unrecognizable to the reader familiar with only the historic/modern Inuit.

PALEOESKIMO CULTURAL TRADITION

Although there are several competing views on the exact area in which Paleoeskimo culture originally developed, most archaeologists would agree that it originated somewhere in the Bering Strait region of Siberia and Alaska between approximately 4,700 and 4,500 years ago, and very quickly spread throughout the Canadian Arctic coastal and island regions (including northern Quebec and Labrador) and into Greenland in one or perhaps several migration waves. There are several local variants of Paleoeskimo culture within the Canadian Arctic and Greenland (earlier Independence 1, Pre-Dorset, and Sarqaq, often collectively referred to as the Arctic Small Tool tradition, and the later Dorset culture). For the purposes of this chapter, following much recent usage and emphasizing apparent cultural continuity, Paleoeskimo tradition cultures will simply be referred to as Pre-Dorset and Dorset.

Pre-Dorset Culture: The Kapuivik Site, Jens Munk Island, Nunavut

Following the migration of earliest Pre-Dorset people from the Bering Strait region, they very rapidly colonized the then-uninhabited areas of most of the Canadian Arctic. Although archaeological surveys and excavations over the past four decades have greatly increased our knowledge of the nature and geographical extent of Pre-Dorset culture, some of the

A series of raised beaches in the Canadian Arctic. Post-glacial uplift of the land has resulted in a sequence of progressively higher and older beaches inland from the modern beach. Paleoeskimo sites are often dated according to the beach level on which they are located, so that the higher the beach elevation, the older the site.   [James Savelle]

earliest sites recorded and excavated remain in many respects still the most important. One example is the site of Kapuivik on Jens Munk Island in Foxe Basin, immediately north of Hudson Bay. This site is one of the largest Pre-Dorset sites recorded and includes most of the full temporal range of Pre-Dorset occupation, as well as transitional Pre-Dorset and Dorset, and Neoeskimo occupations. Because of the uplift of the land in the region following the melting of glaciers at the end of the last glaciation, this entire occupation sequence is represented by a series of sites on a succession of raised beaches. The oldest sites of these occupations are on the highest beaches, adjacent to what would have then been the contemporaneous shoreline, and successively younger occupations are on successively lower beaches. At Kapuivik, the earliest Pre-Dorset occupations are found on beaches at approximately 52 meters above sea level, whereas the latest Pre-Dorset occupations are found on beaches at approximately 23 meters above sea level.

Kapuivik and neighboring Pre-Dorset sites were first recorded and excavated by the Danish archaeologist Jorgen Meldgaard in the 1950s and 1960s. Because of the essentially

continuous occupation of the site throughout the Paleoeskimo period, it figured prominently in Meldgaard's interpretation of Foxe Basin as a Paleoeskimo "core area" in which cultural developments, and to an extent geographic population expansions, considerably influenced other Paleoeskimo groups throughout the Canadian Arctic and Greenland. The site is impressive in size, consisting of 352 dwelling features, of which 279 relate to Paleoeskimo occupations and the remainder to Dorset and Neoeskimo occupations; the site was remapped and several test excavations were undertaken by Arthur Dyke and James Savelle in 2003. The Pre-Dorset dwelling features are typically boulder tent rings or amorphous boulder piles or loosely scattered stone arrangements, often with stone central axial hearths and associated food preparation/storage areas. Given the extreme climate of the area, preservation of organic materials tends to be generally good, at least for buried deposits.

As large and impressive a site as Kapuivik is, the overall lifeway of Pre-Dorset peoples based on the archaeological evidence from the Arctic presents a picture of generally small,

Kapuivik

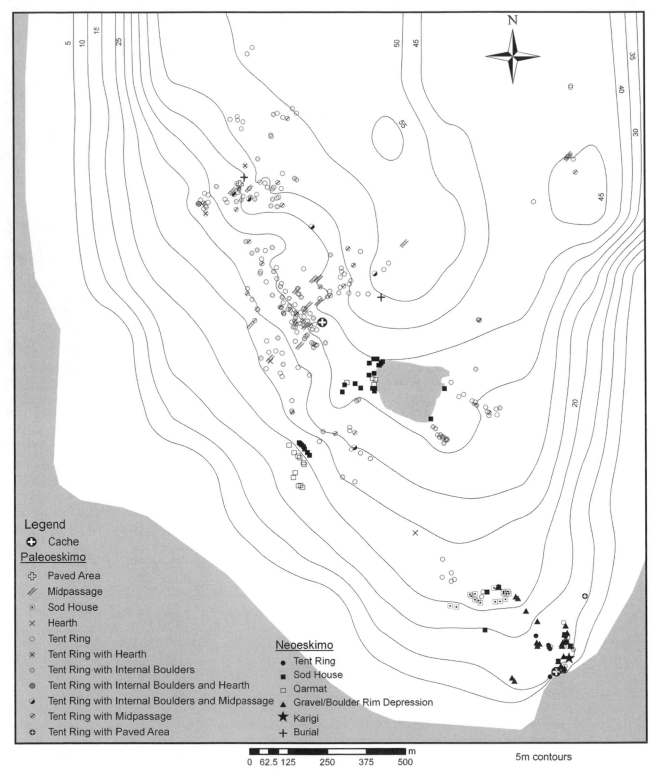

Map of the Kapuivik site on Jens Munk Island, Foxe Basin, Nunavut. Pre-Dorset dwellings are situated on beaches at elevations between approximately 52 meters and 23 meters. [Map produced by Melanie Poupart based on data collected by Arthur Dyke and James Savelle, 2003]

Typical Pre-Dorset dwelling of amorphous stone arrangement and a cluster of smaller boiling stones associated with hearth area. [James Savelle, 2004]

technology-impoverished (relative to later Neoeskimo groups) bands of perhaps one or two families moving from place to place according to the availability of food sources, and congregating in groups of perhaps 50–100 individuals semi-annually or annually at sites such as Kapuivik. Dwellings would have consisted of simple small skin tents made of caribou, musk ox, or seal hides, which were heated by small hearths in which dwarf willow or driftwood would have been burned. It was only later during the Dorset period that sea-mammal oil lamps were used extensively, and Pre-Dorset peoples appear to have relied heavily on stones heated over hearths and immersed in blood or water containing various raw animal parts. Although igloos may have been used during the winter, there is no archaeological evidence of artifacts that would have been associated with the construction of such features; instead, skin tents were probably banked with snow during the winter. Harpoons were the main sea-mammal-hunting weapons, while the bow and arrow and lances would have been used primarily for caribou, and fish spears for Arctic char and other fish species. Most of these tools would have been made of bone and wood, ivory was for harpoons, and bone- and wood-working tools, knives, scrapers, and end blades for various weapons were constructed

primarily from chert. There is some evidence of dogs in the form of skeletal material, but there is little evidence for dog traction gear (i.e., sleds, harness toggles). Similarly, evidence for boats (kayaks or umiaks, the latter large open skin boats) is also extremely rare.

With such apparent limited mobility on either ice or snow or in open water, it is surprising that Pre-Dorset peoples were able to survive, let alone colonize vast areas of the Arctic. But what is certain is that they did just that, relying extensively on ringed seals and locally including Kapuivik, walrus, and bearded seal. Other animals in their diet included various fish and wildfowl, harp seals, and musk ox and caribou (especially in interior regions and coastal caribou migration crossing points).

The original early Paleoeskimo migration into the Canadian Arctic and subsequent expansion took place during a period in which the climate was warmer than present. However, within about 500 years of their first arrival, the climate began to cool such that by about 2,500 years ago conditions were now considerably colder than present. During this cooling trend, much of the geographic periphery of Pre-Dorset occupation was apparently abandoned, such that the Foxe Basin core area remained one of the few continuously inhabited areas

Dorset shallow sod-covered winter dwelling in Foxe Basin. Arthur Dyke provides scale.   [James Savelle, 2003]

Late Dorset longhouse on Victoria Island, Canadian Arctic, first recorded by Robert McGhee. Arthur Dyke provides scale.
[James Savelle, 2000]

Dorset ivory carving of head of polar bear immediately after excavation.   [James Savelle, 1978]

with apparently relatively stable human populations. It was also during this cooling period that important changes occurred in Pre-Dorset culture, leading to what archaeologists refer to as Dorset culture.

Dorset Culture: The Alarnerk site, Melville Peninsula, Nunavut

The Alarnerk site on Melville Peninsula, geographically close to the Pre-Dorset Kapuivik site and within the Foxe Basin Paleoeskimo core area, was first recorded and excavated by Jorgen Meldgaard (who was also responsible for the recording and excavation of the Kapuivik site, as mentioned earlier). The Alarnerk site consists of 208 Dorset dwellings on raised beaches from 22 meters above sea level (earliest Dorset) to 8 meters above sea level (latest or terminal Dorset). Recall that the 23-meter level at Kapuivik contained the latest, or terminal, Pre-Dorset occupations there. Meldgaard considered Alarnerk as the type site for Dorset, and indeed,

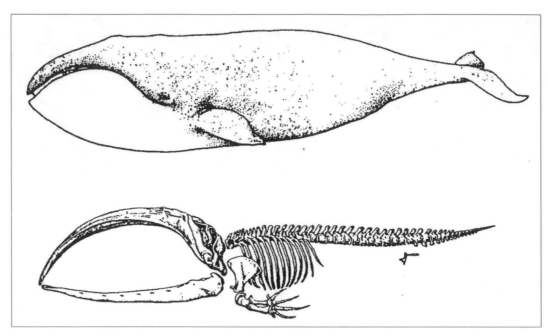

Bowhead whale and skeleton.   [Sketch produced by Allen McCartney and James Savelle]

despite extensive surveys and excavation of Dorset sites else-where in the Canadian Arctic, much of what is known about Dorset culture can be traced back to Alarnerk (although, as with Kapuivik, a detailed monograph of the site was never published). The site was occupied for about 1,800–2,000 years, from approximately 800–600 BC to AD 1000–1200, thus spanning the entire Dorset continuum.

Even within the core area, this site is unique not only for being the largest but also for having the only known Dorset burials (eighteen in total) within the Paleoeskimo core area, although several other Dorset burials have been reported out-side of the core area in northern Quebec and Newfoundland.

The cooling climate during the later Pre-Dorset period has traditionally been directly related to the transition from Pre-Dorset to Dorset. The likely increase in extent and seasonal persistence of shore-fast sea ice is seen as catalyst for a change from a varied sea mammal and terrestrial mammal diet to one focused extensively on sea mammals (but with local variations where caribou and/or musk ox still played prominent roles in the diet). This increasing focus on sea mammals led to significant changes in technology, to some extent, but more important were changes in the size and per-manency of Dorset settlements, and in social structure and ideology. Most of these changes are evidenced at Alarnerk.

Changes in technology are the most easily observed, but to some extent the most puzzling. For example, whereas Pre-Dorset used small drills to produce circular holes as small as eyeholes in needles, Dorset replaced this technology with gouged elongated groves that penetrated from one side of the object to the other. In addition, the bow and arrow appear to

have disappeared from Dorset hunting technology to be replaced by large lance heads. The tool technology continues to be dominated by bone, wood, and chert, although ground slate emerges as a common material for weapon points. Finally, there is evidence of a "snow technology" in the form of snow knives; however, these are rare, and whether they were associated with igloo construction is a matter of debate. Otherwise, definite evidence of dog traction and kayaks or umiaks, as with Pre-Dorset, are extremely rare at Dorset sites.

New and very characteristically "Arctic" technologies, however, do appear with the emergence of Dorset, including the extensive use of stone lamps for heating and cooking with sea-mammal oil, a much more efficient technique relative to burning dwarf willow or driftwood. In conjunction with this development is the construction of much more substantial dwellings, indicating a more sedentary lifestyle. These dwellings are relatively large, typically measuring 4 × 5 meters and dug into the soil down to 30–50 centimeters. They pre-sumably consisted of wood supports over which skins were placed. The lower walls would have been braced by stones and perhaps sod, and the entire structure covered in snow for added insulation. Typically, these dwellings retained the axial hearth arrangements of Pre-Dorset culture.

Another type of dwelling, however, also appears in Dorset, and is unique to this culture. Although small com-munal dwellings appear in earlier Dorset times, it is the late Dorset longhouse, which, while not yet recorded in the Paleoeskimo core area, nevertheless is relatively common in other areas occupied by Dorset peoples. These long-houses are impressive structures; rectangular in shape,

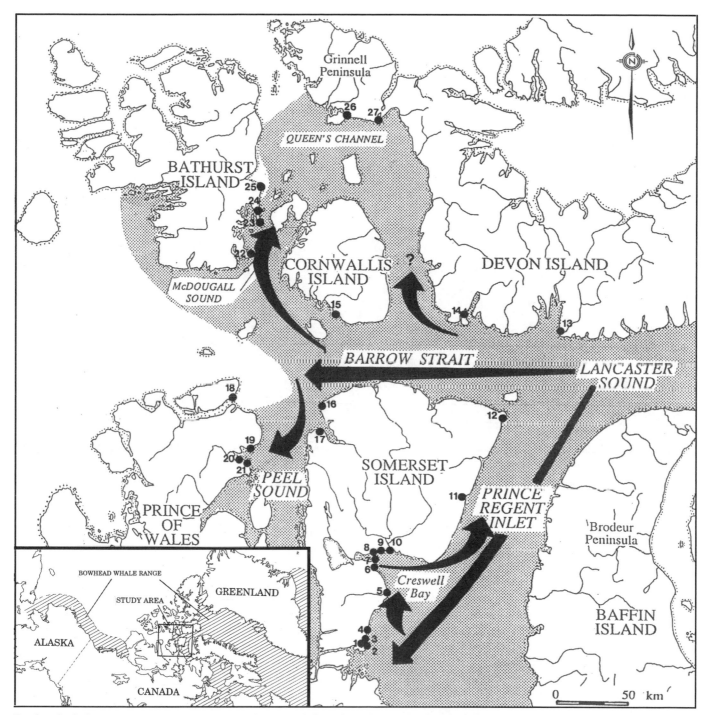

Bowhead whale summer migration routes in the central Canadian Arctic. Bowheads follow retreating ice edges according to the routes indicated. Numbered dots indicate locations of Thule winter sites in the area. Sites 1–4 indicate the Hazard Inlet Thule sites. [Diagram produced by James Savelle]

often with high stone walls and entrances at each end, they range from 8 to 45 meters long and 4 to 6 meters wide. Typically, each longhouse has a series of hearths running down the center of the structure. They also commonly have one or more series of external hearths running parallel to the major longhouse. The specific function of longhouses is of

considerable debate in Arctic archaeology, but there is no doubt they represent a new type of social gathering of otherwise dispersed smaller groups on a probable annual basis, and thus suggest new social relationships amongst local groups not previously seen amongst earlier Dorset or Pre-Dorset societies.

Row of Thule winter houses at Hazard Inlet, Somerset Island, Nunavut.   [James Savelle, 1988]

Turning now to Dorset ideology, one aspect of Dorset material culture that has a particular fascination is that of "art" in such forms as carved animal effigies, human faces, and masks, many realistic and others abstract. Typically carved from antler or ivory, often the animal carvings will exhibit a skeletal motif, whereas human faces are often found in clusters on antler wands. Animal effigies include just about every animal type present in the Arctic—walrus, polar bear, wolf, hawks, geese, seal, caribou, fish, and beluga whale. To this may be added human faces carved on soapstone outcrops in the Hudson Strait region. The reason for this artistic florescence among Dorset peoples is a topic of considerable debate among Arctic archaeologists. Certainly it must relate to the spiritual world of Dorset peoples and their shamans, but in what way is a matter of speculation.

The overall picture of Dorset culture, then, is one of a highly sea-ice-adapted society that was seasonally sedentary (presumably made possible by the stockpiling of surplus food resources), and in which social cohesion and the spirit world played important roles. However, as with the ancestral Pre-Dorset culture, Dorset societies were very likely essentially egalitarian, with extended family "elders" providing informal social leadership and possibly spiritual leadership as well.

The demise of Dorset culture, and indeed the extinction of the Dorset people themselves, deserves some discussion. By approximately 900 years ago, Dorset disappeared from most of their former geographical range, while remnant populations remained in peripheral areas for a few additional 100–200 years. The demise does not appear to have been gradual, but rather, in archaeological terms, quite sudden. The Dorset demise and geographic range constriction coincides with the expansion of the whale-hunting Thule Inuit out of Alaska into the Canadian Arctic, and it is difficult not to see at least some connection between the two events. Nonetheless, recent DNA studies by Geoffrey Hayes and colleagues suggest that Dorset did not contribute to the gene pool of the Thule but probably did to the Sadlermuit, an isolated Inuit group in Hudson Bay that died out during the winter of AD 1902–03 and that had been considered by some archaeologists to have been a remnant Dorset group. In any event, the Pre-Dorset and Dorset were remarkable in their adaptive persistence over an approximately 3,500-year period in one of the earth's most hostile environments, in the absence of the more sophisticated technologies associated with the incoming Thule Inuit.

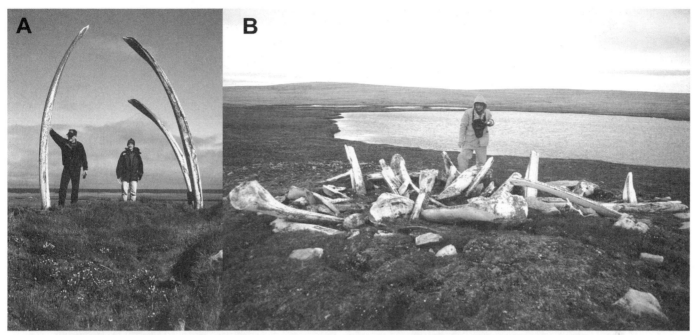

A: Example of probable "conspicuous consumption" relating to use of whalebone as an indicator of social status at an Alaska Thule whaling village. Amanda Crandall and Allen McCartney provide scale. [Photograph by James Savelle 1996] *B*: Thule whalebone house in the Canadian Arctic illustrating extent of the use of bowhead whalebone in Thule house construction. House is undisturbed other than natural collapse of whalebone roof supports. Allen McCartney provides scale. [James Savelle, 1988]

Finally, although space limits a lengthy discussion of the topic, it is appropriate to note here that recent research by Patricia Sutherland and colleagues would suggest that the first European–Native American contact took place between late Dorset peoples and Icelandic and Greenlandic Norse explorers/colonizers apparently on more than simply a chance, intermittent basis.

NEOESKIMO CULTURAL TRADITION

A group of peoples biologically and culturally distinct from the Paleoeskimos first migrated to the Canadian Arctic from Alaska approximately 1,000 years ago, and those peoples and their historic descendents are referred to as Neoeskimo. These first Neoeskimo migrants, however, the Thule, were very different from historic Neoeskimo groups (the seal-hunting, igloo-dwelling, dog-sled driving, highly nomadic Inuit referred to in the introduction). Instead, they arrived from Alaska with a very sophisticated sea-mammal-hunting technology, including one designed for large bow-head whale hunting, kayaks and umiaks (large open skin boats using for large sea-mammal hunting), a sophisticated dog-sled technology, and certainly a much more (albeit informally) socially stratified society than the Dorset peoples. In addition, they developed a sophisticated snow-related technology associated with the construction of igloos and other snow structures shortly after their arrival in the Canadian Arctic.

As noted earlier, there is some overlap between Dorset and Thule peoples in the Canadian Arctic as evidenced by radiocarbon dates, but the nature of contact or cultural exchange during this contact period is a matter of continuing debate. Nevertheless, it has been well established that within a few centuries or less, following the arrival of the first Thule peoples from Alaska, Dorset peoples had essentially become extinct throughout the Canadian Arctic.

Thule Culture: Hazard Inlet, Somerset Island, Nunavut

Thule culture sites are found throughout most of the coastal and island regions of the Canadian Arctic. However, there is certainly no other series of archaeological sites that provides a better example of the technological, social, and ideological aspects of the Thule culture in the Canadian Arctic than those at Hazard Inlet, Somerset Island. Thule culture as represented at Hazard Inlet has the highest concentration of winter settlements and bowhead whaling camps, bowhead whale product storage, and bowhead whalebone use anywhere outside of the directly ancestral Thule Alaskan or Siberian culture areas. This area was occupied for about 300 years, from approximately AD 1200 to 1500. The Thule sites in this area were first examined in detail by Allen McCartney in the mid-1970s, and extensive mapping and excavation at the sites were carried out by the author and Peter Whitridge between 1989 and 1994.

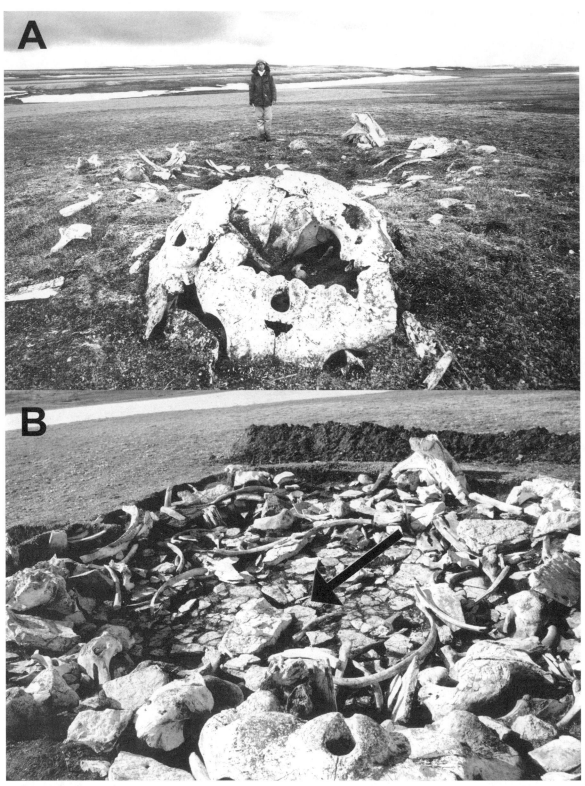

A: Karigi at Thule winter village site, Hazard Inlet, prior to excavation. Note the entrance composed of six bowhead whale skulls in the foreground, through which Thule Inuit would have symbolically "entered the whale" through its mouth. Junko Habu provides scale.   [Photograph by James Savelle, 1991] *B*: Karigi shown in 11 A during excavation. Note the amount of whalebone on the house floor resulting from collapse of the roof. Arrow points to pit beneath house floor, which probably originally contained various whaling-related ceremonial artifacts.   [Junko Habu, 1991]

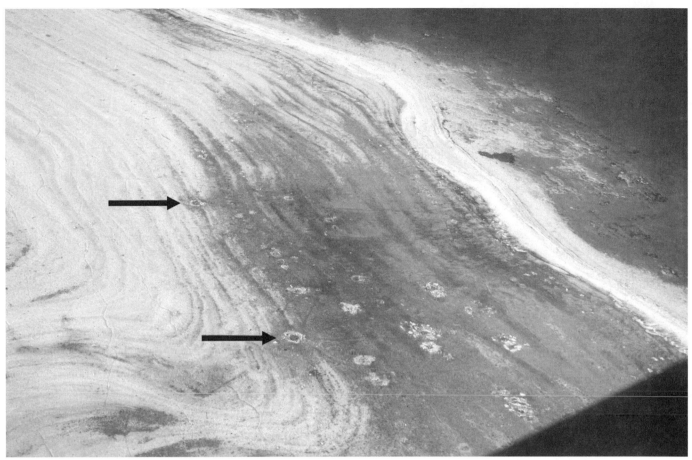

Fall Thule whaling camp at Hazard Inlet. Arrows indicate two karigis, seaward of which are a number of whaling crew house clusters. Note footpaths leading from the karigi in the foreground to whaling crew house clusters associated with that particular karigi. [James Savelle, 1991]

At Hazard Inlet, within a coastal expanse of approximately 12 kilometers, there are four winter villages with a minimum of 64, 13, 11, 7 dwellings each, as well as several large fall whaling villages consisting of up to 56 dwellings and a number of summer non-whaling (sealing/fishing) camps totaling at least 150 dwellings, in addition to several thousand above-ground stone bin and beach gravel meat caches. The winter villages and adjacent fall whaling camps here are perfectly situated to intercept bowhead whales during their northern summer migration, and this is characteristic of most Thule winter/whaling village sites in the general region.

Thule winter houses are impressive semi-subterranean features, typically occurring in one or several rows on raised beach ridges, and consist of sod and stone walls and roof built around and over a framework of bowhead whalebones (primarily skulls, jaws, and ribs), after which they would have been covered with snow for additional insulation. The interior would have been heated by sea-mammal oil burned in stone lamps. Dwellings contained one to three raised stone sleeping platforms and were entered through a low tunnel constructed from stone, sod, and whalebone.

Based on analogy with historic north Alaskan Eskimo societies, and the archaeological evidence at Hazard Inlet, each of the villages would have consisted of a number of extended families. Adult male members of these villages would have served as members of a whaling crew, which in turn would have been under the control of a whaling crew captain. The whaling crew captain would have had a higher social status than others in the crew and would have been responsible not only for directing the whaling operations but also for distributing products of the whale hung among his and other crew members. At Hazard Inlet, the smaller villages of seven and eleven dwellings probably consisted of single whaling crews, the village of thirteen houses possibly two whaling crews, and the village of sixty-four houses six to seven or more whaling crews. In the largest multi-crew villages, it is very likely that one or two of the whaling captains would have had an elevated status relative to the other whaling captains, and presumably would have been responsible for the overall organization of the village whaling activities. Several houses at the larger sites contain an inordinate amount of whalebone relative to other houses as well as a disproportionate amount of exotic iron, copper, and ivory artifacts, and these are interpreted as having been occupied by high-status whaling captain families. In addition to the conspicuous consumption of whalebone by the highest-status whaling crew leaders, these individuals typically owned a ceremonial house referred to as a *kairigi*. These served as centers for whaling ceremonies and general "men's" activities, and in the larger villages a number of whaling crews would have been associated with each karigi.

There is considerable symbolism associated with the karigis, as well as many of the residential houses. Specifically, the entrance was often constructed primarily from whale skulls, with the interior, as noted earlier, constructed from jaw bones, ribs, and other bones. This whalebone arrangement symbolically represented a whale, such that a person entering the house or karigi was symbolically entering the whale through its mouth (entrance) and into the whale's body. In addition, one of the karigis excavated at Hazard Inlet had a small chamber constructed beneath the original house floor, which, based on similar structures excavated at Alaskan Thule whaling sites, may have contained various whaling-related charms and other objects and which has been referred to as "buried symbolism."

Some whaling would probably have been carried out from these winter villages, but most whaling activities appear to have been carried out at the specialized fall whaling camps, noted earlier. The houses at these localities were less substantial than the winter houses, consisting of low stone and sod walls over which skins would have been laid on a few wood or whalebone vertical supports. These whaling camps typically consisted of several house groups of five to seven houses per group. Each house group was probably occupied by members of specific whaling crews (which would have consisted of six to nine individuals) and their families. Furthermore, each of the fall whaling camps at Hazard Inlet contained one or more karigis. As in the case of the winter villages, these karigis would have been owned by a high-status whaling crew leader, and a number of whaling crews would be associated with each one. This arrangement is readily apparent at one of the Hazard Inlet fall whaling camps. Two karigis, indicated by arrows, occur on the highest beach levels at the site, and a number of shallow pit house groups are associated with each of the two karigis. There are a series of footpaths radiating out from the karigi to the house groups associated with it.

Finally, mention should be made of the extent of whaling that took place at Hazard Inlet. There are literally thousands of whale bones present at the site, both as structural material and on the beaches immediately in front of the winter villages and whaling camps where the whales were butchered. Based on surface bone counts and extrapolating from the probable numbers of bones in unexcavated houses (less than 10 percent of the houses in the area have been excavated), a conservative estimate of the numbers of bowhead whales killed by Thule peoples during occupation of the sites at Hazard Inlet is 1,500–2,000, or an average of 5–7 whales per year during the occupation of the site.

The Demise of Thule Culture

Beginning approximately AD 1400–50 and generally coinciding with a cooling trend that led to the little ice age, many areas of the Canadian Arctic where bowhead whales formed the basis of the Thule diet were completely abandoned by Thule peoples. The reason for this abandonment favored by archaeologists is that the cooling trend resulted in a decrease in the abundance and predictability of bowhead whales in the area, due to much more extended and extensive summer sea ice cover. While many village populations presumably gradually decreased and eventually died out during the cooling period, others apparently moved farther south into areas rich in food resources such as seals, caribou, and walrus, perhaps joining non-whaling Thule peoples who already lived in these areas. In the absence of a diet based on bowhead whale that provided abundant food surpluses, these Thule peoples eventually developed the characteristic Inuit lifeways documented historically by nineteenth-century explorers and early twentieth-century ethnographers. They became relatively small, highly nomadic groups that relied on dogs for transportation; hunted seals on the sea ice in winter and musk ox, caribou, fish, and other smaller animals during other seasons; and lived in igloos during the winter and skin tents during the summer.

SITE ACCESSIBILITY

Generally speaking, the vast majority Canadian Arctic archaeological sites are relatively inaccessible. To visit the sites, it is first necessary to fly to the nearest Inuit settlement by commercial airlines, after which local guides are typically hired as guides and as polar bear monitors, and the sites are flown to by chartered aircraft or boat. In the case of the Paleoeskimo sites of Kapuivik and Alarnerk, interested individuals would first have to fly to the settlement of Igloolik (which itself has a considerable number of Paleoeskimo features in the immediate vicinity, some of which have been excavated and reconstructed), and from there charter aircraft or boats would be required to transport them to the sites. Cold-weather clothing and camping gear would be a definite requirement. In the case of Hazard Inlet, individuals would first have to fly to Resolute and from there charter an aircraft to take them to sites in that area; again, a local guide and cold-weather clothing and camping gear are essential. However, there is a Thule village near Resolute where several whalebone houses were excavated and reconstructed by Robert McGhee several years ago, and where presently excavation and reconstruction of several additional houses is being undertaken by Sarah Hazell.

Further Reading: Maxwell, Moreau S., *Prehistory of the Eastern Arctic* (Orlando, FL: Academic Press, 1985); McGhee, Robert, *Ancient People of the Arctic* (Vancouver: University of British Columbia Press, 1996); McGhee, Robert, *The Last Imaginary Place: A Human History of the Arctic World* (Toronto, ON: Key Porter Books, 2004); Schledermann, Peter, *Voices in Stone: A Personal Journey into the Arctic Past* (Calgary, AB: Arctic Institute of North America, 1996).

James Savelle

HAMILTON INLET REGION SITES

Hamilton Inlet, Coastal Eastern Labrador
Cultural Boundary Shifts along a Forest-Tundra Frontier

Among all the Native peoples of the Americas, two groups stand out as being different from each other in almost all respects: Indians and Eskimos. These differences are seen in language and folklore; in genetics, physical features, blood types, and other biological features; and in their adaptations and cultural history as seen in archaeology. American Indian origins can be traced back to peoples who emigrated from northeast Asia 15,000 or more years ago and spread throughout temperate and tropical regions of North and South America. Eskimos, whose more recent Asian ancestry is evident in their stronger "Asian" physical features, occupy only the Arctic regions of North America. In Canada and Greenland, Eskimo culture arrived from Alaska only 4,000 years ago. Before that, Arctic regions of Canada and Greenland were uninhabited and blocked by ice. However, Alaska and the Bering Strait region were ice-free throughout the Ice Age, and in this region Eskimo and Aleut cultures can be traced back to 6,000–8,000 years. Today archaeologists know Beringia as the source of Eskimo cultures that developed under Asian influence thousands of years after the proto-American Indians entered the New World.

Although archaeologists debate the origins of American Indians and Eskimos and their interrelationships in the Bering Strait region, the distinction between Indian and Eskimo cultures, languages, and biology is sharply defined across northern Canada. At least two major "Eskimo" migrations originating in the Bering Strait region moved into Canada and Greenland. The first, known as Paleoeskimos, founded the seal- and walrus-hunting Pre-Dorset and Dorset Paleoeskimo cultures of Canada and Greenland; and the second, known as Thule culture, brought a more advanced whale-hunting Neoeskimo culture into these regions from the Bering Strait. Paleoeskimos arrived in the eastern Arctic about 4,000 years ago and spread as far east as Labrador, Newfoundland, and eastern Quebec. The Thule Neoeskimo culture expanded out of northern Alaska in a warm climate period about AD 1000, replacing or absorbing Dorset peoples and occupied the eastern Arctic from the time of Viking contacts about AD 1200 until the arrival of modern Europeans in the 1500s. Probably their contacts with Vikings were still remembered when Eskimos in Baffin Island, now called Inuit by their own designation, met members of Martin Frobisher's English expedition searching for the Northwest Passage in 1576.

Spreading around the continent of North America from Alaska in different directions, Indians and Eskimos (a collective term used for all Arctic-adapted peoples, whether Paleoeskimo, Neoeskimo, or historic Inuit) did not meet again until Eskimos, moving east across the Canadian Arctic, reached subarctic Labrador about 4,000 years ago. This meeting was a historically momentous event, when peoples who had diverged for thousands of years met face-to-face for the first time somewhere in central or northern Labrador. After that, their histories became closely entwined until the present. Four thousand years is a long time for two groups living side-by-side to maintain distinct identities; but, remarkably, Indian and Eskimo groups in Labrador remained separate, territorially distinct cultures throughout this entire period, with little cultural exchange or convergence. Archaeologically each group can be identified by its artifacts, settlement patterns, house types, and even the types of stone they chose as raw materials to make tools; and over the long period during which they shared frontiers and hunting zones, each maintained its distinct cultural identity, even into the present. By contrast, in Alaska, Indian and Eskimo cultures shared many features and influenced each other considerably over the past several thousand years.

Exploring the Eskimo-Indian boundary in Labrador has produced a remarkable history of cultures and their relationships with environment during the 10,000 years that humans have lived in this part of North America. Most of Labrador was covered by glacial ice until about 8,000 years ago, when the continental ice sheet began retreating into central Labrador-Quebec. Mountainous northern Labrador remained ice-free through the late glacial era, but its central and southern regions were covered with thick ice sheets. As this ice began to melt 12,000 years ago, a wedge of land appeared first along the southern coast, expanding gradually north. Late Paleoindian peoples followed this expanding wedge of coastal tundra north into the central Labrador coast, reaching Hamilton Inlet by about 8,000–9,000 years ago. Pollen cores taken from the bottoms of lakes show that the environment at that time was Arctic tundra and that Indian groups moved north as the northern forest fringe expanded with the warming climate. By 6,000 years ago the forest boundary had reached its present northern limit near Okak, where it has remained ever since, even though cooling climates resulted in periodic expansions of Arctic pack ice south along the coast as far as Newfoundland.

This dichotomy between a warmer and stable interior and a cold-sensitive coastal region has dominated the history of

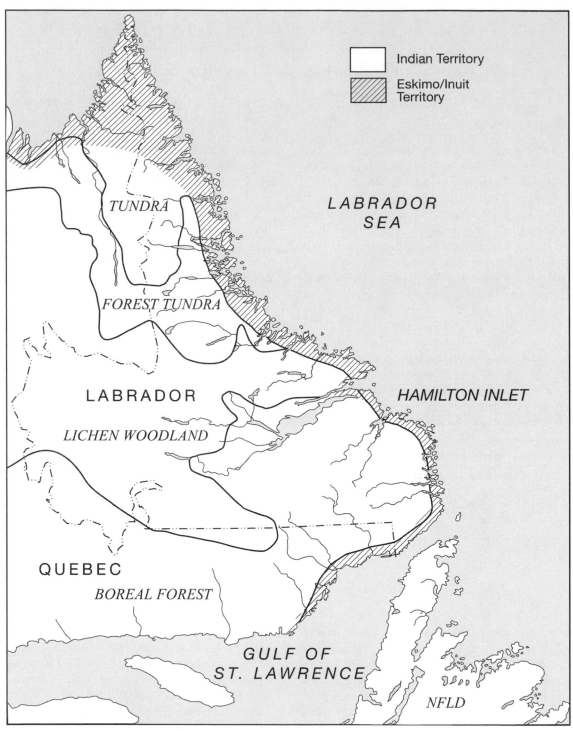

A map of Hamilton Inlet.   [Illustration by Marcia Bakry]

vegetation and human cultures in Labrador for thousands of years. In warmer periods Indian cultures have been able to move north along the coast into northern Labrador due to a relative lack of sea ice. During these warm periods, the major hazard to Indian culture was the threat of forest fires that decimated caribou and other land game on the interior. During cold periods, Arctic ice spread south to Newfoundland and beyond. As the ice spread, Indian groups could not sustain life on the coast and lost advantage to Eskimo groups that were better adapted to utilizing the seals, walrus, and other northern marine mammals associated with cool summers and icy coasts.

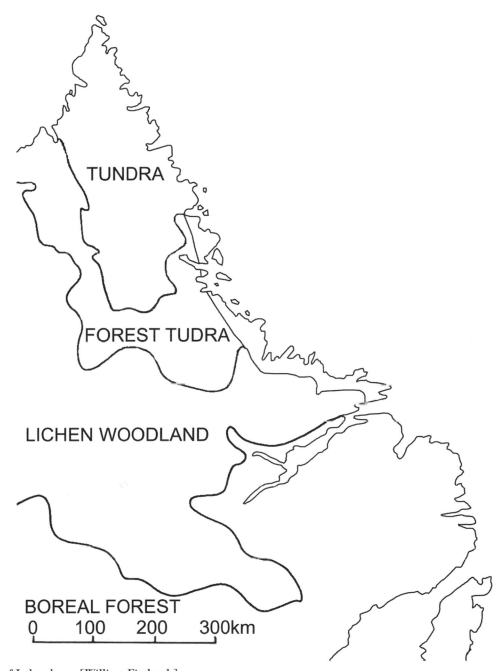

TUNDRA

FOREST TUDRA

LICHEN WOODLAND

BOREAL FOREST
0   100   200   300km

Ecological zones of Labrador.   [William Fitzhugh]

The archaeology of Hamilton Inlet and neighboring areas of central Labrador demonstrates this dynamic relationship between cultures and environments in a dramatic fashion. The prehistory of Hamilton Inlet, located at the boundary between the northern tundra and the subarctic forest, revealed an 8,000-year history of Indian cultures, from the first arrival of people until the historical era. The first 4,000 years of this period was a time of relative warmth and was paralleled by the development of a long maritime-adapted Indian cultural tradition known as the Maritime

Archaic. Related to the early Indian cultures of Maine and the Northeast, the Labrador Maritime Archaic developed a culture utilizing the rich resources of the marine zone, as well as caribou and other land game. During this long period they developed an increasingly elaborate ceremonial tradition evolving from individual burial mounds dating to 7,500 years ago to large cemeteries with burials containing large deposits of tools covered with red ocher. As these developments occurred, houses evolved from single-family pit dwellings to 100-meter longhouses containing rooms for twenty to twenty-five families,

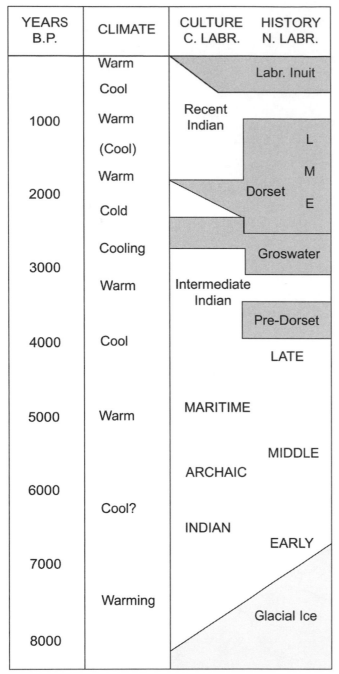

YEARS B.P.	CLIMATE	CULTURE C. LABR.	HISTORY N. LABR.

Climate and culture change in Labrador prehistory. Indian cultures shown in white, Eskimo cultures in gray. [Illustration by Marcia Bakry]

and trade in exotic materials linked communities over hundreds and even thousands of miles, as seen by tools made from northern Labrador Ramah chert found in red paint cemeteries in Maine.

All this changed when Eskimo peoples from Alaska migrated into northern Labrador 4,000 years ago. By 3,500 years ago these Pre-Dorset Paleoeskimos moved south into central Labrador, displacing the Maritime Archaic

Indians in Labrador, and by 3,200 years ago Maritime Archaic Indians disappeared from their last stronghold in Newfoundland. Meanwhile, under warming conditions, a new Indian culture moved into central Labrador from Quebec about 3,500 years ago, pushing the Pre-Dorset Eskimo peoples north and taking over their coastal territories in Labrador.

Shortly after 3,000 years ago the tables turned again, and under a cooling regime, with Arctic pack ice expanding south along the Labrador with seals, walrus, and polar bears, a new Paleoeskimo culture appeared, known as Groswater. Groswater Paleoeskimos spread south into Newfoundland and west along the north shore of the Gulf of St. Lawrence, apparently without strong resistance from Indians, who were not adapted to the new Arctic maritime conditions and made light use of coastal resources. Groswater Paleoeskimos came to occupy the largest territory of any Eskimo group in eastern North America, and their culture lasted in Labrador, Quebec, and Newfoundland until the arrival of a new Arctic culture, the Dorset people. All of these early cultures passed through Hamilton Inlet and left archaeological traces that allow archaeologists to identify and date more than twenty different cultural phases and traditions, and their territorial movements over 8,000 years.

While the coast was occupied by these Paleoeskimo groups, a succession of different Indian cultures continued life on the Labrador interior, hunting caribou, fishing, and capturing birds and small mammals. Life on the interior, in the boreal forest, was not easy and was subject to periodic bouts of starvation when caribou populations declined or forest fires interrupted animal cycles. Compared with the larger populations seen at Indian coastal sites, Indian settlements on the Labrador interior were small and left faint archaeological traces.

After AD 600 the disappearance of Dorset Paleoeskimos from the central Labrador coast brought a new Indian culture into prominence. First identified as Daniel Rattle and later as the successor Point Revenge culture, these Indians were probably Algonquian speakers who expanded onto the coast and occupied it as far north as Okak and Ramah Bay. Here they obtained Ramah chert for making tools and traded this lithic material far south across the Gulf of St. Lawrence into the Maritimes and Maine, where it appears in Middle and Late Woodland sites between AD 1000 and 1300. This is also the period when Vikings explored and briefly settled the Labrador and Newfoundland coasts, and although no Viking artifacts have been found in Labrador, the L'Anse aux Meadows site in northern Newfoundland is an authentic Norse site with three houses and several outbuildings and may have been occupied by Leif Eriksson. A Norwegian coin dating to AD 1065, artifacts of Ramah chert, and a Dorset culture tool have also been found at the Goddard site in Penobscot Bay, Maine, which archaeologists believe is indicative of Indian trade with Newfoundland rather than direct Viking presence in Maine.

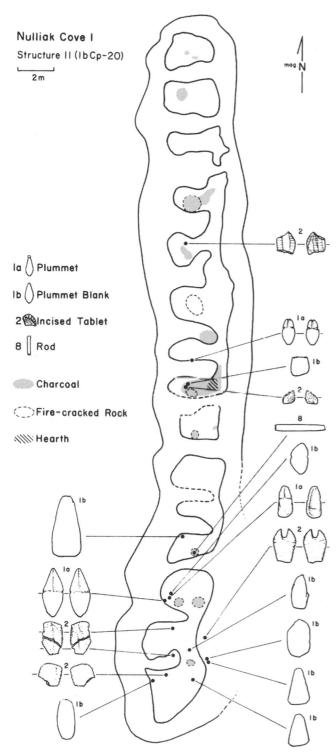

Nulliak Cove 1

Structure II (IbCp-20)

2m

mag N

Ia   Plummet

Ib   Plummet Blank

2   Incised Tablet

8   Rod

  Charcoal

  Fire-cracked Rock

  Hearth

Plan of Nulliak Cove 1, Structure 11 longhouse on northern Labrador coast, around 4,200 years ago, illustrating family dwelling spaces and unusual carved soapstone pendants. [Illustration by Marcia Bakry]

Soapstone carving of Dorset figure in high-collared garment from Shuldham Island, Saglek, Labrador. [William Fitzhugh]

Point Revenge Indian culture lasted on the Labrador coast until a new Eskimo group began migrating south about AD 1200. The new arrivals were Thule Eskimos, a whale-hunting people who had developed the technology for hunting large whales in the Bering Sea and expanded east across Arctic Canada during a warm climate period when a marked reduction in Arctic ice permitted whales to trans-migrate between the Atlantic and the Pacific oceans. Thule people, the ancestors of the modern Inuit, quickly replaced the Dorset culture in northern Labrador and Point Revenge Indians on the central Labrador coast and pushed south between AD 1300 and 1600, eventually reaching southern Labrador, where they met Spanish Basque whalers. Retreating from the coast, most Point Revenge Indians, by this time identified by their own name, Innu, retired to the interior, although they maintained coastal enclaves where they met Jesuit missionaries and traded with Europeans during the summer. For the next several hundred years the Inuit and Innu maintained separate lives—the Inuit on the coast and the Innu largely on the interior—generally avoiding contact with each other, but occasionally engaging in skirmishes over hunting territories or access to European traders and missionaries.

Throughout history, Hamilton Inlet remained a tension point between Arctic and subarctic cultures of Labrador. Lying at the intersection of Arctic tundra along the coast and the subarctic boreal forest on the interior, the inlet not only served as an east-west corridor between the forested interior and the tundra coast, but it also was the boundary between a more heavily forested southern coast and a more tundra-dominated northern coast. As such it remained a long-term fulcrum point in Labrador culture history. In colder periods Arctic-adapted Eskimo cultures tended to move south of Hamilton Inlet and its outer extension, Groswater Bay, to occupy Newfoundland and occasionally the Quebec lower north shore. In warmer periods, Indian groups found it advantageous to expand into northern Labrador to take advantage of the rich caribou and Ramah chert resources of the northern coast, driving out or replacing resident Eskimos in the process.

Today, outer Hamilton Inlet is home to the southernmost Inuit community in the world at the town of Rigolet, while at the western end of Lake Melville, Indians live in Seshashit and farther north along the coast at Davis Inlet. In addition to dynamics stimulated by climate and environmental change, the presence of Europeans and opportunities for trade during the historic period have been strong forces attracting Inuit peoples south from Arctic regions. Conversely, the opportunity to trade caribou skins to the Hudson's Bay Company in northern Ungava lured Innu north into the rich but unpredictable northern forest fringe. Both attractions had their hazards. Armed conflicts with Europeans in southern Labrador and epidemic diseases caused large losses for the Inuit, while hunger and starvation when caribou hunting failed resulted in heavy losses for Innu in the northern interior. For the past 4,000 years, as climate changes produced shifts in animal populations and sea ice, Indian and Inuit cultures on the central Labrador coast have had to compete for both resources and territory. Archaeology has demonstrated many rapid, large shifts in the Indian-Eskimo boundary over hundreds of miles.

Today this coast is peaceful, except for the roar of road graders and mining machines. Indian and Inuit groups still live largely separated in different villages, but as the Native populations decline in a rising tide of European immigration, the old days of Labrador, lying at the farthest geographic extreme of humanity's expansion around the globe east and west, are passing.

Further Reading: Fitzhugh, William, *Environmental Archaeology and Cultural Systems in Hamilton Inlet, Labrador*, Contributions to Smithsonian Anthropology, No. 16 (Washington, DC: Government Printing Office, 1972); Fitzhugh, William, "Population Movement and Culture Change on the Central Labrador Coast," *Annals of the New York Academy of Sciences* 288 (1977): 481–497; Fitzhugh, William, ed., *Cultures in Contact: the European Impact on Native Cultural Institutions in Eastern North America, A.D. 1000–1800*, Anthropological Society of Washington Series (Washington, DC: Smithsonian Institution Press, 1985); Tuck, James, *Newfoundland and Labrador Prehistory* (Ottawa, ON: National Museum of Man, 1974).

William W. Fitzhugh

MARTIN FROBISHER SITE

Baffin Island, Canada

The Sixteenth-Century English Search for the Northwest Passage

Starting with the sixteenth century, the English and other European nations saw the Spaniards coming back from Mesoamerica with their boats full of precious metals. Realizing the same was within reach for all, the English first attempted to sail to China by the northeast of England in 1553; when met with failure, they made a second try by the northwest in 1576. Based on an ambiguous map showing the existence of an ice-free passage in a temperate zone through the Arctic Archipelago, Captain Martin Frobisher was enlisted by London merchants to explore that new route. This route would allow the English to avoid the Portuguese on the African coast and the Spaniards roaming the Caribbean seas. Although the initial venture was for the discovery of a passage to China, the recovery of an unknown type of black rock, which they thought contained precious metals, soon forced them to abandon the idea of sailing to China. The English immediately identified on a map Canada's Frobisher Bay as the "way trending to Cathaia" and turned their attention to exploiting what they believed to be precious-metal-bearing ore. They built two assay shops on a small island in Frobisher Bay, which they used as their center of operation for testing various rocks in 1577 and 1578.

From an archaeological point of view, the Frobisher written accounts of the travels and archaeological remains provide an extraordinary window into the first encounters between Europeans and Inuit. Published records of the voyages contain descriptions of Inuit life and customs, housing, and the behavior the English observed of the Inuit. They also relate peculiar details of skirmishes between them and the Inuit, and of the establishment of shore camps, mines, and general operations. Edward Fenton's journal contains valuable details of the 1578 voyage and mining activities, including assays of supposedly precious-metal-bearing ore they collected in the Countess of Warwick's Sound and thereabout. The accounts

Leftovers intended for the colony that were never buried in the 1577 mine on the Countess of Warwick Island. Besides the recovered food and wood remains archaeologists were able to identify evidence of boat building and determine that someone had used that sheltered spot to light a fire for food preparation.　[Réginald Auger]

contain information about hostage taking, on both parties, and the fate of the Inuit hostages that can be traced to their graves in England. Although the disappearance and presumed loss of a group of five sailors and the ship's shore boat in 1576 leads to ambiguous conclusion in the records, oral tradition transmitted to an American journalist Charles Francis Hall in the 1860s finds support in the archaeological data. In short, the ethnographic details provided in the various accounts have been under investigation since 1981 as part of an archaeological investigation of the English impact on Native cultures of the eastern Arctic.

MARTIN FROBISHER'S VOYAGES OF DISCOVERY

The first English voyage for the discovery of a Northwest Passage set out from London in June 1576; the small fleet of two barks and one pinnace was manned with thirty-seven people. On July 26 the captain came in sight of a promontory that he named Queen Elizabeth Foreland on southeast Baffin Island. From the appearance of Native people, the difference in duration of the flow and ebb tides, and an underestimation of the size of the earth, Frobisher and company concluded they were in a strait at the entrance to the Orient: Asia lay to the north and the Americas to the south. The minerals the expedition brought back to England were at the root of two subsequent expeditions. That rock raised curiosity among financial backers, notably Michael Lok, former secretary of the Company of Muscovy, who after initial assays of the rocks believed it to be a rich ore that graded 25 ounces of gold to the ton. Lok was fast to put forth the idea of mounting a second expedition to Baffin Island.

The following year, an expedition under the sponsorship of the Company of Cathay was to bring back as much ore as possible and to survey for new sources of that coveted ore. The exploration for a passage to Cathay received only minor consideration from the 1577 expedition. Instructions were given to survey only if the ore discovered and assayed by German alchemists did not yield enough precious metal. The miners discovered at the mouth of Frobisher Bay a rich deposit of the type of ore sought after. Approximately 5 leagues to the north, a new bay sheltered by a string of islands offered protection against the pack ice. Frobisher noted in his journal: "Upon this iland was found good store of the ore, which in the washing helde golde plainly to be seen: whereupon it was thoughte beste rather to loade here, where there was store and indifferent good, than to seek further for better, and spend time with jeopardie." Following their arrival in England late in the fall, funding had to be raised in order to build furnaces large enough to process the three shiploads of the ore they had brought back. A delay in finding sufficient funding prevented the enterprise from processing the ore, and it was not treated until a master plan for a third expedition was moving ahead.

A most impressive expedition was underway in 1578, a flotilla that included fifteen vessels manned with 400 people had a twofold objective: to bring back as much ore as possible and to establish a permanent colony of 100 people. Miners, soldiers, carpenters, and boat builders were to be left in the Countess of Warwick's Sound with enough provisions for eighteen months. However, an early May departure with severe weather conditions hampered navigation; ships were cast adrift in all directions and eventually twelve of them reached their destination, but not without damage to their

In the industrial zone of the site, two shops were tested. It appears that one was used for melting ore in crucibles and in the other there is evidence of attempts to part gold and silver using cupels.   [Réginald Auger]

hulls and content. After taking stock of his flotilla, Captain Frobisher realized he could not establish the proposed colony that year for lack of essential supplies such as drink and fuel. Essential goods had not arrived; the bark *Dennys*, which was transporting parts for the barracks and other provisions for the colony, was drowned. Designs to build a colony were quickly abandoned, and the Frobisher expedition spent a few weeks mining for ore and assaying at the center of operation on the Countess of Warwick's Island. Before journeying back to England, Frobisher ordered the building of a cottage on the island and leftover supplies were buried with the expectation that another expedition would return the following year. The entry for August 30, 1578, reads, "We buried the timber of our pretended forte, with manye barrels of meale, pease, griste, and sundrie other good things, which was of the provisions of those whych should inhabite, if occasion served. And insteede therof we fraight oure ships full of ore, whiche we holde of farre greater price. Also here we sowed pease, corne, and other graine, to prove the fruitfulnesse of the soyle against the next yeare" (Stefansson and McCaskill 1938).

ARCHAEOLOGICAL RESEARCH AT THE SITE

The actual research at the Frobisher site was stimulated by the 1960s experimentations into carbon-14 (C-14) dating methods by Jacqueline S. Olin, a research scientist at the Conservation Analytical Laboratory in Washington, D.C. Following her dating results on a bloom stored at the Smithsonian Institution that Charles Francis Hall had brought back from

his visit to the site with the Inuit in 1861, she got results that far exceeded expectations. Olin obtained C-14 dates that placed the site in the tenth and eleventh centuries. New fieldwork was pursued by Arctic specialist William W. Fitzhugh, her colleague at the Smithsonian, in order to test some of the unanswered questions regarding those unexpected early dates from the blooms. Cultural interactions between the Englishmen and the Inuit of southern Baffin Island in Elizabethan time and technological data of the voyages became the focus of the research program started in 1990. Although the archaeological investigations of this project consumed a lot of energy, concomitant archival research in the Frobisher-related papers in England and France has also yielded a wealth of new data on Elizabethan cultural contacts, provisioning of an Arctic expedition, pyrotechnology, economy, exploration, and characters.

Archaeological excavations have recovered remnants of supplies left on the island for later use. Archaeologists recovered the 1578 expedition supplies buried in a trench described by Hall during the 1860s. He referred to the Frobisher mine site on the north shore of the island as a place interpreted by Inuit where ships were refitted: "On the shore on the north side of the island I found also an excavation which I called a ship's trench, for the Innuits said that was where a ship had been built by the white men. It had been dug out of stone, which was of such nature as to yield to the persevering use of pickaxe, sledge-hammer, and the crow-bar. The bottom of the trench, which was one hundred and ten feet in length, was an inclined plane, running from the surface of the ground to a depth of twenty-five feet at the water's edge." Archaeologists tested that feature over two field seasons and recovered large quantities of goods buried in a soil that reverted to permafrost for another 400 years after the leftover provisions were buried. Unusual preservation conditions allowed researchers to unearth German-made stove tiles, a wicker basket used for loading ore onboard, coarse flour, peas, bread, barrel parts, squared timbers, and other such remains. It appears that the Inuit never touched those English supplies, which remained buried on site for over four centuries. Informants told archaeologists in 1994 that Inuits would have perceived it as wrong if anyone had touched provisions that were intended for later use by someone else.

Research in microstratigraphy and the study of wood remains have allowed archaeologists to highlight discrepancies between Inuit oral history and the published accounts of the Frobisher voyages. Thus, although the accounts of the 1576 voyage refer to five Englishmen being taken captive by Inuit, and accounts of the 1577 voyage relate how they discovered traces of the people they had lost the previous year, the entry ends up speculating on the obvious death of their countrymen at the hands of the Inuit: "But amongst sundrie straunge things whiche in these tents they founde there was rawe and newe killed fleshe of unknown sortes, with dead carcasses and bones of dogs, and I know not what. They also beheld (to their greatest marvaile) a dublet of canvas, made after the Englishe fashion, a shirt, a girdle, three shoes for contrarie feete and of unequal bigenesse, which they well conjectured to be the apparell of our five poore contriemen whiche were intercepted the laste yeare by these countrie people, aboute fifty leagues from this place further within the straightes."

In opposition to that quote, the 1860s oral history enquiry by Hall and other work on oral tradition in 1993–1994 make reference to Inuit feeding white men and helping them to build a watercraft. As it was revealed to Hall, archaeologists believe that oral tradition brings to light another version of the "lost sailors" incident that is considered as valid. Inuit oral tradition claims that a group of white men were abandoned in Frobisher Bay, that the Inuit helped them survive through the winter, and that in the spring they built a watercraft (presumably from timbers cached by Frobisher on Countess of Warwick's Island). Furthermore, oral history informs that the sailors tried to sail away before the ice had cleared and perished in a storm. When asked how they knew that story, Hall's informants replied, "all the old people knew about it." It is unclear whether those oral traditions relate to the same or to separate incidents; notwithstanding, documentary accounts speak of a single group of sailors taken captives by Inuit during the 1576 voyage. It is believed that the Inuit accounts tell another version of the same incident.

Since Frobisher could not leave people for lack of sufficient building material and provisions, before journeying back to England at the end of the 1578 season, the captain ordered the building of a cottage on the island. He dictated on August 30, 1578, "This daye the masons finished a house whiche Captaine Fenton caused to be made of lyme and stone upon the Countesse of Warwickes Ilande, to the ende we mighte prove against the nexte yeare, whether the snow coulde overwhelm it, the frosts break uppe, or the people dismember the same. By the construction of that little cottage, members of the expedition intended to befriend Inuit. Thus, it is mentioned: And the better to allure those brutish and uncivill people to courtesie, againste others times of our comming, we lefte therein dyvers of our countrie toyes, as bells, and knives, wherein they specially delight, . . . Also pictures of men and women in lead, men a horsebacke, lookinglasses, whistles, and pipes. Also in the house was made an oven, and breade left baked therein, for them to se and taste."

The second area of archaeological field investigations was the industrial sector of the site where Frobisher's men assayed ores. Testing of two features revealed the presence of fuel such as coal and charcoal, slag, crucible, cupels, and lead scraps. Archaeologists were able to define two distinct features related to ore assaying; they were shops used in the transformation of the ore. The first shop measured approximately 7 × 4 meters, and its limited sampling did not allow for determining its original interior organization. However, archaeologists were able to clearly identify the inside and the outside of the shop. In addition to a store of coal located outside of the shop used to roast the ore, partial excavation of its interior revealed a concentration of material related to assaying: crucibles, slag, coal, charcoal, brick fragments, and clay stains. It is interesting to note that there is no, or at least very little, evidence of blacksmithing that may be witnessed by the presence of scales or tiny droplets of iron resulting from welding. However, it was peculiar to have thousands of crucible fragments form a site that was so short lived; this alone suggests that Frobisher's alchemists were testing a wide range of rocks of which they were unsure of the content in precious metals.

Thirteen meters to the northwest of the first shop, archaeologists sampled another feature that was defined by three walls meeting at right angles and forming a structure measuring approximately 5 × 5 meters in size. The most obvious of the three walls revealed that the building was made of rows of stones apparently held together by mortar. Excavations revealed an assemblage that was very different from that recovered from the first shop: it contained a smaller amount of slag, and the slag fragments tended to be much smaller in size. There was wood charcoal found rather than anthracite, and red-stained soil was uncovered along with brick fragments, refractory ceramics, and crucible shards in the 1-square-meter unit excavated in the midden. Obviously, the color of the soil and the cultural content of the layers identified can be attributed to the use of fire nearby. However, the activities involving pyrotechnology were undoubtedly different from those observed in the first shop.

Table 1 Comparison of the Assemblages between the Two Shops

	Shop 1	Shop 2
Charcoal	149	539*
Coal	2376	7
Coke	918	8
Slag	7300	767
Lead	4	3
Crucible	472	1080
Cupel	0	73
Scorifier	38	97
Muffle fragment	0	475
Refractory ceramic	0	64
Brick	896	508

*The amounts of charcoal, coal, coke, slag, and lead are given in grams. Other items are given in number of fragments recovered.

Comparisons of the two assemblages highlight differences in the function of those two shops. Differences are most notable in the type of fuel used and the hardware each feature contained. Wood charcoal was used in one shop much more extensively than in the other. There is a preference for coal and coke in the shop where ore was melted in crucibles; slag is ten times more abundant in that feature as well. Crucibles and scorifiers, which have basically the same function, were found in both features. It is supposed that their large number in the second shop may be because archaeologists excavated into its midden where garbage was discarded. Cupels, which are usually associated with the second step in the process of assaying minerals, were found essentially in the second shop. Another marked difference between the two features is the 539 pieces of refractory ceramics found in the shop where wood charcoal is predominant; the other shop did not yield any such remains. Refractory ceramics come from the use of muffles, which serve as shelters in the assaying process to protect the crucibles and the cupels from the falling soot present in the oven.

Analysis of the assemblage composition shows remains associated to the transformation of the minerals, such as crucibles and slag, whereas the space outside the buildings shows an abundance of fuel and little in terms of the assaying of the minerals. Although it is clear that the space inside the shop has yielded a greater quantity of material than the space outside, it is believed that the lack of a sharp distinction between the three sectors may be due to a certain amount of salvage of the site by the Inuit, since they confided to Hall in 1862 that they used to go to the island to pick up pieces of red ceramics (either roof tiles or bricks), which they used to polish their brass ornaments.

CONCLUSIONS

Although archaeologists initially tended to put a lot of faith in written sources, the field research has taught that such sources have much the same sort of one-sided perspective as oral tradition does. Comparisons between three sources of information (written accounts, oral tradition, and archaeological data) have provided a somewhat more balanced interpretation of what went on when Englishmen and Inuit encountered at the end of the sixteenth century. For example, accounts of the 1576 voyage refer to five sailors taken captive by the Inuit, while those of the 1577 voyage relate that their traces were discovered and claim that they must have died at the hands of the Inuit. In contrast to the hostage-taking interpretation found in the accounts, oral traditions collected talk about the Inuit feeding white men and helping them to build a watercraft. Comparisons of the written and Inuit accounts together with archaeological data, such as that from the ship's trench, provide clues to resolve diverging versions of history.

Even though the study of the food remains used for provisioning the 1578 expedition is not yet complete, archaeologists have been able to present a number of results derived from the analysis of wood and ceramic remains. The knowledge acquired through a combination of archaeology, oral history, and analysis of written documents has provided alternative interpretations of the data obtained so far by historians working on written records alone. These studies have enabled archaeologists to add a new chapter to the history of sixteenth-century English explorations of the New World, which, until recently, were studied mainly from published sources. By analyzing Inuit oral traditions collected during the nineteenth century and new information gathered through oral inquiries and archaeological excavations, archaeologists have been able to critically examine the principal source of information on the voyages. The originality of this approach is that it has combined diverse sources of data to investigate a 400-year-old event.

Although archaeological excavations on Kodlunarn Island and oral tradition have shed light on some of the provisions that were used by the Elizabethan explorers and the technology employed by Frobisher's men to extract and assay minerals, archival research by a team based in London has allowed for a better understanding of the way in which the assayers employed the technology at their disposal in testing minerals for precious metals. Similarly, interdisciplinary studies of the documents have produced a whole new set of speculations about the outcome of the voyages. Another discovery made while working on the archaeology of the Frobisher voyages is the richness of Inuit oral tradition. Inuit oral history regarding the Elizabethan presence in the region, as well as information transmitted by informants, has convinced archaeologists of the importance of that data and has renewed their interest in conducting systematic research on oral history in conjunction with future archaeological work.

A last conclusion is that once all the plans were assembled into a master plan of the site, archaeologists realized that all the buildings identified on that small Arctic island were laid out according to a precise grid or development plan of the island: they all met at right angles. This alone indicates that, had the plan for a colony been successful, the little island would eventually have been filled with tightly set rows of habitations and industrial buildings. However, this grand scheme never materialized. Archaeologists have barely scratched the surface of that site, nevertheless, an understanding of the site has been gained through the unflagging efforts of the researchers who worked on the pyrotechnology aspects of Frobisher's operation, and have generated more questions than answers. A similar observation applies to the results gained from digging in the ship's trench. Although archaeologists are confident about the validity of the results regarding the use of this feature after provisions were stored on August 30, 1578, the interpretation remains a speculation with what knowledge is at hand.

Further Reading: Auger, R., W. W. Fitzhugh, L. Gullason, A. Henshaw, D. Hogarth, and D. Laeyendecker, "De-Centering Icons of History: Exploring the Archeology of the Frobisher Voyages and Early European-Inuit Contact," in *De-Centring the Renaissance: Canada and Europe in Multi-Disciplinary Perspective, 1500–1700*, edited by Germaine Warkentin and Carolyn Podruchny (Toronto: University of Toronto Press, 2001), 262–286; Collinson, R., ed., *The Three Voyages of Martin Frobisher in Search of a Passage to Cathaia*

and India by the North-west, Ser. 1, No. 38 (London: Hakluyt Society, 1867); Fitzhugh, William W., and Jacqueline S. Olin, eds., *Archeology of the Frobisher Voyages* (Washington, DC: Smithsonian Institution Press, 1993); Hakluyt, Richard, *The Principal Voyages, Traffiques and Discoveries of the English Nation*, 3rd ed., 8 vols. (London: J. M. Dent and Sons, 1927); Hall, Charles F., *Life with the Esquimaux: A Narrative of Arctic Experience in Search of Survivors of Sir John Franklin's Expedition* (London: Sampson Low, Son and Marston, 1864); Hogarth, D. D., P. W. Boreman, and J. G. Mitchell, *Mines, Minerals Metallurgy*, Canadian Museum of Civilization Directorate Paper No. 7, Mercury Series (Hull, QC: Canadian Museum of Civilization, 1994); Hoover, Herbert Clark, and Lou Henry Hoover, *Agricola, Georg, 1494–1555. De re metallica / tr. from the 1st Latin ed. of 1556, with biographical introd., annotations and appendices upon the development of mining methods, metallurgical process, geology, mineralogy & mining law, from the earliest times to the 16th century* (New York: Dover, 1950); Stefansson, V., and E. McCaskill, eds., *The Three Voyages of Martin Frobisher*, 2 vols. (London: Argonaut Press, 1938; facsimile ed. West Germany: Da Capo Press, 1971); Symons, Thomas H. B., ed., *Meta Incognita: A Discourse of Discovery Martin Frobisher's Arctic Expeditions, 1576–1578*, with the assistance of Stephen Alsford and Chris Kitzan, Canadian Museum of Civilization Directorate Paper No. 10, 2 vols., Mercury Series (Hull, QC: Canadian Museum of Civilization, 1999).

Réginald Auger

SKAGWAY, DYEA, AND THE CHILKOOT TRAIL SITES

Southeastern Alaska and Northwestern British Columbia
Archaeology of the Klondike Gold Rush

Dyea and Skagway are located at the head of Taiya Inlet in upper Lynn Canal, a deep fjord at the foot of southeast Alaska's Coast Ranges. Historically, the Taiya and Skagway River valleys were important subsistence grounds and trade routes for the Chilkoot and Chilkat Tlingit settled in permanent villages farther down the canal. The coastal Tlingit tribes established trade routes through these glacier-free valleys and fostered relationships with other Natives in the Alaska and Yukon interior. The discovery of gold on tributaries of the Yukon River in the late nineteenth century forever changed the trail dynamics and demographics at the head of Lynn Canal. Two town sites arose at the edge of the wilderness, each competing for the gold rush traffic that ensued. The majority of archaeological sites within Klondike Gold Rush International Historical Park contain information that relates to the successes and failures of Euro-American expansion into this western subarctic region.

DYEA AND CHILKOOT TRAIL SITES, DYEA, ALASKA, TO BENNETT, BRITISH COLUMBIA

Throughout the nineteenth century, Dyea served as a Tlingit seasonal subsistence camp and the start of the Chilkoot Trail. From the camp the Tlingit harvested eulachon, salmon, and berries at the mouth of the Taiya River while the inlet provided waterfowl, marine mammals, shellfish, and seaweed resources. An abundance of these resources presented the Tlingit trading opportunities with interior Natives who provided, among other things, moose and caribou skins, beaded clothing, and raw copper resources. Both indigenous groups benefited from western goods, such as iron implements, guns, and ammunition, gained through opportunistic trade during the Hudson's Bay Company's advance into northwestern North America, and with Boston whalers plying Alaska's vast coastline. Test excavations at a rock shelter located on the Chilkoot Trail revealed a small assemblage of chipped-stone flakes, trade beads, lead shot, and burned animal bone, demonstrating the flow of western goods from Dyea to the interior.

In 1884 Euro-Americans established a trading post at Dyea to supply merchandise directly to the Tlingits, interior Natives, and an ever-increasing flow of prospectors using the Chilkoot Trail. The 33-mile trail offered the shortest of several strenuous routes from the coast to the headwaters of the mighty Yukon River, where prospectors sought gold along its many tributaries. Tlingit groups profited from sporadic packing and guiding services they provided to prospectors and explorers attempting to reach the Yukon River. The 1896 discovery of large quantities of gold on the Klondike River in the Yukon Territory created a rush of westerners to the gold fields. Hoards of seasoned and novice prospectors began funneling their way to the head of the Taiya Inlet and Dyea. Ambitious merchants and freighting companies quickly overwhelmed the Tlingit village, creating a boom town that sprang up on the river floodplain. Transient camps, with names like Canyon City, Sheep Camp, Lindeman City, and Bennett, sprang up along logistical points of the Chilkoot Trail. However, the stampede fizzled within three years. Dyea entrepreneurs abandoned their interests there and either moved on to other gold strikes or invested in the neighboring town of Skagway.

Today, the dynamic Taiya River has eroded portions of historic Dyea, but visitors may still roam through the former town site viewing interpretative displays, structural ruins, and isolated artifacts. Park visitors who wish to experience the terrain and trials of the Tlingit traders and gold rush stampeders have the opportunity to hike and camp along the international Chilkoot Trail. Hikers may view lost or abandoned sleds, boots, cans, bottles, and a variety of other stampede artifacts and features throughout their Chilkoot adventure, and while they stay overnight at former stampeder camps in Alaska and British Columbia.

SKAGWAY AND WHITE PASS DISTRICT SITES, SKAGWAY, ALASKA

In 1887 father and son homesteaders William and Bernard Moore made plans for the construction of an alternative pedestrian route across White Pass and into Canada in anticipation of the gold rush that would occur ten years later. They chose the start of their trail at the mouth of the Skagway River, a 3-mile canoe trip south of Dyea. There on the deep floodplain sands and gravel beds, they maintained a seasonal cabin from 1887 to 1896 while they constructed a wharf and started developing the White Pass Trail. News of the 1896 Klondike gold strike brought thousands of prospectors to their doorstep, creating a rivalry between Skagway and Dyea. The White Pass Trail rapidly evolved from an arduous winter pedestrian route into a year-round pack train and wagon trail. Skagway's tent city blossomed into a boom town, complete with false-front buildings hastily erected on a block and lot street grid. The new city soon took on an elegantly detailed Victorian appearance as entrepreneurs built multistory hotels

with corner towers and filled their stores with mass-produced commercial goods. The last stage of trail evolution culminated with the completion of the White Pass and Yukon Route railway to the top of White Pass in 1899, and on to Whitehorse, Yukon Territory, by 1900. The railroad effectively ended the commercial viability of the Chilkoot Trail and turned Dyea into a ghost town.

Modern Skagway is a thriving tourist destination and host to the Klondike Gold Rush International Historical Park where visitors can view many restored gold-rush period buildings within its historic district. The White Pass and Yukon Route railroad is a privately owned and operated attraction, and the restored railroad depot and office buildings serve as the U.S. park's headquarters, visitors' center, and museum dedicated to interpreting gold rush history and archaeology. The White Pass unit of the park is not yet open to the public, but cursory archaeology surveys located remnants of trail and wagon road features and archaeological remains of White Pass City, a short-lived boom town once utilized by stampeders and railroad construction workers.

The Moore Homestead is one of Skagway's premier sites. In 1890 Bernard Moore married and started a family with Klingit-sai-yat, a prominent Tlingit woman. As their family grew, Bernard built a balloon-frame home adjacent to the original one-room log cabin. Located in the town's historic district, the National Park Service administers the house museum that includes a parlor room decorated with an eclectic mix of late Victorian era and Alaskan material goods. Archaeological excavations at the homestead have revealed tantalizing details into the lifestyle of the town's founding family. Fragments of undecorated dishes, unrefined glassware, numerous medicine bottles, and children's toys recovered from privies, dumps, and the yard reflect the Moore's modest social standing and domesticity. After the gold rush subsided, the Moore's sold their residence to a jeweler who ran a nearby curio shop. Alaska Native-themed jewelry and dishware recovered from post–gold rush features represent souvenirs and materials associated with Skagway's early tourist trade.

Besides domestic households, the National Park Service restoration of several saloons lead to excavations associated with commercial establishments once common during Skagway's gold rush and up to prohibition periods. These dens of solace offered men of all walks of life an acceptable place to communicate their mutual hardships and celebrations, politics and polemics. Artifacts such as poker chips, dice, tokens, whiskey and beer bottles, drinking and shot glass fragments, and tobacco pipes are tangible remains of the vices they shared. While excavations under the saloon buildings offered a contextual glimpse of culinary preparation, service, and container products, privy excavations presented a broader picture of saloon life. Shellfish remains and animal bones draw attention to the types of food and meat cuts saloon proprietors offered their patrons, whereas artifacts such as buttons, garter clips, textiles, earrings, and a ring are material reminders of the patrons themselves. Maintained as an interpretative exhibit, the park recreated a 1900 diorama in the rehabilitated Mascot Saloon complete with artifact displays of saloon material culture.

Further Reading: Chilkoot Trail National Historic Site of Canada, Parks Canada Web site, http://www.pc.gc.ca/lhn-nhs/yt/chilkoot (online January 2007); Cooper, Doreen C., *A Century at the Moore/Kirmse House: Archeological Investigations in Skagway, Alaska*, vol. 8 (Anchorage, AK: National Park Service, 2001); Griffin, Eve, and Karl Gurcke, "An Overview of Chilkoot Trail Archaeology," in *Eldorado! The Historical Archaeology of Gold Mining in the Far North*, edited by Catherine H. Spude, Robin O. Mills, Karl Gurcke, and Roderick Sprague (Lincoln: University of Nebraska Press, 2008 in press); Johnson, Julie, *A Wild Discouraging Mess: The History of the White Pass Unit of the Klondike Gold Rush National Historical Park* (Anchorage, AK: National Park Service, 2003); Klondike Gold Rush National Historical Park, National Park Service Web site, http://www.nps.gov/klgo (online February 2007); Spude, Catherine Holder, *The Mascot Saloon: Archeological Investigations in Skagway, Alaska*, vol. 10 (Anchorage, AK: National Park Service, 2006); Thornton, Thomas F., *Klondike Gold Rush National Historical Park Ethnographic Overview and Assessment* (Anchorage, AK: National Park Service, 2004).

Andrew Higgs

GLOSSARY

Accelerator Mass Spectrometric (AMS) Dating. A method of radiocarbon dating precise enough to count the proportion of carbon isotope (carbon 14) atoms directly and reducing the size of the sample of material required for accurate dating dramatically.

Anasazi (Ancestral Puebloan) Cultural Tradition. A well-known ancient cultural tradition that existed in the "Four Corners" area of the Colorado Plateau, around the common corners of Colorado, Utah, Arizona, and New Mexico, beginning about AD 900 and lasting until about AD 1300. Anasazi is the older and more traditional term used by archaeologists to refer to Ancestral Puebloan people. Many well-known sites are associated with this tradition, for example, the ancient architectural sites of Mesa Verde, Chaco Canyon, and Canyons of the Ancients National Monument (see the essays by Steve Lekson, Wirt Wills [on Shabik'eschee Village site], Paul Reed [Overview of Chaco Canyon], Jill Neitzel, Tom Windes, LouAnn Jacobson, John Kantner, Cathy Cameron, and Mark Varien in the Southwest section).

Archaic. A general term used to refer to a time period that encompasses the early Holocene from about 10,000 to 3,000 years ago, but varying in different regions. Developments during the Archaic included the manufacture of ground stone tools, the beginnings of food cultivation, and initial settled life. In some parts of North America this time period is divided into three sub-periods: the Early, Middle, and Late portions.

Assemblage. A group of artifacts recurring together at different places or times. Assemblages may be associated with particular activities or with a cultural tradition.

Atl atl. A spear-, arrow-, or dart-throwing tool. These are composite tools usually with several parts, including an antler or wood handle, a weight, and a hooked end. The atl atl works as a lever to propel the projectile for greater distance and with greater force.

Avocational archaeologist. Individuals with a serious interest in archaeology, but who do not engage in the discipline as their profession. Many avocational archaeologists have made important archaeological discoveries and contributions to our understanding of the ancient or historic pasts.

Basketmaker. A term used to refer to the early portion of the Ancestral Puebloan cultural tradition. Early Basketmaker people relied on hunting and gathering for much of their food, but during this period, domesticated plants, such as corn, beans, and squash, were added to the diet. During this period, ways of life became more settled and more permanent houses, called "pithouses" because they were dug partly below ground became common. Coiled and twined basketry also is common, and people began to make plain pottery for the first time.

Biface. A stone tool that has been chipped on both sides to shape and thin it.

Blade tool manufacture and technology. Blade manufacture is a quite different method of making flaked stone cutting and piercing tools than that employed in making chipped stone tools, such as a bifacial point or knife. The latter involves shaping, thinning, and sharpening a single piece of stone. In blade manufacture, a nodule of stone is carefully prepared to form a core so that multiple, long, narrow, parallel-sided flakes with very sharp edges can be struck. These "blades" then are used as knives for cutting, or snapped into segments that can be inserted into slots on the sides of antler or wooden points to form the cutting edges. Knives can also be made this way. One advantage of this technique over biface manufacture is that large cutting and piercing tools can be made using small pieces of stone when large pieces are not available.

Cation ratio dating. Cation ratio dating is used to date rocks that have a modified surface such as prehistoric rock carvings (petroglyphs). This is a relative dating technique that is not considered an accurate method of dating by some professional archaeologists.

Rocks are covered by a kind of varnish, a chemically-changed layer caused by weathering that builds up over time. The change in the rock varnish is due to calcium and potassium seeping out of the rock. The cation ratio is determined by scraping the varnish from the carved or petroglyph surface back to the original rock surface and making a comparison of the two. The technique relies on change due to weathering of the stone over long periods of time, so geographically distinctive patterns are needed to compare the original surfaces with the modern suface that show the results of weathering.

Chert. A type of very fine-grained stone rich in silica. It is often found in or weathered from limestone deposits. It was shaped into chipped stone tools, and sometimes for blade tools, using stone and bone or antler hammers.

Chipped Stone tools. Tools shaped and thinned by systematically flaking exterior portions off. Typically this manufacturing technique is used with very fine-grained stone (e.g., obsidian, chert, or flint) that can be flaked relatively easily because it fractures smoothly in a way that can be controlled manufacturing techniques skillfully applied.

Clovis. Clovis is a term used to name an archaeological culture, a time period, and a particular variety of fluted stone spear points or knives. The name derives from Clovis, New Mexico, near which is located the type site, Blackwater Draw. Clovis spear points have been found in direct association with extinct megafauna in ice age gravel deposits The Clovis culture is known to have occupied many parts of North America during the Paleoindian period. The distinctive Clovis spear point has a vertical flake scar or flute on both faces of the point that extends about 1/3 its length. Sites containing Clovis points have been dated across North America to between 13,500 and 10,800 years ago. In western North America Clovis points have been found with the killed and butchered remains of large animals like mammoth or mastodon. As a result, Clovis peoples are assumed to have targeted large game animals, although how much of their diet actually came from hunting, much less from large game, is unknown (see the essays by David Anderson in the Southeast section and Bonnie Pitblado and Dennis Stanford in the Great Plains and Rocky Mountain section).

Component. A culturally homogenous stratigraphic unit within an archaeological site.

Core. A lithic artifact used as the source from which other tools, flakes, or blades are struck.

CRM (Cultural Resource Management). This activity includes archaeological investigations done as part of public project planning required by federal or state laws to ensure that important archaeological sites are not wantonly destroyed by public undertakings. CRM also includes the long term management of archaeological resources that are on public lands and for which legal protections and preservation is required of the public agencies that administer these lands (see the general introduction for more details abut contemporary CRM in North America).

Dalton. Term used to refer to an archaeological culture dating to the end of the Paleoindian period and the beginning of the Archaic time period. Dalton artifacts and sites are recognized in the Midwest, Southeast, and Northeast of North America. The point distribution shows that there was a widespread Dalton lifeway oriented toward streams and deciduous forests. Dalton culture people were hunters and gatherers using a variety of wild animal and plant foods over the course of each year. Timber and nuts were important as raw materials and food. Like Paleoindians, Dalton groups probably consisted of families related by kinship and mutual dependence (see the essay by Dan Morse in the Southeast section).

Debitage. Stone debris from chipped-stone tool manufacturing or maintenance activities.

Desert Culture. Ancient cultural groups that occupied the present-day Great Basin and Plateau regions. They created a distinctive cultural adaptation to the dry, relatively impoverished environments of these regions. The Cochise or Desert Archaic culture began by about 7000 BC and persisted until about AD 500.

Earthfast foundation. Earthfast (also known as "post-in-the-ground") architecture was the most prevalent building tradition of 17th-century Virginia and Maryland. At its core, the typical "Virginia House" (as dwellings of this type were sometimes called) consisted of pairs of hewn wooden posts set into deep, regularly-spaced holes dug into the ground. Once set in the ground and backfilled, these posts were either pegged on nailed together with cross beams to form the sides and gables of a rectangular, A-framed structure. The exterior "skins" of such earthfast structures varied. Some were both roofed and sided with riven wooden clapboards. Others were sided in wattle-and-daub and roofed with thatch. Irrespective of their construction, earthfast structures tended to be rather impermanent, lasting no more than perhaps a decade or two at most in the hot, humid Chesapeake region.

Effigy pipes. A variation on the plain stone tube pipe carved in the likeness of an animal. A wide variety of animal images—birds, mammals, and reptiles—are used for these pipes which are frequently associated with the Adena and Hopewell cultures in the Midwest region.

Feature. Usually refers to types of archaeological deposits related to a particular focused activity or event. For example, hearths, garbage or trash pits, storage pits, and foundations or other architectural remnants are referred to generally as features.

Flotation. A technique for recovering very small organic remains, such as tiny pieces of charcoal, seeds, bone, wood, and other items. A soil sample is placed in a drum of water, sometimes mixed with other liquids. The liquid is agitated to loosen any soil from the organic material. This material, being lighter than water, floats to the surface and can be skimmed off using a fine mesh screen. The organic materials can be used in a variety of analyses, for example, to interpret diet, subsistence activities, for dating, and to determine use of wood for tools or structures.

Gorgets. Made of copper, shell or polished or smoothed stone these thin, often oval artifacts were often perforated by two or more holes and worn around the neck.

Hohokam Cultural Tradition. Hohokam refers to the Sonoran Desert region of Phoenix and Tucson in southern Arizona and further south. The Hohokam region witnessed remarkable cultural developments beginning about AD 900. In this general area, about 200 sites with large oval, earthen features (interpreted as local expressions of Mesoamerican ball courts) have been found. A distinctive cluster of large sites in the area of modern Phoenix clearly represent the Hohokam center. Hohokam had red-on-buff pottery, large towns composed of scores of courtyard groups (three to five single-room thatch houses facing inward into a small courtyard or patio), and ball courts. There were regular markets for the exchange of goods supported by canal-irrigated farming (see Steve Lekson's essay on the classic period ancient Southwest).

Holocene. The most recent geological epoch, which began about 10,000 years ago. The period after the last glaciation in North America.

Hopewell Cultural Traditon. An archaeological tradition of the Midwest dated to the Middle Woodland period (about 50 BC to AD 400). The Hopewell tradition is known for a distinctive burial patterns and a wide-ranging exchange among communities. Communities hundreds, even thousands, of miles from one another participated in this exchange system and raw materials, as well as finished products were exported and imported. The Hopewell tradition also is known for the mounds that they built for ceremonial and burial purposes. It is known to be one of the most considerable achievements of Native Americans throughout the ancient past. These mounds, especially in the Ohio River valley are large complexes incorporating a variety of geometric shapes and rise to impressive heights (see essays in the Midwest section by George Milner, Douglas Charles, N'omi Greber, William Dancey, and Bradley Lepper).

Horizon. A set of cultural characteristics or traits that has a brief time depth but is found across multiple areas or regions.

Kiva. Among modern Pueblo Indian communities in the Southwest, a kiva is a nonresidential structure or room that is owned and used by specific social groups, such as clans or religious societies. The activities that take place in kivas are different than the daily, domestic activities—such as food preparation and pottery manufacture—that occur in dwellings. Because of this historic affiliation of sociopolitical functions with kivas, archaeologists use this term to refer to large pit structures lacking evidence for domestic functions that may have been used as public buildings, rather than household dwellings.

Lithic. Stone.

Loess. Fine-grained windblown sediment deposited as soil layers on areas not ice-covered during the last glaciation.

Megafauna. Large mammal species, such as mammoth, mastodon, bison, giant beaver, giant ground sloth, and stag elk that lived in North America during the late glacial and early post-glacial time periods. Many megafauna species have become extinct.

Midden. The archaeological remains of a human settlement's garbage and trash deposits. Middens typically are an accumulation of decomposed organic refuse usually very dark colored that frequently also contains thousands of discarded pieces of stone artifacts and ceramics, animal bones, nutshells, and other remains.

Mimbres Cultural Tradition. The Mimbres cultural development occurred in the Mogollon region of western New Mexico between about AD 900 and 1150. It is most famous for its remarkable black-on-white pottery. While the majority of Mimbres bowls are painted with striking geometric designs, images include depictions of people and events using an artistic style that merits inclusion in the world's major art museums. Images also show Mimbres' wide interests: Pacific Ocean fish, tropical birds from western Mexico (and, perhaps, monkeys from the same area), and armadillos (see essays by Steve Lekson [Classic Period Cultural and Social Interaction], Karen Schollmeyer, Steve Swanson, and Margaret Nelson, and J. J. Brody in the Southwest section).

Mississippian Cultural Tradition. A widespread tradition centered on Midwestern and Southeastern North America beginning about AD 1000 and lasting in some places until AD 1600. Typically societies that were part of this cultural tradition had chiefdom level political organizations, had subsistence systems based on intensive agricultural production of corn, beans, squash, and other domesticated plants, and built settlements that incorporated earthen architecture, typically various kinds and sizes of mound architecture. Mississippian chiefdoms flourished across much of the Eastern Woodlands: as far north as Illinois and southern Wisconsin; as far west as eastern Oklahoma; as far east as the Carolinas and Georgia; and south to Florida and the Gulf Coast (see essays by Robin Beck in the Southeast section and Mary Beth Turbot in the Midwest section).

Mogollon Cultural Tradition. An ancient Southwestern cultural tradition dating between about A.D. 200 and 1450. The tradition is found in a vast, ecologically diverse geographic area in southwestern New Mexico, southeastern Arizona and northwestern Mexico. Mogollon takes its name from the mountain range and highlands that separate the Anasazi and Hohokam regions. The Mogollon area witnessed remarkable cultural development referred to as the Mimbres after the river in southwest New Mexico where this development was centered (see essays by Steve Lekson [Classic Period Cultural and Social Interaction] and Wirt Wills [the SU site] in the Southwest section).

Paleoindian (Paleoamerican) Cultural Tradition. The Paleoindian time frame extends from approximately 13,500 to 9,000 BC and is found in almost all parts of North America. It is the earliest widely recognized archaeological cultural tradition in North America. The Clovis culture is the earliest Paleoindian culture, but there are increasing numbers of investigations of sites that are purported to be older than the Clovis or Paleoindian tradition.

Pit. A hole in the earth constructed and used for cooking, storage, or garbage or trash disposal. Pits are a common kind of archaeological feature.

Pithouse. Pithouses typically are single room dwellings, although some have antechambers. Pithouses are semi-subterranean dwellings in which some portions of the walls consist of the sides of an excavated pit. They are constructed by excavating a large hole or pit, building a timber framework inside the pit, then covering the framework with the excavated dirt, resulting in a house that is very thermally efficient, but prone to rapid deterioration, depending on the climate, from the effects of moisture, as well as vermin infestation.

Pleistocene. The geological epoch dating from 1.8 million to 10,000 years ago. During the last part of the Pleistocene human populations began to migrate into North America. The end of this epoch is a period of repeated glaciations in North America. It is succeeded by the Holocene era.

Postmolds. The archaeological remains of timbers, posts, saplings, or other wood structural elements of former buildings or dwellings. Depending on the age and soil conditions, posts placed in the ground ultimately will decay into fragments or mere stains indicating where these portions of buildings once existed.

Prehistory, prehistoric. Regarded by some as a demeaning term indicating primitive, but, most often used simply to refer to the general period of time prior to written records. As such, the length of the prehistoric period for different parts of North America varies according to when written records are available, generally associated with the beginning of European contact with aboriginal cultures.

Radiocarbon Dating (also known as Carbon-14 [^{14}C] Dating). An absolute dating method that measures the decay of the radioactive isotope of carbon (^{14}C) in organic material.

Steatite (Soapstone). A metamorphic rock, composed largely of the mineral talc and relatively soft. Steatite has been used as a medium for carving for thousands of years. Steatite also was carved out in ancient times to create bowls, in particular in places and at times before pottery had begun to be produced.

Taphonomy. The study of the process of fossilization. Used in archaeology to examine the human and natural changes that produce the archaeological record. For example, changes to organic materials after the death of the organism, such as how bone is changed by chemical, mechanical or animal processes after burial.

Tradition. An archaeological concept indicating a consistent set of cultural characteristics and traits that has great time depth and covers a recognized area.

Wattle-and-daub construction. A building technique using poles placed vertically in the ground and then plastered over with mud to construct the walls. Usually structures of wattle and daub were topped with thatched roofs.

Woodland Time Period. A time period term used mainly in the eastern North America south of Canada between roughly 1000 BC and AD 1000. In the Midwest region the Woodland period is regarded as the centuries between Archaic times and the Mississippian period. During this long period, the technology of pottery developed and spread, social and political complexity increased, cultivated plants changed from a supplemental part of diet to dietary staples, and settlements grew from small groups of residences to some of the largest cities in the world at that time.

Younger Dryas. A cold climatic event that took place from 12,900–11,600 years ago. It was a rapid return to glacial conditions during the longer term transition from the last glacial maximum to modern climatic conditions.

Sources used for definitions: The definitions in this glossary are derived from a number of sources, including essays in this encyclopedia, and the following texts:

Renfrew, Colin and Paul Bahn (2000). *Archaeology: Theories, Methods, and Practice*, third edition. Thames and Hudson, London and New York.

Thomas, David Hurst (1991). *Archaeology: Down to Earth*. Harcourt Brace Jovanovich College Publishers, Fort Worth and New York.

ABOUT THE EDITORIAL BOARD

FRANCIS P. McMANAMON is the author of many articles, commentaries, and reviews on a variety of topics related to American archaeology. He is coeditor of *The Antiquities Act: A Century of American Archaeology, Historic Preservation, and Nature Conservation* (2006) and *Cultural Resource Management in Contemporary Society* (2000). He has been involved in archaeological investigations in eastern North America, Western Europe, and Micronesia. He played a key role in the investigation of the Kennewick Man skeletal remains from Washington State. Dr. McManamon is an Adjunct Professor in the Department of Anthropology at the University of Maryland. He is the Chief Archaeologist of the National Park Service, Departmental Consulting Archaeologist for the Department of the Interior, and Manager of the Archaeology Program of the NPS national office in Washington, DC.

LINDA S. CORDELL, former Director of the University of Colorado Museum, Boulder, is a Senior Scholar at the School for Advanced Research in Santa Fe and Professor Emeritus of Anthropology at the University of Colorado, Boulder. Her research in the American Southwest focuses on Ancestral Pueblo settlement and agricultural strategies with excavations in the Upper Pecos and Rio Grande Valley areas and complementary analysis of museum collections. Her most recent research includes elemental analyses of archaeological maize from Chaco Canyon and materials analysis of fifteenth-century Ancestral Pueblo pottery. She is author of *Archaeology of the Southwest* (1997), and coeditor, with Don D. Fowler, of *Southwest Archaeology in the Twentieth Century* (2005). She serves on the Galisteo Basin Archaeological Sites Protection Act Coordinating Committee and as an advisor to the Friends of Tijeras Pueblo, organizations focused on the protection and interpretation of archaeological sites.

KENT G. LIGHTFOOT is Professor in the Anthropology Department at the University of California, Berkeley. As an archaeologist who has spent the last 30 years working in New England, the American Southwest, and the Pacific Coast of North America, he specializes in the study of coastal hunter-gatherer peoples, culture contact research, and the archaeology of colonialism. Since joining the Berkeley faculty in 1987, much of his research has focused on prehistoric Native Californian peoples and their later encounters with early European explorers and colonists. His recent book, *Indians, Missionaries, and Merchants: The Legacy of Colonial Encounters on the California Frontiers* (2005), presents the results of some of this research. His recent work has centered on the archaeology of the greater San Francisco Bay Area.

GEORGE R. MILNER is Professor of Anthropology at Pennsylvania State University. He specializes in archaeology and human osteology, focusing on the prehistoric peoples of the

American Midwest and Southeast. He has taken part in archaeological excavations of villages and cemeteries in the eastern United States, Micronesia, and Egypt, and has studied collections, mostly ancient and modern human skeletons, from these areas as well as Denmark and Switzerland. His recent book, *The Moundbuilders* (2004), is an overview of the prehistoric societies of eastern North America. An earlier book, *The Cahokia Chiefdom* (1998; reprinted 2006), covers the development and organizational structure of the Mississippian period society centered on the largest prehistoric mound center in the United States.

ABOUT THE CONTRIBUTORS

Elliot M. Abrams
Ohio University
Athens, OH

E. Charles Adams
Arizona State Museum, University of
   Arizona
Tucson, AZ

J. M. Adovasio
Mercyhurst College
Erie, PA

C. Melvin Aikens
University of Oregon
Eugene, OR

James M. Allan
William Self Associates, Inc.; St. Mary's
   College of California
Orinda, CA; Moraga, CA

Rebecca Allen
Past Forward, Inc.
Garden Valley, CA

Stacy D. Allen
National Park Service
Shiloh, TN

Kenneth M. Ames
Portland State University
Portland, OR

David G. Anderson
University of Tennessee
Knoxville, TN

Douglas D. Anderson
Brown University
Providence, RI

Lisa Anderson
California State University, Fresno
Fresno, CA

Bill Angelbeck
University of British Columbia
Vancouver, BC, Canada

Herbert O. Anungazuk
National Park Service
Anchorage, AK

Jeanne E. Arnold
University of California, Los Angeles
Los Angeles, CA

Réginald Auger
Université Laval
Québec City, QC, Canada

Jennifer J. Babiarz
University of Texas at Austin (Ph.D.
   Candidate)
Austin, TX

Jesse Ballenger
University of Arizona
Tucson, AZ

Janet R. Balsom
National Park Service
Grand Canyon, AZ

Douglas B. Bamforth
University of Colorado
Boulder, CO

Marc L. Banks
Marc L. Banks, Ph.D., LLC
Weatogue, CT

James F. Barnett, Jr.
Mississippi Department of Archives and
   History
Natchez, MS

Mark Barron
Hardy, Heck, Moore, Inc.
Austin, TX

James M. Bayman
University of Hawaii
Honolulu, HI

Robin Beck
University of Oklahoma
Norman, OK

Leland C. Bement
Oklahoma Archeological Survey
Norman, OK

Ellen P. Berkland
Boston Landmarks Commission
Boston, MA

David J. Bernstein
Stony Brook University
Stony Brook, NY

Michael S. Berry
Bureau of Reclamation
Salt Lake City, UT

Brandon S. Bies
National Park Service
Washington, DC

Ted Birkedal
National Park Service
Anchorage, AK

Dennis B. Blanton
Fernbank Museum of Natural History
Atlanta, GA

Eric Brandan Blind
Presidio Trust; University of California,
   Berkeley
San Francisco, CA

Mark A. Boatwright
Bureau of Land Management
Las Vegas, NV

Todd W. Bostwick
City Archaeologist
Phoenix, AZ

Edmond A. Boudreaux, III
East Carolina University
Greenville, NC

Jeffrey P. Brain
Peabody Essex Museum
Salem, MA

Jack W. Brink
Royal Alberta Museum
Edmonton, AB, Canada

John D. Broadwater
National Oceanic and Atmospheric
   Administration
Newport News, VA

J. J. Brody
University of New Mexico (professor
   emeritus)
Albuquerque, NM

Robert L. Brooks
Oklahoma Archeological Survey,
   University of Oklahoma
Norman, OK

David S. Brose
Imprints from the Past, LLC
Kalamazoo, MI

Emily J. Brown
Aspen CRM Solutions
Santa Fe, NM

Maureen J. Brown
Texas Historical Commission
Austin, TX

James. E. Bruseth
Texas Historical Commission
Austin, TX

Greg C. Burtchard
Mount Rainier National Park
Ashford, WA

Jeff Burton
Trans-Sierran Archaeological
   Research
Tucson, AZ

Brian M. Butler
Southern Illinois University
Carbondale, IL

Catherine M. Cameron
University of Colorado
Boulder, CO

Amanda Cannon
Statistical Research, Inc.
Redlands, CA

Aubrey Cannon
McMaster University
Hamilton, ON, Canada

Roy L. Carlson
Simon Fraser University
Burnaby, BC, Canada

Jefferson Chapman
Frank H. McClung Museum, The
   University of Tennessee
Knoxville, TN

Douglas K. Charles
Wesleyan University
Middletown, CT

Elizabeth S. Chilton
University of Massachusetts Amherst
Amherst, MA

Amelia Chisholm
Archaeology in Annapolis
College Park, MD

Rudolf Berle Clay
Cultural Resource Analysts, Inc.
Lexington, KY

Liz N. Clevenger
Presidio Trust
San Francisco, CA

Charles R. Cobb
South Carolina Institute of Archaeology
   and Anthropology, University of
   South Carolina
Columbia, SC

Arthur B. Cohn
Lake Champlain Maritime Museum
Ferrisburgh, VT

Thomas J. Connolly
UO Museum of Natural & Cultural History and State Museum of Anthropology, University of Oregon
Eugene, OR

Ann S. Cordell
Florida Museum of Natural History
Gainesville, FL

Ross Cordy
University of Hawai'i–West O'ahu
Pearl City, HI

Pamela J. Cressey
Alexandria Archaeology/City of Alexan-
   dria
Alexandria, VA

George M. Crothers
University of Kentucky
Lexington, KY

Aron L. Crowell
National Museum of Natural History,
   Smithsonian Institution
Anchorage, AK

J. Brett Cruse
Texas Historical Commission
Austin, TX

William S. Dancey
The Ohio State University
Columbus, OH

I. Randolph Daniel, Jr.
East Carolina University
Greenville, NC

Loren G. Davis
Oregon State University
Corvallis, OR

R. P. Stephen Davis, Jr.
University of North Carolina
Chapel Hill, NC

Neill De Paoli
Colonial Pemaquid State Historic Site;
    Southern Maine Community College
New Harbor, ME; South Portland, ME

Glenna Dean
Historic Preservation Division, Depart-
    ment of Cultural Affairs, State of New
    Mexico
Santa Fe, NM

Albert A. Dekin, Jr.
Binghamton University, State University
    of New York
Binghamton, NY

Richard J. Dent
American University
Washington, DC

Chester B. DePratter
South Carolina Institute of Archaeology
    and Anthropology, University of
    South Carolina
Columbia, SC

E. James Dixon
Maxwell Museum of Anthropology, Uni-
    versity of New Mexico
Albuquerque, NM

Clark A. Dobbs
Institute for Minnesota Archaeology
Minneapolis, MN

Glen H. Doran
Florida State University
Tallahassee, FL

Christian E. Downum
Northern Arizona University
Flagstaff, AZ

Boyce C. Driskell
University of Tennessee, Knoxville
Knoxville, TN

Penelope B. Drooker
New York State Museum
Albany, NY

Don E. Dumond
University of Oregon
Eugene, OR

Jeffrey J. Durst
Texas Historical Commission
Austin, TX

David H. Dye
University of Memphis
Memphis, TN

Ann M. Early
Arkansas Archeological Survey
Fayetteville, AR

Suzanne L. Eckert
Texas A&M University
College Station, TX

Steven Eminger
University of Hawaii
Molokai, HI

Jon M. Erlandson
Museum of Natural and Cultural
    History, University of Oregon
Eugene, OR

Charles R. Ewen
East Carolina University
Greenville, NC

Glenn Farris
California State Parks
Sacramento, CA

Kenneth L. Feder
Central Connecticut State University
New Britain, CT

Christopher C. Fennell
University of Illinois
Urbana, IL

Shannon M. Fie
Beloit College
Beloit, WI

Paul R. Fish
University of Arizona
Tucson, AZ

Suzanne K. Fish
University of Arizona
Tucson, AZ

Charles L. Fisher (deceased)
New York State Museum
Albany, NY

Richard T. Fitzgerald
California Department of Parks and
    Recreation
Sacramento, CA

William W. Fitzhugh
Smithsonian Institution
Washington, DC

Catherine S. Fowler
University of Nevada, Reno (emerita)
Reno, NV

Don D. Fowler
University of Nevada, Reno
Reno, NV

Richard A. Fox
The University of South Dakota
Vermillion, SD

Noreen R. Fritz
National Park Service
Blanding, UT

Eugene M. Futato
University of Alabama Museums
Moundville, AL

Dennis R. Gallegos
Gallegos & Associates
Carlsbad, CA

Lynn H. Gamble
San Diego State University
San Diego, CA

S. Craig Gerlach
University of Alaska, Fairbanks
Fairbanks, AK

Donna L. Gillette
University of California, Berkeley
Berkeley, CA

Amy J. Gilreath
Far Western Anthropological Research
    Group, Inc.
Las Vegas, NV

Lynne G. Goldstein
Michigan State University
East Lansing, MI

Anthony P. Graesch
University of California, Los Angeles
Los Angeles, CA

N'omi B. Greber
Cleveland Museum of Natural History
Cleveland, OH

Diana M. Greenlee
Poverty Point State Historic Site
Epps, LA

Roberta S. Greenwood
Greenwood and Associates
Pacific Palisades, CA

Kristen Griffin
National Park Service
Sitka, AK

Steven Hackenberger
Central Washington University
Ellensburg, WA

Charles M. Haecker
National Park Service
Santa Fe, NM

David J. Hally
University of Georgia
Athens, GA

Jeffrey L. Hantman
University of Virginia
Charlottesville, VA

Robert J. Hard
University of Texas at San Antonio
San Antonio, TX

Donald L. Hardesty
University of Nevada, Reno
Reno, NV

Michael L. Hargrave
U.S. Army Engineer Research and
    Development Center, Construction
Engineering Research Laboratory
Champaign, IL

Alan D. Harn
Dickson Mounds Museum
Lewistown, IL

Marlin Francis Hawley
Wisconsin Historical Society
Madison, WI

Holly Herbster
The Public Archaeology Laboratory, Inc.
Pawtucket, RI

Brent A. Hicks
Historical Research Associates
Seattle, WA

Andrew Higgs
National Park Service
Skagway, AK

William Hildebrandt
Far Western Anthropological Group, Inc.
Davis, CA

Robert J. Hoard
Kansas Historical Society
Topeka, KS

S. Homes Hogue
Ball State University
Muncie, IN

Lisa Holm
Pacific Legacy, Inc.
Berkeley, CA

Logan W. Hovis
National Park Service
Anchorage, AK

Bruce B. Huckell
University of New Mexico
Albuquerque, NM

Kathleen L. Hull
University of California, Merced
Merced, CA

William J. Hunt, Jr.
National Park Service
Lincoln, NE

Mark G. Hylkema
California State Parks
Santa Cruz District, CA

Jack B. Irion
Minerals Management Service
New Orleans, LA

James E. Ivey
National Park Service
Santa Fe, NM

David Jacobs
Arizona State Historic Preservation Office
Phoenix, AZ

LouAnn Jacobson
Bureau of Land Management, Canyons
    of Ancients National
    Monument/Anasazi Heritage Center-
    Dolores, CO

Richard W. Jefferies
University of Kentucky
Lexington, KY

Dennis L. Jenkins
Museum of Natural and Cultural
    History, University of Oregon
Eugene, Oregon

Ann M. Johnson
Yellowstone National Park
Mammoth Hot Springs, WY

John R. Johnson
Santa Barbara Museum of Natural History
Santa Barbara, CA

Michael F. Johnson
Fairfax County Park Authority
Falls Church, VA

Timothy W. Jones
Consulting Anthropologist
Tucson, AZ

Russell L. Kaldenberg
ASM Affiliates, Inc.
Cheyenne, WY

John Kantner
School for Advanced Research
Santa Fe, NM

Kathleen L. Kawelu
University of California, Berkeley
Berkeley, CA

John E. Kelly
Washington University
St. Louis, MO

Robert Kelly
University of Wyoming
Laramie, WY

James D. Keyser
USDA Forest Service (retired)
Portland, OR

Adam King
South Carolina Institute of Archaeology
and Anthropology, University of
South Carolina
Columbia, SC

Robert E. King
Bureau of Land Management
Anchorage, AK

Timothy A. Kohler
Washington State University
Pullman, WA

Lisa Kraus
The Louis Berger Group
Washington, DC

Lee Ann Kreutzer
National Park Service
Salt Lake City, UT

Kristin A. Kuckelman
Crow Canyon Archaeological Center
Cortez, CO

Michael Kunz
Bureau of Land Management
Fairbanks, AK

Mary L. Kwas
Arkansas Archeological Survey
Fayetteville, AR

Joseph E. Labadie
National Park Service (retired)
Del Rio, TX

Jason M. LaBelle
Colorado State University
Fort Collins, CO

Stephen H. Lekson
University of Colorado
Boulder, CO

Mark P. Leone
University of Maryland
College Park, MD

Bradley T. Lepper
Ohio Historical Society
Columbus, OH

Jed Levin
National Park Service
Philadelphia, PA

Owen Lindauer
Federal Highway Administration
Washington, DC

William D. Lipe
Washington State University
Pullman, WA

Barbara J. Little
National Park Service
Washington, DC

William A. Lovis
Michigan State University
East Lansing, MI

Edward M. Luby
San Francisco State University
San Francisco, CA

Wayne R. Lusardi
Thunder Bay National Marine Sanctuary
Alpena, MI

Mark T. Lycett
University of Chicago
Chicago, IL

Margaret M. Lyneis
University of Nevada, Las Vegas;
Museum of Northern Arizona
Flagstaff, AZ

Jonathan B. Mabry
City of Tucson, Cultural Resources and
Historic Preservation
Tucson, AZ

Robert I. MacDonald
Archaeological Services Inc.
Kitchener, ON, Canada

Robert C. Mainfort, Jr.
Arkansas Archeological Survey
Fayetteville, AR

Seth Mallios
San Diego State University
San Diego, CA

Mary L. Maniery
PAR Environmental Services, Inc.
Sacramento, CA

William Marquardt
Florida Museum of Natural History
Gainesville, FL

Susan R. Martin
Michigan Technological University
Houghton, MI

Terrance J. Martin
Illinois State Museum
Springfield, IL

Antoinette Martinez
California State University, Chico
Chico, CA

Desireé Reneé Martinez
Harvard University (Ph.D. candidate)
Cambridge, MA

Patricia A. Martz
California State University, Los Angeles
Los Angeles, CA

Robert F. Maslowski
Marshall University Graduate College
South Charleston, WV

R. G. Matson
University of British Columbia
Vancouver, BC, Canada

Mark D. McCoy
San Jose State University
San Jose, CA

Windy K. McElroy
University of Hawai'i at Manoa
Honolulu, HI

Bonnie G. McEwan
Mission San Luis
Tallahassee, FL

Chip McGimsey
Louisiana Division of Archaeology, State
    Historic Preservation Office
Baton Rouge, LA

J. David McMahan
Alaska Office of History and Archaeol-
    ogy
Anchorage, AK

R. Bruce McMillan
University of Missouri
Columbia, MO

Patricia A. Mercado-Allinger
Texas Historical Commission
Austin, TX

Robert R. Mierendorf
National Park Service
Marblemount, WA

Peter R. Mills
University of Hawaii at Hilo
Hilo, HI

Paul E. Minnis
University of Oklahoma
Norman, OK

Jeffrey M. Mitchem
Arkansas Archeological Survey
Parkin, AR

Daniel Monteith
University of Alaska Southeast
Juneau, AK

Juliet E. Morrow
Arkansas Archeological Survey
Jonesboro, AR

Dan F. Morse
University of Arkansas (retired)
Panacea, FL; Cashiers, NC

Jeremy M. Moss
National Park Service
Tumacacori, AZ

Stephen A. Mrozowski
Andrew Fiske Memorial Center for
    Archaeological Research, University
    of Massachusetts Boston
Boston, MA

Paul R. Mullins
Indiana University-Purdue University,
    Indianapolis
Indianapolis, IN

Larry E. Murphy
National Park Service
Santa Fe, NM

Stephen E. Nash
Denver Museum of Nature & Science
Denver, CO

Michael S. Nassaney
Western Michigan University
Kalamazoo, MI

Jill E. Neitzel
University of Delaware
Newark, DE

Margaret C. Nelson
Arizona State University
Tempe, AZ

Robert S. Neyland
Department of the Navy, Naval Histori-
    cal Center
Washington, DC

Vergil E. Noble
National Park Service
Lincoln, NE

Larry Nordby
Mesa Verde National Park (retired)
Placitas, NM

Michael J. O'Brien
University of Missouri
Columbia, MO

Jeff Oliver
University of Sheffield
Sheffield, UK

David G. Orr
Temple University
Philadelphia, PA

Sannie Kenton Osborn
Presidio Trust
San Francisco, CA

Marshall D. Owens
U.S. Fish & Wildlife Service (retired)
Council Bluffs, IA

Matthew Palus
Columbia University
New York, NY

E. Breck Parkman
California State Parks
Petaluma, CA

Virginia Parks
U.S. Fish and Wildlife Service
Sherwood, OR

Mia T. Parsons
National Park Service
Harpers Ferry, WV

Robert Paynter
University of Massachusetts Amherst
Amherst, MA

Christopher S. Peebles
Glenn A. Black Laboratory of Archaeology, Indiana University
Bloomington, IN

Steven R. Pendery
National Park Service
Lowell, MA

James B. Petersen (deceased)
University of Vermont
Burlington, VT

Staffan D. Peterson
Glenn A. Black Laboratory of Archaeology, Indiana University
Bloomington, IN

Paul Picha
State Historical Society of North Dakota
Bismarck, ND

Arnold Pickman
Archaeological Consultant
New York, NY

Peter J. Pilles, Jr.
Coconino National Forest
Flagstaff, AZ

Bonnie L. Pitblado
Utah State University
Logan, UT

Thomas J. Pluckhahn
University of South Florida
Tampa, FL

Stephen S. Post
Museum of New Mexico
Santa Fe, NM

Louise Pothier
Pointe-à-Callière, Montréal Museum of Archaeology and History
Montréal, QC, Canada

Ben A. Potter
University of Alaska Fairbanks
Fairbanks, AK

Robert W. Preucel
University of Pennsylvania
Philadelphia, PA

Angus R. Quinlan
Nevada Rock Art Foundation
Reno, NV

John C. Ravesloot
William Self Associates, Inc.
Tucson, AZ

Brian G. Redmond
The Cleveland Museum of Natural History
Cleveland, OH

Judyth E. Reed
Bureau of Land Management
Cheyenne, WY

Paul F. Reed
Center for Desert Archaeology, Salmon Ruins Museum
Bloomfield, NM

Mark A. Rees
University of Louisiana at Lafayette
Lafayette, LA

J. Jefferson Reid
University of Arizona
Tucson, AZ

Glen E. Rice
Rio Salado Archaeology, LLC; Arizona State University
Tempe, AZ

Christina B. Rieth
New York State Museum
Albany, NY

Robert V. Riordan
Wright State University
Dayton, OH

Paul A. Robinson
Rhode Island Historical Preservation & Heritage Commission
Providence, RI

J. Daniel Rogers
National Museum of Natural History, Smithsonian Institution
Washington, DC

Martha Ann Rolingson
Arkansas Archeological Survey (emeritus)
Alvin, TX

John Roney
Colinas Cultural Resource Consulting
Albuquerque, NM

Jeffrey S. Rosenthal
Far Western Anthropological Research Group, Inc.
Davis, CA

Patricia E. Rubertone
Brown University
Providence, RI

Allika Ruby
Far Western Anthropological Research Group, Inc.
Davis, CA

Matthew A. Russell
National Park Service; University of California, Berkeley
Berkeley, CA

Michael Russo
National Park Service
Tallahassee, FL

Patrick G. Saltonstall
Alutiiq Museum & Archaeological Repository
Kodiak, AK

David Sanger
University of Maine
Orono, ME

Robert Lee Sappington
University of Idaho
Moscow, ID

Robert F. Sasso
University of Wisconsin–Parkside
Kenosha, WI

Joe Saunders
University of Louisiana at Monroe
Monroe, LA

James Savelle
McGill University
Montreal PQ, Canada

C. Margaret Scarry
University of North Carolina at Chapel
   Hill
Chapel Hill, NC

John Scarry
University of North Carolina at Chapel
   Hill
Chapel Hill, NC

Jeanne Schaaf
Lake Clark National Park and Preserve;
   Katmai National Park and Preserve;
   Aniakchak National Monument and
   Preserve
Anchorage, AK

Polly Schaafsma
Museum of Indian Arts and
   Culture/Laboratory of Anthropology
Santa Fe, NM

Tsim D. Schneider
University of California, Berkeley
Berkeley, CA

Karen Gust Schollmeyer
Arizona State University
Tempe, AZ

Sissel Schroeder
University of Wisconsin
Madison, WI

Gerald F. Schroedl
University of Tennessee
Knoxville, TN

Margo Schwadron
National Park Service
Tallahassee, FL

Douglas D. Scott
University of Nebraska–Lincoln
Lincoln, NE

Erika K. Martin Seibert
National Park Service
Washington, DC

Paul A. Shackel
University of Maryland
College Park, MD

Paul R. Sheppard
University of Arizona
Tucson, AZ

Michael J. Shott
University of Akron
Akron, OH

Arleyn W. Simon
Arizona State University
Tempe, AZ

Brona G. Simon
Massachusetts Historical Commission
Boston, MA

Steven D. Smith
South Carolina Institute of Archaeology
   and Anthropology, University of
   South Carolina
Columbia, SC

David H. Snow
Independent Scholar
Albuquerque, NM

Dean R. Snow
The Pennsylvania State University
University Park, PA

Susan Snow
National Park Service
San Antonio, TX

Elizabeth Sobel
Missouri State University
Springfield, MO

Stanley South
South Carolina Institute of Archaeology
   and Anthropology, University of
   South Carolina
Columbia, SC

Katherine A. Spielmann
Arizona State University
Tempe, AZ

Dennis Stanford
National Museum of Natural History,
   Smithsonian Institution
Washington, DC

Edward Staski
New Mexico State University
Las Cruces, NM

Amy F. Steffian
Alutiiq Museum & Archaeological
   Repository
Kodiak, AK

Julie Stein
Burke Museum, University of Washington
Seattle, WA

Connie L. Stone
U.S. Bureau of Land Management
Phoenix, AZ

Bonnie W. Styles
Illinois State Museum
Springfield, IL

Lynne P. Sullivan
Frank H. McClung Museum, University
   of Tennessee
Knoxville, TN

Steve Swanson
Arizona State University
Tempe, AZ

Amanda K. Taylor
University of Washington
Seattle, WA

Wendy Giddens Teeter
Fowler Museum at UCLA
Los Angeles, CA

Thomas D. Thiessen
National Park Service (retired)
Pleasant Dale, NE

David Hurst Thomas
American Museum of Natural History
New York, NY

Mary Beth Trubitt
Arkansas Archeological Survey
Arkadelphia, AR

David Tuggle
International Archaeological Research
   Institute, Inc.
Honolulu, HI

E. Randolph Turner, III
Virginia Department of Historic
    Resources
Newport News, VA

Shannon Tushingham
University of California, Davis
Davis, CA

Mark Tveskov
Southern Oregon University
Ashland, OR

Douglas H. Ubelaker
Smithsonian Institution
Washington, DC

Mark D. Varien
Crow Canyon Archaeological Center
Cortez, CO

Andrew Veech
National Park Service
Omaha, NE

René L. Vellanoweth
Humboldt State University
Arcata, CA

Douglas W. Veltre
University of Alaska Anchorage
Anchorage, AK

Nina M. Versaggi
Binghamton University, State University
    of New York
Binghamton, NY

Bradley Vierra
Statistical Research Inc.
Albuquerque, NM

Barbara L. Voss
Stanford University
Stanford, CA

Sharon A. Waechter
Far Western Anthropological Research
    Group, Inc.
Davis, CA

Birgitta Wallace
Parks Canada (retired)
Halifax, NS, Canada

Joe Watkins
University of Oklahoma
Norman, OK

Carol S. Weed
Vanasse Hangen Brustlin, Inc.
Watertown, MA

Kit W. Wesler
Murray State University
Murray, KY

Gary C. Wessen
Makah Cultural and Research Center
Neah Bay, WA

Michael E. Whalen
University of Tulsa
Tulsa, OK

Gregory G. White
Pacific Legacy, North Coast to Cascades
    Office
Chico, CA

Robert Whitlam
Washington State Department of
    Archaeology & Historic Preservation
Olympia, WA

Stephanie M. Whittlesey
SWCA Environmental Consultants
Flagstaff, AZ

Michael D. Wiant
Illinois State Museum–Dickson Mounds
Lewistown, IL

David R. Wilcox
Museum of Northern Arizona
Flagstaff, AZ

Scott S. Williams
Department of Archaeology and Historic
    Preservation
Olympia, WA

W. H. Wills
University of New Mexico
Albuquerque, NM

Douglas C. Wilson
National Park Service
Vancouver, WA

Thomas C. Windes
University of New Mexico; National
    Park Service
Albquerque, NM

Mona Wright
Army Corps of Engineers
Richland, WA

DeeAnne Wymer
Bloomsburg University
Bloomsburg, PA

Rebecca Yamin
John Milner Associates, Inc.
Philadelphia, PA

Jason T. Younker
Coquille Indian Tribe; Rochester Insti-
    tute of Technology
Rochester, NY

Larry J. Zimmerman
IUPUI; Eiteljorg Museum
Indianapolis, IN

INDEX

A page number followed by *i* indicates an illustration; *m* indicates a map; *t* indicates a table.